"Nowt but a fleein' thing"

A history of climbing on Scafell

This edition published in 2016 by The Fell and Rock Climbing Club of the English Lake District Limited.

ISBN 978-0-85028-059-3

www.frcc.co.uk

Design, layout and patience by Chris Sherwin – Pepperdog Press, FRCC.
Printed and bound in Europe by Latitude Press Ltd.

"Nowt but a fleein' thing"

A history of climbing on Scafell

by Al Phizacklea and Mike Cocker

with additional contributions from Brian Davison and John McMMoore.

FELL & ROCK CLIMBING CLUB

Photo: Al Phizacklea

Contents
"Nowt but a fleein' thing"

Introduction

Foreword - Chris Bonington Page IV - V
Message from the FRCC President
Area Map VI
Introduction Page 1 - 7
Detail Map Page 8
A Short Walk Page 9 - 19
Climate & Conditions Page 20 - 25
Wasdale Head Page 26 - 30

Early Years 1802 – 1914

1802 - 1880 Page 31 - 40
1881 - 1888 Page 41 - 54
1889 - 1895 Page 55 - 68
1896 - 1899 Page 69 - 80
1900 - 1903 Page 81 - 90
1904 - 1913 Page 91 - 102
1914 Page 103 - 114

Middle Years 1915 – 1973

1915 - 1929 Page 115 - 130
1930 - 1935 Page 131 - 150
1936 - 1948 Page 151 - 164
1949 - 1957 Page 165 - 176
1958 - 1964 Page 177 - 198
1965 - 1973 Page 199 - 220

Recent Years 1974 – 2015

1974 - 1976 Page 221 - 236
1977 - 1981 Page 237 - 252
1982 - 1986 Page 253 - 260
1984 - 1987 Page 261 - 276 *winter*
1987 - 1997 Page 277 - 294
1998 - 2006 Page 295 - 308
1990 - 2015 Page 309 - 320 *winter*
2007 - 2015 Page 321 - 334

Geology Page 335 - 350

Crag Diagrams Page 351 - 374

First Ascents Page 375 - 380

Biographies Page 381 - 391

Accidents Page 392 - 393

Acknowledgements Page 394 - 398

Andy Mitchell on Ringwraith, Scafell Crag.

Foreword
Chris Bonington

Photo: Al Phizacklea

It was over seven years ago that Al Phizacklea called in at my house with Mark Scott, the oral archivist from the Fell and Rock Climbing Club, to interview me about my part in the history of Scafell climbing. Whilst I was only involved in a handful of new routes on Scafell, it reminded me of some of the best days climbing I have ever had in The Lakes on what is not just it's finest crag, but one of the best in the British Isles. It's one of the highest crags south of the Border, and whichever route you take to reach it entails a slog. The routes on the crag have the combined attributes of length, quality and a richness of history that make them memorable. I found myself fondly reminiscing over those days with Nick Estcourt and Mike Thompson. They were wonderfully happy-go-lucky, when we were young and fit, when climbing seemed more spontaneous and carefree than it is today.

This book, which covers the entire history of just about every route on Scafell and The East Buttress from 1802 to 2015, is a tremendous feat of work by a dedicated team from the Fell and Rock. The early years have been superbly researched by Mike Cocker, and his meticulous details are full of interest and wonder. The tone of this book subtly changes through the decades and the more recent history is supported by oral recordings and quotes which give character to the writing. I am so pleased time was taken to talk to those climbers who were involved with developing these crags, because the result is a timeless account full of anecdotes, incidents and epics that would have otherwise been lost.

Al Phizacklea is the main author and he has an unequalled knowledge of Scafell gained through his 37 years of climbing there. He made his initial first ascents of routes in 1984 and has continued to do so into 2015. He is the Fell and Rock guidebook writer to three of the Scafell editions and he produced new crag diagrams to illustrate these.

Al took it upon himself to gather together a fantastic collection of photographs, from the well-documented Abraham collection to those he took himself which adorn these pages throughout. There are many shots of routes that have never been published before, and many that were carefully choreographed to take advantage of the sun, I never realised it shone so much up there! In particular, I have never seen the cross carved at the foot of Lord's Rake to commemorate the tragedy from 1903 so clearly defined as in his early morning photograph.

It is not just climbing that is covered here, there is a very interesting geological section written for the climber and not just for students of geology by John Moore; a comprehensive set of diagrams depicting the routes in both summer and winter, an intriguing map depicting the accident black spots on the hill and some fascinating facts about life at Wasdale Head and its hotel.

Take time to look through this book, it is full of interest, historical snippets and facts, all gathered together in a volume that will grace the shelves of anyone who has visited these crags and who wants to learn more about a route and its history. The Fell and Rock team have created a masterpiece of climbing literature that will become a classic source of inspiration for generations to come. But it's more than that, it will also become a lasting memorial to those friends and characters that have graced the greatest climbing ground in England.

Chris Bonington, December 2015.

Photo: Ron Kenyon

The Fell and Rock Climbing Club has had a long association with Wasdale Head and Scafell. The crags here have, for many years, been and still are at the forefront of climbing in The Lake District and the history of the exploration and climbing of these is such an integral part of The Lake District and British climbing heritage.

It is so important not to lose this history and it is good to see this being brought together by such a fine team as Al Phizacklea and Mike Cocker and everyone else involved. On behalf of the Fell and Rock Climbing Club and the rest of the climbing fraternity I would like to thank them all for bringing this book together.

Ron Kenyon
FRCC President

Chris Bonington on The Lord of the Rings.

The Scafell Massif and surrounding area.

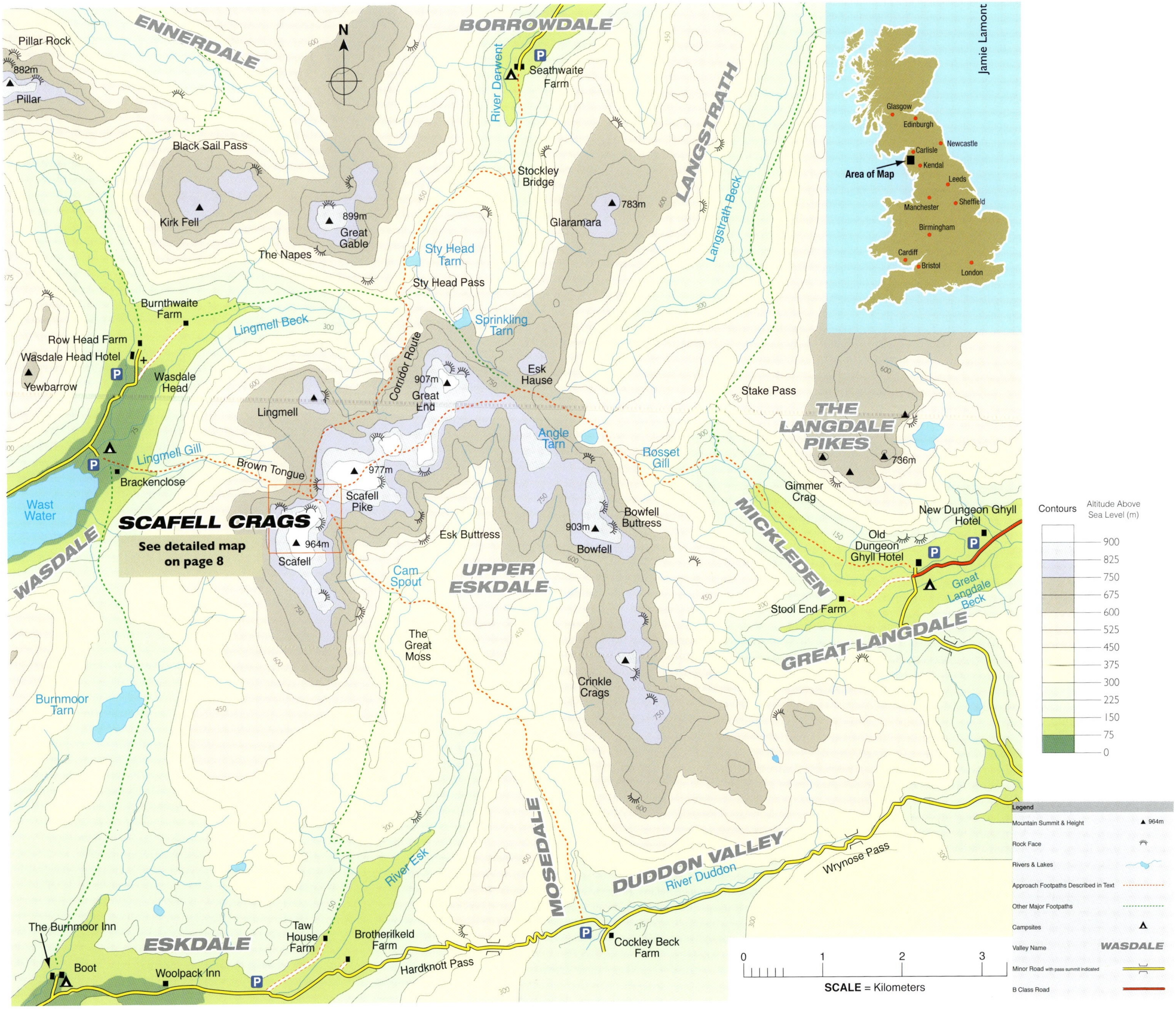

Introduction

A full moon rises above the vertical profile of Scafell Crag.
Photo Al Phizacklea

Scafell

Scafell is many things to many people. It is the highest crag in England, it has the longest climbing history and possibly the most famous route, and some of the hardest lines ever established on a high mountain crag in the country. Scafell is one of those climbing grounds that you either love or hate, it all depends on your personal experiences. Catch the crags on a cold, greasy day when the wind saps your enthusiasm and you may wish you'd gone to a crag within easy reach of a pub and you may never want to return. On the other hand, if you ever catch one of those long days of unbroken sunshine when you romp up three or four routes near the limit of your grade, then you will be taken in by the magic of the place, you will become infected with a yearning to return which lasts a lifetime; believe me. Most climbers will have their favourite crags, Gogarth, Stanage, The Cuillins, but I am writing this book because, for me, my favourite crags are those around Scafell, The East Buttress and the main crag, which is commonly referred to by its most famous route, The Central Buttress. I have known climbers who hate the place, but that is their opinion and I respect that, in return I hope they understand the reasons why I hate Kilnsey. It all depends on your personal experiences. Happily, because my friends and I live fairly locally, we can pick and choose when to visit Scafell, and therefore we have only climbed there when the conditions have been favourable, be it either summer or winter. I've never known a bad day on Scafell!

This is a book devoted to the history of climbing on the cliffs of Scafell. There have been hundreds of books written about climbing and its history in the Lake District. Some have attempted to record the events and characters with respect to the entire area, some detail the personal achievements of famous pioneers, and others are the reminiscences of those famous pioneers. I have found that many of these historical books have either incorrect or misleading references to the Scafell crags, and I hope this volume will be free of errors. Most of the famous ascents on Scafell have been well documented in the past, and Central Buttress springs to mind here. I believe it is the only single route in the country to have an entire book devoted to it, yet there is so much of this history that remains unrecorded. The last time the full climbing history of the Lake District appeared in print was around 1986, when both *A Century on the Crags* and *Cumbrian Rock* were produced to commemorate the centenary of the first ascent of Napes Needle. Bill Birkett's 2006 volume of *Scafell, Portrait of a Mountain* covered the history of climbing on Scafell and Esk Buttress in 12 pages, which covered this area better than any previous work. You will note that by devoting over 300 pages to the climbing history on Scafell we have managed to record more incidents and details, and to allow the contributors to tell of their experiences for the first time. I have tried to mention every route established on these crags in both summer and winter, which may seem tedious when it comes to the minor lines, but they all go together to create the story of this fine mountain.

There is another reason for writing this book, because it is a hundred years since a group of men dressed in tweed and nailed boots first climbed the formidable Central Buttress on Scafell, which was the hardest route in the country at the time and according to some possibly the world. This was achieved at the height of the post-Edwardian era, a time when the future was bright and exciting due to a host of new and amazing inventions that brought revolution to the lives of these people over the previous decade. These developments such as the motor car, radio, electricity, the aeroplane and the telephone created the biggest change in society and social culture since the birth of civilisation. These were optimistic times when scientists believed that any problem presented by the natural world could be overcome by the application of some form of technology.

It was also a time of distinct social hierarchy, with the poor very much at the bottom of the pile with little chance of improving their lot, and the privileged upper class lording it over everyone; and they knew it. It was the time when The British Empire was at its most oppressive height, and Britannia ruled the waves. What great times they were for some.

A typical Victorian scene at the second col of Lord's Rake in heavy snow conditions.

Photo: © abrahamphotographic / FFRCC archive

However, the times, as the song goes, were a-changing. The sinking of the Titanic in 1912 forced a revision of this dream, for the first time those privileged people were forced to recognise that when man was pitched against nature, they were all in the same boat, so to speak. Two other inventions were also improved during these times, but these were not designed to benefit mankind and they cast a deadly dark shadow over the entire globe; these were the machine gun and barbed wire. When these two items were pitched together against flesh and bone, you had a combination that was to change history forever. Amongst the millions that perished in the war that started just months after the ascent of Central Buttress was the pioneer of that very route, Siegfried Herford.

This is more than a historical record of rock climbing; it is a story of achievement, heartbreak and ambition that was played out on this mighty vertical stage. The performers who played their part in the history of this place tell their own story, be it from old written records to recent recordings. I thought I knew everything there was to know about Scafell, but how wrong I was. The research for this book unearthed so many new stories and interesting facts; I hope you enjoy these as much as we did in compiling this work.

The idea for this book was mooted many years ago when I tried to persuade several of the older members of the Fell and Rock Climbing Club to each write a section of the history of Scafell. The common reply was that whilst it was a good idea in principle, it should fall upon the shoulders of a younger and more active member to write, whilst they nodded approvingly in my general direction. I did not set out to write this book single handedly, indeed the thought of spending hundreds o f hours in front of a computer after spending hundreds of hours researching through old books, journals and magazines certainly did not appeal. Spare time for me was precious, it was the pressure of work and a growing family which led me to decline the editor's role for the Fell and Rock guidebooks, and I wanted to spend my time climbing; not writing!

Mark Scott.

It was following a particularly severe accident in the spring of 2008 that I realised that with the prospect of seven months off work, I needed something to stimulate the mind and focus my energies; in fear that I would otherwise go around the bend. So I started to write the history of the crags, starting with the 1980's and 1990's, the era in which I had been involved and knew well. So the history was written backwards from this point, each chapter stepping back in the mists of time, each demanding more research from books borrowed from Doug Elliott and Mark Scott, who both have impressive personal libraries. I then decided that direct research was required, so I embarked on a mission to contact and interview as many of the first ascentionists as possible. This became a fascinating and satisfying part of the work, meeting people who I had only ever read about, getting them in groups and letting the stories flow. I am hugely indebted to Mark Scott for his support with recording these people; he had the right equipment in his capacity of Oral Archivist for the Fell and Rock, and also to his insistence on chauffeuring me in my incapacitated state around the country to meet these characters.

Time has been a cruel mistress to me in regards to the publication date. I originally set a date of 2013 to ensure this book would be released to commemorate the centenary of the first ascent of Central Buttress, probably the most famous route in the country. Therefore I had 5 years to research, write and accumulate photographs, at a pleasantly leisurely pace to prepare this work, but it still ended up being three years late with a mad dash at the end to meet the deadline.

An explanation must be made over the photographs and what influenced their choice of inclusion. It is not possible to illustrate any book that covers the history of climbing without the use of the Abraham Collection. Despite being used throughout many publications, these images are still under the copyright of the family, and we would like to extend our gratitude to Sue Steinberg for permission to reproduce these iconic images. We were also fortunate to be presented with a set of previously unpublished photos from the early years of the twentieth century by Albert Holmes which adds considerable charm to the early chapters. I would also like to thank Roonie Wood-Johnson for use of her father's photographs from the 1920's, and again many of these have been published here for the first time.

I have called upon the likes of Ken Wilson, Bob Allen, Ian Roper and John Hartley to use their classic black and white photographs from the sixties and seventies. More recently, you cannot fail to be impressed by the work of young Ed Luke, who has endeavoured to abseil down the main buttreses in both summer and winter to capture his remarkable images, a labour of love undertaken in difficult conditions.

It was not my intention to photograph every route on the crag, but I believe many of those depicted in this book have never been photographed before, and I was pleased to obtain photos of well known routes from new and unusual angles. Many of the shots were arranged especially to make the best use of sunlight, and I would like to thank those climbers who either put up with my requests, or who tolerated that idiot on an abseil rope when they were embarking on a long-anticipated route.

Some of the first ascent photographs are lacking in clarity and finesse, but they have been included because of their historical importance, certainly not for their aesthetic values. The last thing I wanted was to fill the book with 'bum shots' of climbers taken from the base of Scafell Crag, which seems to have been a common trait with many books including the older Fell and Rock guidebooks, and I hope you appreciate the results.

Iain Small climbing Borderline. This was one of the first routes to overcome the impressively overhanging rock on The East Buttress of Scafell.

Photo: Al Phizacklea

Mike Cocker.

Photo: John Holden

Al Phizacklea.

The chronology of climbing on these crags falls into three distinct phases, each defined by a major change in attitudes of society and within the climbing world. These phases have been subtly defined throughout the book by changing the coloured banding which accompanies the text. There are no formal boundaries between these periods; they just seem to form their own natural progression. The first phase, which encompasses the time between the first cautious investigations around the periphery of the crags to the start of the First World War, is defined by bold climbing with minimal protection methods or equipment. The pioneers of this era were generally professional or well-heeled middle class people, united by a common rule that 'The leader must not fall'. I requested the help of Michael Cocker to write about these early years because he had spent years delving into archive material to research the story and characters from those days, as part of his superb study of the *Wasdale Climbing Book*, (Ernest Press, 2006). There is no-one better qualified to cover that period and I am hugely indebted for his support and assistance.

The second phase, which I have defined between 1915 and 1974, is a time of improving equipment such as rubbers, pitons, nylon ropes, karabiners and early nuts, which ensured a gradual increase in standards on the crags. Socially, climbing became the preserve of the working class, which along with better transportation led to a huge increase in the popularity of the sport. The leading activists of this time were pushing the limits of what was possible and some of these became household names.

It took a shift in the attitude of climbers to define the modern era since 1974, where training and a more professional approach, along with the development of 'modern' gear such as micro-nuts, Friends, chalk and sticky boots allowed the remaining lines on the crags to be developed. Climbing itself became more specialised, with bouldering, winter and sports climbing becoming almost divorced from climbing on traditional crags such as Scafell. It is somewhat ironic that the hardest climbs on these crags have brought us round full circle, where a tremendous degree of boldness ensures the old adage that 'The leader must not fall' is the only way to guarantee a safe ascent. You will notice a subtle change in the style throughout this book. The older material has been filtered from the hundreds of old written sources, old books, journals and newspaper cuttings, and hence it has been written in the third person. Once the history passes the period of the Second World War, the style of the book changes as interviews with living climbers are included, and I have chosen to concentrate on these to tell the story. However, there came a problem when it was the time to tell of my own involvement with the history, in order to maintain a consistent style throughout the section, some of these were written in conversational speech.

I have taken the liberty of selecting the best bits from the recorded conversations with the climbers; in effect the written versions you read are my own interpretations of what they said. I have not altered what was said, just spliced it together in a way that becomes relevant, as many of these conversations rambled about from one topic to another in a random fashion. I apologise to any of those people whom I interviewed if I have misinterpreted their valuable stories.

I would also like to thank the other friends who have contributed to this book, John Moore and Brian Davison require a special mention for their writings that cover the geological and winter climbing sections. Dave Miller, Tony Greenbank, Julian Carradice, Paddy Cave and Chris Bonington have all written some pieces to support this work, while Don Sargeant, Ben Ransom and Jamie Lamont all added some semblence to the hand drawn sketches, maps and crag diagrams that you see. To all those who wrote to me, answered their phones or simply talked to me in the pub, you have all contributed in some small way to make this book as interesting as possible. This is your book, and my final vote of thanks go to you all who are reading these words, because you have all supported this venture by buying a copy.

I hope you enjoy the story.

Al Phizacklea, July 2016.

Ed Cleasby captured on the first ascent of Shere Khan on The East Buttress of Scafell. Note how their inspection abseil rope hangs ineffectively out in fresh air.

Detailed plan on the crags of Scafell.
Based upon satellite photograph and local survey.

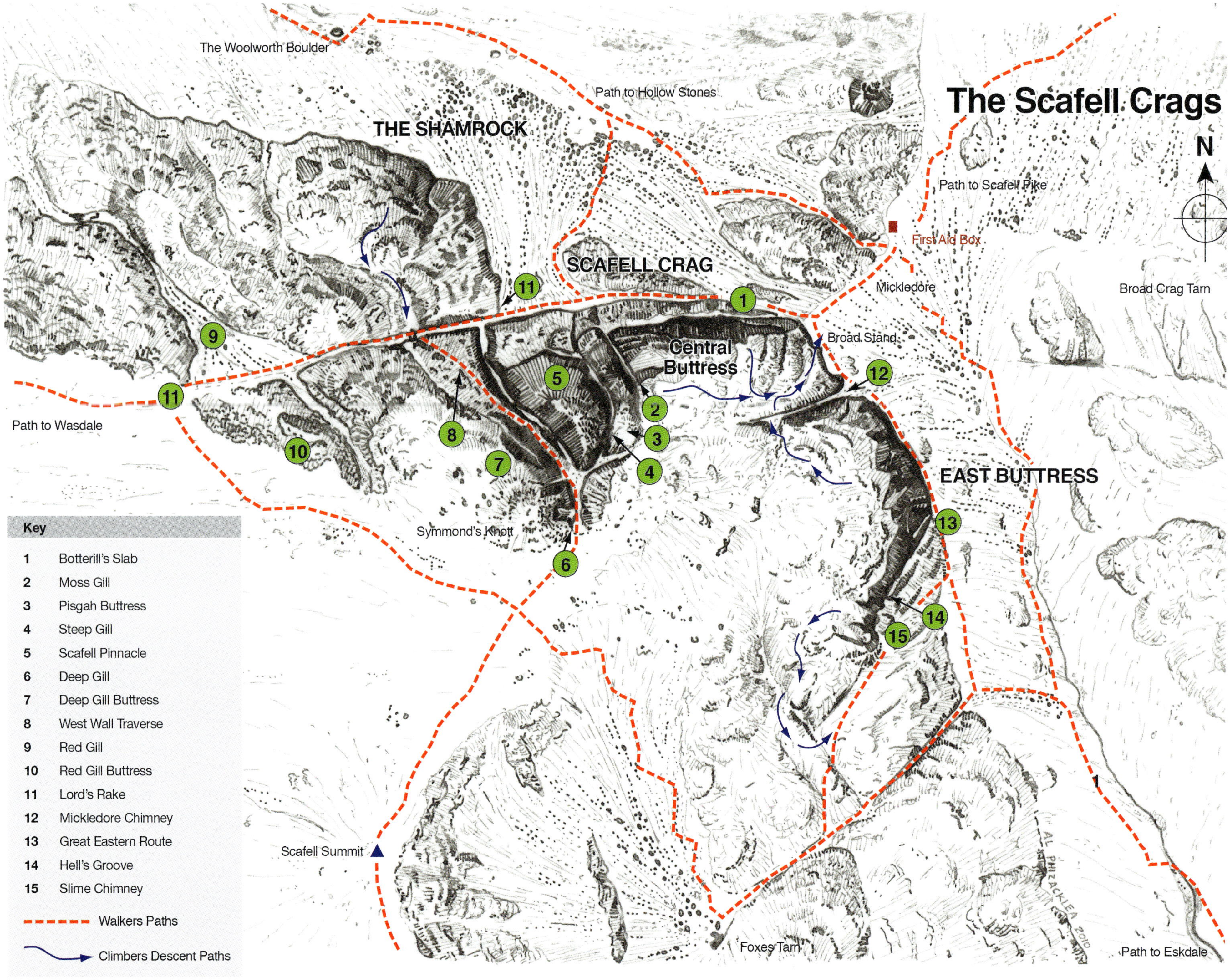

A short walk around the crags of Scafell

Scafell and its crags are located slightly south-west of the central hub of The Lake District, having four main approaches aligned roughly with the four main points of the compass. Wasdale provides the shortest and quickest approach from the west, but this approach is steep and taxing. Borrowdale is the normal starting point from the north, a long walk through interesting scenery. The approach from the east, starting in Langdale, is the longest and most strenuous because the summit of Scafell Pike must be crossed on the way there, and re-crossed on the return. The southern approach from the Duddon is probably the least popular; it is a long, wet, easy walk with a steep finale.

The entire north and east sides of Scafell Mountain are ringed by a continuous line of crags that cannot be crossed without the co-ordinated action of hands and feet. This ring of crags forms a formidable obstruction between the two highest mountain tops in England, Scafell Pike (977 metres or 3210 feet) and Scafell (964 metres or 3162 feet), and indeed it is the most difficult barrier between any two peaks south of the Scottish Highlands. The crags of Scafell force walkers into making long and tiring detours which involve much hard graft due to considerable loss of altitude. A scrambling route, Broad Stand, provides a direct link between the two mountains starting from Mickledore, but it is a serious undertaking for fellwalkers.

The insignificance of man is well portrayed when seen against the backdrop of Scafell Crag.

Mickledore

The narrow, notched arête of Mickledore forms a steep sided col linking Scafell and Scafell Pike, and at 831 metres, or 2726 feet, it is the highest pass in The Lakes, and therefore the highest in England. The height of this col is widely disputed; the old 6 inch maps from the early twentieth century give a spot height of 2666 feet, or 813 metres, whereas Wikipedia gives the height as 840 metres, or 2755 feet. The 831 metre point on the new 1:10 000 O.S. map is clearly at the lowest point of the pass, therefore this should be regarded as the correct height.

Scree on either side of Mickledore is shattered and loose, leaving an unstable and unpleasant final struggle to reach the col, but it is a satisfying moment when reached. For a climber, in fine weather, Mickledore is a superb location with major crags all around. Looking left and down towards Eskdale, The East Buttress curves away in a sweeping mass of overhanging rock; looking right, the main Scafell Crag rises as a plumb vertical wall of over 100 metres height.

The spectacular location of Mickledore has been described as the best place in the country for observing the vertical from the comfort of the horizontal. It is the starting point for a descriptive tour of the Scafell crags.

Mickledore.

Scafell Crag

From the Wasdale approach, the impressive north facing main area of the crag is usually the first section to be seen. Trending right from Mickledore, Scafell Crag starts as a low wall, no more than 8 metres high, running rightwards towards the main mass of the crag. Below this low wall is a continuous ledge system, too narrow and with a considerable drop of steep vegetated rock beneath to make it suitable for walkers. However for climbers it forms the starting point for routes on Scafell Crag with the full height of the crag rising above. Known as Rakes Progress, the ledges rise slightly on leaving Mickledore and then run diagonally down to the foot of Lord's Rake.The first breach in this low wall of crag is a notch forming North Climb, beyond which the crag increases in height and steepness to form a vertical wall still awaiting development.

Scafell Crag (continued)

On its right is the distinctive feature of The Hanging Chimney, after which the crag reduces in steepness to form a stepped recess taken by Collier's and Keswick Brothers' Climbs, with what was originally known as Tricouni Slab to its right. The latter is the first facet of Scafell to follow the most distinct feature of the crag, a series of diagonal breaks set at 65 degrees and forming parallel features across the face. Right again the crag forms a vertical wall, seamed with thin cracks at the same 65 degrees angle. This is the Shadowfax wall which stops abruptly at another major slanting slab, Botterill's Slab, the most distinct feature of the left side of Scafell Crag.

The full extent of Scafell Crag indicating the main features.

Photo: Al Phizacklea

The Central Buttress.

Photo: Al Phizacklea

Scafell Crag (continued)

The magnificent main face then rises to its full height, and it continues in an unbroken wall until the cleft of Moss Gill is reached as a fissure running vertically up the crag and extending deep into its heart. Between Botterill's and Moss Gill, the wall continually overhangs towards its left side, as anyone who has abseiled down Ringwraith can testify, with the rest only slightly off-vertical. The main edifice, like a masterpiece of architecture set directly in the centre of this wall, is The Great Flake - the focal point of the Central Buttress. Close up it seems to be a large structure, and though it extends only one sixth of the height of the crag, its presence is emphasised by the surrounding clean, featureless rock. At the right end of this main face, another series of parallel diagonal breaks slash upwards from their source in Moss Gill. From below these look to be mere crack lines, but each is a distinctive slab, forming the lines of Moss Ghyll Grooves and Slab and Groove.

Beyond Moss Gill the predominant diagonal breaks of the main wall are lost, and the next feature is the tapering, rounded pillar of Pisgah Buttress. The right side of Pisgah ends in Steep Gill, a second dividing gully that is steeper, wetter and looser than Moss Gill, and unpopular, except in a harsh winter.

The main features of Pisgah Buttress and The Pinnacle.

Scafell Pinnacle and Deep Gill

To the right of Steep Gill is Scafell Pinnacle, a wide-based cone which tapers throughout its 80 metre height to a distinct summit called Low Man. This is connected to the higher top of High Man by a sharp ridge, the Knife-Edge Arête. High Man is the summit of Scafell Pinnacle, cut off from the main mountain by a vertical 8 metre slot, Jordan Gap, formed by the upper section of Steep Gill. The lower section of the Pinnacle consists of superb clean slabs sweeping across to end abruptly at their right side, forming a rising arête dropping vertically into a third major gully, the wide, scree filled Deep Gill. The Deep Gill side of the Pinnacle rises up steeply, finally ending in a sunny band of slabs which ascend to the summit of High Man.

Deep Gill forms the only passage through the cliffs that is possible to ascend by walking, although this is encumbered by vast quantities of shifting scree. Deep Gill can be reached from the foot of the main crag by following a diagonal trench rising in the same line as the base of the crag, a feature known as Lord's Rake. This continues in a straight fault-line rightwards across a series of cols for some considerable distance before it merges into the main hillside of Scafell.

Nomenclature

It is interesting to note how the names High Man, Low Man, Shamrock, Pisgah and Jordan Gap are all repeated on Pillar Rock, which was the first crag to have been developed in The Lakes. The names of Pisgah and Jordan on Pillar were first used by the redoubtable pioneer Walter Parry Haskett Smith. He explained this in a letter to Harry Kelly in 1936 when he was in his seventy-sixth year:

"Dear Kelly,
You ask about the naming of these climbs. You must blame me for Pisgah and Jordan. In those days people mainly reached the rock via the fell top and were apt to march up to the former in the belief that it led to the top [of Pillar Rock], but found, like Moses, that Jordan cut them off from the Promised Land." (1)

Naming of features from biblical themes was quite common in the Victorian days. Haskett Smith was the son of a clergyman and he was typical of the well-educated middle to upper class pioneers of those days, and biblical quotes would have been a subtle notification of a good, well rounded upbringing.
In those Victorian days deference was given to the Church and Christian observance, and for example O.G. Jones was reputed to have chastised the Abraham brothers for climbing on the Sabbath! Pisgah was a prominence, or high point, said to be the modern Mount Nebo, to the east of the River Jordan. From its summit, Moses could see The Promised Land where God told the Israelites to settle. First they had the issue of crossing the River Jordan which runs along a deep ravine for much of its length; hence the Jordan Gap. (2)

It is uncertain whether it was Haskett Smith who used these same names on Scafell, or whether they were copied by his contemporaries. However, in the case of Scafell crags, 'The Promised Land' would refer to Scafell Pinnacle. The common use for High Man and Low Man, referring to the highest points of both Scafell Pinnacle and Pillar Rock, and a lower subsidiary top, was probably a similar case of copying the named features from Pillar.

Nomenclature (continued)

High Man and Low Man were once terms commonly used throughout The Lakes, for instance Skiddaw has now lost its High Man label for the main summit, but still retains the name of Skiddaw Low Man for its subsidiary top. 'Man' is an ancient word for an eminence on the side of a mountain, and its best association nowadays is with Coniston Old Man.

The name Lord's Rake is intriguing. The term Rake implies a path which rises diagonally across a steep precipice, which is found in several places in The Lake District, such as Jack's Rake on Pavey Ark and Fisher's Wife Rake on Clough Head. Lord's Rake would suggest it was the best way up created by God, as opposed to a way discovered by a titled person. Religious nomenclature is likely to have been bestowed by one of the early pioneers rather than by the local shepherds or hunters. There is no record of why the feature is named Lord's Rake.

In Green's Guide, the very first guide written in 1815 for travellers in The Lake District to detail passages across the fells, there is reference to the name 'Mickle Door'. This implies the feature was already named by shepherds. 'Mickle Door' means literally Great Door, and 'door' is the local dialect name for a pass, so Mickledore derives from the local naming of the Great Pass between Wasdale and Eskdale. Green then makes a record of the passage up 'Scawfell from the Wastdale side of Mickle Door' by two local men, there was no naming of this way as 'The Lord's Rake'. From this, we can assume that the term 'Lord's Rake' was not used by the locals, at least not in 1815 when Green wrote his guide.

The name of Scafell itself was originally spelt 'Scofell', before being changed to 'Scawfell'. It derives from the Old Norse for Bald Hill, referring to the lack of vegetation on the tops of these fells. It is interesting to note that a local newspaper, The Whitehaven News, used the spelling 'Scawfell' right into the 1960's, whereas the newspaper from Barrow-in-Furness, only 40 miles down the road, has used the name 'Scafell' from the end of the nineteenth century. Locals still consider the inclusion of the 'w' to be the correct way of spelling the name. It is certainly the correct way of pronouncing the name, unlike a reference made recently on the BBC news, which used the awful pronunciation of 'Scay-fell'. Honestly, would expect the BBC to get these things right!

The first col on Lord's Rake was recently the scene of a landslide where a large block fell across the gully bed and came to rest in a precariously bridged position. This gradually became accepted as an obstacle to be circumvented with care by walkers for over a decade, but it collapsed without warning in July 2016 and it now forms an unstable obstacle in the main gully of the Rake. It is too soon to assess whether this can still be used as a passage to access the Deep Gill area of the crag.

An exposed path ascends leftwards from just below the first col of Lords Rake to the upper section of Deep Gill and so avoids the lower steep section of the main Deep Gill gully. This path, the West Wall Traverse, forms a convenient access point for the routes on Deep Gill Buttress. It leads upwards to the highest point of Deep Gill, and eventually emerges on the summit plateau of the mountain. About 80 metres below this exit, opposite the summit of High Man, Deep Gill Buttress rises as a prominent curving arête which forms the line of Upper Deep Ghyll Buttress. On the right is a vicious overhanging prow of excellent rock appropriately called Death Arête. This feature dominates the scene and is formed by the intersection of two major fault-lines cutting across the gully bed and is evident as a narrow slot cutting deeply into the crag, The Great Chimney. The fault-line forming this chimney can be traced across the mountain to where it creates the feature on The East Buttress we call Mickledore Chimney.

Below The Great Chimney, the crag consists of a series of mossy grooves with cleaner rock between, home to Grey Bastion and Xerxes. Continuing rightwards beyond this point leads back to the bridged block in Lord's Rake, and from here the crag lies back in a broken series of easy angled grassy rock of little interest to climbers. A wide shallow gully, Red Gill, separates this from the final area of rock, the easy angled pillar called Red Gill Buttress. From here, the crag merges into the easy western slopes of Scafell Mountain.

The Shamrock

This is the lower buttress of Scafell Crag, lying below the line of Lord's Rake in a structurally supporting role for the main crag. The Shamrock is the poor relation of Scafell as it consists of generally easy angled and grassy rock with wetness often seeping down the routes. However, it steepens towards the left end of the crag where a handful of quality routes lie, but these suffer badly from a veneer of algae. The attractions of The Shamrock frequently entice those unwilling to flog up the final hundred metres of shifting scree to reach the main crag! An often overlooked fact is that The Shamrock actually supports the longest routes on Scafell's crags. The name derives from the early pioneers who noted it was a 'sham', a deceptive buttress which is prominent on the approach, yet had to be passed by to get to the main crag. When pulling over the steep rise of Brown Tongue towards Hollow Stones there is little of the main crag visible, but the 'sham rock' is prominently in view. As with the other features on Scafell, the name was first coined on Pillar Rock, where the early pioneers descended from the main ridge of the mountain into a cove called Great Doup, from where the 'sham rock' was the first section of the crag to be encountered.

Photo: Al Phizacklea

The Woolworth Boulder.

The East Buttress

This magnificent crag lies over on the Eskdale side of Mickledore, and it comes strikingly into view as the col is crossed. The surroundings were beautifully described by Allan Austin, who wrote:

> "The East Buttress of Scafell – the finest crag in the lakes. A great lonely crag. Its walls overhang. Water drips out from the crag instead of down. Greenery is almost non-existent. The sheer bulk of its sweeping grey rock and barrel shape induces in a climber a feeling of insignificance. Massively constructed in iron-hard rock, it possesses a string of the finest lines in the district." (4)

The Woolworth Boulder

Many climbers pause by a large boulder lying at the top of the steep rise above Hollow Stones at the foot of the scree and directly opposite The Shamrock. It is known locally as The Woolworth Boulder but the origin of this name is rather uncertain. It possibly derives from the earlier climbers who used to boulder on here in their climbing plimsolls to get used to the feel of the rock. As most of these plimsolls were obtained from Woolworths stores the name could have been transferred to the boulder. Graham MacPhee sheds a different light on the origin. He wrote, 'Woolworth Nails are made from angle-irons obtained for a penny each at a certain well-known store, hence the name, which has been handed on to a popular boulder in Hollow Stones on Scafell, where the nails were first tried on rock.' (3)
Local guru and previous leader of the Wasdale Mountain Rescue team, Bill Pattinson, once suggested that when seen from above the boulder takes on a 'W' shape along its crest which resembles the 'W'-shaped logo used by the old stores. Any such resemblance seems just a bit too vague to be credible!

Broad Stand

There has been an increase in walkers tackling Broad Stand due to the restrictions on Lord's Rake, and it is well known as being the most formidable obstacle to runners attempting the classic 'Bob Graham' fell-running round of The Lake District. For assistance, support teams often rig a knotted rope down Broad Stand (runners clearly have no qualms over use of direct aid!), but in 2009 there was uproar when three bolts appeared! Bolts on Scafell! On the easiest route on the crag! Once word got around, they were quickly removed by a couple of local climbers, but whoever placed the bolts has never come forward to admit their crime. The bolts had evidently not been placed by anyone with previous experience as they were badly positioned, and one had been placed in a loose block. The finger of accusation was pointed at the fell-running community, but this was adamantly denied to an extent that risked causing serious offence. Even so, there was a clue to identification of the perpetrators of this misdemeanour. The rope left hanging on the bolts was a static rope, a black static rope no less; the type that is commonly used by the military for abseiling. Whoever placed these bolts is certainly not welcomed in the mountains, and it is very much hoped this incident will never be repeated.

Photo: Al Phizacklea

There are very good reasons why Broad Stand is the biggest mountain accident black spot in the country!

From the col of Mickledore The East Buttress starts to drop down leftwards towards Eskdale as a low steep wall. After 20 metres, a narrow gap behind an immense block leads to the only break in this initial section; the stepped scramble of Broad Stand. This is the main descent line from most of the climbs on Scafell Crag and The East Buttress. It may be classified as only a scramble, but Broad Stand in reality contains a move of 'Very Difficult' standard. The pull over the final step is awkward and polished, and it requires the use of a small hold where there is evidence of a once useful hold having broken off. In ascent it can be made to feel easier by removing any rucksack, but in descent it always feels precarious. It is the only breach in the entire crags where an agile scrambler may ascend, but it should not be attempted by walkers with no experience of climbing, as failure can be fatal.

It is acknowledged Broad Stand can be potentially lethal, particularly in greasy or icy conditions. However, when used for descent by climbers, the final drop (and for many, it has literally been their final drop!) can be avoided easily by walking left from its top towards Mickledore, where a large boulder supporting a plethora of threads can be used for a short abseil to easy ground. This is by far the best way of descending to Mickledore in winter.

Thirty metres beyond Broad Stand is the deep cut, mossy fissure of Mickledore Chimney cutting back into the hillside. This fissure actually runs parallel to the line of the main Scafell Crag, and though useless as a climb it defines the right extremity of The East Buttres; the finest crag in The Lakes for climbers operating above the 'Very Severe' grade.

The first major East Buttress feature is the wide, smooth slab taken by Midnight Express, which rises from the foot of Mickledore Chimney. Continuing leftwards there is a series of steep grooves and cracks until the level path below the crag ends at the spectacular protruding arête of Edge of Eriador. Beyond, the path drops more steeply down towards Eskdale, and the character of the crag also changes here. It becomes steeper, initially breached by a series of ramps, until a permanently wet zone around the line of Armageddon, left of which lies the huge overhanging brown wall taken by Siege Perilous. The next features encountered are a series of impressively leaning corners separated by sharp-edged arêtes. The main corner is Lost Horizons with New Horizons and Talbot Horizon on either side, two of hardest climbs in the country

A path follows the scree down towards Eskdale, but a steep scramble up leftwards leads onto a delightful grassy terrace below the left end of the crag. The East Buttress turns thirty degrees south at this point, and the rest of the crag remains in the sun until around two o'clock in summer. The point of this bend in the buttress is taken by the classic Centaur, and beyond this point the lower part of the crag forms a clean wall, drastically overhanging at a measured 25 degrees beyond the vertical, with the only break being the large flake line of Overhanging Grooves Direct. The awesome thin groove of Borderline serves as a dramatic eye-opener to the highest 'Extreme' grades, yet the next breach in this wall gives the more amenable classic lines of Phoenix and Ichabod. Beyond, the steepness continues to guard the base of the crag, but a number of diagonal breaks allows for routes like Morning Wall and Pegasus.

The large corner of Hell's Groove defines the end of the steepness, after which a succession of grooves and chimneys lets the crag peter out at its left end with an easy descent. Beyond The East Buttress, broken ground and scree lead back to the domain of the fellwalker.

The East Buttress in full winter cover, as seen from Eskdale on the day of the first attempt on 'Never Ever say Never'.

Footnotes

1. Walter Parry Haskett Smith, Letter to HM Kelly 1936, FRCC archives.
2. As clarification for those agnostics amongst the readers of this book, the names Pisgah and Jordan Gap come from the 5th book of the ancient Hebrew Bible, since incorporated into the Old Testament under Deuteronomy, Chapter 34.
3. Graham MacPhee, 'Nails', *SMC Journal* 1933.
4. Allan Austin, Ichabod, *Hard Rock* 1974.

The name gill originates from the Old Norse 'gil', which described a steep, narrow ravine or valley, which often included a stream, from which the naming of the stream is frequently suffixed with 'gill'. Its origin is definitely Scandanavian, and can be traced throughout various settlements around the Lakes such as Rosgill and Sadgill.

What's in a name – Gill or Ghyll?

One particular issue has bothered the author since the conception of this book, and that is the spelling of the word gill, or should it be ghyll? Both versions appear in this book, and to the casual reader this may seem a little strange, maybe confusing, and the rules of inclusion are seemingly inconsistent when reading this text.

Many of the routes in the Scafell guidebook were originally spelt Ghyll, such as Moss Ghyll, Steep Ghyll and Deep Ghyll, but they are now spelt Gill. Where did the original spelling originate and why has it changed recently?

It is often thought that the first recorded version of the spelling ghyll was by the Lakes poet William Wordsworth in his poem 'Evening Walk'. This appeared as gill when first published in 1793, but in a later edition from 1820 it had been changed to:

> 'Then, while I wandered where the huddling rill
> Brightens with water-breaks the hollow ghyll
> As by enchantment, ...'

It is thought he spelt it this way to ensure the hard sounding 'g' was used, as opposed to the soft version which would have resulted in something sounding like 'jill'. In those days, that pronunciation of gill was used to describe a quantity of liquid of around two pints, such as milk, which was commonly sold in these measures.

Certainly the local dales men of the nineteenth century would have used gill to describe any ravine in the district. The older O.S. maps, dating from 1860's named every ravine in the Lakes as 'gill', even the famous Dungeon Gill in Langdale was thus named, although the early name for the hotel itself was 'Dungeon Ghyll Hotel'. The early written records by the guide Green, and poet Colderidge, both used 'gill', and even Wordsworth used both versions in some of his later works, so obviously the alternative 'ghyll' was slow to catch on.

It was the influx of the highly educated adventurers and climbers who first introduced the spelling ghyll to the rock features of the area. Looking through the writings inside the *Wasdale Climbing Book* we can see that the early visitors used the local term gill when referring to the feature, for instance the entry from 1869 where T.L. Murray-Browne made a note of a 'remarkable gill which cleaves the rocks of Scawfell, it looks stiff' (Deep Gill). The first recorded use of 'ghyll' in this book was by Hermann Woolley and Charles Hopkinson in 1879 when they referred to 'Piers Ghyll' by this name. Even so, the nomenclature gill was still widely used thereafter; Haskett Smith used the version gill when referring to his original ascent of Scafell Pinnacle from Deep Gill in 1884. Norman Collie was the first to give this feature the alternative spelling of Deep Ghyll in 1891, and in 1892 Collie used the name Moss Ghyll when recording his first ascent, and subsequently this version of the spelling stuck. Even the local statesman farmer John Robinson became influenced by the 'in-crowd' at Wasdale Head, and from 1892 he started to refer to the gills as ghylls.

It is interesting to note that the adoption of the name 'gill' to describe a crag gully occurs almost exclusively to the Scafell area, whereas on The Napes, Pillar Rock, Dow Crag these features are all always named gullies or chimneys even though they were initially developed by the same climbers. You will notice that apart from Hopkinson's Gully (which is not a true gully) there are no 'gullies' on Scafell.

O.G. Jones used ghyll for the Scafell route names in his book *Rock Climbing in the English Lake District* and the only other gullies given the same spelling Ghyll were two on Haystacks and Mouse Ghyll in Borrowdale. The spelling ghyll was used for route names on Scafell for nearly a century until the eighth edition of the Scafell guide when author Al Phizacklea reverted to the original spelling gill for all the routes. He was worried that such improper and unsolicited changes to tradition would have caused a backlash from the old guard, but he actually received no letters or comments of condemnation and, apart from a distant observation by Ken Wilson in the latest version of *Classic Rock*, it passed without comment.

Interestingly, Alfred Wainwright names all the gullies on Scafell with the spelling gill in his fourth fell walking guide to The Lakes, and whilst this book has no influence on the climbing world he was clearly keeping in line with the Ordnance Survey stance which stated back in 1859 that ghyll was 'evidently incorrect and in contrast to all northern glossaries.' Even today, you will only find two streams named with the version 'ghyll' on the four 1 : 25 000 Ordnance Survey maps which cover The Lake District area.

In this book, I have chosen to retain the original descriptions as written, so the spelling ghyll is used throughout when referring to the old routes. To change the historical spelling of the route would necessitate altering the spelling of hundreds of original documents and this would change the spirit of the age, but when referring to the feature itself (i.e. the gully) I have used the correct term 'gill'. Therefore the terms gill and ghyll appear side by side in the text, in reality there is no difference between them and the spelling should be considered to be interchangeable.

Climate and Climbing Conditions

The mighty Scafell crags are at a height above everything else in England, and in addition the nearby farm of Seathwaite is recognised as the wettest place in the country. It is something of a wonder anyone bothered to go at all, but there wouldn't be lakes without the rain! Past generations, especially the Victorian and Edwardian visitors from before The Great War, visited Wasdale on their fixed holidays and they climbed upon Pillar, The Napes and Scafell irrespective of the weather. These early pioneers relished demanding climatic challenges, especially snow and ice, for being the closest they could find to enable them to practice under Alpine conditions. In those days there was no such notion as the crags being 'in condition', they took things as they came - wet, greasy or frozen – it was simply climbing to them.

Scafell and The East Buttress as viewed from the Three Tarns, Bowfell.

The modern climbing activists seems to have outgrown the older traditional upbringing amongst the mountains involving roaming around the fells or climbing classic easy lines in bad weather, possibly because in older times that was it; there was nothing else to do!

Nowadays climbers are raised on warm, dry walls, they travel extensively to Europe or further afield to climb on sunny, bolt-protected rock, and they prefer the clean, cosy and friendly outcrops and edges to practice their sport. A stage has been reached whereby, for many, climbing on high mountain crags is an alien activity. Excuses include cold, windy and wet weather, and greasy rock, and climbing in anything less than perfect conditions that means either a big reduction in standards or a hard, frightening struggle, and in reality it is usually both. The first time a route, any route, receives an ascent each spring, the climber will encounter a fine veneer of algae on the rocks, which makes it feel slippery and insecure. Climbing in poor conditions on the high crags is not for the faint-hearted. It appears true that the big crags are becoming dirtier and more vegetated, and there are several reasons; the lack of climbers, global warming and the reduction in atmospheric pollution are amongst the most frequently cited theories. It is not that there are less climbers today, indeed there are many more as compared with thirty years ago, it is just that for the top echelon, climbing bolted rock is an easier way to get publicity and recognition in the sport's magazines. In the future, there needs to be a cultural shift to turn climbers back to the big naturally protected crags. Older generations tell of days out climbing before the 1980s, when the big crags were popular and there were frequent queues for the classic routes. Nowadays it is rare to see more than two or three teams on Scafell on a fine day, the long walk keeping the riff-raff at bay. This may be better for the locals(!) but it is a sad reflection of modern attitudes.

Climbing on these high crags has evolved into two distinct factions, winter and summer. Winter climbing is notoriously unreliable and it can take place under a huge variety of conditions, which are outlined below. Large snowfalls take some time to consolidate before the gullies are firm enough to climb, although some of the buttress routes such as Pisgah Buttress can be exciting under heavy snow.
The author was part of a team that decided to attempt Moss Gill on a day of atrocious weather, where the forecast warned people not to venture into the mountains due to storm force winds. We wanted to experience a true epic and we got one; the retreat down a constantly avalanching gully and the blinding spindrift put an end to any further desire for challenging conditions.

Photo: Laurence Monkton

Climbers on the lower part of Moss Gill (left) and on pitch 3 of Pisgah Buttress (right).

A harsh prolonged frost enables the ice to form, but temperatures that are too low often locks the water at its source so the build-up can be limited and the ice becomes brittle. The best conditions are a frost at night and a slight thaw through the day, this allows a constant trickle of water to freeze and build up the best ice for climbing. The crag can look spectacular when coated with a rime of hoar frost. It may look in condition but this is often misleading as the frost breaks off easily leaving only the bare rock to climb. The best condition the author has encountered on Scafell was following a brief warm front that passed through during a cold spell. This plastered the crag with slushy wet snow that quickly froze into a mantle of solid ice that covered the entire face, brilliant for delicately front pointing up the rock, but these are rare conditions indeed.

Many climbers visit the crag year after year hoping that the right conditions have formed, but judging by the many tales in the past of the legendary 'East Buttress icefall', these are very rare. The one that forms below Armageddon has been described to the author as being a huge column of ice, as thick as an old tree and one that you could walk right around. No-one who has the equipment or ability to tackle such a feature has ever seen this form to such an extent. It's probably a once in fifty year formation, and perfectly illustrates the fickle nature of winter conditions, but when they are good, the rewards are fantastic and the memories last a lifetime.

For the rock climbers, the wait for good conditions and dry warm rock can be just as frustrating. A good week of fine, breezy weather is required to ensure the crags will be dry and, with the exception of the major drainage lines, much of The East Buttress is well known to come into condition quickly. The East Buttress can be strange as it appears to dry off in the mid-summer morning sun, but then there can often be small areas of dampness that start to trickle again once the sun goes off the crag. A good example of this type of seepage affecting a route was the fall by Martin Berzins from The Siege Perilous. The line had been dry when he cleaned the route in the morning, but later when he was climbing the wetness came as a surprise and he fell earthwards at the usual velocity.

On the main crag, Botterill's Slab, protruding away from the main body of the crag, is the first to dry out, as do the lower slabs of The Pinnacle. The slowest regions to dry are generally the grooves that see little sun; White Wizard, Leftovers and Xerxes are typical of the lines that unfortunately harbour the most tenacious lichens.

Scafell Pinnacle and Deep Gill in misty conditions.

The best advice for visitors to Scafell is to try and choose a time to coincide with a spell of good, clear weather; somewhat unrealistic but weather forecasts have improved recently. Also it is of no comfort for those on fixed holidays, or who have booked accommodation in the area making it just pot luck. Experience over the past few years indicates that the best time to climb on Scafell is during the spring months with statistics confirming the period between late April and mid-June to be the driest. Following this, the summers generally detriorate to coincide with the height of Lakeland's tourist season, this perception is usually reinforced when there is a long settled period of fine weather in September.

Weather records show that Sprinkling Tarn, 4 kilometres north of Scafell, has an average annual rainfall of 196 inches (about 5 metres!) whilst Keswick, about another 15 kilometres distant, only experiences an annual rainfall of 55 inches (1.5 metres). This does not mean the Scafell region gets more than three times as many wet days as Keswick, but it demonstrates how when it rains up on the fells, it really does rain. The floods of December 2015 saw 13½ inches (341mm) of rain falling at Honister in 24 hours, an almighty drenching that caused widespread flooding and chaos in Keswick, Cockermouth, Kendal and Carlisle. A similar downpour in 2009 was referred to then as a 'once in a thousand year event', how wrong they were, it has happened twice in six years. Clearly the people of Cumbria and the Environment Agency have their work cut out in future years, especially if this provides proof for the theory that rainfall will become heavier as a result of climate change.

When assessing rainfall records from the 1940's, it is as well to know how Bill Peascod and Bill Rushworth used to leave the Scafell Hotel in Rosthwaite and wander up the fells to top up the rain gauges with their 'processed' Jennings beer!

Severe thunderstorms can occur at anytime of the year but they are most likely to be encountered in the summer months. A particularly violent thunderstorm occurred in August 1958, causing an astonishing rainfall rate which was estimated at 6 inches (152mm) per hour over the central Scafell area! Masses of fresh scree were literally flowing down the fells, gouging out gullies and causing flash floods that re-shaped the beds of the local becks, and there are tales of boulders weighing over 50 tonnes being shifted by washout during the storm! Luckily, such events are extremely rare.

Joe Griffin was once caught by a tremendous thunderstorm as he was taking a novice up Botterill's Slab. He witnessed a most unusual phenomenon, and recalls:

> "We were two thirds of the way up the route when I noticed these large black clouds coming fast towards us from over Pillar, but this was so unusual because they were approaching against the wind. We were soon enveloped by this enormous electrical thunderstorm, the likes of which I have never experienced before, it was worse than the Alps. There was lightning striking all around, boom, boom, and the air was filled with a gunpowder smell of breaking rocks, it was so violent, and the downpour was relentless. We managed to find shelter below a small overhang near the top, but I was glad we didn't get to the top, as I later learned that Gof Francis was killed by lightning on Pillar by the very same storm". (1)

Dave Birkett also recalled the excitement of being caught in one of these sudden storms. He described this in his usual animated manner as:

> "I remember back in 2004 when I did Borderline and Ichabod with Mary on one of the hottest days of the summer, when this huge thunderstorm broke and it pissed it down. We sheltered under Lucius which was the driest place, but unfortunately my camera packed up because there were three huge waterfalls pouring over the lip of the crag, and it was fantastic!" (2)

Rainfall

When we hear weather reports informing us of 'six, eight or twelve inches of rain' in a 24 hour period, have you ever paused to consider what that means? Take The Lake District as a whole. It covers an area of 2292 square kilometres. That's 2292 million square metres. If there has been an average rainfall of say six inches across this entire area (which is 152mm, or 0.15 metres), then the volume of water falling on the ground is an astounding 343.8 million cubic metres. That's 343.8 million tonnes of water, enough to fill 1.6 Olympic-sized swimming pools every second, all of it falling from the sky. If we placed all this rain in a water tank that covers a full square kilometre (The size of a single square on an Ordnance Survey map) the water tank would have to be 344 metres high – that's 1125 feet – which is more than twice the height of Blackpool Tower, (if I can be forgiven for using this tourist landmark as a standard measuring unit). As the people of Keswick and Kendal know, this has to flow past their houses to reach the sea, the sad fact is that during these spells of heavy rain some areas cannot cope with the devastating results.

If this is what you see when you look over your shoulder at the end of the day, you've had a good day.

On the topic of good-weather-only climbers, Dave Birkett admits to frustration at the attitude of some of the top performers. He held forth with:

> "I met two good climbers who'd been trying Welcome to the Cruel World, but had failed to do the moves, and they said they didn't want to come back to have another go. They said it was wet, but there's like a little hole that weeps, and I've never been there when the bottom's been dry and you've got to avoid that section by being half a move to the right. I think people just search for so many excuses not to climb. These things are hard, and you've also got to be prepared for disappointment. Just going up to the crag is part of the day, I can walk up to any mountain crag and if it's wet I've still had a good day because I have enjoyed the walk, whereas other people would see it as a wasted day. No, a lot of people find excuses like its green or wet, but that's the nature of the crags, especially Scafell Crag, they're always a bit wet or green and if you wait for perfect conditions then no one will do them. Too many climbers are number orientated, and they think there's no glory if you fail on an E5 on Scafell. Well take Ringwraith, it's such a bloody fantastic pitch, and it's a shame to give these things numbers because it's all about the fight, and if you fight and fail its better than not fighting at all.

> "When I did Ringwraith it was a fight, but it was a fight I wanted to win and I really had to put the effort in, it felt like climbing an E7 on sight. It bothers me when people go on about poor conditions because it shows their inexperience of what these places are going to be like, you know. You've got to adjust your climbing style to suit the conditions; these crags are not climbing walls and they never will be climbing walls. People don't want to fail on things, but British climbing is a big day out, walking up to Scafell takes a lot of effort and when you get back down and driving home you're really tired, but you've had a bloody fantastic outing." (3)

Dave Birkett's commentary endorses the sentiments hinted at with the Introduction. The Scafell crags are unequalled in their provision of top grade quality climbing of character and for delivering stimulus to those prepared to apply themselves; those who wish to fight on a route, and those who are not afraid to fail. Such climbers will gain the greatest satisfaction and get the best from Scafell.

Footnotes

1). Joe Griffin, FRCC audio recording 2008
2). Dave Birkett, FRCC audio recording 2008
3). Dave Birkett, FRCC audio recording 2008

The Wood-Johnson family larking about on the Packhorse Bridge behind The Wasdale Head Inn.

Wasdale Head

The tiny community of Wasdale Head which lies at the head of the Wasdale valley in West Cumbria has changed little over the past century and a half, since it first came to the notice of the mountaineering world. The area can only be reached by car along a single track road that runs alongside Wast Water, but despite its relative remoteness the valley can be reached in an hour and a half from the motorway.

There used to be 7 farms at Wasdale head; Row Foot farm was converted into the hotel and three small farmsteads at Down-in-the-Dale were uneconomical and were amalgamated into the remaining valley head farms, the buildings being demolished in the 1930's. There are now only 3 working farms in the valley head, Middle Row, Row Head and Burnthwaite. The community supports a church, St. Olaf's, which is reputed to be the smallest in England. It is said to be over 1000 years old and the roof beams are reputedly from a Viking long ship. There may well have been an original church that was founded around that time, but there is no record of a place of worship in the valley before 1550. The church we see today was restored into its current layout in 1892.

The tiny building (which now supports the visitor's toilet block) was originally a school which opened in August 1888. It was regarded by the school inspector as 'isolated, absolutely necessary and probably the poorest we have', as the school fees were only 1 penny a week. There were so few children in the valley that this closed in 1931, by which time cars were reliable enough to transport the three remaining pupils to the nearest school at Nether Wasdale. This school was itself closed due to lack of pupils in 1935, and following this the children attended the school at Gosforth.

There are two recognised campsites, a small field adjacent to the inn and the larger National Trust campsite which is found closer to the lake and which has full facilities including a small shop.

Then and now - these two photographs, taken over 100 years apart illustrate how little change there has been at Wasdale Head since the days of the Victorian pioneers. In both views, the Wasdale Head Inn is behind the trees on the right of the picture. You will note that the path leading to Sty Head across the lower slopes of Great Gable is very noticable on the Abraham picture. This has been enhanced by marking up the negative of the shot.

Photo: © abrahamphotographic / FFRCC archive

Photo: Al Phizacklea

The tradition of the Wasdale Shepherds' Meets goes back for hundreds of years, where farmers used to gather together to buy, sell or exchange tups (rams) to prevent inbreeding of their flock, and to exchange sheep that had strayed from their heaf. (These upland grazing lands are rarely defined by physical boundaries; the sheep naturally confine themselves to the valley. This is passed down through generations of lambs, so the grazing pastures, or heafs, become ingrained into their way of life.) The main meet is always in October, which was in time for the ewes to be tupped in November, and there was a smaller gathering in the spring to return the tups to their owners. These were important social meetings for the farmers, who rarely met together under one roof, so there was plenty of ale and 'tatie pot' suppers consumed. (Before the Huntsman's Inn was opened, the gatherings used to take place at one of the farms. It was a fine from the local magistrates for selling unlicensed alcohol in 1851 that prompted Will Ritson to apply to convert Row Foot farm into an inn.) The modern meet is still celebrated as the Wasdale show, but the emphasis is now centred more on sheep judging, hound trailing, fell running and of course the beer tent!

The most disturbing aspect of life in Wasdale is the almost parasitic influx of those taking part in the Three Peaks Challenge. They cause disruption with traffic at all hours of the day, create noise, litter and excrement in abundance but contribute little or nothing to the local economy or welfare. The local Mountain Rescue teams are kept busy (read 'out of their beds') throughout the summer nights to assist those who require it but, despite receiving donations from the fundraising, one team member confessed "We don't need their money, what we want is some peace in our lives." To finish this section I will paraphrase Sansom's famous poem and bring it up to date with 'There's nowhere as unquiet as Wasdale when spring comes up the dale'.

Sheep judging is still the most competetive aspect of the Wasdale Show for the farmers, whilst the direct ascent of Kirk Fell presents the most punishing and challenging of all the fell races.

Taken late in a summers evening, this picture shows scores of three-peak eventers heading up Brown Tongue towards Scafell Pike and certain nightfall before they return to Wasdale. The author noted that few of them seemed to be properly equipped or prepared for such an eventuality.

The field system of Wasdale Head as seen from Yewbarrow. The farm, upper left, is Burnthwaite Farm and the dark clump of trees (lower centre) is St. Olaf's Church. Note the field clearance cairns to the right of the farm.

The Walls of Wasdale

Few visitors to Wasdale Head will fail to notice the rambling nature of the field boundary walls which form a unique arrangement across the dale head. These follow no pattern and they seem to have evolved in an organic manner due to their lack of straight lines, and their substantial girth, up to 10 metres wide in places, make these a remarkable sight. Similar walls exist across other valleys in The Lakes, but none dominate the landscape in such a noticeable manner as do the walls of Wasdale Head. These walls are the result of a millennium of hard field clearance work. The first settlers to Wasdale were the Vikings and in those days there would have been little flat grassland, there would have been a mixture of bog, reed and boulders similar to what still exists higher up the valley bottom.

There wouldn't have been lots of boulders; there would have been millions of boulders. At first, the surface stones would have been dug up and moved to create a better grazing potential for their livestock. These stones would have been piled in heaps which are now recognised as the field clearance cairns and these would have been scattered in a rather random pattern across the valley. There would have been little planning or organisation of these, the cairns are there simply because there was no mechanical assistance and the stones would have been carried by hand or cart, so the least distance you move stones the better. Over generations, these would have evolved into the massive mounds that form the basis for the thick blisters in the current wall layout. The settlers would have also discarded more stones in lines between the existing cairns and thus formed the basic footings for the drystone walls we see today, the random patterns being a result of some whim of a man in the field over 1000 years ago.

Once the surface had been cleared, any attempt to plough the land for crops would have brought another carpet of stones to the surface. Again these would have been cleared by hand and added to the walls, this process would have been repeated each time a patch of land was ploughed. Full scale field ploughing as we see today would have not been possible; the ground would have been too rough for that. The fields would have been ploughed in sections, at maybe 10 or more year intervals over the centuries. Even after multiple ploughings of the same piece of ground, stones still rise to the surface, and clearing these has been part of farming life ever since. The author recalls his youth on his farm near Ulverston, when he assisted in the obligatory clearance of the fields after ploughing; the stones were picked by hand and placed in heaps, to be cleared by loading them onto a trailer. These stones seem to emerge from the ground even though the same field had been ploughed and cleared dozens of times in the past. This laborious work is rarely carried out on modern farms these days; it is a task that is difficult to mechanise and it is too expensive to conduct this work manually.

Farmer Wilson ploughing the fields between Middle Row and the church, circa1928.

Wasdale Head from Lingmell
The three white buildings in the middle distance are from left to right: The Wasdale Head Inn, (Formally the site of Row Foot Farm); Middle Row Farm and Row Head Farm, which was often known as Row Farm by the early climbers. The building in the left foreground is the old vicarage and the cluster of yew trees on the right obscures St. Olaf's Church. Burnthwaite Farm lies 400 metres further up the valley off the right side of the photograph. The valley in the background is Mosedale, which leads up over Black Sail Pass to Ennerdale for Pillar Rock, and eventually continues to Buttermere via Scarth Gap Pass.

These huge field clearance cairns are a unique feature of the Wasdale valley.

This is a detail of the 1: 10, 000 O. S. map from 1861. The only changes to the valley are that the building cluster at Down in the Dale have been demolished, and the course of Lingmell Gill was re-routed in 1920 using German prisoners of war.

Note the old course of the beck which ran through Lizaholme Wood, this is now the location of the National Trust campsite.

1802 - 1880

The Romantic Vision (Early Scrambles)

Portrait of Samuel Coleridge from 1795.

Overleaf:
Mickledore and Broad Stand.
Photo: Al Phizacklea

On Thursday morning 5th August 1802 a man in his late twenties, with a knap-sack on his back and carrying a broom handle for a fell pole, set off from Wasdale Head to climb Scafell. He had spent the previous night at Burnthwaite Farm and was on his way to Eskdale. It was a bright day with clear summits but cloud was gathering to the west, threatening rain later. He walked down to the lakeshore, followed the trail to Burnmoor Tarn and clambered up the easy angled slopes to the summit where he found a sheltered spot and sat down to write a letter. "Surely," he wrote, "the first letter ever written from the summit of Sca'fell." Around 3:00pm he started looking for a direct way down to the col at Mickledore and, quite by chance, struck upon practically the only line of weakness in the steep band of cliffs that run for almost half a mile in either direction. He gave himself a serious fright but managed to complete the descent, inadvertently making the first recorded rock climb in The English Lake District. His name was Samuel Taylor Coleridge, already an acknowledged poet, but at the time he was struggling with his writing and his marriage and, despite his relatively young age, was afflicted with a variety of physical ailments and already addicted to opium. In a bid to escape these problems and wanting to explore the surrounding mountains he had left his home in Keswick the previous Sunday and embarked on a nine day walking tour; a journey that, for the period, was unusually adventurous and probably unprecedented.

Just a few decades earlier The Lake District, in common with other mountainous areas, had been viewed with disdain and suspicion. The enclosure of common land, changes to traditional forms of agriculture and the rapid expansion of industry and urbanisation, had prompted a re-evaluation and new appreciation of the natural world. No longer to be feared and tamed, this was now regarded with awe and wonder. Influential and effective communicators of this new aesthetic were the Romantic poets Coleridge and his friend William Wordsworth, who were amongst the very first to walk the fells for pleasure and inspiration. Coleridge, in particular, was drawn to the steeper ground and plunging waterfalls, well away from the established paths, where the experiences sharpened his perception and "intensity of the feeling of life". Shepherds and dalesmen had occasionally ventured onto the crags to rescue stranded sheep or to collect birds eggs, but not for sport. Coleridge was, in all probability, the first recreational scrambler.

The line that Coleridge used to descend from Scafell is known today as Broad Stand, a rock climb graded Difficult that has been the scene of a number of serious accidents over the years. Coleridge was lucky to get through unscathed, for there is no indication that he had any prior knowledge that a way could be found. At one point, after hanging from his hands and dropping down several short sections of vertical cliff onto ledges below, he suddenly realised that he was totally committed, unable to return and barely able to control his fear. He left an account of the descent in a continuation of the letter he started on the summit:

> "There is one sort of Gambling, to which I am much addicted… It is this. When I find it convenient to descend from a mountain, I am too confident & too indolent to look round about and wind about 'till I find a track or other symptom of safety; but I wander on, and where it is first possible to descend, there I go - relying upon fortune for how far down this possibility will continue. So it was yesterday afternoon. I passed down from Broad-crag, skirted the Precipices, and found myself cut off from the most sublime Crag-summit, that seemed to rival Sca'Fell Man in height, and to outdo it in fierceness. A Ridge of Hill lay low down, and divided this Crag (Called Doe-crag) and Broad-crag - even as the Hyphen divides the words broad & crag.

"I determined to go thither; the first place I came to, that was not direct Rock, I slipped down, and went on for a while with tolerable ease - but now I came (it was midway down) to a smooth perpendicular Rock about 7 feet high - this was nothing - I put my hands on the ledge, and dropped down - in a few yards came just such another - I dropped that too - and yet another, seemed not higher - I would not stand for a trifle - so I dropped that too - but the stretching of the muscles of my hands and arms, and the jolt of the Fall on my Feet, put my whole Limbs in a Tremble, and I paused, and looking down, saw that I had little else to encounter but a succession of these little Precipices - it was a Path that in a very hard rain is, no doubt, the channel of the most splendid waterfall. - So I began to suspect that I ought not to go on but then unfortunately tho' I could with ease drop down a smooth Rock 7 feet high, I could not climb up it, so go on I must and on I went, the next three drops were not half a Foot, at least not a foot more than my own height, but every Drop increased the Palsy of my Limbs - I shook all over, Heaven knows without the least influence of Fear, and now I had only two more to drop down, to return was impossible - but of these two the first was tremendous, it was twice my own height, and the Ledge at the bottom was so exceedingly narrow, that if I dropt down upon it I must of necessity have fallen backwards and of course killed myself. My limbs were all in a tremble - I lay upon my Back to rest myself, and was beginning according to my Custom to laugh at myself for a Madman, when the sight of the crags above me on each side, and the impetuous Clouds just above them, posting so luridly and so rapidly northward, overawed me. I lay in a state of almost prophetic Trance and Delight - and blessed God aloud, for the powers of Reason and Will, which remaining no danger can overpower us! …I exclaimed aloud - how calm, how blessed I am now - I know not how to proceed, how to return, but I am calm and fearless and confident … [after further contemplation on his situation] - I arose, and looking down and saw at the bottom a heap of Stones - which had fallen from abroad - and rendered the narrow Ledge on which they had been piled, doubly dangerous - at the bottom of the third Rock that I dropt from, I met a dead sheep quite rotten. This heap of stones, I guessed, and have since found that I guessed aright, had been piled up by the Shepherd to enable him to climb up and free the poor creature whom he had observed to be crag fast - but seeing nothing but rock over rock, he had desisted and gone for help - and in the mean time the poor creature had fallen down and killed itself. As I was looking at these I glanced my eye to my left, and observed that the Rock was rent from top to bottom - I measured the breadth of the Rent, and found that there was no danger of my being wedged in, so I put my knap-sac round to my side, and slipped down as between two walls, without any danger or difficulty - the next drop brought me down on the Ridge called the How. I hunted out my Besom Stick, which I had flung before me when I first came to the rocks."

On reaching safe ground Coleridge collected his stick and, in a state of high elation, hurried on down Eskdale where he stayed the night with John Vickers Towers and his family at Taw (Toes) House. Although the nomenclature is a little shaky and the height and number of drops appear slightly exaggerated, there is little doubt that the line Coleridge followed was Broad Stand.

Some researchers have cast doubt over the authenticity of this account, citing the exaggerated number of drops described and Coleridge's desire to impress his reader Sarah Hutchinson. It is easy to understand this uncertainty because today Broad Stand is generally known to refer to the initial 12 metres of scrambling above the Eskdale side of Mickledore, and there are only two large steps to negotiate. Coleridge actually starts his description from much higher, from the ridge immediately behind the top of Scafell Crag, and thus the initial part of his account are of the upper rocks, he only starts to descend the true Broad Stand from the point where he describes 'but of these two the first was tremendous, it was twice my own height' which perfectly depicts this point. We don't know for certain if Coleridge described his descent to Towers, but this seems probable and can be inferred from his notebook, which records that Towers confirmed that the pile of stones at the bottom of Broad Stand had been made by a shepherd trying to free his sheep.

The line depicted is the usual descent down Broad Stand from the top of Scafell Crag. The exact line of Coleridge's descent cannot be determined, but any deviation to the line above leads over difficult ground, perhaps Coleridge took a more direct descent?

Broad Stand in the early 1900s; it starts up the right-hand vertical slot known as 'Fat Man's Agony'.

Climber - George Abraham.

There is no suggestion that Towers or Thomas Tyson, Coleridge's host at Burnthwaite the previous night, knew anything about a direct route between Scafell and Mickledore, and it appears likely that it was Coleridge's account to Towers that evening that drew their attention to it, for sometime in the early years of the nineteenth century, tradition has it, Towers and Tyson made an ascent of Broad Stand together. The only record of this appears in William Green's *The Tourist's New Guide* (1819):

> "The Crags on the south west [of Mickledore], though seeming frightfully to oppose all passage, have been ascended as the readiest way to the top of Scafell, and, amongst other adventures, by Mr Thomas Tyson, of Wastdale Head, and Mr Towers, of Toes."

It is not clear if the Towers that Green mentions is John Vickers Towers (1746 - 1817) or his son Thomas Towers; much depends on the year of the ascent and Green gives no clue to this. The account also suggests that there were other ascents of Broad Stand. For the shepherds this would have saved a long detour round either side, and once established one can imagine the route developing into something of a sporting challenge for the bolder and more agile amongst them.

William Green was a surveyor and artist from Manchester who moved to Ambleside in 1800. He developed an interest in fell walking and his delightful two-volume *The Tourist's New Guide* included the first descriptions of the high fells. One of Green's regular walking companions was Jonathan Otley, a clockmaker from Keswick and the author of another guide: *A Concise Description of the Lakes*, first published in 1823. Otley's book ran to several editions and was the first to unequivocally state that Scafell Pike was the highest mountain in England:

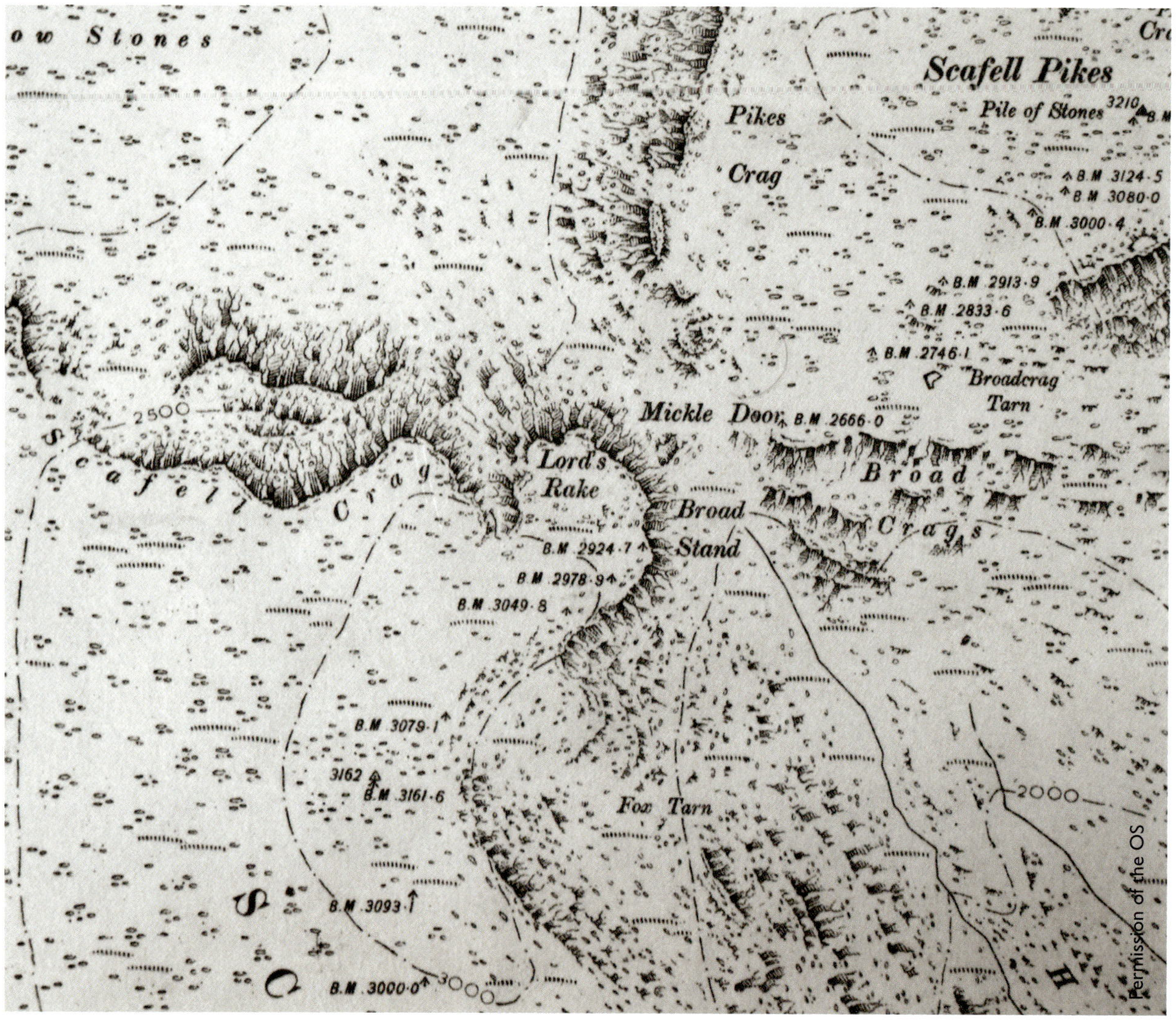

Sample of the 6" to the mile OS map from 1861 which covers the Scafell Crags.

"Scawfell is the name that has generally been given in maps, to the mountains connecting the heads of Borrowdale, Eskdale and Wasdale. It is the highest ground in all this mountainous district and indeed in that part of the united kingdom called England. The several lofty peaks by which it is distinguished are known in the neighbourhood by different names.... The lower of these points, lying to the south-west, is a bulky mountain - the proper Scawfell; the higher raising from a narrower base, has been called the Pikes [or High Man]. For want of a designation sufficiently explicit, strangers have sometimes been mistakenly directed to the secondary point; and to cross the deep chasm of Mickle Door, by which they are separated, is a work of considerable difficulty; although the direct distance does not exceed three quarters of a mile. Latterly however it seems by common consent, the highest point is called Scawfell Pike; and since the erection of a large pile and staff upon it in 1826, there is no danger of mistaking the place."

Green's guide contains an account of an excursion made by Otley and Edward Birkett, the latter a local guide and fisherman, on 7th June 1815. The pair left Keswick at five in the morning and, after breakfasting at Rosthwaite, walked over Scafell Pike to Mickledore and then continued:

"for some distance in the direction of Eskdale, to a deep fissure, through which they scrambled to the top of Scafell and thence descended to Wastdale Head."

The "fissure" they ascended might be taken to be Mickledore Chimney, but Haskett Smith, when writing about this in *Climbing in the British Isles: England* (1894), thought it "more likely that this was another and easier gully a good way further down". This feature would be the wide gulley that leads to Foxes Tarn. Interestingly there are no other obvious breaks in the crags of The East Buttress and it is not clear where Otley and Birkett went. Nevertheless, the present writer is inclined to agree with Haskett Smith in thinking it unlikely that they ascended via Mickledore Chimney, based on the fact that Green emphasised the distance they descended towards Eskdale and that there has never been any tradition suggesting this course was taken at such an early date.

Knowledge of a direct route between Mickledore and Scafell may, indirectly, have stimulated interest in the virgin summit of Pillar Rock, which was first ascended by John Atkinson, a local shepherd, in 1826 and repeated later the same year by three others, one of whom was W. Tyson of Burnthwaite Farm at Wasdale Head. These early ascents of Broad Stand and Pillar Rock, although marking the start of rock climbing in The Lake District, were essentially isolated incidents and only loosely connected with the emergence and development of an organised sport more than 60 years later.

In the early nineteenth century the only other way up the Scafell Crags was via Lord's Rake. This is not a climb in the same way that Broad Stand is, but a straightforward scramble up a scree shoot. The first ascent is unknown. Men like Tyson, Towers, Otley or Birkett may have ascended it, but, equally, it could have been done centuries earlier by an adventurous shepherd or fox-hunter. It is first mentioned in the *Penny Magazine* for 1837, when an anonymous tourist and shepherd took this course on their way to Eskdale, the writer telling us that the "shepherd was very proud of having brought me through the Lord's Rake, and the people much surprised. It seems to be rather a feat in the country."

Charles Baumgartner (1), an Oxford graduate of Swiss extraction, was one of the first people to seek out and climb the more challenging features on British mountains. He made the first recorded traverse of the Crib Goch Ridge, in Snowdonia, in 1848. Two years later, he visited Wasdale Head and stayed at Row Foot Farm, owned by Will Ritson. On 28th August 1850 he made the fourth ascent of Pillar Rock and a few days later the first known tourist ascent of Broad Stand.

Burnthwaite Farm, Wasdale Head, the home of W. Tyson in 1826. The farms at the head of Wasdale all took in visitors with bed and breakfast accommodation. This would have provided much needed income in the late 19th century.

Charles Baumgartner

A brief account of these climbs appeared in a local paper:

> "Great as the number of tourists visiting the wild and magnificent scenery of Wastdale Head and neighbourhood within the last few years, we have heard of but one who has ascended the Pillar Stone on Ennerdale Fell… The same gentleman, a few days afterwards,… ascended Scawfell Pikes, when he climbed the Broad Stand, a rocky and dangerous precipice, situated between Scawfell and the Pikes, an ascent which is perhaps more difficult than even that of the Pillar Stone."

The only outsider who may have preceded him in the ascent of Broad Stand is Professor John Wilson who lived at Elleray, near Windermere. Wilson was a Professor of Moral Philosophy at Edinburgh University who used to write critical and satirical articles under the pen name 'Christopher North'. He was friendly with Wordsworth and Coleridge and other Lakes poets and often used to stay at Row Foot Farm with Will Ritson, where he enjoyed taking part in the local field sports. Edmund Hodge, in *Enjoying the Lakes* (1957), writes that Wilson "learned from the shepherds the scrambling route up Broad Stand and ascended Scafell from practically every direction". Whilst he doesn't indicate when these events took place, they must have occurred before Baumgartner's ascent as Wilson died in 1854. Exactly when the name Broad Stand became associated with the direct route between Mickledore and Scafell remains obscure but it was clearly well established by 1850. Haskett Smith thought the title a misnomer for there are a number of other places in the surrounding area with names that include the word 'stand', which, he believed, indicates "a large grassy plot of ground awkward of access". He suggests that the name Broad Stand would originally have referred to the substantial grassy platform above the difficult section of the climb, that is also reached by Mickledore Chimney and North Climb, and that the oldest and best known route erroneously became associated with the name of this feature. The first time the name Broad Stand appeared in print was when a local paper used it to report Baumgartner's ascent.

Photo: FRCC Archive

The Huntsman's Inn from 1870. Note the barn on the right already had 'Post Horses' painted above the door.

The establishment of the railways and improvement in road conditions in the mid nineteenth century made access to The Lake District much easier. Visitors from the surrounding towns started to come regularly for day trips or short holidays and fell walking grew steadily in popularity as attitudes to mountains changed. Around 1856, in response to the increasing number of visitors to Wasdale Head, Will Ritson acquired a license to sell alcohol and added an extension to Row Foot Farm, which he opened up as the Huntsman's Inn.

Will and Dinah Ritson, hosts of The Huntsman's Inn.

The Wasdale Head Inn

Originally this was a small farm called Row Foot. Around 1856, in response to an increasing number of visitors to the valley, the owner, Will Ritson, acquired a licence to sell alcohol, although it is likely that his father and grandfather, being well in with the local smugglers, had been doing this illegally for years. Ritson built an extension to the southern end of the farm buildings and started providing basic accommodation, food and beer. He re-named it the Huntsman's Inn, which quickly acquired a reputation as a lively and hospitable venue. Ritson also owned the adjacent Row Head Farm which he rented to Tom and Anne Tyson, who, sometime in the early 1870s, established this as a guesthouse. This rival concern was teetotal but equally popular with a reputation for good home cooking.

Will Ritson and his wife Dinah retired in 1879 and the business was taken over by Dan Tyson, who changed the name to the Wastwater Hotel. Tyson was an easy going tolerant landlord who became well acquainted with the pioneer climbers, although he had no interest in the sport himself. Around 1890 the hotel was substantially rebuilt resulting in what is essentially its present day layout. The current entrance hall and dining room are in the same position and similar in appearance to how they would have been in the 1890s.

This establishment quickly acquired a reputation as a lively and hospitable venue and in the years to come would play an important part in the development of the sport of rock climbing. Ritson, or 'Auld Will', as he was generally known, knew the surrounding hills intimately and would occasionally act as a mountain guide for visitors, but he had no interest in rock climbing and usually tried to dissuade tourists from attempting it.

The Alpine Club was formed in 1857 and, although the majority of its members, most of whom lived in London or other large cities remote from The Lake District, had no interest in British mountains, an enlightened few began to make occasional visits to The Lake District for some 'off-season' practice, finding, in the winter months, that the snow covered domestic hills could provide a comparable, although shorter, experience to that in the Alps. At first they simply walked up the mountains, or climbed them on their steeper sides or by the narrow ridges, where they could get practice in step-cutting. By the start of the 1870s they were beginning to turn their attention to the easier and more obvious gully lines; initially because these offered practice in Alpine snow-craft, but later because they had shape, identity and technical interest.

In 1859 Professor John Tyndall and an unnamed friend spent a week walking in The Lake District and, on 19th April, crossed Mickledore and ascended Broad Stand when it was partially covered in snow and ice. They had spent the previous night at one of the farmhouses at Wasdale Head (he omits to mention which one) and had been given some general directions by their host. Tyndall, a prominent scientist and one of the leading lights in the Alpine Club, published an account of this holiday in *The Saturday Review* in which he suggests that the correct line up Broad Strand was not easy to identify although once embarked he didn't find any significant difficulty.

> "We tried the cliffs at one point, reached a platform, rounded a crag, and found ourselves upon a ledge with smooth vertical walls above and below us. We retreated and tried at a neighbouring point. The mountain was broken into rocky ledges, from the edge of which long icicles hung like stalactites, while stalagmitic heaps lay upon the ledges beneath them. These we were obliged to remove to render our footing secure, but, this being once effected, the danger was very trifling. Fifteen minutes effort carried us over all serious difficulty; and the ascent afterwards, though steep, and sometimes demanding both hands and feet was perfectly easy... To any ordinary cragsman it presents a pleasant bit of mountain practice, and nothing more."

The visitors' books from the Huntsman's Inn still survive and it is in these that some of the earliest records of scrambling and climbing in the area are to be found. In 1869 T.L. Murray Browne, a London barrister, and his brother W.R. Browne, an engineer from Kidderminster, both members of the Alpine Club, left a significant note drawing the attention of climbers to the challenge posed by Deep Gill and Scafell Pinnacle:

> "Aug. 1869. The attention of mountaineers is called to a rock on Scafell on the right (looking down) of a remarkable gill which cleaves the rocks of Scafell and descends into Lingmell Gill. It looks stiff."

During their stay the brothers climbed "Scafell by the direct route from Mickledore" [Broad Stand] and Pillar Rock, but, as far as we know, did not attempt Deep Gill or the Pinnacle, although they were clearly interested and capable. Three years later, in August 1872, they made the first, but ultimately unsuccessful, attempt to climb the north facing cliffs on Lliwedd, in Snowdonia.

The Wasdale Head Inn

The old smoking room was on the left of the entrance and on the far side of this used to be the billiard room, where various gymnastic and acrobatic feats were performed by the early climbers as well as the game unique to Wasdale Head called Billiard Fives. There were two baths but only one was plumbed in and visitors often found it easier to wash in the Mosedale Beck. If the weather was poor the whole place would be filled with the odour of drying garments.

The Wasdale Head Inn today. Photo: Al Phizacklea

When Dan Tyson retired in 1901, John Ritson Whiting, Will Ritson's great nephew, took over the business. Whiting retained the relaxed atmosphere of his predecessors and employed a French mountain guide, Joseph Gaspard, in the winter months to take visitors climbing and help with the running of the place. Up until the First World War the hotel was one of the main focal points of British mountaineering. During the 1920s and 30s it continued to be a popular venue with climbers, but its position was diminished as other climbing centres developed and alternative types of accommodation became available.

Whiting retired in 1951 and the hotel was sold to William Wilson Pharaoh who continued to run it until 1974 when Edwin and Carolyn Hammond bought the business. The property was substantially refurbished and the public bar extended in 1977, the same year that mains electricity was brought to Wasdale Head. Around 1980 the name was changed to the Wasdale Head Inn, ostensibly to be consistent with the OS maps which had always shown it as an inn. In 1999 the hotel was acquired by it present owners who are very conscious of its place in British mountaineering history. It remains a popular venue with walkers and climbers.

North or Penrith Climb.

In the same year, 1869, Major John Ponsonby Cundill of the Royal Artillery climbed a route on Scafell that later became known as North or Penrith Climb. There is no surviving record of the ascent and all we know is that he left a stick in the deep crack that was subsequently found by Oxford University reading party member, Christopher Cookson, in August 1884. The climb starts a few yards right (when facing the crag) of Mickledore Ridge and it is likely that Cundill made the ascent in the erroneous belief that this was Broad Stand. George Seatree and Stanley Martin, who lived in Penrith and made the second ascent on 12th September 1874, made the same mistake. With no detailed description available, Seatree and Martin failed to locate the true start to Broad Stand and took the easiest and most direct line they could find and only later discovered that this was a separate route. The pair were staying at Burnthwaite Farm and that evening went to the Huntsman's Inn where they described their ascent to Will Ritson, who received the story with incredulity, declaring in broad Cumbrian:

> "There's nobbut ya way up't Scaafell Crags that's be't Broad Stand on't Essgill [Eskdale] side of Mickledoore ridge an nowt but a fleein thing could git up't crags on't Wasdale Head side. Nivver neahbody hed gitten up theer, and neahbody nivver wad."

Seatree published an article describing this climb in the *Cumberland and Westmorland Advertiser*, which was later reprinted in pamphlet form:

> "From the ridge we traversed a ledge of grass covered rock [Rake's Progress] to the right, until we reached a detached boulder, stepping upon which we were enabled to get hand-hold of a crevice six or seven feet from where we stood. To draw ourselves up so as to get our feet upon this was the difficulty; there is only one small foot-hold in that distance, and to have slipped here would have precipitated the climber many feet below. Having succeeded in gaining this foothold, we found ourselves in a small rectangular recess, with barely room to turn round. From here it was necessary to draw ourselves carefully over two other ledges into a small rift in the rocks, and then traverse on our hands and knees another ledge of about eight feet to the left, which brought us nearly in line with Mickledore Ridge. From here was comparatively smooth sailing."

The route became known as Penrith Climb in recognition of Seatree and Martin's ascent. Seatree, when reminiscing about his climbing exploits in the 1870s, recalled that there were no details or published information available about climbs and that each party had to find its own way. He also commented on how difficult it was to find any companions willing to spend whole days on the hills and that for youngsters living in the area fear of the unknown and parental disapproval were still major deterrents. The name North Climb was first coined by C.N. Williamson who, presumably unaware of the other title, "for want of a better name", used it in his two-part article "The Climbs of The English Lake District", which appeared in the November 1884 issue of the magazine *All The Year Round*.

C.W. Dymond made the first ascent of Mickledore Chimney, around 1869, and wrote a description of this that was included in Herman Prior's *Ascents and Passes in the Lake District*:

> "Pass the fissure leading to Broad Stand, and continue descending steeply for two minutes, which brings you to a narrow gully in the rock with a thread of water trickling down it over moss. This is the Cheminée to be ascended: it is very steeply pitched, rather wet and slippery, and needs to be climbed with care, especially at one or two points where a slip might result in a fractured limb. Near the top, the gully is effectively blocked by two flat slabs of rock wedged in a fissure a little overhead, and impending so much that the only alternative is to climb out of it by the rock which is about 12 feet high, the lower six vertical and the upper a steep slant. This, which can only be scaled à la chimney-sweep is exceedingly difficult, as is also the gymnastic feat of escaping to terra firma from the narrow shelf on which the shoulder-and-hip-work lands you. Assuming the obstacle overcome you are on the broad grassy slope mentioned in the last ascent [Broad Stand] and will proceed as there indicated, following the course of the upper gully from which the chimney descends."

Dymond climbed Pillar Rock in 1866 but aside from this nothing else is known about him, although an archaeologist with the same name drew the first accurate plan of Castle Rigg stone circle and it may have been the same individual.

In the 1870s Alpine climbing was beginning to enter a new phase. All the major peaks had been climbed and there was a move towards guideless climbing and new ascents up previously unclimbed ridges and faces. At the forefront of this were Charles and Lawrence Pilkington, from Lancashire, and Richard and William Pendlebury, from Liverpool. All four were also regular visitors to The Lake District; the Pilkingtons in particular attributed much of their success in the Alps to having wandered regularly over the Lakeland fells at all times of year, especially in the winter months. At this time, upper middle-class distaste for publicity and any behaviour that might appear boastful meant that most left no record of their mountaineering activities, and it is possible that some of the easier gullies and more exposed scrambles, the first ascents of which are now attributed to a later generation may have been made during this period. There was also a widely held view that to put even the briefest account of a climb on record was to deny those that followed the experience and excitement of exploratory mountaineering. They wanted the crags to retain their mysteries, and for those that came later to be able to uncover them for themselves.

The main objective of a mountain day was still the summit or perhaps several summits; any features - gullies, ridges or faces - taken on the way were seen only as areas of interest and not normally as objectives in their own right. In the early days in the Alps the lines of ascent were mainly made on snow and although there were sometimes unavoidable sections of rock climbing it was a minor part of the activity; the concept of scaling a rock feature as a worthwhile objective in itself had yet to be discovered. So although no rock climbing as such was yet being attempted in The Lake District, there was a growing awareness that, aside from the standard test pieces of Broad Stand and Pillar Rock, problems of mountaineering interest could be found on the cliff faces even when the hills were not snow covered.

This then was the level at which mountaineering was being practiced in The Lake District at the beginning of the 1880s. The events of the previous eighty years were a necessary prelude, both technically and psychologically, from which the separate activity of rock climbing was to emerge.

Footnotes

1) Baumgartner lived and worked in Australia for a number of years but returned to Wasdale in the 1880s when he climbed with Walter Parry Haskett Smith and John Robinson. In 1907 he was made an Honorary Member of the newly formed Fell and Rock Climbing Club.

George Seatree (1850 - 1928).
An early visitor to Wasdale, he climbed regularly with John Robinson and Walter Parry Haskett Smith.

Looking up Mickledore Chimney.

Scafell Crag in winter.

1881 - 1888

An Age of Iron (The First Rock Climbs)

Walter Parry Haskett Smith.

Frederick H. Bowring. Bottom: John Maitland

Photo: © abrahamphotographic / FRCC Archives

Previous page: Richard Hargreaves, Mike and Pippa Cocker on top of Low Man, Scafell Pinnacle after an ascent of Slingsby's Chimney. Hargreaves is the great grandson of the first ascentionist, Cecil Slingsby. Photo: Al Phizacklea

Will Ritson retired in 1879 and Dan Tyson took over the licensed premises and changed the name from the Huntsman's Inn to The Wastwater Hotel. Tyson was to witness the birth of rock climbing and, until his retirement in 1901, played host to the men and women who invented and shaped the sport. He was an easy-going, tolerant man who also had an interest in the Row Farm Guest House.

Walter Parry Haskett Smith made his first visit to Wasdale Head in the summer of 1881, when he was twenty-two years old, studying classics at Oxford and already acknowledged as an outstanding athlete. He had been asked by friends to choose the location for a university reading party and, after acquiring a map of Cumberland, had selected Wasdale because it appeared to be the remotest place that had an inn. They spent a month at the Row Farm Guest House, a temperance establishment adjacent to the inn, where they met Frederick Bowring, a barrister and veteran hill walker with an encyclopaedic knowledge of the fells. Bowring was almost sixty years old, but, despite the age difference, Haskett Smith found they had much in common. In the mornings the students read Plato and Aristotle; in the afternoons Bowring took them for long walks on little known tracks well-away from the main paths. No real climbing was attempted that summer, but years later, when writing Bowring's obituary, Haskett Smith acknowledged the pivotal role that he had played in introducing him to the hills and more particularly to the concept of gill scrambling and seeking out the lines of weakness on crags that might provide sporting interest (1).

In September 1881 Frederick Bowring, John Maitland (a London architect of a similar age) and another unnamed companion made the first recorded traverse of Rake's Progress on Scafell Crag and the first recorded descent of Deep Gill via the West Wall Traverse. Maitland sent the following report to the *West Cumbrian Times*:

> "After getting well past the foot of that portion of the Lord's Rake visible from Mickledore, we turned sharply to the right between some grass covered rocks, and then going left, stepped onto the ledge leading directly up to the Mickledore ridge. The first part was easy enough; but very soon care and caution became the order of the day, and though all three of us had climbed the Pillar Rock, and two of us several times, we found the 'Rake's Progress' (as a barrister watching the climb from below happily named it - running as it does from Lord's Rake to Mickledore) VERY MUCH more difficult. On our right shoulder rose the vertical face of Scawfell, while to the left there was a steep descent of 50 or to 100 feet. Still the ledge was wide enough for those accustomed to crag-climbing; and with alpenstock in the left hand, and grasping all available bits of rock with the right, we slowly accomplished three-fourths of the climb and arrived at the hardest part, where stands up some twenty high, a pile of detached blocks, with a truly formidable look. However, by passing the right hand, between the blocks, and the vertical wall of Scawfell, and grasping most firmly, while freely using both knees and feet in turn, we attained its summit, and from its centre found a thinnish slab of rock standing up edgeways. We passed between this and the cliff on our right, and felt the great value of the alpenstock in the left hand, as it enabled us to descend slowly, but safely, to the main ledge, along which we soon travelled to Mickledore. On the first two occasions I had passed under this pile of blocks; but, though more arduous, I think to go over safer, and have so gone the last three times.After the Rake's Progress, we found the familiar Broad Stand unusually easy, and were soon on the grand crags forming the northern summit of Scawfell. We then for the first time descended into Deep Ghyll - a wonderous place with the most glorious perpendicular cliffs on all sides - and steering left came out, as I expected, on the first limb of Lord's Rake."

This is a good example of the kind of adventurous scrambling that was being practised in the era immediately prior to the discovery of rock-climbing. The party carried alpenstocks for clearing away loose rock and earth and to improvise as the occasional handhold, but didn't use a rope.

It is clear from the article that the name Rake's Progress dates from this ascent and that Maitland had already made four earlier traverses. It also indicates that their descent of Deep Gill was made by the line that would later become known as the West Wall Traverse and that this was the first time any of the party had been there. This is the earliest recorded passage of Deep Gill; what we don't know is if Maitland or his companions had knowledge of any other climbers having preceded them.

In late March 1882 large quantities of snow fell and Deep Gill was filled to the extent that all the normal obstacles were buried. Taking advantage of the unusual conditions Arnold Mumm and John King made a direct descent of the gully without experiencing any difficulty. They were staying at the Row Farm Guest House attending an Oxford University reading party. The visitors' book shows that Mumm stayed from 22nd March to 7th April, the others to 13th April. Mumm was an experienced mountaineer having already spent several summers climbing in the Alps. This was his second vacation at Wasdale. During his earlier visit, at Easter 1881, he had rather recklessly descended Mickledore Chimney when it was covered in snow and ice, wearing ordinary boots without nails and carrying a walking stick - the first recorded descent. This time they came armed with ice axes, but it never occurred to them to bring a rope for they were mainly interested in finding steep slopes of snow and ice upon which to practise step cutting and glissading. Later in life Mumm took part in expeditions to the Himalayas, the Canadian Rockies and the Mountains of the Moon. King became headmaster of Clifton College, Bristol.

Sometime during the early months of 1882 Charles Pilkington, Lawrence Pilkington and Eustace Hulton made the first ascent of Deep Gill when it was in winter condition. This undertaking would have remained unknown had Ashley Abraham, who had presumably been told about it by one of the first ascent party, not recorded it in a brief editorial note in the *Fell and Rock Climbing Club Journal* (1908); the only detail being that "wintry conditions prevailed and an hour and a half was taken over the second pitch". There is no record of the Pilkingtons' visit, but Hulton signed the guest book at Row Farm on 8th April 1882 so the climb may have been made a few days after Mumm and King descended the gully. The only gullies known to have been ascended in winter, prior to this, were South Gully on Bowfell (1870) and Cust's Gully on Great End (1880), although an obvious feature such as Deep Gill could have had earlier, unrecorded, winter ascents.

In August 1882 Haskett Smith returned to Wasdale with his brother Edmund. He stayed for nine weeks and during this time made the first ascents of Central Gully on Great End, North Gully on Bowfell, Great Gully on Pavey Ark, North West Gully on Gimmer Crag, West and Central Jordan Climbs on Pillar Rock and what he described as a 'piecemeal' ascent of Deep Gill on Scafell Crag, climbing individual sections on different days. What distinguished these from earlier climbs is the attitude in which they were approached: they had no utilitarian value, were not intended to provide practise for the Alps or greater ranges and were not merely distractions on the way to the summits; these climbs were seen as interesting and worthwhile objectives in themselves and it is this new perspective that marks the beginning of the sport of rock climbing in Britain.

A party descending Deep Gill, the lower figure is cutting steps in the snow.

View looking up Deep Gill from Lord's Rake, 2010.

A bronze effect resin statue of Walter Perry Haskett Smith as commissioned by the FRCC to commemorate the centenary of his first ascent of Napes Needle. The statue stands 31cm high, and it is thought to be the only one made of a Lake District climber.

Courtesy of Mark Scott.

A team cautiously traversing into Deep Gill along the West Wall Traverse.

Haskett Smith went to the Pyrenees the following year and didn't return to Wasdale until the summer of 1884. During this visit he and Oxford colleague Christopher Cookson made the first summer ascent of Deep Gill as a continuous climb.

In summary, the history of Deep Gill, as far as we know, is that the first descent by the West Wall Traverse was made by F. Bowring, J. Maitland and one other in September 1881; the first ascent in winter conditions by C. Pilkington, L. Pilkington and E. Hulton in early 1882; the first descent in winter conditions, by A. Mumm and J. King in late March or early April 1882; and the first complete ascent (in summer conditions) by Haskett Smith and C. Cookson in late August or early September 1884.

In the summer of 1884 Fredrick Bowring introduced Haskett Smith to John Robinson. Robinson was a 'statesman' or yeoman farmer who lived at Whinfell Hall near Lorton. He was a devout Quaker with a deep love of nature and a comprehensive knowledge of the fells. Robinson was unusual in that he was one of the few local inhabitants who showed an interest in climbing and had already ascended Pillar Rock. It was an important meeting for their combined knowledge, natural ability and shared outlook was a major influence in shaping and accelerating the development of Lakeland climbing over the next few years.

On Monday 1st September 1884 Robinson walked from Whinfell Hall to help Haskett Smith move an injured climber, Michael Petty (2), from Burnthwaite Farm to the road head where a carriage was waiting, using a wheelbarrow to transport him as this was the only means of conveyance available. Petty was a medical student from Edinburgh and had made the first ascent of the short cleft immediately left of North Climb, a variation known since as Petty's Rift, before taking a serious fall from the Broad Stand area a few days later. After assisting Petty, Robinson and Haskett Smith walked up to the Napes together and, having inspected Napes Needle, made the first ascent of Needle Ridge.

On 3rd September Haskett Smith made the first ascent of the High Man on Scafell Pinnacle, or Scafell Pillar as it was generally known then, and built a cairn on top. He climbed solo up the short side from Jordan Gap and had to reverse the route to descend because he didn't have a rope or any other means of assistance. He left the following account in the hotel visitors' book:

> "The Scafell Pillar. This rock, which for the last year or two has attracted a good deal of attention from climbers, and has by some been considered to be inaccessible, bears a striking resemblance in structure and cleavage to the larger and better known Pillar in Ennerdale. It forms with its two summits one side of the fine ravine called Deep Gill which owes to it much of its amazing rock scenery. It is readily got at by turning to the right after ascending from Mickledore by any one of the usual ways - The Broad Stand, The Chimney (now becoming better known) or the Penrith Climb on Rake's Progress... Here, as in Ennerdale, there is a 'Pisgah' from which the summit is almost within jumping distance but in order to be duly appreciated the rock should be viewed from Deep Ghyll or from the second summit. It was climbed by a gentleman staying at this Inn on Wednesday last - probably a first ascent since above the foot of the rock no signs of previous attack could be detected of course no ropes or other illegimate means were resorted to.
> W.P.H.S. "

Haskett Smith doesn't describe the way he went, perhaps thinking that this was obvious as any other approach would have been much longer and more committing. It was his first climbing entry in the hotel visitors' book, although he had left earlier ones in the visitors' book at Row Farm, and it marks a deliberate shift away from the earlier reticence, made with the specific intention of leaving a record that would be of interest and assistance to other like-minded individuals. The pejorative tone of his qualification "no ropes or other illegitimate means were resorted to" gives an insight into the way climbs were approached at this time; i.e. un-roped, in nailed country boots, often encumbered with a fell pole or ice axe. Haskett Smith later wrote that when he first started climbing he didn't have a rope and was inclined to "scoff at those who had", believing their use to be a form of cheating that enabled bad climbers to go where none but the best had any business to be. Ropes didn't come into general use in British climbing until the end of the decade.

The Pinnacle, High Man from Jordan Gap. John Robinson guiding two clients up the short side of The Pinnacle, which is the route line first climbed by Haskett Smith in 1884. Note the lack of any belay by Robinson.

John Robinson.

Photos: © abrahamphotographic / FRCC Archives

This is the Knife Edge Arête first climbed by Haskett Smith and Robinson. This famous photograph by the Abrahams shows evidence of tampering during the printing - the gap between the Pinnacle and the hillside behind has been enhanced, as can be seen by a modern photograph of the same point with climber John Holden.

Later that month, on 20th September, Haskett Smith and John Robinson made the first ascent of Scafell Pinnacle via Steep Gill and the Low Man. It was the second overall ascent of the Pinnacle and the first to approach it from the long side overlooking Hollow Stones. Haskett Smith left details of their ascent in the hotel visitors' book and John Robinson left the following account in the book at Row Farm:

> "Yesterday in company with Mr. W.P. Haskett Smith climbed from the 'Lord's Rake' end of the 'Rake's Progress' straight up to the top of the 'Pinnacle Rock' of Scawfell, being the second recorded ascent of this Rock, the first ascent was made by W.P.H.S., Esq., some weeks ago by the short 'slab' route near the top by which way we descended. You enter our climb of yesterday about 60 yards from the (? North) end of the 'Rake's Progress', a slight detour to the right hand lands you at the foot of a steep, narrow gorge, up which no difficulty is experienced to a height of about 300 feet, you are then faced by a 150 feet of almost perpendicular chimney in which the holds are small, but sound as far as they go. Arriving at a point, where the chimney is lined with rotten moss, a few careful steps to the right bring you out onto a broad ledge, pass along about 20 yards onto the arête, which leads up to the 'Pinnacle' rock above. A short scramble from this point lands you on the lower summit of the Pinnacle Ridge from which you look down a perpendicular wall into 'Deep Ghyll'. Here we built a good sized cairn of stones. Nothing now remains but a good scramble up a very steep arête to the top, where you observe a cairn built by W.P. Haskett Smith on his first ascent from what may be called the Pisgah Rock and Pisgah Gap side, a few weeks ago. This name is rather a good one, as the resemblance to the Pillar Rock 'Pisgah' is striking. The climb up the latter part of the arête is charming, as the holds are splendid in comparison to the previous experience in the chimney below. On the top you will observe in a hole in the cairn a bottle, in which to deposit visiting cards. To descend from here into the Pisgah Gap there is no great difficulty, as the holds, if not numerous, are sound.
> J.W. Robinson, Whinfell Hall, Cockermouth."

In his climbing diary Robinson noted that there was rain and mist when they were ascending the main chimney, which they christened 'Steep Gill', and that the whole climb took them two and a half hours. Fred Jackson and Haskett Smith's brother Edmund watched the ascent and joined the climbers at the top, after which they all descended Mickledore Chimney and returned to the valley via Piers Gill.

It is apparent from Robinson's records that some of the current nomenclature - Pisgah, Pisgah Gap and Steep Gill - date from this time. The line they discovered is rarely, if ever, climbed today, but it is still included in the Scafell Guide, mainly for historical interest, and graded Mild Severe. It was an exceptionally bold and technically difficult undertaking for the time, especially when one considers that they were climbing into the unknown without a rope or any effective means of retreat on terrain that held a good deal of loose and vegetated rock.

Photo: © abrahamphotographic / FRCC Archives

Steep Gill, an early ascent. The leader is in the narrow 'Perpendicular Chimney' as described by Robinson. The first true ascent of the entire Gill was by Hermann Woolley, who soloed it in 1888.

Cecil Slingsby.

Deep Gill. The climbers are on O.G. Jones' variation to the second pitch, which follows a very difficult slab, thus avoiding the awkward chockstone cave. Jones climbed the first ascent of this variation on Christmas day 1896 in the company of a Mrs Hill.

A.H. Stocker (who made the first ascent of the West Buttress of Lliwedd, in Snowdonia, in 1883) made the second ascent with C. Bragg on 17th August 1885. Hermann Woolley made the first direct ascent of Steep Gill solo, following the crux chimney directly to the Jordan Gap, on 15th May 1888. He probably did this accidentally, unintentionally overlooking the point where Haskett Smith and Robinson traversed out of the gill to reach the Low Man and arête leading to the summit. Woolley's note in the visitors' book at the hotel says that the portion which lies above the main chimney is not to be recommended "as it is very steep, and the rocks for the most part covered with moss". In November 1884 C.N. Williamson (3) gave a significant impetus to the sport when he published a lengthy two-part article, "The Climbs of the English Lake District", in the popular magazine *All The Year Round*. This was the first comprehensive survey of rock climbing in the area and included detailed route descriptions for most of the existing climbs. It was a welcome source of reference for the few who were already active and, more significantly, stimulated an initial interest in many of those who were later to become enthusiastic and well-known climbers themselves. Williamson's articles became a sort of textbook for mountaineers visiting Wasdale, for prior to this the only sources of information on climbing were the accounts of how to climb Pillar Rock and Broad Stand in Prior's *Ascents and Passes in the Lake District*, the notes in the Wastwater Hotel and Row Farm visitors' books, occasional pieces in local newspapers and contact with other climbers.

William Cecil Slingsby was a Yorkshire squire and textile manufacturer closely related to two other mountaineering families; the Hopkinsons and the Tribes. He started walking and scrambling in his teens and by the mid-1880s had acquired considerable mountaineering experience in Norway and the Alps. In March 1885 Slingsby attempted to climb Deep Gill in winter conditions, but failed on the first ice-glazed chockstone. He returned the following year and, on 28th March 1886, and with better conditions, made a successful ascent with Geoffrey Hastings and J. Mason. Unaware of the earlier ascents Slingsby wrote a two-page account of this climb in the visitors' book at the hotel and a couple of months later published a paper in the *Alpine Club Journal* entitled "A New Ascent on Scaw Fell":

> "After a couple of hundred steps had been cut in the snow in Lord's Rake and at the bottom of Deep Ghyll, we reached the first block - a large rock perhaps 15 feet square, which overhangs the ghyll and so forms a cave. Below the rock the snow was moulded into the most fantastic shapes by occasional water drips from above. At the right hand of the big rock a few small stones are jammed fast between it and the side of the ravine, and they afford the only route up above the rock... Hastings and I got on the stones... He then stood on my shoulders and, by the aid of long arms and being steadied by me, he reached a tiny ledge and drew himself up. Mason and I found it no child's play to follow him with the rope. Some 200 hundred more steps in hard snow brought us to the only place where we could attack the second block. Here three fallen rocks stop the way, and on the left hand is the well-nigh ledge-less cliff which terminates far away overhead in the Scaw Fell Pinnacle. On the right a high perpendicular wall effectively cuts off the ghyll from the terraces of Lord's Rake. On the left hand of the ghyll, a small tongue of rock, very steep, juts out perhaps 40 feet down the gully from the fallen block nearest to the Pinnacle wall, and forms a small crack, and this crack is the only way upwards. From a mountaineers point of view, the stratification of the rocks here is all wrong. The crack ends in a chimney about 20 feet high, between the wall and a smoothly polished boss of rock. Hastings, still leading, found the crack to be difficult, but climbed it in a most masterly way. All loose stones, tufts of grass and moss had to be thrown down, and, in the absence of hand and footholds, the knees, elbows, thighs and other parts of the body had to do the holding on, whilst, caterpillar-like, we drew ourselves upwards bit by bit. The chimney is best climbed by leaning against the pinnacle wall with ones back and elbows, and, at the same time, by walking with the feet fly-like up the boss opposite. From the top of the boss a narrow sloping traverse, perhaps 12 feet long, leads in to the trough of the ghyll. With a rope this is an easy run; without one it would not be nice.

"A stone thrown down from here falls over both blocks and rolls down the snow out of the mouth of Lord's Rake on to the screes far away below. The crack, chimney, and traverse, short distance though it is, took us an hour to pass. Just beyond this place the ordinary route from Lord's Rake joins Deep Ghyll, and for the ascent of Scaw Fell there is no further difficulty. We wished, however, to climb the Scaw Fell Pinnacle…The climb from Deep Ghyll to the gap from which the pinnacle is ascended is a very good one, where two men can do much better than one."

Slingsby's party made the second recorded winter ascent of Deep Gill. The last sentence is tantalising for it suggests that they may have climbed the Professor's Chimney to reach the gap between the Pisgah and Scafell Pinnacle, which, if they did, predates the first ascent, by John Robinson and H.R. Procter, in August 1887. The reference to "the ordinary route from Lord's Rake" into Deep Gill - the West Wall Traverse - is also interesting for it suggests that by 1886 this had already become an established course. Deep Gill soon became one of the most popular climbs in the Wasdale area, for both summer and winter ascents. John Robinson's diary records that he climbed the gill over twenty times, the first of these being an early winter ascent, probably the third, made in January 1887 with T. Creek when it was filled with soft snow and all the difficulties buried. The hotel visitors' books and later the Climbing Book record a number of minor variations, made by different parties, to the lower pitches of Deep Gill during the next decade. Slingsby's paper helped to raise awareness of the opportunities for climbing in The Lake District, particularly amongst the Alpine Club members, who in the next few years would play a significant role in its development.

However, the event, which perhaps more than any other, stimulated interest in British rock climbing, was Haskett Smith's solo ascent of Napes Needle in 1886. The story is well known and many take this to mark the beginning of the sport of rock climbing. It was both the timing of the ascent and the striking shape of the Needle that caused this to have such an impact. In June 1890 a drawing and an accompanying article on how to climb the Needle, by Walter Brunskill, appeared in the *Pall Mall Budget* magazine. This, along with a photograph of the Needle taken by Professor Harold Dixon, on sale in a photographer's shop in London, did much to raise the profile of Lakeland climbing.

On 17th August 1887 John Robinson, H.R. Proctor and W.S. Corder climbed Deep Gill and made the first recorded ascent of the Professor's Chimney. The latter is the deep cleft high on the left at the top of Deep Gill that leads directly up to the Jordan Gap, between Scafell Pinnacle and the Pisgah. The name originally applied to the main left branch that passes to the right of the Pisgah - the Hopkinson brothers had christened it after one of them had recently been made a professor - but it was so often erroneously applied to the chimney below the Jordan Gap, that this eventually stuck and became the accepted title. The branch passing to the right of the Pisgah subsequently became known as the New Professor's Chimney. Three ladies - Miss Alice Corder, Miss Effie Corder and Miss Watson - accompanied Robinson's party. They climbed Deep Gill independently, by the West Wall Traverse, and joined the others higher up where Alice Corder made the first ladies ascent of Scafell Pinnacle. Robinson left a detailed account in the hotel visitors' book of which the following is an extract:

"Having been joined by the ladies, who crossed from Lord's Rake by the grassy traverse [West Wall Traverse], they climbed in company to near the head of the Gill, at which point Proctor led the way up the narrow chimney (which leads direct to the 'neck' connecting the Deep Ghyll Pillar with the rest of the mountain), and was followed by Robinson and Corder. Having been joined by Miss Corder they now made the ascent of the Deep Ghyll Pillar in the following order. Robinson mounted the slab & with Corder assisting below, helped up Miss Corder over the first step which rather overhangs, Miss C now took the lead with R close behind to prevent a slip. This is believed to be the first ascent of this rock by a lady."

Photo: © abrahamphotographic / FRCC Archives

Napes Needle on Great Gable. Haskett Smith's solo ascent of this pinnacle was one of the most significant events in the history of British climbing.

Photo: FRCC Archives

The first pitch of Deep Gill as seen from Lord's Rake, c. 1900.

Charles Hopkinson.

Around this time the unclimbed face of Scafell Pinnacle, standing between Deep Gill and Steep Gill, started to attract the attention of climbers and three significant attempts were made on this in less than a year. The first, at the end of September 1887, was by the Hopkinson brothers Edward, Charles and Albert and their cousin Wilberforce Tribe. They descended the upper part of the Pinnacle, by the line known today as the Low Man from Hopkinson's Cairn, as far as a prominent ledge overlooking Deep Gill, but were unable to make further progress and returned by the same route. Edward built a cairn on the ledge, known ever since as Hopkinson's Cairn, which for the next 25 years acted as a magnet for climbers, challenging them to find a direct way up from the foot of the Pinnacle.

A modern team finishing up 'Low Man from Hopkinson's Cairn' which is the line taken by the Hopkinson team to descend to Hopkinson's Cairn ledge (at the foot of the photograph). Climbers: Phil Blanshard, Penny Excell and John Ellerton.

Charles Hopkinson, Hermann Woolley, Henry Holder and E.W. Bury were the first to attempt this direct ascent, when, on 30th December 1887, with Hopkinson in the lead, they endeavoured to climb the face in winter conditions. Their entry in the hotel visitors' book, probably made by Woolley, states the party climbed 150 to 200 feet up the Pinnacle until stopped by a heavily iced slab where they were forced to traverse leftwards into an icy gully, which they subsequently descended. For years this attempt was regarded with awe, it being assumed that the party had climbed some distance up the smooth and technically difficult rock of the Pinnacle face and then traversed into the shallow corner known ever since as Hopkinson's Gully, all in desperate winter conditions that would be a least grade V I today. However, it is much more likely that they climbed the first rock buttress, near the start of Lord's Rake, to the Pinnacle Terrace, where they were stopped by ice-sheathed slabs on the face above, and traversed leftwards into Steep Gill, which they ascended as far as the main chimney and then retreated. Their entry in the visitors' book is quoted in full (4) :

> "Three of the party led by Hopkinson made an attempt on the Deep Ghyll Pillar (Pinnacle) from the entrance to Lord's Rake. They succeeded in climbing 150 to 200 feet but were stopped by a steep slab of rock coated with ice. From this point however a good traverse was made to the first gully (or chimney) on the left (apparently that referred to by Mr Haskett Smith). They forced their way up this gully to the top of the chimney. At the top of the chimney there was a trough of ice about 30 feet long surrounded by steep rocks glazed with ice which brought the party to a stop. They descended the chimney again and returned to Wastdale being unanimous of opinion that the days excursion had afforded one of the finest climbs the party had ever accomplished."

Sunday, 15th July 1888, was wet and unseasonably cold but this didn't deter Cecil Slingsby, Haskett Smith, Geoffrey Hastings and Edward Hopkinson from venturing out to attempt a new route on Scafell Pinnacle. They entered the lower section of Steep Gill and, at the first opportunity traversed out onto the Pinnacle face where they soon found themselves at the foot of a steep and narrow chimney. Robinson's entry in the hotel visitors' book dramatically describes the difficulties they encountered:

> "An extremely narrow gully on the front face of the precipice was unavailingly assaulted by two of the party and it was found necessary to call W.C.S [Slingsby] to the front. The issue was no longer in doubt. After a brief war dance on the heads and shoulders of his less dextrous companions the new comer started on his wild career, gliding up improbable inclines and wriggling over streaming slabs with the swift and sinuous motion of a partially inebriated eel! Nearly 120 feet of rope had run out before he paused in an easy chimney within sight of the low man, and with the certainty that the climb was practically accomplished. The rest of the party followed in due course and drenched as they were with rain and benumbed by the bitter cold were glad enough to have the benefit of a friendly rope."

The route became known as Steep Gill via Slingsby's Chimney and is currently graded Very Difficult. It was one of the first routes to break away from the traditional gully lines and, for the period, involved an exceptionally long and exposed run out. This was an important ascent, completed in less than ideal conditions that heralded the beginning of a bolder and more adventurous approach to climbing.

This illustrates the probable line taken by Hopkinson's team during their winter attempt on The Pinnacle in 1887. The line XX represents the later line of Hopkinson's Gully.

Photo: FRCC Archive

(L to R) W. P. Haskett Smith, W. C. Slingsby and G. Hastings. The driving force behind the ascent of Slingsby's Chimney route.

The Chimney Pitch of Slingsby's Chimney Route, taken in 1931.

Photo: Eric Radcliffe

The close of the decade marked the end of the first period of the sport's evolution. The exploration of the crags had started to move out of the wet and moss-filled gullies onto the cleaner but more exposed ridges and faces. A rope was routinely being used, and many of the identifiable features on the crags now had names. The number of active participants was increasing each year and a feeling of fraternity began to arise as they met regularly but informally, particularly at Christmas and Easter. Norman Collie, who was to play a significant role in the next stage of development, suggested that climbing in Cumbria, in the 1880s should be referred to as the 'Age of Iron', the hard metal symbolizing the sterner, more committing approach to the fells than had previously been practiced (5).

Footnotes

1) Haskett Smith joined a second reading party coincidentally based at the Wastwater Hotel and, in total, spent two months at Wasdale Head in the summer of 1881.

2) Petty was lucky to survive and spent two weeks at Burnthwaite Farm before he was considered well enough to travel. He eventually made a good recovery and went on to practise medicine.

3) Williamson was an engineer turned journalist who made a number of visits to Wasdale in the late 1870s and early 1880s. He was a keen climber but was never involved in any first ascents.

4) It is likely that the misunderstanding of the line taken by Charles Hopkinson's party was due to O.G. Jones. In the second edition of *Rock Climbing in the English Lake District* (there is no mention of this ascent in the first edition) Jones suggests that in December 1887 the Hopkinson's climbed some way up the feature now referred to as Hopkinson's Gully until stopped by the icy conditions. This, almost certainly, is incorrect and Jones is mistaken in his interpretation of the account in the visitors book. In the second edition of *Rock Climbing in the English Lake District* (p. 86) Jones refers to Hopkinson's Gully by name and this is probably the origin of the name for there is no earlier written reference to it.

5) Collie's label echoes the appellations of Golden and Silver Ages that had been applied to climbing in the Alps.

Photo: Eric Radcliffe

View looking down onto the upper section of Slingsby's Chimney.

The Victorian climbers relished climbing the gullies of Scafell such as Deep Gill under harsh winter conditions, it was said that Scafell gave perfect practice for The Alps without the crevasses.

Photo: © abrahamphotographic / FRCC Archives

1889 - 1895

Putting Down New Routes (An Evolving Fraternity)

Photo: Mike Cocker

The Wasdale Climbing Book was held at The Wastwater Hotel between 1890 and 1919. A facsimile of the book with accompanying notes was published in 2006, written by Michael Cocker with the help of the Fell and Rock Climbing Club.

Photo: © abrahamphotographic / FRCC Archives

Owen Glynne Jones - the nearest thing to a rock star in the Victorian era..

Overleaf: Unknown climbers above Tennis Court Wall, illustrating the typical lack of belaying technique for the time.
Photo: Albert Holmes.

The increasing number of individuals seeking information about climbs, and of climbing entries in the hotel visitors' books, had created a need for the existing records to be catalogued into a more convenient and accessible format. Robert Cary Gilson, a fellow of Trinity College Cambridge and a regular visitor to Wasdale Head, undertook the task and purchased a substantial leather-bound volume into which he transcribed all the climbing notices in the visitors' books. He presented this to the hotel proprietor, Dan Tyson, in January 1890, and for the next 30 years this book, referred to as the Wasdale Climbing Book, the Hotel Climbing Book or simply the Climbing Book, was used exclusively for climbing reports. Before the advent of club journals and climbing guides, it was the only continuous and up to date record of activity in and around Wasdale, and practically the sole source of route descriptions for parties wanting to repeat climbs. Initially, it was freely available for anyone to review or to which they could contribute, but in later years it was kept under lock and key and only accessible to those considered suitably qualified.

Widening interest in rock climbing drew a number of talented individuals to Wasdale around the start of the new decade. Some of these had a background in Alpine climbing, others had little or no previous experience. The most focused and driven of them, and the man who more than any other was to influence the development of rock climbing over the next few years, was Owen Glynne Jones.

Jones grew up in London, where his father worked as a carpenter and a builder. Academically gifted he did well at school and became a physics teacher. As a teenager he had read the classic books from the 'Golden Age' of Alpine climbing and it was these that stimulated his initial interest in climbing. Jones started scrambling on a family holiday in Mid Wales, in 1888, and had made the first ascent, solo, of the Cyfrwy Arête on Cader Idris. This, however, was an isolated event and he didn't climb again until he visited Wasdale in April 1890. His first Cumbrian climb was an icy ascent of Broad Stand with his friend and teaching colleague Dr W. Sumpner; an ill-equipped and reckless endeavour, as they had no rope, ice axe or nails in their boots. A few days later the pair joined W.M. Crook, an experienced Alpine climber, to make an ascent of Pillar Rock, and it seems that even at this early stage Jones showed considerable aptitude, for Crook later wrote that Jones "was no ordinary climber" but one who moved "with great confidence and speed" and that he had never before seen "a man to whom rock climbing seemed so natural and easy".

Jones and Sumpner returned to Wasdale in the spring of 1891. In the interim, Arthur Milnes Marshall, Harold Dixon and W.I. Beaumont made the first recorded winter ascent of the Professor's Chimney on 3rd April 1891 (1). There had been a storm the previous day and the party struggled up deep powder snow and ice glazed rocks in Deep Gill to the foot of the chimney, which, compared to the ground they had just covered, they found "comparatively easy". Marshall and Dixon were both academics at Owens College in Manchester and regular visitors to Wasdale (2).

On 19th April 1891 Jones and Sumpner climbed Cust's Gully on Great End with Dr. C. Munro. They had no significant experience of winter climbing and with the gully filled with snow and ice, Munro had to teach them how to cut steps. The party continued over Scafell Pike to the foot of Mickledore Chimney, which was also full of snow. Munro initially took the lead but it was Jones who completed the climb and made the first winter ascent. Jones included the following account in his book *Rock Climbing in the English Lake District*:

> "Munro took the lead and hopefully ploughed through heavy wet snow as a preliminary. Unfortunately, the snow became softer and deeper as we advanced, until at last we were up to our waists in slush, and wet through. The pitch was not very far to seek. We saw long dripping icicles barring our direct route onwards. Both sides of the gully were heavily glazed with wet ice, and we foresaw an anxious time of waiting while the leader prospected. At the time we were not aware that the usual exit was upon the right-hand side of the pitch, by a couple of broad easy ledges. Nor could we see that the pitch was in two parts, cave upon cave, with a large resting place between; for the icicles hung in an impenetrable curtain.

"Munro attacked the icicles valiantly. Twice he succeeded in working half way up between the centre and left wall, but twice he was repulsed vigorously, and found himself landed in the snow below. I was getting cold and impatient. Munro was willing to take a breathing space. I unroped and made for the left wall. Cutting little steps for hands and feet in the ice that covered the wall, and using the fingers for all they were worth, in some ungainly fashion I reached the level of the top of the pitch and traversed on to the snow above. The axe had been used, I suspect, more like a croquet mallet than anything else and introduced its own particular dangers. But it was of no consequence, the pitch was climbed. The shivering pair below tried to fling the rope up to me. This was a matter of much difficulty, placed as we were, but by approaching each other as far as we dared, a happy fling brought the end of the rope into my hand, and I responded by throwing down, to their extreme peril, the ice axe that they needed to effect their ascent. We managed the rest badly. My position was insecure in the upper snow of the gully, or at any rate it seemed to be so. The others were benumbed with cold and wet, unable to feel the holds or to rely on getting any help from me. We certainly were not a strong party, and there was no possibility of mutual aid. The only consolation was in the fact that all danger was absent; a fall could only result in a plunge into ten feet of soft snow, but we never afterwards spoke with pride of that afternoon's work. The other two decided to give it up, and go down to Mickledore again. My own feelings were not consulted, but what matter? The Broad Stand was somewhere about. I might descend that way and shout when in trouble. We joined again at Mickledore, and rather gloomily glissaded to Hollow Stones".

Two days later, on 21st April, the same party made the first recorded winter ascent of the New Professor's Chimney, at the head of Deep Gill, cutting their way through "a fine ice cornice" to gain the summit plateau.

John Norman Collie started climbing on the Isle of Skye in 1886 and was unaware of the opportunities for climbing in The Lake District until he read Walter Brunskill's article on Napes Needle in the June 1890 edition of the *Pall Mall Budget.* He arranged to make a visit at the first opportunity and arrived at Wasdale Head on 22nd December 1891, with two friends, E.W. Marshall and W.L. Brodie. The weather was unsettled and the hills snow covered. Their luggage had been delayed but nevertheless they decided to climb Napes Needle which shocked the hotel landlord, Dan Tyson, who thought they were going out in their "Sunday clothes". Collie was 32 years old at the time and a lecturer in Organic Chemistry at London University. On 25th December Collie, Brodie and Marshall climbed Steep Gill when it was covered with snow and ice: the first winter ascent. This was an astonishingly bold undertaking for the time and, almost certainly, the first grade V winter climb ever made in Britain. The party were probably deceived by the relatively easy start to the gully and climbed into a position from which they were unable to retreat and had no choice but to force the difficult upper section. We don't know who led the crux chimney pitch, but it is likely to have been Collie. A brief note recording their ascent was placed in the Wasdale Climbing Book, but this contained no detail regarding the conditions or difficulties encountered only the suggestion that "a much better way to the top is by the rock arête between Steep Ghyll and Deep Ghyll". Many years later, in a reflective article in the *Fell and Rock Climbing Club Journal (1926)*, Collie wrote that he thought Steep Gill in snow and ice was one of the most dangerous climbs he ever made. Collie's reticent nature and the lack of differentiation between summer and winter climbs, at that time, meant that this outstanding achievement went almost unnoticed for more than a century.

Norman Collie.

Peter Ashworth seconding the main pitch of Steep Gill.

Photo: Steve Ashworth

It cannot be emphasised enough just how significant Collie's ascent of Steep Gill was for its time, it was not only the most difficult and daring lead of its day, but it remained so for almost half a century. It still retains a grade of V to this day, more for its sustained and unprotected nature, rather than for technical difficulty. The article "Steep Ghyll" in Wilson, Alcock and Barry's excellent book, *Cold Climbs* by Paul Nunn clearly shows the difficulty of an ascent as late as the 1960's:

> "In some sections the gully was too flat-backed to allow a bridging technique. Straight ice-axes sculptured narrow and fragile hand holds which consolidated under mitten pressure, and the feet followed into those slots always wondering if the snow would hold. It was a delicate and balancy form of progress. I have no idea how long it took; picking and chipping for little holds, teetering from one to the other, holding some rock or icy nubbin with one hand whilst poking around with the ice axe in the other. Front-points often broke through to the rock underneath, scraping and scratching. Once or twice dubious slings draped over even more dubious spikes created an illusion of protection… Spreading the weight on the snow pockets became even more strenuous after 50ft. Spindrift from a wind sweeping across Scafell summit occasionally burst in a flurry down the scoop, filling face, anorak and holds. Progress got even slower but it looked harder still to go down. Legs and nerves tired at the endless chipping and balancing and hanging on with one mitten. A final steep section of ice at least promised an easing beyond. But with maximum rope-drag and no security beyond a good sense of balance it was the trickiest movement of all; the final move onto easy ground, the point of relaxation where so many leaders fall."

This remained the hardest route in England and in all probability the world for many years, and it wasn't until the second ascentionists of this route Bert Hargreaves, Ruth Hargreaves, Sid Cross and Alice Nelson climbed a winter ascent of Bowfell Buttress (grade VI) in 1936 that the level of difficulty was surpassed in The Lakes. Even in Scotland, the first time that the difficulty of Steep Gill was matched was probably by Raeburn with his ascent of Green Gully on Ben Nevis in 1906.

The early climbers made no real distinction between summer and winter conditions and, as a consequence, it is possible that a number of impressive attempts, first ascents and early repeats of routes, done under difficult winter or semi-winter conditions, remain unacknowledged because they would not have been recorded as a separate category of climb. There are several reasons for this; firstly climbing rock partly covered in snow and ice was normal practice in the Alps, so no great division was made when routes were encountered in similar conditions in the British hills. Secondly, the winters were generally much colder a century ago; snow frequently covered the Lakeland fells from December through to March or April, and the largest gatherings of climbers at Wasdale occurred at Christmas and Easter - periods when winter conditions were likely to be encountered. Finally, the equipment used on summer and winter climbs was the same; a hemp rope, nailed boots and an ice axe, so there was no separation of activities in terms of the necessary equipment in the way that there is today.

Moss Gill must have presented an obvious challenge to the pioneer climbers and it is slightly surprising that this remarkable cleft remained undisturbed for so long. Haskett Smith, Geoffrey Hastings, Cecil Slingsby and John Robinson made the first approach on the 4th June 1889, and succeeded in climbing as far as the Great Cave, but could find no way of continuing. Slingsby later wrote:

> "The wall below the Tennis Court Ledge was curtained with lovely moss, in some cases in long sprays. This suggested the name Moss Ghyll. With ruthless energy we stripped away the green covering off the line of ascent and then found the loosest of loose walls. After making ourselves into a sort of human pyramid, Robinson climbed up it, and then came the real work. It is not too easy even now, but it is child's play compared with what it was when it was first tackled. When, with the help of the rope I reached the grass ledge I was so delighted that I shouted out, 'There's a tennis court here'. Of course we were beaten at the 'window', which was also my poor fortune on a second occasion, and had to descend the wall. Robinson again took the post of honour and came down last."

Haskett Smith's party left a note in the hotel visitors' book recommending Moss Gill to anyone looking for a new and difficult climb. Cary Gilson, his brother J.P. Gilson and F. Wellford were the next to try when, on 19th June 1889, they climbed as far as the Tennis Court Ledge but were unable to progress any further. Cary Gilson suggested the name Sweep Gill because euphonically it matched Deep Gill and Steep Gill and indicated the "probable profession of the future first climber of its extraordinary vertical chimneys". A couple of days later, and to get a better look at the difficulties involved, the same party descended the upper part of the Gill as far as the Amphitheatre, lying above the Great Cave, but could see no possible connection. Discouraged by the failure of acknowledged experts, three and half years were to pass before anyone attempted Moss Gill again.

Curtains of moss near Tennis Court Wall gave the name to Moss Gill.

The Victorian gentlemen

If we pause to consider what life was like for the pioneers from the Victorian era, we can conclude that it would have been very different to what is the norm for today. At home they would have been expected to wear formal dress for dinner, especially if guests were invited. Conversation would have been muted and polite, particularly in mixed company, and one can imagine that any laughter or jokes were reserved until after the gentlemen had retired to the smoking room with a glass of port. Their guests would have inevitably been of a similar social standing, so it would have been unseemly to display any raucous behaviour or to say anything contentious in case talk of such leaked out into the wider community. Social morals and fear of being ostracised from the rest of society would have been the factors that prevented any conduct that was beyond the realm of the strict etiquette that was normal in those days.

But at Wasdale, while these gentlemen were away from their social peers, it was a gathering of like-minded individuals who shared a common passion and its associated dangers. They could wear flannel shirts for dinner, and sit in stocking feet and drink beer like a working class man, (although drunkenness seemed rare, evidence suggests that they imbibed alcohol in moderation). In effect, they could let their hair down and enjoy boisterous games, such as Billiard Fives or traversing the table with their feet on the walls. Such behaviour would cause outrage at home, but they were all together in a clique which could be described as a 'Band of Brothers.' You will notice from the writing of that era that any reference to this behaviour was always covered by pseudonyms such as 'The Athlete' or 'The Professor' to ensure that those involved were not identifiable to the outside world. In modern parlance, we would say 'What goes on tour stays on tour,' these guys were true Victorian rock stars, and hats off to them.

The days leading up to Christmas 1892 were cold and dry. Norman Collie, Geoffrey Hastings and John Robinson were amongst the guests staying at the hotel and on 26th December they set out for Moss Gill. Collie takes up the story:

Photo: Abert Holmes/ FRCC Archive

Right: Climbers admiring the view from Tennis Court Ledge just above Tennis Court Wall of Moss Gill.

"When we attacked it, this ghyll had not been climbed, although several parties had been up a considerable distance. The highest point attained was just underneath a huge overhanging block of rock, weighing hundreds of tons, which formed the roof of a great cave. Robinson, Hastings, and I were anxious to see whether it was not possible in some way to circumvent this objectionable block. We had already carefully prospected the upper part of the ghyll from above, finding that there was no difficulty once this obstacle was passed. We therefore next attacked the ghyll from the bottom, hoping that we should be able to discover a way where others had failed.

"Starting from below we chose the easiest route up the rock face on the right hand of the ghyll. Here the climbing chiefly consisted in getting from one ledge to another, up slabs of rock. We soon, however, got into the gully itself, where we found a perpendicular wall, up which we had to climb, before reaching a ledge, which the first party of exploration had called the 'Tennis Court' on account of its large size when compared with those lower down. If it were to grow vigorously, perhaps in its manhood it might become just large enough to run about on, but when we first made its acquaintance it must have been in its early childhood. From here we traversed back into the ghyll and got underneath the great overhanging block.

"We found that below the great slab which formed the roof another smaller one spanned the ghyll, forming the top of a great door to the cave behind. Under this we passed, and clambered up on to the top of it. Over our heads the great rock roof stretched some distance over the ghyll. Our only chance was to traverse straight out to the right, over the side of the ghyll, till one was no longer overshadowed by the roof above, and then, if possible, climb up the face of rock, and traverse back again above the obstacle into the ghyll once more.

"This was easier to plan than to carry out; absolutely no hand hold could be found, but only one little projecting ledge jutting out about a quarter of an inch and about a couple of inches long to stand on; moreover, a lip of rock overhung this little ledge, making it impossible to grip it satisfactorily with one's foot. Beyond this there were six or eight feet of the nearly perpendicular rock wall to traverse. I was asked to try it. So, being highly pleased at being entrusted with such delicate operations, I, with great deliberation, stretched out my foot and tried to grip the little edge with the side nails of my boot. Just as I was going to put my whole weight on to this right foot, the nails, unable to hold on such a minute surface, gave way, and if Hastings had not instantly with a mighty pull jerked me back, I should have been swinging on the rope in mid-air. But we were determined not to be beaten. Hastings's ice axe was next brought into requisition, and what followed I have no doubt will be severely criticised by more orthodox mountaineers than ourselves.

"As it was my suggestion I must take the blame. Peccavi! I hacked a step in the rock! It was very hard work, but, that upper lip to the step had to go, and Hastings's ice axe, being an extraordinary one, performed its work admirably, and without damage to anything else than the rock.. But I should not advise anyone to try and do the same thing with an ordinary axe. Hastings' axe is an extraordinary one, and was none the worse for the experiment. I was then able to get a much firmer foothold, and stepped across the mauvais pas, clambered up the rock till I had reached a spot where a capital hitch could be got over a jutting pin of rock, and the rest of the party followed. We then climbed out of the ghyll on the left up some slabs of rock." (3)

By the time they emerged at the top of the gill the sun had set and they experienced an evening of unusual light and clarity with the peaks of Snowdonia rising above a sea of cloud:

"The sun-god had plunged once more into the baths of ocean, leaving behind him the golden splendour of a perfect evening. In the far distance lay the sea, with banks of sullen mist brooding over it; nearer, like a purple curtain, stretched the low hills by the coast; whilst far away in the south, towering into the sunset glow, out of a level surface of sea mist rose the peaks of Snowdon and the two Carnedds in Wales."

The next day the same party made the first ascent of Great Gully on the Screes - "hoar frost covered the ground", the trees were "a mass of silver" and the waterfalls in the gully "frozen solid". There was no snow in the gully, but this was certainly a winter ascent for they were forced to cut steps in the ice and made good use of the frozen turf. (4)

John Robinson wrote the contemporary account of the ascent of Moss Gill in the Wasdale Climbing Book, but his inaccurate description, Collie tells us, was directly responsible for the second ascent party, led by Joseph Collier, climbing a new and more direct finish:

"That Collier did not follow our route was, I believe, entirely due to Robinson, who, being so excessively delighted with having at last conquered Moss Ghyll, wrote a long account of it in the climbing book at the inn, and being in this particular instance far more capable of successfully climbing Moss Ghyll than describing how it was done, produced a tale where the points of the compass got, so to speak, 'snarked'."

Photo: Albert Holmes /FRCC Archive

The leader, belayed by a companion hidden behind the chock-stones, makes the delicate move onto the Collie Step.

Photo FRCC Archive

Joseph Collier.

Sketch of Moss Gill by Arthur Marshall which was drawn following the third ascent. This is probably the first topo sketch of a route in climbing history. It can still be used to this day.
His notes are as follows:

I A-A Moss Ghyll B Pisgah C Deep Ghyll Pillar D Tennis Court Ledge

II A sketch of Moss Ghyll showing details of the climb. The sketch is partly from memory and is only approximately correct.

1 Commencement of Moss Ghyll, at the Rake's Progress
2 Snow patch
2a Chimney with cave and jammed stone
3 Rock face below Tennis Court Ledge
4 Tennis Court Ledge
5 The lower of the two large stones blocking the gulley: below this stone is an archway leading to a cavern behind the stone.
6 The upper of two large stones
7 Window between the two large stones through which the climb is continued
8 Dr. Collie's Step: the dots right and left of this which represent natural steps
9 The 'Belaying Pin' around which the rope may be secured very firmly during the passage of the party from the window
10 Stone over which the traverse back into the gulley is completed
11 Snow patch
12 Bottom of the Great Chimney
13 First traverse from the chimney
14 Jammed stone forming floor of the 'Sentry Box', holding 3 people
15 Second traverse from the chimney
16 Jammed stone forming top of the chimney
17 Snow patch: gentle incline
18 Steep pitch
19 Top of Moss Ghyll
E -E Route taken by Messers Robinson, Collie and Hastings after leaving the gully.

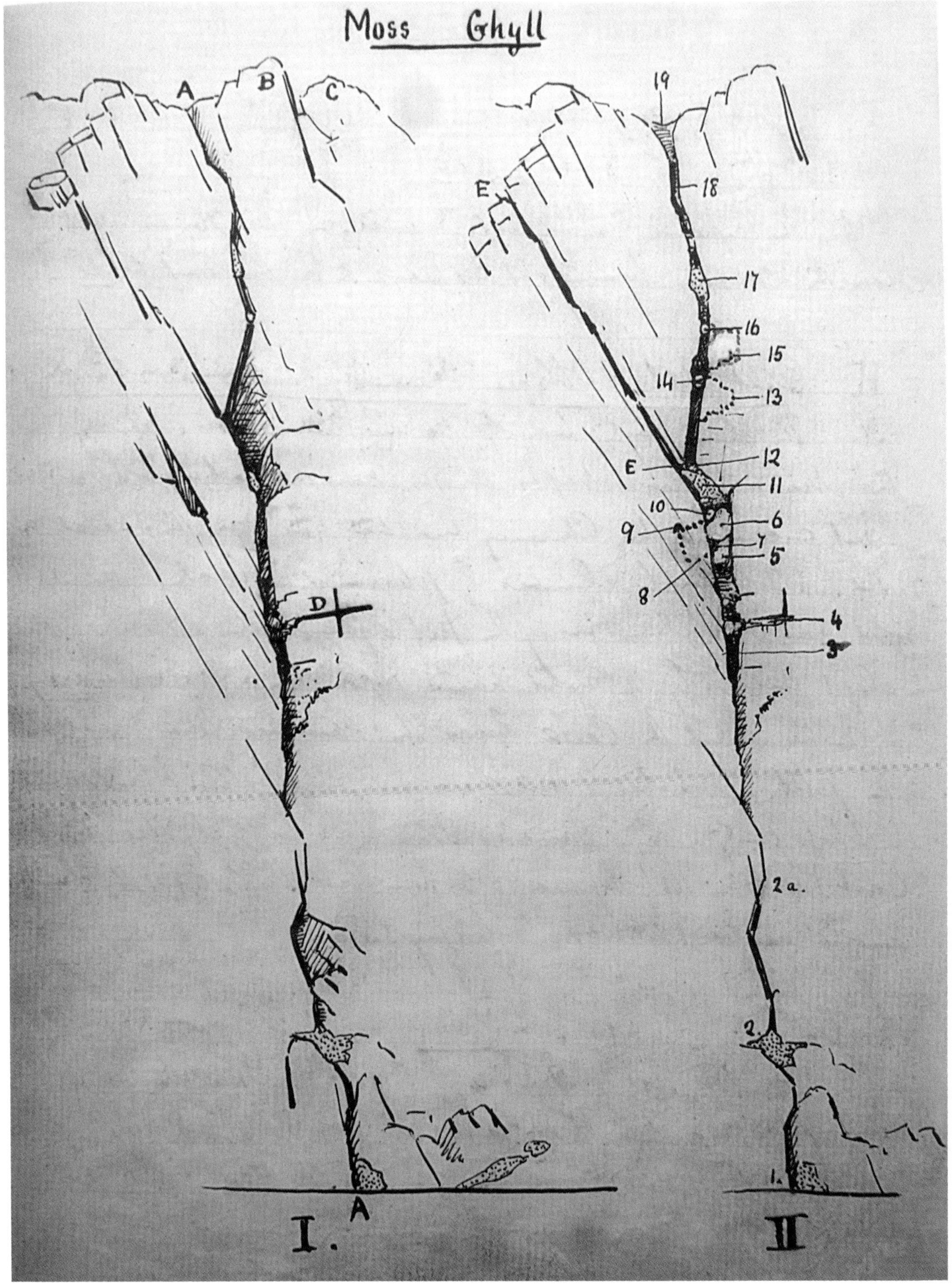

Dr. Joseph Collier was a surgeon from Manchester who excelled at sports and had already done some climbing in the Alps. On 30th December 1892, with E. L. Woolley, B. Goodfellow, E. Talbot, and S. B. Winser he made the second ascent of Moss Gill adding a new variation finish. The party followed the original route as far as the Amphitheatre and then climbed the steep moss-covered chimney that forms the direct continuation of the gill, under the impression that the previous party had followed the same line. They thought this was the most difficult section of the climb and only later discovered that it was a new variation - Collier's Chimney. This direct finish is currently graded Severe but rarely climbed today.

Collier made the third ascent of Moss Gill, including his own direct finish, with Harold Dixon and Arthur Marshall, on New Years Day 1893, after which Marshall drew a fine sketch of Moss Gill with a detailed route description in the Climbing Book. The following April he produced a drawing of the whole of Scafell Crag that included significant topographical features and the lines of all the routes climbed so far. Aside from a useful but crude outline of Gable Crag, made by John Robinson, this was the first time illustration was used as a guide to assist other climbers.

The weather deteriorated after New Year and all the residents departed except for Owen Glynne Jones. On 9th January 1893 Jones ploughed his way through deep snow to the foot of Moss Gill and at 12.45 p.m. started up the first pitch. He was climbing alone and, wanting to establish the altitude of prominent features on the climb, encumbered with an aneroid barometer:

Photo: Abert Holmes/ FRCC Archive

A typical ascent of Collier's Chimney involving unbelayed climbers moving together, which illustrates the precarious and dangerous climbing style used prior to the advent of belaying methods.

> "It was distinctly a day of adventure, and I learnt a great deal concerning the ghyll. The passage across the Collie step appeared to me the most difficult, but the loose slabs over which one has to walk adroitly were then covered with fresh snow. The famous step was invisible, and I had to stoop and scrape in order to determine its exact shape and position. At the first attempt on the traverse I slipped, and fell into the snow–bed of the gully below. The result was scarcely surprising, though eminently uncomfortable. But the falling was, under the circumstances, almost part of the programme, and a rope had been fixed in the interior of the cavern, passed out through the 'window', and then attached to my waist, to eliminate the danger of plunging some 400 feet down to the foot of the gully. The second attempt was successful, though I confess to a feeling of lively apprehension as the critical point was being passed."

Jones cracked two ribs in the fall and was badly bruised. He finished by Collie's exit, but having left his ice axe in the cave and with almost every hold having to be scraped clear of snow, it was 5.45 p.m. and pitch dark when he reached the top.

Two days later Jones repeated the climb to retrieve his rope and ice axe and to re-check some measurements. These solo ascents were also the first and second winter ascents and extraordinary undertakings; ones that caused his contemporaries to comment, not always approvingly, on Jones' phenomenal confidence and ability. Today Moss Gill is considered to 'go' in almost any conditions, but a heavy covering of powder snow, as it had when Jones tackled it, is probably the most taxing.

A month later a strong team consisting of Geoffrey Hastings, Alfred Mummery, William Cecil Slingsby, Hermann Woolley and Roderick Williams assembled at the hotel. On 11th February Hastings and Mummery made the second ascent of Great Gully on the Screes when it was free of snow and ice. Higher up, winter conditions prevailed and, on the same day, Williams, Woolley and Slingsby made the third winter and sixth overall ascent of Moss Gill, when the floor and side-walls of the gully were coated in ice. They clearly had a struggle, for Slingsby, an experienced winter climber, when recording their ascent in the Climbing Book stressed that the gully should not be attempted in future "except when the rocks are dry and quite free from ice". Mummery, who was the outstanding Alpinist of the era, found that he disliked gully climbing, considering it to be "both difficult and dangerous", and this was his only visit to Wasdale.

On 1st April 1893 Norman Collie, Geoffrey Hastings and John Robinson made the first ascent of a route on Deep Gill Buttress that starts up a shallow groove, 100 feet (30 metres) above the Great Chimney, and follows a left to right diagonal line across the crag. Robinson left a brief note in the Climbing Book saying he considered it "an interesting way of leaving the ghyll and so missing the loose scree near the top". Technically the climb is probably only moderate but it has never been included in any guidebook and remains unnamed.

The following day, 2nd April 1893, Joseph Collier and S.B. Winser made the first ascent of Collier's Climb. This was the first route to breach the steep ground between North Climb and Moss Gill, which had previously been regarded as unclimbable. Their account in the Climbing Book was matter of fact and gave little indication of the difficulties encountered. Unlike Moss Gill, which immediately became popular, Collier's Climb remained practically untouched for three years. O. G. Jones, who made the second ascent with George and Ashley Abraham in April 1896, wrote:

> "The unknown is always the most terrible, and the brief note in the Wastdale Climbing Book recording its first ascent left much to an anxious imagination. Queer tales were told round at the inn of men who were flung back over Rake's Progress after rising only ten feet. Even Dr. Collier was reported to have said he never wished to see the place again."

Collier started up a steep, mossy and rather loose corner to reach a grass ledge at 30 feet, above which the difficulties eased. For many years this first pitch was graded Very Severe, but, after a rock fall occurred at the hardest section, reducing the difficulty, it was re-graded Hard Severe. The route description in the modern guidebooks now avoid this start to give a more balanced climb with an overall grade of Difficult.

After completing Collier's Climb, the pair joined Max Schintz and Godfrey Solly to make the first descent of Moss Gill, with Collier coming down last. Schintz, who was a member of the Alpine Club, worked at his father's merchant's business in Liverpool. Solly, also a member of the Alpine Club, was a solicitor from Birkenhead who climbed regularly at Wasdale. The year before he had led the first ascent of Eagles Nest Ridge Direct on the Napes, one of the outstanding climbs of the decade.

After descending Moss Gill Collier and Winser teamed up with Arthur Marshall and four of the Hopkinson brothers to descend the upper part of Scafell Pinnacle. They followed the line the Hopkinsons had discovered in September 1887, and twenty feet above the cairn met Charles Hopkinson and his cousin Wilberforce Tribe, who had just made the first ascent of a steep curving crack on the wall of the Pinnacle overlooking Deep Gill — Hopkinson and Tribe's Route. Tribe included an account of this ascent in a retrospective article written for *the Fell and Rock Climbing Club Journal* (1927):

> "In April 1893, our party were staying at Rosthwaite and our destination one day was Scawfell, but, as often happens on these occasions, by starting at different times we missed connections, and Chas Hopkinson and I found ourselves separated from the others. We tried the north face of the Pinnacle from its base, but after advancing a short distance were driven back by the coldness and wetness of the rocks. We then walked up Deep Ghyll, and just above the second obstacle we noticed a shallow crack curving up to the north arête of the Low Man which seemed to have possibilities, so I crept up, followed by C. H., till I reached a small stance on the arête, where the latter joined me. Directly above, the arête rose almost perpendicularly, the only handholds were at the extreme length of our reach and they and the rocks sloped the wrong way. After several attempts to advance we gave it up. What conduced to our defeat was that the other members of the party had all the food and we were feeling rather weak and empty. However, rather than submit to a complete failure, we found a good belay and descended some distance towards Hopkinson's Cairn, the last man on a doubled rope, and found our way up the face to the Low Man."

While they were gathered at Hopkinson's Cairn, John Hopkinson, with the security of a top rope, climbed down the lower half of the Pinnacle Face, completing the first descent. The others returned to the summit by the normal route.

The Direct Finish to Mickledore Chimney is blocked by two chockstones stacked one above the other, with a small cave in between and a large quantity of loose material lodged above. Munro, Jones and Sumpner had attempted this in winter conditions in April 1891, but it remained unclimbed until 12th September 1893 when William Henry Fowler, an engineer from Manchester, managed to surmount it by standing on the shoulders of a tall companion. The other five in the party, because of the risk of dislodging some of the loose stones above the chockstones, finished by the usual exit. Fowler was involved in a number of first ascents around this time including the Arête Route on Napes Needle, which he climbed solo, Kern Knotts Crack and several gullies on Pikes Crag.

New Years Eve 1893 was marred by tragedy. Arthur Milnes Marshall, who was professor of Zoology at Owens College in Manchester, was killed in a fall near the bottom of Deep Gill. Marshall didn't begin climbing until he was in his thirties but had had several seasons in the Alps and had been a regular visitor to Wasdale Head during the previous eight years.

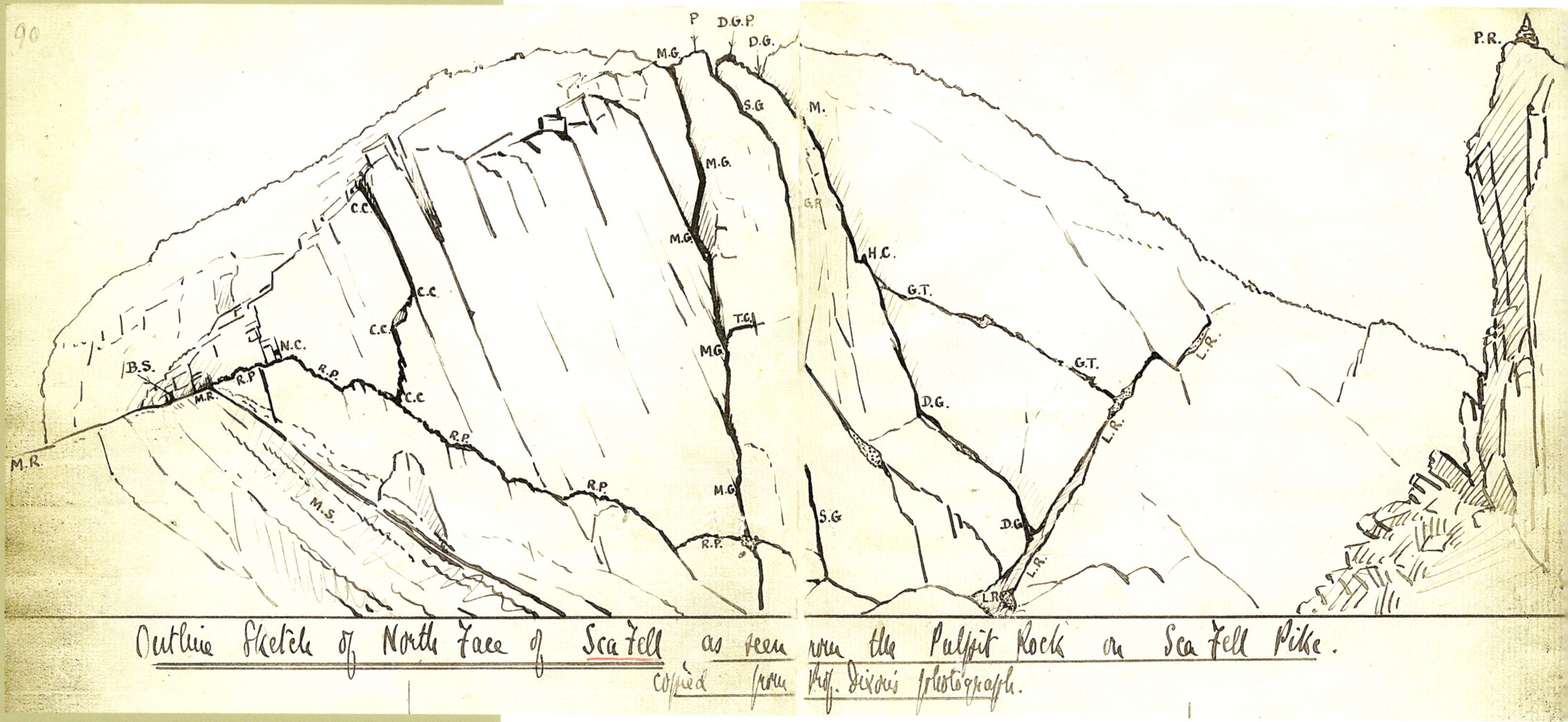

A sketch of Scafell Crag by Arthur Marshall from the Pulpit Rock which set the standard for all susequent crag diagrams.

MR	Mickledore Ridge
BS	Broad Stand
RP	Rakes Progress
NC	North Climb
CC	Collier's Climb
MS	Mickledore Scree
MG	Moss Ghyll
TC	Tennis Court Ledge
SG	Steep Ghyll
DG	Deep Ghyll
HC	Hopkinson's Cairn
M	Low Man - *part of diagram is missing*
DGP	Deep Ghyll Pinnacle (Scafell Pinnacle)
P	Pisgah Butress
GT	West Wall Traverse
LR	Lord's Rake
PR	Pulpit Rock

He was a talented artist and after making the two excellent drawings of Moss Gill and Scafell Crag in the Wasdale Climbing Book, Haskett Smith had asked him to produce the illustrations for his forthcoming guidebook, *Climbing in the British Isles*. Marshall was keen to make some further sketches of Scafell Crag and had arrived at Wasdale Head with Joseph Collier, on Thursday 28th December. On the Sunday, New Years Eve, O.G. Jones joined them and they climbed Steep Gill via Slingsby's Chimney together and then descended Deep Gill to Lord's Rake where Marshall wanted to take a photograph. He had found the position he was looking for on the low ridge above Lord's Rake, opposite the first pitch of Deep Gill, and asked Collier and Jones to join him. A few moments later the sound of falling stones caused Collier to look up and see Marshall tumbling down the ridge and disappear out of view. They rushed down to the spot where Marshall had landed but found that he had sustained extensive head injuries and was already dead. A simple slip seems to have been the cause of fall. Jones and Collier gave evidence at the inquest held at the Wastwater Hotel the following Tuesday, which returned a verdict of accidental death.

Haskett Smith's book, *Climbing in the British Isles*, was published in 1894. This described climbing in England with the bulk of it being devoted to the Lake District. A second volume came out the following year and covered Wales and Ireland. Ellis Carr replaced Arthur Marshall in providing the illustrations. Designed to be carried in a rucksack or on the crag, these were small, slim, pocket-sized editions, a lot of the information being taken directly from the visitors' books or climbing books kept at Wasdale Head and the Pen-y-Gwryd Hotel in North Wales. Haskett Smith also drew extensively from his own climbing experience and those of friends as well as from newspaper and magazine articles. They were the first guides to climbing in Britain ever produced and effectively brought together all the available data on climbing south of Scotland. They were a welcome and convenient source of reference for those already active but, being produced for the specialist, did little to attract the uninitiated.

Probably the strangest character active at Wasdale, in the mid 1890s, was Aleister Crowley. He was a student at Cambridge, intellectually gifted and an outstanding chess player, but also prickly, quick to take offence and generally not popular with his contemporaries.

He was a competent climber who recorded several new routes in the area, including one on Napes Needle that still bears his name. In later years he climbed in the Alps, Mexico and the Himalayas. He also acquired a considerable degree of notoriety due to his interest in drugs and the occult. On 9th May 1894 Crowley soloed the short cracked wall, above the start to Broad Stand, where the Mickledore Ridge abuts the crags. He wore 'rope-soled slippers', to improve adhesion on the mossy damp rock, and wedged an ice axe half way up to use as a foot hold. No one witnessed the ascent and, after he had written it up in the Climbing Book that evening, he was accused of lying. To refute his critics he repeated the ascent the following day in front of an audience. Crowley gave his own account of this in his autobiography *Confessions*:

> "Scafell is separated from Scafell Pike by a pass called Mickledoor… It had always been the ambition of every climber to start from the exact top of the ridge. This was called the direct climb of Mickledoor; and nobody had done it. That seemed to be a shame, so I did it. This time the fat was in the fire. My good faith was openly challenged in the smoking-room. I shrugged my shoulders, but offered to repeat the climb the following day before witnesses - which I accordingly did. I suppose I am a very innocent ass, but I could not understand why anyone calling himself human should start a series of malicious intrigues on such a cause of a quarrel. I must admit my methods were sometimes calculated to annoy; but I had no patience with the idiotic vanity of mediocrities."

There is only one vague, and possibly inaccurate, reference to Mickledore Direct in the Wasdale Climbing Book and Crowley probably overstates the case when he says, "it had always been the ambition of every climber". Indeed, the fact that neither Haskett Smith nor O. G. Jones refer to Mickledore Direct in their books suggests it was not generally considered to be of significant interest. The climb, known today as Crowley Direct, is short, 24 feet (8 metres) and technically Severe. The first unaided ascent was made in 1907; the following notice appeared in the first issue of the *Fell and Rock Climbing Club Journal*:

> "We are informed that one of our members, Mr H. B. Gibson, climbed the 'Direct Mickledore'… on 12th September of this year [1907]. His ascent recalls the fact that no record exists in the Wasdale Climbing Book of this having been accomplished before, except by the aid of an ice axe. It would be interesting to know if any other members have used this route. It was discussed a good deal sometime ago, but seems to have escaped notice of recent years."

During the same month (probably on 7th May) the Reverend T.C.V. Bastow climbed Parson's Gully, on The East Buttress of Scafell. He ascended this alone and afterwards left an account in the Climbing Book in which he comments on the curious neglect of The East Buttress. Unfortunately Bastow's climbing ethic was somewhat suspect as he was reputed to wander about the crags with a three-pronged claw attached to the end of a length of rope, which he would throw up the rocks till it caught on something and then swarm up the rope. (5)

Vernon Blake and A.W. Southall made the first ascent of the Great Chimney, on the west wall of Deep Gill, on 23rd September 1895. They made a note of this in the Climbing Book but didn't include any description or comment on the technically difficulty. The climb is straightforward apart from a large chockstone that is awkward and strenuous to overcome. For a short period thereafter the route was referred to as "Blake's Chimney".

It was still a long journey to Wasdale Head, usually entailing an overnight train to Drigg or Seascale followed by a thirteen mile walk or ride in a horse and trap. Accommodation was limited to the Wastwater Hotel, Row Farm Guest House and Burnthwaite Farm, all of which would be full at the popular times of year and those that hadn't booked months in advance might find themselves sleeping in a chair or with the rats in the barn.

Haskett Smith's book *Climbing in the British Isles* from 1894.
Photo: Mike Cocker

George Abraham climbing whilst being watched by A. E. Field. The Barn Door Traverse was a favourite problem in its day. Modern climbers have been prevented from repeating this traverse by some very conscientious pointing work between the stones, no doubt a result of some health and safety review. The crack in the original glass plate of the negative perfectly illustrates the fragile nature of the early photographic materials.

Claude Barton described the following way of attaining a standing position in the doorway in an article from 1900.

"Another method of ascent is to spring from the ground and seize the stone sill of the doorway with the hands and pull up the rest, but if the lower doors are open so that a kick off with the feet is not permitted, and the upper door closed so that the hands are unable to grip the inside of the sill, this will be found exceedingly difficult, and has, I believe, only once been successfully accomplished." (6)

The hotel was the main social centre with climbers moving freely between the different venues. The majority rose early and would climb in all but the very worst weather. The barn wall, outside the hotel, was often used for practice and the traverse of the stable door was a favourite problem. The Climbing Book was kept in the Smoking Room at the hotel, which was an area generally reserved for conversation. The younger and more boisterous residents tended to frequent the Billiard Room next door, where various gymnastic feats would be performed on or around the billiard table. There was much singing, joviality and generally high-spirited behaviour. Alcohol was used in moderation; the majority it seems preferred soft drinks or water. The only rule they had was that the Billiard Room must be vacated by midnight so that the person sleeping on the table was able to get to bed.

Almost without exception the loosely knit and homogenous group that gathered at Wasdale Head during the 1890s were well educated and financially secure. The majority came from the professional middle classes, and were doctors, lawyers, university professors or successful businessmen, with responsibilities and family commitments. A few, like Haskett Smith and Aleister Crowley, were bachelors with independent means. Climbing was a holiday activity, most could only manage a week or two a year, and it was mainly, but not exclusively, a masculine gathering. Climbing, for them, provided an escape from the constraints and formalities of the late Victorian era and was an activity where they could let off steam, make new friends and enjoy the pursuit of a common objective. It was a relaxed and tolerant community without conscious organisation or regulation but with a strong feeling of camaraderie and a sense that they were in some indefinable way unique and the undertaking special.

Footnotes

1) The winter of 1891 was unusually severe with snow and ice remaining in the gullies until the beginning of May.

2) A few days earlier they had made the first winter ascent of Central Gully on Gable Crag and during the previous New Year period the first winter ascent of Grainy Gill.

3) There is no suggestion that Collie's party were ever criticised for "improving" the crucial foothold in Moss Gill, which, according to George Abraham, soon became so nail scratched that within a few years it was impossible to tell which bit of rock had been worked.

4) It is interesting to note the unusual conditions with a high route like Moss Gill being essentially a rock climb whereas a much lower route was filled with ice. This must have been as a consequence of a period of sustained high pressure with hard overnight frosts but little or no precipitation.

5) According to Aleister Crowley, Bastow claimed to possess a rudimentary tail and was "credited with a readiness to demonstrate the Darwinian theory to any young anatomist who might be in the offing".

6) 'A Wet Day at Wasdale' - C. Barton, *Climber's Club Journal*, 1900.

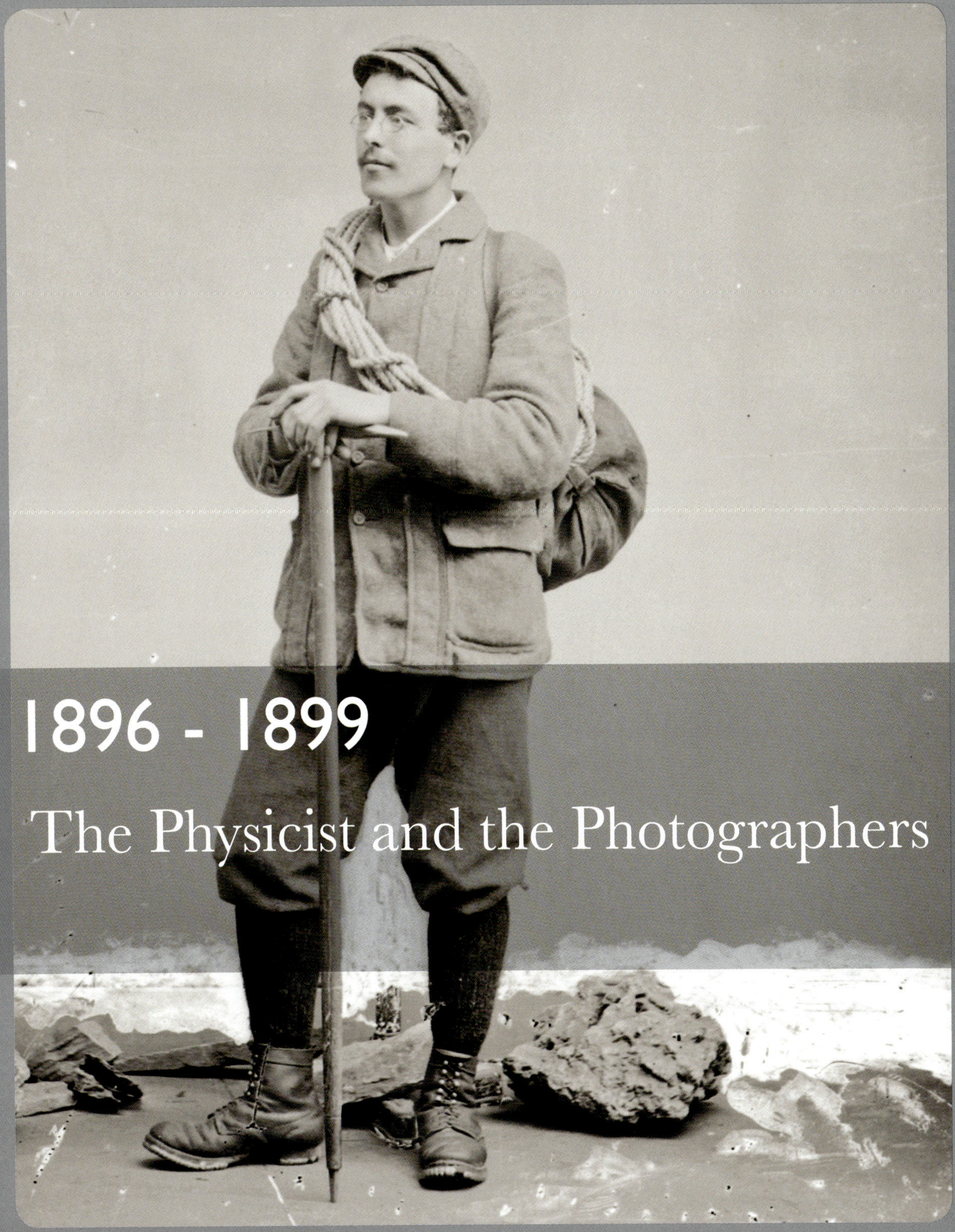

1896 - 1899

The Physicist and the Photographers

Ashley (left) and George Abraham's pioneering photography provides a unique perspective of Victorian climbing.

By the middle of the decade Owen Glynne Jones was generally acknowledged to be the outstanding climber of his generation (1). During the Easter of 1896 he travelled by train from London to The Lake District and early one morning called, unannounced, at George and Ashley Abraham's home in Keswick. George was 24 years old and Ashley 20, and both were photographers (2). They had been dabbling in climbing for several years but were still relatively inexperienced. Jones and Ashley had met briefly at Wasdale Head the previous year but barely knew each other, and so it is slightly surprising that Jones, at such short notice, managed to overcome parental misgivings and persuade the two brothers to accompany him to Wasdale for a few days. Jones probably had an ulterior motive for he was preparing a book on climbing and may well have been looking for original ways to illustrate this. George and Ashley were, no doubt, flattered by the invitation and delighted to find someone willing to pose for them in difficult and exposed situations. In the event they became great friends and for the next three years formed one of the most successful climbing partnerships active in The Lake District in the years before the First World War.

They spent their first day climbing the ridges on the Napes then, on 20th April, went up to Scafell Crag where they made the first ascent of Jones' Route from Deep Ghyll. The climb started up the curving crack first ascended by Tribe and Hopkinson in 1893 and continued directly up the steep and exposed arête above (3). Ashley took a photograph of Jones and his brother climbing the initial curving crack; it was the first photograph ever taken of a new route being made in Britain. Jones, who was belayed at the top of the crack with George following, takes up the story:

> "My companions were holding an animated discussion below on the subject of photography. The light was excellent, and our positions most artistic. The cameras were left in the cave at the foot of the ghyll. Ashley was afraid I meant to go up without him; but his professional instinct got the better of his desire to climb, and, shouting out to us to stay where we were for five minutes, he ran round to the high-level traverse on the other side of the ghyll, and down the Lord's Rake to the cavern. George had the tripod screw and could not hand it to his brother; so, asking me to hold him firmly with the rope, he practised throwing stones across the gully to the traverse. Then, tying the screw to a stone, he managed to project this over successfully. We composed our limbs to a photographic quiescence. Ashley had a splendid wide-angled lens, which, from his elevated position on the traverse opposite, could take in 400 feet of the cliff, showing the entire route to the summit. It was his turn to take the lead. 'Mr. Jones! I can't see you, your clothes are so dark.' I apologised. 'Will you step out a foot or two from that hole?' I was in a cheerful mood and ready to oblige a friend, but the platform was scarcely two feet square, and to acquiesce was to step out a few hundred feet into Deep Ghyll. For this I had not made adequate preparation and told him so. 'Well, will you take off your coat?' That I could do with pleasure, and for a while his instructions were levelled at George. He was in an awkward place and was much cramped in ensuring safety, but Ashley was dissatisfied and insisted on him lifting the left leg. This gave him no foothold to speak of, but in the cause of photography he had been trained to manage without such ordinary aids. He grumbled a little at the inconvenience but obeyed, resolving that if he were living when the next slide was to be exposed he himself would be the manipulator and his brother the centre of the picture. The ghyll had become rather gloomy and we had a lengthy exposure. I was glad to slip on my jacket again and draw in the rope for George's ascent… Then came the question of getting our third man up. We tried to throw the rope-end to him, but it persisted in clinging to the face vertically below us and would not be caught. I had to return to firma loca and throw the rope from there. Ashley now reached it safely, tied himself on, and hastened up to our level, having left his camera on the traverse below. In this way we found ourselves together again, on the corner of the arête. The others fixed themselves to a little belaying-pin while I attempted to swarm up the vertical corner. A couple of feet above their heads I found that the only available holds were sloping the wrong way. They could be easily reached, but were unsafe for hauling, and after clinging for some minutes without advancing an inch I was compelled to descend and reconsider the problem."

Overleaf: O.G. Jones.
Photo: © abrahamphotographic / FRCC Archives

The first ascent of Jones' Route from Deep Ghyll, probably the first time that a new route had been recorded by a photograph. Note how the profile of the crag has been altered at the top right side of the picture.

This is the remarkably bold top pitch of Jones' Route from Deep Ghyll, now known simply as Jones' Arête. This pitch is now used as the final pitch of Moss Ledge Direct Route.

Jones tried a variation further right, but found this even more difficult and so returned for a further attempt on the arête. Another party of climbers, at the top of Deep Gill, watched their manoeuvres with interest.

> "This time Ashley gave me a shoulder at a slightly lower level on the ghyll side of the ridge. A trying drag upwards with very scanty fingerholds brought my knees on to a satisfying hollow in a little ledge, and steadied by the two side faces of the sloping slab I stepped up and on to it. The cheers of the observing party told us that our mauvais pas was practically overcome. The other two men came up with a little assistance from the rope, and we cleared away the loose stones from our platform. It shelved badly downwards and offered no guarantee of safety in case I fell from the next vertical bit. But George sturdily rammed his brother close against the wall and intimated that the two would accept the responsibility of fielding me if necessary. I mounted their shoulders, and reached up at arm's length to a sharp and firm edge of rock. A preliminary grind of my boot into a shoulder-blade and then a clear swing out on the arms, a desperate pull-up with knees and toes vainly seeking support, and at last the upper shelf was mounted. But we were all breathless. The lower edge of the broken crest of rock that marks the Low Man was now close at hand. Close by was the fine cairn built when the pinnacle was first climbed from Lord's Rake. A few yards off to the east the edge of the cliff was cut by the top of Slingsby's Chimney, and before us remained the magnificent ridge up to the summit."

The 22nd April was George and Ashley's last day. The weather was still fine so Jones, thinking it "imprudent to take their votes" on the matter, announced that they were returning to Scafell to reconnoitre the start to Collier's Climb:

> "There could be no possible doubt of the place. A thin crack rose direct from the Progress, overhanging for the first ten feet, then leaning back a trifle towards the left. A yard or two to the left of this a square corner led directly up so as to join the crack just below a thin chimney, that started some twenty feet above our heads. To get to this chimney was the difficulty. Either the cleft or the corner should be taken. Which was the easier? I first tried the cleft, but it overhung so seriously that I dared not venture further... We decided to take the corner. A. was to stand on a small ledge about a foot above the Progress, and brace himself firmly enough to hold my weight. G. acted as a sort of flying buttress for his brother, and paid out my rope with extreme care. From A's shoulders I could just reach a high hand-hold with the left. But one grip at that height was useless, as the body had to be lifted up on to the rib of rock separating the two clefts. A. then padded his head with a handkerchief beneath his cap, and begged me to stand on it. However steady a young man may be, there are times when his friends think him weak in the head. Such a time was this, and I anxiously asked him if he could hold it perfectly still while I used it. 'You may do anything except waltz on it,' was the encouraging rejoinder, and I promptly placed my left foot on his parietal. 'That's all right,' the tough young head called out, 'you may stay there all day if you like.' This was reassuring, but I had come out to climb and meant to move on. Yet for the life of me I could not see what to do next. The left foot required a lift before the high handhold could be employed, and there was nothing for it to rest against except the square corner of the recess. Two or three times I tried hard to grip the corner with the toe of my boot, but ineffectually. Then A., seeing my trouble, reached up a hand and held my boot on an infinitesimal ledge. It felt firm, and I trusted to it. With the first movement upwards my right hand felt a charmingly secure depression in the rib above, and swinging clear from A.'s head I dragged up on to the buttress and felt that the game was half won already. The rib was easy to ascend for a foot or two, till indeed it terminated at the small chimney above. But caution was the instinct uppermost in my mind, and the climb to the grassy platform above might, in spite of appearances, prove nasty. Casting around for some means of anchoring on my own rope, I saw that in the crack to my right a bunch of small stones were firmly jammed, and that daylight could be seen behind them down a hole that pointed through to the Progress, fifteen feet below. Here was a chance that, if we had known of it at first, might have been used to conserve our strength and nerve from the start. The others were as yet unroped.

"Calling to them to let go the rope, I drew up the free end by my teeth and 'unemployed' hand, and let it fall straight down the hole to them. If a fall occurred now in trying the next few feet I could only tumble three or four yards, and should not pass over my friends' heads and the Rake's Progress… Now was the time to appreciate the joy of climbing, in perfect health, with perfect weather, and in a difficult place without danger, and I secretly laughed as I called to the others that the outlook was terribly bad and that our enterprise must be given up. But they also laughed, and told me to go higher and change my mind, for they knew by the tone that my temper was unruffled. A few feet more and I drew up to the platform. It was about a yard wide and three yards in length, reminding us strongly of the Tennis Court ledge, a similar formation half way up Moss Ghyll. Between the ledge and the wall rising above it a fissure cut down into the mountain. It still held some old winter snow, and its depths were cold as a refrigerator. Shouting to the others to rope up at a distance of thirty feet apart, I sat down on the grass with my legs dangling in the frigid fissure, bracing myself to stand any jerks that might be given to the rope by a sudden slip of the second man at the rounding of the rib."

Above the ledge where Jones belayed the climbing was easier and they managed to complete the second ascent of Collier's Climb without further incident. In *Mountain Adventures At Home and Abroad* George writes that he and Ashley invented the threading technique that Jones used to protect the difficult upper section of the first pitch and that they had already used it to good effect on several occasions (4).

Jim Puttrell lived in Sheffield and worked as a manager in a silversmiths. He was one of the first people to explore the gritstone outcrops in the Peak District where he made numerous first ascents. In July 1896, when he was 27 years old and on an early visit to The Lake District, he managed to climbed 65 feet up the virgin rock to the right of Collier's Climb, reaching the grass ledge at the top of the first pitch, and in doing so created an easier alternative start. Jones and the Abraham brothers had independently come to the conclusion that a feasible route could be made in this area, so when the Abrahams heard about Puttrell's ascent they wrote to him asking for further information. They subsequently arranged to meet at Sty Head Tarn at 11:00am on 12th July 1897 and arrived within two minutes of each other - the Abrahams walking from Keswick and Puttrell from Langdale. They climbed Central Gully on Great End as a preliminary then made their way over to Scafell. At the foot of the steep wall they roped up and, with George Abraham in the lead, made short work of Puttrell's variation leading to the grass ledge on Collier's Climb. They continued up a short chimney then traversed rightwards over narrow ledges to a pinnacle half way up the crag where they stopped for a break and started singing. Puttrell's account of the day, in the *Yorkshire Rambler's Club Journal* (1900), says that their chorus drew the attention of some passing walkers who thought they might be in trouble and shouted up to ask if they needed assistance. The climbers replied, to the bewilderment of the party below, that the only thing they required was a cup of tea (5). In jocular spirits and with Puttrell now in the lead, they continued more easily to the final deep cleft which they named "Puttrell's Chimney". Owen Glynne Jones made the second ascent the following Christmas, adding a variation finish and, in recognition of George and Ashley's contribution, christened the route Keswick Brothers' Climb. George, in *British Mountain Climbs*, recalls a slightly different version of their encounter with the passing tourists:

"The first party who visited the place were watched from Mickledore Ridge by a lady and a gentleman immaculately clad in attire more suited to Piccadilly than Mickledore. At this pinnacle [half way up the climb] it seemed that the pioneers had arrived at a standstill; the route up the buttress looked impossible. At that moment a thin voice was wafted up from the Ridge, "If you please, is there a road up there?" The irony of the situation was so overpoweringly amusing, and the answer may have seemed discourteous, for the climbers simply roared with laughter. A peep around the corner to the right revealed a surprisingly easy exit into the now well-known wide crack, and the climbers disappeared by that "road", whence the summit was soon reached."

Photo: © abrahamphotographic / FRCC Archives

The Keswick Brothers' Climb, first climbed with Jim Putterell.

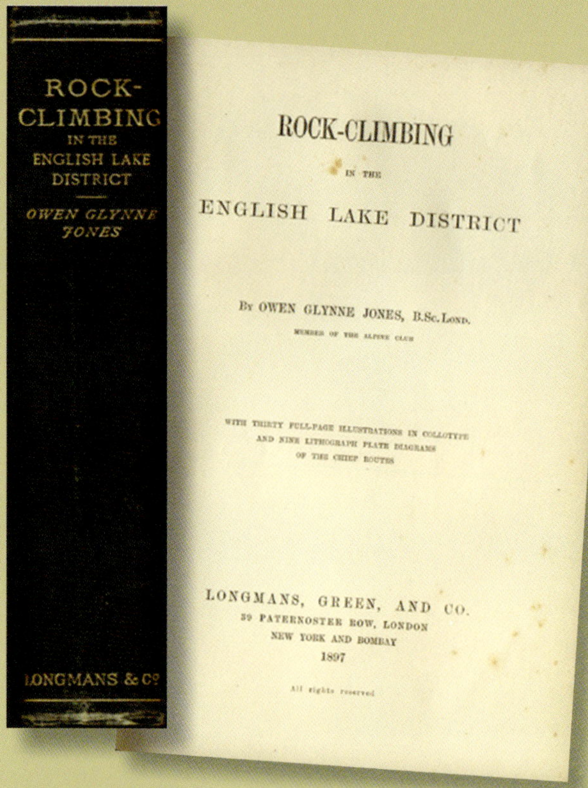

Photo: Mike Cocker

The spine and fronticepiece of Jones' *Rock Climbing in the English Lake District.*

Owen Glynne Jones kept detailed records of all his climbs in a series of notebooks. Unfortunately the originals have been lost but much of the information contained in these was incorporated into his book *Rock Climbing in the English Lake District*, which was published in December 1897. This was a substantial volume, richly illustrated with photographs by the Abraham brothers and completely different in concept to Haskett Smith's climbing guides. Much of the book describes Jones' own experiences and reads more like a series of adventure stories than a guidebook. It appealed to a wider audience, and for the first time the general public was able to get an insight into the activity of the British rock climber. In his introduction, Jones listed all the climbs described in order of difficulty, classifying them as: Easy, Moderate, Difficult or Exceptionally Severe. This was done so that anyone coming to the district for the first time, and not having the advantage of being in the company of an experienced climber, would be able to select a route to match their ability. It was the first adjectival grading system. It is still being used today, although the number of categories has had to be extended to accommodate the increasing levels of difficulty encountered on the new climbs made by later generations. Jones' book was well received by the climbing fraternity at Wasdale Head and it soon became a popular objective to attempt to complete all the routes he described (6).

O.G. Jones returned to Wasdale Head the following spring and stayed for two weeks. On 19th April 1898 he teamed up with G.C. Walker (7), who appears to have been a chance companion, and made the first ascent of Jones' Route Direct from Lord's Rake; the first really difficult face climb ever made in Britain. They climbed in socks with their boots strung round their necks:

> "We had spent a long and exciting day in the neighbourhood, and were descending Slingsby's Chimney late in the afternoon, when we were suddenly struck with the idea of descending the fissure behind the nose and prospecting the face of rock between it and Deep Ghyll. A rough inspection of the first fifty feet below us proving satisfactory, we hastened down Steep Ghyll and traversed across to the top of the first pitch in Deep Ghyll. In spite of the late hour I could not refrain from a trial trip on the edge of the great Low Man buttress. At the point where the earlier party found the direct ascent barred by smooth ice on the wall, and decided to traverse off to the gully on the left, we had a council of war. It resulted in my throwing down my boots to Walker, and then crawling up fifty feet of, perhaps, the steepest and smoothest slabs to which I have ever trusted myself. This brought me to a tiny corner where I essayed to haul in the rope attached to my companion. But he also had to remove his boots and traverse to a point vertically below me before he could follow up in safety. We were now some distance to the left of the edge of Deep Ghyll, and straight up above us we could distinguish the crack where our new route was to terminate. Getting Walker to lodge firmly in a notch somewhat larger than mine, six feet away on the Steep Ghyll side, I went off again up another forty feet of smooth rock, aided by a zig-zagging crack an inch or so in width, that supplied sufficient lodgement for the toes, and a moderate grip for the finger-tips. After both had arrived thus far, we were able, with extreme care, to reach the side wall of the nose itself, and at a point, perhaps, fifty feet from its crest we turned round its main outside buttress and found ourselves in a spacious chamber with a flat floor and a considerable roof, the first and only genuine resting-place worthy the name that we found along our route. We could look straight down Hopkinson's Gully, and would gladly have descended into it and 'passed the time of day' with a little speculative scrambling thereabouts. But darkness was coming on apace, and we had yet a most awkward corner to negotiate before finishing our appointed business. Standing on Walker's shoulders I screwed myself out at the right-hand top corner of our waiting-room, and started along a traverse across the right face of the nose. The toes of the feet were in a horizontal crack, the heels had no support, and the hands no grip. It was only by pressing the body close to the wall, which was fortunately a few degrees away from the perpendicular, and by sliding the feet along almost inch by inch, that the operation could be effected. It was with no small sense of relief that the end was reached in a few yards, and a narrow vertical fissure entered that gave easy access to the top of the nose. Then we put on our boots again and hurried. *Rock Climbing in the English Lake District*, 1900."

Photo: Walter Brunskill

Siegfried Herford and George Sansom on the second ascent of Jones' Route Direct from Lords Rake. Herford is poised on the delicate narrow ledge called The Gangway.

Photo: Gordon Stainforth

Gavin Brown embarks on The Mantleshelf move above The Waiting Room on Jones' Route Direct from Lord's Rake. This is the celebrated traditional crux of the route; it is also the location of Eva Bailey's fatal accident in 1938.

The earlier party referred to was Charles Hopkinson's attempt on the Pinnacle Face in December 1887. Jones is almost certainly incorrect in what he says, but only repeating a widespread misunderstanding of the time. It is much more likely that Hopkinson's party only climbed the lower buttress to the snow covered grass ledge at the foot of the face and then traversed left into Steep Gill (8). Jones and Walker's ascent broke a psychological barrier and was an inspiration to a whole generation of climbers. It made conceivable the possibility of climbing the exposed and unprotected faces that had previously been avoided (9). Their entry in the Climbing Book was brief and lacking detail; a full account of the climb wasn't available until the Abraham brothers published a second and enlarged edition of *Rock Climbing in the English Lakes District* in 1900.

During the ascent described above, Jones looked across to the steep slabs below Hopkinson's Cairn and thought it might be possible to find a way up these. This line, the Direct from Lord's Rake to Hopkinson's Cairn, was the scene of an appalling accident when four men were killed attempting it in September 1903. Had Jones lived longer he may well have been the first to conquer this coveted route; he was certainly capable of it.

Three days after his successful ascent of the Pinnacle face, on 22nd April, Jones made a solo ascent of a new route on the Deep Gill side of Scafell Pinnacle. This became known as Jones and Collier's Climb; an obscure, grassy route that is rarely climbed today. The current guidebook lists O.G. Jones and J. Collier as having made the first ascent together, but in fact Jones climbed this alone, crediting the idea to "Dr Collier, who told me some years ago that the only real difficulties were concentrated in the first thirty feet of ascent" (10). Jones included the following account in his article 'English Climbing: Considered Mainly from An Alpine Standpoint', which was amongst the first articles published in *The Climbers' Club Journal* (1898):

> "The first part overhung considerably, and the footholds - such as they were - sloped the wrong way. But the rocks were dry and warm, in the best possible condition, and the finger tips could find an abundance of encouraging little roughnesses on the slabs. Scarcely two minutes of uncertainty, and the route was assured. An upward traverse to the left, away from the forbidding buttress that figures so prominently in the best views of the pinnacle, led to a slight chimney that conducted me easily to the Low Man ridge in ten minutes from Deep Ghyll. An equal interval sufficed to allow a traverse of the pinnacle, and a descent by the Professor's Chimney to the starting point."

Jones continued on to Mickledore where he had arranged to meet George and Ashley Abraham for an attempt on the unclimbed Pisgah Buttress.

The Abrahams, who were also staying at the Wastwater Hotel, had examined the lower section of Pisgah Buttress in the morning, but being unable to find a practical way up climbed the adjacent Moss Gill as far as Tennis Court Ledge, to try to gain access to the upper half of the buttress. Jones arrived at Mickledore at the appointed hour expecting company, only to receive a call from the depths of Moss Gill. Ten minutes later he joined George and Ashley on Tennis Court Ledge and, after tying onto the rope, started to inspect the slightly overhanging crack above. This is currently graded 5a, and Jones had to use a shoulder and steadying hand for his feet to get established on the grassy ledge above, which they named the Fives Court. Above this a large and precariously poised block barred access to the obvious chimney on the left and Jones was forced to climb directly up to the outer edge of the buttress. Beyond, the route was straightforward and they soon found themselves on the easier ground near the top of the ridge, which they reached less than an hour after leaving Tennis Court Ledge (11).

In December 1897 The Climbers' Club was founded with C.E. Mathews (12) elected as the first President and F. Morshead and F.H. Bowring as Vice Presidents. Two hundred members enrolled and O.G. Jones, W.P. Haskett Smith and Cecil Slingsby were on the original committee.

Dave Woods and Joe Holden on the first pitch of Jones and Collier's Climb.

The object was to encourage mountaineering, particularly in England, Wales and Ireland, and to provide a forum through which climbers could meet and exchange information. The first journal was published in August 1898 and informal meets were held that year, simultaneously at the Wastwater Hotel and the Pen-y-Gwryd Hotel in Snowdonia, from mid August to mid September (13).

John Robinson had been aware of the potential for a new climb on the west wall of Deep Gill for several years and had made an attempt with H.W. Blunt and another Oxford don in autumn 1897, when he was forced to retreat due to poor conditions. Robinson returned for a further attempt with Blunt and J.H. Doncaster, the latter from Sheffield, on 10th September 1898. The trio left the hotel at 7:45am and approached the climb by way of Red Gill. Robinson down climbed the upper section with the support of a top rope to inspect an undercut pinnacle that he thought might be problematic, but after clearing away some loose rock and convincing himself that this was climbable, returned to his companions and they descended to the foot of the climb. The route, West Wall Climb, starts at a chimney and is currently graded Very Difficult. Blunt left a route description in the Climbing Book and Robinson published an expanded account in the *Yorkshire Ramblers' Club Journal* (1899), of which the following is an extract:

> "The chimney was tackled at once - Dalesman [Robinson] leading as before, until the upper ledge above the chimney was reached, when he decided to pass over a corner of rock round to the right. To make this possible, it was necessary to pull out a number of loose stones which rested in the crack of the ledge above, which done, he planted himself firmly on the rock ledge, and, with the Don [Blunt] holding onto the rope, he gave the Alpine Expert [Doncaster] a shoulder. The Expert, thinking he was on the face of the Za [Aiguille de la Za, in Switzerland] once more, went up the rocks like a chamois, until a halt was called on a ledge about 20 feet above. There the others joined him, and having passed a detached rock slab arrived at the foot of the undercut pinnacle. The Dalesman again took the lead and went up the left-hand side for about 10 feet, then passed over the nose of the pinnacle into a little gully on the right-hand side. Here a rock shelf led to a small recess from which the climb could be finished direct up the arête, or by a traverse on the left to and along the edge of Blake's Chimney [The Great Chimney]. Both finishes were taken."

One of the curious facts about the early history of Lakeland climbing is the number of leading teams that were brothers who operated together. The Pilkingtons, Pendleburys, Hopkinsons and the Abrahams have already been mentioned. The Barton, Broadrick and Thompson brothers, who all made their earliest visits to Wasdale in the late 1890s, continued this tradition leaving their own impressions on the crags surrounding Wasdale Head.

Claude Barton was an estate manager and his brother Guy a doctor. They were both strong climbers but Claude usually did the leading. Their first new route together was a variation finish to Moss Gill, which they climbed on 5th September 1898. This followed the oblique vegetated crack up the corner to the right of Collie's Exit and is currently graded Very Severe but rarely climbed today. More impressive were their winter ascents of North (Penrith) Climb and Steep Gill via Slingsby's Chimney, made with F. Cowley and C. Davey, on 8th and 11th April 1899, respectively. Details are sparse for the only record is the brief entry in their personal climbing diary where they noted: "the wind had gone due north and with the snow as well things were moderately Alpine". This was their "first encounter with snow and ice" and they found "North Climb proved moderately hard under the present conditions". Of Steep Gill and Slingsby's Chimney, they recorded that "our position on the Pinnacle wall was chilling in the extreme" and that "it was quite by chance that we did not get frost bitten". Despite this they completed the route in three and a half hours and concluded that it was "nowhere really difficult barring the 60 feet in the middle of the climb which includes the Slingsby Chimney" (14). They descended via Deep Gill where they took a photograph, which shows old hard snow in the bed of the gully and their clothes white with frost. The speed with which they overcame the technical difficulties indicates the high level of inherent skill they had in undertaking what today would still be considered hard mixed climbing.

Owen Glynne Jones was killed in a climbing accident in the Alps, on 28th August 1899 (15). He was 32 years old at the time and at the height of his powers. The climbing community was shocked by this and the Abrahams, who practically worshipped Jones, were devastated. His passing took some of the impetus out of Lakeland climbing and for a decade after his death, Jones' personality, through the legacy of his book and his climbs, continued to exert a powerful restraining influence on the psyche of many Lake District climbers. It took a new generation, sufficiently distant and free from preconceptions, to transcend these inhibitions. Had Jones lived longer it is likely that some of the routes climbed later by Botterill, Herford, Sansom and even Kelly might have fallen earlier under his impetus.

'That there's some corner of a foreign graveyard that is forever England'.
O. G. Jones' resting place in Evolena, Switzerland seems a little neglected for one of the best climbers of his day.

Footnotes

1) Although not everyone agreed with this. Aleister Crowley, for example, thought him reckless and vain, and Norman Collie once recalled an uncomplimentary episode when he had to help Jones down from the top of Napes Needle.
2) George and Ashley worked in a photography business owned by their father G.P. Abraham, which was located in the premises now occupied by George Fisher Ltd, on Borrowdale Road, in Keswick.
3) Known today as Jones' Arête. Tribe and Hopkinson had attempted the arête in 1893 but retreated and escaped by a short abseil and traverse to Hopkinson's Cairn
4) Jones and the Abrahams were probably the first climbers to experiment with techniques to improve belaying and protection.
5) This meeting was the start of a lasting friendship between Puttrell and the Abraham brothers. In later years they would climb together in the Peak District, Wales, Scotland and the Alps. Their most notable achievement, with the addition of E.A. Baker, was the first ascent of Crowberry Ridge Direct, Severe, on Buachaille Etive Mor, in May 1900.
6) Jones' book remains a classic of British mountaineering literature. The Abraham brothers published a revised and extended second edition in 1900 and a further edition in 1911.
7) In the second edition of *Rock Climbing in the English Lake District* Walkers initials are printed as G.T., but in Jones' entry in the Wasdale Climbing Book these are clearly written as G.C. It seems that Walker was a chance companion for his name doesn't appear in the hotel visitors' book or in any other records and we know nothing more about him.
8) See chapter 1881-1888, footnote 4, page 52 for further comment on this.
9) Jones' Route Direct remained unrepeated until Siegfried Herford climbed it with either Walter Brunskill or George Sansom in April 1912.
10) This was probably Dr Joseph Collier of Collier's Climb, but could refer to Dr William Collier who was also a medical man active at Wasdale in the 1890s.
11) Siegfried Herford and F.M.J. McConechy made the first direct ascent of the lower part of the buttress on the 6th July 1911.
12) Charles Edward Mathews (1834-1905) was a solicitor from Birmingham and an original member of the Alpine Club. In 1870 he founded the 'Society of Welsh Rabbits' with Frederick Morshead and others, its object being the exploration of Snowdonia in winter.
13) The formation of The Climbers' Club gave a degree of recognition and respectability to the sport. Not everyone approved and some of the ultra-conservative members of the Alpine Club chided Mathews for giving his support to a new club "for chimney sweeps".
14) Low Man via Slingsby's Chimney, which is currently grade IV, 5, didn't receive a second winter ascent until 1985.
15) Jones was attempting the third ascent of the Ferpecle Ridge, on Dent Blanche, with his friend F.W. Hill and three guides. One of the guides fell killing himself and three others. Only Hill survived, and being unable to retreat had to complete the climb alone. Jones' last major climb in The Lake District was the first ascent of Walker's Gully, on Pillar Rock, done in desperate semi-winter conditions with George Abraham and A.E. Field, on 7th January 1899.

Photo: © abrahamphotographic / FRCC Archives

This classic image of the entrance hallway of the Wastwater Hotel was probably set up for the photograph. It does illustrate well the equipment of those days, the ice axes, knapsacks and the thick hemp ropes. The boots, which are mainly edged with clinker nails, were derived from the working boots worn by local farmers. This type of footwear, complete with identical nailing patterns, was still widely used by farmers well into the the 1970s.

1900 - 1903

Conquest and Loss

Photo: Douglas-Milner collection

Looking down Thompsons' Route to the depths of Deep Gill.

Right: Thompsons' Route takes a steep traverse rising leftwards from the gully near the lower left part of the picture.
This photograph, by the Abraham brothers, illustrates a remarkable innovation - the lake in the distance does not exist. It has been created by the brothers to look like Derwent Water backed by Skiddaw. It is not possible to see these features from where the photograph is taken. The Abrahams had effectively photo-shopped this image over 100 years ago!

Overleaf: Dave Carr on the crack splitting the upper section of Botterill's Slab.
Photo: Al Phizacklea

On 1st June 1901 two brothers from Cardiff, Philip and Peter Thompson, discovered a new route on the Deep Gill face of Scafell Pinnacle. They had recently made the second ascent of the New West Climb on Pillar Rock and the fifth ascent of the upper half of Pisgah Buttress, and were climbing confidently together. From the top of the first pitch of the Professor's Chimney, they traversed out onto the steep and exposed wall of the High Man overlooking the upper part Deep Gill and "worked upwards with excellent handhold [sic] to a grass ledge from which a short stiff exit led up to [a] slight chimney" which they followed to the summit. They thought the climb to be "rather easier and not nearly as fine" as Jones' Route from Deep Gill and the rock "not everywhere reliable". Thompsons' Route is currently graded Very Difficult and, although short (45 metres) with the occasional loose hold, it has exceptional impact.

Nevertheless by the beginning of the new century it was widely held that the crags around Wasdale were becoming exhausted and that all the worthwhile lines had already been discovered. Other climbing areas had started to come to prominence in The Lake District, new crags had been discovered in Buttermere and Langdale and in Snowdonia, Archer Thompson and friends were creating routes as difficult as any in The Lakes. In the Peak District, on the gritstone edges, a new style of climbing was evolving, one that required more poise and balance than the traditional muscular grip and pull approach. And so, for the first time, the advancement of British rock climbing began to be more diverse and less exclusively focused on the activities at Wasdale.

Photo: © abrahamphotographic, FRCC Archives

The only person who had the skill and mental equilibrium to rival O.G. Jones and advance the standard of rock climbing in The Lake District was Fred Botterill. Botterill was from Leeds and a member of the Yorkshire Ramblers' Club. He had done relatively little climbing in The Lake District, but found that he could easily apply the delicate techniques of balance and friction climbing acquired on his native gritstone to the volcanic rock of the high mountain crags above Wasdale. The weather was settled over the 1903 Whitsuntide holiday and the rock on Scafell in good climbing condition. Fred Botterill arrived at Wasdale Head with three friends - H. Williamson, J.E. Grant and an unnamed novice climber who was an expert gymnast. On their first day, Saturday 30th May, they climbed Moss Gill by the direct finish and Steep Gill via Slingsby's Chimney and, over the next two days, Kern Knotts Crack, Kern Knotts West Chimney, Napes Needle and on Pillar Rock, North Climb by The Hand Traverse. The gymnast appeared to be holding his own so they agreed that on Tuesday, 2nd June, they would attempt the second ascent of Jones' Route Direct from Lord's Rake, on Scafell Pinnacle. However, in the morning, Botterill felt unwell and was reluctant to undertake any hard climbing, so they ascended Deep Gill and the Pinnacle from the Jordan Gap instead and then descended Broad Stand to Mickledore. Botterill had now recovered his usual form so they decided to try Keswick Brothers' Climb while the gymnast walked to the summit of Scafell Pike. During their search for the start they noticed a mossy corner that looked unclimbed and so ventured up this instead and made the first ascent of a route that remained unrecorded for over 100 years, it was described for the first time in the latest *Scafell and Wasdale* guidebook (2014). Botterill, however, wrote an article, 'Two New Climbs On Scafell Crags', published later that year in *The Yorkshire Ramblers' Club Journal* (1903), that included the following account:

> "The idea of a new climb of any importance in the Wasdale district had never crossed our minds, and the suggestion of one on Scafell Crags - perhaps the most frequented rocks of all - would, if proposed, have been received with derision. Nevertheless, whilst looking for the foot of Keswick Brothers' Climb we chanced upon a square opening which, judging by the quantity of moss and grass in it, seemed to denote something new. The leader had by then quite recovered his spirits, and although the others protested there was nothing new to do on Scafell the party started up, H. Williamson being second and J. E. Grant third.
>
> "We soon found ourselves facing a crack some six inches wide which leaned away to the left at an angle of about 70°. It was decidedly rotten, but after clearing away a few loose boulders up went the leader with both hands in the crack for about 40ft. until he was stopped for want of hand or footholds. He then bore away to the left and upwards until the ledge of Keswick Brothers' traverse was reached, and three yards along this the leader found a cairn. Whilst trying to locate the ledge Williamson attacked the continuation of the crack and managed to lead up what proved to be the second mauvais pas (the first is at the commencement) - a hand-over-hand climb of about 12ft. After this we entered a good sized chimney with a large chockstone overhead and by the aid of back and knee we passed up the chimney, underneath the chockstone, and then up into the final gully. From here the ascent was easy, and coming for the first time across nail marks, we rightly concluded this was the upper part of Collier's Climb.
>
> "Our second and third were now convinced that something new had been done, and entered heartily into the task of building a cairn at the head of the gully. We again descended by the Broad Stand and were joined by the gymnast, to whom we somewhat boastfully announced the news. He was not adequately impressed however - mere gymnasts never are - but only made some discouraging remarks. He said we were as excited about it as a party of school boys who had found a sixpence; but then he didn't understand."

Photo:, FRCC Archive

Fred Botterill.

The climb followed the first pitch of what would later become Tricouni Slab, as far as the ledge shared by Keswick Brothers' Climb, and then continued up a slabby corner to join the upper section of Collier's Climb. Botterill left a sketch and description in the Wasdale Climbing Book, but the route seems to have been overshadowed by subsequent events and forgotten (1).

The next day, Wednesday 3rd June, the same party returned to Scafell where, without prior inspection and wearing nailed boots, Botterill made the historic first ascent of the route known ever since as Botterill's Slab:

This photograph shows Fred Botterill on the first ascent of his eponymous slab. The first ascent details in the previous Scafell guidebooks have included the comment '*climbed in nailed boots with a rucksack and an ice axe*'. This is erroneous as the photograph clearly shows that he was not carrying a rucksack.

Photo: J H Taylor

"We arranged to spend another day on the Crags in order to examine the crack to the right of the new climb, and see if a way could be found connecting it with the finish of Keswick Brothers' Climb. Business called the gymnast away, and he left us to proceed to Boot, via Burnmoor, thence to be whirled away into civilisation. During the whole of our visit we had had perfect weather, and that day was no exception. We slowly made our way up Brown Tongue, and leaving our rucksack at the foot of Deep Ghyll walked along the Rake's Progress, taking with us a light axe, which judging by the previous day's experience we were sure would be useful.

"At the foot of the climb we roped up and noticed that the time was 12.15 p.m. The going, over grass ledges, was found fairly easy, until we reached the narrow crack which may be seen from the Progress. The bottom of this was entirely hidden by grass and earth, which when vigorously attacked with the pick, was dislodged in such quantities as to seriously alarm a party coming over Hollow Stones. The removal of some boulders uncovered a large sloping slab which afforded excellent hand and foot holds and enabled the leader to proceed about 15ft up the narrow crack. Clearly no one had been here before, so we made greater efforts to advance; it was absolutely impossible however to do so in the crack, it being only 6 inches wide and about 12 inches deep, and the sides almost as smooth as the inside of a teacup. The leader reluctantly descended to the afore-mentioned slab and examined the projetcing face of the crack, which leans away towards Scafell Pike at about the same angle as the crack we had ascended the day before. This seemed equally hopeless, the ledges being all inverted and the slabs too smooth to climb with safety. Traversing about 12ft outwards to the edge formed by one side of the crack and the face of the crags, I saw that with care we could advance some distance up this nose. Clearing away the moss from little cracks here and there I managed to climb slowly upwards for about 60ft. The holds then dwindled down to little more than finger-end cracks. I looked about me and saw, some 12ft higher, a little nest about a foot square covered with dried grass. Eight feet higher still was another nest and a traverse leading back to where the crack opened into a respectable chimney. If I could only reach hold of that first nest what remained would be comparatively easy. It seemed to be a more difficult thing than I had ever done but I was anxious to tackle it. Not wishing to part with the axe I seized it between my teeth and with my fingers in the best available cracks I advanced. I cannot tell with certainty how many holds there were; but I distinctly remember that when within 2ft of the nest I had a good hold with my right hand on the face, and so ventured with my left to tear away the dried grass on the nest. I also remembered my brother Ramblers, who were at that moment exploring the depths of Gaping Ghyll, and wondered which of us were in the more comfortable situation. However, the grass removed from the ledge, a nice little resting place was exposed - painfully small, but level and quite safe. I scrambled on to it, but on account of the weight of the rope behind me, it was only with great care and some difficulty that I was able to turn round. At last I could sit down on the nest and look around me.

"The view was glorious. I could see Scafell Pike and a party round the cairn. Far below was another group intent on watching our movements, a lady being amongst the party. I once read in a book on etiquette that a gentleman in whatever situation of life should never forget his manners towards the other sex, so I raised my hat, though I wondered if the author had ever dreamed of a situation like mine. I now discovered that our 80ft of rope had quite run out and that my companions had already attached an additional 60ft. Further, I began to wonder what had become of my axe, and concluded I must unthinkingly have placed it somewhere lower down. There it was, stuck in a little crack about 5ft below me. Not knowing what was yet to come I felt I must recover it, so I lowered myself until I could reach it with my foot.

Joe Holden reaches for the upper crack on Botterill's Slab, as viewed from the stance on the Girdle of Central Buttress.

"I succeeded in balancing it on my boot, but in bringing it up it slipped and clattering on the rocks for a few feet took a final leap and stuck point downwards in the Rake's Progress. Standing up again I recommenced the ascent and climbed on to the second nest à cheval, from where, after a brief rest, I began the traverse back to the crack. This was sensational but perfectly safe. As usual I started with the wrong foot, and after taking two steps was obliged to go back. The next time I started with the left foot, then came the right, again the left, and lastly a long stride with the right brought me into the chimney. The performance was what might have been called a pas-de-quatre. Complimentary sounds came from my companions below, but without stopping to acknowledge these I pulled myself up 10ft higher on to a good grass-covered ledge to the right of the crack, smaller but very similar to Tennis Court Ledge of Moss Ghyll. 'How is it now?' my companions enquired, 'Excellent,' I replied, 'a good belaying pin and just room for three. Do you feel like following?' Without answering me the second man commenced the traverse to the chimney edge whilst I carefully belayed the rope. Up he came in splendid style and without stopping, taking only a quarter the time it had taken me. He then untied and we threw down the 140ft of rope to our third, who soon joined us. We hailed a climbing friend who was watching from the Progress and invited him to join us, but he very generously refused and said he would hover near lest we might not be able to advance further and so require the aid of a rope from above. We next christened our berth 'Coffin Ledge,' built a cairn on it and left our names on a card.

"Starting off again a long stride with the left foot took the leader back into the crack, and a stiff climb of 20 to 30 feet landed us all into an extraordinary chimney, which though only wide enough to comfortably admit the body sideways ran right into the crag for about 15ft. Like the crack below it leaned to the left at an angle of 70° or so. About 23ft up, chockstones and debris formed a roof, and suspended in the middle, some 6 or 7ft below it, were three more chockstones. When the second man had joined me he exclaimed with astonishment: 'What a place! How can we get out?' 'Wait a bit,' I answered, although for the life of me I could not then see a way. However, I went as far as I could into the crack and with restricted use of back and knee climbed upwards until the level of the suspended chockstones was reached; from there a narrow ledge rendered these easily accessible. They were securely wedged and safe to stand upon. The ledge continued along out of the crack until the most outward chockstone of the roof was within reach. This I seized with both hands, and a steady pull upwards landed me into the Puttrell Chimney of Keswick Brothers' Climb.

"Our main difficulties now being over, the comparatively easy upper gully was soon finished, and as we clambered out at the top at 3.45 p.m., our climbing friend met us with congratulations on what we all agreed was the hardest three and a half hours' work we had ever done. During the descent we recovered the axe and built a cairn at the foot of the climb.

"On our return to the Hotel at night we received cordial congratulations from our friends."

W.E. Webb, Dr J.H. Taylor and the unidentified lady to whom Botterill raised his hat, watched the climb and Taylor took a photograph showing Botterill a third of the way up the main pitch. The ice axe he carried is not visible in the photograph but was probably hidden by his body. George Abraham, when referring to Botterill's Slab in *British Mountain Climbs*, suggests that the lack of footholds forced Botterill to use the ice-axe for direct aid:

"At one point the daring pioneer's footsteps are not there, for upward progress was made by using a quaint form of ice axe plunged into some doubtful turf."

Peter Graham and Hazel Findlay enjoying the evening sun on Botterill's Slab.

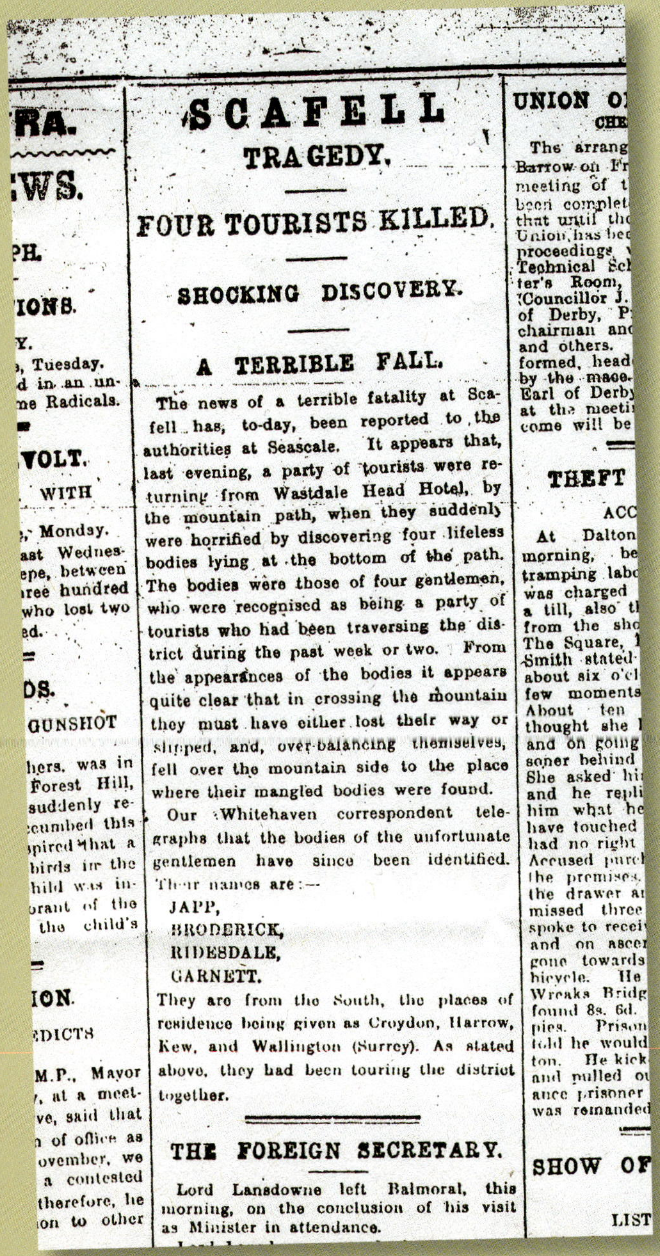

SCAFELL TRAGEDY.

FOUR TOURISTS KILLED.

SHOCKING DISCOVERY.

A TERRIBLE FALL.

The news of a terrible fatality at Scafell has, to-day, been reported to the authorities at Seascale. It appears that, last evening, a party of tourists were returning from Wastdale Head Hotel, by the mountain path, when they suddenly were horrified by discovering four lifeless bodies lying at the bottom of the path. The bodies were those of four gentlemen, who were recognised as being a party of tourists who had been traversing the district during the past week or two. From the appearances of the bodies it appears quite clear that in crossing the mountain they must have either lost their way or slipped, and, over-balancing themselves, fell over the mountain side to the place where their mangled bodies were found.

Our Whitehaven correspondent telegraphs that the bodies of the unfortunate gentlemen have since been identified. Their names are:—

JAPP,
BRODERICK,
RIDESDALE,
GARNETT.

They are from the South, the places of residence being given as Croydon, Harrow, Kew, and Wallington (Surrey). As stated above, they had been touring the district together.

THE FOREIGN SECRETARY.

Lord Lansdowne left Balmoral, this morning, on the conclusion of his visit as Minister in attendance.

Courtesey of Barrow Evening Mail.

Botterill doesn't mention this in his account, but he is rather vague about how the ice axe ended up below his feet. Abraham's suggestion may well be true for it is likely that he would have had a first hand account of the climb from its creator. Botterill wrote a detailed description in the Wasdale Climbing Book to which Webb added a note suggesting that the climb should be "named after its daring leader". Over the next couple of days Botterill, Williamson, Grant and Webb, climbed Eagle's Nest Ridge Direct (Mild Very Severe) on the Napes, and Savage Gully (Mild Very Severe) on Pillar Rock, the third ascent of the latter, in order to assess the difficulties of their new climb in comparison to other routes in the area, and concluded unanimously that Botterill's Slab was the hardest.

Botterill's Slab was the first climb made in Britain that is still graded Very Severe (2). It set a new standard for technical difficulty and effectively demonstrated what was possible if climbers were prepared to accept longer run-outs and greater exposure on areas of unexplored rock. It must also have been one of the last routes, made in the summer months, where an ice axe was routinely carried to clear away grass and loose rock or to improvise as an occasional handhold. Botterill's Slab was only the second climb in Britain to venture onto the blank-looking faces and slabs that had been shunned by the earlier pioneers (the first was Jones' Route Direct from Lord's Rake) and remains one of the great milestones in British climbing history. A.J. Slade, W.E. Webb and H. Williamson attempted a second ascent later that summer. They left no details, only a stern warning in the Wasdale Climbing Book that the route should be "left alone" because "it is impossible to belay or assist the leader in any way" (3). Botterill wasn't an ambitious climber and although he made other new routes, most notably North West Climb on Pillar Rock, in 1906, and Abbey Buttress on the Napes, in 1909, in all probability he never realised his full potential and the eponymous slab, made early in his climbing career, remains his greatest achievement.

At 9:40a.m. on Monday 21st September 1903, Algernon Garrett, Wilfred Broadrick, Stanley Ridsdale and Henry Jupp left the Wastwater Hotel and walked up to Scafell Crag. A strong wind was blowing from the southeast, but the rock remained sheltered, warm and dry. They climbed Jones' Route from Deep Gill without difficulty and after descending met W.E. Webb, A.J. Slade and H. Williamson around 1:30p.m. near the foot of Collier's Climb. They had lunch together and went their separate ways. Webb's party returned to Rake's Progress around 5:00p.m. when they heard a faint call from some climbers on Pikes Crag. Thinking they might be in trouble Slade traversed further along the Progress to get a better view but on looking down into Hollow Stones saw four figures stretched out on the screes below lying quite still. At first he thought they were resting, then the awful reality dawned on him. After alerting the others he descended quickly to the foot of the crag, but found that Garrett, Broadrick and Jupp were already dead and that Ridsdale, although alive and semi-conscious, had sustained appalling injuries. Williamson ran down to the valley to get help while Webb and Slade tried to comfort Ridsdale. A rescue party, made up of hotel guests and dalesmen, carried Ridsdale down on a makeshift stretcher but he died before they reached the hotel.
The bodies of the other three were brought down the following day.

Before he died Ridsdale was able to give some account of what had happened, and this was recalled by Webb at the coroner's inquest. "Mr. Ridsdale was the only one alive, he was conscious. He did tell us a little of what happened, but we did not like to ask him, he was in such awful pain; but he did tell us a little about it. What he said was, of course spoken rather indistinctly."

They had agreed to attempt the first ascent of Scafell Pinnacle Direct from Lord's Rake to Hopkinson's Cairn. Initially Broadrick was in the lead with Garrett second, Ridsdale third and Jupp last. It transpires that Broadrick led the team as far as Moss Ledge, which lies at the foot of the steep slab (now called Herford's Slab) about thirty feet below Hopkinson's Cairn. Broadrick became tired and exchanged places with Garrett, and it was whilst attempting the slab that Garrett slipped, and not being properly belayed, they were all pulled to their deaths (4).

After the inquest, which concluded "accidental death", Ridsdale, Garret and Jupp were buried in the little churchyard at Wasdale Head. Broadrick's body was taken to Windermere and buried at St. Mary's Church. Sometime later a cross was carved into the rock at the foot of Scafell Pinnacle, with the date of the accident and the initials of those killed. It is still discernible and marks the spot close to where the bodies were found. All four were experienced climbers; Broadrick, especially so. Broadrick's family home was in Windermere and from an early age he had been a strong and enthusiastic hill walker. He had climbed in the Alps and, with his brother Henry, had made some notable new routes on Dow Crag. At the time of his death he was a schoolmaster at Fettes College, near Edinburgh. Garrett, Jupp and Ridsdale all lived in the southeast and had been climbing together for several years.

The shock of this accident led to several of the curious leading activists visiting the scene in a bid to understand its cause. They climbed down from the top of Low Man to reach Hopkinson's Cairn ledge in a similar manner to Hopkinson's team some 16 years earlier. One such investigation was described by Ashley Abraham, who noted:

> "…those ominous scratches which marked the place where the unfortunate leader slipped and fell. These were on the slab above the left-hand side of the Moss Ledge, which is a mere wrinkle, a few feet long and a few inches wide, high up on the smooth front of the Pinnacle. The place, before the weather blotted out the traces of the accident, was marked from end to end with scars of nailed boots. The party had evidently spent a long time and many vain endeavors to climb the short but vital section that separated them from the safety of Hopkinson's Cairn An attempt had been made to climb up from the right-hand edge of Moss Ledge." (5)

The accident received extensive coverage in the local and national press, prompting many to question if the risks were justifiable. Up until this point no roped party had ever been fatally injured, but it must have been as much luck as skill that had spared them so long for there had been several narrow escapes. This was the first serious climbing accident to occur in Britain (6) and the climbing community was badly shaken by it. Although there is no mention of the accident in the Wasdale Climbing Book, it is evident that the number of new entries drops off markedly after this date.

A further fatal accident occurred on Scafell on Boxing Day, 1903. Alex Goodall, a journalist from Keswick, lost control whilst trying to glissade down a snow slope at the top of Deep Gill and fell the length of the gully. His body came to rest on the scree close to the spot where Broadrick and his companions had been found and where, ten years earlier, Professor Miles Marshall had been killed. The two accidents, occurring so close together, caused Harold Spender, a prominent member of the Alpine Club, to write the following letter in the *Manchester City News*:

> "The greatest peril of all is the absence of any guides. In 1902 and 1903 two of us took a young Dauphine guide (7) to Wastdale Head, and he pronounced the climbing to be more difficult than any in the Dauphine, where few English climbers would go without guides. And yet on these English heights dozens of young fellows without any experience of mountains or real respect for their dangers, risk their lives every Christmas and Easter in gay adventure on the heights. There is a very strong and partly a healthy prejudice against the importation of guides, and, of course, there are no natives who possess the necessary capacity. But if guides are not employed, the parties ought at least to observe some proportion between their experience and their climbs. As far as I have observed, there is no sense of any such obligation, and it is simply due to good fortune that there have not been many more accidents. How long is this to go on, and how many more young lives are to be lost?"

An illustration showing the location of the 1903 accident and the two routes that existed at the time; Slingsby's Chimney Route (white) and Jones' Route Direct from Lord's Rake (yellow).

Photos: Al Phizacklea

The cross carved into the rock at the foot of Lord's Rake. The date of the accident (SEP. 21 1903) and the initials of the four deceased climbers (RWB; AEWG; SR AND HLJ). as inscribed alongside. This feature is only illuminated by the sun's rays between 6.30 and 7a.m. for a couple of weeks either side of midsummer's day.

The gravestone of Jupp, Risdale and Garrett at Wasdale Head Church.

Spender's letter is interesting in that it reveals not only the general attitude towards rock climbing in Britain at the time, but also a residual hostility in the minds of the more conservative members of the Alpine Club.

The Scafell accidents, combined with the untimely death of O.G. Jones and the belief that all the worthwhile climbs around Wasdale had already been discovered, took much of the impetus out of Lakeland climbing, particularly at Wasdale Head. And although the traditional Christmas and Easter gatherings continued to be held at the Wastwater Hotel, and the popular climbs received regular ascents, for a number of years exploration became more cautious and circumspect.

Photo: Al Phizacklea

A detail of the gravestone at Wasdale Head Church.

Footnotes

1) This climb was rediscovered by the present author when researching the *Wasdale Climbing Book* (2006). It was included in the latest Scafell rock climbing guide as Botterill's Corner.

2) O.G. Jones attempted the slab on Christmas Day 1897 and managed to climb forty feet up the corner crack before being forced to retreat due to ice and a lack of positive holds.

3) Botterill's Slab didn't receive a second ascent until Siegfried Herford and Walter Brunskill climbed it in August 1912.

4) The Scafell accident remained the biggest loss of life on British crags until five climbers were killed on Ben Nevis in 1954.

5) *On Alpine Peaks and ~British Crags* by G.D. Abraham, Meuthen & Co., London 1919.

6) Lehmann Oppenheimer (1868 -1916), author of *Heart of Lakeland*, estimated that prior to this disaster well over 10,000 ascents had been made on the Lakeland crags,

7) The young Dauphine guide was Joseph Gaspard. From 1902 to 1914 Gaspard spent every winter at the Wastwater Hotel working as a guide, mainly with novices. He also did odd jobs around the hotel, like greasing and re-nailing climbing boots. Each year, in June, he returned to the Alps to visit his family and work the summer season as a mountain guide.

1904 - 1913

Regeneration
(Siegfried Herford and George Sansom)

The Fell and Rock Climbing Club held its first meet at the Wastwater Hotel on 30th March 1907. It was a mixed club from the start, formed with the aim of facilitating both rock climbing and hill walking in The Lake District, and by August 1907 it had 164 members, eight of whom were women. Ashley Abraham was the first president and John Robinson and George Seatree vice presidents. Honorary membership was given to many of the pioneers of Lakeland climbing including: C.A.O. Baumgartner, Charles Pilkington, Haskett Smith, Cecil Slingsby, Norman Collie and Geoffrey Hastings. The idea of forming a Lake District based climbing club had initially been proposed by John Robinson some twenty years earlier and it is curious that, although Wasdale Head had been the main centre for the development of British climbing throughout that period, it was one of the last of the major clubs to be formed (1). The reason for this may have been that the spark and vitality that pervaded the climbing scene at Wasdale throughout the 1890s arose from the unshackled, spontaneous and unplanned nature of the events, and that the need for more formal organisation only became apparent after this first phase had passed. Like the other clubs The Fell and Rock Climbing Club produced a regular journal, which helped to disseminate knowledge of old and new climbs as well as technique, especially in relation to safety, and the early editions contained several articles on rope-work and belaying.

However, the Wasdale Climbing Book was to remain an important repository of new routes and variations for another decade or more:

The 1907 meet at The Wastwater Hotel.

Photo: FRCC Archive

Overleaf: Susan Jensen on Herford's Direct Finish to Woodhead's climb.
Photo: Al Phizacklea

"At the end of June, 1907, I found a variation of Jones' route from the top of the 2nd pitch of the Ghyll, which avoids the exceptionally severe piece up the arête, & affords a much safer way to the top of the Low Man."

This was the first sentence in the lengthy account H.O.S. Gibson wrote in The Wasdale Climbing Book describing a solo ascent of Gibson's Chimney as an alternative finish to Jones' Route from Deep Gill. Harry Gibson was a school friend of George Mallory (2) and was rather pleased that he had managed to ascend a line that O.G. Jones had dismissed as "hopeless". However, unbeknown to Gibson, the route had already been climbed by A.H. Binns (3) who had made a solo ascent of the chimney in August 1904 but, because Binns never recorded this, it is Gibson's name that has remained associated with this feature. George Mallory and H.E.L. Porter made the third ascent of Gibson's Chimney, in September 1908, and thought it "a great improvement" on Joness' original finish up the arête; a curious assessment considering the chimney is a loose and mossy Severe that is hardly ever climbed today and Jones' Arête, a superb and exhilarating pitch leading directly up to the Low Man. Their opinion though may have been coloured the by seriousness of the arête finish, which is very exposed with difficult starting moves and, at that time, no form of protection.

Woodhead's Climb looking across Deep Gill to The Great Chimney in the background. Climbers: Susan Jensen and Brian Davison.

Photo: Al Phizacklea

Pisgah Buttress Direct, Tommy Moore joins Joe Holden at the Crevasse Belay.

On 24th August 1907 Arthur Woodhead and Leonard Collinson made the first ascent of the vertical southern face of Scafell Pinnacle. It was a "reasonably fine day" and they had already climbed the Great Chimney on the West Wall of Deep Gill and were on their way back down the gill when they were "suddenly seized" with "the wild idea" of climbing directly up to the High Man. They initially ascended the curving crack and arête of Jones' Route to the top of the Pinnacle and then descended the upper half of their intended route to inspect the difficulties and clear away any loose rock and moss. Encouraged by the "unexpectedly easy character of the upper part of the climb" they returned to the foot of the Pinnacle and roped up at the base of the blunt arête formed by the junction of the Deep Gill face and the wall descending from the Professor's Chimney:

> "We were confronted by a very steep slab with only the most rudimentary holds, while twenty feet above was a miniature chimney, the counterpart of the crack on the southern face. Twice while by balancing by toes and fingers on the tiny ledges of the slab did I despair of reaching the foot of the chimney. But with a little pertinacity the necessary holds were gradually found, and eventually access was obtained to the very corner of the buttress by a flight of three steps... Securing myself by a couple of turns of rope round the top 'step', I called out that I was ready for the next man, and C. attacked the slab. Very unfavourable comments upon the character of the route were soon to be heard, followed by an injunction not to pull so hard. It was not long however before he was ready to take my place, and the climb was continued by standing on the top 'step' as a take off, and doing some peculiar work on ledges, rather wider certainly, than those below, but at the same time further apart. I should have called this "mantelshelf" climbing, but the veriest [sic] jerry-builder would scarcely dare to furnish his most ramshackle cottage with mantle-pieces two inches wide. Perhaps they are more aptly described as 'window-ledges'.
>
> "We had now joined the route surveyed from above, and knew the rest to be comparatively easy. A short chimney above the 'window-ledge' section is capped by an overhanging rock, necessitating a long stride to the right round a rib of rock, a small notch in which served as a belay. Next, a scramble of fifteen or twenty feet brought us to another overhang, underneath which we traversed back to the left, and down onto a good broad ledge. To climb from this ledge over the projecting rocks above was the only remaining difficulty. Having discovered by our preliminary trip which was the right place for attack, we built a small cairn to indicate the spot to any future climbers who might chance that way, and an arm-pull, followed by a few feet of easy climbing, brought a good belay within reach. This was fortunate, as projecting rocks at that height up the wall, should receive due respect. Finally, a scramble up the grassy gully down which I first reconnoitred brought us again to the summit of the High Man. The climb occupied about 40 minutes."

Woodhead's account of the climb, of which the above is an extract, appeared in the first edition of the *Fell and Rock Climbing Club Journal*. Only the lower half of the climb was new, for above the belay at the rock rib they were following the line already taken by Thompsons' Route. Woodhead doesn't mention this and probably didn't realise that most of the terrain they inspected on a top rope had already been climbed.

At the end of March 1909, Fred Botterill took a career break (4) and bought a caravan called 'The Bertol'. He established himself at Wasdale Head and stayed for nine months dividing the time between walking, climbing and generally involving himself in the life of the valley. His account of this period, "The Log of Bertol", published in the *Yorkshire Ramblers' Club Journal* (1909), paints a delightful picture of a halcyon summer (5). On the 10th June, Botterill climbed a variation finish to Moss Gill with Ernest E.Roberts and H.B.Gibson (6), that ascended the cracked wall to the right of Collier's Chimney - a 17 metre pitch that is currently graded Mild Very Severe. They recorded this in the Wasdale Climbing Book, remarking that they thought it "slightly more difficult than the Chimney exit".

Snow and ice covered the fells at the end of March 1910 and it was late one Easter afternoon when T.C. Ormiston-Chant and E.H.P. Scantlebury started up Keswick Brothers' Climb. They managed to get as far as the section above Botterill's Slab but there found the exit blocked by a "huge fringe of ice". Ormiston-Chant had dropped their only ice axe on the way up so they spent a difficult hour trying to cut steps in the ice with a wedge of rock. They made little progress and with the light fading fast were reluctantly considering trying to descend when a friendly call from the Hollow Stones alerted them to the presence of other climbers, through which a rescue was effected. C.S. Worthington and J.D. Gemmel went to the top of Keswick Brothers' Climb and spent an hour cutting steps down to a position where they could lower a rope and haul them up. Although not a complete winter ascent this was the first time Keswick Brothers' Climb had been attempted in icy conditions and is a good example of the difficult mixed climbing occasionally undertaken during this period (7).

The only other event of any note during this year was Nigel Madan and Hugh Rose Pope's discovery of a variation pitch linking the Tennis Court and Fives Court Ledges on Pisgah Buttress (8). On 1st September 1910 the leader (their entry in the Wasdale Climbing Book doesn't say who this was) took the normal way up the corner crack, originally climbed by O.G. Jones, and the second traversed from the Tennis Court onto the steep and exposed face on the right of the ledge and climbed directly up to the Fives Court, clearing away some loose rock on the way. This was technically easier than the original route but much more exposed. Pope returned on 6th September and led this variation with Erik Addyman seconding.

Siegfried Herford and F.M.J. McConechy climbed the lower half of Pisgah Buttress, up to the Tennis Court Ledge, on the 6th July 1911 (9). This was Herford's first venture onto virgin rock at Wasdale and a modest start for the man who, over the next three years, would make a series of remarkable first ascents, most notably on Scafell Crag, that would once again put Lakeland climbing at the forefront of the sport.

Herford was athletic and strikingly good looking with a mop of blond hair. His mother was German and his father professor of English Literature at Manchester University. He was brought up in an atmosphere of liberal minded Unitarianism and studied physics at Manchester University where he was a student at the same time as Ludwig Wittgenstein. The family used to take holidays in The Lake District and it was during these that he first discovered walking and scrambling. It is not known exactly when he started rock climbing, but he certainly visited Wasdale in August 1909 and, around the same time, began climbing regularly on the gritstone edges of the Peak District with Stanley Jeffcoat, John Laycock and others (10).

Left to right: Stanley Jeffcoat, John Laycock, Arthur Thompson, Siegfried Herford in typical Edwardian climbing attire.
Photo Goerge Sansom

In early September 1911, Herford, Laycock and H.B. Gibson made the first ascent of Upper West Wall Climb, above Deep Gill - a rather wandering line of no particular merit that is currently graded Severe. They found nail scratches on the higher rocks but were "almost certain" the lower slab had never been climbed before (11).

Sometime in 1911 Laycock introduced George Sansom to Seigfried Herford. Sansom was a zoology student at University College, London, whose interest in climbing was initially sparked by reading A.E.W. Mason's evocative novel *Running Water* (12). In 1907, when he was nineteen and on holiday in Keswick with his mother, he called in at the Abrahams' photography shop where he told George Abraham he would like to try some rock climbing. Sometime later Sansom and John Abraham, the youngest of the Abraham brothers, walked over Styhead Pass to Wasdale where they stayed a few days and Sansom was introduced to the sport. Being a naturally good climber with an agreeable personality he was welcomed into the fold and in a short time was climbing in the company of Walter Brunskill, Fred Botterill, H.B. Gibson and other notable individuals. However, it was with Herford that, within a few months, he was making first and second ascents of the hardest routes in the area.

The traverse to the Fives Court ledge on Pisgah Buttress Direct.

In April 1912, Herford made the second ascent of Jones' Route Direct from Lord's Rake, on Scafell Pinnacle. Unfortunately he didn't record this in the Wasdale Climbing Book so, although it is likely that either Brunskill or Sansom seconded him, this isn't certain and we don't know exactly when this ascent occurred (13). Nevertheless, it was a significant event as it was only the second time the Pinnacle Face had successfully been ascended and the first time anyone had ventured onto it since the appalling accident when four climbers were killed in September 1903 – an event so shocking that it not only stopped any further attempts on the Pinnacle Face, but took the impetus out of Lakeland climbing for nearly a decade.

Climbers on Direct from Lord's Rake to Hopkinson's Cairn.

On 17th April 1912, Herford and Sansom made the first ascent of the Direct from Lord's Rake to Hopkinson's Cairn on Scafell Pinnacle. This is the route that had repulsed all attempts since the first by Charles Hopkinson's party in December 1887 and was the scene of the tragic accident in 1903. Herford and Sansom had been climbing together for several days and Herford had probably already made the second ascent of Joness' Direct from Lord's Rake during which he would have had an opportunity to survey the unclimbed slabs leading up to the cairn. One of the spectators in the small group watching the ascent was Walter Brunskill, who wrote the following account (14):

The middle climber is poised on the delicate section of what is now named as Herford's Slab. This is the point from where Garrett slipped in the1903 accident.
Climbers: Phil Blanshard, John Ellerton and Penny Excell.

> "Soon after Easter this year a climber, young but experienced in many ascents, started alone from Lord's Rake. His boots are left below, and soon he is passing silently from the Gangway out on to the broad face beyond. With skilled eye he scans the rock, searching out every hold around, and seeming to make swift mental trial of each, before he makes an upward movement, lightly and without apparent effort. It is a weird exhibition of the cat-like. To his companions, watching from below, it is but a short time till he comes to the final difficulty. From some tiny holds, an arm pull and a neat press up brings his feet to the safe hold. He must next project himself against the rock, it is rough and slopes back a little) until he can rise on the finger ledge, and get upon it. It is done, and he is ready for the stretch across. A second or so for breath, and he swings over to the crack, and slowly hand over hand, goes up. Good holds are waiting for him at the top, and the next moment he is by the Cairn. A coil of rope is lying there. He drops an end into Deep Ghyll, hauls up his boots; and then a companion, safeguarded by the rope, follows up the way he has come."

It is clear from Brunskill's description that Herford climbed the route solo in socks and only dropped a rope down to Sansom after he had reached Hopkinson's Cairn. They had probably climbed down from the top of the Pinnacle to the cairn earlier in the day to enable Herford to inspect the unclimbed slab and leave a rope in position. Even with prior inspection this was an exceptionally daring lead, for Herford not only had to overcome the technical difficulties of the climb, but also the psychological barrier that surrounded it. The crux pitch leading to the cairn is still known as Herford's Slab.

Hopkinson's Gully is something of a misnomer for it isn't really a gully at all but more an open corner or groove in the front face of the Pinnacle. The name derives from Charles Hopkinson's December 1887 venture after which it was erroneously believed that the party had climbed some way up this feature in winter conditions (15). Still under this misapprehension, Herford and Sansom made the first ascent of Hopkinson's Gully on 19th June 1912. They climbed in socks and at the junction with Jones' Route followed this to the ledge at the foot of Slingsby's Chimney. From here they ascended the unclimbed rounded slabs to the left of the chimney and then traversed back right, crossing a steep corner, to re-join the normal route (16). The day after their ascent of Hopkinson's Gully, Herford and Sansom were joined by Walter Brunskill and the three of them made the second ascent of Thompsons' Route on the Deep Gill face of the Pinnacle.

First ascent photograph of Siegfried Herford looking down the upper section of Hopkinson's Gully.

Botterill's Slab had retained its reputation as an extremely difficult and serious undertaking and the only attempt to repeat it was the one by Slade, Webb and Williamson in the summer of 1903. This position remained unaltered until the 27th August 1912 when Herford and Brunskill completed the second ascent. Herford led the climb, probably in stockinged feet as this was his normal practice on steep rock with small sloping holds, and Brunskill followed. They were both of the opinion that this climb stood in a class of its own and that no one should attempt to lead it without prior inspection on a top rope.

In an article, 'Notes on Some Recent New Climbs in the Lake District' (*FRCCJ*, 1914), Herford mentions that there were "several subsequent ascents" of Botterill's Slab shortly after he and Brunskill had made the second. These probably only involved Herford, Sansom, Brunskill or other trusted companions and are unlikely to have been made by climbers outside of this elite group (17). There is, however, a strong possibility that Geoffrey Winthrop Young and Herbert Reade made a winter ascent of Botterill's Slab sometime before the First World War for in *Mountains with a Difference* Young wrote:

> "And a little later another lesson was driven home, when we came upon Fred Botterill, upon whose eponymous slab on Scafell, H.V. Reade and I had just made the first winter ascent cautiously and admiringly, much adrift upon the iced holds of the Professor's Chimney, which gave our Alpine technique no pause."

The clean corner of Hopkinson's Gully highlighted by the morning sun.

In the early years of the twentieth century, Young was at the forefront of Alpine climbing and spent several Christmas holidays at Wasdale Head. His reference to the alleged first winter ascent is both tantalizing and puzzling. The mention of the Professor's Chimney, for example, which lies at the head of Deep Gill, is inconsistent. Perhaps he meant Puttrell's Chimney, which is an optional finish to Botterill's Slab. This certainly fits the quote that this chimney gave their alpine technique 'no pause', as the interior of this is very tight and awkward. The inscription also suggests that he and Reade met Botterill shortly after their ascent. It is known that Young and Botterill were both staying at the Wastwater Hotel in December 1907 ('The Club Meets', *FRCC Journal*, 1908), and they may have met earlier, which would place the date of the winter ascent at least five years before the acknowledged second ascent by Herford and Brunskill and around eighty years before the first recorded winter ascent by Phizacklea and Kay in 1984.

George Sansom worked out a possible route for a girdle traverse of Scafell Crag and suggested the idea to Herford. They arranged a visit to Wasdale and arrived to find H. B. Gibson and Walter Brunskill already staying at the hotel and keen to join them. On the 12th September 1912, the party started at the top of the first pitch of the Professor's Chimney in Deep Gill and followed sections of Thompson's, Woodhead's and Jones and Collier's climbs to reach Jones' Arête; they then doubled the rope around a block and abseiled down the 'Bad Corner' to Hopkinson's Cairn. From there they climbed down to Moss Ledge and traversed the face to the Waiting Room and Crevasse below Slingsby's Chimney. Crossing Steep Gill and Pisgah Buttress via the Fives Court and Tennis Court ledges, they entered Moss Gill and traversed onto the Central Buttress as far as the broad ledge below the Great Flake. They christened this 'The Oval' – an acknowledgement of Sansom's interest in cricket. Herford tried to continue along this line, but the ledge soon tapered off and the climbing became delicate and he soon found himself out of balance. By this time it was starting to get dark and so they called it a day and retreated down Moss Gill.

The Girdle Traverse started at the top of the crag and this shows the climbers on the initial traverse out of the Professor's Chimney. This is another example of the re-touching of photographs, carrying on the tradition started by the Abraham brothers.
Climbers: George Sansom, H.B. Gibson and Siegfried Herford.

The next day was wet but the following one, 14th September, was fine. They had decided to try and cross Central Buttress at a higher level and so started by ascending Moss Gill to a belay above the Collie Step. Brunskill, rather eccentrically, had decided to wear "a long female garment showing an elegant waist" which he had found in Walker's Gully. At one point, as he swung rounded a particularly exposed corner, the tails of this garment flew up in the air causing great amusement to the rest of the party. They were, however, unable to continue this traverse line and eventually climbed up to the top of the crag.. They returned to the Oval where, after some probing, they managed to find a secure belay and a way down to the foot of Botterill's Slab. They ascended the slab, the most difficult pitch on the Girdle Traverse, with the aid of a top-rope and completed the route by descending part of Keswick Brothers' Climb and finishing up the broken rocks to the east of Collier's Climb.

Waller Eden-Smith and C.J. Astley Cooper on Sansom's Traverse across the face of The Pinnacle on the Girdle of Scafell.

Photo: Ernest Wood-Johnson

The Girdle Traverse was over two hundred and fifty metres in length and technically Very Severe. It was the longest expedition in the Lake District and the first time a Lakeland crag had been treated in this manner (18).

Herford is sometimes credited with having invented the concept of the girdle traverse on a gritstone outcrop in the Peak District called Castle Naze. In fact, J.M.A. Thompson and E.S. Reynolds made the first girdle traverse on Lliwedd, in North Wales, in 1907. Herford may have devised this independently, but it is more likely that he adopted the notion, putting it to good effect on Castle Naze and Scafell Crag. Sansom recalls that when Gibson wrote the account in the Wasdale Climbing Book he put Herford's name first and that Herford protested saying that "Sansom planned the whole thing, he ought to come first". Two days after completing the route Herford was in Farnborough about to start a postgraduate scholarship in aeronautical research at the Royal Aircraft Factory. Sitting in front of the fire in his rented accommodation he read an account of their exploits on the Girdle Traverse in *The Manchester Guardian*, which, at the time, was co-edited by his friend and fellow climber C.E. Montague.

On 1st June 1913, Herford and Sansom made the second ascents of Hopkinson's Gully and the Direct Route from Lord's Rake to Hopkinson's Cairn. The next day they were joined by Brunskill and made the second ascent of the Girdle Traverse in five hours. During the course of the latter excursion Sansom found a variation connecting Hopkinson's Cairn with the easy chimney leading up to the Crevasse; known since as Sansom's Traverse and graded Very Difficult this is an exposed but logical way of tackling this section.

Shortly after this, Sansom left Wasdale to join a zoological expedition in Brazil and was absent for the rest of the summer. With Sansom away, Herford joined forces with Stanley Jeffcoat and on 10th July they repeated Woodhead's Climb on Scafell Pinnacle. After they had finished the route and were sitting on the top of the Pinnacle, Herford wondered if it might be possible to create a new direct finish and asked Jeffcoat to lower him down to what today is the belay at the top of the first pitch.

With the reassurance of a top rope he climbed directly back up removing a number of loose blocks on the way. The two of them then descended the upper half of Woodhead's Climb to the start of the Direct Finish. Herford then led this, which, in a letter to Sansom, he described as "very steep and sensational, but not really very hard as there are good in-cut holds for the fingers all the way up". He also remarked that he thought it was "a far finer finish that the rather tame one of the ordinary route". The Woodhead start combined with Herford's Direct finish is technically Mild Severe and one of the best climbs of that standard in the area.

Footnotes

1) The Cairngorm Club was founded in 1887 and the Scottish Mountaineering Club in 1889. In England the Yorkshire Ramblers' Club was formed in 1892, The Climbers' Club in 1898, and The Rucksack Club in 1902.
2) Gibson and Mallory were school friends from Winchester Collage where they had been introduced to climbing by one of the masters, R.L.G. Irving. After his usual climbing partner had been killed in an accident Graham Irving was looking for new recruits and had started the Winchester Ice Club. He took pupils to Wales, Scotland and the Alps, to introduce them to mountaineering. Gibson and Mallory climbed in the Alps with Irvine in August 1904 and at Easter 1906 Irvine, Mallory and Gordon Leach made the second winter ascent of the North East Buttress on Ben Nevis.
3) Alfred Henry Binns started walking and climbing in the Lake District in 1888. His mountaineering career spanned 60 years and included 7 Alpine seasons. He was a lifelong friend of Ashley Abraham and much of the climbing they did together in Skye formed the basis for the Abraham's book *Rock Climbing in Skye*. Binns joined the Fell and Rock in 1907 but was not an original member. He died in 1960 aged 89.
4) Botterill's occupation at this time is unknown.
5) Botterill doesn't mention this in his article, but the autumn was overshadowed by tragedy. On 27th September, T. J. Rennison tried to lead Eagle's Nest Ridge Direct on the Napes with Botterill holding his rope. Rennison fell and was killed. Botterill never climbed seriously again.
6) Roberts was editor of the *Yorkshire Ramblers' Club Journal* for many years and later climbed with Frank Smythe and J.H.B. Bell. Gibson was a member of the FRCC and involved in a number of first ascents on the crags around Wasdale Head prior to the First World War, most notably Central Buttress with Herford and Sansom.
7) Worthington and Gemmel made the first ascent of Engineers Chimney (Grade V/4) Easter 1910.
8) Madan and Pope were both friends of George Mallory and Geoffrey Winthrop Young. Pope was killed solo climbing on the Pic Du Midi d'Ossau in the Pyrenees in 1912. Madan died in the First World War.
9) Herford and McConechy's start to Pisgah Buttress was superseded by the one discovered by C.D. Frankland and V. W. Brown in 1920.
10) Stanley Jeffcoat was from Buxton and one of the first people to climb on Castle Naze in the Peak District. He was killed in the First World War. His name is inscribed next to Herford's on the memorial plaque on Great Gable. John Laycock wrote *Some Gritstone Climbs: Shorter Climbs in Derbyshire and Elsewhere*, the first guidebook to climbing in the Peak District, that was privately published in 1913. Laycock and Jeffcoat were both members of the Manchester based Rucksack Club. Laycock was so traumatised by the loss of his friends in the war that he gave up climbing and took a job with the administrative service in Singapore.
11) Collie, Hastings and Robinson climbed a route on this buttress in April 1893 and, as there is no record of any other ascent, the nail scratches may have been theirs.
12) Mason was a popular novelist who climbed at Wasdale Head in the 1890s. The climax of *Running Water* is a gripping account of an ascent of the Brenva Spur on Mont Blanc. Mason's other works include *A Romance of Wastdale* and *The Four Feathers*.
13) Brunskill took a photograph of Herford, protected by a top rope, on the crux mantelshelf pitch of this climb. The photograph still survives, but it isn't known if this was taken when Herford was practicing this section prior to making the second ascent or, as is more likely, at a later date.
14) Brunskill's article was titled 'The Finest Rock Climber in England'. He sent a copy to Herford, who objected to the title and made some other amendments. It is reproduced in Keith Treacher's *Siegfried Herford An Edwardian Climber*, but there is no record of it ever being published prior to this.
15) For further detail on this misinterpretation and the origin of the name Hopkinson's Gully see chapter 1881-1888, footnote 4.
16) Hopkinson's Gully remained one of George Sansom's favourite climbs and he often repeated it in the years when he returned to Wasdale after the First World War.
17) In July 1913 Herford ascended Botterill's Slab in 4 minutes and then descended it in 12 minutes.
18) The original line is no longer followed. In the modern guidebooks it is described in the opposite direction, starting up the first pitch of Botterill's Slab and finishing on Jones' Arête.

After
Jeffco
now c
the to

Herfo
attem
ice. C
leadi
their
Holla

A da
Walk

Ceci
he di
West
beca
enco
year
How
outli

Her
snov
the a
Gre

1914

Central Buttress

Stanley Jeffcoat fror
the war, but left bel
Central Buttress wi

Photo: George Sansom

Siegfried Herford attempting the Great Flake without any assistance on the first attempt, 19th April 1914.

Overleaf:
The Central Buttre
Photo: Al Phizacklea

"As far as the bulge, above mentioned, the climbing was comparatively simple but from this point to a large jammed stone 20ft higher it was extremely difficult, as the crack is practically holdless and just too wide to permit a secure arm wedge. Two fairly good footholds permit of a position of comparative comfort just below the jammed stone, and I noted, as Herford had suggested, that it was possible to thread a rope there. The stone itself afforded quite a good handhold, but the crack above overhung to such a shocking extent that the ascent of the remaining 12ft proved excessively difficult. My arms gave out long before the top was reached and a very considerable amount of pulling from Gibson was required before I joined him. Herford then tried the ascent on a rope and just succeeded in getting up without assistance. We thereupon decided to attempt the ascent in the orthodox manner, and preparatory to this we descended by Broad Stand and re-joined Holland on the Oval.

"Our plan of attack was to climb up the crack and thread a loop behind the jammed stone, and I undertook to do this if Herford would lead the upper part which he was quite prepared to do. My first procedure was to soak two feet of the end of a rope in wet moss to render it stiff and to facilitate the threading. I then attempted the ascent but 6ft below the jammed stone I found my position too precarious to be pleasant and called to Herford for a shoulder. He came up without the least hesitation and standing on the bulge of the foot of the crack steadied my feet on small holds until I attained a safer position and was able to climb up to the chockstone. The stiff rope threaded very easily and making a double loop I ran my own rope through it for the descent which was, under those conditions, quite safe. After a brief rest, Herford tied on to the threaded rope and speedily reached the level of the chockstone. He made a splendid effort to climb the upper part but his strength gave out and he returned for a rest. A second equally fine effort was also unsuccessful and he climbed down to the Oval. I then made the attempt but soon abandoned it and we unanimously agreed to postpone the ascent until the morrow, leaving the threaded rope in situ. As Holland had already spent seven hours on the Oval, we decided to waste no more time and accordingly descended via the traverse into Moss Ghyll.

"The next day [20th April], we climbed to the Oval direct from the Progress and one member ascended to the chockstone to renew the loop, which showed slight signs of wear from the previous day's use. We decided that combined tactics would be necessary and accordingly ran a second rope through the loop. Herford tied on one rope and I on the other whilst Gibson and Holland manipulated the respective ropes. I followed Herford closely up the crack and hung on to the loop whilst he used my shoulders as footholds. Directly he vacated them, I climbed 3 ft higher and hung by my hands from the top of the chockstone whilst he again employed me as footholds which were most sorely needed at this point, for the crack is practically holdless and overhangs about 20°. A minute or two of severe struggling and he reached the top to the great joy of all members of the party. Hereford thoughtfully hung a short loop over the tip of the flake to assist us in the ascent but even then we required much help from above and it was with a sense of great relief that we found ourselves on the crest of the flake. Murray (3) who had been observing us from the recess, with some interest, was delighted with an invitation to join the party, so we lowered him a rope down the crack and induced him to remove the threaded loop on the way up."

After they were all assembled Sansom took a photograph of Herford astride the top of the Great Flake. No further climbing was attempted that day as they were all tired and well satisfied with their achievement. That evening, back at the hotel, Herford wrote a route description in the Wasdale Climbing Book and each member of the party signed it.

Photo: © abrahamphotographic/ FRCC Archives

This photograph was taken shortly after the first ascent of Central Buttress to re-enact the ascent for the camera. The climbers, Seigfried Herford, belayed by H.C. Bowen have traversed to the top of the Great Flake from the Keswick Brothers' Climb and can be seen top roping the Flake.

Sansom's iconic photograph of Siegfried Herford on top of the Great Flake, on the first ascent of Central Buttress.

The next day Gibson added the following comment:

> "The extraordinary nature of the difficulties of this climb can hardly be over emphasised. The safe ascent of the crack was rendered possible only by most daring combined tactics on the part of the leader and second. The work of the second in threading the rope and afterwards giving a shoulder at the most exposed part was only less remarkable than the actual leading of the crack."

Photo: George Sansom

Holland, in an article on the events surrounding the first ascent of Central Buttress (*FRCC Journal*, 1921), included an incident that Sansom probably enjoyed describing to his friends after they had finished the climb, but omitted to mention in his account:

"A most remarkable incident had occurred while the crack was being led. Sansom was hanging on by indifferent sloping handholds on or near the lower end of the great chockstone, and Herford was standing on his shoulders, about to make the first step of the last tremendous solo effort. The initial difficulty confronting him was that of getting a purchase with his left foot in a groove unsuitably shaped for that purpose. Sansom's left hand began to slip under the great strain, and must inevitably have given way very soon, in which case he would have come off, though only for a foot or two, onto the loops. Herford's fall, unavoidable if this had happened, would have been a very serious affair indeed, and even if his rope had held it is impossible to see how we below could have given any assistance, beyond keeping the ropes tight, if either had been injured in any way. At this moment, however, the great Goddess of Luck took a hand in the game. I call it 'Luck'; there are those who would name it differently. Finding himself unable to get his foot as he wanted it, Herford stepped back and accidentally put his foot on the slipping hand, thus holding it in position; and the difficult step was made so quickly at the second attempt that Sansom was able to support the double weight till that of the leader was removed. So it may well be said that "Luck" was the sixth member of the party, and no inefficient one either."

George Sansom.

The delicate traverse to reach the V ledge on Central Buttress.

Although delighted that they had unlocked the key passage up the Great Flake, Herford and Sansom regarded the buttress as still only half climbed, for the difficult looking upper section remained untouched, and so two days later, on the 22nd April, they set out again. Unfortunately Gibson had to return home and was replaced by Edward V. Slater, a schoolmaster from Eton, who assisted with some of the belaying but didn't follow them up the climb. Sansom continues:

> "Two days later, therefore, we set out – greatly regretting Gibson's absence from the party – to explore the upper part of the face. 50 ft above the top of the Great Flake on the Central buttress is an irregular 'V' shaped grass ledge, from the western end of which springs a wide chimney which is the lower section of the conspicuous Bayonet-Shaped Crack running up to the very top of the crags. The upper section of this crack was, we knew, easy. The lower portion looked very unpleasant but we hoped to avoid it by climbing the steep face on the left with Holland and Slater belaying us. We climbed down steep rocks to the 'V' shaped ledge, 100 ft below, and from there we were able to look down a remarkably smooth and almost vertical wall to the top of the Great Flake, 50 ft lower. The wall was broken at one point by a right angled arête, which in spite of the fact that it overhung slightly, possessed sufficiently good holds to permit of a comfortable descent of 25 ft. From its foot, a wonderfully exposed traverse across the almost vertical face on the left enabled us to pass behind a large detached pinnacle and to climb slightly downwards to the shattered ridge against the foot of which the Great Flake abuts.

'Charles' Holland belayed on the V-Ledge below the Bayonet-Shaped Crack on the first ascent of Central Buttress..

"Much elated at this discovery, we climbed back to Holland, and Slater and the three of us at once descended the easy rocks to the Cannon. Belayed from this point, I led across the traverse and up to the 'V' ledge. Herford then took the lead, Holland going second. Now the way by which we had descended necessitated an extremely difficult hand traverse on bad holds in an exposed situation and we therefore cast about for a better route. Herford first tried the Bayonet-Shaped Crack but it looked repulsively difficult and he abandoned it in favour of a most exhilarating traverse across its foot on to the vertical wall beyond and upwards across the latter 30 ft to a steep slab which he followed for another 25 ft to a good belay at the top of the lower section of the crack. We soon joined him here and climbed easily up the left wall of the upper portion of the Bayonet-Shaped Crack, to the top of the crags." (4)

The first ascent of Central Buttress was now complete. Both in terms of the concept and the technical difficulty that had to be overcome it was way ahead of its time and certainly the hardest climb ever made in Britain and possibly the world (5). The first guide to Scafell (Holland, 1924) didn't attempt to grade it, presumably because it went beyond O.G. Jones' conception of "Exceptionally Severe" and described it simply as "the most arduous ascent in the Lake District" and with the difficulties so great "that the expedition ranks among the world's hardest". In later years Hard Very Severe 5b became the accepted grade, a standard that was not regularly being attained until after the Second World War. The modern guidebook still describes this ascent as "the biggest single breakthrough in standard in the history of Lakeland climbing". It was the pinnacle of achievement for the pre-war climbers and remains one of the great milestones in British climbing. However, although they didn't realise this at the time, it also marked the end of a Golden Age. Herford and Sansom had planned to repeat the ascent in September 1914, hoping to find a better and more direct approach to the Oval, but they were overtaken by events and Sansom's entry in the Wasdale Climbing Book, describing the direct finish, was the last to be made for five years. Ten weeks after the first ascent of Central Buttress, two shots rang out of a Sarajevo street, two shots that were to change the world for ever.

Siegfried Herford.

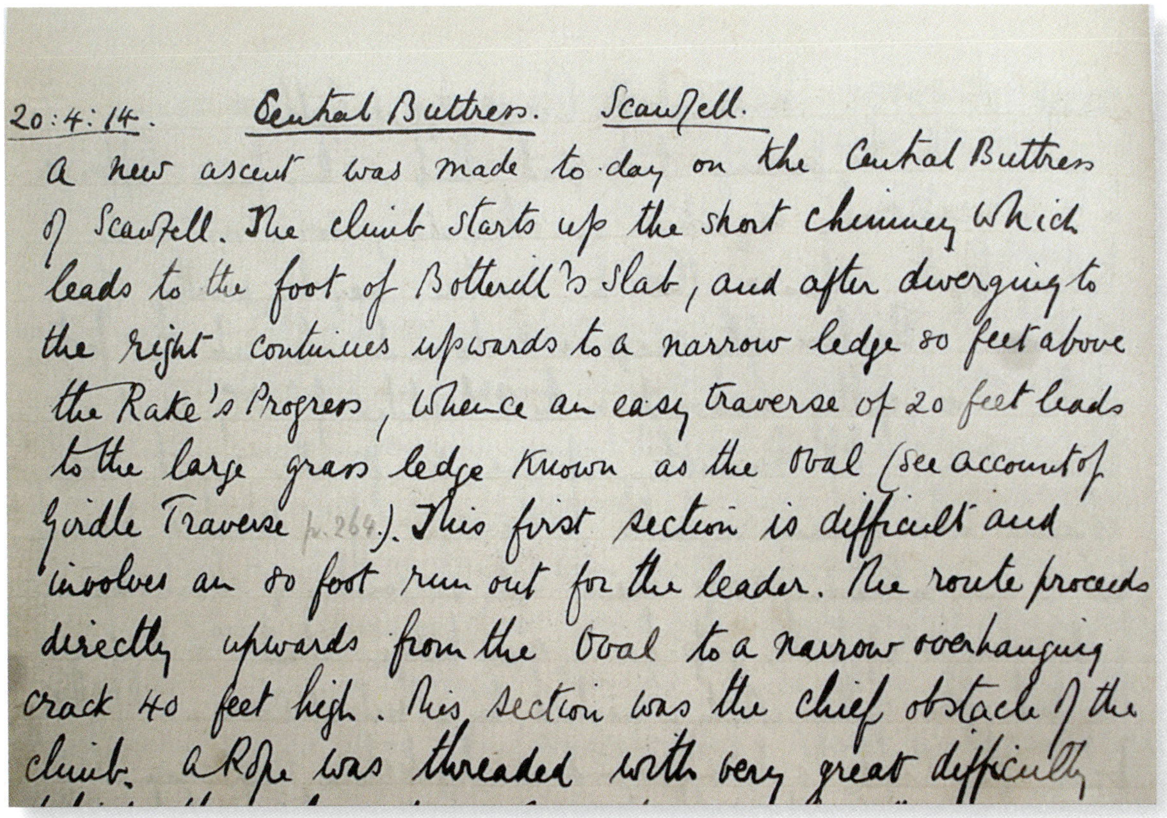

20:4:14. Central Buttress. Scawfell.

A new ascent was made to-day on the Central Buttress of Scawfell. The climb starts up the short chimney which leads to the foot of Botterill's Slab, and after diverging to the right continues upwards to a narrow ledge 80 feet above the Rake's Progress, whence an easy traverse of 20 feet leads to the large grass ledge known as the Oval (see account of Girdle Traverse p. 264). This first section is difficult and involves an 80 foot run out for the leader. The route proceeds directly upwards from the Oval to a narrow overhanging crack 40 feet high. This section was the chief obstacle of the climb. A Rope was threaded with very great difficulty

Herford's account of the first ascent of Central Buttress as written in the climbing book at the Wastwater Hotel.

The First World War more or less put a complete stop to climbing. Many climbers volunteered or were called up for active service. Those that were deemed unfit or held in reserved occupations were busy supporting the war effort in other ways. Even when leave or leisure time was available, it was difficult to get to the hills due to limited transport. Sansom initially worked with the St. John Ambulance Brigade and later transferred to the Royal Flying Corps. He was shot down three times but survived the war and was awarded the M.C. and D.F.C. for gallantry. Herford started as an ambulance driver and then applied for a commission. For reasons that remain unclear this was delayed so he fought as a private in the Sportsmen's Battalion of the Royal Fusiliers. Herford was killed by a rifle grenade at Festubert on 28th January 1916. Had he lived British rock climbing may have taken a more accelerated course and he would in all probability have been considered for the early Everest expeditions.

There is a curious story linked to Herford's passing. The well-known legend is that, in January 1916, 'Charles' Holland was walking alone below Scafell Crag, somewhere near Hollow Stones, when he met Herford who appeared unexpectedly. They talked for a while until Herford said something to the effect that he must be on his way as he had an appointment in the next valley. A few days later Holland heard that Herford had been killed in France on the same day that he believed they had been talking together. Holland never wrote specifically about this, but alluded to it in later writing and occasionally spoke about it with friends. In the early 1930s, when he was walking back from Pillar Rock with the Lakeland author Arthur Harry Griffin and George Basterfield, Holland related this tale and, according to Griffin, was convinced that Herford had "come back" at the moment of his death to speak with an old friend and to see the hills he loved. Griffin refers to this event in two of his books (6) and may be the primary source for what has become the established version of this story.

However, a letter from Herford's mother, Marie, to her sister Augusta, dated 7th June 1921, has recently come to light and tells a different but equally strange story (7). She describes, in detail, the content of a letter the family had recently received from 'Charles' Holland that refers to an event that occurred in August 1918. Holland, who was still in the army, had three days leave and without telling anyone or making prior arrangement, went to Burnthwaite Farm, at Wasdale Head. That evening he met a friend who appeared shocked and upset, but not surprised to see him. It transpired that the friend, who in the letter is only referred to as 'A', had been out walking earlier in the day on Scafell and encountered a tall young man, wearing a white sweater with fair hair and striking blue eyes. They talked for a while about climbing and shared one of 'A's' sandwiches. During the course of the conversation the stranger asked 'A' if he knew that Holland would be arriving at Burnthwaite that evening, which, of course, he didn't. The stranger then, quite suddenly, disappeared leaving 'A' alone on the hillside feeling very uneasy and unable to explain what had happened. According to Holland, 'A' had never met Herford and was normally calm and rational with no interest in religion or the occult. Holland was convinced from the description that it was Herford that 'A' had encountered and that accepting one of his sandwiches was characteristic as Herford rarely carried any of his own and was always inclined to share other peoples. The identity of 'A' is uncertain and, unfortunately, Holland's letter to Herford's parents is not amongst the family papers. Holland was known to be religious and something of a mystic and, for the rest of his life remained convinced that, at times, Herford's spirit was abroad on the Lakeland fells.

The story doesn't end there for in the late 1920s Arthur B. Reynolds, a cabinet maker from Windermere who associated with the leading post war climbers in The Lakes, had an unusual experience. During a solitary walk he had stopped to rest at Esk Hause when a stranger with fair hair and blue eyes dressed in a white roll neck sweater approached and sat down next to him. They exchanged polite conversation for a while before Reynolds got up and started to walk away. After a few moments and for no particular reason, he stopped to look back and saw that the young man had unaccountably disappeared. A few days later Reynolds was in a local inn, probably the Wastwater Hotel, where he saw a picture of a climber hanging on the wall and immediately recognized it as the person he had spoken to at Esk Hause - the picture was of Siegfried Herford (8).

Photo: Al Phizacklea

Dave Parton and Scott Young on the Great Flake of Central Buttress. This picture was taken after the loss of the chock-stone, which was wedged into the widest part of the crack.

Photo: David Stephenson

The gravestone of Seigfried Herford in Brown's Road Cemetery Festubert The inscription reads: "I will lift mine eyes to the hills from whence cometh my help'.

G.R. Speaker, who was a friend of Holland's and a one-time president of the Fell and Rock Climbing Club, also believed that he had an encounter with Herford on a misty day near the top of Scafell Crag. Odd experiences of this kind continue to be reported to this day.

While there is no easy explanation for these stories, it is, perhaps, significant that they occurred towards the end of an era when spiritualism and ghost stories were popular. This context combined with a nation trying to come to terms with the recent carnage and unprecedented loss of life in The Great War may have made some individuals psychologically more susceptible to assuming super-natural explanations for unusual experiences. And once a phenomena has been reported by a credible witness others may have had a lowered threshold for accepting similar interpretations of events. However, in spite of this, it remains a strange tale and the only example of what might be considered a ghost story in British climbing history.

The war created a watershed, effectively dividing the period before it from what came after. The unprecedented loss of life – one million British dead and two million more wounded – combined with crippling expenditure had left the country traumatized and economically ruined. Life had been cheapened by the carnage and the earlier bonds of convention and tradition that had sustained social and economic progress though the Victorian and Edwardian years were called into question and the old barriers of class, money and sex eroded. Changes in the political and economic climate also saw a broadening of the social classes attracted to the outdoors, and climbing was no longer to be a holiday activity for the literary and learned upper middle-classes but a weekend activity that was progressively open to people from all walks of life.

For Lakeland climbing the halcyon days of the Wastwater Hotel were over. Wasdale was no longer the focal point of development and, although it remained a popular venue, it shared its position as a climbing centre with a number of other bases in The Lake District and other parts of the country. Many climbers never returned from the war, and a good proportion of those that did were struggling to rebuild their lives and careers and had no desire for further danger and hard living.
A connection had been broken and although small parties did regroup and resume their pre-war activities the climbing movement as a whole faltered and took a number years to recover. A new generation, less influenced by the older traditions than would have been the case had there been more direct continuity, were about to take climbing into its next phase of development.

Footnotes

1) The first of these would later become Moss Ghyll Grooves

2) O.G. Jones made the first ascent of Walker's Gully in January 1899 with George Abraham and A.E. Field in desperate semi-winter conditions. The ascent by Herford, Sansom and Holland at New Year 1914 was the first in full winter conditions.

3) Dennis Murray was an engineer from Barrow. In 1918 he made the first ascent of the classic Murray's Route on Dow Crag.

4) The line they discovered up the upper section of the buttress is no longer used, and a more direct variation, climbed by F.G. Balcombe, J. Wright and J. Files in 1934, is incorporated in the modern route description. The Original Finish lies to the right of 1934 variation and the upper section of this now forms the last pitch of Moss Ghyll Grooves.

5) In the 1960s Central Buttress was still considered to be a major undertaking and something of a milestone in any up-and-coming climber's career. Its inclusion in Ken Wilson's book *Hard Rock* helped to maintain its profile and popularity until the chockstone unexpectedly fell out in 1994 tragically killing the climber involved.

6) *The Coniston Tigers* (p. 52) and *In Mountain Lakeland* (p. 155). The writer also had personal correspondence with Griffin on this subject.

7) Recently donated to the Mountain Heritage Trust, Penrith.

8) 'Barefoot in the Twenties: A.B. Reynolds and the story of Gimmer Crack', Ken Smith, *Climber and Rambler*, Jan 1983, (p. 47).

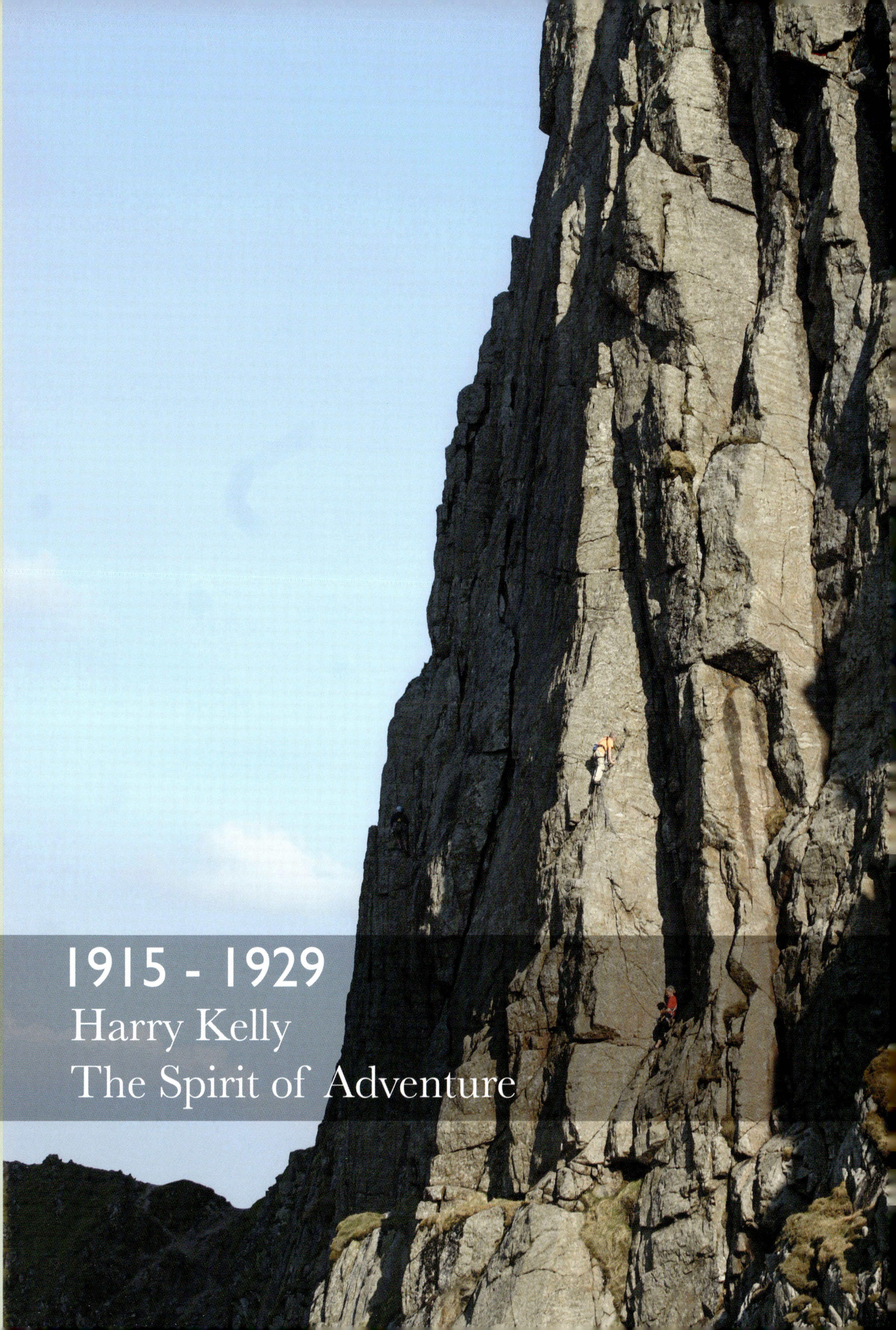

1915 - 1929

Harry Kelly

The Spirit of Adventure

Above: Harry Kelly, Below: Kelly relaxing on a gritstone slab.

Photo: FRCC Archive

Photo: Rucksack Club Collection

Right: There were many types of nails and many variations in style. It was said you could tell who had passed from the distinctive patterns of nails in boots. From a 1932 advert.

Overleaf: Al Davies and Mary Grace Brown on the main pitch of Moss Ghyll Grooves.
Photo: Al Phizacklea

During the confusion and social upheaval of the First World War in 1916 came the first visit to Wasdale of Harry Mills Kelly, who was to become one of the most dominant climbers over the next decade. Kelly had been climbing for many years on the gritstone edges to the east of his home town of Manchester, and he even used the buildings of his home town to practice climbing, including a traverse across the roof of his local Police Station. He was 32 years old when he first visited the valley and Wasdale was to become his favourite climbing centre.

Kelly was a radical figure in the climbing world and he developed several original concepts to bring about subtle changes in the sport, both practically and inspirationally, and he certainly became one of the most influential climbers to grace the crags of Cumbria. One innovation was the inspection of potential new routes from above, which usually involved cleaning as well as checking the rock before actual climbing. These were untested methods at the time, not least because abseiling devices and harnesses were still half a century away. Kelly's usual approach was to be lowered by hand down the crag by an accomplice making him an early practitioner of top-roping investigation and gardening of routes. He repeated this process over several months or years, and interestingly in the 1920s no-one stood up to decry the practice, even though Kelly never kept it secret. Pre-inspection and cleaning were fairly standard practices on the gritsone edges, where protection for a leader would have been non-existent. There was none of the frenzy of the climbing press at that time; none of the competitive spirit of the later years; and little concern for environmental issues.

It is often thought that Kelly was responsible for introducing a new type of footwear; lightweight gym plimsolls which were referred to as 'rubbers', although the first recorded use of gym shoes for climbing was by W.A. Andrews sometime before World War I. Kelly first realised they were excellent on slabs whilst climbing in Skye, and afterwards he spent some time comparing these rubbers with nails by repeating climbs on gritstone using both types of footwear. He noted with satisfaction that rubbers offered superior friction on dry, sloping rock, and he set about wholeheartedly promoting their use. Within years they were widely accepted and rubbers became synonymous with the hard routes of the day, and were widely preferred to nails by many. However, this new footwear was not universally accepted by the older climbers, as Kelly recalled many years later in an article titled Memorabilia, written for the Fell & Rock Climbing Club in 1976:

> "Recalling the earliest days, he considered himself fortunate that he started climbing when the development of the sport was taking the climber away from gullies and chimneys onto the open faces of crags where the tiny footholds and mere rugosities demanded another type of footwear which ultimately was found to be the rubber soled gym shoe. The introduction of these was largely frowned upon. They were considered to lower the standard of climbing – a fallacy in this case as they actually raised it. What the objections were could hardly have been that of a climber of the later generation who mordantly stated that their use 'didn't give the rocks a chance." (1)

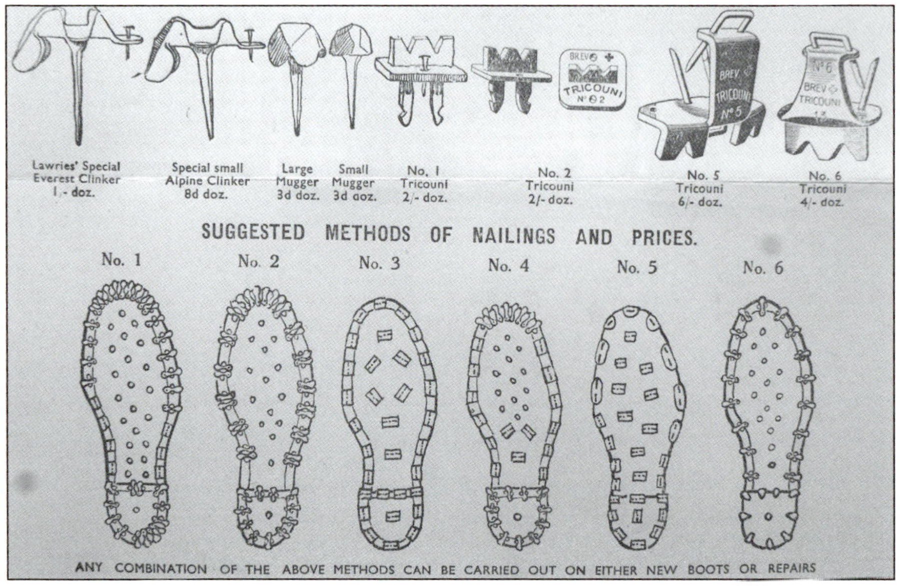

A second stimulation to this drive to get climbers to accept rubbers for climbing was the erosion of the holds on the climbs, which was evident as early as 1919, when Kelly wrote:

> "To the unconverted may I plead that they should don some less destructive footwear than nailed boots when doing some of the climbs (e.g. South West Climb [Pillar]). It only needs a few passages over the routes in such footwear to eradicate the holds thereon. This is not an attempt to humour, but as statement of fact made in all sincerity. Our climbs are too precious to be worn away for a fetish."

Kelly was a large and imposing figure, 'a powerfully built man of average height, with a russet-red face adorned with a dark, upturned moustache', and his dictatorial manner rather intimidated his fellow climbers. *In A Century on the Crags*, Alan Hankinson paints a complex portrait:

> "Those who met him in the 1920s and 1930s retain vivid impressions. Ivan Waller says he was terrified of him: 'He seemed to be like a sergeant-major to me. Actually he wasn't like that but he did give the impression of being a terrific disciplinarian.' Harry Griffin also remembers him as a rather frightening figure with a brusque commanding manner. A.B. Hargreaves found him difficult: 'I didn't dislike him but I didn't really get on with him and a lot of others had the same experience.' Certainly there was another side to Kelly. He had many close climbing friends and he kept them for many years. He was a good and loyal club man – both with the Rucksack Club and the Fell & Rock. His writings show a laconic wit and he had, by all accounts, a lively sense of fun, – and with children unlimited patience and gentleness. Kelly was a very private man, secretive about his personal life; and this has left some intriguing mysteries. Why, for example, did he play no part in the First World War? He was 30 years old when it started and, as far as is known, more than usually fit and strong. Another even greater mystery is what, if anything, he did for a living. No one seems to know. Some thought he might be a school teacher, others suspected banking - maybe he had independent means. He could afford to run a car in the 1920s and had several holidays to the Alps and Norway and one trip to Russia. The pattern of his life revealed in his diaries suggests that some responsibility kept him in Manchester on weekdays. We shall probably never know what it was." (2)

With a little detective work, the Rucksack Club reviewed Kelly's original application for membership, and on this he gave the description of 'Cashier' in the section describing his profession. It is interesting to note that he is described as being an insurance clerk in Wikipedia, although the source of this information is not referenced. Both these careers seem somewhat improbable for a man of such means, and it can be assumed he used them as a cover for his real occupation.

Kelly's avoidance of conscription and the horrors of the trenches, for whatever reason, set him in a position to take advantage of the great outdoors revival following the end of The Great War, and he wrote of this period:

> "With the close of hostilities in 1918 a great renaissance in climbing was naturally to be expected. For four long years the big majority of active climbers had been able to pay but brief, furtive visits to their happy hunting grounds; and now they returned with an avidity sharpened by the lengthy period of rock-starvation, and the spirit of adventure which the searing experiences of the war has intensified rather than dulled." (3)

Kelly became a regular visitor to Wasdale, and soon became familiar with the crags of the area, forming a close partnership with 'Charles' Holland and Charles Crawford, and driving the pace of exploration forward.

Clinkers, Muggers and Tricouni nails, a classic combination!

'Charles' Holland, one of the most influential climbers of his day. Below: The Bad Corner on Scafell Pinnacle, first climbed by Kelly in 1919.

It took some years for the equivalent Welsh and Scottish climbing groups to recover from the war and reach a similar level of development to match what this Wasdale-centred group established. Typically for the time, on one occasion just before Kelly departed to Wasdale for one of his climbing holidays, he received the following telegram: "Please bring one pound of 'Capstan' or similar strong tobacco and two pairs of rubbers. Holland". Holland was still recovering from his wartime wounds when a bullet shattered his upper arm, but this obviously wasn't going to stop him from climbing. Again Kelly notes:

> "Holland was a great climber, an even greater inspirer; he has probably exerted more influence on ambitious youth in the climbing world than any other man of our time. His knowledge of the crags was extensive, his courage boundless, his temperament ideal. Holland's eye for a route, Crawford's cheery optimism in conjunction with his remarkable aptitude for the sport, and Kelly's technical skills in leadership formed an irresistible combination when these three got together. They first swept clean the face of Scafell Pinnacle, climbing every route upon it and making numerous variations of great merit." (4)

On this first trip in 1919 they made the first recorded descent of Botterill's Slab, which he described as being 'harder than ascent, lower section very trying'. This was an impressive achievement as the route had only received its second ascent seven years earlier.

During a later holiday in the valley in June 1919, Kelly and his wife Emily, George Bower and Reginald Pritchard made the first ascent of The Bad Corner, a short blank groove high on the arête above Hopkinson's Cairn. This had been a notorious feature for some time; and it had first been descended down the rope hand-over-hand by Charles Hopkinson and Wilfred Tribe in 1893. It is uncertain who christened this feature, but Kelly realised the ascent of this feature 'solves the problem of doing the Girdle Traverse in reverse'. Even the advent of modern equipment has not diminished the reputation of this feature as it is only possible to fix a single poor nut, which inevitably lifts out as it is passed. It is currently graded 4c. Kelly described the ascent thus:

> "The problem requires a big stride towards the right [away from the corner] first. Next, a foothold is reached with left foot crossing right leg followed by a pull up an edge overlooking Deep Ghyll." (5)

Also on this holiday he attempted the coveted second ascent of Central Buttress with Harry Gibson and Charles Crawford. Gibson and Kelly both took turns to lead up to the chockstone, but Kelly's diary stated that neither of them had the enthusiasm for threading it, so they retreated back down to Moss Gill. They then reversed the initial section of the Girdle Traverse of Scafell, incorporating his 'Bad Corner' solution to reach the top of High Man, which has since become the standard way of doing the girdle traverse.

The following day they once again explored the possibility of the Central Buttress, gaining the top of the Great Flake by traversing in from Keswick Brothers' Climb in similar manner to inspection by the first ascent team. Kelly traversed along the top edge of the Flake and reversed the crux until he notes 'Self just touched chockstone with toe'. Once again the aura surrounding the Central Buttress and its tremendously intimidating situation forced the team to retreat the way they had come.

Returning to Scafell in July of that year, Kelly wandered up the lower part of Steep Gill with Crawford and Holland, where they started to investigate the unclimbed right-hand side of Pisgah Buttress. Holland was regarded by Kelly as 'the moving spirit for the adventure', and he persuaded Kelly to explore the steep wall above. He managed to reach a ledge about 60 feet above the gully from where two large blocks were sent earthward, but there he was faced with an area of steep blank rock

Kelly untied and dropped his end of the rope to the ground, showing blind faith that he could be reached from above. Crawford coiled the rope and soloed up Slingsby's Chimney Route, traversed around the head of the gill and scrambled down from the top of Pisgah Buttress. He successfully lowered one end of the rope to Kelly, who attempted to finish the route on a top-rope, but he reached "an impossible 8ft groove, the rocks looked easier beyond this but there was no way of reaching them, so I gave up the job". He was then lowered to Holland in the bed of the gill. Kelly had probably been attempting a line that was to become known as Pisgah Ya Bas, and with a modern grade of HVS it is little wonder he backed off. Crawford descended Deep Gill to rejoin Kelly and Holland, and from this point they made the first ascent of The Right Wall of Steep Ghyll, Mild Severe, which wanders up the right side of the gully to the top of High Man via a series of mossy rock and grassy ledges. In fact, Holland later described how the route suffered from the following defects:

> "Loose rock, an excess of moisture, an all pervading air of gloom, and a lack of definition!" (6)

Photo: Al Phizacklea

The parallel system of grooves and slabs rising out of Moss Gill became known as Moss Ghyll Grooves, first named by Herford and Sansom in 1912.

Photo: Ernest Wood-Johnson

The first pitch of Central Buttress, which was added as 'a new and superior start' by C. D. Frankland and B. Beetham on the second ascent in 1921.

Two days later, again with Holland and Crawford, Kelly made his first investigation of what was to become Moss Ghyll Grooves. An initial appraisal of this area came as early as 1912 when George Sansom and Siegfried Herford climbed about 30ft. up one pitch before turning back. They had been trying to reach the ledge system high on the face of the crag, christened The 'V' Ledge during exploration for the Girdle Traverse. It was Holland who named this batch of slanting slabs rising out of the bed of Moss Gill gully the plural title of Moss Ghyll Grooves. When Kelly referred to Moss Ghyll Grooves it was not to the classic route we know today, but to the entire area on the left side of Moss Gill.

Kelly was also interested in finding a way of reaching The V-Ledge because he wanted to avoid what he called "That awful Great Flake on the Central Buttress"; the earlier attempts on that feature obviously had a profound effect on him. He initially set off up what he called "The number two groove line" (which was possibly the line of the Variation Start to the modern route), past a good thread until it became blank, from here he stepped sensationally right into another groove, which was named "Groove number three," but again found awkward climbing with neither ledge nor belay. He retreated with difficulty back to the gill, from where they moved up to investigate what they called "The number one groove."
This was described as being:

> "The kind of slab work met with on the previous route, with the same hopeless stretch of rock after fifty feet. The leader reported a possible forty feet of further progress, but ahead of this was an abominable overhang and no apparent means of overcoming it." (7)

Holland was naturally rather worried by these daring attempts, and wrote:

> "Kelly made a series of determined efforts to force a way up, but was in every case faced with climbing of such severity that any advance without the certainty of a resting place within a reasonable distance would have been more than risky. As it was, he had great difficulty in returning from one point." (8)

Kelly was to become somewhat obsessed with this area which was obviously the major unclimbed feature of the crag at the time. It is apparent from his writings that this first reconnaissance did not attempt what is now regarded as the true line of Moss Ghyll Grooves. Such a line seemed so improbable it did not even warrant a number during this first attempt, and it is not hard to understand why he avoided the true line of Moss Ghyll Grooves. The main slab on that route appears to fade into the main face, whereas the other groove lines seem to present some potential for reaching the upper part of the face.

Following the abortive attempt at Moss Ghyll Grooves, Crawford took the lead and climbed the steep rock of the lower part of the Pinnacle which was to become a fine MVS pragmatically named Waiting Room from Steep Ghyll. Holland later wrote:

> "Crawford chose the centre line and made steady progress for fifty feet when he reached a belay. Kelly did not seem to agree with the leader's statement that the holds were good and so I was prepared for something unusually arduous. In fact the holds were not satisfactory and for nearly thirty feet the climbing seemed to me to be in the first order of desperation and to be much harder than Hopkinson's Gully." (9)

The first guidebook description of this route pulls no punches, (although it was written by Holland):

> "In tackling this pitch the leader is confronted with a most formidable and exacting task, and its successful negotiation requires considerable strength and exceptional powers of balance." (10)

They then finished their climbing by traversing across the Pinnacle Face to finish up Jones' Arête; once again repeating the Bad Corner.

Climbing above Hopkinson's Cairn Ledge towards Bad Corner.

Above: Starting the top pitch of Upper Deep Ghyll Buttress. Climbers A. Wood-Johnson, C. J. Astley-Cooper.

Below: The final exposed arete of Upper Deep Ghyll Buttress. Climbers A. Wood-Johnson, C. J .Astley-Cooper.

Photos: E Wood-Johnson

After Kelly's departure to his home in Manchester, Crawford and Holland added Pinnacle Face from Steep Ghyll, a wandering line that traversed rightwards across the lower left face of the Pinnacle at Hard Severe. As Holland commented: "It is the easiest of the four ways onto the Pinnacle from the base, and can be used to access any of the routes on The Pinnacle face." (11)

This old variation is now only of historical interest, as is the case for several minor variations they made to existing routes on the Pinnacle which have since disappeared from the record, such as an alternative line from Hopkinson's Gully to the Crevasse, and a variation just right of Hopkinson and Tribe's Route.

The following year Claude Frankland and V.W. Brown climbed the lower slabs of Pisgah Buttress by a more direct variation, which is now the recommended line of Pisgah Buttress Direct. The notable feature of this ascent was that it was made under a heavy covering of snow, and thus presumably climbed in nailed boots to suit the conditions.

Also in 1920, Kelly returned with George Bower and Reginald Pritchard, when they climbed the rather intimidating route Upper Deep Ghyll Buttress, which still retains a MVS grade today. It follows the left-hand arête of the buttress overlooking the narrow upper slot of Deep Gill, and it finishes just below the summit rocks of Symmonds Knott, the small peaked top above the crag. This is another neglected route simply because of its relatively remote location, though the quality is all there and it is just that very few people have bothered to try it. The group noticed the possibility offered by the steep headwall during an ascent of Herford's Upper West Wall Climb. The key third pitch which traverses around the arête was the crux, and it gave them some trying problems. Kelly had attempted a delicate traverse leftwards to the rounded arête on the left, but he was defeated by a lack of holds just below a belay ledge, which entailed a tricky retreat to his team. This obstacle was overcome by the following tactic as later described by Pritchard:

> "The second man should climb round and on to the top of the large detached block to belay the leader, who climbs the wall to a small recess underneath an overhang by inserting his fingers in a thin diagonal crack, the feet finding support on minute ledges." (12)

The impending nature of this pitch made for a difficult and technical lead in its day, which Kelly curiously admitted to "being laid under contribution" during its ascent. This is a rather quaint description for finding oneself in a taxing situation and it seems that Kelly found this pitch rather difficult. The modern guidebook description for pitch 3 now follows Kelly's earlier attempt by traversing out to the arête; which was not climbed until 1946 by Arthur Dolphin and John Cook.

Later that year, Kelly explored the sweep of slabs on the Deep Gill side of the upper Pinnacle with Dorothy Pilley and Morley Wood. They reached a point in the centre of the slabs by reversing the old Hopkinson and Tribe's route, from where Kelly attempted a direct ascent of the slabs above. The smooth and unprotected nature of the climbing obviously unsettled him, as he asked Morley Wood to solo across to the Low Man in order to lower him a top-rope to finish the route. This might have seemed to be an ordinary epic, until you refer to Dorothy Pilley's memoirs in which she notes the incessant heavy rain. Kelly hadn't even bothered to mention in his diary that it had been pouring down.

Several weeks later, Kelly returned with Pritchard and Bower to climb this route in fine style, which was named Central Route, Deep Ghyll Slabs, a rather pleasant and clean Hard Severe. Before the ascent Kelly had asked Pritchard to lower him on a rope down the lower section of the slabs until he was "stopped within twelve feet from the bed of the gill by the undercut base of the cliff. These last few feet were also tried from below but they proved hopeless, – a few deep incut holds are necessary to overcome such a bulge of rock". In fact this start was not climbed until 1962 when Allinson and Mansfield added Slab Climb.

Photo: Al Phizacklea

Dave Woods and Joe Holden on Central Route, Deep Ghyll Slabs.

Kelly once again returned in 1921 with George Bower for his third attempt at climbing Central Buttress, and unwittingly became involved with the eventual second ascent. His diary for that day records:

> "Found Frankland and Beetham already on the job. Went up Keswick Brothers' and across to top of the flake, where Frankland had already threaded a rope around the chockstone. Beetham then climbed up and lashed himself to the chockstone. Frankland then followed and climbed over B. to top of the flake. He asked us to join them from Jeffcoat's and we did so finishing the rest of the climb with them." (13)

This incident seemed to satisfy Kelly with C.B. as he never returned to climb the route in its entirety, so he never did climb 'that awful Great Flake'.

Claude Frankland and Bentley Beetham climbed the prestigious second ascent of Central Buttress on the 20th August, 1921. The brief comment in the FRCC journal of that year said "It was led throughout, without previous inspection from above". Nuff said! Frankland was a Yorkshire climber; nowadays best known for his awkward Frankland's Green Crack at Almsscliff, whilst Beetham is well known for developing the lower valley crags in Borrowdale - the classic Little Chamonix at Shepherds is his most popular route. The pair reached the Oval ledge by climbing directly up a shallow ramp from the base of the crag, which has since become the standard start to the route.

This photo taken in 1928 illustrates the tactics used to climb the Great Flake on Central Buttress. The leader is belayed to the chockstone. Climbers A Wood-Johnson, C J Astley-Cooper.

Photo: E Wood-Johnson

The First Scafell Guidebook

The first guidebook to cover the 'Scawfell [sic] Group' was produced by the Fell & Rock Climbing Club, 1924, and it was simultaneously published in the Club's Journal. The actual guidebook had a thin, flexible red cover of Crimson Basil Cloth as used for all of the 'First Series' of guidebooks which became known as the 'Red Series', and they were renowned for leaching red dye when they became wet.

Photo: Al Phizackea

This series were the first in The Lake District to utilise photo-topos to illustrate where the routes lay. The guide included some remarkable diagrams and photographs, including several photo-diagrams to clarify the confusion of routes on The Pinnacle. These were all marked-up by hand, as the example opposite from the first Scafell guidebook shows. There was a ninety year period before the next photo diagram of Scafell was used in a FRCC guidebook.

The team proudly display their wounds after an ascent of Central Buttress, 1928. From left to right; C. J. Astley Cooper, Ernest Wood-Johnson and Arthur Wood-Johnson.

Frankland's account of the second ascent remains one of the best pieces of descriptive writing of its time:

> "Beetham invited me to use him as freely as I would any jammed boulder, and I tried to grace my compunction in grating over his frame by calling attention to my rubber shoes. Without further ado, Beetham trussed his near side leg with both hands and made a fine stirrup from which I mounted to his equally firm shoulders. It was fortunate that my friend was staunch, as he sat there dangling in the loops, or our escapade would have been March Madness. Both hands were needed to maintain a very unstable balance as I straightened my knees on each side of a steady head. The grip of the hands upon the tapering edges of the Flake was enough to prevent a backward crash, but the sharp, hollowed crest was still out of reach, Beetham offered his head. Agitation immediately gave way to complacency. Very carefully, very confidently, the left hand slid up the outside face of the Flake until the fingers curled over and hooked the sharp crest. Then, with feelings unbecoming of expression to a man who has reached my side of middle age, I enjoyed the luxury of lusty hauling, which was sheer joy with such a hold and such a space below to spur one's efforts." (14)

Tragedy struck Harry Kelly in 1922 when his wife Emily was killed on Tryfan whilst descending the Heather Terrace. Emily, or 'Pat' as she was also known, was an excellent climber in her own right and she was the driving force behind the founding of the ladies' The Pinnacle Club. Following her death, Kelly spent much time with his good friends the Eden-Smiths, who lived at Grange-over-Sands. Over the years he formed a strong partnership with Mrs. Blanche Eden-Smith, whom he referred to simply as 'G' in his diaries (reputedly short for Gabriel, as he looked upon her as his guardian angel). And for the record, this relationship was regarded by most at the time as being platonic. Not that it has stopped any of the smutty rumours down the years!

Five months after Emily's accident, Kelly and Waller Eden-Smith climbed an isolated pinnacle of good clean rock found close to where Lord's Rake crosses the ruddy-coloured scree run of Red Gill. Red Ghyll Buttress is hardly ever climbed nowadays due to its remote location, but it contains some delightful climbing on clean, rough rock at the amenable grade of Very Difficult. Waller Eden-Smith was Blanche's brother in law, his name has been incorrectly spelled as Walter in some other publications.

Aside from the exploits of Harry Kelly, around this time in 1923 the third ascent of C. B. was made by Alf Piggott, Morley Wood and Bernard Meldrum. The following year, Claude Frankland and Mabel Barker claimed the fourth ascent. At the age of 38 years, Barker became the first woman to climb the route, and Frankland became the first person to climb the route twice.

Photo: A. Wood-Johnson

In the traditional style Frankland tied himself to the chockstone and Barker climbed up to him, recording the following:

> "I got onto and over my partner and off his head as quickly as possible. He says he felt for my foot to hold it if necessary, but could not find it, and I do not know where it went. Probably, being slimmer than former climbers, I got further into the crack, and chimneyed it. I faced out, and I think there was a small hold far up on the inside wall. Almost at once, I felt the top of the flake with the left hand. 'I've got it!' I said, thrilled with the realisation that the thing was virtually done, and there was probably not a happier woman living at that moment!" (15)

It is clear that Mabel was the first woman to climb Central Buttress and that she had led the crux of the route, and it is also interesting to note that she was also part of the first team to descend the route. It is still a commonly held belief that the first woman to lead the Flake pitch was Alice Nelson in 1939, but this confusion derives from the fact that Alice was the first woman to lead the route in it's entirity.

Photo: FRCC Archive

Mabel Barker, an extraordinary climber.

Over the following years Kelly concentrated his pioneering around The Napes and Pillar Rock areas. Pillar was his favourite crag; here he led the first ascents of Sodom, Gomorrah, (which were originally named Routes 1 and 2), Grooved Wall and The Appian Way amongst others. Apart from two further attempts at the true line of Moss Ghyll Grooves in 1923, one of which entailed being lowered down on a rope from above, he never returned to Scafell until 1925 when he added several minor routes on the broken rocks between Deep Gill Buttress and Red Gill Buttress. These are Castor, M, and Pollux, VD, which he climbed in the company of Reginald Pritchard; and The Bannister, a fine line easy route up the crest of Red Gill Buttress giving one of the few lines of Difficult standard that can be recommended on the crag. This was led by Blanche Eden-Smith, and significantly this is the only first ascent of a route on Scafell that was led by a woman.

Kelly had yet another determined look at Moss Ghyll Grooves in 1925, again in the company of Blanche Eden-Smith. He climbed up to the crux slab, but concluded that a party of two was insufficient in number for a serious attempt to be made, and they made their way to the top of the crag by way of Moss Gill. Kelly and Blanche then made an audacious investigation from above, climbing down the upper slabs of the Grooves until they came to a point which is now known as the Lookout. From here Kelly could study the crux slab from above, and by climbing back up the way they descended it left only a fifty foot section of the route remaining to be climbed.

The First Scafell Guidebook

This first guide was written by Charles Holland with editing undertaken by Theo Chorley. It contained almost fifty routes and variations, the hardest of course being the magnificent Central Buttress.
It was priced at two shillings (10p), which seems ludicrously low nowadays. If one compares this with the price of the latest rubbers these were only one shilling a pair. It is difficult to imagine paying twice the cost of a pair of modern rock boots for a new guide.

B-B	Hopkinson's Cairn Direct from Lord's Rake.	S	Hopkinson & Tribe's Route
A-A	Hopkinson's Gully	SI	H & T Variation
G	Gangway	V	Gibson's traverse
N	Moss Ledge	K	Waiting Room
H	Herford's Slab	M	Toe Traverse Mantleshelf
R	Hopkinson's Cairn	C	Crevasse
		T	Sansom's Traverse

It is interesting to note the Climbers' Club had been intending to publish guidebooks to the Lakeland Crags when as early as 1913 Geoffrey Winthrop Young had asked Siegfried Herford to write a guide to Scafell for the C.C. The carnage of the trenches prevented this project ever coming to fruition, and growing dominance of the Fell & Rock in The Lake District enabled the Club to take control of guide-book production in the area.

The rudimentary form of protection used in the 1920s is well illustrated with this shot of Tower Buttress on The Shamrock.

Ascending the short length of mossy slab to Herford's Ledge which gave the name to Moss Ledge Direct Route.

The following day the pair made the first investigation of Shamrock, the large rambling buttress below Lord's Rake which was unclimbed at this time. Kelly tried the prominent deep recess in the lower part of the crag, but backed off. He returned a couple of months later with Blanche Eden-Smith and Reginald Pritchard and made significant progress up the crag for eight pitches to a point where they were forced off leftwards due to a heavy shower and the cold wind. They escaped up a set of broken chimneys and followed a wretched line of grassy slots which led to the top of the buttress. This same team returned a couple of days later to complete their route which was named Tower Buttress, HS, and with a length in excess of 200 metres over 11 pitches it is the longest route on the Scafell crags. It has not proved popular, but some considered it to have redeeming features, and even Arthur Dolphin recorded it as "A magnificent climb!". The same cannot be said for what is one of the worst routes on the crag, Intermittent Chimneys, which was later a complete ascent of the broken chimneys they had used earlier for their escape.

Two further routes were climbed in 1925, both of them being significant for different reasons. The first, Slime Chimney, is the short, greasy chimney line at the extreme left end of The East Buttress, and although it only takes the form of a flanking attack, it was the first route on The East Buttress since Mickledore Chimney nearly sixty years earlier. This was climbed by the large team of Claude Frankland, Bentley Beetham, Arthur Wakefield and Jerry Wright.

The second route was a direct ascent up the front face of the Pinnacle which led to Moss Ledge, thus creating the best route of its grade in The Lakes when combined with Herford's eponymous slab and the upper pitches of The Bad Corner and Jones' Arête. Fergus Graham and G. Wellburn slowly crawled their way up these delicate, unprotected slabs which are now known as Moss Ledge Direct, VS. Graham wrote:

> "For some considerable time I remained gracefully poised on one toe and glared fiercely at the rock in endeavour to conjure up a ledge, but there was no response." (16)

This route is still the firm favourite with many climbers, and is best appreciated on a warm, sunny evening in late spring. The rock is clean and rough, and the line followed is continually interesting and sustained at uniform standard. It is a route of outstanding quality in a district overflowing with excellent climbing.

Following the 1903 accident this part of the crag had retained its reputation of being somewhere that only the most experienced climbers should venture. A fine example of this prevailing attitude from the 'Old Establishment' was noted by Alan (A.B.) Hargreaves, when he recalled the day that Colin Kirkus and he first climbed on this face during their first trip to The Lakes in 1929:

> "Now, in those days no-one ventured onto the Pinnacle Face of Scafell, not since Herford and Sansom wrote it up. It had a big hoodoo on it following the terrible accident in 1904 [sic] when four climbers were killed on the thing. It was most definitely taboo for most Fell & Rock people. I remember that Colin and I had been all over the Pinnacle Face, we'd done Jones' Route, Hopkinson's Gully, the Direct Route by Herford's Slab which everyone fell off, and another out to the right – we did the lot! We were two cocky young climbers! Anyway, we met this chap in the village pub in Wasdale who was Vice-President (17) of the Fell & Rock, and we said what we'd done and he was absolutely horrified, horrified! He said it was a job for experts with twenty years experience behind them. 'You silly young buggers', he said, 'you'll cause another fatal accident'. Anyway, we went off and did Botterill's Slab. We were using line of course, and we'd discovered that you could do funny things with line; it hooked over things well for belays." (18)

Harry Kelly returned in 1926 and renewed his obsession with Moss Ghyll Grooves. During a hot, dry spell of weather his diary entry for 1st July notes:

> "Explored Moss Ghyll Grooves from above, self climbed down to first groove and descended it about 15 to 20 feet gardening en-route. Saw enough to satisfy me that lower portion may be linked up with this – a matter of about 30 feet. Rejoined others." (19)

Photo: Al Phizacklea

Woodhead's Climb Variation.

There is a variation finish to Woodhead's Climb on the upper reaches of Scafell Pinnacle that is named after the first ascentionist Michael de Selincourt.

It is currently graded MVS and the description in the guide contains the advice that 'difficulties are short and loose', which has ensured that it has been completely ignored ever since. Details of the ascent are sketchy, it was not included in the 1924 guide, but it appears in the 1936 guide. It is recorded that de Selincourt was active on Scafell between 1924 and 1926, and in 1926 he had attempted an ascent of Central Buttress with Ivan Waller. This followed the fourth ascent of the route by Mabel Barker and Frankland and they had commented that 'If a woman can climb that route, so can we.'

Well it turned out they couldn't. Waller fell off the crux and was held by de Selincourt, the second instance in a short space of time that he had held a falling leader. This shook him up so much that he gave up climbing shortly after, saying, 'If it was easy it bored him and if it was difficult it frightened him and he did not like being bored or frightened'. It was recorded that he took up cooking instead.

Al Davies on the 'Damson Stone' traverse on Moss Ghyll Grooves. He is belayed by Mary Grace Brown who is standing at the same point where Blanche Eden-Smith perched without a belay on the first ascent.

After this inspection from above, Kelly, Blanche Eden-Smith and a young accomplice, J. B. Kilshaw, were dismayed during their lunch at the top of the crag when a vicious little thunderstorm drenched the rock. However, by the time they had descended Keswick Brothers' Climb and gathered in the depths of Moss Gill the sun had dried the rocks, and they set about the new route. The first pitch was familiar to Kelly and Blanche as they had previously been up this many times. Kelly's diary describes the crux section of the second pitch:

> "The slab is climbed for a few feet in the corner. A sensational 'holdless' step across it to the left leads to a perch (The Pedestal) at the foot of another facet of the slab. This is followed and shortly a basin hold in the corner is thankfully reached. Although the slab is narrowing to an apex, three delightful but narrow ledges are encountered and give approach to the Lookout by way of some welcome blocks." (20)

Blanche Eden-Smith watches Harry Kelly making notes at the foot of an unidentified crag, sometime around the late 1920's. According to Anne Greedy, Blanche's granddaughter, Blanche was very fond of Harry, and although she never heard of any inappropriate behaviour between the two, she remembers that Grandpa was not very happy with Kelly making frequent visits to the house and spiriting Blanche away when they climbed together.

Kelly was aided by Blanche on this ascent by an act that was bordering on being either exceedingly brave or lethally reckless. He made this known via her obituary some fifty years later:

> "In order that the leader might avoid a run-out of about 80ft., she undertook a precarious and belay-less stance some 15ft. higher, thereby boosting the morale of the leader. How much easier it was, with someone at hand, to take that delicate step across to the Pedestal." (21)

Below, Blanche, from her insecure perch was holding his rope in anticipation. She recorded her own version:

> "From a very narrow foothold on the centre of the slab, a left-hand movement had to be made upward and outward to a small level stance (The Pedestal) on the extreme edge, about two strides away. The difficulty lay in the fact that there was nothing to stride across on except a small protuberance about the size of a damson stone, on which, moreover, hands had to be changed somehow. Twice Kelly tried it and came down to the grass for a rest from the toe-cramping footholds from which the movement must start. The third time he went straight for it and seemed to flow over those two 'holdless' strides to The Pedestal, where, at last, both feet could rest at once. The earnest pathos in his voice, as he besought his followers to do their best when their turn came, was ominously indicative of what he thought of the place." (22)

Thus after a period of seven years of trying this plum line Kelly had stamped his name on Scafell with an incredible classic contribution; Moss Ghyll Grooves. This became Kelly's favourite climb, and every time he visited Scafell with a new partner, part of the day's itinerary was an ascent of his much-loved route. He gave the route a VS grade, and noted that it was the same calibre as Botterill's Slab. By the 1936 guidebook it had been downgraded to Severe (exposed), it was then upgraded to Hard Severe in the 1956 guide where it stayed until it was further promoted to Mild VS in the 1996 guidebook.

After Moss Ghyll Grooves Kelly went on to pioneer further routes on Pillar and Gable, but he was not involved with any more major first ascents on Scafell, apart from one insignificant line on The Shamrock. Following the ascent of Moss Ghyll Grooves, activity faded away and there was no further exploration on the crags during the rest of the decade. Perhaps this reflected the social upheaval and anxiety caused by the Great Depression, with uncertainty and fear over unemployment and poverty affecting everyone, and even the well-to-do middle classes were forced to tighten their belts. Such a hiatus marks one of those periods in the crag's history when the 'Old Guard' took stock, and wondered when and from where the next wave of progress might come.

Luckily they didn't have too long to wait, for there was a 'new breed of climbers' (possibly an overworked phrase demanding an apology) cutting their teeth on the Welsh cliffs, and they came to Scafell looking for unclimbed rock. They found plenty around the corner on the east side of the mountain which heralded a whole new phase of development.

Footnotes

1. H. M. Kelly, 'Memorabilia' *FRCC Journal*, 1976
2. Alan Hankinson, extract from '*A Century on the Crags*' 1986
3. H. M. Kelly '*New Climbs and Old*' *Rucksack Club Journal*, 1920
4. H. M. Kelly '*New Climbs and Old*' *Rucksack Club Journal*, 1920
5. H. M. Kelly's Personal diary
6. C. F. Holland *New Climbs in the Wasdale District* *FRCC Journal*, 1919
7. H. M. Kelly *New Climbs and Old*' *Rucksack Club Journal*, 1920
8. C. F. Holland *New Climbs in the Wasdale District* *FRCC Journal*, 1919
9. C. F. Holland *New Climbs in the Wasdale District* *FRCC Journal*, 1919
10. C. F. Holland, Scafell guidebook, 1924
11. C. F. Holland, Scafell guidebook, 1924
12. R. E. W. Pritchard, 'Further Ascents in Wasdale' *Rucksack Club Journal*,1922
13. H. M. Kelly's Personal diary
14. C. D. Frankland, excerpt from '*The Central Buttress of Scafell*' by G. Wilson
15. Jan Levi '*And Nobody Woke Up Dead*' 2006
16. F. Graham, first ascent comment
17. This would have either been R. T. S. Chorley or L. W. Somervell
18. A. B. Hargreaves, extract from '*Hands of a Climber*' by S. Dean
19. H. M. Kelly's personal diary
20. H. M. Kelly's personal diary
21. H. M. Kelly, Obituary of Blanche Eden-Smith *FRCC Journal*, 1963
22. Blanche Eden-Smith, 'MGG' *FRCC Journal*, 1926

Left: Middle Row Farm in 1928 with the Wood-Johnson family on the wall and C. J. Astley-Cooper alongside. Note the sign above the door which says

WILSONS
MIDDLE ROW
TEMPERANCE HOTEL
REFRESHMENTS, BEDS

Which seems to make a positive spin on the fact that they had no licence to sell alcohol! Old Dick Wilson, who was a champion Cumberland wrestler with over one hundred trophies to his name, retired later in this year and the farm was taken over by Joe Naylor, who's son Joss went on to become the most famous fell runner in the country.

Middle Row Farm today. The farm used to be the unofficial headquarters of the Fell and Rock Climbing Club at Wasdale in the 1920s, mainly because it was favoured by H. M. Kelly over the hotel, which seemed to have lost its appeal by this time. Although only a small house, the farm was the largest in the valley with a flock of over 2000 sheep.

The upper slabs of Moss Ghyll Grooves, above the belay ledge known as 'The Look-Out'.

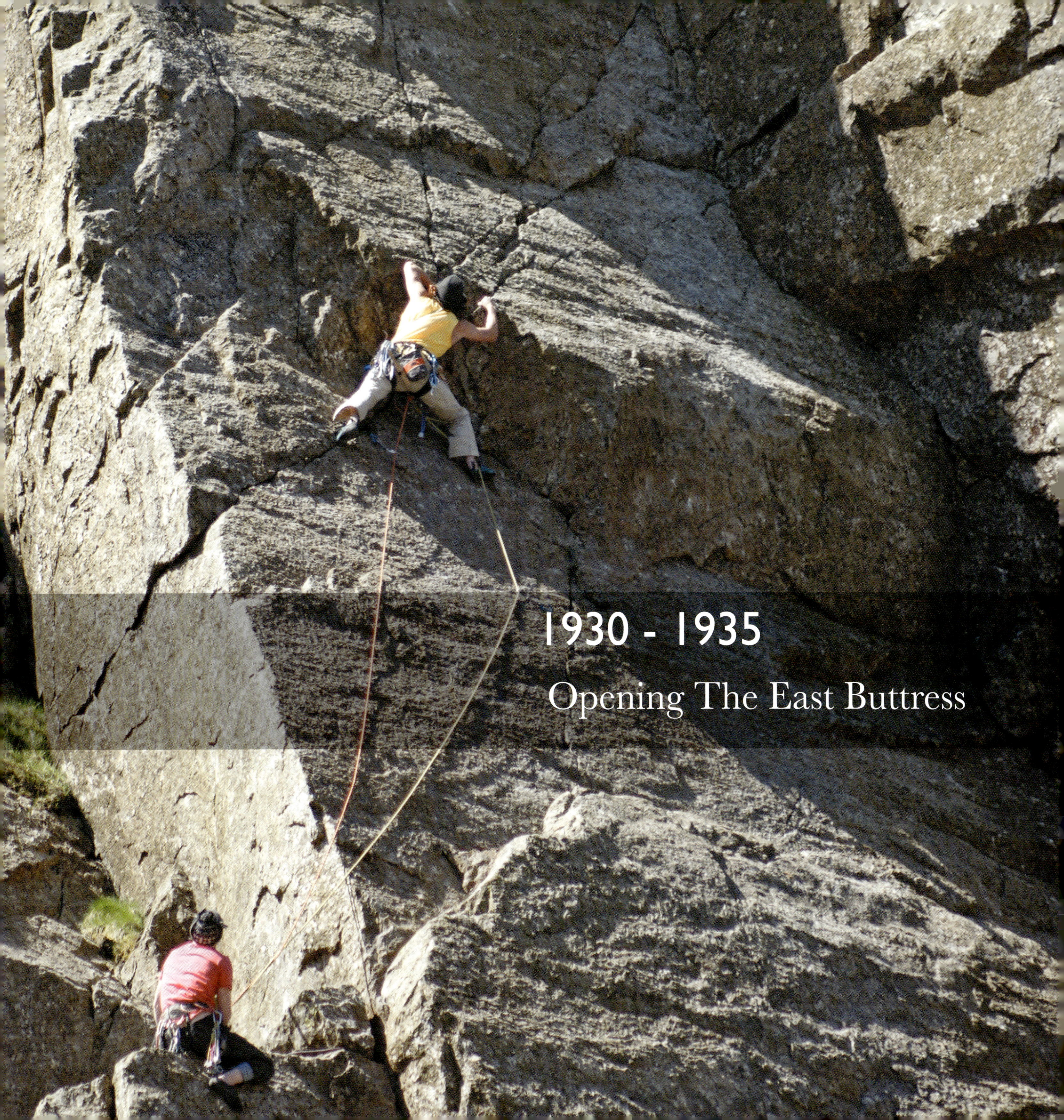

1930 - 1935

Opening The East Buttress

Clogwyn Du'r Arddu

In terms of notoriety, the big, bad twin of The East Buttress on Scafell is a crag in North Wales which exhibits similar difficulty and seriousness; Clogwyn Du'r Arddu, also known as The Black Cliff, nestling under the northern slopes of Snowdon. In 1927 Alf Piggott climbed the breakthrough line of Piggott's Route, the first to assail the walls between the obvious chimney courses. This was followed by further impressive lines by Colin Kirkus, Jack Longland and Maurice Linnell. Apart from the early reputations enjoyed by both crags for being utterly unclimbable due to steepness, inaccessibility and wetness, there was little else they had in common. 'Cloggy,' as it was christened by Kirkus, has an intricate topography and though it is more than twice the height of The East Buttress it suffers double deterrents of loose rock and excessive vegetation. The sheer majesty of the architecture may not be matched by Scafell, but The East Buttress is generally steeper than Cloggy. It is made up of better rock, and because it faces east, it has less lichen and other vegetation. It is somewhat fitting that these two majestic rock faces were initially developed by the same climber; Colin Kirkus.

Overleaf:
Joe Holden and Craig Spence on the main pitch of Mickledore Grooves.

Right:
The East Buttress as viewed from Broad Crag Tarn.

Photos: Al Phizacklea

With its mass of bulging rock and dripping bleakness, The East Buttress forms a formidable sight as it leans above upper Eskdale in a manner that defies the laws of gravity. Until 1930 the only routes that ventured anywhere near this face followed unpopular chimney weaknesses at either end of the crag. In between lay a quarter of a mile of deeply impressive lines barring any attempts at exploration. The earliest recorded reconnaissance came in 1919 from Harry Kelly, Charles Crawford and Charles Holland. Kelly started at the foot of Mickledore Chimney and:

> " ... explored a terrific slab at the bottom of the chimney. Self went up about 60ft, looked hopeless. Perhaps will repay prospecting from above." (1)

He never did return, but what he was attempting is now known as the Barry's Slab start to Mickledore Grooves. The East Buttress had a massive reputation in these early days; it was steep, wet, and hugely intimidating.

The first serious route to breach The East Buttress was Mickledore Grooves, climbed in May 1930 (2) by Colin Kirkus, a young climber from Liverpool and one of the best of his generation, matched only by Menlove Edwards and Maurice Linnell. Mickledore Grooves was a profound psychological breakthrough for climbing in that era. The team of Kirkus, Ivan Waller, Marco Pallis and their photo-grapher for the day Richard Nicholson approached from Langdale, pausing for a bathe in Angle Tarn before making for the secluded East Buttress of Scafell.

Mickledore Grooves is the first weakness left of Mickledore Chimney following a series of rising grooves which peter out against the left side of the slab originally attempted by Kelly. It is little wonder they chose this line; at the right end of the crag it is not as steep or intimidating as it becomes further left, a factor which must have appealed as they examined the possibility of breaching this formidable wall. Waller recalled the ascent in a *Fell & Rock Climbing Club Journal*:

> "Colin was an untidy-looking lad with wiry hair and slightly sunken features. He looked neither strong nor athletic, and quite unprepossessing. In fact he was incredibly tough, determined and completely dedicated to the mountains. On arrival at The East Buttress, then unclimbed, Colin led the first two pitches just as if he was on a well-trodden route. Each pitch had a strenuous fingery move which I thoroughly enjoyed. For the main pitch the second man sits on a good ledge with an overhanging wall above, behind which goes the slab up where the pitch starts. After about a quarter of an hour Colin made an excursion to the left edge of the slab and his head appeared above me. He was happy and relaxed and assured me that all was going well. After a further half hour all the rope was out and it was my turn to follow." (3)

This final pitch was a huge affair; a full 140 feet long, crossing the upper stretches of the big slab and following a corner line running up the right side of the slab. The entire pitch was completely unprotected apart from the moral support of passing the rope behind a loose looking spike on the left wall of the crux groove. Kirkus described this groove as being climbed with great difficulty for 30 or 40 feet, with the hardest move being a tricky pull at the top to gain a grass ledge. No-one in those days climbed with a 150 foot long rope and he only managed to reach the belay ledge by tying two ropes together. This was an amazing lead from a young man not yet 20 years old, on rock that was lichenous with cracks full of grass that left the outcome in doubt until the very end.

The East Buttress had been conquered at last; the route has stood the test of time and is now regarded as one of the great classic Very Severes of the area, but it can only be expected to be found at that grade in perfect conditions. Ivan Waller appreciated this was a hugely significant and quite superb route, and he later said that this had been the best day he ever had in The Lakes.

On return to Liverpool, Kirkus phoned his close friend Alan (A.B.) Hargreaves with the news of this huge new route. (Hargreaves was never called Alan by his friends, he was always known as A.B. even throughout his old age, it was a term of endearment in the climbing world.) The following year, on the day after the first free ascent of Central Buttress, Hargreaves led the second ascent of Mickledore Grooves with Bill Stallybrass in perfect dry conditions. What isn't widely known is that this second ascent contained a twist that was kept hidden for over 60 years. Stallybrass was then a young and rather impetuous lad, and he had found the climbing on the blunt end of the rope quite straightforward. In the evening of this second ascent A.B. returned to Barrow, and the following day Stallybrass tried without success to persuade one of his family holiday group to join him climbing. Undeterred, he wandered back up to Scafell alone in the hope that he could join with another climbing team, with the intention that he might actually lead Mickledore Grooves himself. Bill found the crag deserted, and he sat on the grass at Mickledore pondering the superb dry conditions when an audacious idea entered his mind. He stepped up to Mickledore Grooves and soloed the third ascent in twenty minutes. At the time, soloing was almost unheard of, especially at such a high grade and on an almost virgin crag.

Above: Colin Kirkus.
Below: Craig Spence and Joe Holden on the intial grooves of Mickledore Grooves.

Above: Marco Pallis on the first ascent of Mickledore Grooves.

Right: Joe Holden on the final pitch of Mickledore Grooves.

> "Courage did not come into it; there was not a single moment of fear, just an amazing sense of freedom without a rope in front or behind me….I was inordinately proud of myself." (4)

Upon returning home, he wrote a rather boastful letter to A.B., who replied with 'a most awful bollocking' accusing Stallybrass of being totally irresponsible; he had demeaned Kirkus' achievement and exploited their second ascent in order to boost his own ego. Bill had always looked up to A.B. with tremendous respect, and was so horrified over this rebuke that he never mentioned the tale to anyone. Hargreaves was apparently so infuriated that he never climbed with him again – A.B. was well known for his ferocious temper and long-term memory! Stallybrass went on to become Kirkus' best man at his wedding, but he never confessed this incident until shortly before his death when he wrote to Steve Dean, finally laying the episode to rest. He was eventually reconciled with A.B. when they met at the 1994 Climbers' Club AGM dinner.

In 1937 Mickledore Grooves route was to be the scene of a horrific accident involving Kirkus' cousin Wilf Noyce and his partner Menlove Edwards. The best description of this epic occurence was written by John Wilkinson in his article for *Mountain* magazine:

> "Noyce and Edwards had walked to The East Buttress from Buttermere where they were staying at Professor Pigou's house. It had been raining, the lower grooves were awash and even the great slab was shining with water. Climbing in socks, Noyce led across the great slab and into the big groove. Near the top, there was a very awkward move out to grass ledges out right, and Noyce had to change his grease-choked socks for another pair let down by friends. As he moved onto the grass ledge, the entire ledge slid off. A hundred feet below Edwards was belayed on a grass ledge at the top of the first groove pitches, and there were no runners. As Noyce fell down the groove Edwards took in some slack, and with the rope running behind the grass ledge, took the strain. The 170ft. rope, which consisted of two lengths of hemp tied together stretched, and two strands parted; Noyce touched-down on the ground. He was fortunate to survive a fall of 200ft. with only a few broken bones to his face and hand. Professor Pigou had a charming habit of awarding medals to his house guests who had accomplished stirring deeds on the crags. Noyce was presented with a leather medal for his exploits on Mickledore Grooves." (5)

An impromptu rescue party managed to get the unconscious Noyce to Whitehaven Hospital, where an emergency operation skilfully patched his smashed face, and after three days he regained consciousness and went on to recover fully. Noyce seems to have been an accident-prone character. He was injured whilst winter climbing on Ben Nevis, broke his leg falling off Tophet Bastion on Great Gable, and he confided to a friend, John Jackson, that he seriously considered giving up climbing 'as it was clear that the mountains did not want him as they kept throwing him off!' Ironically, Noyce was to lose his life in the Pamir Mountains in the company of another fine East Buttress pioneer, Robin Smith. Allan Austin rates this incident, in particular the lightning reactions and sheer strength of Edwards, as the greatest individual action ever in British climbing. He commented:

> "It was a monstrous effort, it still takes my breath away when I think about it". (6)

By strange coincidence a very similar accident happened from the same place in parallel circumstances thirteen years later, when the artist 'Ginger' Cain fell from the same delicate move high in the crux groove. He was then a young student and had been climbing in socks over his rubbers due to the greasy conditions, but the slime from the rock had built up on his socks, rendering them as slippery as the rock itself. The main difference between this and Noyce's accident was that he was stopped after eighty feet by a peg runner which was by then in place at the foot of the groove. Cain had been incensed when he first saw this peg, and had spent some time attempting to remove it before finally admitting defeat and clipping his rope through it.

Menlove Edwards, the first to climb the Great Flake of Central Buttress without assistance.

Maurice Linnell.

Fortuitously he only sustained an extensive friction rash which he colourfully described as:

> "I took the skin right off one cheek of my arse!".

After scraping down the slab he was left dangling from the end of the rope, and just at that point a family group which included a young daughter arrived below the crag, and viewed the scene of carnage above: 'Ooh look, Mummy,' cried the little girl, 'Climbers!' (7)

Ginger was top-roped off the route by Pete Moffatt and Peter Hogg (who later became notorious for disposing of his wife's body in Wastwater; becoming the first of the infamous 'Lady in the Lake' villains). His companions, Ron Miller and Tony Greenbank, assisted him back down to the Brackenclose hut where they cleaned out his abrasions and administered an iodine lotion, which caused Ginger to hop around the hut screaming in agony as the stinging unguent took effect. Sid Cross later spiced up the story by claiming his screams could be heard from the bar of the Old Dungeon Ghyll in Langdale!

Following the ascent of Mickledore Grooves, 1931 saw the first free ascent of Central Buttress (C.B.). This had been a long-term undertaking with several teams showing interest in the prize. During a dry spell in August, one such team comprising of Alf Bridge, Maurice Linnell and Bert (A.T.) Hargreaves bivouaced below the crag, and in a confident mood they soloed to the Oval. Bridge led the Great Flake pitch, and without even pausing to thread the chockstone, he attacked the upper layback with determination. Suddenly, when he was committed to the move, his feet shot off the opposite wall and he fell. By sheer determination and luck, he made a grab for the chockstone as he fell past it, and he held on, absolutely drained and quite shaken by his near miss. He tied himself to the stone and the others climbed over him to complete the pitch in conventional style.

Waiting and watching in the wings was a second team of Menlove Edwards, Março Pallis and Bill Stallybrass. Having witnessed Bridge's near disaster, Edwards threaded his rope through a sling left around the chockstone by Bridge and returned to the foot of the Flake where Stallybrass was arranging a better belay. Edwards suddenly announced that he was going to have a go, and with Stallybrass still fumbling about with the rope, he laybacked confidently to the top of the Flake. It was an astonishing feat of climbing, especially as Edwards was climbing in nailed boots.

Edwards was a brilliant climber, and the first free ascent of the greatest route in The Lakes was a huge success and a major historical achievement. However, the institutionalised intolerance of his private life meant that he was not universally liked, and his ascent of C.B. did not feature in any of the *Fell & Rock* journals of the time. Edwards was completely ignored by the establishment, and whether this was simply due to an oversight or homophobia is still a debating point today.

The next character to grace the walls of Scafell was a young man born in Stockport but raised at Kendal in The Lakes; the talented and determined Maurice Linnell. Linnell was a formidable climber, but his appearance at the crag caused much amusement amongst his contemporaries. He wore large, round metal-rimmed spectacles under a floppy shock of dark hair and he was always attired in an old suit whilst climbing. He said that last year's office suit is this year's climbing suit and he cut a smart figure whenever he appeared on the scene.

Linnell had already made a name for himself with the 28 pitch girdle traverse of Pillar Rock, but in 1932 he visited The East Buttress with fellow Kendal climber Sid Cross, who was four years his junior. Linnell picked up Cross from his school where Sid had been playing a game of rugby and drove to Langdale on his motorbike and sidecar. They had a few drinks in The Old Dungeon Ghyll before walking up Mickleden in the dark and enduring a cold, uncomfortable bivouac near Angle Tarn, particularly so for Cross who did not possess a sleeping bag.

The cold night air caused them to rise early and walk on to see the sunrise from the summit of Scafell Pike. Once underneath The East Buttress, Cross managed to catch some sleep in the sun whilst Linnell inspected the base of the crag, looking for a suitable breach in its redoubtable defences. At the lowest point of the crag, where it bends around between the east and south-east facets, he noticed a line of grooves slanting leftwards across the overhanging rock which offered the best possibility for a route. The start proved to be the most difficult section, where a short overhanging corner had to be overcome by an awkward layback move. Grooves were followed to a short corner where a wet yellow-coloured slab continues leftwards across the crag. Instead of tackling this they climbed along a delicate ramp line rising back rightwards above the centre of the crag, emerging at the top of a large white-coloured slab. This delightful climb was originally called East Buttress Climb, but it was later changed to Great Eastern Route, and it became a classic line up an uncompromising area of rock that fully deserves its VS grade. Some derisive comments written about this route in the past refer to the fact it wanders from right to left and back right again, following the easiest line on this part of the crag. Surely these are classic features for a route finding the easiest way through difficult and intimidating surroundings. There is no other way at this grade, and Great Eastern Route is recognised as being a superb lead for its time.

Photo: Al Phizacklea

Joe Holden on the steep section of Great Eastern Route.

They followed this climb with breakfast, which typically for Linnell consisted only of a bag of sugar, before wandering around to the main face of Scafell Crag. First, Cross led Botterill's Slab, and then they scrambled up Moss Gill where Linnell attempted a new variation start to Moss Ghyll Grooves. Cross described the situation in *A Century on the Crags*:

> "Linnell tackled the second groove out of the gill. I saw very little of him after he left me, with a belay that kept slipping off, but I could hear him. It was very slimy in places and he was having a desperate struggle. I spent about an hour whistling and singing and being bombarded with sods. Now and again I put my belay back on the rounded knob. Very near the top, Linnell was really struggling. A.B. Hargreaves, who was watching from above, [from Moss Ghyll Grooves] insisted on giving him a top rope. I think he felt that 'the young bugger down below' couldn't be trusted to hold a fall." (8)

So Linnell couldn't claim a first ascent, but all the same it was a terrific lead and completely on-sight. He had attempted the Variation Start to Moss Ghyll Grooves, which was not properly climbed until 1946 (The original article suggested that he had attempted Narrow Stand, but it would not have been possible to drop a rope to him if he was on that route).

One of Linnell's best achievements followed a rather amusing episode, best described in Trevor Jones' *Cumbrian Rock*:

> "As the autumn mists started to swirl around Hollow Stones, A.B. [Hargreaves] decided to try to lead Flake Crack by conventional means. He assembled a support team of mighty strength – Jack Longland, conqueror of the West Buttress of Clogwyn Du'r Arddu, Ivan Waller and Alf Bridge. Bridge climbed up and secured himself to the chockstone so that when the others followed they could use him as a ladder. Unfortunately as each man climbed over Alf his trousers parted company from him and they slid to his ankles. Suddenly Maurice Linnell appeared on the scene looking neat and immaculate as if he had just come out of the tailors. He viewed the bizarre scene with distaste and announced: 'I'm not going to be buggered about by you lot.' He then soloed up Keswick Brothers', traversed onto Central Buttress and to their astonishment he soloed the virgin Bayonet-Shaped Crack, named by Ashley Abraham more than a quarter of a century before. It is still [Grade] 5b but Linnell made light of its difficulties and produced the first pitch of that standard to be soloed on sight on mountain crags." (9)

The performance was indeed impressive and Longland was concerned about Linnell's safety, commenting: 'Quite frankly, Maurice used to frighten the life out of me sometimes'. The crack would have been dirty with soil and lichen, and to solo this, close on to being two hundred and fifty feet (70 metres) above the base of the crag at a time when the 5b grade had only just been established on other mountain crags, is truly amazing. This achievement has probably never been matched – it could be the equivalent of Pete Livesey walking up to a crag and on-sight soloing an E4 or Dave Birkett soloing an E8 ground up – it is a little-known event that deserves respect.

The name 'Bayonet-Shaped Crack' was first coined by Ashley Abraham , who was representing 'The Old Guard' during a long discussion with a group of younger activists in the private bar of the Wasdale Hotel back at the start of the century:

> "Have any of you ever noticed a bayonet-shaped crack descending from the skyline about midway between Moss Ghyll and Botterill's Crack [Slab] on Scafell? No? Has it ever occurred to you that between these two climbs there is a stretch of nearly two hundred feet of unclimbed rock?" (10)

Marice Linnell on the first ascent of Overhanging Wall.

1933 turned out to be a momentous year for Scafell with four new routes pioneered on The East Buttress, all involving Maurice Linnell. He and A.T. (Bert) Hargreaves, no relation to A.B. (Alan) Hargreaves, started this campaign with the aptly named Overhanging Wall which found an improbable chink of weakness in the bastion of the crag between Mickledore Grooves and Great Eastern Route. It started up an awkward corner leading to an obvious little ramp running up and right following the angle of the slanting base of the crag, so they gained little actual height from the floor. A deft traverse over a protruding block led to a thin crack, where Linnell commented:

> "From here the fun begins, and on the first ascent several ways were tried without success before the objective on the right was reached. This consists of a formation resembling a gable-end, only that the roof ridge slopes as well as the tiles, and above there is nothing but overhang and a few scanty holds; but to the right is a sort of scoop, with a holdless, vertical back-wall, and a quite inadequate crack at the far side to pull across into. There was only one thing for it; and it was an eventuality to which I had come prepared. I inserted a piton in the little crack, and inserted it well and truly with a hammer. Nor was it only put there as a safeguard; by pulling on it sideways, downwards, outwards and upwards, and finally planting a foot on it, I was able with a struggle to reach a little ledge. I offer no apologies; those who prefer to climb the place unaided are cordially invited to remove the piton and do so." (11)

The rest of the pitch weaved a way up the slimy, mossy groove and through a steep bulge above to emerge at the foot of a large wet slab from which an easy angled, dirty chimney offered the line of least resistance to the top. Linnell had pioneered an audacious route up some of the steepest rock yet climbed in The Lakes, and despite the use of aid, it still earned a HVS grade. To endorse this impressive ascent even further it was climbed in greasy conditions. 'Charles' Holland commented that even the Central Buttress has to bend the knee as far as technical difficulty is concerned.

The piton remained in use for 12 years until the first confirmed free ascent was made by a youthful schoolboy team of Des Birch and John Wilkinson in 1945. This achievement is not generally recognised – it has always been thought that the talented team of Martin Boysen and Dave Alcock were the first to climb it free in 1972. Also Stan Thompson recently disclosed how Jim Birkett and Len Muscroft wouldn't use the peg, but without it had climbed the route, not even holding on to it or using it as a thread for protection. Stan was Jim Birkett's best man when he got married for the first time. Unfortunately Stan couldn't verify which year Jim climbed the route, but in all probability this would have been before Birch climbed it free.

Dave Alcock on the crux of Overhanging Wall, at the site of the original piton.

Photo: Ken Wilson

Bert Hargreaves then took the lead on their next project, a line starting up an easy angled ramp across the left side of The East Buttress (later the start of Ichabod). They dropped down to a lower ramp which swung around left into a steeper part of the crag, where a short corner caused some difficulty for the leader. Here Linnell inserted a small chockstone into a crack and tied himself to it, thus allowing Hargreaves to stand on his shoulder and overcome the problem. This may be the first record of inserting stones for belays in The Lakes. Linnell probably picked up this method from climbing in Wales. Hargreaves' two partners, Linnell and Bill Clegg, were both forced to pull up on the rope when seconding this pitch; such is the intimidating nature of the route. A stomach traverse and a thin slab followed, all gradually rising above an increasingly imposing drop to create the first ascent of Morning Wall, so called because the early sun warmed the rock for them. The first recorded free ascent of this route was made by Arthur Dolphin and A Gilchrist in April 1945, and it is now regarded at MVS as one of the easiest lines on The East Buttress.

To illustrate Linnell's foresight, skill and determination, another day on The East Buttress commenced with an attempt on one of the great right-angled grooves to the right of the lower part of Great Eastern Route, but he could make nothing of it and climbed Mickledore Grooves instead. Some accounts have suggested Linnell had attempted what was later to become May Day Climb, but this does not really tally with his description. When standing off the base of the crag in the vicinity of Great Eastern, the huge slanting corner of Lost Horizons is evident, but it is the easier-angled corner of The Centaur which appears to offer greater accessibility, and it was probably this route he had attempted. It was not climbed for another quarter of a century.

Linnell's last contributions to Scafell were a couple of variation finishes to two of his own existing routes; Overhanging Wall and Great Eastern Route. These were both linked in one long trip, and in fact the route followed on this day was to form a significant part of the final seven pitches of Jim Birkett's East Buttress Girdle five years later. Linnell and Harry Pearson commenced by repeating the start of Overhanging Wall and in passing they further drove the piton into the rock with a slater's hammer, to make it more secure. The original finish to this route had followed an open chimney line forming the right branch of a prominent 'V' in the structure of the crag, the left branch being a wide light-coloured slab. Linnell later wrote:

> "From the base of the 'V' we made for the White Slab which gave a magnificent climb right up to the finishing point of the Great Eastern Route. In spite of the drought the top pitch of the slab was running with water, but was successfully overcome in socks. This makes a far finer finish to the Overhanging Wall than the original chimney route." (12)

They then reversed down the upper section of Great Eastern Route to a point where Linnell had spotted a large yellow slab running up leftwards during the first ascent of that route. He noted:

> "This day it was perfectly dry. Before the slab is reached there is a bulge and then a short vertical crack. I must confess to having used another piton to overcome the bulge; but once up I was not sure that I might not have got there without it, so I took it out again." (13)

Photo: FRCC Archive

Bert Hargreaves.

Photo: FRCC Archive

Linnell and Hargreaves on the first ascent of Morning Wall.

Right: Joe Holden on the Yellow Slab.

Below: A climber on the crack above the Yellow Slab.

Photos: Al Phizacklea

Pearson avoided the piton move by standing on the belay spike and stepping left into the crack. The first ascent notes do not mention the piton, but do state that it requires strength and skill to gain the slab. Their only belay available at the foot of the Yellow Slab was a thin line over a poor sloping spike; totally inadequate to hold a falling leader. With Pearson attached to this psychological belay, Linnell climbed to the top of the slab where it merged into the base of a corner which appeared to offer no escape. He overcame this trap by traversing left where he found a crack line in a shallow vertical corner in a phenomenally exposed position. He climbed this with difficulty and without any vestige of protection, noting:

> "This is best started as a lay-back, but the top section calls for wedging of the arms and legs, and is very hard work. I only succeeded at the third attempt." (14)

The Yellow Slab is no mere variation; it was without doubt one of the most serious leads of the period, following a fantastic line above the steepest part of the crag. Fittingly, it is now one of the most popular routes on the crag. Allan Austin praised the route as:

> "This is the best bottom end HVS in the country. The last crack is mindblowing, with two hundred feet of overhanging rock below you, and an overhang above you. It's wonderful; it's one of the greatest achievements, in my view." (15)

It was to be Linnell's final route in Lakeland; unfortunately in the following spring Linnell and Colin Kirkus had an accident in the snows of Ben Nevis where Kirkus fell from the top of The Castle, and pulled Linnell from his belay. Kirkus survived but Linnell broke his neck in the fall and was found dead with the rope wrapped tightly around his throat. He was buried in Glen Nevis. Following the loss of his friend Kirkus gave up climbing harder routes.

The first photograph of The East Buttress with routes indicated appeared in the 1934 *FRCC* Journal

GER	Great Eastern Route
OW	Overhanging Wall
WS	White Slab
MG	Mickledore Grooves
M	Mickledore Chimney
P	Piton on Overhanging Wall

The diagram omits the Yellow Slab route.

1934 was uneventful except for the first ascent of the Direct Finish to Central Buttress by Graham Balcombe, Jerry Wright and Bobby Files. The team was forced to climb Central Buttress in stockinged feet because the rock was so greasy, and Balcombe initially failed on the Great Flake. Using the chockstone as a runner, he down climbed a short way and attempted to bypass the crux by pulling leftwards onto the front of the Flake, but after a short probe he retreated back to the Flake. A second assault of the Flake using the more traditional combined tactics proved more successful and they soon found themselves on Jeffcoat's Ledge, but without a guidebook they were uncertain of the true line of the route.

Higher up, Balcombe climbed a new direct finish, which at the time he considered to be an escape route; he was astonished to find out later that he had caused some clamour in the national press. This was entirely due to Wright, by profession a journalist for the Daily Telegraph, who characteristically exaggerated the account:

> "I have just heard the story of one of the most daring and arduous rock climbing expeditions ever undertaken in the British Isles. Anyone who has been on Scafell Pike will have seen the gigantic precipice which towers for a thousand feet above the Mickledore chasm … but it was the finest bit of leadership I have ever seen and the greatest rock climbing day of my life." (16)

Ironically the only time Balcombe ever climbed in The Lakes again was when he took some German visitors up C. B. and its Direct Finish in 1936. The weather had been poor, and the Germans knocked in two pitons for aid on the finish, commenting that it was too dangerous given the conditions. This dastardly deed was made worse by the fact that it was the same German team of H. Teufel and H. Sedlmayr that caused consternation in Wales when they climbed Munich Climb on Tryfan, on which they added two pegs for aid. It was probably these two events that prompted Frank Smythe to write his unrestrained outburst on pitons and the damned continental style of climbing (See Pitons in the 1930s, page 156). To give them some credit, though, this incident should not be simply viewed as one of bad old Germans desecrating our great crags, because it appears they were sandbagged from the start. Keith Treacher explains:

> "Unfortunately, the bad weather which had characterised North Wales continued into The Lakes. In appalling conditions, a German rope had been encouraged onto C. B. which they climbed, but not without considerable trouble. It was just an awful day. Had the German climbers been deliberately 'set up'? There is no real answer to that, but more to the point, they were furious because they believed they had been. It was unfortunate business, and as the British were to discover, revenge is an ancient appetite." (17)

It seemed they were well and truly sandbagged!

Climbing Down Gracefully

The ability to climb down in control has always been a demonstration of a climber's skill and nerve. With early climbers it was expected that one must have the ability to reverse anything that had been ascended; necessary in the days when protection was non-existent. Probably the earliest example of down climbing was by the Hopkinson party when they reached the ledge now bearing their cairn. In the *1914 Fell & Rock Journal*, Siegfried Herford wrote his 'Doctrine of Descent', in which he notes that an ascent of a crack entails:

> "A drawn-out scheme of caterpillar-like wriggling – arm-wedge, leg-wedge, arm-wedge, leg-wedge, and so on, the monotony being broken by an occasional backsliding. Now let us watch a man come down the place. He may very well have taken ten minutes in getting up; if he knows his business it can be done in not much more than ten seconds.

Climbing Down Gracefully (continued)

> "There need be no relative motion of different parts of the body; he can slide down keeping himself quite rigid, merely adjusting his speed by suitable side-pressure. The more delicate method of descending steep, open rocks dictates a more precise technique. This is where balance comes in. Since it implies an instinctive valuation of prospective changes of attitude, it gives confidence, and this is the secret of good footwork, particularly when descending. It enables the sloping holds to be boldly stepped down to, the hands being used to push the body away from, instead of holding onto the rock. The body is held in a graceful and more or less upright position." (18)

Shortly after World War I, Holland, Kelly and Bower all recorded descents of their own recent new routes including South-West Climb on Pillar and Kern Knotts Buttress (now graded HVS!) The recording of first descents became a popular pastime, and these were published in the Fell & Rock's journals alongside the more conventional new routes.

Another remarkable descent was of Moss Ghyll Grooves in 1928 just two years after the first ascent by a team 'led' (as last man) by Graham G. Macphee. Macphee was said to have been a conceited person, who ruled his private and public life in a very controlled manner. He was an intimidating character; if he took a dislike to anyone he said nothing, he just stared at them in a most disconcerting manner in order to get rid of them. This uncompromising attitude also applied to climbing. Moss Ghyll Grooves had been said by some to be 'irreversible', but Macphee was determined to achieve the first descent in order to write in the climbers' book at Wasdale the enigmatic entry 'M.G.G. ▼ G.G.M.'

The first descent of Central Buttress was planned by a young Workington engineer, Jack Carswell, who with Mabel Barker and Ieuan Banner-Mendus achieved the feat on a glorious but windy day in 1936. Carswell recently explained that whilst they were at the top of the crag searching for the exit of the route, they came across Stanley Watson, a local guide who tried to find out what they were up to, but they never let on to him as they wanted to keep their plans secret. It took them a while to find the top of the route, and once they were confident that they had identified the exit correctly, Mabel Barker went down first. She was at this time 50 years old, but she led down all the pitches confidently, the only awkward moment was the start of the upper traverse. The traverses were no more difficult in reverse than in ascent, but they found communication difficult due to the wind. However, they all knew the descent of the Great Flake would be the most difficult part of the venture. In a recent interview Carswell recalls:

> "A.T. Hargreaves, Sid Cross and their two wives had got to the Oval just at the same time we got down to Jeffcoat's Ledge; they had just completed a new route out of Deep Gill [Grey Bastion] and typically of A.T., they were climbing C. B. as part of their way of getting back to Langdale! They were clued up as to what we were up to and they waited there to see how we coped with the Flake. We didn't want anybody to see because we were still trying to work it out, so we finally sat them out. Hargreaves' team successfully climbed the Flake and they passed each other on Jeffcoat's Ledge, where Mabel swapped a cigarette for a toffee from them. I sent Banner-Mendus down first, I kept the rope as slack as possible and he got to the thread at the chockstone. Mabel Barker went down and she went right down to the bottom at the Oval, where she held my rope.

Graham McPhee and H. G. Knight relax following their descent of Moss Ghyll Grooves.

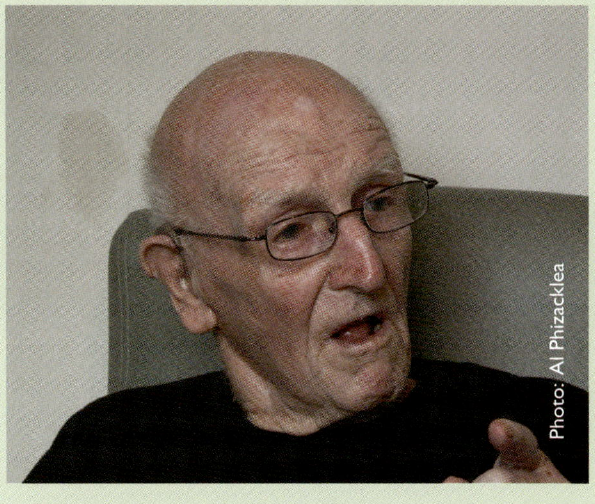

Jack Carswell still in fine form in 2008.

Climbing Down Gracefully (continued)

> "I had been perched on the Flake for so long that I was quite stiff, so I had to rest awhile before starting the descent. I came down last and managed to thread a rope through the chockstone and I came down from there on a double rope. In fact, in those days there was a little thing which I think has gone now, a hook that you could put a double rope on there, and I came down on a double rope. I said at the time it wouldn't be sensible without this, but mind, things have changed since, and don't forget you can see the gear we had in those days [he pointed to a faded monochrome print of himself with the rope tied around his waist and a rope sling around his shoulder] – we had no gear at all. Mabel Barker was rather pleased about the fact that she was the first woman up C.B. and the first woman down. She was a bold climber, she led Eliminate A on Doe [sic] Crag in 1928, and after we had climbed down C.B. she said to me that she was in her 51st year." (19)

An article by Carswell in a *Fell & Rock Journal* describes the method of descent:

> "I found the descent less trying than the ascent, because by getting the right shoulder in the Crack one can use sundry small holds on the inside, sufficient to control a descent but not much help when overcoming the excessive friction of an ascent. On looking back we agreed that in the previous 5½ hours we had savoured the essence of climbing to the full, and that C.B. had no rival. Ieuan and I were proud to have had the company of Mabel Barker. We had read her account of her ascent with Frankland in 1925 many times before we had the pleasure of meeting her. She was the first woman up the climb, and it was appropriate she should also be the first down it. As we sat in Mrs. Edmondson's at midnight that night quaffing tea, Mabel said to us, 'Only one thing remains for you boys.'
> 'Yes?' we replied.
> 'To repeat the climb when you are in your 51st year.'
> Truly a chastening thought." (20)

The reference to a hook by Carswell is puzzling. Jack later explained that this was a small spike of rock about 3 or 4 fingers in size which protruded from a horizontal crack in the front face of the Flake, just above and left of the chockstone. He said it was suitable for putting a loop of rope over, which could be used for standing in, or in the case of the descent, for a back-rope. It was a very fragile feature and Jack wondered whether it was broken off by some clumsy climber in boots. The truth about the spike was discovered from an entry in the Brackenclose logbook dated June 1951:

> "C. B. Combined tactics were being used and just as the second man was standing on the leader's shoulders the spike belay broke off, but the party remained attached to loops around the chockstone." (21)

This descent of C. B. appears to have been a high point in the doctrine of down climbing, because following this there are very few recorded descents of routes. Perhaps the climbers of the era had realised that there was nothing further to be gained from recording of descents. When Jack was asked whether he realised that the descent of C. B. marked the end of the trend of down climbing hard routes in The Lakes, he replied:

> "I don't know, I never thought of that. Don't forget, if anything went wrong you had to downclimb. The thing what we tried to do was not go up anything we couldn't climb down or do any moves that were impossible to reverse. That gradually wore away with equipment, so it's not the same as it was then." (22)

Winter Climbing, 1930s Style

The early pioneers of the Victorian and Edwardian era, such as Collie, Collier and O.G. Jones, were typical of the trailblazers of the sport. They were generally wealthy men of professional or independent means, enjoying a privileged lifestyle and towards the top of the social hierarchy. Conditions for the working class was somewhat different. For many workers it was simply a struggle to survive. Wages were low and hours were long; the typical working week was five and a half days and there was little hope of a holiday apart from perhaps a single week at the seaside, which they considered to be a luxury. There were no climbers who came from the working class during the Edwardian period, principally because any money spent towards climbing meant less food for their families. The climbing classes in those days tended to enjoy lengthy holidays at Christmas and Easter in mountainous centres such as Wasdale Head. During these times they frequently encountered winter conditions and records show winters were generally harsher than those of today.
The conditions were regarded as normal for rock climbing; indeed they were preferred because these holidays were used as training for the greater Alpine peaks, so in those days there was little differentiation between rock and ice climbing and many of the routes from this time were climbed under true winter conditions.

Stirrings of a revival in winter climbing came in the mid-1930s, when climbers started to appreciate how this aspect of the sport provided difficult and challenging offerings. Men such as Bill Peascod, Sid Cross and Bert Hargreaves came to the fore, ascending routes such as Steep Gill and Bowfell Buttress in conditions that would be considered technical Grade V today. These pioneers were not the rich sons of society who frequented the crags throughout the winters before World War I; these were local climbers at the forefront of a socio-economic revolution. They were the first of the working class climbers to enter climbing; men who found that a change in the conditions of employment allowed them to take Saturday afternoons off work. The nature of public transport at that time meant there was little possibility of weekend visits to The Lakes from far afield; hence the increase in winter activity was primarily from local climbers.

There was surprisingly little to separate the equipment of Victorian climbers and those of the 1930s when it came to climbing snow and ice. Nailed boots and long-handled, straight-picked ice axes were the norm as there had been no development in equipment over this forty year period.

Jack Carswell was archetypal and he pointed out that all winter climbing in The Lakes was then done in nails, as crampons could only be purchased in the Alpine regions. The working class man in those days typically had only one week of (unpaid) holiday per year, so it wasn't possible to travel abroad to obtain crampons. Jack remembers buying a pair of hand-made nailed boots from Birkett's shop in Keswick for two pounds and ten shillings (£2.50) which was a week's wages in those days. He noted:

> "The problem with the leather soles of these boots was that the snow used to freeze up on the sole, worse than on a rubber 'Vibram' sole. The main use of the ice axe in those days was to pick the ice out from between your nails." (23)

3 grainy stills from Barton's original 1930s film of Jack Carswell climbing the Barn Door in Buttermere.

Illustration of a Hargreaves Nail.

Winter Climbing, 1930s Style (continued)

The style of winter climbing of this era was recently brought to life with the discovery of a canister of film shot around 1935 by Austin Barton. It had been rescued from the ravages of decomposition by his nephew Eric Ivison, who had it transferred to digital format with the help of his friends in the Fell & Rock Climbing Club. After restoration, the film was shown to Jack Carswell who was able to add a narration to the finished version.

The grainy, flickering film shows Carswell climbing the first ascent of The Barn Door on Eagle Crag in Buttermere, a relatively easy route, in bitter winter conditions. He climbed in nailed boots and his only equipment was a hemp rope tied around his waist trailing uselessly down to his second man as there were no runners. Neither did he carry an ice axe, and a most astonishing thing about the grainy scenes on the screen was the clothing – Jack wore neither hat nor gloves, and his outer clothing was just a heavy woollen jumper – no jacket or coat in those days! The film was an amazing insight to a forgotten style of climbing gear in the years between the wars.

The partnerships of Sid Cross, Alice Nelson, Bert Hargreaves and Ruth Hargreaves were unusual in that the women were an integral part of those winter climbing teams, often leading through on the hard pitches. Such teams made the first winter ascent of Pisgah Buttress, and the second winter ascent of Steep Gill in 1938 in typically thin conditions; unprotected, runnerless and using hemp ropes; and it would have been little different to Collie's ascent 47 years earlier. It still took skill and nerves of steel to climb the harder routes, as well as massive stamina. Step cutting was still the order of the day. Stan Thompson recalled that the average climber had to cut steps using alternative hands as they tired, whereas Jim Birkett and Bill Peascod, who were used to swinging hammers at work, were able to chop a line of steps with one hand all day long.

Hargreaves was inventive when it came to adapting his gear for the winter; he developed 'The Hargreaves Nail', a tooth-serrated plate similar to an overlarge tricouni nail which he had specially manufactured in Ulverston. Unlike tricounis, which were just nailed around the edge of the sole, several of these nails were screwed to the underside of the boot to create a similar pattern to the modern Vibram sole. This type of nail never became popular, as one critic noted:

> "This type of nail has two very distinct drawbacks, one of which I am certain renders this type of nail definitely dangerous. Firstly, the nails being so soft wear down very rapidly and have to be constantly renewed. The second disadvantage – and to my mind the dangerous one – is that the screws constantly come loose and even after one climb it is usually necessary to take out a screwdriver and tighten up the whole of the boot. I am quite convinced that it is well within the bounds of possibility that some of the nails might work loose during the climb, and possibly cause the climber to slip". (24)

Winter Climbing, 1930s Style (continued)

Ice axes had changed little since the Victorian days when the straight pick and long shaft still held sway. Axes were heavy, cumbersome and totally unsuitable for the harder climbs, so Hargreaves and Cross experimented by cutting down the shaft to create shorter axes, but they proved to be unbalanced and unwieldy. They found that trenching tools were better suited for the steeper confined spaces of the harder lines. These innovative adoptions and adaptations of gear for climbing in winter were never widely appreciated, and commercially available gear stuck to traditional styles. Over the years, other climbers would improve on these ideas and the design of the gear evolved. Eventually curved and drop-pick short axes became available in the early 1970s and when combined with front point crampons, it allowed a revolution in Scottish winter climbing, and caused a burst in popularity for this crazy game which has continued to this day.

Footnotes

1. H.M. Kelly – Personal diary
2. The year of the ascent of Mickledore Grooves has been erroneously recored as 1931 in every FRCC Scafell Guidebook until it was corrected in the 2014 Scafell Guide. The date of 1930 is clearly noted in Kirkus' first ascent entry in the Rucksack Club logbook.
3. I. Waller 'Cat Amoung the Pidgeons' – *FRCC Journal 1978*
4. Bill Stallybrass, by Steve Dean, 'Bill Stallybrass', as sent to the author
5. John Wilkinson, *Mountain 30,* 1974
6. Allan Austin, FRCC audio recording, 2007
7. 'Ginger' Cain, Telephone conversation with author, 2008
8. Sid Cross, extract from *A Century on the Crags*, 1986
9. Trevor Jones, extract from *Cumbrian Rock*, 1986
10. Ashley Abraham 'An hour in the Smoke Room at Wasdale' *FRCC Journal* no.1, 1907

11-14. M. Linnell 'Scawfell Revisited' *Rucksack Club Journal* 1934

15. Allan Austin, FRCC audio recording, 2007
16. J.E.B Wright, *Daily Telegraph* article
17. Keith Treacher 'The Anglo-German Exchange' *Rucksack Club Journal* 1989
18. S.W. Herford 'Doctrine of Descent' *FRCC Journal* 1914
19. J. Carswell, FRCC audio recording, 2008
20. J. Carswell 'B.C.' *FRCC Journal* Vol 11 1936
21. Brackenclose log book, 1937-1959
22. J. Carswell Telephone conversation with author, 2008
23. J. Carswell FRCC audio recording, 2008
24. G. Brumming '*Rock Climbing and Mountaineering*', 1946

'Owd' Joe Thompson was one of the farmers at Wasdale Head in the early part of the 20th century. The clothing and personal appearance were typical of the farming community at that time.

Photo: FRCC Archive

1936 - 1948

The Jim Birkett Years

The Second Guidebook

The second guidebook to Scafell was published by the FRCC in 1936 and it differed in style to the 'First Series'. The book was produced in a smaller format, so it may be slipped into a pocket and referred to when climbing.

The cover was changed to a buff coloured rigid board intended to be hard wearing. The author of this guidebook was A. T. (Bert) Hargreaves, and as Harry Kelly had taken over as editor of these guide-books he had Hargreaves adopt a terse style of writing that encouraged brevity in descriptions. Kelly was a stickler for correct English, and he was aware that a vague or lengthy description could be subject to the wrong interpretation. Gone were the florid metaphors and also the photographs and photo-diagrams; these were replaced by beautiful pencil sketches by the artist William Heaton Cooper. This new format for the guides portrayed an overall effect of neatness and business-like efficiency, a style Kelly sustained with an irascible stubbornness for almost three decades. From the first to the second guidebook there were nineteen additional routes in the Scafell section, and the second guide contained the first descriptions for The East Buttress routes.

Cover of the second Scafell Guidebook.

W. Heaton Cooper's beautifully simple diagram of the East Buttress is an example of his artwork in this new guide.

S	Slime Chimney	OW	Overhanging Wall	BS	Broad Stand
MW	Morning Wall	W	The White Slab Variation	M	Mickledore Ridge
GER	Great Eastern Route	MG	Mickledore Grooves		
Y	Yellow Slab	MC	Mickledore Chimney		

The walls on the right of Deep Gill above Lord's Rake attracted Bert Hargreaves and Sid Cross in 1936. Their first route, Jacob's Ladder, followed a series of short, vertical corners climbing up the tower to the right of The Great Chimney. Sometime later Hargreaves wrote:

> "Cross and I collected this climb on a sunny afternoon in June and were so astonished at the ease with which we had surmounted the steepest bits that some sort of ladder was the only possible name for it. We were climbing well, and almost having romped up the magic stairway, we built a cairn, then without hurrying we descended the West Wall Climb close by – to find on arrival at our starting point that we had taken exactly 30 minutes. A second visit to introduce our wives was made on a day that was not so sunny and was certainly not in June this year [which was 1943]. And we suffered many jibes from our companions when, instead of dancing upwards over the steep brown rocks, the leader had the greatest difficulty in even maintaining the 'status quo' and only just managed to avoid making another record, this time in descent." (1)

Overleaf:
Unknown leader at the top of the main pitch of Slab and Groove Route.

Photo: Al Phizacklea

Their route turned out to be a delightful Hard Severe, with a particularly impressive third pitch making an awkward pull into a sentry box high on the slim, exposed pillar. It has since been given a 4a grade in the guidebook. Bill Peascod said of this pitch:

> "It gives a delightful zig-zag on adequate handholds but not such satisfying footholds. The climbing is continuously steep with good ledges and belays, and the views out to the Pinnacle add further enjoyment to this pleasant route." (2)

The next route was Grey Bastion, climbed the following day in the company of Ruth Hargreaves, and this was an altogether more serious proposition. They had previously sat on the Hopkinson's Cairn ledge, directly opposite, and studied the line of their imagined route in detail and it became exactly the line they eventually climbed. The route starts from the base of a prominent protruding corner which forces the West Wall Traverse into a narrow passage, a well known landmark for all who pass this way. Again in the words of Hargreaves:

> "It is a fine climb on good rock, steep with excellent situations. The hardest pitch is a grey wall about half its height, and here we spent many trying moments before the leader eventually reached a capacious stance under a great overhang. Fortunately, like other similar places which seemed to have been designed for climbers, an easy slab led out of its forbidding shadow onto a very airy wall where it was finally necessary to traverse left across a steep crack to easier ground, avoiding on the way a large block lying on a sloping ledge." (3)

Above: A mature Sid Cross photographed in 1978. When he was president of the FRCC.

Photo: John Holden

Al Phizacklea on the first pitch of Grey Bastion.

William Heaton Cooper sketches a crag for the second series of FRCC guidebooks under the scrutiny of Harry Kelly.

Above: Sid Cross, Ruth Hargreaves, Jammie Cross, Evelyn Price, Bert Hargreaves and Frank Heap gathered outside Brackenclose just after it was opened.

Below: Bert. and Ruth Hargreaves below Central Buttress.

The first pitch, a steep thin crack, is currently graded 5a, and the thin, precarious wall that gave them their troubles is still 4c. Altogether this is a fine VS route, not one to be taken lightly but neither should it be overlooked.

There is an aside to this route as Ruth Hargreaves should actually be referred to as Ruth Heap for the first ascent. Ruth was married to Frank Heap, a Blackpool hotel proprietor at the time; but this was by all accounts a very open marriage. She had been 'romantically associated' with Bert Hargreaves for some time, and in the summer of 1934 they both moved into a house in Cark-in-Cartmel and from that point onwards she called herself by the surname Hargreaves. This was confirmed by entries from the Parkhead visitors' book, where before April 1934 Ruth signed herself R. E. Heap and on her following visit in September she signed herself in as R. E.Hargreaves. One would assume from this evidence that they started their new life together as if they were a married couple, without disclosing their secret.

Furthermore, there is a remarkable twist to this tale that could grace the pages of a Barbara Cartland novel. Hargreaves' wife had returned the favour and was herself in a relationship with Frank Heap (who said swinging was a modern fad?). This was a convenient arrangement that was not widely known, even amongst other members of the FRCC where Ruth, Frank and Bert were all full members of the club. Despite the unusual situation the two couples still remained good friends and they all regularly climbed together over the years.

This arrangement was made obvious to the wider public some time later. It came to the author's notice when Stan Thompson told the tale of how he and Bill Peascod applied to join the FRCC during Christmas 1940. As part of their initiation to the club they joined the Hargreaves and Heap couples on an appraisal climb on Pikes Crag. Bill and Stan were much perplexed by their mentors and were unsure whether the ladies were Mrs Hargreaves or Mrs Heap; it was a conundrum that was cleared when they finished the route as Stan explained some seventy years later:

> "When we got to the top, Bert was up there with Heap himself, and they said 'Well, we have to tell you two something. You may not know, but we have changed wives.' 'What, just now?' I asked. 'Oh no,' they replied, 'It happened a week or two ago!' I responded with 'Well, I didn't know', which was countered by 'We know, it must be very confusing, but there you were, Mrs Heaping and Mrs Hargreaving all up the route. So now you know!'" (4)

Utilising Ruth's previous experience in the hotel trade, Bert and Ruth later moved into the Burnmoor Inn at Boot which they ran as a joint venture until Bert's death in 1952.

In 1936, a rather overlooked variation start to Mickledore Grooves was climbed by Geoffrey Collin and a South African, Richard Barry. Climbing starts from the bottom right corner of the big slab rising from the foot of Mickledore Chimney as the line that had first been attempted by Kelly in 1919. It ascends the corner a short while before traversing the smooth slab left to the belay below the top pitch of Mickledore Grooves. This start, now known as Barry's Traverse, was later used as the opening pitch of the East Buttress Girdle, and was neatly summed up by Arthur Dolphin on the third ascent:

> "It was necessary to make a simple traverse about thirty feet to the left along an obvious line of holds, or so it appeared from the ground. That nothing could be further from the truth I realised in full measure when my turn came to follow. The 'obvious line of holds' dwindled as I approached as though viewed through reversed binoculars. This was balance work indeed! I thought of boots - and shivered!" (5)

Brackenclose under construction in 1936.

In 2012, the FRCC celebrated the 75th Anniversary of the opening of Brackenclose.

1938 was to be a notable year for two reasons. In this year Harry Kelly ascended his final new route on Scafell, and Jim Birkett climbed his first. Kelly was by now 54 years old yet he was in the company of Sid Cross, Alice Nelson and C. J. Astley-Cooper for the first ascent of The Rampart. This long Hard Severe weaves its way up from the base of Shamrock, and Kelly was originally going to call it Tower Slabs, until Cross persuaded him to change the name. There is little to recommend about this route, and Kelly describes the ascent in his diary as 'a concoction of grass interspersed with sensational climbing', though he noted that 'with some gardening, it could become a first-class route'. Unfortunately, Kelly's gardening days were over and the route never was cleaned, so it remains firmly a second-class route.

Jim Birkett was a local lad, born and raised in Little Langdale where he worked in the slate quarries, but despite his hard working life he also had an immense passion for the birds and plants of the region. Ironically his earliest forays on the cliffs were to satisfy his passion for collecting birds' eggs, where he would lower himself down the crags on a borrowed cart rope. Later in life, he was repentant of his egg-stealing days and he devoted himself to the protection of wildlife and especially the birds and their nests, becoming a champion for their protection. Jim was a remarkably strong climber and was renowned as being one of the greatest exponents of the long lost art of nailed-boot climbing. Harry Griffin recalled:

> "He climbed with such balance and poise, moving with easy confidence, applying the edge nails to the tiniest wrinkles in the rock, using smooth momentum to keep in contact in places where the rock was unreliable or covered in slime".

However, his son Bill disclosed that Jim often climbed in rubbers when the weather was fine, dispelling the myth that he only ever climbed in nails. Jim is remembered as an intensely quiet man throughout his life; he kept his private affairs to himself and was famously reluctant to talk about climbing to anyone. Even his own son Bill was unaware how his father had been a famous climber; until he noted the name of Jim Birkett in guidebooks.

Brackenclose

In October 1937 the FRCC opened its first climbers' hut in The Lakes, at the foot of Scafell close to the shore of Wastwater. The triangle of land known as Brackenclose Wood had been purchased in a rather hurried private deal in the previous year by an ex-FRCC President W.G. Milligan for £150, after he discovered that the YHA had expressed interest in the land. The building of a hut almost caused a schism within the club; one of the wealthier members thought that it would attract the common class of climber who couldn't afford to stay in the hotels! Jack Carswell recalls that Milligan had said:

> "I bought this land for the Club, you can please your bloody selves what you do with it. You can build a hut or camp on it". There was a lot of apathy about the hut at the time. (6)

The Committee eventually agreed on the project and a hut was built over seven months by a team of local men with stones obtained from Lingmell Gill. The timber work was completed by local joiner and cabinet maker, John Moffatt, helped by his young son Peter, who would later become a President and Honorary Member of the Club. When it was opened the only facilities provided were primus stoves and paraffin lamps for cooking and lighting, showers (but only cold ones!), and dormitories for both men and women. This cost the Club a total of £2,337, and the first fee for a stay was two shillings (10p) per night. Bert Hargreaves was the first warden, and Harry Kelly kept the accounts. The purchase and building of such a superb facility in the centre of The Lake District could never be repeated in the modern world with the current batch of legislation and restrictions on property. What far-sighted members there were on FRCC committees in those days!

Hargreaves ran the hut with strong and forceful determination, and some of his comments against members who had left the hut in an untidy mess made it clear that his word was final. Hargreaves also instigated the 'no dogs' rule in the huts following an incident during the opening ceremony when Frank Heap's carefully acquired chicken disappeared inside another guest's hound. Things were hard during the war; by 1941 the following note was added to the hut book: 'Paraffin is now unobtainable in the district so cooking has to be done by fire'. Amenities quickly improved after the war and the first hot water system was installed in 1945 by Club member, J. Blackshaw, who owned a hardware shop in Barrow. However, electricity was not introduced to the Wasdale Valley until 1977.

Jim Birkett .

'Up "very severes" he goes at a toot,'cos he only drinks diluted grapefruit,!! He's "Boots Birkett". Charlie Wilson's caricature captures the reverence that Jim Birkett held over his peers.

Rob Matheson on the awkward initial pitch of May Day Climb.

Jim's first new route was on The East Buttress which he visited on the first day of May 1938, so inspiring the name May Day Climb. This line had first been proposed by Charlie Wilson of Carlisle, who with Chuck Hudson from Ambleside accompanied Jim to the crag. Wilson had brought several pegs with him, made from an axle of an old Ford by his blacksmith uncle who had a forge in Thirlmere. On the first pitch Charlie climbed a short way up to a ledge no larger than a foothold where he belayed to a peg hammered in with a stone. Birkett joined him, and according to some of the written accounts of this epic, he stood on Wilson's shoulders before continuing up the pitch. This was a fiercely smooth slab, and near the top, he hammered in a second peg for a runner with a stone carried up from the base of the crag. He then traversed right to a ledge where he used a third peg to belay. A short, hard second pitch led to the base of a huge corner (the Direct Finish), but this was probably wet (it usually is), so they continued the route out left, crossing several ribs of rock before finishing up a hanging slab that they described as being 'harder than the White Slab on Overhanging Wall'. Birkett had completed a magnificent route that was considerably harder than anything yet climbed on Scafell; originally given VS, later raised to HVS, it is now regarded as an E1, 5b. Some reckon this was the first true E1 in the Lakes; it was certainly the hardest route on Scafell at the time, and Birkett's first ascent description actually suggested that it is considerably harder than Central Buttress.

Photo: Hartley collection

John Hartley on the second pitch of May Day Climb, the open corner of May Day Direct beckons above the climber.

Being famously reticent in discussing his climbing or his personal life allowed malicious rumours and tales about how the route was climbed, and some suppositions became accepted as historical fact. However, in his later years, Jim opened up to his son Bill, who recalled that:

> "Dad was hurt by the criticism over this route. He had been accused by a number of people who had no first-hand experience of the event who wrote some time later that he used the pegs for aid. He said that these tales told about him were untrue, and was absolutely adamant that he climbed the route free and he categorically stated that he never even stood on Charlie's shoulders. He was badly affected by this criticism, and after that incident he always underplayed what he said, and he never used pegs again. It actually took me some time to get the full story from him, because Dad never volunteered any information, he only answered to a direct question." (7)

Pitons in the 1930s

The use of pitons, or pegs, in climbing has evoked many passions in climbing over the decades. The first recorded use of what would be classified as a peg came from Steeple Jackson who hammered iron spikes into Pillar Rock for assistance in 1875. It is unclear if there were any pegs driven into Scafell before Linnell's on Overhanging Wall, but his was the first to be used for direct aid. It certainly wasn't to be the last. Over time the practice of using pegs for protection slowly became accepted, and in 1942 'Charles' Holland comments:

> "I can see no necessity for their use except in positions where no other belay can by any method be devised and a piton will make the second's stance secure, and probably save the life of the leader should he come off. In the case of the expert who knows exactly how to insert and secure them, and can be trusted to make use of them only when absolutely essential to safeguard further progress or retreat, I can see no possible objection by any reasonable person." (9)

Frank Smythe mirrors this opinion in a later article. He starts mildly before turning somewhat xenophobic, and continues in rather jingoistic prose; written as it was during World War II:

> "The piton is permissible only as a safeguard on climbable faces, and is undesirable as a means of climbing otherwise unclimbable rock. The German technicians think otherwise. To them nature only exists to be bludgeoned into submission, and if a precipice is reputed to be unscaleable then it must be climbed by fair means or foul. One may admire the courage of the performers, while deprecating the spirit in which the performance is undertaken; it is the same spirit as that which dynamites a trout pool or massacres tame pigeons. It is neither mountaineering, nor is it sport. Worse than this, the German technique in the years before the present war became tainted with nationalism. Desperate ascents in which pitons were driven into otherwise unclimbable rock were undertaken for the honour and glory of Germany, to prove that Germans were not only good sportsmen, but the best sportsmen.

The Italians who, it would appear, are ever imitative of the worst practices in others, have vied with the German technicians in scaling otherwise impossible rock faces by means of enormous numbers of pitons, these 'conquests' being acclaimed in the Italian Press as another great achievement of Fascism." (10)

Quality ranting indeed! Smythe had obviously been inflamed by the so-called 'Munich Mechanics' who had used pitons on the Direct Finish to Central Buttress in 1936.

Colin Kirkus also wrote on this issue, in his excellent article entitled 'Ethics of Ironmongery':

"It is hard to see how the use of the piton on an old climb can be excused. Any climb belongs in part to its pioneers; it should be climbed as they climbed it. If an ascent has already been made it is safe to assume that there are some leaders who can repeat it in perfect safety, whatever the run-out. And the climber who cannot manage the long lead in safety had no right to spoil it for those who can by sticking in his offensive ironmongery. He should instead choose a climb which is within his capacity." (11)

These sentiments are still upheld as strongly now as they were then. Unfortunately, as the popularity of climbing expanded in the 1960s many routes were to suffer from pegs inserted by leaders who found themselves in difficulties beyond their capabilities. This situation only ended with the introduction of the nut runner, and especially the micro-wires in the mid 1970s.

The use of the pegs did not go un-noticed amongst the close-knit climbing world. Alan Hankinson notes in *A Century on the Crags*:

> "It was not clear from subsequent accounts how many pitons Birkett banged into the cracks. One says there were four, another says three, yet another mentions only two. But pitons were undoubtedly used, though only for protection, not to help the climbing. Perhaps he was influenced by the knowledge that Linnell had used a piton on the nearby Overhanging Wall. Whatever the reason, he regretted the action: 'I was young and daft and thought I'd have a go at this pegging business. Perhaps I was a bit overwhelmed by the occasion. Because there was certainly no need for them. They didn't help the climbing at any point'. He never used pitons again." (8)

The pitons remained in place until 1953 when Harold Drasdo repeated the route. He noted they were so badly corroded that he twisted and snapped off all three pegs with his hand. This act did not prevent a less talented leader from replacing one of them at a later date. It remained there for another thirty years before rusting away; it is these relics that have filled the crack, thus preventing later climbers from placing any modern protection at this point.

This first day of May 1938 did not pass without further incident on Scafell. Eva Bailey, a 27 year old from Edinburgh, fell whilst leading Jones' Route Direct on the Pinnacle, and was killed. Her partner, Annie Hamilton of Carlisle was belayed in the Waiting Room, from where Bailey climbed past onto the feature known as The Mantleshelf, when she suddenly fell without warning. A report in the Whitehaven News states that 'Hamilton had belayed the rope to a rock. The rope snapped as it caught the sharp edge of the stance'. Bailey fell to her death, and Hamilton was brought to safety by two climbers from Whitehaven who were following them on the route. Bailey's body was brought down the valley on an improvised stretcher by climbers at the crag, including Birkett, Hudson and Wilson. This accident illustrates the weakness of the hemp ropes that were in use at the time. However, the notion that 'They belayed the rope to a rock' suggests that perhaps the technique of passing the rope directly over a spike of rock, instead of around the body, may have been employed in this case, a distressing reminder of the primitive belaying methods of the time.

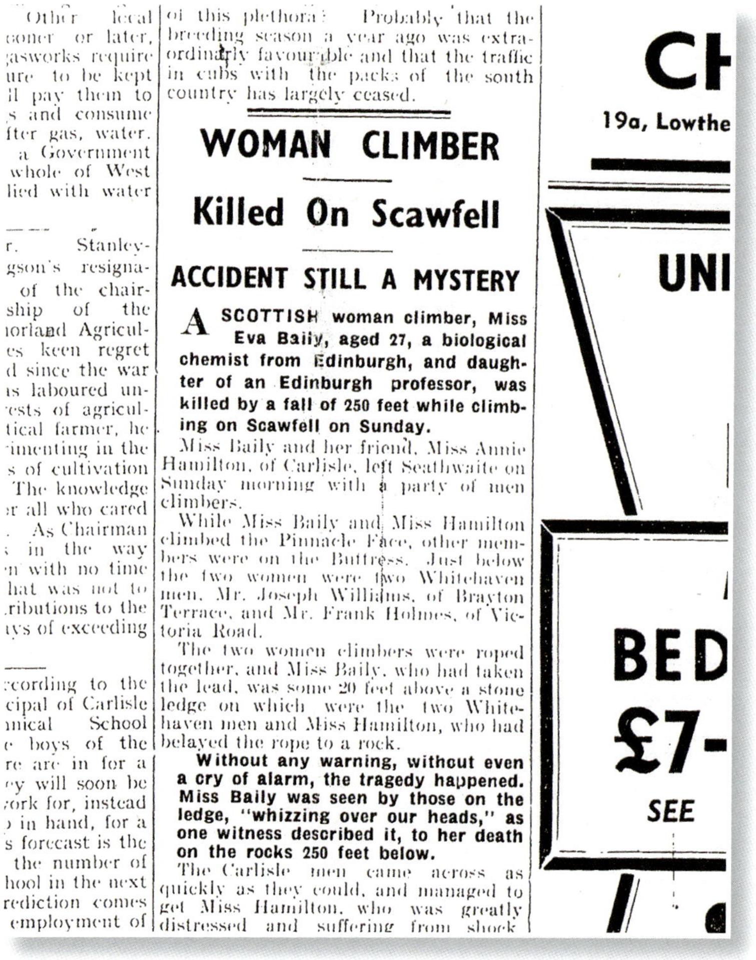

of this plethora? Probably that the breeding season a year ago was extraordinarily favourable and that the traffic in cubs with the packs of the south country has largely ceased.

WOMAN CLIMBER

Killed On Scawfell

ACCIDENT STILL A MYSTERY

A SCOTTISH woman climber, Miss Eva Baily, aged 27, a biological chemist from Edinburgh, and daughter of an Edinburgh professor, was killed by a fall of 250 feet while climbing on Scawfell on Sunday.

Miss Baily and her friend, Miss Annie Hamilton, of Carlisle, left Seathwaite on Sunday morning with a party of men climbers.

While Miss Baily and Miss Hamilton climbed the Pinnacle Face, other members were on the Buttress. Just below the two women were two Whitehaven men, Mr. Joseph Williams, of Brayton Terrace, and Mr. Frank Holmes, of Victoria Road.

The two women climbers were roped together, and Miss Baily, who had taken the lead, was some 20 feet above a stone ledge on which were the two Whitehaven men and Miss Hamilton, who had belayed the rope to a rock.

Without any warning, without even a cry of alarm, the tragedy happened. Miss Baily was seen by those on the ledge, "whizzing over our heads," as one witness described it, to her death on the rocks 250 feet below.

The Carlisle men came across as quickly as they could, and managed to get Miss Hamilton, who was greatly distressed and suffering from shock

Coutesy of Whitehaven News

Photo: © abrahamphotographic / FRCC Archives

An unusual photograph from the Abrahams set in a slate quarry to illustrate a book on climbing techniques, *Modern Mountaineering* by George Abraham from 1933.

The caption in the book reads:

'Is the next step possible? The newest modern climbing methods. Using pitons and Karabiners on a steep, difficult rock face. The leader is securely placed and carries a hammer in his pocket to drive in a higher piton.'

It seems incredulous that this illustrates what was considered a safe and modern practice – the fact that the rope passes directly through the eye of the peg and the excessive protrusion of the pegs from the rock prove that Abraham hadn't a clue about practical or safe peg placements or what happens when these pegs become loaded. One could cynically say that this book was an attempt by an old 'has-been' to generate income from his good name in climbing, but the fact is that he was so far out of touch with the activists of the time (which included the likes of Linnell and Kirkus) that this reveals a sad and dangerous lack of knowledge. However, the majority of climbers of those years must have also been ignorant of the subject, because the book went on to have a third reprint in 1948!

Jim Birkett (centre) with his close friends Len Muscroft (left) and Charlie Wilson (right), who partnered Birkett on many of his Scafell ascents. The photo was taken at the top of Castle Rock, following the first ascent of Overhaging Bastion in 1939.

What do you do if you couldn't purchase karabiners, because none were available? Lt. Com. G. K. Ryland O.B.E. had an answer to this conundrum - he was director of Rylands Bros., wire manufacturer of Warrington, who got his workforce to make karabiners for his own personal use. This is a rare example of a model from 1949 which was produced in its own presentation box.

Birkett followed his ascent of May Day Climb by climbing the East Buttress Girdle from right to left with Len Muscroft. This was a long, elaborate route across an intimidating and little explored crag, with the prospect of retreat (in those days via the classic abseil with the rope wrapped around the torso) being a worrying prospect. He would have had the details of the existing routes already established, but it is not known whether he had climbed any of these before embarking on the traverse.

They began up Barry's Traverse start to Mickledore Grooves, from which point a difficult and intricate traverse left across a series of corners and grooves (which would later become The Fulcrum, Leverage and Dyad) led to the top of the big corner on May Day Direct. The traverse continued across the severely undercut upper slab crossed by the top of May Day Climb and followed by a long descent down the upper chimney of Overhanging Wall to the base of the White Slab. Here they made their way across to the exit of Great Eastern Route, and by reversing the upper part of this route they linked up with the Yellow Slab Variation. This was used to finish the route as there was no natural continuation of the girdle across the lower part of the crag where the modern routes such as Borderline are found. Despite the length of the expedition, and with much of the earlier part of the route previously unexplored, they took only four and a half hours to complete this sustained HVS.

A second ascent two years later, by Sid and Jammie Cross with Bert and Ruth Hargreaves, followed a slightly different line between Mickledore Grooves and May Day Climb, which has since been incorporated into the guidebook description. They then adopted a large variation to Birkett's route by abseiling down the line of May Day Direct and using a lower traverse line to link up with the White Slab. This abseil variation is no longer described in the guidebook.

A further addition to the main face of Scafell Crag in 1938 was Tricouni Slab, climbed by Alf Mullen and L. Mack. This is a smaller twin of Botterill's Slab about twenty metres left of that route. Mullen was considered an expert at climbing in nails and he was probably the only climber to equal Jim Birkett and Ron Jackson in these techniques. The tiny edges of the thin holds on this slab formed perfect lodgements for the sharp edged tricouni nails that gave the slab its name. His description was fairly specific for the time, an extract says:

> "Higher up a very thin perpendicular crack will accommodate one nail of the left boot, while the right shoulder and the hand work on the inside wall." He claimed it would be "very doubtful if either clinker nails or rubbers would be of any use on this climb. A very interesting example of nail technique." (12)

The following year this prediction was proved wrong when the route was repeated by a Rucksack Club team led by W. J. K. Pearson, who shot down Mullen's boastful claim with the comment:

> "Considered to be only Severe in rubbers. The description of the first ascent as VS and possible only in tricounis is decidedly exaggerated." (13)

The upper portion of this route cannot be followed with any certainty. The original finish followed by Mullen was never described in the guidebooks and a new variation finish was added to the 1984 guide. It must be noted that that the main section of this slab pitch was first climbed in 1903 by Fred Botterill along with H. Williamson and E. Grant on the day before he climbed his superb slab. Botterill wrote up this climb in the *Wasdale Climbing Book* and George Abraham mentions it in the FRCC 1908 Journal, but it never made the guidebook that was published in 1924. Mullen would have been unaware of this earlier ascent when he claimed Tricouni Slab in 1938. This information was recently re-discovered following scrutiny of the *Wasdale Climbing Book* as part of the research for this book. So in spite of Mullen's rather indulgent boast about the difficulty of the route, he was beaten to the first ascent by some 35 years, which indicates that the technical level of nail climbing achieved by the earlier generation was at a greater level than is generally appreciated.

The War Years

The Second World War was not as devastating in terms of overall casualties as the First, but many of the leading climbers were called up for active duties. This kept them away from the area, and in first ascent records through the war it can be seen how the only active pioneers who could gain regular access to the crags were the locals such as Sid Cross, or those too old to be called up, such as Bentley Beetham. Jim Birkett's and Bill Peascod's work in the reserve occupations of quarrying and mining kept them away from military duty and they became the two main activists in The Lakes during this period.

The major effect of the war on the sport of climbing was the development and availability of equipment. A major revolution in equipment created during the war was that of nylon rope; it was stronger, more elastic and less likely to absorb water than the old hemp rope. This fantastic new material that was to revolutionise safety in the mountains was originally developed for towing gliders during airborne attacks. The use of nylon ropes did not filter through to the climbing world until the late 1940s, and the first were imported from America.

The Commando corps trained heavily on sea cliffs and mountain crags for their assaults on coastal targets, and for this they utilised large amounts of pitons and karabiners. These original karabiners were crude and made from steel, and had little strength in their design, apart from the inherent structural resistance from deformation within the steel itself. Karabiners became openly available after the war and were eagerly sought by climbers, where as previously they were only available in small numbers from the Alpine regions. Another innovation was the commando soled boot, made with a single moulded rubber sole that was quieter than the old hob-nailed soldiers' boot. This was a development of the invention of the Italian climber Vito Bramanti, who made lighter and more comfortable mountaineering boots just before the war.
The rubber sole gave exceptional grip on clean, dry rock, but its main drawback was the poor adhesion to wet and greasy rock. All modern mountain boots are now derived from this original commando boot and are referred to by the trade name of Vibram.

Derek Kenyon and Stuart Holmes on the Direct Start start to Central Buttress, first climbed by Mullen.

The War Years (continued)

Another less well known creation from those war years was the Standing Advisory Committee, which later evolved and matured into the British Mountaineering Council. This organisation came into being because training for the commandos and paratroopers on coastal cliffs and in the mountains had no central advisors from the civilian world of mountaineering. Geoffrey Winthrop Young, President of the Alpine Club at the time, arranged a meeting between representatives of the leading clubs to form the body that advised the armed forces on mountaineering matters. So the next time the question arises in a pub quiz of 'who was responsible for the creation of the BMC?', it can be answered with confidence – 'Adolph Hitler'.

Joe Holden and Dave Woods on the second pitch of Gremlin's Groove.

On the same day they made the third ascent of May Day Climb in 1939, Mullen also climbed a new start to Central Buttress with Harry Thompson. This was described as a direct start, but was in fact more indirect than the normal start. The route commences at the foot of Moss Gill, and climbs a rounded arête to a prominent triangular roof. Mullen took a belay here on a peg, which was the only protection he used on the entire climb. For a 5a pitch it was a very bold lead for the time, and the pitch, now considered to be a healthy HVS, has subsequently been described as the normal start to Central Buttress.

During the six years of the Second World War, the main climbing activities and developments were restricted to local valley crags which were easily accessible, as petrol was rationed. The only climb added to Scafell during the period of hostilities was on the obscure section of the crag Red Gill Buttress, close to the end of Lord's Rake. Here the Cross couple, Sid and Jammie, and the Hargreaves couple, Bert and Ruth, added a Mild Severe called Red Gill Wall, which wanders up the left side of the buttress and has long since been relegated to the mists of obscurity.

One notable visitor to the crag in 1944 was a young Arthur Dolphin. He had overcome the wartime travelling restrictions by cycling to Langdale from Clapham in Yorkshire, and on this first visit he led Botterill's Slab, Overhanging Wall, Moss Ledge Direct, Central Buttress and Moss Ghyll Grooves. Arthur Dolphin was then only 19 years old and already a force to be recognised.

Jim Birkett returned to the main face of Scafell shortly after the end of the war; he and Tom Hill explored the steep right side of Pisgah Buttress by scrambling up Steep Gill to a point directly opposite the start of Slingsby's Chimney Route. On climbing up this rarely visited part of the crag they passed an area of shattered rock to reach a wet chimney, which provided the crux of the route. They called their unsatisfactory result Steep Ghyll Grooves (VS), now possibly the least popular of Birkett's routes. in The Lakes.

The following day, and in the company of Len Muscroft, Birkett and Hill wandered around to the left-hand end of The East Buttress where they investigated a large corner line guarded by a viciously overhanging crack. They tried to climb this without success but they still gave it a name: Hell's Groove. Moving further left along the buttress, they spotted an obvious groove to the right of Frankland's Slime Chimney, which forms the first natural break at this end of the crag. This rather mossy groove was followed by an interesting line trending rightwards up some lovely delicate ramps sandwiched between steep rocks to give the pleasant Gremlin's Groove (VS). Again, this is a little frequented line today, but some modern climbers will be familiar with its first pitch, as it forms the start of The Lord of the Rings girdle of The East Buttress.

To the left of Gremlin's Groove and Slime Chimney lies another steep fissure, the line of South Chimney, first climbed by Birkett and Hill. The first pitch proved to be quite difficult, and Birkett recommends that 'a thread can be arranged about 8 feet above the start of the pitch to protect the leader on the overhang'. Tom Hill led the top pitch, a 30 metre chimney protected by only a single spike runner at 8 metres, making it a considerable lead for an on-sight first ascent. This was a rather popular route in its day and many of the older climbers interviewed for this book had enjoyed it, stating it was an airy, first class piece of climbing. However, with such a splendid choice of modern routes, nobody gives it much thought in today's world. It must be acknowledged that in the 1940s there were only ten routes on The East Buttress, so it was an easy task for a good team to climb them all in a couple of seasons. Now there are so many good routes to choose from on the crag that these older 'out-of-the-way' climbs remain neglected, unloved and overgrown.

Another lull in Scafell popularity set in, and apart from a variation start to Moss Ghyll Grooves in July 1946, by T.G. Peirson and M.H. McFarlane, little was achieved on the crag over the next few years leading to 1948. This variation start takes the slabby groove to the right of the main route, joining it at the belay at the top of the second pitch. It was the line first inspected by Kelly in 1919, and possibly the same pitch first climbed with top-rope assistance by Linnell in 1933. Although it gives good, clean climbing with an unusual layback section, the pitch now sees few repeats.

In 1948 Jim Birkett, with Len Muscroft, returned for a final new route on the crag. This started opposite the famous Tennis Court Wall of Moss Gill where a large, smooth slab sweeps up leftwards, capped by a formidable overhang. Muscroft must have shown the potential of this route to Birkett as he had held the rope for Joe Williams of Whitehaven during an attempt on this line several years before. Williams had climbed the corner of the slab to the roof, but unable to make any progress, had calmly climbed back down again, without runners and in nailed boots.

Birkett started up the right-hand corner for a short distance before traversing boldly leftwards to reach a thin crack in the left edge of the slab. This led directly up to the top of the slab, passing to the left side of the capping roof and thus avoiding Williams' blind alley. The upper pitch following the groove was easier by comparison, and their resultant route, Slab and Groove (VS) was probably the last major route to be pioneered on Scafell in nailed boots. It was a remarkable lead; completely unprotectable until wired nuts became available twenty years later. Jim could have used pegs for runners, but following the May Day controversy he chose not to carry them.

Local climber and raconteur Tony Greenbank recalled the time he first climbed the route, which he considered to be one of the very best pitches around. He was so thrilled, he rang Jim Birkett to tell him the news and was met with a quiet, dry reply: "Aye, well when we first climbed it, we thought it was only Severe", which deflated Greenbank like bursting a balloon. (14)

With Slab and Groove, at the relatively young age of 34 years, Jim had climbed his last new route on Scafell, but it was only the beginning of the Birkett dynasty. Son Bill and grandson Dave were still to follow.

Above: Mel Michon on the variation start to Moss Ghyll Grooves, the grass ledge up and left of her is the 'Lookout' belay ledge on Moss Ghyll Grooves.

Below: The main pitch of Slab and Groove - an unprotected lead in Birkett's day.

Footnotes

1. A.T. Hargreaves, 'Land of Plenty' *FRCC Journal* 1943
2. W. Peascod 'Old and New' *FRCC Journal* 1945
3. A.T. Hargreaves 'Land of Plenty' *FRCC Journal* 1943
4. Stan Thompson, FRCC audio recording 2008
5. A.R. Dolphin 'Recent Developments in Lakeland' *FRCC Journal* 1947
6. Jack Carswell, FRCC audio recording 2008
7. Bill Birkett, FRCC audio recording 2008
8. Extract from '*A Century on the Crags*' by Alan Hankinson 1986
9. C.F. Holland 'Pitons – A Middle View' *FRCC Journal* 1942
10. F.W. Smythe 'Mechanised Mountaineering' *FRCC Journal* 1942
11. C.F. Kirkus 'Ethics of Ironmongery' *Wayfarers Club Journal* 1939
12. Alf Mullen, first ascent notes.
13. W. J. K. Pearson, *Rucksack Club Journal* 1939
14. Tony Greenbank, telephone conversation with the author, 2008

Looking at Hollow Stones from Wasdale, with Pikes Crag on the left and Scafell Shamrock in the centre.

1949 to 1957

Dolphin and The Rock and Ice

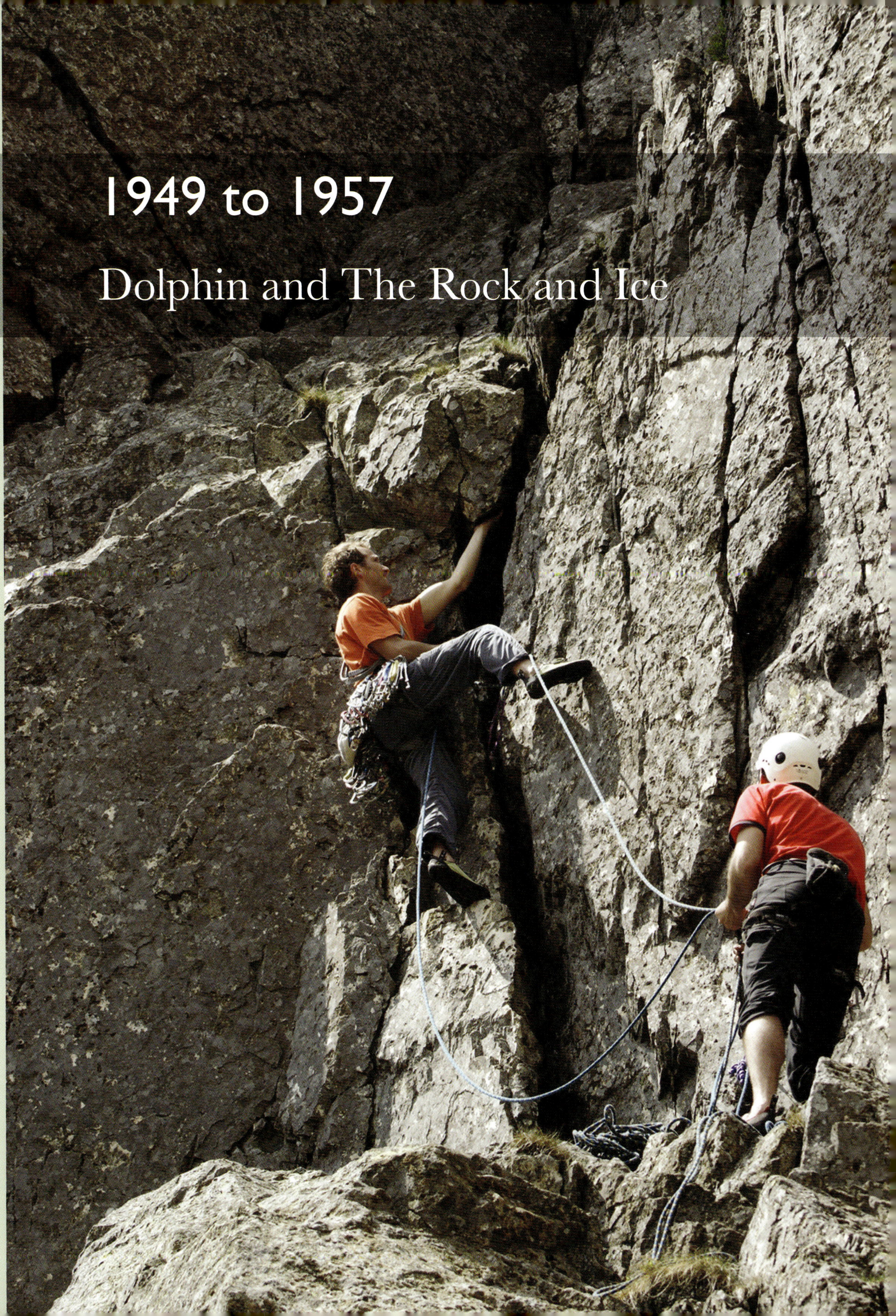

In the mid-1940s, a young student from Baildon near Bradford started to make his mark in The Lake District. By 1951, Arthur Dolphin had established a series of impressively hard routes such as Kipling Groove, Deer Bield Buttress and Sword of Damocles and he was regarded as one of the best young climbers around. His appearance was unmistakable; tall, thin and topped by a distinctive head of blonde hair, he was extremely fit and had an intense desire to climb steep, untrodden rock.
Jim Birkett said of him

> "Arthur was a super bloke. I liked him a lot. He was one of the best. I admired him because he was dead straight, never sponged. He was the most unlikely looking climber ever, long, thin and anaemic. He always had a drip at the end of his nose. But could he climb!" (1)

Arthur had an ex-W.D. motorbike, a 350 Gold Star, that apparently sounded like a "bag of nails because it had an alloy engine", which made it rather unreliable as it kept breaking down. (2) Arthur was a notoriously late riser in the mornings, but this didn't delay his partners because his experience as a cross-country runner soon enabled him to catch up to the others at the crag.

Arthur had teamed up with another son of Bradford, Peter Greenwood, who was an extroverted, hard drinking, heavy smoking lad with a rather pugnacious approach to confrontations. Greenwood was a short, powerful but extremely supple climber, who had a determined drive fuelled by competitive ambition. During the interview for this book, when Pete was struggling with the effect of a long-term illness, he fondly recalled those days with a smile and a simple economy of words. Although it had been 55 years since Arthur died, the adoration of his old partner was still profound and eloquently stated.

Dolphin paid three visits to The East Buttress in 1952. On his first of these, he was with his fiancée, Marie Ball, Don Hopkins and Peter Greenwood. They climbed Morning Wall and Gremlin's Groove, and attempted "the groove left of Hell's Groove, but it was abandoned pending further exploration from above", a line which would eventually become Trinity. Two weeks later, on a hot, spring day they climbed Pegasus, a prominent diagonal line below and left of Morning Wall, which rises across the crag just above the steep lower wall, giving it an intimidating style of climbing which is liberally coated with black, dusty moss. Greenwood recalled:

> "We walked in from Langdale, it was a long way, you know. There was no transport in those days, just the odd motorbike knocking about. It made a big difference to the routes when you had to walk all that way. Arthur set off on this route but I couldn't see him from where I was belayed. He thought at first that it was going to be Severe, because he found the start of it was so easy, when suddenly he came up against something a bit harder. Anyhow, he put a piton in and did a swing move or something, I dunno, I couldn't see him. But that's why he called it Pegasus, because of the peg assistance. I can remember it was such a red hot day which made Arthur very hoarse because his throat was so dry. The route wasn't too dirty, but there was a lot of loose rock on the hard pitch, I cleaned that out, I was on it for quite a long time cleaning it out then I came back down again and said 'you have a go'. So he went up and actually lassoed a little flake above and that's how it was first climbed, he pulled up on this sling, but when I came up I did it free, so it went all right, you know." (3)

Keith Phizacklea prepares to pull onto the mossy ramp on pitch 2 of Pegasus,

Overleaf:
Dave Parton and Scott Young on the initial crack of Hell's Groove.

Photos: Al Phizacklea

Dolphin had used a tension move on the second pitch, which involved a delicate traverse into a shallow, mossy groove. When he got to the stance at the top of it, he wedged his peg hammer into a crack and passed the rope around it for the belay thus creating a hammer thread. He also used an aid point on the third pitch, probably because it held a quantity of loose rock as noted above. It may seem unusual for the Yorkshire Wonderkid (as he was known) to use aid here when he had climbed many harder routes in The Lakes, but this substantiates the intimidating nature of climbing on The East Buttress, and leading this on sight would have taken some courage. Dolphin's diary states that the route had taken them "Six long hours" to complete. Ron Miller and Pete Moffatt were the first team to climb this route free in 1955 during their investigations for the guidebook; it still deserves a grade of HVS. Dolphin and Greenwood were evidently late back when they returned to Langdale, as Greenwood later commented,

> "I felt that the walk back in the dark was more dangerous than the climbing we did that day!"

The following weekend they returned to the same area and climbed Hell's Groove, the prominent undercut corner that had been a major project for many years. This is guarded by a short over-hanging crack that suited Greenwood's squat but lithe frame. He records that:

> "Arthur already had Hell's Groove in mind and said 'If you can get up this overhang, I'll climb the rest'. He had tried it a couple of times beforehand but couldn't get up, and so had Birkett as well. It was Birkett that named it Hell's Groove, so it was already named when we did it.
>
> "On the first pitch I was finding it hard when – bang! I got in this knee-jam; I could take my hands off and lean backwards and look for holds above (gesturing with both hands wiggling above his head). It was easy actually, once you had the knee-jam, a bit exciting probably, but you don't think about that, do you?
>
> "I had in all these little bits for a belay, a little line here and a little line there, I had about 4 or 5 belays on, all on little knobs, but it was nothing at all. Then Arthur led the rest of the route which was runnerless, there were no real runners at all. He did have some pitons with him and he placed two for runners, but he didn't have a piton hammer. There's two good ledges on the way up with a crack down the back, and he just stuck them in with his hand. Whether they'd have come out I dunno, they probably would have done had he fallen. So really the entire route was done unprotected from bottom to top, the standard was all right, apart from the overhanging crack which I had found hard until I had found the knee-jam, but there was no way that Arthur could get the knee-jam in; he did try, mind." (4)

The second pitch of Hell's Groove did not follow the deep corner above the belay; instead Dolphin carefully eased his way up the steep wall to its right. It must have been a tremendously bold lead, as the final pull onto the belay was described by Dolphin as being "rather awkward". The upper three pitches of Pegasus were followed to the top of the crag on the first ascent, but in 1971 Johnny Adams and Colin Read added a direct finish which included an overhanging green crack, which is only recommended in dry conditions! This route is now a classic, three star E1. It was to be Dolphin's final contribution to Scafell, as he was killed the following year during the descent of the Dent du Géant in the Alps. This accident happened the year after the death of Bert Hargreaves, who had perished in an avalanche in Austria. Both Hargreaves and Dolphin had been in the process of re-writing the guidebook to Scafell at this time. This was not published for some years until Ron Miller completed their work.

Arthur Dolphin.

Peter Greenwood.

Hell's Groove; Dave Parton on the second pitch.

John Wilkinson accurately observed that the deaths of these two prominent climbers caused the pace of exploration in The Lakes to slow down. The next group to become dominant in the area were mainly north of England climbers who based themselves around Keswick, led by Paul Ross.

The focus of hard British rock climbing by this time had well and truly moved from The Lakes to the mountains of Wales. The activities of Menlove Edwards and Peter Harding were soon superseded by the intense Rock and Ice Climbing Club men, spearheaded by Joe Brown, Don Whillans and Ron Moseley. They built upon the earlier development of their predecessors and brought a new degree of difficulty to the crags of Llanberis Pass and Cloggy with a string of hard, new extreme climbs. This new order was never challenged by climbers based in The Lake District because the death of Dolphin robbed the area of the one person who was capable of equalling this Welsh dominance. The situation remained unchanged for many decades and some still argue that Welsh-based activists still dominate the British climbing scene, a ludicrous claim according to the Cumbrian fraternity.

Another tragic accident occurred on Central Buttress, in June 1953. The author first found out about this accident when he was looking around the graveyard of Wasdale Church. Amongst the old and faded headstones lies a simple slate block as shown alongside.

Gunter Franz was a young forestry worker of German parentage who was climbing C.B. with Des Birch, who was an instructor at Eskdale Outward Bound School. They were both experienced climbers, as Birch had already climbed C.B. five times. Birch was belayed to a peg on the 'V' ledge, and Franz was horizontally left of Birch, possibly 20 to 25 feet away, and was trying to avoid the awkward start to the Direct Finish by hand-traversing into it from the left, a variation that had not been climbed before.

According to the newspaper report, Birch told the Coroner that Franz had already made one attempt at the line and returned to the belay. He said:

> "This time Franz managed to get his fingers over the top. Then he pulled himself up to the full extensions of his flexed arms, but found he had no strength to finish the climb. He had been trying this pitch for ten to fifteen minutes. He then lowered himself to full stretch, let go with one hand and tried to reach the footholds by stretching the full length of his fingers. He could not do it and had to let go with his hand. He dropped about six inches into the footholds, over-balanced and fell. " (5)

Birch later commented:

> "When I saw him falling, I took in a few feet of the slack rope. He swung below me like a pendulum. The weight came on the rope gradually and the rope started to run out, then it broke. I thought the rope might have been caught in a groove of rock and then snapped under the weight. At the time of the break, Franz was directly below me." (6)

Birch managed to attract the attention of a fellow instructor and was faced with a harrowing solo up the Bayonet-Shaped Crack before descending to the foot of the crag, where they found Franz's body. The cause of the fatality was not Franz's attempt at a new variation, and had nothing to do with the team or their techniques; it was the tragic cutting of the rope over a sharp edge of rock as he swung across the face. (In a later conversation, Birch said that the rope had caught behind the upper left edge of The Great Flake when it snapped.) They had been using a nylon rope, the remains of which were independently examined and found to be in a sound and safe condition.

Gunter Franz's grave in Wasdale.

NORTH-WESTERN EVENING MAIL,

AUSTRIAN'S DEATH FALL ON SCAFELL

Trying to retrace his steps

A YOUNG Austrian who went climbing on Scafell with a friend from the Outward Bound School, on Saturday evening, was fatally injured in a fall on Central Buttress.

The victim was Max Philip Gunter Franz (23), who had been employed at Braithwaite with the Forestry Commission, and it is understood he was a member of the Keswick Mountain Rescue Team.

Franz went climbing on Central Buttress with Desmond Cornell Birch, a teacher at the Outward Bound School. They were attempting one particular stretch with Franz in the lead when the Austrian apparently decided it was too difficult. In trying to retrace his steps, Franz fell past Birch and the rope broke. Franz was thrown to his death.

Assistance was called and members of the Fell and Rock Climbing Club who were staying at Bracken Close went up with a stretcher. The body was brought down to Bracken Close in the early hours of Sunday morning, and Dr. J. Loudon, of Gosforth, certified that Franz was dead. Later the body was taken to Whitehaven.

Franz had been staying at the Outward Bound School for the past fortnight. His parents are believed to be living at Wupperthal in the Western Zone of Germany.

BARROW H.F. RAMBLERS

Over a lesser known ridge in Lakeland

Barrow H.F. Ramblers walked over one of the lesser known mountain ridges of the Lake District — between Ennerdale Water and Buttermere—yesterday.

The ramblers left the bus at Ennerdale Bridge, and proceeded in rather overcast weather to climb the lower slopes of Banna Fell, where lunch was eaten before tackling the main ascent. After lunch, the ramblers crossed Gill Beck and climbed Great Borne, from which point all the Loweswater and Ennerdale Fells were partially obscured from view by mist hanging over the fells. The main party then walked over Starling Dodd before climbing the highest peak on the ridge, which was Red Pike (2,479ft.). The ramblers then walked over High Stile to High Crag, down the screes to Scarth Gap and thence along the shore of Buttermere village.

A second party, after climbing Great Borne, broke away from the main party and descended

Celebration was favoured by the weather

Newspaper report on the accident to Gunter Franz in 1953. North West Evening Mail.

The year of 1954 became notorious as the wettest year ever recorded in Britain, with almost 14 feet of rain (a staggering 4.35 metres!) falling on Seathwaite in Borrowdale. Little wonder that anyone managed to climb that year, but it did not stop another Bradford lad, Harold Drasdo, from making a rare foray up to Scafell with Ken Finlay. Here they noticed a prominent crackline running up the steep wall which rises above the foot of Mickledore Chimney. This turned out to be a pleasant clean VS which they named Tia Maria, after Ken's liking for exotic drinks, thus starting a liqueur based naming theme for subsequent routes in this area. Harold states that the route went without incident at the end of a long day of climbing at the higher grades, but he felt satisfied that this route would appeal to the mid-grade climbers. A couple of years later, following some advice from Harold, Geoff Sutton and Geoff Roberts climbed the inferior grassy crack to its right at VS, naming it Tio Pepe.

At Whitsuntide in 1955 a legendary figure from the Rock and Ice Climbing Club, Don Whillans, stopped off at Wasdale on his return from ascending the Old Man of Storr on the Isle of Skye. Whillans was a renowned hard man - hard climbing, hard drinking and hard hitting, his reputation always preceding him, but under the hard exterior was an exceptional climber. His tally of new routes in the Peak District and Wales was matched by his exploits abroad; he was involved in first ascents on The Central Pillar of Freney in the Alps, Cerro Torre in Patagonia, and the south face of Annapurna. It was typical of the man that he met John Sullivan not at the crag, but in the pub at Wasdale Head, and together they climbed Trinity on The East Buttress.

Craig Spence on the first pitch of Trinity.

The Third Scafell Guide

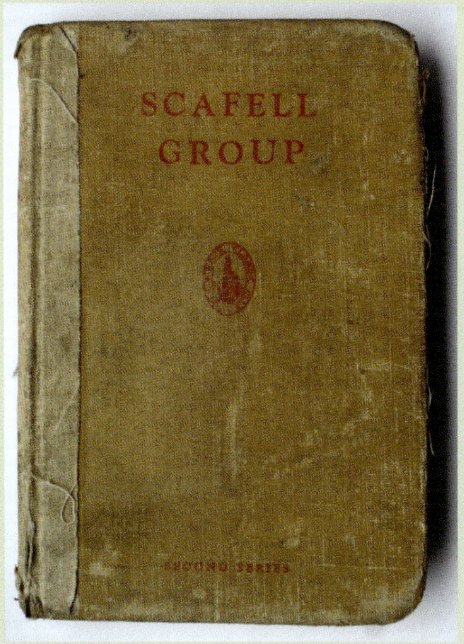

The third guidebook to Scafell was produced in 1956. There was little to distinguish between this edition and the second guide from 1936. The guide had the confusing sub-heading of Second Series on its cover. This may have been because it was the second series produced by Harry Kelly, and was this his way of stating that his version of the guide was superior to that from Holland in 1924? It retained the same rigid buff-coloured cover, but it was also inhibited by the stifling effect of Harry Kelly's dictatorial editing style. Despite this, he was still a well respected editor, and as was usual for the times he undertook all his correspondence by letter.

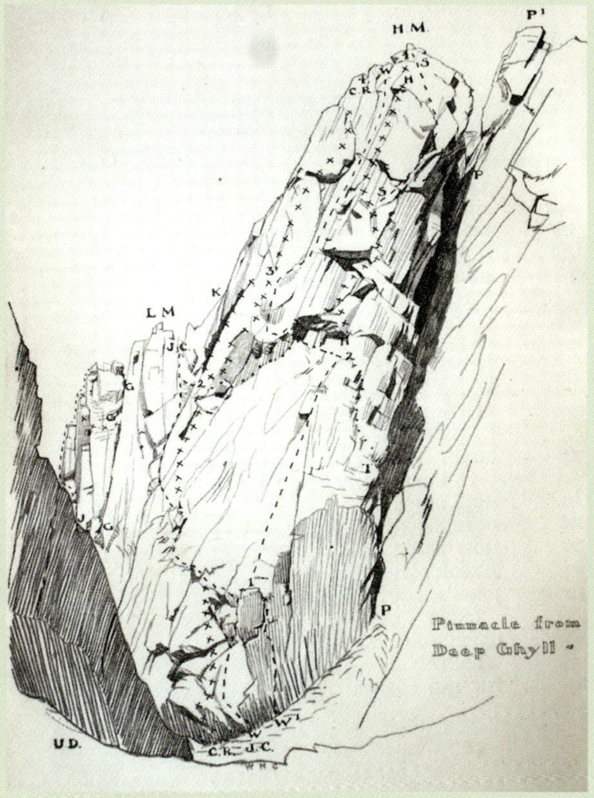

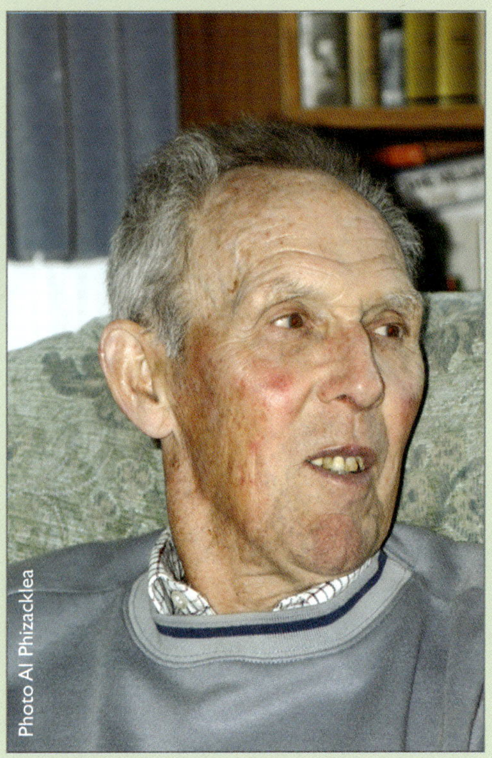

Ron Miller.

Ron Miller picked up the writing of the guide after the deaths of Arthur Dolphin and Bert Hargreaves. He was given little scope to alter any of the older descriptions and Kelly even refused to allow an increase in the grades above VS. In the twenty years since the previous guide there were only 16 routes added to Scafell. The most recent route, Trinity, was climbed late in the production of the guide and only appeared as an addendum. One description from the guide brought the following disparaging comment from local climber John Temple:

"The description of The Great Flake on Central Buttress contained the instruction 'The leader ties into the chock-stone, the second man now climbs up to and past the leader. A tall man can reach the perfect holds at the top of the flake from the leader's shoulders…' Well, Rocker Dave came up and surely being 6'4" qualified him as a tall man. He stood on my shoulders – not even close! My guidebook later sported the comment 'lying sod!!' next to this statement, but I would like to unreservedly withdraw my comment and belatedly apologise to the author. It seems that 6'4" was simply just not tall enough!"

Although this comment was aimed at Miller, Temple was unaware that the comment had been inserted by Hargreaves in the 1936 guidebook, and this typifies the unchanging style of the guides of the time.

This takes the series of steep grooves and corners forming a strong natural line to the left of Hell's Groove. The route is constantly interesting, with a succession of jamming, bridging and strenuous layback moves typical of the type of climbing that defines a Whillans route.

There is a lovely description of an ascent of Trinity by Ken Jackson in his autobiography *Climbing in the Dark*. In this, he claims there is a mistake in the guidebook regarding the description for the second pitch:

> "The guidebook said, 'layback up the crack,' so I took this to mean exactly what it said and it was necessary for me to layback for twenty feet or more, up this ferocious, bulging crack, two hundred feet above the ground, in an exposed position and not too well protected. Add to that my cold fingers and the lack of experience of my young companion, and you have a recipe for disaster.
>
> "To make matters worse, the guidebook went on to say, 'step on to the slab on the left,' when what it should have said was, 'step onto the slab on the right!' In retrospect, I should have noticed a small clue that would have made me realise the guidebook was in error – there was no ledge on the left! Taking a deep breath and grasping the edge of the crack with my hands, I faced the wall on the right and placed one foot flat against it, pulling hard to increase the friction on the sole of my boot. I started to move up, hand over hand, until my arms threatened to pull out of their sockets and my fingers began to uncurl. 'You bastard, Whillans,' I gasped, 'You bastard!'
>
> "Now I'm not given to swearing much, but when my life depended on it, I let rip with all the venom I could muster. And somehow the swearing and fear seemed to release enough adrenalin to give the extra strength needed to reach the tiny ledge at the top of that fearsome crack. Breathing heavily and drained emotionally, I looped one of the ropes around a spike. This gave me some protection whilst I regained sufficient energy to fix a runner, the first one for thirty feet – God knows what would have happened if I had fallen. This was by far the hardest pitch I had ever climbed on Scafell East Buttress, or anywhere else for that matter. By no stretch of the imagination was this thing Hard Very Severe – not the way I did it, anyway. But of course I didn't know that the guidebook had mixed up right and left! By bridging up the slab on the right, I could easily have rested safely, less than half-way up the crack. Fancy that!" (7)

This accusation worried the author, because he was also the guidebook writer, and Trinity was one of the routes that was checked before publication of the 1995 guide. The description Jackson followed in the earlier guides was a little longer than that used today, it read: 'Continue over the bulge in the corner on to a slab. Go straight up the slab to an overhanging corner crack. Layback up the crack, and step onto a slab on the left. Move diagonally leftwards to the foot of a short wall…'

Jackson's accusation of erroneousness sent the author scrambling up under The East Buttress at the earliest opportunity, because the FRCC pride itself on accuracy in its guides. It comes down to a matter of interpretation. As the author of Scafell guidebooks, I would like to state that the description is absolutely correct; there is a huge ledge on the left above the finish of the layback crack. Ken is also correct when he says there is no slab on the left whilst lay-backing, you've just got to grit your teeth and get on with it until you reach the top. There may well be a small foot-hold on the right wall that he later took to mean as a ledge, but that wasn't part of the description.

Considering this is an excellent Whillans route that is only HVS, it sees little traffic nowadays but it is one of the best of its grade on the crag. This seems a little puzzling, but consideration must be given to the accident of 1962, detailed in the next chapter, when two young climbers were killed on Trinity. This accident gave the route a certain notoriety amongst the climbers of the day.

Ron Moseley, another Rock and Ice star, was responsible for the next big route on The East Buttress when he climbed Phoenix in August, 1957, at the age of 26. Moseley had already developed classic routes in Wales such as the White Slab on Cloggy and Left Wall on The Cromlech, and in The Lakes he had pioneered routes such as Dight on Gimmer and Pendulum on Deer Bield Crag.

Phoenix followed the easy, initial ramp of Morning Wall to its terminus with the overhanging rock, where a belay was taken. The rock above this point is rather intimidating, steep and hard. There is a niche a few metres above the belay and it is known that Moseley and Eric Metcalfe had spent the previous two days attempting to traverse rightwards from here to gain a line that would eventually become known as Ichabod.

Photo Al Phizacklea

Mark Gorin on the initial crack on Phoenix.

Photo courtesy of the internet

Ron Moseley in 2008. After leaving climbing in 1958 he became a renowned artist.

He returned on the third day and used a peg for aid to tension left from the niche onto the arête where a steep and very strenuous crack rises with difficulty to a recess higher up. This was an impressive lead in those days where the only protection came from a couple of chockstones (hand inserted) and a peg runner, and it wasn't realised at the time that this was the hardest line on the crag; it still retains a grade of E2 today with modern gear. Moseley was accompanied on the route by a young partner called Dave Adcock, whose career in climbing was a short one.

Shortly after he had climbed this route, Moseley gave up climbing completely. His form was astonishingly sporadic, unstoppable one week, failing on a VS the following, and this inconsistency probably led to his decision to quit climbing. He resigned from his post as secretary of the Rock and Ice Club which caused it to be disbanded, stating that that part of his life was over for good. He emigrated to Canada and South Africa for many decades, ignored his climbing friends and it is said that he never talked about climbing again, apart from saying that those had been wasted years.

A little known fact about Moseley is that he was a commercial artist by trade and his work was seen by millions of people every day, even unknowingly worshipped by some. Part of Ron's artistic work was to design the intricate patterns and swirls on banknotes in the days before computer graphics took over that task. (8.) He currently lives near Blackpool and still paints beautiful landscape scenes which have earned him a reputation as a successful artist.

The aid point on Phoenix was found to be unnecessary if the traverse leftwards was made from the belay, thereby avoiding the niche, and this was first achieved by David Miller in 1962. The upper pitch of the route originally followed the left-slanting gangway to the top of the crag, but a new second pitch, a direct finish, was climbed in 1967 by Geoff Cram and Bill Young. This pitch utilised a sling for aid, but this was freed shortly afterwards by Ken Wood to give another superb route on The East Buttress. The direct finish was put up just before the guide was published, hence the aid was never mentioned in the description.

Footnotes

1. T.W. Birkett, '*Lakeland's Greatest Pioneers*' 1983
2. Arthur Brookes, FRCC audio recording, 2008
3. Peter Greenwood, FRCC audio recording, 2008
4. Peter Greenwood, FRCC audio recording, 2008
5. Coroner's report from the *Whitehaven News*, 1953
6. Des Birch, telephone conversation with the author, 2008
7. Ken Jackson, *Climbing in the Dark* 2008
8. Valerie Brown, conversation with the author, 2009

Photo: Al Phizacklea

Robin Whitworth and Mark Gorin on what is now regarded as the regular finish to Phoenix, steep and exposed climbing on excellent rock. This variation was climbed in 1967 by Geoff Cram and Bill Young.

Wasdale Head with Pillar behind.

Photo Al Phizacklea

1958 - 1964

Scottish Raiders Revive the Locals

Photo: Jimmy Marshall

Robin Smith.

In May1958 a visit by Robin Smith and Derek Leaver, two climbers from Edinburgh, shook the local climbers out of their complacency and set off a major wave of development on Scafell. In a single day they climbed two new routes in the area of Mickledore Grooves; a remarkable and rather provocative feat at the time. The last occasion the Scots crossed the border and raided Cumberland was when they were ruled by a Prince everyone called 'Bonnie'! What was the world coming to? It was not Robin's and Derek's first visit to Scafell; they had spent a week at the Fell & Rock Climbing Club's Brackenclose hut the previous year and climbed many of the existing routes, no doubt spotting the remaining potential. Smith was a superbly talented climber who had made a name for himself in Scotland with first ascents such as Shibboleth in Glencoe and The Bat on Ben Nevis. It must be conceded that some of Smith's Scottish routes were harder than anything yet climbed in The Lakes, and they were on a par with the top climbs in Wales.

The first of the Scafell routes, Leverage named after Derek Leaver, follows the obvious thin crack in the steep wall above the start of Mickledore Grooves. The disproportionately hard start still perplexes many climbers; being a short boulder problem onto the initial ramp of Mickledore Grooves. The rest of the main pitch was also a fierce lead considering only jammed knots and spike runners were available for protection, and the route is currently graded E1 even with the full gamut of modern gear. The second ascent of Leverage came five years later from Allan Austin, who is reputed to have had a hard time on it; so endorsing the standing of Robin Smith. It took a third ascent from Rod Valentine to dispel the mythical status, and afterwards Leverage became one of the most popular routes of its grade, though not everyone could agree on what that was, and it has bounced between HVS and E1 ever since.

Their second success on that day, Chartreuse, continues the liquor-themed route names around this area of the crag. Chartreuse takes a delicate and very bold line up the lower left edge of the huge slab at the right end of the crag to the belay on Mickledore Grooves. Even today there are few runners available on this pitch; it must have been a remarkable, completely unprotected lead. The second pitch moves up to the headwall, where it finishes up a wide awkward crack; an obvious feature when viewed from ground level.

The route's final section was the reason Al Phizacklea refused to climb Chartreuse for over twenty years of visiting the crag, but one busy day he realised as writer of the next guidebook to the area he had to do it. His ascent turned into a bit of an epic, and Al recalls:

> "The top crack felt really awkward because it was fist-wide and smooth. I struggled up it until I got close to the top, where I slotted in my right knee and flexed my leg to wedge it in place. I then put my weight on this knee and it slipped down slightly where the crack narrowed and it seemed to get stuck in a vice. I struggled a bit, then I realised that I had to get my weight off my knee to get it out. The problem was the crack above me was quite wide, and I tried to get a double stacked hand jam in, but it was that awkward width where nothing worked. I couldn't move, so I called quietly down to John [Holden] that I was stuck. Unfortunately some of my mates who were watching a team on Midnight Express overheard me. Those buggers then went and broadcast the news loudly around the crag, and before long there seemed to be a throng of mocking climbers gathered at the bottom of the crag just to take the piss. It felt just like that tale when Martin Boysen got his knee jammed high on the Trango Tower, except this wasn't the mighty Himalaya; it was on a classic E1 on Scafell.

Overleaf:
Dave Parton and Scott Young take advantage of a 5.30 am start on Leverage, The East Buttress.

Photo: Al Phizacklea

Photo: Al Phizacklea

Scott Young seconding Leverage, leader Dave Parton belays after climbing the full route in a single pitch.

I struggled for another five minutes before I realised I would have to ask someone for a top-rope, so I sat back on my knee and looked up, and that's when I noticed the crack narrowed quite a bit a metre above my reach. So I clipped my biggest nut to a sling, and after a few goes I managed to swing it into the narrows where it wedged in place. By this time the mocking taunts from below had increased in intensity, but I managed to clip my harness into the sling and get both hands under my knee and eventually wriggle it free." (1)

Iain Turnbull on the lower, bold slab of Chartreuse, the route finishes up the short wide crack at the top; the scene of the Author's epic.

There seems to be an error in *High Endeavour*, Jimmy Cruickshank's biography of Robin Smith. In his book Jimmy states that Geoff Oliver witnessed Robin in action during his audacious border raid on Scafell that resulted in two new routes. Geoff did meet Robin upon Scafell, but it was not then; it was during the winter following a near miss when Smith was avalanched down Deep Gill. Geoff is adamant he didn't see him up there when he did Leverage and Chartreuse. An interesting aside regarding Robin Smith also came from Les Brown:

> "It was amazing, but Robin had failed on Hell's Groove; he couldn't get up the overhanging crack at the start, which I found surprising. He said to me that he had too big a belly for an overhanging crack, and when I gave this information to Jimmy Cruickshank, he refused to put it into his book because he said that Robin was thin, but I remember him as being rather pod-shaped really. Anyhow, Robin did loads of harder routes than that." (2)

During the research for this book an unrecorded route came to light during an interview with Ron Miller. Sometime during 1958, Ron climbed the large corner directly above the Barry's Traverse start of Mickledore Grooves and continued up a direct continuation to the top. Somehow it remained unrecorded and forgotten, and in 1959 the upper section of this route was claimed as the Direct Finish to Mickledore Grooves by Dennis English. Moving forward to 1974, K. Rudd, A. Brown and Ian Angell re-climbed Miller's line, but they used a nut for aid to overcome the bulge guarding the upper groove, which they called Strider. Miller had originally climbed this free simply because there were no nuts in his day! This route was first recorded in the 1996 guidebook, but in the recent edition the first ascent details have been amended to credit Miller for the route.

Following the raid from Robin Smith, the locals awoke to the fact that there was still plenty of potential left on Scafell. Les Brown looks back with:

> "Smith's visit from Scotland made us all aware that there was still a lot of scope for routes up on Scafell. I remember thinking: Bloody hell, here I am right underneath Scafell, and Robin comes down and does a couple of routes up there. So that's what sent me up to the crag." (6)

The arid conditions of that 1959 summer ensured that many of the natural drainage lines that normally glistened with running water were starting to dry out. One of the most obvious features to come into condition was the huge, open groove above the start of May Day Climb. Paul Ross spotted the potential and made a serious attempt on this direct line; claiming to have free climbed two thirds of the way up the difficult corner before encountering a wet streak. He was not far from easy ground, so he put in a piton which he intended to use for aid. His second, Frank Carrol, suggested that instead of using aid, he should retreat and come back the next weekend when it might have dried even more. Ross considered this option before agreeing with the proposal, so he abseiled off the peg and leaving a sling in place. (7) However, Geoff Oliver was also up at the crag that day and realised the significance of the sling swinging in the breeze. That night he met Ross in the Wasdale Head Inn, and recalled the following conversation:

> "I asked whether he was going back up there the following day, but Paul said it was too sunny to walk back up there, so I might have said to him 'Do you mind if I could have a go?' I'm not usually that pushy, so I think I might have asked him that. So I went up the following day to complete the route with Les Willis, and Paul later reckoned I was a bad bugger for doing that." (8)

Ross admitted that he got excessively drunk that night, and the following day he was so hung-over he couldn't face the walk back up to Scafell, so he went climbing on Kern Knotts instead. When discussing this incident with Paul some fifty years later, he still regretted the fact that he let this route slip through his grasp, asserting Oliver had sneaked up and finished it. Ross never forgot the loss of this line, especially since he claims his first attempt was done without using any slings for aid.

The Great Footwear Revolution

The use of nailed boots finally faded from the upper echelon of climbers during the 1950s and, after Jim Birkett's ascent of Slab and Groove, there were no further routes pioneered in nails on Scafell. Nevertheless nailed boots were still occasionally used by traditionalists throughout the 1960s when conditions were wet. The 'Vibram' boot with its moulded rubber sole became the popular choice of footwear, especially for the approach walk to the crag, but these were never widely used for climbing except on the easier lines.

Following the hiatus of the First World War, the leading climbers generally used soft-soled, black gym shoes as were widely available from Woolworths, and which acted very much like the lightweight slippers of today. Some climbers even rounded off the edges of the soles to reduce the tendency for them to roll off the holds. The price of these was a shilling (5p) in the 1920s but, by the time the mid-fifties came around, the price had gone up to 'two shillings and sixpence' (12½ p). It is incredible to realise that for forty years, these old gym shoes remained the primary footwear amongst the climbing fraternity. Some climbers experimented with alternative footwear in attempts to find a better solution to the old gym shoes. Pete Greenwood never climbed in nails; preferring women's field hockey boots with the studs shaved off, because as he said they felt nice and had a good ankle support, and they had a similar fit to the 'E. B.' boot of the 1960s and 1970s. He also reminisced:

> "Arthur Dolphin used those white tennis shoes, Dunlop Green Flash; they were posh things. That's what the University boys wore, not like us common lads." (3)

Paul Ross recalls that Pete Greenwood once persuaded him to try the field hockey boots minus studs, but he never liked them. He always climbed in rubbers but looks back on how the Manchester based Rock and Ice climbers started to climb in a new type of rock boot known as 'P.A.s' almost two years before they became known by the lads from The Lakes. He first saw Don Whillans use them on an early attempt at Vertigo on Black Crag in Borrowdale in about 1957. When he asked Whillans what were those shoes he was wearing, the reply in a disparaging manner was that they were some French rubbish he had picked up in Paris, and Ross never gave them a second thought.

The Great Footwear Revolution (continued)

He hadn't appreciated that he was looking at a new style of boot that would revolutionise climbing. Whillans had pulled the wool over his eyes, and it was only some time later that he realised that 'the Rock and Ice had a great advantage for at least two years over us thick buggers from The Lakes'. (4)

The original P.A.'s and E.B.'s were much loved by climbers and were usually worn to destruction before they were replaced.

The 'P.A.' was a smooth soled, lightweight canvas boot developed by Frenchman Pierre Alain, and it first became available on the continent around 1956. Astute alpinists returning to Britain used to call into Alain's equipment shop in Paris to purchase these boot, as initially they were unavailable in Britain. By 1958 they were imported and became widely available in the UK, with an immediate and noticeable impact on climbing standards. The rock boot design allowed flexibility along the boot for use on friction holds, but it was rigid across the sole, which enabled it to be used with great confidence on small, sharp edged holds. This boot and its later successor the 'E.B.' (named after the manufacturer Edouard Bourdonneau) were to revolutionise the sport of climbing in Britain. The age of the nailed boot was well and truly over, but perhaps this section should end with a quote from the master of nail climbing, Jim Birkett. When Jack Soper first showed him a pair of 'P.A.s', Jim studied them thoughtfully, turning them over in his rough hands, and said with a shrewd smile, 'Nay, they're as slape as a bottle! (5)

Steve Merry taking advantage of the dry conditions to climb the main corner of May Day Direct.

Nowadays, May Day Direct provides a superb E2 when it is dry, but this is always a bit of a lottery. Oliver's first ascent description of May Day Direct states he used slings threaded behind two inserted chockstones and Ross' peg for aid to climb it. He claims he can't remember using the slings for aid, but as he wrote them into the first ascent description, he conceded that he must have used them;

> "In my defence, I did have a terrible hangover that day. I was nearly puking up on the route and I wasn't really caring about it. I don't want to get involved whether Rossy did the bottom bit free or not. Les Brown did the first proper ascent when he did the second ascent, and he took the peg out." (9)

Many years later Ross got partial revenge when he grabbed the first ascent of a route that Oliver had gardened on Castle Rock in Thirlmere, cheekily calling it The Last Laugh. Ross never managed to achieve his ambition of climbing a new route on Scafell until 35 years later when he added Swansong to Deep Gill Buttress.

Two further lines were added to Scafell Crag over one fine weekend in August 1959 by Joe Griffin and the Merseyside based Welsh activist Hugh Banner. This was a long-established partnership with them climbing together since the early 1950s when they were both based at Bristol University. Griffin explained how he noticed the first of these lines:

> "It would have been around 1944 when there was no-one around. I was staying at Brackenclose and was soloing around the Pinnacle face when I saw the line. There was a lot of rock with precious little on it, so I had it in mind for a long time, but I didn't fancy my chances then. I pointed Hugh up it; he climbed it easily. I can't remember anything difficult about it, but it was an enjoyable route." (10)

The result was Bos'n's Buttress, an amiable VS which climbs a series of steep cracks, shallow grooves and a tight little chimney that closely follows the right edge of Pisgah Buttress. The name derives from an old rugby song, which contains the phrase: 'The Bosun, cunning bugger that he was;' because, according to Griffin, Banner had been a cunning bugger to find his way around all the steep bits.

Whilst on that route, Banner had looked across Moss Gill and noticed another line that rises leftwards out of the gully; its initial slab and crack striking up the wall just left of and below the main pitch of Slab and Groove Route. The following day together with Jim O'Neil they climbed this rather delicate but interesting crack-line to a junction with Slab and Groove. They then moved leftwards and followed a slender slab and wide open chimney to eventually link up with Moss Ghyll Grooves. The route is more apparent from below the crag than from a distance, and it turned out to be a pleasant HVS. Interestingly it was originally named Narrow Slab, but in the 1967 guide Griffin changed its name to Narrow Stand.

At the very right-hand end of the Scafell Crag, as far right as anyone is willing to go, there will be found a steep crack-line at the point just before Deep Gill Buttress starts to deteriorate into broken ground. This is obvious from Hollow Stones, and it became the first new route to be climbed on Scafell by a tall, rather cumbersome, bespectacled physics graduate who worked at the nearby Sellafield nuclear plant; Les Brown. Les seemed to have a permanent stoop, presumably from ducking under doorways for all his adult life, but he was an elegant and powerful climber. In the company of Mike Yates, a fellow student from Manchester University, Brown led the prominent V-groove and the sustained crack which Yates called Xerxes, an interesting and sustained HVS. This is not the usual classic Brown route, being rather spoiled by some suspect rock and vegetation. Les muses:

> "I chose this line because it was the first bit of unclimbed rock I saw, and there was very little on this buttress, and I remember thinking 'There's bugger all on that', so we went up and pinched the most obvious line. At that point I hadn't cottoned on to The East Buttress." (11)

Above: The initial pitch of Bos'n's Buttress is surprisingly steep, as Joe Holden discovers.
Below: Keith Phizacklea on the pleasant first pitch of Narrow Stand, which was Hugh Banner's best contribution to the crags of Scafell.

Les Brown, legendary Lake District pioneer.

Geoff Oliver.

It wasn't long before Les Brown turned his attention to The East Buttress. Walking leftwards from Overhanging Wall, he spotted a steep brown wall which normally spouts water from a huge green mossy carpet. The crag at this point has an easy angled base, inviting inspection from curious suitors, but then it rises steeply where it oozes spittle and snot from the overhangs above. The situation is impressive; this is an intimidating part of the crag that has a certain degree of attraction for those who strive for a bit of adventure after their breakfast. Taking advantage of the summer drought, Les and Tom Gerrard wove their way up the lower slabs, moving around bulges to reach a grass ledge after two pitches. They examined the steep wall above which was wet, and they were unable to climb any further. To make matters worse, they became aware the weather was clouding in, and so decided to retreat. Unfortunately their two 100ft. ropes didn't quite reach the ground and they were forced to make use of a spike right on the lip of an over-hanging wall to complete the descent. By all accounts this was a real nightmare!

Les returned with Gerald Lund to complete the route. The steep wall that stopped his earlier attempt required a peg for aid to overcome a particularly awkward bulge and the line continued rightwards over easier ground to reach the base of the White Slab. The route originally finished up the final corner line of Overhanging Wall, but the guidebook now describes it as following a later independent variation called The Doomwatch Finish. Brown called this now neglected line Moonday, because he thought it was climbed on the day that the Soviet Luna 2 space probe became the first man-made object to impact on the surface of the moon. (Pedantic readers will note the route was climbed the day after the rocket was launched, two days before it actually crashed onto the moon). When asked why he selected this rather unappealing line for his first new route on The East Buttress, Brown replied with a refreshing admission of naivety that it was the first large unclimbed piece of rock you met as you walked under the crag.

The most influential route climbed on The East Buttress in 1960 was Ichabod, which was destined to be one of the great classic lines of The Lakes. It was such an obvious unclimbed feature that it had been pre-named by Pete Greenwood many years earlier; taking his inspiration from the final words of the 1924 guidebook by C. F. Holland, which read: "And so we leave the history of Scafell at a time when the future is bright with the possibility of great developments, a time when there is no danger of the call of Ichabod, a time when we may feel that the best is yet to come." (12) Ichabod is an ancient Hebrew saying, said to mean 'The Glory has departed' or literally 'Inglorious'. Holland used the term to signify that there was no chance of Scafell falling into obscurity, and the best had not yet been climbed. It is obvious Holland recognised the huge outstanding potential of The East Buttress, even though there was little he could have done about it with the gear of 1936.

Early in 1960 the Newcastle based team of Geoff Oliver and Maurice St John Jarre went up to The East Buttress in thick mist to have a go at Hell's Groove, but they became disorientated and inadvertently ended up attempting instead the line of Ichabod. It was only later when they checked the guide did they realise they had not failed on Hell's Groove at all; they had been trying something new. Oliver had seen the potential and realised that here was his chance, so he soon returned with Geoff Arkless and Len Willis for another attempt on Ichabod. It follows an obvious corner line which is the first natural break to the left of Great Eastern Route. The upper corner line peters out at its base and is guarded by a large overhanging wall, leaving a difficult section of climbing at the start of the route. Oliver wrote his hair-raising first ascent account in a Fell & Rock Journal:

> "Above the belay a short overhanging corner crack followed and this led to a large niche below the roof, ten feet to the right was the corner I hoped to attain, and this was the immediate problem. On a rickety flake in the corner of the niche I arranged a line runner and tensioned to the right to reach a handhold at shoulder height. The hold was not big and the angle bulged slightly, but it seemed as though it might be just possible to mantelshelf on it. One hour and ten attempts later I realised it was not feasible, so I called in science in the form of a thin-bladed piton. At the side of the crucial hold was a crack, and a few gentle taps of the hammer pushed home the peg, jeopardising the existence of the hold by widening the crack.

"With a sling on this flimsy support, I straightened up to reach a good hold for the step across to the corner, and the first obstacle was overcome. The going was easier for 10 feet, then the angle steepened and I had to leave the corner for a diversion on the right wall. My route from here was dictated more by the position of the holds than by my own wishes and I progressed diagonally right by a succession of delicate mantleshelves. My objective was the foot of a V-chimney above and 20 feet to my left, but the few holds available still led me to the right. However, the prospect of reversing the moves I'd just made was appalling, so the only possible course was to push on. Eventually I came to a crack with reasonable handholds and here I rested after a fashion. The rope snaked down for 70 feet and dragged abominably through the pitons, but I was cheered by the sight of the V-chimney with which I was now level. The approach to it was via a narrow sloping ledge with no handholds at all in evidence. I dearly wanted a piton in the shallow crack which I was about to leave, but the best I could arrange was a combination of two pegs jammed side by side. The rope running through these helped to hold me in balance as I inched across the traverse. On reaching the chimney I found an ideal thread belay and the gravity of the situation disappeared completely. I was not at all surprised to learn that the ascent of this 110-foot pitch had taken three hours." (13)

Geoff explained a little more about the day:

"Of course, the thing that always gets mentioned nowadays is the infamous peg; the only thing I can say in my defence is when you get up there it looks a lonely way ahead without any prospects, you can't see anything else to come. Maybe I chickened out a bit, and I would have something to retreat from, but it was only an 'Ace of Hearts' peg that was tapped in, because nothing else would go in; but fair enough. I did manage to do it free at the age of 65 when I followed Chris Bonington up it; he led it really well and just put a nice little wire in it." (14)

After completing this first pitch, Oliver abseiled off, and returned to complete the route the following day. He actually abseiled down to the stance and dropped a rope for his second to follow, which must have been a daunting experience without the rope passing through the runners. The second pitch climbs a short V-chimney above, and gives the 5c crux of the route; this was well described by Allan Austin in *Hard Rock*:

"It was a delightful corner: lots of cunning moves and delicate bridging. True, it was wet and greasy – but that didn't detract from the enjoyment. Then came the crunch. I couldn't for the life of me find anything to pull. Something would have to be done quickly. I couldn't let the young whippersnappers above think that I was in difficulties. It wouldn't do at all. I was the one who was supposed to be showing them the way. I finished up trying to mantelshelf out onto the left-hand rib. It was a round, sloping boss and threatened to precipitate me into the truly awesome depths. An extra coil or two dropped around my knees – slack to enable me to appreciate the situation! By dint of getting a knee on, wedging a shoulder against the wall, and pushing my finger into the moss on the bulge above, I managed to achieve a position of verticality above that evil little glacis." (15)

Oliver had created a classic climb of considerable merit and Ichabod firmly put the E2 grade on the crag. It received a second ascent in 1962 by Chris Bonington and the third by Dave Miller in 1963, and it was repeated twice more later that year, including, according to local myth, an ascent by Don Whillans; by which time its status was confirmed as a true classic.

Above: Susan Jensen on the initial traverse of Ichabod.
Below: Geoff Oliver as seen on the only known first ascent photograph of Ichabod, he is on the traverse out right before he reached the first thread belay. Note the first pitch started from the ground, not from the ramp.

Robin Whitworth about to make the committing move on the initial traverse of Ichabod. The flake out right is where Oliver placed a peg for tension.

Photo: Al Phizacklea

There was an interesting incident on the third ascent, led by David Miller with guidebook writers Joe Griffin and John Wilkinson in tow. Miller passed the first peg, which he used for aid, and continued straight up to the thread belay at the base of the V-chimney, but he wasn't aware that he had completed the pitch. On the first ascent, Oliver had started from the grass terrace at the base of the crag, not from the top of the ramp as Miller had, which resulted in a pitch length of 110 feet. Miller had barely reached the mid-point of the rope and, with so much rope remaining, thought the belay must lay somewhere above. In continuing up the route he inadvertently ran both pitches together, and became the first leader to climb the route in what is now considered to be the modern style. When Griffin came to second the route he reached out to grab the sling on the aid peg, but Miller had only draped the sling over the top of the peg. As Griffin grabbed the sling it slipped off taking him with it, and he swung down below into the area of overhanging blank rock with the sling in his hand. To exacerbate the situation, the karabiner on his waist belt slipped around his back, and Joe was unable to swing upright. Despite many attempts he was unable to regain contact with the rock, so Miller tried to lower him to the ground. He was slumped in an agonising doubled-up position, but the rope wouldn't reach. It was fortunate that Wilkinson managed to start a pendulum motion towards the belay with his end of the rope and grab hold of Griffin's foot. They abandoned their attempt to follow the route, and they rescued Miller from his perch with a top-rope. (16)

Notwithstanding Ichabod becoming the classic of the crag, Oliver declined to mention its ascent in the historical section of the next Scafell guidebook; perhaps indicating a little too much modesty!

It was noted in Trevor Jones' *Cumbrian Rock* that Les Brown had abseiled down the line of Ichabod and had declined to lead it, stating that it would take too many pitons to force the climb. This is incorrect; the route Brown was actually referring to was the then unclimbed Central Pillar on Esk Buttress, and his reference to pegs was made about a direct finish of that route which wasn't climbed until 1979. (It was later to be called Strontium Dog.) Brown had intended to go and attempt Ichabod on the very same weekend as Oliver first climbed it, but was persuaded by his Langdale-based mates to attend the Isle of Man T.T. Races instead. When he returned to the mainland, he found that Oliver had beaten him to it! This was not the end of Les' association with Ichabod, because in September 1964 Terry Sullivan and he climbed the route free. This earliest free ascent of Ichabod was unearthed during the research for this book.

As dry conditions continued to stifle the usual stream of water down this part of the crag, Les Brown returned with Gerald Lund to tackle the steep bastion he had noticed to the left of Moonday. From the end of the second pitch of Moonday, he traversed further left into an area of even steeper rock with some tension from the rope to reach a ledge and belay. Then followed a difficult and quite precarious traverse across the steepest part of the buttress to below an overhanging crack. To climb this took three pegs for aid until the steepness relented and the upper section of Great Eastern Route could be reached. This route, appropriately named Armageddon, soon achieved notoriety for difficulty and inaccessibility, as normally there is a considerable wet section on the traverse. As usual for the time, it was originally given a grade of VS, but even in perfectly dry conditions in its free state, it is considered to be a tough E2.

Les used this route as an example of how modern guidebooks devalue the achievements of the earlier generation:

> "One thing that irritates me is when you see in the guidebooks the letters FFA at the bottom – First Free Ascent. There should be a DBN on these routes – Done Before Nuts! There's no concept now how these routes were done at the time, in most cases the only protection you had was a peg, you'd put it in for protection, and now there's a runner every 5 feet and they're a lot easier – so we should introduce a DBN in the guides. Had we known that we would be put on trial about the ethics of these routes twenty years later, we might have been a bit more cautious!" (17)

Above: The crux of Ichabod is emerging from this constricted groove on what used to be the second pitch, climber George Ullrich.

Scott Young climbing the second pitch of The Centaur. The open corner above belayer Dave Parton gives the direct version of the route.

Brown's final route on The East Buttress was also in 1960 and it is undoubtedly his best. The Centaur is an appropriately named line directly up the centre of the buttress, at the point where the angle of the crag changes between its left and right flanks. In fact, this route starts at the lowest point of the crag and finishes at the highest, making it one of the longest on The East Buttress. The lower portion of the route is steep, and it roughly follows a shallow groove line, but it cautiously steps left and right around any awkward sections encountered. Because of this wandering nature of the climbing, many climbers over the years have lost the original line and many subtle variations have been added, and many now climb the main groove directly at E1.

Above, the line trends left to finish with a spectacular layback in a very exposed position up the final split blocks. The result is a long, sustained HVS that has become a true classic climb.

The Centaur had previously been inspected in the 'thirties by Linnell and it had defeated Paul Ross, who left a piton in place to retreat following a torrential downpour. Ross got to theorising whether Les Brown got some of his new routes from hearing casual pub chatter about his abortive attempts! They certainly used to frequent the same pubs, and he considered the likelihood that these happened by coincidence was too great. Les confirmed that in the case of The Centaur he had heard of Ross' attempt, but he didn't notice his peg when he climbed the route. There is nothing unusual about this, as the line of Brown's route weaved around – so who knows? Ross may have been trying the more direct line which was avoided by Brown. Les recalled the day with a satisfied grin across his genial face:

> "The day I climbed Centaur was a wonderful day, but it started with bad omens. We were up really early, I had persuaded Steve Read to come and stay in my digs near Gosforth, because at the time I was working at Sellafield. We rode up the side of Wasdale on my motorbike full of the joys of spring, it was a perfect day and the crags were warm and dry. Anyhow, we were just coming into that part of the road where the walls narrow just before the turn off to Brackenclose when we met the bloody bread van coming the other way. I was on the wrong side of the road and realised we couldn't make it onto the right side; so I aimed to pass him on the inside and luckily he realised what I was doing at the last minute. I just managed to get through the gap between him and the drystone wall by kicking the van with one foot and the wall with my other, and I came out of the other end; he screeched to a stop, but I thought I'm not stopping, so I carried on to the hut.
>
> "We got the gear sorted and set off, and Steve hadn't said a word! When we got up to Brown Tongue, he broke the silence and said 'Les', and I said 'Yes', then he said with deadly seriousness, 'Do you always drive like that?' Anyhow, it was one of those days where I couldn't put a foot wrong, Centaur was a complicated thing, but everything just went like a dream from beginning to end and we got to the top. I hadn't inspected the route beforehand, and was amazed to find the layback crack at the top; it was a fantastic way to finish a superb route. Steve asked to do Central Buttress, so we did that and Moss Ghyll Grooves before we came down – and the pub was still open! [In those days the lunchtime drinking session closed at 3 p.m.] It was one of those days when you could do anything; it was the best days' climbing I ever had in Britain.
>
> "I'd tried Centaur once before with Richard McHardy, but I couldn't get up the first groove, and it was a very cold day. I know Paul Ross had tried it but I don't recall his peg, I might have just forgotten it. One thing that annoyed me later was that Bill Birkett once wrote an article saying I had put my own peg in and it really infuriated me, so I rang him and gave him a bloody earful. I was so pleased when I did it, there was no frigging or nothing, everything went in sequence." (17)

Les Kendall and Dennis English added a route on the front of the Pinnacle Face to the left of Hopkinson's Gully; The Left Edge. They had enjoyed a long day on The East Buttress, and were attracted by the sunshine on The Pinnacle where they intended to climb Hopkinson's Gully. It was only when Les was committed and a long way up the initial corner that he realised what he was on hadn't been climbed before. He moved right to overlook Hopkinson's, and continued up to join the Waiting Room in one long pitch. (He was climbing on a 300 foot [90 metre] rope). He was puzzled as to why a clean, steep flake chimney to the left of The Mantelshelf move had not been climbed, so he used this as the finish of his route. The Left Edge has since become somewhat neglected to Les' dismay, for he thought it was a rather fine climb.

Les Kendall.

Dennis English.

Dave Parton on the immaculate layback which forms the final pitch of The Centaur.

In the pub at Wasdale Head that night, someone amongst the large group of climbers stood up in a rather volubly inebriated state and announced they had witnessed 'the first new route to have been added to the Pinnacle for 42 years', and asked who the climber was. Les raised his hand, but was surprised to find another climber raised his at the same time. It was soon established this was Jeff Allison who unknown to Les had also climbed a new route on the Pinnacle that day. (18)

Jeff Allison and Gerry Rawbotham had just added Right-Hand Edge and Pinnacle Face Direct Finish, a delightful, varied route that starts from the gangway of Jones' Route Direct. Here it moves rightwards across the slabs to reach a sloping stance below a band of overhangs. Skirting these on the left, the route moves back delicately to the very edge of the buttress overlooking the lower part of Deep Gill. A second large overhang above this slab then forces the climber spectacularly out right onto the steep gully wall, and up a series of overlapping sloping shelves which are poorly protected and very exposed, until the Hopkinson's Cairn Ledge is gained. The top pitches weave across the upper part of The Pinnacle, taking in the two little niches noted as obvious features of the face. Allison recalled the day:

> "There was nothing on that side of the Pinnacle in those days; that part of the crag probably wasn't popular in the sixties; those climbs seemed to be from the Victorian age. It was a good example of slab climbing, but the bit above Deep Gill was awkward; it slopes out on a series of little ledges and I had to stand about a while; there was no gear in those days. From Hopkinson's Ledge we traversed across to Slingsby's Chimney to a belay, and then traversed back right into what seemed like a couple of slabby grooves. I remember stepping up on nothing to get onto this second slab, again there was no protection, but it was a fine, spectacular finish." (19)

To this day, Right Hand Edge is the best route of HVS standard on the main face of Scafell Crag. Interestingly, the earlier guidebooks split it into two separate routes, and the first ascent section dates the lower section as 1960, whilst the upper part was dated 1961.

Photo: Al Phizacklea

Photo: Gordon Stainforth

Above: This view depicts Martin Bagness on the intimidating section of Right-Hand Edge Route where it ascends the steep, fluted wall above the depths of Deep Gill.

Left: This photograph depicts Colin Beechey moving on to the initial slab above The Gangway on Right-Hand Edge, the route continues diagonally to the top right of the picture. This photograph originally appeared in '*Eyes to the Hills*' where it was captioned as 'Moss Ledge Direct', being described as 'rather serious for the grade.' This was obviously the result of route finding error, as Beechey is on a HVS 5a pitch, not the expected MVS 4b of Moss Ledge Direct.

Russian Climbers on Scafell

Following the 1958 British Caucasus expedition the leader, Sir John Hunt, invited an official group of five Russian mountaineers to visit Britain. During their visit the Russians visited Wasdale on 1 June 1960 as guests of the Fell & Rock Climbing Club. This was during the 'cold war' when the 'iron curtain' was a very real barrier to any travel or contact between the peoples of the Soviet Union and the West, so the hosts had no idea what the Russians would be like, how well they could climb, and if they would be friendly.

Anatoli Ouchinnikov and Eugine Tur compare gear with Joe Griffin (centre rear) at Mickledore during the Russian visit to Scafell.

Two of the Russian climbers, Anatoli Ouchinnikov and Eugene Tur, walked over from Langdale and were met by their hosts on Mickledore. The weather was perfect for climbing and the rocks were dry. They spoke no English, and as their translator had remained with the others, communication was very limited. However, they were very relaxed and friendly. Their equipment was basic, with 'baseball type' boots for climbing, but they did have a webbing waist belt to tie on to the rope. At this time the hosts had just started using P.A. rock boots, but still tied the rope round the waist.

Photo: FRCC Archives

FRCC members gather with their guests from the USSR on the wall behind Brackenclose, from left to right (back row) Joe Griffin, Anatoli Ouchinnikov, Albert Ashworth, Dennis English; (front row) Dave Thomas, Michail Borushko (President of the USSR Mountain Federation), Misha Kergiani (Translator and presumably KGB minder), Joseph Kakhiani (Role unknown, presumably a second KGB minder), Eugine Tur, Peter Moffat and David Miller.

Winter climbing adventures, early 1960's

By the 1950s, the main gullies of Scafell had been climbed but no one had ventured onto the steeper face routes. Les Kendall was to change that in December 1960. Riding high from just completing the first winter ascent of North-West Climb on Pillar, Les called on John Douglas. His infectious enthusiasm persuaded John, who owned a car, to drive to Wasdale the following day to try Great Eastern on The East Buttress of Scafell. Its summer line zigzags along ramps; first left then right through the steep imposing walls of The East Buttress at a very amenable VS grade. Climbing was in nailed boots with a traditional ice axe plus a slater's hammer where the narrow pick was a good substitute for an ice hammer; yet to be generally recognised as a second ice tool. The winter crux of the route is the few moves where the ramp steepens and narrows before the zag back right. These thinly covered mixed climbs were an excellent choice of route for the more primitive straight pointed axe picks of the day, which had limited holding power in pure ice but could be torqued effectively in cracks. Only two days later Les, with Jeff Allison, made an ascent of Mickledore Chimney by the icefall start and finish.

The legendary winter of 1963 saw Kendal and Allison again in action, this time on the chimney Direct Start to Steep Gill. Unrecorded at the time, this waited 27 years for its next ascent by Davison and Hewitt who thought they were doing the first ascent.

The Shamrock Cascade Route saw its first winter ascent by Bob Bennett and Royanne Lavender in January 1969, the pair returning in 1972 to add the Lost Arrow Variation while Bill Pattison and A. Dunn added The Pillar.

These notes illustrate difficulties surrounding recording of the earlier winter routes. Knowledge of ascents was mainly spread by word of mouth and with time the details became forgotten, and subsequent ascentionists were led to assume they were on a first ascent.

Climbers on the start of the Shamrock Cascade route in the winter of 2010. The Pillar climbs the obvious monolithic icicle up the centre.

Russian Climbers (continued)

Each Russian was accompanied by two hosts on the climbs, which made communication easier, and initially the climbs were led by the hosts. Anatoli was accompanied by David Miller and Peter Moffat and Eugene by Dennis English and Des Birch. The Russians had little difficulty climbing the routes; they enjoyed the climbing and were good company. The first climb was the classic Central Buttress, with the Direct Finish. This was followed by Great Eastern Route, with the Yellow Slab finish and it was here that Anatoli indicated he wanted to lead. The Yellow Slab crosses an impressive and serious part of The East Buttress and at that time belays and protection were poor. It was not possible to describe the line of the route to Anatoli, so it was with some trepidation that the hosts held his rope while he led the pitches. They should not have worried; they later found out that Anatoli was a Master of Sport of the Soviet Union and one of their top mountaineers.

That evening the visitors were invited to meet the Fell & Rock President and many members of the club at a celebration dinner at the Wasdale Head Hotel. A commemorative banner presented to the club from the Russians hangs in the entrance hall of the Brackenclose hut. (20)

Photo: Al Phizacklea

The banner presented to the FRCC by the visiting Soviet team hangs proudly inside Brackenclose.

Gear of the early 1960s

Climbing gear used in the early sixties was primitive and little better than it was thirty years before. Instead of tying the rope directly round the waist, most people wrapped a long nylon sling several times around the waist into which the rope was tied directly, or with a karabiner, to create a waist loop.
Paul Ross used a typical rack of the period; 4 or 5 Goldline slings which were ¼ inch thick, each with a steel karabiner. He remembers there were only two sizes of peg that were available; a ½ inch Simond channel piton and a vertical ex-army blade, and he normally carried two of each. It was a case of finding a crack to fit the peg, rather than finding a peg to fit the crack! It is also interesting to note how the rope was usually clipped directly into the peg, which often caused severe rope drag.

Photo: Al Phizacklea

A selection of early Clog tapered chocks and two drilled out machine nuts show a typical rack from the early 1960's.

In certain circumstances, it had been noted how the knot in a sling could be jammed into a crack just above a narrow section. This could be used as a runner or a belay, but its application was strictly limited. The art of slotting pebbles into cracks and threading a rope behind them had been developed in Wales and was practised for many years; climbers would often carry a few pebbles in their pockets for this purpose. In the early part of the decade, the use of engineering nuts instead of pebbles for wedging in cracks became commonplace.
This practice is widely believed to have been developed in Wales by Jack Soper and Dave Gregory, who picked up spare hexagonal nuts found alongside the Snowdon railway track.

During the early 1960's, two teams added a variety of routes around the flanks of the main crags after a search for lines that had been overlooked during the recent spate of exploration. Jeff Allison and Roger Mansfield discovered Slab Climb (VS) on the upper flank of The Pinnacle, starting from the left end of the grass ledge cutting across the base of the upper pinnacle, and separating the slabs from the steep broken ground that drops into Deep Gill. It is a rather unbalanced route; a short hard wall leads to slabs which lead leftwards with ease to join the top of Low Man. This was the line below Central Route on the Deep Gill Slabs that was initially top-roped by Harry Kelly in 1919.

Photo: Al Phizacklea

Jeff Allison, climber and sailor.

Jeff continued with his climbing activities until 1967, when a serious alpine accident caused him to re-assess his priorities. He became a long distance sailor, but one who took to the more adventurous aspect of that sport. In 2007 he and his 2 man crew became the second team to sail a fibreglass yacht through the North-West Passage, through arctic Canada. (They were only beaten to second place by a single day by a team from the USA). In 2009 he requested to navigate the North-East Passage, above Siberia to become the first ever person to sail around the Arctic Ocean in a yacht but the Russian authorities denied him permission. Undaunted, Jeff simply turned to starboard when he left Murmansk and sailed east undetected to the most northerly point of Russia. Here the sea ice threatened to trap his boat, so he returned only to be arrested by the Russian navy.
The authorities must have been impressed by his spirit, because they only imposed a paltry £5 fine and told him not to enter Russian waters for another five years.

This same pair also climbed The Hanging Chimney, a long-neglected line on the front face of Scafell Crag. At the extreme left end of the main crag, well left of Collier's and The Keswick Brothers' Climb, it is hardly ever noticed by visitors.

> "You had to traverse right to get into the groove, it was a bit more than a groove really; it was a big sentry box, but you're getting a decent drop under you by then. I put in a peg for protection because there was a loose stone about this big [gestures with hands held 18 inches apart] on a sloping shelf, probably someone has kicked it out by now. It was just another one of those little gaps between wherever, and we gave it VS because everything was VS in those days." (24)

On a recent ascent, the neglected and unpopular nature of The Hanging Chimney was very evident. The loose block (of a similar size as this book) was still precariously lying at the foot of the chimney, and the route itself, awkward and poorly protected, was considered to be more like E2 than HVS! However, the steep wall that encloses the chimney is seamed by several thin cracks, and may still become attractive to the modern climber armed with a brush. For present day extremists it may be that this historical section could make rewarding reading!

On the 17th June1962, the very same day that the classic Central Pillar was climbed on the nearby Esk Buttress, there was a fearsome accident on The East Buttress. An early reference was in *Hard Rock*, where Paul Nunn noted in his article on Central Pillar: "The 'first team' off from Langdale picked the plum while, less than a mile away, two other climbers of the '59 generation died below The East Buttress." (24) The climbers were Alban Crowther, 22, and Derek Turner, 24; both students and members of Liverpool University Climbing Club, who were enjoying a meet on Scafell. They were climbing Trinity, and according to witness Richard Courchee:

Courtesy of The Whitehaven News.

Three Men Killed in Lake District Fells Accidents

BLISTERS ON THEIR FEET

Wigton Dustmen Blame Gumboots

DUSTMEN who work for Wigton Rural Council are rebelling against wear ing gumboots with steel toe-caps. They are tired of throbbing feet and blisters and hours spent soaking their feet in warm water at home. They want the Council to stop issuing the boots. The Council is to discuss the matter.

DECLINED

The trouble started when two men declined a recent offer to have a pair of steel-tipped boots. The two are Mr. Joseph Armstrong, 49, of Greenacres, Wigton, who has been a dust-man for five years, and Mr. John Coulthard, 32, of Brindle-field, Wigton.

Mr. Armstrong said: "These steel-tipped boots were issued a year ago. I don't wear them because they are too heavy—three times heavier than an ordinary shoe and they give you very tired feet. I was asked recently if I wanted a pair at the time of re-issue. I refused—I would rather wear my own boots.

THREE young men, all of them experienced climbers, were killed on the Lake District fells at the week-end. Two of them were climbing together on one of the most difficult climbs on Scawfell on Sunday when they crashed 500 feet to their death. The other victim lost his life on Saturday when he was descending an easy gully on Dow Crag, near Coniston.

The Scawfell accident was the result of a stone being dislodged while two members of the Liverpool University Climbing Club were tackling one of the Lake District's most difficult climbs, "The Trinity" — a sheer wall on Scawfell (3,162ft.) which faces towards Eskdale. The rumble of falling stones was heard by nearby climbers and the bodies of the two men were seen flying through the air, bouncing several times as they fell 500 feet to their deaths.

While one climber went to Wasdale Head to get stretcher parties, others went to the foot of East Buttress where they found the two climbers — one dead and the other dying. With the aid of members of the Out-

piece falling, followed by a larger piece about 4ft. wide and two bodies flying through the air," he added.

Mr. Courchee said he could not say for certain whether the two men were still roped together as they fell. He thought that after finishing their meal one of them had just moved off and must have dislodged a loose rock accidentally.

Calculated Risk

Dr. Charles I. Jones, of Seascale, said both men died from skull fractures and brain lacerations. Crowther would die instantly but Turner may have survived for a short while.

Mr. Gough said he was satisfied that the two men were

Visiting Whi Delle Stivire have set up Tuesday, Mr.

SIR JOI

"They were about 150 feet up sitting on a ledge, apparently eating, just before the accident. There was a shout that loose rock was coming down. I saw one small piece falling followed by a larger stone about four feet wide and two bodies falling through the air."

Crowther was killed instantly, and as Courchee ran down to Wasdale for assistance, Turner died shortly afterwards cradled in the arms of his distraught friend, Hugh Banner. (26)

It is not certain exactly what happened. Perhaps the pair had sat on a belay ledge, eaten a snack, and when one of them moved off he disturbed a loose rock that sent him tumbling off the crag, pulling his partner and his belay block after him. The evidence of 'a larger stone' points to the possibility of belay failure. They were still roped together, although another witness at the inquest stated that he was uncertain whether the two had been roped together at the time of the accident. Questions were even raised at the inquest by the coroner as to whether the newly introduced 'P.A.s' were suitable footwear for such a difficult climb! This accident certainly had an effect on the climbers of that generation; little wonder Trinity was avoided, albeit subconsciously, for many years afterwards.

In 1963 Allison, partnered by Dave Moy, ascended Overhanging Grooves on The East Buttress, but this turned out to be a disappointing route. The huge overhanging flake dominating this part of the crag which forms the modern first pitch of Overhanging Grooves Direct is a prominent feature, too obvious to ignore.

Gear - early 1960s (continued)

A sling was threaded directly through the hole, but it was soon realised there was benefit in drilling out the sharp-edged threaded portion of the nut to give a smooth inner hole, through which the rope was threaded. Various sized nuts were often used on the same sling; the smallest were commonly called 'Meccano' nuts. (21)

The first 'wedge' shaped nut was developed in 1961 by a Sheffield blacksmith, John Brailsford, who developed a taper-sided wedge of aluminium which was named after the Mountain Activity import company, and the 'MOAC' was born. This became the classic design of nut, and it was developed in several different sizes. These are still occasionally carried by older climbers today, probably for sentimental reasons.

A selection of MOAC nuts available from the mid-sixties, clockwise from the top:- Baby MOAC, MOAC 2, original MOAC and MOAC 4.

Before long the first nut held by wire was developed by Chas Curtiss, a Professor of Geology at Manchester University, using a method of casting the aluminium nut directly around the ends of a looped piece of wire. However, the heat affected the wire and made the assembly brittle. When Jack Soper attempted the second ascent of Vector at Tremadoc, he fixed a prototype of one of these wires in the final crack and then fell off. Unfortunately the fall stripped the wires out of the aluminium, letting Jack fall a long way. This method of attaching wires to the nuts was superseded by a single loop of wire joined by a swaged joint, thus creating the prototype of the nut we know today.

Gear - early 1960s (continued)

Early versions used thick, rigid wires making them unwieldy, with a tendency to lift out of the cracks by rope drag. The first wires Les Brown ever saw were made by Brian 'Killer' Henderson (So called because he was a karate expert, and once naively claimed in a drunken moment that he could kill a man with his bare hands – sarcasm ensured the nick-name stuck).

Photo: Al Phizacklea

This is a typical rack of wires available in the early 1970's before the micro-wires became available; note the typically rigid wires of the time.

Les recalls:

"I met Killer at Shepherds where we were going to do Fisher's Folly. 'I've got some gear, have a look at these' he said, pulling out these wires. 'What's this, what the hell are you supposed to do with them?' I asked. Anyhow, he put them into the crack for runners, and as he went across the traverse, they all lifted and ended up hanging in a big ball in the middle of his rope. Just at this point, Don Whillans came up to the foot of the crag and shouts up 'Hey up mate, can y' get ITV on that aerial?' (22)

In fact it was the widespread introduction of nuts that was one of the reasons why Whillans abandoned rock climbing to concentrate on the higher mountains of the world. He said to Rod Valentine:

"Aye, when they brought out nuts, that's when I gave up climbing, because it meant that with nuts people could get up the same routes I had climbed without them!" (23)

The modern micro-wire did not appear until 1972, when an American Yvon Chouinard developed the 'Stopper' range. These revolutionised the potential for using thin cracks for protection, and thus made the sport much safer. Using tie offs for extending the nuts and reducing rope drag did not become common practice until the early 1980's.

The crack behind the flake was too narrow to enter and climb by chimneying, but too wide to fit any pegs or nuts for runners; it is truly an intimidating feature. They started up this flake, then as the first ascent description instructs: "Traverse right across the overhanging wall using four pegs, a line sling and a wire sling for aid to reach [a] niche in the central groove. Natural runner. Move right onto a steep wall. Use an ace peg and pull into the little groove on Great Eastern."

Allison and Moy escaped right using seven points of aid; not the sort of climbing that exudes quality. They had spent so long on this pitch that they retreated to the pub. Dave went his separate way, and Jeff went around the bar asking for someone to accompany him on the upper part of his project. Chris Mitchell seemed keen, but announced that he was recovering from a recent broken arm, to which Jeff replied that it didn't matter! They made their way up Great Eastern to the belay, and then climbed a delightful clean pillar above the base of the Yellow Slab to finish. This fine top pitch was the saving grace for the route; and despite use of considerable aid, it was included in the next Scafell guidebook.

Photo: Al Phizacklea

Dave Birkett reaches the base of The Yellow Slab on Overhanging Grooves Route. The current route description follows the sunlit corner above, which is slow to dry and forms the main pitch for the winter climb Never Ever Say Never, first climbed by Birkett in 2010. The original line, taken by Allinson and Mitchell started up this pitch, before traversing right along a small ramp to finish up the crack system up the front of the buttress.

Joe Griffin and John Wilkinson were the other team pioneering routes around this time. In one amazing eleven day session in 1963, they visited Scafell ten times and Esk Buttress on the other day, walking up each day from Brackenclose, demonstrating their dedication to checking the routes for the forthcoming Scafell guidebook. In this spell they climbed four new routes.

Their first was something of a wandering affair, rising from the lower right edge of Pisgah Buttress across to the top left side, and entering Moss Gill before taking a steep crack in the right wall above the Collie Step. Joe Griffin admits that he tried to make use of the untrodden parts of this buttress, but the resulting route was somewhat disappointing. Moses Trod, has since been demoted in the guide to a single paragraph (instead of the usual pitch by pitch description) which includes derogatory comments such as 'unsatisfactory', 'inferior' and 'ill-defined'; not anything to arouse desire!

Griffin and Wilkinson also climbed Absinthe, a rather poor MVS that starts from the dank depths of Mickledore Chimney. This is the furthest-right route to be found on The East Buttress, and its isolation as well as lack of quality has resulted in its neglect. Around on the left end of The East Buttress, they also discovered a variation start to Gremlins Groove which follows a vague groove to its left. Joe thought at the time this was slightly better than the normally greasy start to the route, but again this end of the crag has been left alone by climbers and their variation has seen very few ascents. Their best effort was Shamrock Buttress, a long VS on the same named crag below the main Scafell massif. It starts at the lower right end of the buttress and rises in a delicate line along an exposed diagonal rib cut off from base of the crag by a band of overhangs. The route continues more directly up a chimney line before it merges in with the upper part of Tower Buttress but, along with many of the routes on Shamrock, this has slipped into the realms of obscurity, despite it covering some areas of impressive rock.

Joe Griffin, who was co-author of the 1967 Scafell guidebook.

An unusual rising girdle of Deep Gill Buttress was completed by Don Greenop and Joe Wilson, but it has never been fully described in any guidebook. They climbed from right to left, but it was the manner of the crossing of the deep crevasse of The Great Chimney that led to its exclusion. This crossing had been achieved by lassoing a large block on the opposite side of the gulf; a wild-west manoeuvre that couldn't guarantee any safety. Greenop recalled:

> "We tied a bowline knot in the end of the rope, and managed to lasso a block on the opposite side of the chimney on our second attempt. We tested the rope by abseiling down to the bottom of the chimney and pulled on it, carefully at first, obviously; and then Joe tried his full weight on it. He managed to climb the rope with ease; he was full of confidence at the time." (27)

Prussicking up the rope must have taken some nerve, as there was no guarantee the rope would stay in place, or that the block was solid! Joe Wilson said: "Don got me to try the prussick first. It was pointless letting him weight the rope first because Don had never been more than eight stones in his life!" (28)

Don called this rope manoeuvre the 'Viet Armis' pitch, which is a legal axiom that defines the act of trespass with force and arms that results in the injury to another person or property – take a clue from that! This unique and adventurous outing, named The Inamorata Route (which means someone who is obsessed with an activity, such as climbing), was felt to be too unjustifiably risky for the general public and was left out of the guide. Readers may go and repeat it if they like that sort of thing, but just bear in mind they do so at their own risk!

Keith Phizacklea struggles to enter the flared base of The Hanging Chimney.

Footnotes

1. Al Phizacklea, 2008
2. Les Brown, FRCC audio recording, 2008
3. Peter Greenwood, FRCC audio recording, 2008
4. Paul Ross, email to author, 2011
5. Jack Soper, e-mail to author, 2008
6. Les Brown, FRCC audio recording, 2008
7. Paul Ross, e-mail to author, 2009
8. Geoff Oliver, FRCC audio recording, 2008
9. Geoff Oliver, FRCC audio recording, 2008
   On the occasion mentioned, Les Brown was the first to climb the entire route free.
10. Joe Griffin, FRCC audio recording, 2008
11. Les Brown, FRCC audio recording, 2008
12. A.T. Hargreaves, Scafell guidebook 1936
13. Geoff Oliver 'Recent Developments on Scafell' *FRCC Journal* 1962
14. Geoff Oliver, FRCC audio recording, 2008
15. Allan Austin, from 'Ichabod', *Hard Rock* 1974
16. John Wilkinson, FRCC audio recording, 2008
17. Les Brown, FRCC audio recording, 2008
18. Les Kendall, telephone conversation with the author, 2008
19. Jeff Allison, FRCC audio recording, 2008
20. David Miller, article commissioned for this book
21. Jack Soper, e-mail to author, 2008
22. Les Brown, FRCC audio recording, 2008
23. Don Whillans, as recalled by Rod Valentine, FRCC audio recording, 2008
24. Jeff Allison, FRCC audio recording, 2008
25. Paul Nunn, from 'Central Pillar', *Hard Rock* 1974
26. Richard Courchee, telephone conversation with the author, 2008
27. Don Greenop, telephone conversation with the author, 2009
28. Joe Wilson, telephone conversation with the author, 2009

1965 - 1973

Halcyon Days of Traditional Climbing

Photo: Al Phizacklea

Above: Chris Bonington.
Below: Mike Thompson.

Photo: Ken Wilson

Overleaf:
George Ullrich races against the gathering storm clouds on the sensationally exposed top pitch of the Nazgul.
Photo: Ed Luke

Right: Brian Wright about to commit to the crux move around the arête on Holy Ghost.

In 1965, Chris Bonington and Mike Thompson made an attempt at a left to right girdle traverse of The East Buttress, as one of the biggest unclimbed challenges still left in Cumbria. At this time Bonington was on the verge of becoming one of the best known climbers in the country due to his courtship of the media over his Himalayan expeditions and television broadcasts. Bonington always stated that Thompson was the brains behind the team; he had a knack for spotting the lines, but he always let Chris lead the routes, as he was considered to be the better climber.

They started up Gremlin's Groove and moved across to a belay at the top of the first pitch of Trinity. Climbing up Trinity for a few metres a spike runner then allowed a traverse right onto the steep pillar on undercut holds; the moves felt off balance and he became worried by a lack of protection.
He wrote:

> "No way of reversing those moves; no runners; a long frightening drop; but I just kept going, with a pull over the overlap on small, rounded holds that led on up round the corner with the silent threat of vanishing altogether. I reached a tiny, sloping ledge some 40 feet from my last runner; there were hardly any handholds and my courage quota had oozed out of my 'P.A.s'. I had to get a runner in, but where and how? The way to Hell's Groove was barred by overhanging rock, there seemed to be no line above, and I certainly couldn't retreat or even abseil off. I noticed some climbers coming up from Eskdale, and to my shame I called for a top-rope." (1)

Photo: Al Phizacklea

The 'climbers' approaching the crag were actually three soldiers on exercise (Trevor Jones spices this anecdote up accordingly: 'In his best parade ground voice Bonington orders them to produce a top-rope'). All they could do was pass on the message to the only other climbers on the crag, a party who were halfway up Mickledore Grooves which included John Wilkinson. Bonington would have to wait! He had underestimated the difficulty and seriousness of the pitch; a precarious situation was also noted in a chapter of his own book *Lakeland Rock*: "It was a blind alley and I'd had it, the only thing I could have done was to jump off." However, as he waited for the rescue to arrive, he settled down and discovered a small drilled out hexagonal nut could be wriggled into a crack low down. After another half-hour of deliberating, he made a move upwards and found he was on easier rock. The climbing here consists of steep delicate movements on rounded holds; never desperate, but neither giving any easy moves, and it led further away from that critical runner. Eventually a small alcove was reached and the nightmare was over.

It was interesting to hear a slightly different version of this epic when Chris was interviewed for this book:

> "It was early in the year and it was bitterly cold. I managed to do the hard pitch on Holy Ghost, and I was absolutely and totally freaked. So I brought Mike up to me; we only had a single rope and anyway the belay was lousy, so we couldn't abseil off, so we were stuck. Anyway I'm pretty sure there was a Fell & Rock party who were below us, and I asked them to give us a top rope when they finished their climb, and they said yes. Half an hour later there was no sign of them, and by that time a) we were getting cold, and b) I was getting my courage back, so I led out and finished the route." (2)

Bonington named the route Holy Ghost; at E2, 5c. It had certainly made an impression on him, but it caused controversy at the time as some thought the name was blasphemous. He recalls how they "were castigated left, right and centre for giving it a religious name, but it was merely a variation on Trinity". Although Holy Ghost was a product of a failed attempt at the girdle, Chris considers it to be the thinnest and hardest first ascent he ever made. From out of a frightening failure, Bonington had found an impressive new route, which had been devalued somewhat in the previous guide as 'a meandering line of mostly historical interest'. It is claimed that Ron Mosely climbed a similar but higher line back in 1957, but this was never recorded, and on investigation there seems to be little evidence to support the claim.

1966 was the last year that Les Brown was active in The Lakes, as he was soon to move to Scotland. Before he left he started to secretly investigate the steep crack left of Central Buttress, a long admired project that had been attempted on a top rope by Arthur Dolphin as early as 1945. This line had also been attempted by Paul Ross one wild and windy day sometime around 1961 or 1962. He had almost climbed the initial crack to a point where he was standing in a sling on a peg and his next move to the easier corner which led to the first belay required the aid of a nut. At this time he didn't own any nuts and a sudden downpour of heavy rain forced him to retreat from the peg. Ross was prevented from returning to the line because shortly after he was hospitalised for almost a year with tuberculosis of the spine. Geoff Cram also attempted the line, but got little further than Ross' peg. It was clearly the major unclimbed line of the time.

Les Brown was fully aware of earlier attempts and was keen to attempt the route, but he did not want a crowd witnessing another possible failure. He was strongly quizzed by the close knit circle of Keswick climbers as to where his next big project lay and Brown blandly replied that he was going to have a look at Far East Buzzard Crag. This of course was a non-existent crag but it had a few of his competitors scanning the maps just to make sure … Brown went to Scafell with Ken Jackson and produced The Nazgul, a masterpiece which has now become a superb classic route. The initial steep crack required several attempts and it eventually succumbed to a peg and two nuts for aid. This was one of the few new routes that Les had abseiled down before climbing; he did this merely to remove a loose flake, not to clean or inspect the route.

George Smith on the strenuous initial crack of The Nazgul.

Above: Les Brown captured on the upper pitch of the first ascent of The Nazgul.

Below: Looking down to George Smith climbing the interlinked ramps on the superbly exposed top pitch of The Nazgul.

The following description by John Porter of this pitch was published in Ken Wilson's book *Extreme Rock:*

> "Unlike the situation elsewhere on the main crag, the rock here looks and feels steep as soon as you touch it. Alex and I settle down on the belay, openly pleased that Choe [Brookes] had won the toss. He started up amidst a barrage of encouraging insults. I remember that Jeff Lamb had been going well the day he gave it 5c. After a pause to struggle with wires at 20 feet, Choe continued methodically past the crux. The runners on his harness swung rhythmically in space to the motion of the crack dance: reach, jam, transfer weight and step ... My performance was much like Alex's. The holds are incut and positive to start, but at mid-height there is a bulge to solve on poor jams. As one's strength begins to run out, the holds reappear and the crack widens. Although the mind tells you it's getting easier, arms and lungs tell a different story." (3)

The middle pitch rises from Jeffcoat's ledge on C.B. and follows a surprisingly delicate scoop that makes the lack of protection most noticeable before reaching the upper ledge system on the crag. Brown then followed a ramp out left which reaches right into the centre of the headwall, and where this peters out a second higher ramp fortunately provides further progress to the finish. The result is a superbly exposed pitch, right on the edge of a hundred and twenty metre drop, and it provides an exhilarating finale to this magnificent route. The route wasn't free climbed for another ten years, and it now holds an E3, 5c, 5b, 5a grade. By calling it The Nazgul, Brown became responsible for starting the J.R. Tolkein themed route names from *The Lord of the Rings* books; Nazgul, Ringwraith, Caradhras, Edge of Eriador and Shadowfax are all derived from this source.

The large buttress of Shamrock came under further scrutiny from Dennis English, accompanied by the strong team of John Wilkinson, Rod Valentine and Joe Griffin. They added Silver Lining, another long VS which weaves its way up the left side of the buttress but covers some interesting and impressive ground. As Valentine recalls, he was a young lad raised on gritstone; and the team had intended that he was the one destined to climb the prominent Y-shaped crack up the front of the face:

> "The bottom line was I couldn't, it was too intimidating for the gear we had, it was in 1966 and we were just hanging slings on bits of spikes and stuff like that, and we didn't have the gear to give us the confidence to push on. Dennis also had a look at it and also backed off it, so we went up the groove to the side and bypassed it. That became that cracking pitch on Gilt Edge Eliminate some years later. It was called Silver Lining because it was a really gloomy day, there had been a bit of rain, but just as we finished the clouds parted and there it was; the silver lining." (4)

Joe Griffin fondly remembers this day. He recalls how the three climbers on the belays became so engrossed in conversation that they forgot to watch the rope of the person who was leading the route! He said that it was a very social occasion with excellent company; they were talking and laughing all the way up the route, one of those magic days you get on the hills. The quality continued right to the top; the last pitch followed a steep groove before traversing right under a roof to finish up a gently impending rib, above a huge drop to the screes below. Silver Lining gives the best route of its grade on this buttress, and at 164 metres long; it is over twice the length of other classics such as Moss Ghyll Grooves and Great Eastern Route.

The walls on the right side of Deep Gill were the location for two new routes in 1968; both following the wide central groove right of Grey Bastion. Trevor Martin and Joe Wilson attempted to follow the steep, deep crack in the right side of the groove, but the overhanging nature and increasing dankness of the upper part of the crack forced them into a short detour up the cleaner corner on the left. They finished up the continuation corner above the main groove to give the provocatively named Gobsite, VS. Originally the intention was to call it 'Gobshite', but they realised (correctly) that it wouldn't pass muster with the guidebook editorial team, so they named it as above. Joe explained in his unbridled West Cumbrian accent:

> "We called it that because we wanted to test the mettle of the guidebook team, but they were fuckn' spineless and they ended up changing the name to Gobsite. We went over to that route because there was someone on every route on the crag that day, and we saw this big stunning overhanging crack; but it turned out to be shite really." (5)

Four days later, Geoff Milburn and Dave Gregory climbed the left-hand corner of the same prominent groove throughout which merged with the start of Gobsite. They then swung out right to follow another steep corner line to the top. This route, Sleeping Crack, VS, was omitted from the 1974 guidebook because the writers mistakenly thought it followed the same line as Gobsite; but it was eventually included in the 1984 guide. However, it was not listed in first ascent details, which prompted Milburn to write an article for the 1988 *Fell & Rock Journal*. This brought the error to light and they were finally given credit for the route in the 1988 edition of the guidebook. In his article Milburn described an incident on the ascent where he bypassed a poised block in the steep groove:

> "I arranged a runner on one of the ropes in the line of the groove and held the other out of the danger zone. Fortunately the walls of the groove were as rough as any on the crag and by hitching up the breeches' crutch so that it was in contact with the part of the anatomy which it is designed to cover I was able to bridge past the block without touching it. Another runner above it and the incubus could be surveyed in safety. Its upper surface was horizontal and several smaller fragments, the largest the size of a house brick, rested on it. A tentative disturbance of one of these with a gentle toe set the block swaying, the heart pumping and the wallet cringing, the rope directly below it being my own. That I was not to be the one to disturb it was evident. Even the ropes are expensive, and there is a difference, even if only in degree, between flicking a few grams of pebble at one's companion and giving him the doubtful benefit of a hundredweight or so of best Scafell." (6)

Ken Jackson.

Around on the right-hand end of The East Buttress, north-eastern raider Ken Jackson and Johnny Adams found a surprisingly easy line with The Fulcrum, which finds a direct line up the crag to the right of Leverage.

The first short pitch climbs an awkward corner directly to a cramped stance on the initial ramp of Mickledore Grooves. The second climbs up to gain a hanging slab, which proved rather intimidating and can still give a worrying time for novice VS leaders. Ken Jackson recalled in his autobiography *Climbing in the Dark*:

> "This proved rather awkward and technically difficult, causing Johnny to pause and wrinkle his brow as he worked out the best way to tackle the problem, though once he had decided exactly what to do; he quickly surmounted the obstacle and moved up a slab to an overhung corner on the right.

The Fourth Scafell Guidebook

Joe Griffin took over the task of editing the guidebooks from Harry Kelly in the mid nineteen-sixties. Kelly had stubbornly hung on to the editing job for over thirty years and had reached the grand old age of 80 before he stepped down from the post. He had not been active for almost two decades but his imposing presence still ruled the guidebook committee with a strictness that included reluctance to modernise the guides. For example, he refused to allow an increase of the grades in the guidebooks above VS, he insisted that the old descriptions remained unchanged from those published in previous editions, and he didn't accept that a route which was less than 100 feet long was worth including. (A lot of climbers circumvented this rule by adding on an extra pitch of scrambling to the description, thus achieving the desired route length). Allan Austin and Griffin were the main instigators who finally persuaded him to step down from the post.

Heaton Cooper's diagram is a direct descendent from Arthur Marshall's original sketch of Scafell.

The 4th Scafell Guidebook (contd)

Griffin recalls:

"I wanted to indicate the quality of the route, whether it was good, bad or indifferent, which wasn't done in Kelly's day. The other thing I tried to do was bring grading up to the modern days, I even wrote a paper on advancing the grades, but it was very hard with the guidebook committee and they wouldn't budge. As a fervent soloist, I couldn't care less about the overall grade of the route which took into account protection and the like, this was irrelevant to a soloer, to him the individual technical grade of each pitch was more important. At the time, the FRCC were very entrenched, I couldn't get them to accept that times had changed; especially things like footwear had advanced enormously. The main club committee were a rigid hut-based establishment; it was more of a fellwalking club then, rather than a climbing club. Times have changed for the better, now. Kelly had done a fantastic job with the guide-books, and climbed some good routes in the 'twenties, but he eventually stood aside." (8)

Harry Kelly, captured as a frail old man in 1978.

Unfortunately, Griffin was forced to stick with the existing conventional grades, much against his will. After a frustrating short spell that included editing part of the Langdale guide, his employment commitments proved overwhelming and he stepped down from the post prior to publishing any guides and the job of editing was taken up by John Wilkinson.

"'What now?' he asked, looking at the seemingly impossible rock above him. But when I told him I had intended to traverse left along the slab he said he would rather stay where he was and belay in the corner. He could be strange sometimes, could Johnny. I remember he often wore a black 'sweat-band' around his long and slender neck. At least I thought it was a sweat-band, but it looked to me suspiciously like a lady's garter!" (7)

Keith Phizacklea about to pull over onto the recessed slab on the second pitch of Fulcrum.

Jackson led through to complete the pitch on a sloping stance at the junction with Leverage. From here Leverage follows the open corner above to a small overhang, where it pulls out right. Adams led up to this overhang, but he pulled out left and climbed the steep left wall, where he found a line of good hidden holds and excellent runners in the crack. It was a surprising discovery at the time, because no-one suspected this uncompromising section of crag could have been climbed at such a relatively easy VS grade. But, Johnny Adams remains puzzled at this passage in the book, commenting:

> "I can't disagree with what Ken wrote in his book, because I can't remember too much about the route except that I didn't struggle and belay too soon, as he infers, because the climbing was a romp and I found it easy. The other strange thing he says in his book is that I wore a black band around my neck like a lady's garter, but this is not true at all because I can't stand anything around my neck, I never could, not even a polo-necked jumper. I think he's got me confused with someone else." (9)

Keith Phizacklea on the top pitch of Fulcrum.

Jackson returned with Colin Read and climbed an awkward crack line found just left of the start of Mickledore Grooves. This is Dyad, a steep, entertaining route that starts by teetering up a short delicate ramp to reach the crack, which to avoid failure requires some skill at jamming and gritty determination to access the belay ledge. The first ascent involved several rests on the gear and a point of aid; Jackson states the following in his book:

> "Colin was making an abortive attempt on the first pitch of an unclimbed line, just to the left of Leverage. He had spotted a sling in an overhang and was trying to reach it. Well, he was about twenty feet off the ground and still going strong, when he paused to fix a MOAC wedge into a thin crack.

The 4th Scafell Guidebook (contd)

John Wilkinson succeeded Joe Griffin as editor of the FRCC guidebooks.

Wilkinson revolutionised the production and appearance of the Fell & Rock guides. With the help of Gordon Dyke, the art master at Kirby Stephen School, he introduced a new design of cover to the guide, each coloured according to the area covered (the Scafell area was allocated a purple colour). Guidebooks were encased in sturdy, flexible plastic covers that John had encountered whilst working at his University. It is reputed that he tested a prototype plastic covered guidebook by repeatedly throwing it at a wall for an hour! This style of guidebook cover has remained in production until recently. Another major change thankfully introduced by Wilkinson was the inclusion of the HVS and Extremely Severe grades. In 1967 the fourth edition of the Scafell guide was produced by the FRCC, written jointly by Geoff Oliver and Joe Griffin, with assistance from Bill Young. This was the first guide to the area since 1956, but in that time there had been an additional 35 routes added to Scafell. Geoff Oliver recognised the massive potential remaining on the crags; his final words of the introduction of the guide concluded:

> "There are still new lines to explore on Scafell, protected more by their isolated situation rather than their difficulty, so should the Mickledore chairlift ever become a reality, let Scafell Beware!"

Above: Iain Small maintaining a cool composure whilst on the awkward and very greasy first ramp of Dyad.

Below: The crux section of Dyad is the crack leading to the belay ledge. Climber Iain Small.

Photos: Al Phizacklea

> "And that was that. Already weakened by the fiercely overhanging rock, his fingers could take no more, so he clipped his rope into the MOAC runner and asked to be lowered off. Unfortunately, this left a piece of valuable piece of our property stuck fast in the crack and out of reach – an event that somehow seemed to trap us into completing the first ascent of a climb that is now called Dyad." (10)

However, recently Read recalls:

> "I've read what he'd written, and I looked in my diary, and it seems that his recollection of what happened is different from my recollection of what happened. I'm not saying he's wrong or telling fibs, it's just that my diary says something different; well, it was forty years ago. We were doing Leverage when we saw this line, so we had a go. I can't remember who went first but we kept swapping leads, we got gear in and took rests on it and eventually we got to a belay. It's described as one pitch now, but Ken took a belay on a really poor peg and I led the second half of the first pitch. There were no nut keys in those days, so I took a blade peg and raked the dirt out of the crack until I got more nuts in. In those days, we used to clean only the absolute minimum to enable us to get up, and then the second man would clean it up, sometimes on a tight rope. Anyhow, I took some more rests and then climbed it, at that time it was right at the limit of what we could do. There was a bit of controversy about this at the time, and a group of climbers, I think Roper and Soper were amongst them, happened to come past while we were on it and they stood and laughed for a while." (11)

The second pitch follows an awkward groove and a delicate rib until easier ground can be reached. Dyad is a good example of a route that is just ahead of its time; and several of the local activists recognised that this would be a potential free route. So it proved; within six years it was climbed free by a new generation of fitter and better equipped climbers. Jackson originally wanted to call this route Vector, but this had already been used by Joe Brown for his classic route at Tremadoc. Eventually they chose the name Dyad, because a dyad is supposedly a juxtaposition of two vectors; understandable only to those with knowledge of the science of kinematics.

Down to the left of Dyad, the crag steepens and becomes oppressively wet in places. It was up here that Syd Clark, Geoff Oliver, Hughie Loughram and George Lowes added Minotaur, an interesting climb that branches out of Overhanging Wall in a very exposed situation. Syd takes up the story:

> "The bus went through Whitehaven and Workington and took us to Keswick, and in those days the whole of the top deck was full of climbers. We'd head for the Oasis Café for a brew, where the waitress took kindly to us and she used to save the thicker crusts at the ends of the bread for our beans on toast. We met Geoff Oliver there; he said he had his eye on a line on Scafell, and would we go with him? We felt reet honoured just to be asked. Anyhow, Hughie set off up Overhanging Wall; scrats about for a while and brands this line unclimbable, but we pointed out to him with some derision that he hadn't even left Overhanging Wall yet! So he came down, and Geoff decided it was my turn. I remember there were some bold moves up off Overhanging Wall onto a ramp, and then the crux is the bulge at the top. I probably spent twenty minutes there looking about, scheming, wondering whether to put a peg in or not, and then decided to have a go. It was no more than 15 foot, but I succeeded in getting onto the belay. Just then Geoff Cram appeared over Mickledore, and he shouted 'Hoy! You've just nicked our route!'" (12)

Hughie supplied the name Minotaur, to go with the Centaur based theme. It starts up Overhanging Wall before rising directly up the bulging wall above via a delicate moss-speckled ramp which leads to an exposed pull onto the base of the White Slab. Rarely dry, the route feels tough for the grade of E1, 5b, and the big drop below one's heels concentrates the mind wonderfully; climbers certainly know they are on The East Buttress on this route!

Left: A classic posture of exposure on the ramp of Minotaur.

Below: Syd Clark.

The top pitch follows a ramp across the overhanging headwall, before pulling across left to a rather damp finish. This top pitch never dries out, and cools the climber with a constant cold shower of finest spring water; incidentally the potential for a magnificent icefall in winter.

The final new route of 1968, Long Stand, VS, was climbed out of Moss Gill by Ed Cross, Jack Soper, Gordon Dyke and Gerald Valentine. The first pitch followed the Variation Start to Moss Ghyll Grooves for a while, and then broke out left to climb an awkward crack up to the Lookout stance on M.G.G. The upper pitch traversed right from the belay and followed the shallow, wide open chimney. Soper intriguingly recalled there was much discussion over a rude interpretation of the name, Long Stand, but he couldn't remember any details.

The sixties came to the end with several major routes being climbed on Scafell. Bill Young and Geoff Cram, a West Cumberland team more well-known for their activity on Pillar Rock, climbed Chimera and Gold Rush on The East Buttress.

Chimera climbs a line directly up through Pegasus, but the overhanging first pitch required three pegs and two slings for aid, and it was not climbed free until 1978 by Jeff Lamb. (This first pitch has since been grafted onto Lucius). The upper pitches give pleasant climbing at a HVS standard, and now Chimera is described as starting up Pegasus to maintain an overall HVS grade. This is an under-rated outing and few have enjoyed the excellent jamming crack in the top groove. Cram came up with the name; a Chimera being a mythical Greek monster comprising of several animals, a mixture of lion, goat and snake that breathed fire.

Gold Rush was their next new route; it is a good E1 well known for its inauspicious first pitch. It takes the permanently wet streak to the left of Great Eastern, and it has been described as being akin to swimming up a waterfall, but in normal conditions it can be just described as excessively damp. This feature is offsetting to most suitors, but if they don't want their coiffure to get wet, they can by-pass it by following the first pitch of Great Eastern. The rest of the route is delightful; it trends left-wards across some impressively exposed ground before following a series of clean grooves and excellent cracks that eventually merge with the top of The Yellow Slab. The final pitch follows a direct continuation of the crack, rising up past an overhang to give a steep, satisfying finish. Bill Young said that the route was so naturally clean they only removed one grass sod during the whole of the first ascent. They had used a rest point on both the first and top pitches, but these were climbed free during an early repeat by Johnny Adams and Colin Read around 1970. Incidentally, Cram and Young had gone to Scafell with the intention of climbing a new girdle traverse of The East Buttress, but when they got there, Colin Read and Johnny Adams were already attempting it. (13)

> "It was rather fortuitous that we got started so early, because Geoff and Bill came across shortly after we had started. They hung around to see how we got on, and once we had crossed Hell's Groove, they wandered off to do another climb; I think it was Gold Rush. Interestingly enough I think they had intended to do the girdle from the other way, from right to left." (14)

The Girdle Traverse of The East Buttress is probably the longest Extremely Severe climbed in The Lakes. This had been a long sought after line; Chris Bonington's Holy Ghost was the result of one aborted attempt several years earlier. The girdle was eventually put together by Colin Read and Johnny Adams, whose determination was described by Read:

> "What spurred us on was the *Fell & Rock Journal* of 1968 which had a picture by John Hartley of The East Buttress which said 'Plan your new girdle here' or something.

Above: Bill Young and Geoff Cram used aid to overcome the initial steep wall of Chimera on the first ascent, later freed by Pete Botterill and Jeff Lamb as part of Lucius.

Below: Geoff Cram.

Photo: Al Phizacklea

Photo: John Hartley

John Hartley's classic study of the left-hand side of The East Buttress as depicted in the 1968 FRCC journal, a photo that inspired a brilliant route.

"I did exactly that using the picture, and I took the picture to the crag and took more photographs, then I worked out a line and showed them to John and said 'What do you think of this?' So we went up at Whit weekend but we hadn't checked the weather very well and we bivouacked below the crag with our mate and his girlfriend, the four of us. It absolutely pissed it down that night and it gradually got wetter and wetter, we were bivvied under that bit that's overhanging and keeps the bottom bit dry, but gradually it crept in as it trickled down the crag and we ended up sitting out of our sleeping bags on a ledge just above the floor. As soon as the greyness of dawn came, we just packed up and went back to Borrowdale. We soon went back and bivvied with fine weather, we had to hurry because this was just before Johnny was going on an overland trip to India. We knew about Holy Ghost, and thought it would be a good start to the girdle, but we didn't realise that Bonington had actually been trying to do the girdle. John led the first pitch and I led the second pitch. We actually thought we might be able to get straight across from the traverse of Holy Ghost, but it was only when I got to the thread I realised I couldn't find a way across without doing Holy Ghost, and I didn't want to do that because it would have been too high. I remember getting some gear in there, a small 'Whitworth' nut on some bootlace and something else; I think it was a little thread. I remember climbing down a metre or so and leaning out, and I could see a ledge down below and figured that from there we'd be able to get round the corner. I shouted down to Johnny and said what I'd found, then I climbed down the wall and I managed to get a couple of runners in and got down to the ledge. John had to second it, he came down with a back rope so far to rehearse the moves, then he went back up to unclip the gear and then climbed down. I remember thinking that he should have kept the back rope on, because if he comes off, it would have been a Hell of a mess." (15)

Colin Read.

Above: John Adams

Left: Looking down on the fourth pitch of The Lord of the Rings, at the point where tension was used on the first ascent. Climber Bob Wightman.

Bob Wightman approaches the exposed middle section of The Lord of the Rings.

Colin had earlier described this pitch in more detail in the *Carlisle Mountaineering Club Journal,* which read:

> "Now came the moment of truth, as the descent, on virgin rock, of the wall below began. Down a few feet, then working back a little left to the top of a shallow indefinite groove, down this, not too bad at first, but progressively growing thinner and thinner. A few feet below a poor ledge led rightwards to a possible stance, the next few moves towards it were indescribably thin. Holding my breath as a foot roamed in search of the elusive ledge, gingerly down, then balancing across until being able to see right into Hell's Groove. For John the pitch was utterly serious. As he rounded the edge on Holy Ghost, the situation became alarming – the rope fell away sweeping down across the wall, towards the only two meagre runners on the pitch. He juggled with the 5c moves, for a moment hesitating. I gripped the ropes tightly, watching intently; a fall from there would result in a tremendous pendulum with messy consequences. This must have been spinning through his mind, as he dithered, then braced himself moving very steadily. Things relaxed as the first runner was approached, descending the wall with protection made that part acceptable." (16)

Johnny's recollection of this pitch remains clear to this day:

> "I came across to above where Colin was belayed, there was very little in the way of gear between us, and the crux was near the start of the pitch. The ropes sagged away down to him, and I thought 'Uh, oh!' and I got nervous and frightened, I think it is the only time I've ever been frightened on a route. Fortunately, the climbing went without mishap, because I thought I would hit the ground if I'd have fallen." (17)

This second pitch is still considered the crux of the route, but beware, it's still not over. The route moved into Hell's Groove and crossed a further series of grooves to reach a belay on Phoenix with tension from a nut. The girdle then climbed the pillar before descending to reach Ichabod, and it continued right to The Yellow Slab which is descended. Read continued his reminiscing:

> "I remember one bit before you get to Yellow Slab that's quite tricky which had grass sods in all the holds, but we had realised by then we had cracked it and were both fired up, so we fired the sods out. We could have gone further than we did on that first day but we climbed Great Eastern to the top of the crag, so in that way we'd link in with the old girdle so if it had rained we could claim what we'd done. We were really knackered as we had spent a lot of time on false leads, probing across and coming back to work out the line. We bivvied below the crag again and the next day we went up Great Eastern and went across to Centaur, and what we thought was one of the hardest pitches was getting beyond Centaur. I remember putting in a peg runner and then there's a crack followed by a bit of a slab, a glacis that you land on, I couldn't find any holds to pull onto that. I was scratting the grit out of the cracks and clinging on, there were no runners that I could find so I got a blade peg out and got that in, then with another peg I raked the crack out so you could eventually get your fingers in it. The bit after that wasn't too hard, but it was a bit spooky where you bridge across the top of all those grooves where now the modern classic routes like Lost Horizons come up. We had some kind of a loose idea where we were going, but nothing absolutely firm, but it was magnificent the way it just unfolded." (18)

Near the end of the route Johnny tried climbing across the crag from the ledge below May Day Direct, and he got within sight of the belay, but he had no runners and was forced to retreat back to Colin. The strain of such a long and sustained route was beginning to tell on their tired bodies:

"We were getting quite tired by them, but we still managed to climb May Day Direct free, the route went up there and back down the other side. At the end of the day, there were five or six climbers on Mickledore, Syd Clark was amongst them, and when we finished the route they all gave us a clap." (19)

The first ascent of this girdle took 19 hours of climbing time to complete its fourteen pitches and 342 metres and even now, a competent team can be expected to spend a long eight hour day on it. The superb name of this creation; Lord of the Rings, evokes thoughts of long hot days on the crag. Originally it was to be merely 'The Girdle of The East Buttress', but when Colin wrote his article titled 'Lord of the Rings', the guidebook writer persuaded him to change the name of the route.
At E2 it contains one 5c and six 5b pitches, it is unrivalled in The Lakes for length and consistency of difficulty; it is almost alpine in proportion.

The tension move on pitch 4 was removed by Bill Young and Mike Burbage when checking the route for the forthcoming guidebook. On their first attempt, Young had baulked at the awesome descent on pitch 2, so he returned to the belay and Burbage climbed back up and continued to the top via The Holy Ghost. Returning a couple of weeks later they decided to climb the rest of the route starting from Hell's Groove. Despite a strong wind they traversed as far as Phoenix before retreating. By then they had already inadvertently dispensed with the aid!

Later that summer, another fine route was added to the crag on the much neglected Shamrock, where Colin Read, and partner Rob Lake (Adams was in India) climbed Gilt Edge Eliminate up the front of the crag. They had noticed the line after climbing Silver Lining; and as with Dennis English's team, they had been attracted to the prominent Y-shaped crack up the front of the buttress. This proved to be a stubborn feature and they used an aid nut for gardening, but then climbed the route free. Gilt Edged Eliminate consists of a pleasant series of grooves and cracks in a long and sustained route, some 168 metres over 7 pitches, making it one of the longest E1's in The Lakes.

Above: The diminutive figures on the first section of Gilt Edge Eliminate are dwarfed by the stepped profile of The Shamrock.

Left: Rob Matheson crosses the rather intimidating final pitch of the Girdle of Central Buttress, where a delicate traverse above the stacked overhangs above Slab and Groove route provides a thrilling finish.

Increasing Standards

Note must be made of the growing confidence of some climbers around this time. The fact that emerging teams were willing to tackle the more improbable-looking lines, yet resorting to aid when necessary, indicated that standards were set to rise. Routes being attempted using aid were to become hard free climbs by the mid-seventies. This was a transitional period, fuelled by improvements in gear which made the sport of climbing safer.

A major innovation was the sit-harness, first developed by Don Whillans for high-altitude expeditions, but then rapidly adopted by most rock climbers. Threats to the scrotal area from the strap running between the legs was considered preferable by some to simply having a rope tied around the waist. Others disagreed, preferring to use a 'Swami' belt, a wide strap tied around the waist which dissipated the energy of a fall over a wide area. Notable climbers relying on this belt were Jeff Lamb and Pete Whillance. Improvements to wired nuts, especially the introduction of small stopper nuts from America, allowed protection to be placed wherever cracks existed. These allowed climbers to push their abilities with less fear of hurting themselves if they came off. Growing pressure to reduce the amount of aid used on routes pushed up standards, and over the next few years the old adage that 'the leader must not fall' was gradually eroded as controlled falls became commonplace.

Pete Whillance also noted the following about this period:

"Further signs of rising standards were also evident in the number of hard routes being accomplished in a single day. On Scafell during 1969, Bill Lounds managed The Nazgul, Ichabod, Holy Ghost and Leverage whilst Richard McHardy and Paul Braithwaite paid a rare visit from North Wales to record an even better day. They climbed Leverage, Ichabod, Hell's Groove and another before soloing Mickledore Grooves, Trinity, Chartreuse and Overhanging Wall – all on sight." (20)

All that was now needed was a change in attitude to training to improve fitness and stamina; but for this final piece of the puzzle the climbing community would have to wait for Pete Livesey.

Al Brightman on the initial corner of The White Wizard.

1971 was the year Chris Bonington added two fine routes to the main Scafell face. With Mike Thompson he added The Girdle of the Central Buttress which crossed from left to right at a much higher level than the original Scafell Girdle. This magnificent voyage links several existing pitches taking in some of the best situations on the crag to create a delicate exposed traverse. Interestingly, Chris had completely forgotten that he had climbed this route, which is surprising considering the final pitch traverses above a huge set of overhangs giving precarious climbing with a mind-numbing sense of exposure:

> "I can't remember that. Are you sure I did that route? [He looks at the guidebook] Well, I must have done! You know, I have no recollection of that whatsoever, but we must have had a great time doing it!" (21)

After some consideration he vaguely recalled that it was from this route that he had spotted a potential new line which was to become The White Wizard. The third pitch of the traverse, a mantelshelf onto a small ledge right on the edge of an overhanging arête, is an adrenalin surging udge on the edge of nothing was incorporated into the original line of The White Wizard. The original grade of Extremely Severe was downgraded to HVS by the guidebook writing team, but there are few HVS leaders who could manage the raw terror of that initial mantelshelf. This traverse is recommended to any visitor who has ticked the classics and is looking for something different, it personifies the term adventurous. The following year, Ian Roper and Colin Taylor created a variation to the seventh pitch of the original line of that girdle, but this did little to improve the route.

Bonington's second route was The White Wizard, destined to become the most popular E3 on this side of the crag. It takes a series of steep grooves rising above the foot of Botterill's Slab to finally emerge with a very exposed finish up a bulging headwall. However, the first pitch which forms a steep impending corner was only ascended by using aid from a peg and three nuts. Bonington recalls:

> "You've got to remember that my limit at rock climbing was about E2, and I originally tried to lead this first pitch, but it was too difficult. I handed over the lead to Nick Esctourt who proceeded to frig his way up by resting on the odd nut. It took us all day, it was a bit of a struggle, but we did it on sight from the bottom. It really was too hard for us and I suppose we really shouldn't have been on it, but we were absolutely honest about how we did it." (22)

Their shenanigans on this first pitch were witnessed by two local lads on Botterill's Slab, Tony Stephenson and Chris Sice:

> "We didn't have a camera with us, but I've got this really clear memory as though I'm looking at a photograph. It was quite an electrifying day; we had a grandstand view of Estcourt and Bonington on the crag, and it kind of stays with you. All I'll say is that there was a lot of engineering going on that day, with some very long slings employed!" (23)

The upper pitch, requiring a steep awkward pull onto a ledge above an awesome drop, also utilised two points of aid. It is perched right at the apex of the steepest part of the crag in an astonishingly breathtaking position, and it has possibly the most exposed 5c moves in England. Having such a 'celebrity' forcing a first ascent on Scafell drew scornful remarks from many; accusing Bonington of aiding the route into submission, even though he didn't lead the main pitch. One must remember the route was climbed on sight, and that the wall is naturally lichenous with cracks choked with moss. Chris was asked about the criticism regarding him using his fame to force a new route, to which he replied:

> "That's a load of bollocks. I suppose it was a legitimate criticism, because we should have backed off and left it for someone else to do, but we didn't choose to do that. The really important thing in those circumstances is to be honest, which we were." (24)

Above: Climbers using aid on the difficult top pitch of The White Wizard.

Below: The steep corner of pitch 3 of The White Wizard was first climbed by Pete Botterill and John Taylor in 1977. Pitch 3 originally pulled out right by a difficult mantleshelf onto the ledge just above the belayer, first discovered as part of the traverse of Central Buttress by Bonington and Thompson.

Above: Rod Valentine.

Below: Joe Holden on the crack of The Gripe.

The White Wizard had its aid points gradually reduced over the years; Pete Botterill almost climbed it free in 1976, but admitted to Martin Berzins that he had to resort to one resting point. Realising the first free ascent was up for grabs, Martin and Gordon Higginson flashed the route free a week later. Pete Botterill returned with John Taylor and improved the wandering state of pitch 3 by directly climbing the impending groove, making the route a very sustained outing, and now graded E3, 5c, 5c, 5b, 5c, and confirming it as a classic of Scafell. Just to the left of the final pitch there lies a horrendously overhanging crack, slanting at the same crazy angle as the line of the main corner of the route, but few have been tempted to look at it. It was first climbed by Colin Read and Bill Robinson in 1973, and Colin remembers it as very physical; impending all the way and full of rubble.

Rodney Valentine had been one of the regulars assisting the guidebook team checking routes and had spotted a couple of lines high on the neglected flanks of Pisgah Buttress. The first route, The Gripe, climbs a steep wide crackline on the left side of the buttress on immaculately clean, rough rock. He was accompanied by John Wilkinson and Duncan Pogson on this fine HVS route, which has never become a popular venue due to its rather remote setting. The crack fell to Rod's gritstone upbringing, utilising the full range of jamming techniques in a situation that held no protection. Nowadays a good range of 'Friends' makes the experience a whole lot better, but it still requires some awkward laybacking to overcome the wide section. Valentine explained the origin of the name:

> "We had been staying at Brackenclose, and on Saturday night we were in the Wasdale Head bar, drinking; as you do, and we'd all had a skin full of ale. Anyhow, I was passing the back of the hotel where the door to the kitchen was open, and I saw this container of dehydrated curry mix open on the side, so I thought I'll have a bit of that. I nipped in and shovelled some of this dehydrated curry down me neck, but there was only the beer in my belly to rehydrate it. Consequently, of course, the following morning I was dead rough, and I had the proverbials, and I had to keep stopping to have a turn out all the way up to the crag. I just about managed to come to and do the route, so the name The Gripe seemed appropriate." (25)

Rod's second route, climbed with Wilkinson and Brian Fuller, follows a rather dank groove above the depths of Steep Gill and for this reason is somewhat unpopular. Rod remembers little about this route, except it was rather poorly protected. However it was well within his capabilities, and at the crux groove; rather smooth and blank, but not too steep he could just balance there and work it out. The name for this HVS, Pisgah Ya Bas, was suggested by Wilkinson, who was then working in Scotland and it was inspired by the Glaswegian term of endearment for such 'Effing English Bastards'. (26) It is worth noting that this was probably the same line first attempted by Harry Kelly back in 1919.

In August 1972, Colin Read and Johnny Adams climbed Incubus, which tackled the steep pillar left of Hell's Groove. The line had been noticed as they crossed the pillar during The Lord of the Rings, and Read realised there was a potential route to be climbed. He recalls:

> "I didn't abseil down the route but I climbed it from the ground up and used two points of aid. The interesting thing was that it wasn't free climbed the next week or in six months, it took a few years before it was climbed free, after there had been a leap in standards. I thought it was a good hard route; the free climbing seemed hard and I had lots of goes at it before I actually used the aid, and having got past that point the wall was vertical but felt steeper and I started to get pumped. There was a spike and I eventually managed to get a line on it for a runner then I got past that and arrived on the belay ledge completely burned out. I was on the ledge on my knees, my arms were so pumped that I couldn't stand up until my arms had recovered enough to get a belay on, and Johnny was shouting up to find out what was the matter. I look back and think this was the hardest lead we ever did. Sometime later, I went back to the crag and found Rodney Valentine trying the second ascent, but he was hanging off the sling on the spike having assumed that I had used it for aid, which of course I hadn't." (27)

Above: Dave Armstrong on an early repeat of Incubus.

Left: Rod Valentine above the depths of Steep Gill on the first ascent of Pisgah Ya Bas.

This first pitch was reduced to one point of aid by Martin Berzins and Chris Sowden in 1976; they returned six years later to eventually free climb the full line at E5, 6b. "Incubus free was a bit of an epic! That was totally wild – the gear on the pitch was O.K, but that on the belay was totally crap. I remember being tied onto a load of rubbish, and Chris was leading the second pitch and he wasn't that happy, it was like pretty scary." (28) The name Incubus means nightmare or something oppressive and is derived from a mythical demon which is said to force itself on top of unwary sleepers for sex, thus sustaining itself and draining energy from its victims. It is said to be identified by its unnaturally cold penis!

Read and Adams returned two days later and climbed a direct finish to Hell's Groove, following a crack to the right of the capping roof and a steep green crack above. Needless to say this latter feature was only feasible due to the drought conditions! Their direct variation is now incorporated into the main route, giving it a more sustained line up the buttress. Later on the same day, they moved around the crag to claim the first free ascent of The Doomwatch Finish. Johnny recalled:

> "I recall Sherpa [Ian Roper] saying that this pitch wouldn't go free because if Barley couldn't do it free, then nobody could. Well it was dry when we went and climbed it, it seemed to be quite easy to do it free, and it was a really good pitch. I remember looking down at Colin who was holding the ropes with a waist belay and thinking 'You've gotta keep on going here!'" (29)

Doomwatch was a rather insipid route that was effectively killed off at birth. It was only climbed the year before by A.D. Barley and A. Roach who had been forced to use two points of aid just to leave the ground on the first pitch and three points of aid on the upper section. This is a normally greasy crack on the impressive steep wall to the left of the original finish of Moonday, but when Adams was there he found it to be a superb dry pitch and quickly led it free. The writers of the 1974 guidebook decided not to include the lower pitch of Doomwatch because of the aid, and merely added the top pitch as a variation finish to Moonday. The Doomwatch Finish was to be Colin Read's last contribution to Scafell climbing for the next twenty years. In the late 1970's he suffered a serious accident pursuing his vocation as a joiner – he caught his left hand in a circular saw and lost his thumb and two fingers, and was lucky to save the rest of his severely lacerated hand. It took ten years of rehabilitation before the feeling in his two remaining fingers returned sufficiently to give him the confidence to try climbing again.

Around on the front of the Pinnacle Face, Bob Bennett and Royanne Lavender started up the steep groove line of The Left Edge, but continued directly to the Waiting Room on Jones' Route Direct from Lord's Rake. Their effort was given the rather curt name of Leftovers, which could be a pleasant VS if the veneer of lichens can be removed. Again it is a route that can only be recommended in dry conditions. Finally in 1972, the guidebook checking team of Bill Young, Jeff Lamb and Andy Hunter climbed The Last Stand by a new superior direct start. There is little noteworthy about this, apart from the fact that it was the first time the name of Jeff Lamb appears in the historical list on Scafell. The Last Stand, HVS, is another one of the many crack lines rising leftwards out of Moss Gill and first climbed in 1971 by Hugh Banner and Mike Hatton. Banner had previous connections with this line. Back in 1961 he and Gordon Dyke had added a devious start to his earlier Narrow Stand, but because it weaved across the various groove lines in the vicinity it was given the disparaging name of The Tradesman's Entrance. The Last Stand was an attempt to improve on the original line by following the delightful straight crack, and now it in turn had been usurped by a superior new start. It seems that all Banner's efforts to establish a good route in this vicinity have unfortunately gone to waste as this unbalanced E1 (the hard section is very short) has nowadays lapsed into obscurity. Perhaps this has something to do with the topography of the area, the numerous diagonal lines and similar sounding names making this a confusing and therefore neglected part of the crag.

Photo: Al Phizacklea

Bill Birkett, carrying on the family 'tradition'.

The V-shaped amphitheatre forming the upper section of Moss Gill is dominated by a steep headwall, flanked on the left by the normal slabby Collie's Exit finish of the gill, and the steep, vertical chimney of Collier's Chimney on the right. In 1972 Hugh Banner and Mike Foggan climbed a wandering diagonal line across this headwall which they named Banner's Exit, a rather indirect and soon forgotten VS.

This may be attributed to guidebook writers Mike Burbage and Bill Young usurping the original line the following year when they climbed a superior direct start up a very thin slab that rises leftwards from the base of Collier's Chimney to give friction climbing of the highest quality.

The upper walls follow Banner's Exit for some way, these are easier but they are more exposed and less well protected, which gives an overall impression that this is more like an adventure than a route. Burbage and Young called their line Clockwork Orange, a tough HVS, which is the version that made it into the guidebook. According to Burbage:

> "I'd done Moss Gill many times in the past, and I'd clocked the line from there. There were a couple of prominent features that stood out, especially the big slab, and that's the line we took. We went specifically up there to do that line, I don't remember much about the climbing itself, except that it went well without any epics. We hadn't intended to do a better route than Banner's Exit, it just turned out to be a better line." (30)

Once again, Hugh Banner's contribution to Scafell had been superseded by the locals. Could such action make one suspicious that there was a plot to belittle the routes of a Welsh-based activist who had pioneered many fine routes on Cloggy?

Around in the lower section of Deep Gill, Bill Birkett, son of Jim Birkett, added his only route on Scafell. The route, craftily named Edge Hog, follows a set of intimidating ramps and grooves in the steep wall at the right edge of The Pinnacle overlooking Deep Gill. The line had not received much attention over the years; its unfashionable location and serious climbing has reduced it to obscurity despite Bill adding it to the 1990 reprint of the original Constable selected climbing guide *Rock Climbing in The Lake District*. The unprotected nature of the first pitch gave Bill some worries; he had looked at the line in 1971, but backed off because he thought it would require a peg runner. Being acutely aware of his father's reluctance to use pegs for runners, he vowed to return the following year when the conditions were better. He did return to climb the route in good style in the company of Mike Myers and John Richardson. Ironically, the second ascentionist, Bill Young, had an awkward time on this pitch and, when he wrote the guidebook he recommended a protection peg be used, even though he didn't place one himself. Bill Birkett was rather incensed that his route should be denigrated by such a suggestion. Young accepted his comment was a mistake, and it was removed from later editions of the guide.

The Constable Guide and the Fifth Scafell Guidebook

Two guidebooks were published around this time; both were different for different reasons. The first guide was a new departure for Cumbrian climbing. (A term that can now be used following the 1974 county boundary reshuffle which created a new county of Cumbria from an amalgamation of Cumberland, Westmorland, North Lancashire and Yorkshire). Published by the Constable Company, *Rock Climbing in the Lake District* was a selected guide that cherry picked the best routes from around the area and illustrated them with photo diagrams; some 32 years before the FRCC revived this technique. The guidebook was the inspiration from three young (ish) Fell & Rock members Geoff Cram, Chris Eilbeck and Ian Roper, and it made full use of Roper's fine photographic skills. Initially there was some concern within the club hierarchy, as they worried about how a selected guide would affect the sales of the club's definitive guides.

The second guidebook was the FRCC guide to the Scafell crags, the fifth they had produced covering the area. It followed the usual rather staid style with its plain purple cover, fading Heaton-Cooper sketches in the back and totally devoid of photographs. It was a typical guide of the FRCC genre; it was practical in use but cast in a stoically traditional mould, rather than being a stimulating guide. It was written jointly by Mike Burbage and Bill Young. As Mike was working for much of the time in Scotland, a large amount of the checking fell to Bill to complete. Their edition contained a further 28 new routes or variations to the crags of Scafell, and once again, John Wilkinson remained the editor.

Photo: Al Phizacklea

Right: The fifth FRCC guidebook to Scafell.

The Constable Guide and the Fifth Scafell Guidebook (contd.)

Heaton Cooper's diagrams were looking rather dated by 1974.

At this time on The East Buttress the gaps between the existing routes were blindingly obvious. For instance, between Armageddon and Ichabod there were only five routes, Centaur, Great Eastern and the Yellow Slab Variation, Gold Rush and Overhanging Grooves. (Nowadays there are 22 routes!) Burbage took one last swipe at the growing trend of using aid to force the ascents of routes with a visionary comment in his closing statement in the guidebook's introduction:

"The last two years have been similar in that very few new routes have been climbed. Is it the start of a permanent decline in the Scafell Group or just another lull? One thing is certain however; classic routes which use little or no aid are becoming more of a rarity each year. Will this trend be reversed by a new and more skilful breed of climbers, in the future? Will they be able to overcome the apparently unclimbed expanses of rock that still remain, without having to resort to artificial aid? Time alone will tell." (31)

The Constable selected guide to The Lake District and an example of the photo topos used in that guide.

Photo: Burbage collection

Mike Burbage, guidebook writer and prophet.

Right: Bill Young, joint author of the FRCC guide.

Footnotes

1. Chris Bonington, 'The Lord of the Rings', from *Extreme Rock* 1987
2. Chris Bonington, FRCC audio recording, 2008
3. John Porter, 'Nazgul', from *Extreme Rock* 1967
4. Rod Valentine, FRCC recording, 2008
5. Joe Wilson, telephone conversation with the author, 2009
6. Geoff Milburn, 'A New Route on Scafell' *FRCC Journal*, 1988
7. Ken Jackson, *Climbing in the Dark* 2008
8. Joe Griffin, FRCC audio recording, 2008
9. Johnny Adams, FRCC audio recording, 2008
10. Ken Jackson, *Climbing in the Dark 2008*
11. Colin Read, FRCC audio recording, 2008
12. Syd Clark, FRCC audio recording, 2008
13. Geoff Cram and Bill Young, FRCC audio recordings, 2008
14. Johnny Adams, FRCC audio recording, 2008
15. Colin Read, FRCC audio recording, 2008
16. Colin Read, 'The Lord of the Rings', *Carlisle M.C. Journal*, 1969
17. Johnny Adams, FRCC audio recording, 2008
18. Colin Read, FRCC audio recording, 2008
19. Colin Read, FRCC audio recording, 2008
20. Pete Whillance, 'A short history of climbing, part III', *FRCC Journal*, 1986
21. Chris Bonington, FRCC audio recording, 2008
22. Chris Bonington, FRCC audio recording, 2008
23. Chris Sice, telephone conversation with the author, 2009
24. Chris Bonington, FRCC audio recording, 2008
25. Rod Valentine, FRCC audio recording, 2008
26. John Wilkinson, FRCC audio recording, 2008
27. Colin Read, FRCC audio recording, 2008
28. Martin Berzins, e-mail to author, 2010
29. Johnny Adams, FRCC audio recording, 2008
30. Mike Burbage, telephone conversation with the author, 2009
31. Mike Burbage, Scafell guidebook, 1974
32. Mike Burbage, telephone conversation with the author, 2009

The Constable Guide and the Fifth Scafell Guidebook (contd.)

These comments were written in November 1973; and it begs the question as to whether Burbage had been in possession of a crystal ball? Obviously not, but he had noticed the trend of competition fuelled climbing that was stirring in the dales of Yorkshire and The Peak District.

He was also in touch with the younger local climbers who were starting to emerge; and he climbed extensively with Jeff Lamb in his youth. Burbage also knew of Clegg, Whillance, Matheson and Cleasby, who were his 'new and more skilful breed' on whom he pinned his hopes for the future. He explained:

"I was aware that climbing developed in spurts, and there had been a bit of a lull in the past few years, so I was sat on Mickledore one evening, looking at the massive expanse of unclimbed rock, and I thought we were in for another phase of climbing. I didn't realise it would have gone as quickly as it did, but it was how I felt at the time." (32)

This comment was written only seven months before Pete Livesey burst upon The Lakes scene and raised the standard of climbing in the area from E3 to E5 almost overnight. Mike Burbage's comment was one of the most prophetic ever written, and it heralded the start of a whole new chapter in the history of The Lakes, and in particular of climbing on Scafell.

Photo: Al Phizacklea

Keith Phizacklea tackles the rather thin initial slab of Clockwork Orange, Burbage and Young's adventurous route across the headwall of Moss Gill.

1974 - 1976

The Dawn of a New Age

Photo: Pete Botterill collection

Above: Jeff Lamb and Pete Botterill on the first ascent of Zeus.
Below: Jeff Lamb.

Photo: Ian Roper

Overleaf:
The central section of The East Buttress, with the prominent corner of Lost Horizons at centre and the shorter corner and curving ramp of Shere Khan to the right, two of the major routes of this era.

Photo: Al Phizacklea

The next phase of climbing on Scafell that began in 1974 is probably the most intense and exciting stage of development in the entire history of the crags. It was not just Scafell that witnessed this phenomenon; there was a country-wide revolution in climbing spurred on by new gear, a competitive drive fuelled by the desire to get one's name in print in the magazines, and a realisation how training really improves climbing standards. This 'Cultural Revolution' had its roots in the USA; more specifically as centred in the Yosemite Valley where previously aided routes were being attempted as free climbs. There was a huge shift in the paradigm of climbing. Using aid on existing routes was history; it had become a socially unacceptable practice almost overnight. This attitude was quickly adopted by some of the leading climbers from Britain, and they set about showing the Brits could be just as good as anyone when it came to climbing. The result was a rapid extension to the grades of new routes and the opening of eyes to the potential still available on the steeper crags of Britain - previously assumed to be impossible.

In the summer of 1974 a couple of climbers sat below The East Buttress with their new guidebook; contemplating the line of Dyad which still retained a rest on gear on its first pitch and a point of aid on the second. They were both rising stars of a strong regional group of climbers from Carlisle which was to dominate new routing on Scafell for the next seven years; their names were Jeff Lamb and Pete Botterill. Lamb was a joiner by trade; his stocky, bearded figure formed a powerful frame for a climber who had a reputation for being a proficient crack climber. Botterill was smaller in stature, yet a very talented boulderer who excelled at solving technical problems. Referring to Jeff he admitted:

> "There wasn't a crack he couldn't climb, well, not in The Lakes, anyway." (1)

Pete was a pharmacist who had to work most Saturdays, but he had every Wednesday off. Jeff had a very tolerant boss who allowed him to take any Wednesday off work if the weather was fine. This allowed the very strong and determined pair to forge a powerful partnership. Climbing Dyad free had been Jeff's intention for some time, but this was all a novel experience for Botterill, as this was his first visit to Scafell. Lamb eventually eliminated the aid move from the crack after taking a flyer from just below the belay – and how many other climbers have followed suit? The last couple of moves are on insecure jams in a flared crack which steepens almost without warning, and the lunge for the ledge always seems a bit of a gamble – and anyone saying it's easy should not be believed. Botterill modestly remembers finding the pitch desperate – it was; they had just created the first 6a pitch on the crag.

The following day the pair were back to look at the rock to the left of Phoenix. Here, the main feature is a slim vertical groove linking the lower ramp on Morning Wall to the upper ramp on Phoenix. As a line, it suffers slightly from seepage and is therefore generously cloaked with moss. But, as was the norm for that time, Lamb led the route on sight, sweeping away the black moss as he climbed. The groove is strenuous and surprisingly sustained but he led it in good style. Botterill struggled to follow and needed Jeff to take his weight on the rope to allow him to change hands on a hold. He admitted to finding it hard as he had only started serious climbing the year before. He recalled that Jeff was over the moon at completing his first real new route on Scafell, which he christened Zeus, a respectable E3, 5c. Unfortunately, the current popular vogue for rock to be dry, clean and chalked up means that Zeus is constantly overlooked and neglected, despite it being sustained and providing a superb technical challenge.

Mary Jenner enjoys the main pitch of Zeus, belayed by Dave Birkett.

The Great Ethical Debate

1974 was the year the ethical debate on climbing styles finally blew wide open. Before then traditionally raised climbers had striven to climb new routes from the ground up without any prior inspection, and with as little aid as possible. Diminishing availability of unclimbed lines at easier standards made this increasingly difficult to achieve.

The advent of nuts and wires allowed a form of cheating which was becoming prevalent; the indiscriminate and unreported use of these for aid or illegitimate rests. There are tales of well-practiced teams who used code words or actions (such as the leader nonchalantly scratching his bottom) as secret signals to the second to take the rope in tightly, thus gaining a sly rest, without broadcasting it to the rest of the crag. Ian Roper notes:

"The peg is an honest villain; it proclaims itself not only by the sound of its insertion, but also by the indelible scars that it leaves on the crag. The only difference between a nut and a peg is that they leave fewer marks; it is now standard practice to lace the way up hard climbs such as Cenotaph Corner and Phoenix. The distinction between aid and protection is becoming blurred – a leader held in tension for a rest, or even pulled up by his second is deemed to be 'free climbing' so long as he himself does not pull himself up or stand in a sling." (2)

Major remaining unclimbed lines were on the more challenging areas of rock – still much in abundance; but steep and hard and with no obvious protection, therefore requiring a very bold approach and a new modus operandi. 1974 was also the year that a Yorkshire teacher gave up work for a year to concentrate on improving his climbing. This was Peter Livesey whose unkempt hair gave a demeanour of being a rather scruffy character, but he was a motivated individual who had a fanatical drive to become the best climber in the country through improving his already impressive ability by intensive stamina training. Livesey was influenced by American free-climbing following an eye-opening trip to Yosemite. He trained relentlessly, often utilising circuit training and laps of the early climbing walls to improve his strength and endurance. This fierce attitude to the sport hadn't been seen before, and some people regarded him as being rather ruthless.

The Great Ethical Debate (contd.)

Peter Livesey, taken in 1982.

Peter Livesey had been snapping at the heels of 'the authority' for several years and had already clashed with the FRCC guidebook team; in particular with Allan Austin through his activities in the Langdale Valley. Livesey thrived on kicking against the 'Old Guard'and the climbing establishment in general; this undoubtedly generated a response and stimulated ethical debates. His philosophy was simple; the finished product (the route) was to be ascended in the best style possible, with the minimum assistance from the rope or other equipment. If this meant multiple abseil inspections to clean and prepare the route with pre-placed protection and in certain cases practising the moves on the rock, then so be it. It was a hard-nosed approach, but not a new one, as Harry Kelly had conducted pre-ascent inspections and gardening of some of his hardest routes half a century earlier. What Livesey brought to the fore was a callous professionalism to the sport in a direct challenge to the traditionalist climbers of the time, and his activities predictably raised a stink in the climbing world. Pete Livesey's new routing campaign in The Lakes took a dramatic upturn in 1974. Within the space of a month he had climbed Dry Grasp, E4, and Nagasaki Grooves, E4, in Borrowdale, followed by his greatest breakthrough, Footless Crow on Goat Crag in the same valley, which became the first E5 in the area. With these ascents he burst onto the scene and threw down an unbelievable challenge to the locals, establishing himself as the undisputed 'top dog' almost overnight.

The removal of aid points from existing routes became a way for activists to establish themselves in the climbing hierarchy. Also it sent out a strong signal that aid was not to be tolerated by the younger climbers who were coming to the fore! Aid elimination continued through the dry summer of 1975, when The Nazgul and Moonday were both climbed free. The first of these, Les Brown's The Nazgul received its first recognised free ascent by Pete Botterill and Steve Clegg, another strong Carlisle combination freshly returned from a successful visit to California's Yosemite Valley. It was not only a high degree of fitness they brought back with them, but also chalk, a fine white calcium carbonate powder that helped to remove sweat from hands. The crack of The Nazgul contained several points of rotting aid gear but they led it free; restricting use of chalk to only a single sloping side hold as its use was strictly taboo at the time. Botterill recalls:

> "We had a small paper packet of chalk hidden down the front of our shirts in which we dipped our fingers, because we couldn't allow anyone to see us using it. There was nothing like chalk bags around at the time." (3)

Pete Botterill on the first free ascent of The Nazgul.

In the course of researching for this book, the author was informed of a visiting South African climber, Tony Dick, who claimed a free ascent the year before Botterill and Clegg, but this has never been authenticated. The observation was made by Bill Birkett; but he had no proof of this, he was merely passing on information received by word of mouth.

Clegg returned with Jeff Lamb and removed the single point of aid from Moonday on The East Buttress. Ed Cleasby and Bill Birkett climbed the long awaited second ascent of The Lord of the Rings, but they had not realised that the fourth pitch with a tension move had already been climbed free by Bill Young on his abortive attempt with Mike Burbage. They had a narrow escape whilst on this route which is best described by Cleasby:

> "By 2 o'clock we were at the belay at the foot of the White Slab, which is a bit of a funnel, and I noticed Mike Lynch was above me on Moonday. Bill had just gone around the corner when suddenly Mike unleashed a lot of blocks which fell towards me, and I was sure I was going to die or at least have some limbs sheared off. I was unable to move so I forced myself tight against the rock, and one block bounced off just above me with an awful smell of sulphur, and as I opened my eyes I realised I was completely unscathed. The block had taken all the gear off the right hand side of my Whillans Harness and one rope was sheared right through. I had sleepless nights for a year after that." (4)

Also on The East Buttress Johnny Adams and Chas MacQuarrie climbed a direct version of the old aid route Overhanging Grooves by following the initial large flake line directly to its top. This strenuous feature requires a large amount of effort, especially with the placing of gear which still awaited the 'cow bell' type of large Hexagonal nuts. Despite Johnny's best effort, he had to rest on a peg before he could complete the pitch. He comments:

> "I thought we had just climbed one of the steepest pitches in The Lake District when we did the first pitch. It was a great route, and quite intimidating." (5)

They also added a new variation to the original second pitch up a lovely steep crackline directly above the foot of The Yellow Slab; a pitch that is often damp from the continually dripping slot in the capping roof. Overall, Overhanging Grooves Direct gives a good introduction to the strenuous style of climbing on The East Buttress at E3, 5c,5b.

Down on The Shamrock, Eric Spofforth, partnered by John Wilkinson, found a 81m route on an isolated slab to the right of the buttress to create Silk Cut Slab, a clean and fairly pleasant MVS. He had been aware of this feature for years, and had often wondered why nobody had got around to climbing it. This is not surprising, because the start lies by scrambling for a hundred metres above the scree up slimy, unstable grass and moss and there is no easy way to avoid this. This section of the crag is characterised by a continuous capping roof up to its left, an area completely unexplored until recently but noted by many, even Dave Birkett has cast a speculative eye over the buttress. Spofforth was slightly disappointed the route wasn't any harder, but the advert promising that the named cigarette was so mild inspired its name. Eric returned the following year with Jim Radcliffe to climb the slab to its right at Hard Severe, bestowing the name Sowker; inspired by Jim's love of rather generously endowed women!

Chalk

The sweltering heat of the long summer of 1976 was one of the main reasons why many of the leading climbers in The Lakes started to use chalk on the crags. Chalk is a fine white calcium carbonate powder originally used by gymnastics which has the property of reducing the sweat on the hands, and in certain circumstances improving grip. At the time, the appearance of white dabs on the rock caused apoplectic reactions by many; led by Ken Wilson in *Mountain* magazine. He saw the acceptance of this American import as an erosion of British ethics, devaluing the achievements of the activists, and he held that its use was a form of cheating. Wilson applauded those who declined its use, and gave heroic headlines to those climbers who completed chalk free ascents of existing routes. Martin Berzins wrote into *Mountain*, stating that chalk was the future.
The rebuke from Ken Wilson covered two pages, mainly shouting down the pro-chalk argument and its protagonists, which included Berzins and Ed Cleasby.

Throughout the next years there was still a widespread resentment of chalk; the report of Berzins' first free ascent of The White Wizard in the log book at the Fell & Rock hut at Brackenclose was defaced by an anonymously acerbic comment

'Chalk used for aid!'

Berzins commented that only Livesey took a sane view, stating:

> "Using chalk was about as significant as pissing in the snow in Zero Gully." (6)

There were two opposing factions in what became the great chalk debate. Ian Roper wrote:

> "I have never used chalk and hope I never will.
> It seems to me that this obnoxious stuff is as often used for psychological purposes as it is for its adhesive qualities. It is objectionable for a number of reasons, not at least because the holds are marked out for those to follow." (7)

This was a credible argument which is still relevant today. There are many climbers who are so used to looking for the chalk on the rock above them that they have become dependent upon it for guiding the way. They seem to have lost, or perhaps never even gained, an ability to read the features of the rock on crags free of chalk and so they struggle to on-sight routes, especially in the bigger mountain areas.

Chalk (continued)

Editor Geoff Birtles makes a bold pro-chalk statement with the rear cover from issue 2 of *Crags* magazine.

A new magazine came into circulation that summer; its anarchic style and pro-chalk stance made Geoff Birtles' popular *Crags* magazine, a natural counter to *Mountain*. The radical style of this publication is best summed up by issue number two, where the entire back cover was plain black with only a white hand print slapped across it, with the strap line 'Crags Rules - O.K.' written across in a rushed freehand style. They also produced a large poster of Ron Fawcett leading L'Hora on Curbar Edge, dressed in only a pair of shorts and E.B's, hanging on to the jug with one hand and his other covered with chalk – with the evocative title: 'Remember last summer?'

The image was 'cool' – everyone wanted to be like Ron – complete with chalk bag. Chalk was becoming fashionable, especially with the young; its use was a rebellious, two-fingered reaction to the old establishment akin to the punk movement that was rocking the music world at the time. It was a panacea for the youth, who regarded those who did not use chalk as dinosaurs. The chalk-free campaign could not counter the benefits it offered. Its use became increasingly widespread, and within a couple of years chalk had grudgingly become an accepted part of the climbing scene. There were some notable exceptions to the rule that chalk was necessary in order to climb at a high standard, in particular Pat Littlejohn and Peter Whillance declined to use it for many years. There are still a few climbers who refuse to use it, including Brian Davison, but his stance is seen as an amusing anachronism by most of his peers.

Mary Jenner on the strenuous first pitch of Overhanging Grooves Direct.

The summer of 1976, remembered as 'the summer without end', saw the first ascent of the magnificent Saxon which climbs the beautiful clean wall to the right of Central Buttress. The most obvious feature of this route was the diagonal crack line above and right of the Great Flake, which had attracted the attention of many visitors to the crags. These included Bill Young who recalls:

> "My big regret was not trying Saxon. It was just waiting to be climbed, but I never bothered having a go." (8)

Saxon is inexorably linked with Ed Cleasby, a young teacher from Kirby-in-Furness who was a rather outspoken character and a rising star of the South Lakes group. He described this route with typical immodest assurance as being the best route of its standard in England. Certainly few can match it for superb wall climbing in an unbeatable position. Saxon is often praised as being Cleasby's route, because he had plotted its line from a photograph and it became an obsession with him, but in fact it was led by an old mate from Yorkshire, John Eastham.

It started one Saturday night in the Golden Rule pub in Ambleside; the meeting point for the South Lakes based climbers, and where Cleasby was looking for a partner. His usual mate, Rob Matheson, was at a party that night and they both knew he would be in no fit state for climbing the following day. Spotting John Eastham, Ed soon made arrangements to climb together and told him of this project on Scafell. Eastham was ambivalent; maybe he'd heard other promises of a similar ilk before, but Ed persuaded John with an extra pint of beer and the rash promise that he could have first go at the main pitch. Cleasby explained his rationale:

> "If you've driven over from Leeds to go up to Scafell, you'll have a particular route in mind to do. But to ask someone to take the time to try a project, and this was only a project in my mind's eye, it needed a bit of persuasion. I hadn't even done C.B. so I had no idea how it would go, but I knew it was one of the great unclimbed lines in The Lakes. The only way I could convince John to go there was to offer him the lead of the main pitch, even though I would have loved to lead it". (9)

The following day was fine, and Cleasby led up Mullan's Direct Start to C.B. to gain a small grass patch just right of the Oval ledge, and Eastham set off on the main pitch. This starts up a short corner which merges into the blank looking almost vertical face of rock to the right of the Great Flake. Eastham climbed up on small edges to where these seem to fade and at this point he was forced out right towards Moss Ghyll Grooves to find a runner. Ed did not hide his frustration with John for not climbing straight up to meet the obvious crack, and he was clearly regretting his hasty promise made the previous evening. A short traverse left on tiny ledges soon had John back below the crack, which has slightly offset edges, creating a slender groove. Despite being the start of the driest summer for decades, the crack still contained some moisture and he was finding things distinctly awkward.

Ed recalled:

> "He went up that pitch, but he was quite freaked by it. At one point in the crack, where there was a decent handhold and the crack's fine, he actually rested. He didn't sit on the nut or use it for aid; nothing like that; he just grabbed hold of a wire. I shouted up to him 'Don't spoil it! For God's sake John, don't spoil it!'. Then he got straight back onto the rock and finished the pitch. Sometimes despite the passage of time, you remember some things rather clearly. That's why I went back a week later because I was annoyed with the way he did it; I thought he had flawed the pitch." (10)

Ed Cleasby as seen in 1976.

Ed Cleasby as seen in 2008.

Steve Merry approaches the main crack of Saxon in beautifully atmospheric conditions.

John Porter's account in *Extreme Rock* sums up the style of this pitch:

> "The key traverse back left from the Grooves is difficult to start. A few friable flakes show the way, but the runners in the bottom of the groove seem a long pendulum away, if you were to fall off when seconding. The traverse gets easier near the end, and eventually there is a tiny ledge for a rest. Then the real climbing begins. An awkward mantel gains the bottom of the groove, which in turn is difficult to start and strenuous all the way to the top. The crack at the back oozes green slime even in dry weather, so the jams slip and the footwork on the nearly blank left wall requires care. The angle increases towards the top, making the final surge for the ledge tricky on tired arms. Bridging across the groove, I looked down between my legs, and had the sensation of gazing the wrong way through a telescope. I grappled onto the ledge, and the three of us sat together for a moment, sharing a feeling that the whole of Lakeland climbing had been condensed into one pitch." (11)

To finish the line, Cleasby climbed the lower section of the Bayonet Shaped Crack before traversing out left to a short, but sensationally exposed arête to produce a modern classic E2, 5c,5b climb. But Saxon was still incomplete. The next week, Ed returned with Rob Matheson with the intention of removing John's indiscretion on the main pitch. He also wanted to add a new independent first pitch and to record the route on film.

Matheson and Cleasby formed a strong team, both originating from the Furness area in the south of the county, and both similarly armed with equally strong moustaches. They complemented each other well; Matheson was a superb technician on steep rock, which countered Cleasby's bold and impatient approach to climbing. Rob led the new start on-sight; it rose rightwards across the steep wall from the first pitch of Central Buttress to give an E2, 5c variation that nowadays hardly sees a repeat. This is because it was excluded from the 1984 guidebook, and was relegated as a minor variation in the previous guidebook, but it has now been reinstated as the described start in the 2014 guide. Cleasby then led the main pitch in good style whilst being photographed by Rob, and it was the publication of these pictures that made many people think that Saxon is a Cleasby-Matheson route.

Shortly afterwards the route was repeated by Martin Berzins and Chris Sowden, who only had a rough description of the line. Berzins climbed the wall directly to the crack which had been Cleasby's intended route, thus avoiding the traverse right to the edge of Moss Ghyll Grooves. This involved steep fingery climbing, with a worrying lack of protection to give a bold and probably unrepeated variation. Martin later admitted:

> "That was the scariest thing we ever did, we just climbed straight up the wall of Saxon. There was no gear at all; it would probably be given E4 or E5 now, it was a really serious lead." (12)

Later that day after repeating Saxon, Cleasby and Matheson went around to The East Buttress to look at a crack in the pillar right of Phoenix that Cleasby had noticed earlier whilst on the girdle. They repeated Lamb's Zeus to gain the belay on Phoenix, and then Rob traversed right to the crack which gave a tremendously positioned finish, which is probably finer than the normal finish to the route. They called this The Arête Finish, which was later grafted onto Phoenix to give an exposed and very photogenic variation at E2, 5c.

Photo: Al Phizacklea

Jerry Peel on the main pitch of Saxon, with the Great Flake of C.B. behind.

Photo: Rob Matheson

Ed Cleasby repeating the main pitch of Saxon..

Paul Innes on the outrageously exposed Phoenix Arête Finish.

The next new route climbed that summer was back on the main Scafell crag where the steep frontal wall left of Botterill's Slab is seamed by thin cracks and grooves angled in the same parallel strata as the line of the parent slab. This feature had been inspected in the past by Rob Matheson but it was Pete Botterill and Steve Clegg who cleaned the wall and prepared to do battle. Botterill started across a sloping gangway that runs leftwards to the most prominent groove in the wall, which gradually increased in difficulty to a small overhang, where a thin move stopped him. He was absolutely shattered so he lowered back to the ground where Clegg took the lead. He too could get no further, so they wandered across to Mickledore for a brew leaving the ropes in place. Pete tied back into the ropes and finally reached a good hold, where further neat and sustained climbing led to the finish. The Livesey influence had finally filtered down to the locals, as this was the first time they had used 'yo-yo' tactics to complete a route which they called Shadowfax – they had increased the standard on the crag to E4, 6a. It had been suggested to Pete that he should name the route 'Botterill's Wall', as it lay just below the line of Botterill's Slab. Pete modestly declined the idea as being too pretentious.

Across on the walls left of Moss Gill, a rare raid by the West Cumbrian team of Tony Stephenson, Hillary Charlton and Chris Sice drew attention to this little noticed part of the crag. The classic route on these walls is of course Moss Ghyll Grooves, and the other route that attracts attention is Jim Birkett's Slab and Groove Route. Looking up this latter route, the main slab is seen to be capped by two huge stacked overhangs, and bounded on its right by a steep wall in which is sandwiched a secondary narrow slab as a miniature version of the main slab. Stephenson had attempted to climb the capping roof above the big slab directly some years earlier with Tony Edwards, but the blank slab above the roof forced him to abseil from a jammed knot with his tail between his legs. This line seems to hold some strange attraction for West Cumberland folk, because it was from below this overhang that Joe Williams turned back in 1946.

Returning in 1974, Stephenson padded up the right corner of the main slab until just below the first overhang; then pulled right onto the subsidiary slab and tip-toed up (where there is usually a drainage weep trickling down) until he came across the huge barrier of the upper roof. Here the only way to make progress was to traverse left across the extremely blank slab separating the upper and lower overhangs. This slab is completely devoid of any wrinkles, and neither are there any holds for the hands, so Tony was forced to tension across from his last runner to reach the belay on Slab and Groove. The upper pitch had a lovely airy feel to it, in contrast to the intimidating and claustrophobic environs of the start. The resulting route was called Harvest, after the Neil Young track, and it was to be twelve years before it went free. This was first achieved in 1988 by Al Phizacklea and Bob Wightman, who smeared across the slab by pushing hard up against the underside of the upper roof to maintain balance, a move only made possible because of a new generation of sticky boots. The grade increased from HVS to E2, with a very thin 6b move for the crux.

Another line climbed during this summer was an obscure superdirect version on Pisgah Buttress called Hilarity by the London based team of Mike Morrison and Mick Fowler, who later rose to international fame with a string of audacious Himalayan ascents. This route received a brief mention in *Mountain* magazine but, due to the lack of a description, it never made it into the FRCC 'new routes supplements', and it only warranted a brief mention in the 1984 guidebook, with the contemptuous note that the guide writers could find no further details. Al Phizacklea suspected that a new route he climbed in 1993 could have been the line of Hilarity, and indeed this was confirmed in 2008 when Mick Fowler quickly and efficiently dug out his first ascent notes, finally resolving the issue after 32 years. (Does he file all his own tax returns as competently?) The main part of the climbing is a direct line up the front of the buttress above the large flake belay on Pisgah Buttress Direct, taking a delightful steep wall passing through a band of bulging rock at HVS.

Pete Botterill.

Photo: Brian Cropper

Jill Lawrence and Pete Livesey, Lost Horizons team.

Adam Lincoln about to start the crux moves on Lost Horizons, a difficult traverse to the arête on the left.

Arguably the biggest line to fall during this time was that of Lost Horizons, the huge leaning corner right in the centre of The East Buttress. This was one of only a handful of routes graced with the title of 'the best unclimbed line in The Lakes'. Certainly it is the most prominent feature on the crag; a perfectly clean cut open corner that steepens and closes into a narrow slot right at its top. Often it had been investigated but rarely attempted, and it was to be Pete Livesey and Jill Lawrence who took this mighty prize. It received typical Liveseyan preparation, abseil cleaning, hold inspections and the pre-placement of pegs and wires used for cleaning, a tactic that still raised much controversy at the time. The corner succumbs to sustained bridging which is helped by occasional jams in the crack at the back of the corner, but as the rock slants leftwards and outwards, progress is always strenuous. However, the crux is towards the top of the groove, where a peg was used to initiate a short, sloping traverse out to the left rib; a section that often spits climbers off. Then follows another exposed, delicate move to reach the belay on Great Eastern, an unsettling sequence just when the climber is most tired. Whether Livesey actually used the peg for aid or simply for resting on the first ascent is debatable. A rather pointed section in Bill Birkett's *Scafell, Portrait of a Mountain* includes the following paragraph that
pulls no punches:

Photo: Al Phizacklea

> "Afterwards, relaxing with other climbers on Mickledore, Livesey was asked by Pete Botterill if it had been free. Pete said it had. It was left to Jill to spill the beans with: 'What about the sling, Pete?' Livesey had pre-placed a long sling on a piton and used it to swing around the bulging top arête of the corner – so in fact it was not a free ascent!" (13)

Jill Lawrence recently claimed the ascent was too long ago to recall with certainty; but she vehemently denied that she ever made that quote. Pete Botterill also recalls asking Livesey about the route, but it was some time later and certainly not at Mickledore, and his conversation did not follow the above flow. Any attempt to sympathise with Livesey's account is tainted by the fact that he had an aptitude for stretching the truth, some even hinted that he was an inveterate liar. It seems that Livesey's lasting legacy was one of speculation and strife, and this antagonism was not eliminated by his untimely death due to cancer in 1998.

The following extract by Martin Berzins from the book *Extreme Rock* gives some flavour of an early ascent:

> "It's not as bad as it looks; the first corner is good, honest bridging and laybacking. The sloping ledge above is guarded by a manky peg, so pathetic it could only have been used for cleaning. Above, the corner leans and narrows. Fifteen feet higher is another ledge, and in between is the second peg. A fierce pull enables it to be reached – smashed into the hilt right by the crux, it's obviously not just for decoration. A bit of cunning enables you to free climb until the peg is at waist level but the ledge is still tantalisingly out of reach. The next move, the crux, involves easing up from a precarious bridging position to reach the ledge. There is some dispute about whether Livesey free-climbed the next move on the first ascent. What is certain is that I, for one, grabbed the peg, and that the move was unquestionably free climbed by both Bob Berzins and Alan Murray some five years after the first ascent." (14)

Lost Horizons was Livesey's only contribution to Scafell, and the fact that he may not have climbed it free is testimony to its difficulty. It certainly had a reputation for many years as being one of the hardest lines in The Lakes, with many failed attempts to climb it without aid.

One final achievement from the 1976 summer was the first free ascent of The White Wizard. This route's sustained first pitch still contained several aid points, and it drew the attention of Pete Botterill and Steve Clegg. They attempted the route on-sight with the intention of climbing it as free as possible but despite Pete's best effort, he still retained one point of aid. Pete recalls that during the ascent:

> "There was a narrow edge on the third pitch from where you've got to go up this arête on the right, and there was a small block lying against the rock at the very end of the ledge. I moved it out of the way so I wouldn't knock it off onto Cleggy. I couldn't reach the holds above, then I realised that the block had been placed there on purpose so I replaced it and stood on it, and was able to do the moves". (15)

Pete later mentioned this frustrating failure to Martin Berzins, who promptly returned to the crag with Gordon Higginson and flashed a free ascent on-sight. In this free state, and when it is clean, The White Wizard is one of the most popular E3's on Scafell.

The long drought of 1976 finally came to an end on the 29th August, with a bout of heavy, prolonged rain. This did not deter one party attempting Botterill's Slab the following day, but the wetness had caused the algae to swell rapidly resulting in very greasy rock. The leader, who was making the final move at the top of the slab suddenly found himself in a rapid involuntary descent, to be finally stopped just short of the grass on Rake's Progress!

Once the left arête of Lost Horizons is reached, the climber is faced with a difficult pull to gain a resting place; climber, Adam Lincoln.

The Preparation of Routes

Abseiling down routes to clean them of grass, heather and loose rock had been practised back in the 1920's by early pioneers; notably Harry Kelly, who made the famous comment about Grooved Wall on Pillar Rock:

"There was enough earth sent down into Ennerdale to provide soil for the whole of the reafforestation scheme!"

Another famous route made safe by the trundling, or removal, of loose blocks posing a danger to climbers was The Central Pillar on Esk Buttress, but thereby hangs another cautionary tale – don't boast about it in the pub. Jack Soper, who had removed the blocks, told the landlord of the Old Dungeon Ghyll bar, Sid Cross, about the feat. However, they were overheard by Dave Thomas, a member of Pete Crew's group who made an early start the following day to grab the first ascent of this prized route.

The majority of new routes climbed in the 1960s and early 1970s were done on-sight, without any preparation or inspection of the route. This is considered the most ethical form of climbing; the climber pits himself against the crag without knowing what lies ahead, whether there are any runners or not, nor for that matter whether there are any holds available to climb. The 'Old Guard' were attempting to maintain this ethos of purity and were opposed to the radical changes in ethics beginning to pervade British climbing from abroad. One of the main opponents to this change was Allan Austin, who wrote several caustic comments:

"I do not see crags as impressive backcloths where ruthless men can construct their climbs." and "All the protests come from jumped-up XS men who think their particular brand of ethics should count." (16)

Rob Matheson summed up the time perfectly in an article titled 'Lakeland Climbing in the Seventies' which appeared in *Mountain 54*:

"The conflict derives from the fact that many climbers have begun to adopt a highly 'professional' approach towards the making of first ascents; inspecting new lines in detail by abseil before attempting to climb them. The on-sight principle was discarded by these climbers in the belief that a good job could not otherwise be made ...

Photo: Al Phizacklea

Rob Matheson swings clear of the crag after unclipping from gear placed to clean a new route; this demonstrates the difficulty of reaching overhanging rock for cleaning.

The evolution of the grading system.

The grading of routes according to their level of difficulty stems from the Victorian era, when O.G. Jones published his *Rock Climbing in the English Lake District* in 1897; generally regarded as the very first guide book for climbers. Jones used four categories to determine the difficulty of a route – Easy, Moderate, Difficult and Exceptionally Severe. This primitive form of grading illustrates that in those days, once beyond a Difficult climb, it meant hard climbing with potentially fatal consequences should a slip occur. Over the next twenty years the Exceptionally Severe category was phased out in favour of Severe and Very Severe grades, and this remained the norm in The Lakes until Harry Kelly resigned from his guidebook editing role in the mid-1960s. By that time, the VS grade encompassed routes varying in difficulty from Botterill's Slab and Mickledore Grooves to Ichabod and The Nazgul. Eventually the grading system was extended to include the Hard Very Severe and Extremely Severe grades, and there were instances in the Climbers' Club guides where the grade of Exceptionally Severe was reintroduced to indicate routes harder than Extremely Severe.

By the mid-seventies improved equipment and training, along with competitive drive from the likes of Pete Livesey had increased the level of difficulty to a new level. Livesey wrote an article in *Mountain 39* where he proposed the widespread use of XS, HXS and 'harder still' grades, but this continued reliance on the use of adjectival words.

Many dreamed up new ways of indicating the difficulty of a route. A solution introduced by the Climbers' Club utilised a numerical system to complement the adjectival grade which still exists to this day. For example a VS could be 4c, and an easy XS could be 5c. This numerical arrangement is hard to understand for those not familiar with it; for instance, how to differentiate between a 4c and a 5a? It only becomes clear after prolonged exposure to this system which allows a comparison to be made between routes; it certainly generated many hot arguments in pubs over the years. One man's 4c could easily be 5a to someone of a shorter stature. It's not a foolproof method of grading, but without it the pub scene would not be as lively as it is.

Other new systems were too radical to become accepted by the main body of climbers. Ed Drummond employed a confusing system for the Avon Gorge guide in 1967 that gave a score from 1 to 3 for various aspects of the route such as the number of hard moves, the protection, quality of rock and the type of climbing. For example, a standard HVS 5b would be given the grade of 5b, 3000 – a rather cumbersome system that failed to catch on, though it provided Drummond's rivals with a source for lampooning!

It was the young pretender of the climbing magazines, *Crags*, that published an editorial comment titled 'Super Grades' in early 1977, a title that quickened the heart of the young climber. It noted:

> "Climbers in Britain must want a new grading system like a hole in the head. The whole idea of new grading systems has become somewhat of a hefty joke in the last 15 years, reaching belly-laugh proportions with Drummond's multi-alpha-numerical system. But when the harder climbs get much harder than the XS's we have had established for 20 years, we reach a state of overflow. So what do we do about the traffic jam at the front of the grid? Relax, you don't have to burn your fingers, because the man in the asbestos gloves has already come up with the answer. No, we are not going to have Super-Severe, Supremely severe, Supersonic Severe or any other space age descriptives. The simple proposal is to have Extreme 1, Extreme 2, Extreme 3 and so on." (20)

The individual proposing this scheme was Pete Botterill from Carlisle. The intention was that a grade of E1 to E5 would be allocated to those routes above HVS. This was an open-ended system, capable of increasing to cater for even harder routes of the future. When used in conjunction with the numerical (5b, 5c, etc.) grades, it allows the climber to assess the seriousness of a climb. Over the following years, the perception and acceptance of this system became widespread. Not all climbers grasped the full purpose of the system at first, and Ed Cleasby proposed a strict four-grade scheme from E1 to E4, and then he reserved the final E5 grade for a route that was so unprotected that it would end in fatality for anyone failing on it. This goes some way to explain Cleasby's harsh grading regime through the years. As an example of Cleasby's grades on Scafell, he gave The White Wizard E3; whilst Nazgul, Zeus, Incubus (1 point of aid) and Shadowfax were given E2; with Saxon, Ichabod, Dyad, Holy Ghost, Phoenix and Lord of the Rings all E1. In his world there had been no E5's established, simply because no-one had been killed trying the hardest routes!

The Preparation of Routes (continued)

> "One must remember, however, that in 1968 climbers had little pressure on them; they could afford to climb badly and just have a good time. In the early seventies, growing disapproval of the use of ndiscriminate aid resulted in the trend towards professional methods. In the same way, climbers were led to think about their own ability and, with this as a catalyst, standards improved" (17)

Peter Livesey's ruthless preparation of a potential new route is well known. It allowed him to carry just what gear was required on the route without having to hang around trying various nuts whilst using up his strength. Also he often practised the actual moves from the rope. All this was anathema to the traditionalists, but when it became apparent that Livesey had increased the overall standard of climbing, other climbers realised they had to follow his style, or get left behind. For instance, the majority of the South Lakes lads utilised the full gamut of Livesey's tactics; Cleasby even top-roped one of his new routes, Imagination, prior to the lead. The northern team however, were more restrained in their interpretation of what was acceptable and what was not. Top-roping was definitely not, and they became notorious for only ever placing pegs whilst actually leading the route.

Martin Berzins explained his reason for preparing routes:

> "I gave up on-sighting after a particular harassing ascent of Eclipse on Pavey, which I mistook to be the first ascent. [It was in fact the first free ascent]. I never did see the fuss about pegs; if you have to clean it why not prepare it properly? Eventually on these routes I would figure where the holds are and if it looked possible to reach them. I came to realise it was more fun this way, and inevitably the route felt completely different when climbing it to how I thought it would." (18)

The Preparation of Routes (continued)

SUPER GRADES

EDITORIAL

Prophet of Doom, the groove in shadow, Curbar Edge. Photo Geoff Birtles.

limbers in Britain must want a new grading system like a hole in the head. The whole idea of new systems as become a somewhat hefty joke in the last 15 years, reaching belly-laugh proportions with Drummond's ulti-alpha-numerical system.

The article in *Crags 6* that introduced the concept of E grades to the climbing world.

A more detailed analysis of cleaning routes on The East Buttress is given by Dave Birkett. He observes:

"It's funny, this rock on the East, it's got this kind of algae or lichen over the routes, which they all appear clean but they're not. When you clean them off with a wire brush on that first day, the rock kinds of oozes or sweats, and it's quite hard to hold, but if you go back a week later the rock's got its grip back somehow. So for that first day when you clean something it all feels a little bit slippier than it should, it always takes a week before things feel a lot better." (19)

It was Rob Matheson's article in *Mountain 54* that set the standard for grades in The Lakes; for the routes on Scafell he gave the following suggestions for grades:

Nazgul – E3	Dyad – E2	Phoenix (with Direct finish) – E2
Saxon – E2	Leverage – E1	Zeus (with Arête Finish) – E2
The White Wizard – E4	Gold Rush – E1	Incubus (1 point of aid) – E3
Shadowfax – E4	Lost Horizons – E4	Holy Ghost – E2
Gilt Edge Eliminate – E1	Ichabod – E2	Lord of the Rings – E2

It can be seen that most of these grades still hold true in the current guidebook, so perhaps the perplexing issue of grading is resolved; but the unique British system continues to bewilder and dismay foreign visitors.

Footnotes

1. Pete Botterill, FRCC audio recording, 2008
2. Ian Roper, source unrecorded
3. Pete Botterill, FRCC audio recording, 2008
4. Ed Cleasby, FRCC audio recording, 2008
5. Johnny Adams, FRCC audio recording, 2008
6. Martin Berzins, e-mail correspondence to author, 2009
7. Ian Roper, *Fell & Rock Journal*
8. Bill Young, FRCC audio recording, 2008
9. Ed Cleasby, FRCC audio recording, 2008
10. Ed Cleasby, FRCC audio recording, 2008
11. John Porter, 'Saxon' from *Extreme Rock* 1987
12. Martin Berzins, FRCC audio recording, 2008
13. Bill Birkett, extract from *Scafell, Portrait of a Mountain*
14. Martin Berzins, 'Lost Horizons' from *Extreme Rock*
15. Pete Botterill, FRCC audio recording, 2008
16. Allan Austin, extract from *Mountain 54*
17. Rob Matheson, extract from *Mountain 54*
18. Martin Berzins, FRCC audio recording, 2008
19. Dave Birkett, FRCC audio recording, 2008
20. Geoff Birtles, extract from *Crags 6*

1977 - 1981

The Modern Golden Era of Scafell

Above: The iconic photograph of a young Martin Berzins by John Woodhouse.

Right: Andy Mitchell reaches the 'handrail' hold on Ringwraith, where a semi-rest can be taken before the crux wall above.

Overleaf:
Nathan Pike was pleased to reach the handrail hold on Ringwraith, shortly before he proved the old adage that 'pride cometh before the fall…'

Photo: Al Phizacklea

1977 saw the arrival of the Leeds based team comprising the tall and rather physically intimidating brothers Martin and Bob Berzins, and their smaller but immensely strong friend, Chris Sowden. The reputation of Martin as a powerful climber was suddenly enhanced when a photograph by John Woodhouse was published showing his long hair swept back by a headband, wire framed glasses and a barrel chest rippling under a tiny vest, depicting a rather statuesque physique. They had all trained on the traditional gritstone outcrops and the steep limestone of their home county of Yorkshire which had added considerable strength and technical ability to their climbing style.

The team chose the steep blank wall between The White Wizard and The Nazgul as their first project. This was a rather futuristic line which was given the now customary abseil clean; a task made awkward by the way the wall leaned to the left and overhung slightly. Martin commented later on the reaction he received from the local crowd:

> "I remember getting some gentle grief from the Carlisle lads, who were going on about putting pegs in before leading the route, but there would have been no chance of flashing it if we'd had to carry the pegs and place them on such a steep wall, especially when you'd already be tired from cleaning it. We just used Livesey tactics on it. You've got to remember that we had a lot of pressure to climb these routes on the same day as we cleaned them; if you failed on it and left it, those pesky locals would nip in and do it. There was none of this leaving a route because it was someone else's project; it was fair game in those days. Anyway, you didn't know whether it would be raining the next day, and that could be it for three months or for that year". (2)

Photo: Al Ph zacklea

The route initially climbs a ramp and passes through a bulge, protected by a peg. A stubborn long reach gains a series of awkward layaway holds which lead up to a peg in the centre of the fingery wall. Martin then followed a handrail out right, pulling up with difficulty before a tiring hand traverse led back left to a resting ledge. After composing himself he continued on better holds to complete the pitch in exemplary style. Both his seconds struggled to follow the route – it was an intensely cold day, and they remarked that even with two pairs of gloves they would have had cold hands. Chris had to sit on the second peg for a rest, and Bob cocked up the sequence and sat on the rope to rearrange his hands. His punishment for this failure was being forced to complete the route from the hand traverse section without being given the chance to rest. They noticed a potential second pitch, but lack of time prevented an attempt that day, and they finished up The White Wizard.

Martin and Bob returned the following weekend, when they took the opportunity to climb a hard fingery pitch up the front face of the Great Flake. Two pegs were placed together on the crux bulge from abseil, an act of potential desecration which reminded Gordon Higginson of an old quote from Sir Jack Longland as 'I'd rather shoot a fox than drive a piton in Welsh rock!' This inspired the name of Foxshooter. The first pitch is quite intimidating, and was later felt to be worth E4, 5c, even though it was originally given E2. The brothers then followed the upper section of The Nazgul to the top of the crag, from where they abseiled down the second pitch of their earlier new route. This follows a diagonally slanting groove up the gently overhanging headwall in a similar manner to the underside of the eaves of a house roof. Anyone who thinks the main face of Scafell Crag never becomes steep enough to be called vertical is invited to abseil down this wall where the ropes hang free in space; and for extra spice it should be done in thick mist. This superb pitch can only be overcome by strenuous bridging, as illustrated by Al Phizacklea on the second ascent:

> "After a rest on the ledge I gained my high point, overcoming the awkward section by pinching the right rib of the groove and throwing myself into a wide, high bridge. Gasping for breath I lurched for a finger jug on the tip of the roof with my right hand, then slotted my left next to it. It didn't take long to realise this was a bad mistake – my legs were rattling, and with the fingers slowly creaking open I let out one desperate cry before catapulting through the air." (1)

Martin and Bob laid siege to this pitch by alternating leads. Bob had two attempts to reach the finger slot before Martin completed a clean lead on his third attempt to create the first E5 on the crag, and what many believe is the best E5 in The Lakes. They called it Ringwraith, following Les Brown's theme started with The Nazgul; it was a superb achievement, and was to be the first of many on Scafell. As a footnote to the grade, Martin and Bob cautiously awarded the route E4, because:

> "At the time there were only two E5's in the country, Footless Crow and Right Wall. We couldn't have given it E5 because we hadn't done an E5 at the time, and it just would have seemed too pretentious to pronounce that we were as good as Livesey, so it was given E4." (2)

This undervaluing of route grades was common for the hard routes right across The Lakes in the late seventies for the very reasons Berzins noted above. It was only after these routes were repeated by the younger climbers who had not been in direct competition with Livesey that they were recognised for what they really were – full blown E5s.

On the very same day as the Berzins were completing Ringwraith, Ed Cleasby and Rob Matheson were around the corner under The East Buttress, though neither team were aware of the others existence that day. Ed and Rob had walked in from Cockley Beck at the head of the Duddon valley to investigate a long term project on the brown wall right of Lost Horizons. This had been tried by many others in the past, including Cleasby himself with Bill Birkett, Pete Livesey, Colin Read and Johnny Adams. Read had once led up the initial corner with the aid of a nut and took a hanging belay at the start of the sloping ramp out right, and Adams then reached the end of the sloping ledge before retreating. At the time no-one had bettered his high point.

Photo: Al Phizacklea

The gently overhanging second pitch of Ringwraith, probably the most exposed pitch on the crag.

George Ullrich climbing the awkward initial corner of Shere Khan, at the point where it moves out right onto the ramp.

The initial groove, at a similar leaning angle as Lost Horizons, was adorned by several rusty pegs and a jammed wire from the earlier attempts. Cleasby recalled:

> "Rob abseiled down the crag to have a look at this line, and I thought what a bloody waste of time; he was so far out from the rock because the crag is so steep he couldn't get anywhere near it. I climbed up the first corner, which is overhanging, but there's holds on it and it's not too bad. I would argue that it's psychological because I can't remember it being that hard. I remember thinking that the ledge will be O.K. for belaying on, but when you get there the ledge is like that [holding his hand at a steep angle] and you think 'Wow, this is a wild place to be!' You can rest there, but then you get to its end where it narrows and turns into a vertical shallow groove. There are holds there, and Rob was encouraging me to continue because he convinced me there were better holds above, but it's easy to encourage from a belay ledge. I used a rest point because basically the crag was bloody filthy, so I rested on a nut to clean it. There are reports that it was cold welded to place, well I was pretty good at hammering things, and I know all about cold welding in nuts, but this one was just tapped in. My over-riding impression was that technically it was O.K, but psychologically it blew my mind, and that's why my arms physically turned to jelly. You think 'Oh my God!' and the strength drains away from your fingers through fear." (3)

Cleasby was soon on the ledge and, after Matheson joined him, they abseiled off because the rock above was mossy and the evening was drawing in. They returned the next day and abseiled down to the exposed belay before completing the route up a crack in a mossy groove. This breakthrough became known as Shere Khan, after the tiger in Kipling's *The Jungle Book*, and it has since become one of the most popular routes on The East Buttress thanks to its inclusion in *Extreme Rock*. For the very same reason that Berzins described when defining the grade of Ringwraith, Ed and Rob originally gave this route an E4 grade.

The rest point was dispensed with on the second ascent by another Yorkshire raider Ron Fawcett, and this E5, 6a pitch has since gained a reputation for boldness, as Martin Berzins recorded in *Extreme Rock*:

> "Adams' high point is a typical ledge on The East Buttress – a holdless optical illusion, caused by the eye seeking respite from the overhanging norm. Standing on the ledge only urges you to continue by teetering rightwards to its end, feeling somewhat cheated. The position here is impressive, and the overhanging rock above depressing. The protection at the end of the ramp isn't too good – a collection of tiny wires and the holds all seem to slope the wrong way. The only incentive used to be provided by an in-situ wire sling 20ft. above. Reaching it only made you wish that you hadn't bothered. It was a bashie – cold-welded by fear and panic into a miserable crack. Above is another evil, sloping ledge. What a dilemma! Use the nut for aid to find the holds, or risk a horrendous fall if you fail. The first time I led this pitch I was sufficiently feeble to have no choice. Ron Fawcett's free ascent merely attached guilt to a nut already overloaded by me. I returned much later to get my revenge, and found the nut gone, probably stripped by some falling star. Its absence meant 20ft. of scary groove-climbing with no runners until just before the belay. No place for the faint-hearted, and testing for mind and body." (4)

The crux groove of Shere Khan, climber George Ullrich.

Photo: Al Phizacklea

Above: Rob Matheson.

Below: Ed Cleasby traversing onto the lower section of Edge of Eriador on the first ascent.

Photo: Rob Matheson

Returning to the base of the crag after completing Shere Khan, Matheson and Cleasby immediately eyed up the possibility offered by the prominent protruding arête to the right of May Day Direct; reminiscent of Cloggy's Curving Arête. The lower section of the rib rose above the bivvy shelter at the foot of the crag, but this was evidently too difficult as the holds ran out after 4 metres. A shallow groove just left of this promised little in the way of protection, so Cleasby traversed rightwards across the top of this groove from May Day Climb to reach a small ledge shared with Dyad. Above, the rib loomed menacingly and with the only runners at the level of the ledge, Rob quickly realised that an on-sight lead was not an option and that the pitch needed cleaning. Leaving Cleasby to chill on the ledge, he ascended the second pitch of Dyad and after some effort, managed to brush the rock clean. It was getting late, and despite some dispirited moaning by Cleasby, Rob pulled off a superb lead to complete Edge of Eriador, E4, 6a, which received the praiseworthy comment from Ed that he was 'bloody glad you led that!' The protection on this pitch has not improved over the subsequent thirty years, and in those days, the route had a reputation for being one only suitable for leaders well blessed in the gonad department.

Following their success on the Saturday with Ringwraith, the Berzins Brothers moved round to The East Buttress on the Sunday where they witnessed the Furness lads complete the first ascent of Shere Khan. Not to be outdone, they completed a most remarkable weekend by removing the aid point from Overhanging Groove Direct to leave a sustained but spectacular E3, 5c. Bob recalled:

> "I remember it seemed that Ed and Rob had done a fantastic route [Shere Khan] and I felt as though we'd missed out. You'd look at that wall with the odd peg and bits of tat, and then all of a sudden they'd done it, and we thought that was the route of the crag, and what had we been doing messing about around the corner? I think it was a year or two before we were up to that sort of thing, they were just that bit ahead of everybody, bold enough to have a go at these routes. I take my hat off to them, it was a fantastic achievement, that wall was such a big thing at the time and I thought 'Oh, my God, you wouldn't even think about climbing up there', and they'd done it." (5)

Bob Smith and John Earl on the bold upper pitch of Edge of Eriador.

Photo: Al Phizacklea

Martin added:

> "Mind you, we never admitted to rating Ed in those days. But in one sense, all of our subsequent routes, Cullinan, Zeya and Siege Perilous were just an attempt to recover from them doing that route; it had been that sort of achievement." (6)

A surprisingly good route was added on Shamrock by two Tyneside raiders, Bob Hutchinson and John Earl, who over the previous couple of years had gained a reputation for grabbing new routes all around The Lakes. Shamrock Eliminate, E3 5c,5c,5c,5b, is a long and sustained line right up the main central arête of the buttress. They added a new first pitch to the route the following year, shortly before Bob was tragically killed by a slip from below Eagle Crag in Borrowdale. The route starts up a beautiful delicate scoop in the lower slabs, the second pitch consists of a difficult, shallow groove, but it is the third pitch that lingers long in the memory. This climbs a groove to a bulge in the sharp edged arête, which leans alarmingly to the left. A thin flake right in the edge of the arête is followed in a spectacular position, hanging above the void, to a strenuous, gasping finish on sloping holds. Shamrock Eliminate was once a magnificent route that should be on the tick list of visiting E3 climbers, although a recent attempt floundered under a robust carpet of algae.

Jeff Lamb and Pete Botterill returned to The East Buttress in 1978, a year in which they were to dominate the crag. At the start of an amazing weekend they were joined by John Taylor who pointed them towards a good looking thin crack up a mossy wall between Trinity and Gremlin's Groove at the left end of the crag. An old peg was already part way up the crack; it only became clear many years later that this had been placed on an attempt in the sixties by Paul Ross. Botterill led the route which Taylor named Talisman. Dave Birkett recently described it as "A stonking pitch, I can't believe I over-looked such an amazing pitch before." It gives sustained climbing at E2, 5c, but the return of the moss over the years seems to have deterred all but a handful of suitors. Taylor's involvement with this line had been omitted from the last three editions of the Scafell Guide, and it only came to light following an interview with Pete.

Later that day, Lamb and Botterill inspected a thin flake and a very awkward hanging groove leading directly to the start of The Yellow Slab. This pitch was perfectly suited to Lamb, who demonstrated his superior strength by flashing the first pitch of Caradhras, a powerful 6b pitch. Botterill impressed on spectators the true level of difficulty as he was forced to use two nuts for aid to second him. There was further steep hard climbing to follow which obviously needed cleaning, so they left it for the day and returned to the fray the following morning by abseiling down to the ledge on Great Eastern. Lamb struggled on his first attempt of the second pitch, which followed a thin crack into a bottomless corner which was obviously going to demand a more technical approach. Now it was time for Botterill to come to the fore and seek his revenge for the previous day. The crack overhung at the usual East Buttress angle of around 15° but the intricate crux involved accessing the corner by palming off its smooth left wall. This required desperate bridging to gain easier ground above, which followed the large corner line to the top. This was the first E5 for the Lamb-Botterill team, and its two 6b pitches give a tremendous challenge for the modern climber.

Caradhras wasn't the last of the day's pioneering, for they returned to the base of the crag and inspected the leaning groove which forms a smaller parallel twin to the left of Lost Horizons. This gives a sustained sequence of bridging in a character similar to its bigger neighbour which Lamb led with ease. They retreated from the belay and went home after completing one of the best weekends of their lives. They returned the following weekend, and climbed back up to the belay by way of following The Centaur. Botterill then took the lead, pulling out right from the belay to reach a thin hanging flake on the wall which led with difficulty to the big ramp of Great Eastern. This flake has caused quite a few teams problems in recent years, and it has become apparent that this pitch is actually harder than the groove below. The route Equinox E4 is typical of the excellent but sadly overlooked routes on this part of the crag.

Photo: Al Phizacklea

Above: Steve Merry on the delicate first pitch of Shamrock Eliminate.
Below: Jeff Lamb on the first ascent of Cahadras, pitch 1.

Photo: Pete Botterill

Above: Dai Lampard tackles the initial 6b wall of Cahadras.

Right: Dai Lampard on Cullinan, at the point where it rises off the ramp above Shere Khan.

Around this time, a long dry spell allowed Pete Whillance and Dave Armstrong to free climb Les Brown's Armageddon at E2, 5c. Taken as an isolated event it only deserves a passing mention, but amazingly this is the only contribution to the history of Scafell by this prolific team. Why they never returned when there was so much unclimbed rock up there seemed a bit of a mystery, but Pete explained:

> "We visited Scafell quite a few times over the years because there were so many routes to do; we spent our time repeating these, such as Lost Horizons, S.O.S., Caradhras and Incubus. On the days that we did intend to go up there to have a go at a new route it seemed the weather was against us, and our plans never fell into place. It certainly wasn't the case that we left the crag for Jeff and Pete; although they were our mates, there was never any agreement between us that left certain crags to any one team." (7)

The Berzins brothers gathered again below The East Buttress on a windy day, pondering the direct continuation above the start of Shere Khan. Following a brief clean by abseil and adding a peg (Martin reasoned that it was to show others where the route goes) he set off up the lower corner of Shere Khan, but he made a hash of the sequence and unexpectedly fell through the air, tearing out a fingernail and twisting his shoulder. Eighteen years old Bob wasn't giving him a second chance; this was his opportunity to grab the spoils from his elder sibling and he managed to lead the route in superb style. The climbing is sustained throughout its length, it follows the first groove of Shere Khan to the ramp on the right, then it rises up the leaning wall on the left where a committing move on marginal gear leads to a neat resting perch right on the edge of the wall. Here the climber may study the gently overhanging thin crack above which provides the strength-sapping finish to a fantastic pitch. Bob noted in his diary:

> "My overriding memory of this day was of climbing a steep, impressive route on brilliant rock in the best surroundings I could ever imagine." (8)

The route was named Cullinan (because it's a gem – the Cullinan diamond is the largest gem quality diamond ever found) and although the same grade as Shere Khan, there is a consensus that Cullinan gives better and more sustained climbing than the earlier route. Berzins couldn't resist throwing a taunting comment towards Cleasby by announcing how their new route 'climbs straight up where Shere Khan sneaks off rightwards!' Just for the record, the direct continuation of the initial groove still hasn't been climbed; this will merge back with the main route at the resting ledge, and is one of the few still unclimbed lines left on The East Buttress.

Towards the left end of The East Buttress, to the left of Zeus, Botterill and Lamb had their eyes on a free ascent of Chimera, which still held five points of aid on its first pitch. This starts up a steep fingery wall guarding the awkward entry into a hanging groove via a hard laybacking sequence; the protection consists of an old peg and a providential good wire. They finished up the remainder of Chimera which was only E1, but felt this resulted in an unsatisfactory unbalanced route. Returning the following month they added a more difficult finish to the first pitch by climbing a groove system above the right side of this belay to complete the route, which earned the overall grade of E5, 6b,5c. They called the completed route Lucius after a locally trained horse that had just won The Grand National. They hadn't put a bet on it!

During this memorable year for Jeff Lamb and Pete Botterill they visited The East Buttress sixteen times, mainly via the long walk from Borrowdale. Pete later admitted that as old age and exhaustion caught up with them, they relented and drove down to Wasdale Head, where the approach walk was an hour less. Not all of their visits ended in success, as their early attempt to repeat the free version of Overhanging Grooves Direct illustrates. Pete recalls:

> "The route had only just been climbed free, so I went up there one day with Phil Rigby to attempt it. He led the pitch. In those days there was a chockstone in the flake used to pull on and thread for a runner. It was a hot day, and I was belaying at the bottom dressed only in a pair of shorts, when Phil pulled the chockstone out. It struck me straight in the middle of my back, and Phil came down at once. We had no first aid apart from a single sticking plaster, so I had to go to Whitehaven Hospital to get stitched up. We didn't waste the day though; we later went down to St Bees Head for some bouldering." (9)

Lamb and Botterill's final route of the year was again climbed over two visits, but S.O.S. is a particularly brutal route for its grade of E5, 6b,6b. The first pitch starts from the bivvy shelter where everyone congregates below the crag, from where a mossy groove leads to an incut flake which provides the only hold and runner on the pitch. Passing this proves desperate, yet it is nothing compared to the second pitch. This starts at the foot of May Day Direct, then ascends the overhanging, leaning off-width crack on the left; a fissure designed to repel all suitors due to its lack of holds, protection, friction or compassion. How the Hell Lamb got up this remains a mystery, but he gained the sharp-topped edge of the block from where he could study the overhang above.

A boulder problem move leads to a thin crack that soars up the imposing overhanging wall, but even with protection from a 'Friend' (the first one they had ever used), Lamb found this crack too problematical and came back down to the belay. Swapping leads, Botterill's lighter weight and thinner fingers cracked the starting sequence to reach a good jam, but he was drained of energy. Jeff once again took over the lead, and by utilising the sequence worked out by Pete, he managed to reach the top. This route has been repeated by Pete Whillance and Dave Armstrong, but it has seen little traffic since. Even Dave Birkett has backed off the upper wall, because his sling wasn't long enough to go around the top block to protect the bouldery move to reach the crack. Take a good long sling!

Above: Dai Lampard contemplating the moves on Cullinan.

Right: Jeff Lamb on the first ascent of the difficult S.O.S.

Group Dynamics

History confirms a north-south divide in climbing circles in The Lake District since the 1950's. Paul Ross headed a Keswick-based group which spawned regular disagreements with the Langdale based climbers, led by Allan Austin. During the late 1970s, The Lakes had become entrenched in an almost tribal culture with a strong insular 'us and them' attitude prevailing between the two main camps. The northern group was based around Carlisle; comprising Pete Whillance, Dave Armstrong, Jeff Lamb, Pete Botterill and their friends as a tightly knit group of technically brilliant climbers which formed strong, stable partnerships. They were opposed by a southern and central group based around Furness and Ambleside which did not form such tight knit teams, but they all seemed to gel together to counter threats from the northern group. Ed Cleasby and Rob Matheson were the main pair, but they were allied with Bill Birkett, Rick Graham and Andy Hyslop, supported by Mike Lynch and other friends. Matheson explained his success with Cleasby as a team:
"We worked like brothers on the crag – you could have a go at very hard routes because you knew they were team efforts, and if he couldn't get up the route, maybe I could. We became very good at encouraging and spurring each other on, two strong people focussed on the same thing are stronger than one good climber. Ed and I were equally ambitious." (10)

This distinct grouping was exacerbated by Pete Livesey's activity throughout The Lake District in 1974, where almost overnight he raised the climbing standards from E3 to E5. His ascents of Footless Crow, E5, Nagasaki Grooves, E4, and Dry Grasp, E4, in Borrowdale, Fine Time, E4, and Eastern Hammer, E3, in Langdale, and Rough and Tumble, E4, on Dow Crag forced local climbers to realise that any remaining unclimbed lines were vulnerable to raids from outsiders. They accepted that if they wanted those remaining lines in their areas for themselves, they had to set about increasing their fitness and standards to compete at a similar level. Livesey had increased his ability on the crag by a combination of intensive training including rigorous stamina work and weight training. Previously, training had been an almost accidental by-product of climbing; climbers only became fit if they climbed regularly. Now the locals developed their own training regimes, the northern team used the sandstone outcrops of Armathwaite and the southern team used various venues for training, including Birkrigg Quarry and the Langdale Boulders.

In June 1979 Jeff Lamb teamed up with Bob Berzins to bring together an amalgamation of Cumbrian and Yorkshire strength and talent. There was no rivalry here; there was simply the desire to climb that brought them together. Martin Berzins explained:

> "Jeff and Pete were really rock steady on everything, and very, very strong. They were no-fuss great climbers and really good new-routers." (12)

Jeff Lamb and Bob Berzins teamed up to clean and climb the shallow, vertical groove found between the wall of Ichabod and the rounded pillar to its left. Climbing started by bridging further up the initial corner of Ichabod to gain the large roof, where a fingery swing right across a small flake leaves a difficult move to enter the groove. This is climbed by a sequence of desperately thin technical bridging moves where the narrowness of the groove badly restricts the posture of the body. All movements, including placing gear and climbing, are therefore exceedingly strenuous. This continues until a rest can be made where a horizontal roof on the left increases the width of the groove, allowing for a wider bridging position. The sustained climbing continues for another five metres until the upper corner eases at the point where Ichabod joins it from the right. This superb, underrated route called Mythical Kings after a music album by Dory Previn was graded E4, 6a and it leaves an impression long after an ascent.

Bob remembers how the mist rolled in whilst he was seconding, which made the atmosphere really spooky and quite unnerving. Several years later Dai Lampard was asked about his ascent, whereupon he rolled his eyes to the heavens and uttered 'God, it's desperate, that route!' He later explained:

> "That was possibly the most frightening route I've ever done in retrospect. I remember being so far above any gear the prospect of falling was just death. Somehow, I pulled over the top totally wasted and brought Nige Holmes up, who said he had to leave a 'Friend' in at the overhang – normally I would have gone off in a total tirade, but this time I just said it didn't matter. It's a route I never want to experience again!" (13)

The following day, Lamb was back up to The East Buttress with team-mate Pete Botterill, but it was a quiet day, and the only new line they climbed was the obvious steep crack running directly up through the second pitch of The Fulcrum at E1, 5c.

One memorable day a week later, Jeff Lamb picked up Bob and Martin Berzins from Raw Head in Langdale and they drove to Cockley Beck, where they had abandoned their car with an almost empty fuel tank. Jeff started by inspecting a line around the right end of the crag, so Martin and Bob abseiled down two separate lines, one right of Ichabod and one left of Gold Rush. Bob led his route by starting up the initial wall of Ichabod before traversing delicately right, as Geoff Oliver did, but continuing further to reach a thin crack which led through a bulge on immaculate clean rock. The position here is magnificent with the awesome overhanging wall of Borderline biting at the climber's heels; waiting to pluck any failure right off the face of the crag. With the first welcome runner fixed, the superb exposed crack leads to the penultimate Yellow Slab belay. The first pitch of Roaring Silence is considered one of the best E3 pitches in the entire Lakes; it also has the advantage of being one of the cleanest and fastest drying lines on the crag. Jeff made short work of the second pitch, pulling directly through a niche splitting the capping roof above to give a gymnastic finale to this modern classic route.

Photo: Al Phizacklea

Group Dynamics (continued)

Thus the abilities of the local climbers rapidly improved and subsequently so did their standard of climbing, but it took two years until the standard of their new routes increased to equal those of Livesey. The drive to climb unclimbed lines was intensified by the exposure and kudos derived from reports published in the climbing magazines; Ken Wilson's renowned *Mountain* and Geoff Birtles' new, impertinent *Crags* acting as catalysts for this activity. The undeclared boundary between the two groups ran across Dunmail Raise and Kirkstone passes, but in the west, the border was less clear. Mutual rivalry was intensified each time one team made raids for new routes in the other's territory. Cleasby's and Birkett's route Philistine in Buttermere and the Matheson-Cleasby addition of the classic Grand Alliance in Borrowdale raised the stakes for the southern team. Raids were countered from the north by Whillance, Botterill and Clegg's ascent of Eclipse and Lamb's first free ascent of Fallen Angel on Pavey Ark in Langdale. The northern team's raid into Hodge Close Quarry under the noses of the locals was a particularly bitter event, especially for Cleasby and Matheson.

One crag in particular seemed to focus this rivalry into a clash between the protagonists; this was the steep grey rock of Deer Bield Crag near Grasmere. Here Whillance and Armstrong added the incredibly bold Desperado and the fingery Stiletto, and Botterill removed the aid points from the older Peccadillo. Cleasby and Matheson replied by climbing Imagin-ation, a bold arête which they top roped first. The episode is recorded in Trevor Jones' *Cumbrian Rock*: "Four days later Whillance returned, repeated the route and was enraged when he found out the method of the first ascent. He mutilated Cleasby's written description in the new-route book and renamed it Life in the Fast Lane. The two sides met in the bar of The Golden Rule pub in Ambleside, angry words were exchanged and Botterill said bitterly 'It's like a bloody war', a remark which was distorted in the climbing magazines to 'From now on this is war' to suggest even greater animosity." (11) After the Golden Rule row, Whillance returned to Hodge Close Quarry and established an extremely bold E5 under the watchful eye of Cleasby and with a sense of ironical satisfaction he named the result Life in the Fast Lane.

Alistair Brightman looks for some respite at the end of the intimidating traverse of Roaring Silence.

Group Dynamics (continued)

It was not all serious and bitter rivalry and, as a whole, the atmosphere was one of good competitive spirit and light-hearted banter. It did, however, provide the catalyst for the development of climbing throughout The Lakes that was to last for ten years. Notwithstanding differences elsewhere, the crags of Scafell were regarded as a 'free for all' venue, being neither part of the 'northern' or 'southern' stomping grounds. It was within walking distance from Borrowdale and was therefore at the southern limit of the natural range of the Carlisle team, and it was also easily accessible from the southern area via the Wasdale Valley or Cockley Beck.

Photo: Al Phizacklea

Above: Bob Berzins.

Right: Unknown climber entering the overhanging niche on the top pitch of Roaring Silence.

Bob was rather proud of this line:

> "It was named after an album by Manfred Mann, but I didn't realise that this had become such a classic route until I read a recent article by Dave Birkett in a mag, and there he said that Roaring Silence was fantastic, and he put it in his list of top ten routes in the Lakes." (14)

Photo: Al Phizacklea

This was not a team that rested on its laurels for the day. Martin got stuck into the strenuous initial flake of Overhanging Grooves Direct before traversing left above the impressively steep wall at the first opportunity, following a break that joined up with the second belay on Gold Rush. The next pitch breaks out left to ascend a thin, delicate corner which was followed by a wet crack. Martin ran out of gear at the wet crack, so took a belay and Bob finished off the pitch to the stance on Roaring Silence. Dusk was approaching by the time the team grouped on a ledge, but Bob led up the blunt unprotected arête above to give the top 5c pitch, which he admitted he didn't enjoy because he was knackered and had to push himself so hard to complete it. Martin later credited this as being one of the most inspiring leads he had ever witnessed. This second route is named Forbidden Colours, after a book by Japanese author Mishima; and at E4, 6a,5c it gives a good addition to the crag. It was a tired team that eventually crawled back to the car which fortunately held just enough fuel for them to return to Langdale, but to make sure, Lamb turned off his engine on the downhill sections.

The Shadowfax wall left of Botterill's Slab was the site for the next two lines on the main Scafell face. Lamb and Botterill climbed the impressively steep corner bounding the left side; the right wall of this corner overhangs by 25° though the back wall is merely vertical! This feature can only be overcome by ferocious bridging, a sustained sequence of stretching and pushing, which has the added spice of fiddling wires into the corner with little hope of seeing where they're being placed. A thin coating of algae adds a ball-bearing uncertainty to the procedure, and there is only a single potential resting place on the entire 20m crotch-splitting line. Overall, it is the steepest route on the crag; a memorable outing given the most appropriate name of Burning Bridges, E4, 6a.

Two days later Lamb returned to a rather chilly crag with the Berzins brothers where they abseiled down the right arête of Shadowfax. Bob led the route, which has an awkward boulder problem start to give Subaudition, E3, 5c. Despite some pleasant positions, the route unfortunately remains a rather forgotten line.

Photo: Bob Wightman

Photo: Al Phizacklea

Above: George Smith on the smooth slab of Midnight Express.

Left: Al Phizacklea on the severely overhanging Burning Bridges, a sandbag at E4! Keith Phizacklea recently summed up the grade of this route - 'Shadowfax is E4, Mephisto is also E4 but is much harder. Burning Bridges is a grade harder than either of those'.

Pete Botterill demonstrated his ability on delicate slabs with his ascent of Midnight Express, E3, 6a, which takes a direct line up the smooth clean slab above the entrance to Mickledore Chimney. The line had previously been cleaned by Jeff Lamb, who partnered Pete on the first ascent. This excellent route requires a cool head as protection is spaced, but it has become one of the most popular routes on the East – perhaps because it's not as steep as the usual East Buttress lines? A hanging stance in the right hand corner leads onto the second pitch, a short awkward pull across the steepening headwall to the top jug, with a single 'R.P.' runner for protection. The route was named after Alan Parker's recently released notorious film of a drug smuggler's attempts to escape from a Turkish jail.

The following two years saw little new activity on the crag. The only route climbed in 1980 was an obscure line in the vicinity of Pollux by Steve Dougherty and Tony Glendenning, who called their MVS route Moby Dick. They must have had a whale of a time finding that one – but the guidebook author couldn't match their description to any features on that part of the crag!

After a layoff of two years, Lamb and Botterill returned to The East Buttress in 1981, intent on adding some final new routes before Lamb's planned emigration to Australia. Their first addition was something of an unusual line; Hell's Bells, E4, 6a, following a line of thin flakes up the steep wall right of Hell's Groove. This is not a very obvious line, and difficulties are concentrated in the first twenty metres. Botterill attempted the line first but tired himself out placing the wires before coming back to the ground for a rest. Pulling down the ropes, Lamb casually led the route with nonchalant ease, much to Pete's surprise.

Above: Al Phizacklea shortly before failing on The Almighty.

Right: Mike Lynch follows up Midnight Express.

On their next visit they returned to try the thin and evidently fierce crack to the right of their last line, which climbs directly up the overhanging wall to a belay on the ramp of Pegasus. To Lamb's disappointment, as he emptied his sack below the crag, he discovered his EB's had been left to dry at home after an evening's bouldering at Armathwaite. This left Pete to tackle the crackline alone; a strenuous proposition when it isn't possible to swap leads and rest between attempts. The crack starts on positive holds and solid jams with good protection, but then an awkward section on sloping smears at half height saps the strength, after which it's a fight to the finish between reducing power and increasing gravity. After several attempts Botterill gained the belay, and Lamb seconded the route using Pete's trainers on his feet. These were the type with slick plastic soles and they were two sizes too small. It was an indication of Jeff's great strength that he seconded the route without falling or weighting the rope in any way, which seemed appropriate in view of the chosen name, The Almighty at E5, 6b.

This was to be their hardest and last contribution to the crags of Scafell, as within a month, Jeff had left these shores for Australia, only returning briefly to marry his fiancée Maureen. In a tragic turn of events a few months later, Jeff was involved in a hit-and-run accident which left him hospitalised for some time. He had almost fully recovered from this when he was found dead inside his car with severe head injuries following a visit to a local crag. He had evidently crawled back there from the base of the crag and collapsed. Whether his injury was caused by a falling rock dislodged by his rope or was from a stone thrown from the top of the crag may never be known. Jeff Lamb had been a leading protagonist on Scafell and, in particular, his contributions to The East Buttress are unmatched throughout the history of the crag. Fittingly, his ashes were scattered under its base.

Footnotes

1. Al Phizacklea, 'No Raised Hat' *Fell & Rock Journal* 1984
2. Martin Berzins, FRCC audio recording, 2009
3. Ed Cleasby, interview by author, 2008
4. Martin Berzins, 'Shere Khan' from *Extreme Rock* 1986
5. Bob Berzins, FRCC audio recording, 2009
6. Martin Berzins, FRCC audio recording, 2009
7. Pete Whillance, telephone conversation with author, 2009
8. Bob Berzins, FRCC audio recording, 2009
9. Pete Botterill, FRCC audio recording, 2008
10. Rob Matheson, FRCC audio recording, 2008
11. Trevor Jones, *Cumbrian Rock* 1988
12. Bob Berzins, FRCC audio recording, 2009
13. Dai lampard, e-mail correspondence to author, 2009
14. Bob Berzins, FRCC audio recording, 2009

The End of an Era

When in 1979 Pete Livesey completed his project Das Kapital on Raven Crag, Thirlmere with Pete Gommersall, he left The Lakes scene as quickly as he burst upon it six years earlier. Removing Pete from the equation did not diminish the intensity surrounding the new routes scene, as the Berzins group maintained some external pressure on the two Lakeland factions.

Jeff Lamb's death in 1982 saddened the entire climbing community and it hit the local Carlisle group badly, in particular his long-time partner Pete Botterill never regained the same enthusiasm and he faded from the top of the climbing scene. This single event can be seen as one of the main reasons for the end of the rivalries between The Lakes factions. Lamb had been one of the main inspirations behind the northern group and had been its leading light, and his loss cast a dark shadow over the area.

Maintaining a drive to climb competitively needs determination and bloody-minded disregard to the wellbeing of the family, especially towards spouses and partners. As the protagonists got older, these influences and pressures caused other climbers to reassess their priorities, and more teams broke apart within a few years. Ed Cleasby had found a new challenge in hang-gliding, which he admitted was mercifully free of any bitching and backstabbing which blighted his involvement with the climbing world. This also coincided with the arrival of Rob Matheson's young family and this team broke apart in 1983. Within two years, the prolific Whillance-Armstrong team had also split, when Pete moved away to pursue his academic studies in Liverpool. Though their contribution to the history of Scafell was puzzlingly small, these two were responsible for raising the standards of climbing right across The Lakes. Thus the once intense north-south division seemed to dissolve away without fanfare; it was truly the end of an era for The Lakes.

Even the Berzins became caught up with this general breakdown of partnerships, as Bob dropped out of competitive climbing around this time, leaving Martin and Chris Sowden as the only effective team operating in the area.

It was to be many years before a Cumbrian climber was to again dominate the scene; Dave Birkett made his first mark on Scafell in 1998.

Still as keen as ever in 2013, Rob Matheson and Keith Phizacklea top out of Scafell Crag at the end of another perfect day.

1982 - 1986

The Borderline Breakthrough

Mike Owen high in the corner of Lost Horizons.

Photos: Al Phizacklea

An RAF Sea King helicopter approaches to pick up a casualty from Broad Stand (bottom left), a perfect demonstration of precision flying under difficult conditions.

Overleaf: A study in perfect overhanging rock - Borderline starts up the thin curving flake just left of centre before continuing up the wall just left of the two dark offset grooves.

There was only a trickle of activity over 1982. Martin Berzins and Chris Sowden free climbed the main pitch of Incubus, which gives a tricky section, but which is now regarded as the easiest E5 on The East Buttress. On the same day they added a hard direct start to Zeus by ascending a typically difficult thin crack up the short overhanging wall below the main groove. This raises the overall grade of Zeus to E4, 6a, but unsurprisingly this version is usually avoided by teams intent on climbing the main pitch of that route.

The first free ascent of Lost Horizons was one of the major prizes of the early 1980s. The following note from Dai Lampard perfectly illustrates the competitive element surrounding this coveted challenge:

> "Determined to grab the first free ascent of Lost Horizons we hiked up to Hollow Stones after the pub and woke at 4.00 am. We were climbing at 5.00, and at 5.30 I had just overcome the crux when Geordie Al and his mate came around the corner, absolutely dumbfounded that they had been beaten to the route at 5.30am! The cursing could be heard in Langdale. Unbeknown to all of us was that Bob Berzins had freed the bloody thing a few days before!" (1)

Bob had made his final contribution to the history of Scafell by becoming the first to free climb the main pitch of Lost Horizons, leaving the grade unchanged at E4, 6b. He commented:

> "I remember it being really on/off and lunging for holds, just managed to finish it before it thundered and rained. There had been a bit of history of this route for me and Martin. I remember seeing Pete Livesey at the Leeds University wall and we harangued him for about an hour about all sorts of things including what he'd actually done on Lost Horizons. I didn't have a copy of the original magazine or description, but Pete had been very vague, I think it was something like 'I grabbed the peg' and it took an hour for him to admit, yes this was a peg for aid. So it was great to finally do the route clean, especially as it is such a brilliant natural feature." (2)

1983 was to be the last year available for checking routes for the forthcoming guidebook and for getting in any last minute new routes. Martin Berzins was writing The East Buttress section of the guide and he was accompanied by Chris Sowden throughout the year. Their first new route climbed on a cold and windy day was Aquavit, which is something of a disappointment. Starting just left of the main slab of Chartreuse, it gained a subsidiary arête to the left of that route by an awkward start. Berzins led the second pitch which cranked directly over an overhang to create a very difficult finish at 6b. This unbalanced climb has never become popular, and it may still be unrepeated. Just as Sowden was seconding Berzins, there was a commotion on Broad Stand; a fell walker had fallen and these two instigated the rescue. Whilst Martin was on the belay, he noticed how a throng gathering around the casualty were mulling about like headless chickens, completely clueless as to a course of action. His booming voice from the top of The East Buttress must have sounded like a message from the gods, and it certainly had an effect. He instructed them to "Stop dicking about and go down for the rescue helicopter", and later he commented: "Those RAF lads, they flew so close to the crag, it was frightening. They are the most talented professionals I have ever seen". (3)

Aquavit was followed by Zeya, another bold, strenuous line just right of Shere Khan. Like many of the large, natural features on the East, it had been tried by several teams in the past including Ken Jackson, Andrew Atkinson and Dai Lampard, and it held a set of abandoned nuts and slings. Martin Berzins and Chris Sowden climbed the route; it was to be a long hard day as they first climbed Shere Khan in order to abseil and clean the line. The climb starts up a short, difficult groove parallel to Shere Khan, but this soon peters out, forcing the climber onto the leaning wall on the right, protected by a solitary peg. A stiff pull leads to the base of Shere Khan's crux groove which is followed to the belay.

This is in effect a bold E5 followed immediately by another bold E5; the overall outcome is a pitch offering brilliant sustained climbing. A second pitch traverses leftwards from the belay, across an undercut light-coloured wall before following a crack up to the White Slab. Unclimbed for many years it was in danger of falling into obscurity, but after several recent ascents this line now has the reputation of being one of the best E5s on The East Buttress. Berzins used to be frustrated over the route going unrepeated for so long, but after twenty years of waiting he was satisfied his creation has at last got recognition:

> "I seem to remember the name Zeya comes from a tiger that was once in the paper for escaping from London zoo and mauled some unfortunate keeper or something. That was kind of tragic, but we wanted the name of a real tiger, not like that pesky old thing called Shere Khan out of *The Jungle Book* !" (4)

The East Buttress was to be the venue for the final route climbed by the Cleasby-Matheson team, who signed off their partnership with Shikasta, E4, 5c,6a; named after a Doris Lessing science-fiction novel. The route starts up Armageddon before veering rightwards up a delightful groove to reach the foot of the White Slab, forming the upper section of Overhanging Wall. The uninspiring and often wet start is a poor contrast to the stunning upper pitch. This follows the large square prow which leans over the slab, giving rather bold and strenuous climbing in a very exposed situation. This top pitch had been tried in the past by both Livesey and Pete Whillance, but Cleasby managed the pull into 'a pig of a groove' right in the edge of the arête to claim the prize. Cleasby was well pleased with this route, and later in the pub he gave an illustration of his stiff grading policy by announcing:

> "It's only E3, but no E3 leader could ever lead it!" (5)

The finishing touches to the guide were added by Martin Berzins and Sowden, who added three new lines on the main face of Scafell Crag. Their first contribution was an excellent E4, 6a up the imposing left arête forming the steep front wall of Botterill's Slab. This is a sustained pitch providing an unusual sense of exposure with the arête severely undercut by the corner on its left, leaving the climber's feet right on the edge of the void. However, the thin cracks splitting the wall in the same parallel line as the arête give excellent protection, and despite the veneer of moss coating its strenuous upper half, this route has a reputation of being an outstanding outing on clean holds. Berzins named the route Mephisto, inspired by the Hungarian István Szabó film.

A second contribution by Martin Berzins and Chris Sowden was to add a harder E2 variation to Bonington's Girdle traverse of the Main Buttress; this followed the thin horizontal crack slashing rightwards across the wall above the crest of the Great Flake, a fantastic hand-traverse with nothing for your feet. By combining the excellent mantelshelf and final pitches of the original girdle with this new pitch, it has more impact than anything found on The Lord of the Rings, and it could be said to be the better of the two girdles. Fittingly for such an overlooked classic, in the 2014 guidebook, editor Steve Scott 'upgraded' this route from an un-noticed variation into a fully independent route by giving it the name Ring of Air, which is something he did without consulting the first ascent team.

The steep, blank wall to the right of the Great Flake on Central Buttress was the next target on their list. Although the lower wall was steep, it had reasonable holds and led to a tiny razor-thin peg runner in a horizontal break. From there the climbing becomes harder and it led to two of the smallest 'R.P.' wires in a bulge level with the famous chockstone, but 5 metres to its right. With this marginal protection, the moves through the bulging rock gave a very committing sequence to reach Saxon, at the base of its main crack. Martin commented:

> "It was a really gnarly pitch – you could get very seriously hurt on it. This was another one of those routes where Chris couldn't grade flour; he just followed up Te-tum, te-tum, te-tum, and when he got to the belay I said 'that was really scary, wasn't it?' And he just said 'Nah, barely 6a!'" (6)

Ken Jackson on an early abortive attempt on the lower groove of Zeya.

Bob Wightman climbs 'the pig of a groove' on the upper pitch of Shikasta.

The sixth Scafell Guide

The classic 1984 guidebook to Scafell, Dow Crag and Eskdale.

The new guidebook, produced in 1984, was an innovative change for the Fell & Rock Climbing Club, combining all the routes of Scafell and Esk Buttress together with the Dow Crag area to create a bumper edition. This amalgamation of different guidebooks had been suggested by Ken Wilson many years earlier and it was a major step-change in the attitude of the FRCC. The new guide included all of the recent modern 'classics' climbed on Scafell and, as Berzins noted, half the routes between Botterill's Slab and Moss Ghyll Grooves had been added in the preceding seven years. Indeed the intervening ten years had yielded about 40 new routes and variations, many being in the E5 category.

There were several modernising features inside this guide. Routes were given 'E' grades and technical grades for individual pitches for the first time for Scafell, although these had been used throughout other Lakes guidebooks for many years. A further update in this guide was the use of 'quality' stars to match the expectations of modern climbers. There was even a well received graded list of climbs, but as this covered all the routes in the guide it was difficult to achieve any sense of accurate order.

Although this route, Judas Priest, produced only about 18 metres of new climbing, it is a bold line; the hardest on this face of the crag. It was originally given E4, but it was clear that with the poor state of the peg and the serious nature of the climbing that it was worthy of the E5 grade.

The new guidebook was soon rendered out of date by Chris King and Ron Kenyon during the summer of 1984 with a route taking advantage of the easier portion of Aquavit, which they named Mickledore Arête (HVS, 5a). It starts up The Fulcrum for a couple of metres, and then follows a delicately rising ramp to reach the arête of Aquavit which is followed directly to the belay on Mickledore Grooves. The second pitch climbed the arête above, which was a neglected variation on Chartreuse, before following a steep finish out left of the Chartreuse crack. Although it utilises a good deal of the climbing already taken by other routes, it does give a most gratifying and quite sustained route at a more amenable grade up some impressive ground.

The long neglected slabs on the front of The Pinnacle provided a young Barrow based team of Al Phizacklea and Rob Knight the space to add a pleasantly delicate outing given the name Bushwhacker, at E2, 5c,5b. This started up an awkward shallow scoop just left of the main pitch of Hopkinson's Gully, followed by a fine crack leading to the Waiting Room. Crossing the diagonal slab of Jones' Direct from Lord's Rake the long top pitch follows the left edge of the headwall, looking directly into Slingsby's Chimney at one point before trending out right to finish. The name derives from a brief incident following the previous night's drinking at The Golden Rule in Ambleside. The pair had accepted an offer to crash out on the living room floor of some student friends and, in the morning, Rob was awoken by one of the female students quietly striding over his slumbering body in order to enter the kitchen – and as Rob later recalled with fervour, she was wearing a rather short nightdress and nothing else!

Two variations to existing lines were climbed on one summer day by the immensely tall Dowthwaite brothers, Phil and Joe. Phil was inspired by the picture on the cover of the new guide, portraying the climber on the arête just below the belay of Edge of Eriador. He was so greatly inspired, it turned out, that he never read the description within the guide, and he started up an awkward shallow groove that leads directly to the prominent thread runner. The normal route to reach this thread is via a traverse across from the left side. Half-way up this groove and with only a tiny 'R.P.' runner below his feet, Phil realised belatedly this was not the correct route but was unable to do anything about his situation apart from climbing higher. On reaching the runner he mused: "I've never been so glad to clip a thread. At least I knew I wasn't going to die!" (7)

This steep line was originally given E4, but it has been shunned ever since due to paucity of protection – and may still be unrepeated. Recent interest in the line from Rob and Craig Matheson indicates that the climbing is solid E5. Craig top-roped the route but bad weather prevented a proposed repeat from Rob. The Dowthwaites then climbed the first pitch of the classic Phoenix, where Joe noticed a fine, clean groove between the Direct Finish and the Arête Finish. Again this was led on-sight to give a very good but rather stiff variation they called The Ash Groove Finish, at E3, which has subsequently been grafted onto Lucius to give an independent finish to that route.

The summer of 1986 was not one of the better ones on record, as the low pressure systems rolled in off the Atlantic with depressing regularity. During one brief spell of fine weather in June, Martin Berzins and Chris Sowden set off early from Brackenclose to arrive above The East Buttress. Martin had set his sights on a curving flake rising up the huge leaning wall right of Ichabod, but at the time Chris was totally ignorant of the project. The route had originally been identified by Jeff Lamb and made known to the Berzins some years earlier, but it was a TV programme shown the previous autumn that spurred them on to investigate this major remaining line. Martin explains:

> "There was a final shot where the camera zoomed out of a close-up of The East Buttress, and this unclimbed line was right in the centre of the shot. It was so blatant that we just had to try it on the first spell of decent weather." (8)

The sixth Scafell Guide (contd.)

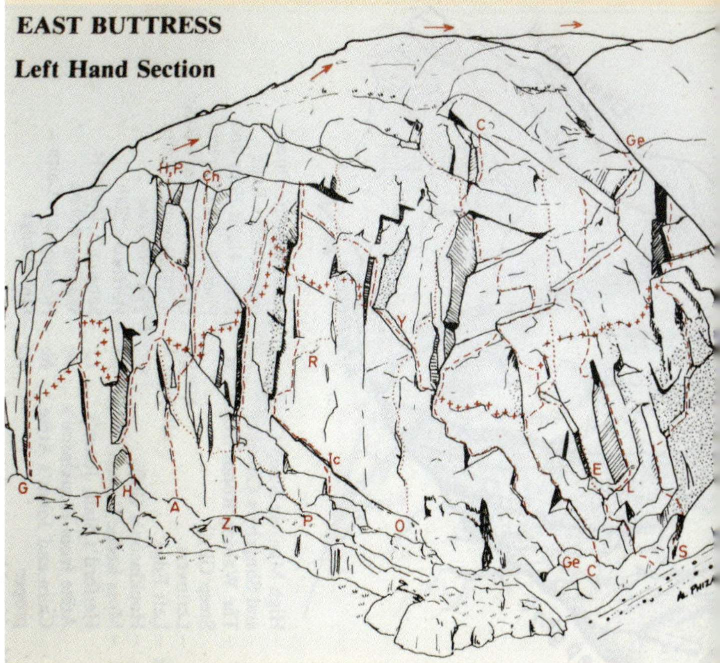

This book included the first diagrams in a FRCC guide from Alan Phizacklea.

The 1984 edition was also the first Fell & Rock guide to include colour photographs, including one on the cover, and the first to be illustrated by a new set of diagrams from Al Phizacklea, which were supplemented with a sketch by Shirley Angel and a couple of the old Heaton Cooper drawings. For the first time the lines of the routes on the crag diagrams were shown in red ink, which greatly enhanced their appeal. This edition contained so much new information it sold very quickly, requiring a re-print only four years later.

Because this new guide combined two of the old areas previously covered by two separate guidebooks, it was given a neutral grey colour for the spine and rear cover. The guidebook was jointly written by Graham Willison, who wrote the Scafell Crag section, (much of this done from a hospital bed following a bad fall at a local crag), Martin Berzins, (East Buttress), Ed Cleasby (Eskdale area) and Rob Matheson, who contributed the Dow Crag and Duddon areas. The editing was a huge achievement by Dave Miller, in particular benefitting from his ability to get such differing factions to coalesce and complete this fine guide.

Left: Breaking out left from the flake on Borderline is the crux of the route. Climber, Iain Small.

The sixth Scafell Guide (contd.)

Graham Willison, joint author of the Scafell guide.

Changes made by Willison included the amalgamation of separate individual pitches to form a single coherent route. One such route was given the incomprehensible name of 'Moss Ledge Direct, Herford's Slab, Jones' Arête from Hopkinson's Cairn and Jones' Arête Proper' which seems a bit of a mouthful for such a good route.

He must also be given credit for reversing the direction of the Girdle Traverse of Scafell Crag from the original right to left description to the left to right version, which is almost all climbed in ascent. This was also the first guidebook to be dedicated to a past member of the Fell & Rock Climbing Club; to the memory of Jeff Lamb.

The steepness of the rock gave them problems during the abseil cleaning as it forced them to insert gear and clip in to maintain contact with the rock, and gear was removed apart from the pegs and a thread runner. The route was obviously going to be harder than anything yet climbed on Scafell; it needed something special – the use of siege tactics. This approach had been used for some time on the steep limestone of Derbyshire and Yorkshire, where climbers had left their ropes into their highest runners whilst repeatedly attempting the moves, thus resulting in an impressive increase in standards.
Martin later commented:

> "I got the initial gear in and we sieged the route, trying it and trying it, falling off lots of times, sitting on gear and having a look at how to do it. I even pulled out one peg placed in the flake when I fell off, but it wasn't replaced because the other gear was good. We tried going a bit higher, then lower, before we worked out the crux, which turned out to be really fingery. Don't forget, we hadn't top-roped it and really only checked it out for a short time whilst brushing. We did frig it to figure out where to go, but when it was Chris' turn to lead it I recall the rope was pulled, so the actual ascent was done in good style. Chris led it because he found the method that worked and his lead was amazing and flawless; the master technician at work. I was dragged up the crux when seconding." (9)

The route starts up the dramatically overhanging curving flake provided with inadequate fingery slots, and it enables a peg to be reached where it is possible to step back down to an unexpected but very contorted jammed-hip rest. An extremely fingery move out left leads to the sanctuary of a second peg runner and a micro cam, but further sustained climbing prolongs the lactic pain until better holds and a welcome thread runner can be reached. Here Sowden hung on by one hand and lowered a loop of rope for some extra gear; they were climbing the route in really light weight style! Just above, the crack line of Roaring Silence is joined which leads to the belay. Chris faced a dilemma – he only had a single small wire on him; all their abseil gear which they had intended to use for the belay, had gone!
As Trevor Jones notes in *Cumbrian Rock* : "They left this gear in place, including two expensive 'Friends', which were gone when they returned. Martin had to threaten the removal men before they would give it back." (10) In reality, this wasn't as confrontational as it seems. They had left the gear on The Yellow Slab belay, including a 'Friend', and the second 'Friend' was used as a directional aid for the ropes.
A team that had just climbed Yellow Slab must have thought that Christmas had come early and had removed the gear without realising its purpose. Berzins left Sowden tied into the single wire as he un-belayed and went off in pursuit, and they apologetically returned the gear when he spotted them on the descent path below the crag.

Above the belay rears a capping overhang with a thin crack splitting the roof left of the niche of Roaring Silence. After a long rest Berzins led this thuggish 6b pitch to reach the haven of the top some 12 hours after they had arrived at the crag. He notes:

> "That top pitch was desperate – brutal. I believe not many people do that pitch, but how can they claim to have done the route without it?" (11)

That is a factual statement. The top pitch is probably still unrepeated to this day, but it would be hard to find anyone who has climbed the first pitch admitting to an incomplete ascent of the route – it's not in climbers' nature to admit such; so the top pitch remains ignored and forgotten. Berzins and Sowden claimed that they called this route Borderline because its existence had been mentioned by Pete Whillance on the 1985 Border TV series Lakeland Rock. This was one of the few unclimbed lines on Scafell that Whillance had actually examined by abseil. There is an alternative theory that Berzins is in fact a closet Madonna fan, as her single of the same name was in the charts earlier in the same year.

It was obviously a breakthrough in standards, and they gave it an E6, 6c grade; the first time an E6 had been established on a high mountain crag in Cumbria. Many suitors have attempted to flash Borderline, but all seemed doomed to failure.

At the time of writing, the author believes there has never been a successful on-sight, first attempt ascent of this route (commonly called a flash ascent) that has been authenticated by an independent witness. Shortly after the first ascent, Alan Murray, Ian Cummings, Mick Lovatt and Paul Cornforth all eventually led the line in good style following earlier attempts. Dave Birkett almost achieved an on-sight flash,but only managed it on his second attempt:

> "I tried it without any cleaning or inspection, and I knew from Corney that getting from the flake to the peg on the headwall was the crux. When I got to the peg, I thought 'Bloody hell, I've done it!', and if I could only have trusted that peg I may have gone and done it, but when I looked at the tat on the peg, it looked terrible. You've got to get something good in there or else you're in the realms of you're going to really hurt yourself, and just above the peg is a slot for a 'Rock 4' or '5'. I tried fiddling this in and getting tired all on one arm, and when I came to do the move, the nut was taking too much of the hold and I blew it. I hung around and realised you need a smaller nut in there so I changed it then went back down for a rest, then pulled the ropes and did it." (12)

The majority of those who have climbed this route confirm it is definitely E7, 6c; it was by far the hardest route on a mountain crag in The Lakes.

So by 1986 Scafell's East Buttress had matured to include an E7 route. However, later in the same year young Johnny Dawes rocked the climbing world with his ascent of The Indian Face on Clogwyn Du'r Arddu, an audacious route given the grade of E9. It took another 14 years and a new generation of climbers before a similar grade was to grace the crags of Scafell.

Got to the peg – by now the pump is beginning to bite.

Chris Sowden, first ascentionist of Borderline.

Footnotes

1. Dai Lampard, e-mail correspondence to author, 2009
2. Bob Berzins, FRCC audio recording, 2009
3. Martin Berzins, FRCC audio recording, 2009
4. Martin Berzins, FRCC audio recording, 2009
5. Ed Cleasby, public house boast, 1983 (as recalled by the author)
6. Martin Berzins, FRCC audio recording, 2009
7. Phil Dowthwaite, telephone conversation with author, 2009
8. Martin Berzins, FRCC audio recording, 2009
9. Martin Berzins, FRCC audio recording, 2009
10. Trevor Jones, extract from *Cumbrian Rock* 1988
11. Martin Berzins, FRCC audio recording, 2009
12. Dave Birket, FRCC audio recording, 2008

Iain Small on the initial flake of Boarderline.

Photo: Al Phizacklea

1984 - 1987

The Great Winter Climbing Revival

Above: The first winter guidebook to The Lakes published by Cicerone Press.

Below: The early sketches merely illustrated the main features of the crag.

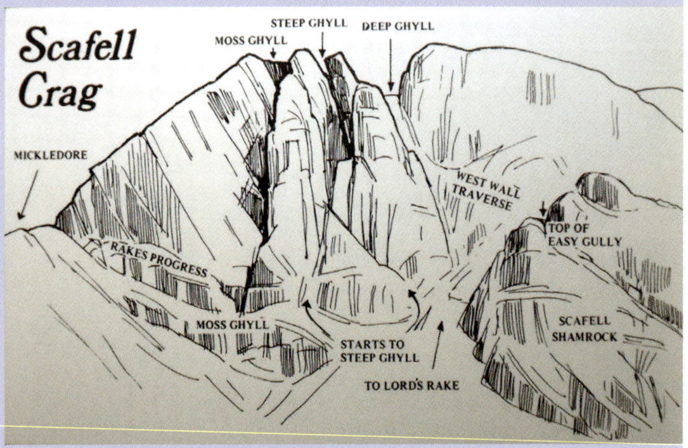

Overleaf:
Scafell Crag and Pikes Crag (left) as seen from Lingmell.

Photo: Eric Shaw

The author is indebted to Brian Davison for writing the winter sections for this book.

The first Lakes guidebook to winter routes, *Winter Climbs in the Lake District* was produced by Bob Bennett, Bill Birkett and Andy Hyslop, and was published by Cicerone Press in 1979. The guide was a collection of the authors' extensive knowledge of winter routes being climbed in the district at the time. The coffee table book *Cold Climbs* published in 1983 by Dave Alcock, John Barry and Ken Wilson selected the best routes in that guide and illustrated the current state of snow and ice climbing in The Lakes. The inclusion of classic gullies such as on Great End, and Moss Gill and Steep Gill on Scafell in the book supported an image that The Lakes was a very traditional area and was lagging behind the rest of Britain in the winter climbing stakes.

Before the 1980s, records of ascents were rarely kept. Some were reported in climbing magazines and other information was archived by keen activists. Matters improved over the years and activists recorded winter routes in the 'new routes' books in climbing shops, and it stayed this way until the advent of the Internet when a site was set up by the FRCC to allow reporting of routes in a more formal manner.

An improvement in ice tools, first with the inclined straight picks of the 'Terrordactyl' in the 1970s and then with the sleek reverse-curved 'banana' picks, such as the Chacal during the 1980s, offering superior performances and holding power. This led, slowly at first, to the ascents of steeper ice falls.

As expected, the Scottish scene set the vanguard for techniques and attitudes with a consolidation of the top grades and new steeper ice pitches being climbed on Ben Nevis and in North-West Scotland. However it was the new mixed buttress lines being established in The Cairngorms that were to push grades and attitudes to what constituted winter conditions.

The breakthrough in what was possible on the open crags in The Lakes came one day in January 1984 and gave rise to a huge jump in standards. Ed Cleasby and Al Phizacklea wandered up to Scafell late in the morning and were disappointed to find two teams already in front of them on their chosen route in Steep Gill. (Winter climbing was more popular in those days as climbing walls were not a common resource and were generally very poor in design and layout, so more teams were out in all weathers on the fells.) There were also three teams cluttering their alternative line up Moss Gill, which at the time only left either the easy icefalls on Shamrock or the snow plod of Deep Gill as recognised routes. They pondered the limited possibilities and were almost resigned to having a wasted day; but even though the rocks were heavily glazed with ice and the snow was crisp and firm – it was too good for simply pottering around!

It was Phizacklea who first noticed a series of snow patches on The Pinnacle scattered across the face like a set of domino spots, and he suggested that they might be linked. The First and Second Nests on Jones' Route Direct from Lord's Rake were the prominent features and snow lay on the Gangway, which almost acted like a pointer up the face. Phizacklea recalls:

> "Ed said 'It's your idea, Al, you can lead it'. I had the distinct impression that he wasn't too keen on the idea. We soloed to the upper right-hand edge of the easier ground below The Pinnacle to a ledge overlooking Deep Gill. Ed belayed around the large block at the start of Jones' Route and I carefully edged up to the Gangway. The larger holds were thickly banked with ice, and I soon found myself with both axes scraping on the Gangway, desperately trying to find some incut hold for purchase with either axe. I got one axe on a nick above the Gangway and then made a rather clumsy half-mantelshelf move up to get my crampon on the shelf, which twisted the axe from its placement. I fell about 15 feet into the deep snow next to Ed which cushioned my fall in a rather amusing fashion – and we laughed at the absurdity of the scene. Taking more care on my next attempt, I managed to get stood on the Gangway, but to my horror there was no possibility of finding any protection, and the thought of reversing a delicate mantelshelf was distinctly unappealing.

Photo: Al Phizacklea

Photo: Al Phizacklea

Above: Scafell Crag in winter, showing the three main gully lines of Moss Gill (left), Steep Gill (centre) and Deep Gill (right). Pisgah Buttress on the left and Scafell Pinnacle on the right had hardly been touched in winter before 1984. Jones' Route Direct takes a diagonal line from the lower right edge of the Pinnacle to the prominent short crack in the centre of the face.

Left: Ed Cleasby at the point just beyond the Gangway on the first winter ascent of Jones' Route Direct.

"I noticed a possible spike at the left end of the Gangway and so I tip-toed carefully across to it, my crampon front points slipping slightly at one point on the rock, the ice being too thin to provide a secure purchase. I was quite relieved to get a sling over the spike, and with this boost to my confidence I quickly made some headway up a series of very delicate icy scoops which led towards the sanctuary of the First Nest. This was a couple of metres beyond my reach, and I frantically scraped away at some vague creases in the rock but there was nothing to hook an axe into, and I was too high above the spike to hold me if I fell, uneasily contemplating the terrifying prospect of a 40 foot fall onto the snow ledges below. I managed to seat a small stopper sideways in a shallow icy placement close by my knee, but couldn't tell whether it was insecurely wedged on ice or firmly against rock. It certainly gave no confidence for lowering off, and this time a fall would generate an awful lot more agony than amusement, and I realised I had got myself into what could only be described as deep shit.

"I remained there for what seemed ages, suppressing the welling sensation of wanting to throw up, incapable of making any move up or down. The Nest was tantalisingly close; I could see thick snow covering its deeply frozen grass, and I realised that this had to be my sanctuary. The only positive placement for the axe was a small undercut sidepull for the right axe; useless for upward momentum, but sufficient to provide balance whilst I raised my left crampon onto the highest sloping icy hold. I held my breath as I slowly rocked over onto my left foot. The points crunched and splintered the ice, but they held, and I straightened up and lunged totally out of control at the Nest with the left axe. The point bit securely into the grass, and I swung wildly across before whacking the second axe alongside with a fantastic roar of relief. To this day I still believe this is the hardest move I ever made on a winter route; it was just total commitment for that one move.

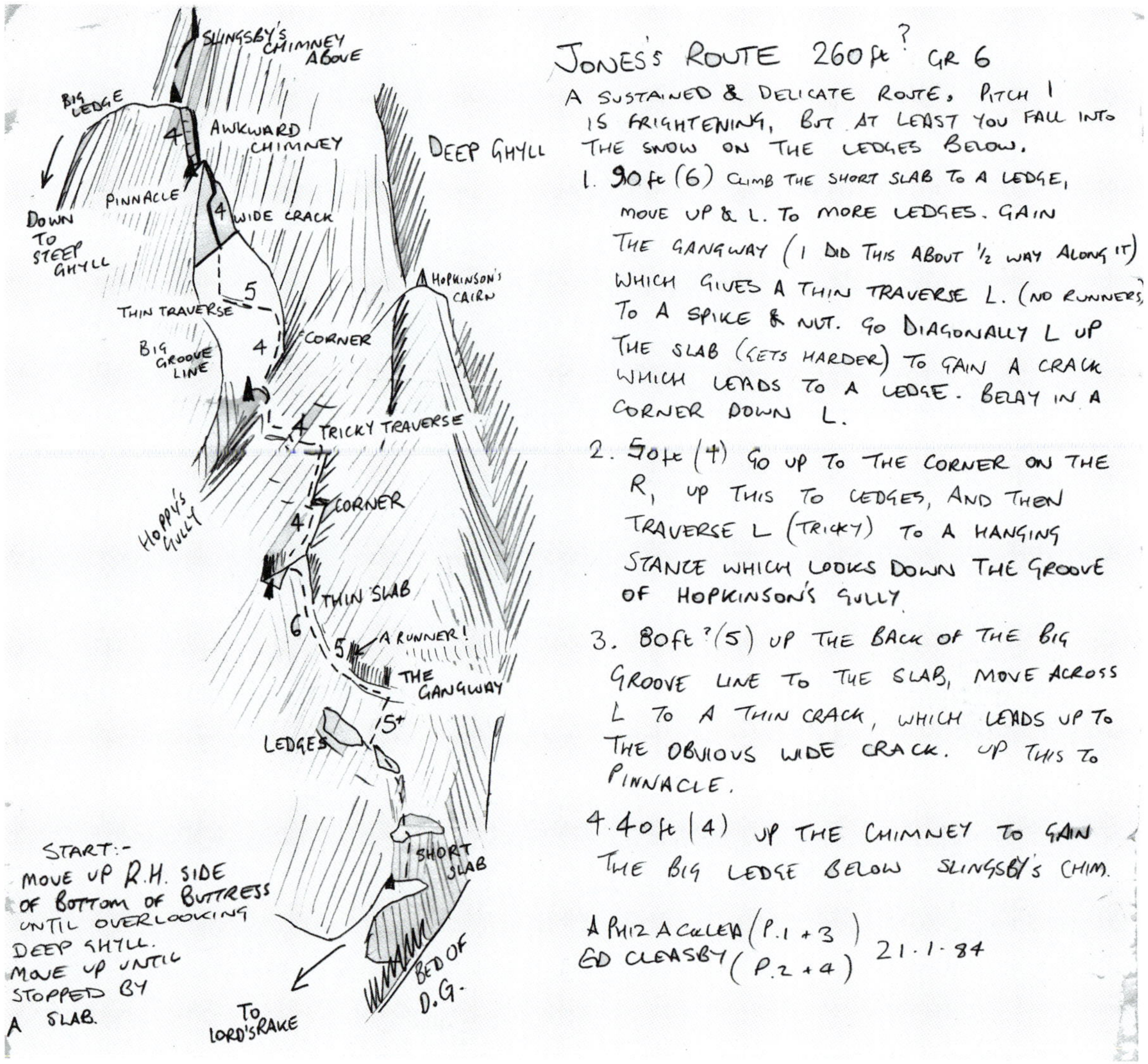

Right: The original sketch Al Phizacklea used to record the ascent of Jones' Route; he recorded many winter routes on Scafell in this fashion.

"Ed led the next pitch to the Second Nest, another awkward lead which was not too easy, and then I continued directly up the open groove on the upper section of Hopkinson's Gully to another belay below the wide crack. We did not go to the Waiting Room and do the mantelshelf pitch, (I once told Ken Wilson that we did; but I got confused with the mantelshelf move onto the Gangway). Ed then led up to the Crevasse stance below the chimney on Slingsby's route. It was now dark; we were surprised to find that it had taken almost six hours to climb this 180 foot route. It was a relief to abseil off into Steep Gill and get down to Wasdale. We never considered it a failure to get to the top of The Pinnacle; we were aware that the climbing we covered was harder than anything done before in winter in The Lakes. I gave it a grade VI, which I believe was the first time it had been used south of the border, but after a few years, it became clear that it was harder than the VIs climbed later, and was subsequently uprated to grade VII." (1)

Phizacklea and Cleasby returned with Rob Matheson the following weekend and climbed Pisgah Buttress Direct, the first occasion it had been climbed in winter for many decades, though at the time they believed it was a first winter ascent. There had been another heavy snowfall that built up on top of the rock until the entire face was thickly plastered, obscuring all small features such as cracks for runners. This was notable for being the very last time that Cleasby and Matheson climbed a route together. The following month Phizacklea was back at Scafell where he met Dave Kay from Penrith, but there had been a thaw stripping the ice from the rock, leaving it dry and clear. Al recalls:

> "We noticed that there was a thin streak of ice down the right corner of Botterill's Slab, and wondered whether it could be climbed. I led easily up some icy cracks and grass to the foot of the slab and Dave soon joined me. The ice at the bottom of the corner was just thick enough to cover the black moss, and I reckoned that the moss would be frozen enough to hold my weight. The ice had built up into bobbly lumps that I could stand on and carefully tip-toe up the moss, which worked well with the axes being used for delicate balance only. After about 25 feet I noticed there was a crack in the right wall, but it felt really insecure to lean across to reach it. I carefully tapped a skyhook into the thickest piece of moss I could find, stepped down and used this as a high runner as I leaned out right to get a nut into the crack. It might sound daft; but I reckoned that the moss would bind everything together, stopping the ice from shattering if the skyhook came under load. (This theory was never tested!) The higher I climbed the thinner and narrower the moss and ice became, but it was easier to fix protection as there were cracks available in the slab itself. It became really delicate towards the top, and I actually had to use a couple of un-iced incut holds on the main slab, which made me wonder whether it would invalidate a winter ascent. The upper pitch continued up a chimney containing thicker ice but because the chimney gradually narrowed, it became increasingly awkward to get any sort of swing to the axes. It's a great route, one that can be frequently found in condition, and it has become one of the most popular of the 'modern' routes on Scafell". (2)

Rob Matheson and Ed Cleasby after their ascent of Pisgah Buttress; this was their last route together.

Below: Ed Cleasby feels his way cautiously across the traverse towards the Fives Court Ledge on Pisgah Buttress Direct, this ascent felt awkward because the snow had obscured the obvious traverse ledge across this face.

Left: Chris Carter seconding the superbly iced Botterill's Slab.

Photo: Al Phizacklea

Above: The right-hand side of The East Buttress taken on the day that May Day Direct was climbed. This takes the right-hand icefall; Minotaur takes the large left-hand icicle, and the vague line up the centre is the original finish to Overhanging Wall.
Below: Al Phizacklea on the controversial winter ascent of May Day Direct.

Photo: Steve Swindells for Phizacklea collection

However, careful scrutiny of the old records has unveiled what could have been an earlier ascent in winter by Geoffery Winthrop Young, which was described in Section 6 on pages 98 - 99.

Phizacklea's next visit was three days later, when he went around to The East Buttress with Ed Cleasby and Steve Swindells in search of the mythical icicle which has been rumoured to form during exceptional conditions. There was plenty of ice high on the crag, but nothing had extended low enough to be accessible from the ground, and it seemed to be another potential day squandered. They admired the ice gripping May Day Direct as a thick bulging mass at the top, tapering and wasting away towards its base. A sudden thought energised them into action.

Abseiling in to climb only the top section seemed eminently commendable, so half an hour later they were pulling down the ropes to their stance below the corner. There was a very lean section at the start which turned out to be very much thinner than it looked from the abseil rope. Phizacklea very tentatively led up this; one slip would have sent him towards his friends 24 points first; but he had been practising. He had been secretly traversing the polished limestone at his home quarry of Birkrigg in his crampons, and had acquired the skill to place front points precisely onto the ice. The first runner was at about 20 feet, but after that the risk diminished leaving just the pure joy of climbing steep ice. This gradually built up the higher he climbed until a short ice screw runner could be place just below the top. Al reckoned it as a very sustained pitch, and one of the best Grade Vs he had ever climbed - but one that troubled him for many years.

Phizacklea came in for some criticism for abseiling down to avoid the steep non-wintry start; a tactic that was said to be unfair as many teams had been watching and waiting for the ice to form down to ground level for many years. It was to be over twenty years before the route saw a ground up ascent when after several attempts Dave Birkett and Mark Edwards finally climbed SOS. as a direct start, though at Grade X this put the route out of the reach of most winter activists! Following the ascent of May Day Direct, Cleasby and Phizacklea abseiled down again to the foot of the White Slab, and were quite intimidated by a couple of steep ice formations above. The slab itself contained a continuous streak of ice, and Ed ran out for a full rope length with only a single runner before finding a suitable belay. It was another tremendous pitch at only Grade III; rather a mild grade for such an exposed and intimidating situation.

On the same day a second local team from the northern end of Cumbria, Tony Furness and Jim Fotheringham, climbed Collier's Chimney; the true direct finish of Moss Gill using a superb steep sheet of ice up the wall just right of the chimney. This had possibly been climbed many years before by Bowers' and Masson who kept within the confines of the chimney. Sadly, poor record keeping will always cast doubt on these possible early ascents. Fotheringham remembered the route fondly:

> "It was a fantastic day; it is by far the best way of finishing the gully. There was about an inch thick layer of translucent ice over the moss, which you could see quite clearly. I pushed my way up this, tapping away through to the moss, thinking 'Fuck me, this is scary' because there was no gear, but with every move I got closer to the chockstone." (3)

Photo: Chris Carter

Robin Beadle high on Collier's Chimney, the superb direct finish to Moss Gill.

Phizacklea returned a fortnight later with Dave Geere and again abseiled down to the base of the White Slab on The East Buttress, but it was rather late in the season and water was running down the rapidly thawing ice. He climbed the steep candle of ice that came down the top pitch of the summer line of Minotaur. This had a steep start, protected by good wires, leading onto an icy ramp below bulging rock where a vertical icicle led to the top. Placing ice screws to protect this move was disconcertingly easy, as the ice was so soft they too readily twisted into place; such was the extent of the thaw. It was not to be the last recorded ascent of this remarkable winter as Jim Fotheringham returned with Steve Howe and climbed Slime Chimney late in March. Their ascent turned out to be what Jim described as a side show that seemed like a good idea – but wasn't. So ended a noteworthy winter season on Scafell which heralded the start of modern mixed climbing in The Lake District – and a significant rise in winter climbing grades.

The first snows of the next winter saw Phizacklea and an inexperienced Rob Knight attempt a line just right of Xerxes on Deep Gill Buttress on the shortest day of the year. It had been noted how this part of Scafell is one of the first areas to come into condition. Without achieving anything in particular it was an interesting event. Phizacklea had decked out next to the feet of his second on his initial attempt when his ice hammer pulled from its placement and struck him squarely in the mouth, sending him backwards and earthbound. He returned to the fray, finding it rather awkward, but Knight refused to follow the first pitch after the earlier shenanigans. They decided to retreat and climb up Steep Gill instead, but only frightened themselves in the process. However Phizacklea returned with George Smith the following day and completed the route, which sported some rather precarious climbing up thinly iced slabs. Their salvation came from a line of providential grass sods, and so gave the name of Sod's Law to the route.

Photo: Al Phizacklea

Brian Davison, the winter guru.

The beginning of 1985 saw a new name appear on the scene, Brian Davison. He had climbed with the Aberdonian activists who were at the forefront of mixed Scottish climbing, and he appreciated how advanced they were in comparison to The Lake District. He was keen to push grades south of the border. Hampered geographically by living in Cambridge and before the days of internet weather forecasts Davison and Richard Jones would test the waters of the Cavendish Physics Laboratory duck pond to assess Lakeland conditions. If they were frozen then The Lakes would be in condition. In some particularly cold mid-1980s winters this involved cycling across the pond!

Moss Gill Grooves had been tried the previous winter by local activists who had failed to pass the summer crux. In mid-January Davison and Jones were to find the grooves covered with a thin layer of snow. As the pair climbed the introductory pitches of Moss Gill to start the Grooves a voice from below introduced himself as Andy Perkins who Brian had met a few weeks earlier. Without a climbing partner, the pair invited him to join them. The summer crux on the first pitch involved a high step onto a sloping foothold covered with crusty snow. Higher up the groove a downward pointing peg was placed more to reduce the feeling of isolation than for its holding power; Richard later removed it by hand. The final pitches passed without any problems and they were in the valley before dark.

The mid-1980s was a transition time for winter grading that was to take another decade to resolve, but only by expansion of the grading system. For several years new hard routes had been shoe-horned into the existing six grades leaving a huge spread of difficulty across the top grade. Davison wrote:

> "The route went without a hitch; the only dilemma I had was with the grade. It was obviously harder than Moss Gill which was Grade III at the time but it was also miles easier than Tough Guy on Lochnagar which I'd climbed only a few weeks before, which had been given a Grade IV. Eventually IV was settled on which was later revised to a V as Tough Guy was later upgraded to VII." (4)

Until the route was repeated it was difficult to tell the grade. The prolonged winter of 2009-2010 saw the slabs often covered with snow and in February 2010 over 25 years after the first ascent Steve Ashworth and Paddy Cave finally repeated Moss Gill Grooves. Their ascent found crusty snow covering the slabs and icy cracks.

Steve Ashworth ascends the upper pitch of Moss Gill Grooves on the second winter ascent.

With the snow too weak for load bearing and runner placements obscured and difficult to find, the pair found the top pitch to offer the hardest climbing as darkness nipped at their heels. Steve thought the climbing bold rather than overtly technical and a grade of VI, 6 felt justifiable for the day. Paddy thought it was VI, 7 demonstrating how subjective opinions affect grades for winter ascents.

But back in 1985 Davison was again on Scafell a week later to look at Central Buttress, this time with Pete Herrold. In summer a seep to the right of the Great Flake had attracted his attention, but sadly in winter this rarely freezes higher on the crag. With heavy hoar frost covering the cliff the conditions were not easy to read. While the chockstone on the Great Flake was reached, little further progress was made – but the pair had been seen and the secret was out!

Jim Fotheringham.

Al Phizacklea on the first pitch of Botterill's Corner; which was formerly known as Tricouni Slab.

The following season started with a late November foray onto The East Buttress by Jim Fotheringham and Gerard Bonington, who is forever in the shadow of his illustrious brother Chris. Their ascent of Overhanging Wall at V, 6 provided ground-up access to Phizacklea's earlier lines and showed an ascent of the entire buttress was possible. However, the use of several aid points and tension from a runner meant the route, which had the potential for becoming the greatest breakthrough in winter climbing, never received any accolades. Fotheringham commented:

> "This was one of the best winter routes I ever did. I walked up and down from the East for three weeks until I eventually found it iced up. The East Buttress is a bit funny with ice, if it is too cold the water trickling down it freezes up too quickly and you never get a build up of ice, but in November or December it is not too cold or too warm, and it freezes well. The lower section was a bit of mixed climbing, scratching on sods and a bit of ice, but higher up there was a blank V-groove which was fucking terrifying, and I was thinking 'Christ, Christ, I'm going to fall a long way here', so I used an étrier clipped into my 'Terror' for aid. We finished up the White Slab, but went back the next day to abseil into the belay to finish up Minotaur, which is a fantastic route – I'll rave about that all day long." (5)

A few days into 1986 the same pair climbed Great Chimney, high up in Deep Gill, and it gave them the usual struggle to pass the great chockstone. The next day a heavily hoar frosted Tricouni Slabs saw an ascent by Al Phizacklea and George Smith who from the top of the slab followed the original, and at that time unknown line of Botterill's Corner, which climbed the open chimney above to finish. Around the same time the complete summer line of Tricouni Slab, which finished out rightwards, was climbed by Fotheringham and Victor Saunders. Activity was heating up and an excellent spell of cold weather in February proved to be highly productive as numerous teams ventured out looking for new winter routes on the crag.

Steve Howe and Joe Grinberg were the first to make use of the excellent conditions as they headed up Deep Gill to try the striking line Jones' Route from Deep Gill; a satisfying route that gives a sense of achievement as it ends on the pinnacle summit of High Man. Meanwhile round the corner Dave Kay and Mike Lynch were discovering that Hopkinson's Gully wasn't in condition. Racing back up Deep Gill they climbed the first pitches of Jones's Route from Deep Gill behind Steve and Joe. With darkness beckoning the pair accepted the offer of a rope from above so became part of the first ascent rather than the second ascent team on what was to be renamed Age Concern for its winter version of the route. This at least helps reduce confusion among the plethora of Jones' routes. While this quartet performed in Deep Gill the trio of Tony Stephenson, Keiran (Keefe) Murphy and Linda Rutland were battling their way out of Steep Gill via the grooves up the left wall at the point where the gully narrows. Steep Gill Grooves V, 6 still has its one aid peg needed to reach the second belay ledge.

A week later Mike Lynch was back; this time with Bob Wightman, and Hopkinson's Gully was again their target. The summer route ends at The Crevasse below Slingsby's Chimney but the pair thrutched their way up the chimney to reach Low Man and then High Man. This was an excellent day out and it was the first of several modern ascents of Slingsby's Chimney. The chimney had received its first winter ascent in 1899, and the thrutching nature of the climbing in the chimney was much more suited to the Victorian style of climbing.

Bob describes the climbing on that day:

> "The verglassed initial wall was the crux and fairly bold; I don't remember getting any gear in until I was stood on a ledge some way up. The upper groove was better but still thinly iced though straightforward. I probably only had three or four runners on the pitch but didn't think too much of it as we didn't carry that much gear anyway. Mike then led across and up the wide cracks on Jones' Route before I finished up the chimney pitch to the summit of the Pinnacle. Not bad for a grade IV!!" (6)

Above: Mike Lynch is following the superb first pitch of Hopkinson's Gully during the first winter ascent.

Left: Dave Kay on Age Concern, the winter version of Jones' Route from Deep Gill.

Photos: Al Phizacklea

Adrian Moore and Tony Brindle as seen during the second day of their contested winter ascent of Central Buttress.

Right: Tony Brindle and below: Adrian Moore.

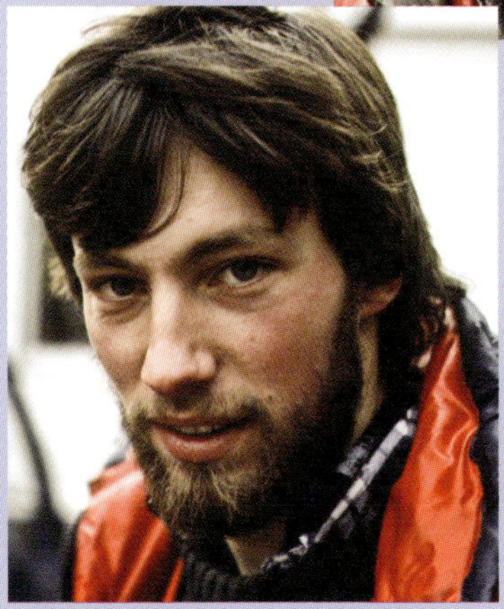

Having spent the previous weekend on Age Concern staring across Deep Gill at Deep Gill Buttress, Dave Kay had had plenty of time to spy out the line up the left edge, West Wall Climb IV, 4 for which he enlisted the help of Steve Howe. Then only three days later Steve Howe, Tony Stephenson and Pamela Andrews took advantage of the conditions to battle their way up the corner system running up from the top left side of the snow bay above the first part of Steep Gill to produce Bridge of Sighs V, 5. Such was the frenzied pace of activity on Scafell that to their left Joe Grinberg and Dave Kay were delicately connecting the slabs and ramps on the right side of the Pisgah Buttress to produce Restless Natives VI, 6.

Wightman's enthusiasm for Hopkinson's Gully persuaded Al Phizacklea and Duncan Richards, full of admiration, to attempt the route which they followed to a junction with Jones' Route Direct. An opportunity arose at this point for further exploration as the ledge of Hopkinson's Cairn was visible about 20 metres away on the crest of the buttress. A delicate, unprotected lead on the perfectly verglassed rock led up and right to the ledge, giving another sustained pitch of Grade 6 quality. Here they could walk around and admire the tremendous vista of snow plastered rock all around them, before tackling the easier groove line of the summer route Low Man from Hopkinson's Cairn. This led, as it suggests, to the Low Man, from where the Knife-edged Arête was followed to the top of The Pinnacle. Dusk was drawing in around them, and the name Moonbathing came from the fact that they made their way down to the valley by the brilliant light from a near full moon – the perfect end to a perfect day.

The longer daylight of early March encouraged climbers to think about trying Central Buttress. This time it was Tony Brindle and Adrian Moore, two young local activists who took up the challenge. On reaching the Oval they decided to remove their crampons and climb the Great Flake in their boots; a fine effort but the style raised doubts over the issue of its winter condition. The new style of climbing snowed up rock routes, by now referred to as mixed climbing, was subjected to extreme criticism with the continuing questioning of what conditions constitute a winter ascent. Joe Brown is often credited with the statement that for a winter ascent the use of axes and crampons must make the climbing easier than without. This seems as good a guideline to winter conditions as any and has been followed by many leading activists over the years. However the controversial ascent of Central Buttress was further compounded when the pair abandoned their intent to bivouac on the route due to possible hypothermia, and retreated from above the Flake to Wasdale. They accepted a friend's invite to a party at the Old Dungeon Ghyll, so the next day they walked in from Langdale and abseiled into their high point to complete the line. News travelled fast and Davison heard about the ascent only a few days later via a radio message relayed to him while he sat tent bound, waiting out a storm in the Antarctic.

Photo: Duncan Richards for Phizacklea Collection

Al Phizacklea on the delicate rising traverse which leads to Hopkinson's Cairn Ledge, during the ascent of Moonbathing.

The Evolution of Winter Ethics

Criticism levelled towards the flawed winter ascent of Central Buttress dates back to the ethically flawed ascent of Point Five Gully on Ben Nevis by Clough, Alexander, Pipper and Shaw in 1959 over six days with returns to their high point, causing a storm in Scottish winter climbing circles. The proof that a more ethical ascent was possible was shown only a year later by Marshall and Smith when they completed the second ascent in only seven hours. In an attempt to preserve ethical standards it was decided that winter ascents must be completed ground up in a single push. Long routes can be difficult to find in complete condition and so require careful planning, early starts and dedication. The message from above the border was if the commitment isn't there don't try the line. Such decision deliberation was further tested in 1976 when Andrew Wielochowski climbed The Fly Direct on Creag Meagaidh over three days, and the ascent of its final pitches saw the bottom of the route ice free. Though the flawed ascent was mentioned in the *Scottish Mountaineering Club Journal* of the time it was not deemed a completed ascent (*SMCJ* 1977). The line was climbed in a single day in 1983 by Mike Fowler and Victor Saunders and it has subsequently seen several ascents.

Thus evolved the Scottish tactics; but while these were regarded as guidelines for the Sassenachs to follow, it didn't mean that these were the supreme law. There are no laws in climbing, and not every English climber recognised or even knew of these guidelines, so some activists think there is some potential for relaxing or ignoring the 'One Day' rule. Not so Brian Davison – he later edited the Scottish Mountaineering Club guidebooks and wholly endorsed their ethics, which he fully promoted when he became the winter guide book writer for The Lake District.

West Wall Climb in Deep Gill, taken on the first winter ascent by Dave Kay and Steve Howe.

As Central Buttress was being finished off Al Phizacklea and Mike Lynch made their way up an obvious rake rising leftwards across the upper section of Deep Gill Buttress from the col on Lord's Rake, later to become part of the Deep Gill Integrale. Half-way along the rake a narrow chimney led to the top of the buttress, giving a rather unassuming route which they called Sod All at Grade III. This may have been the line climbed fourteen years earlier by Bob Bennett and Royanne Lavender, who never recorded it because they were unsure of their location on the crag. Phizacklea finished the day with a solo ascent of the shallow corner running up the slabs to the right of the Old Professor's Chimney to give Impunity Slabs, another Grade III. A few weeks later this excellent 1985-1986 winter closed with that man Phizacklea soloing across the obvious ledge system of Upper Deep Gill Buttress to give the un-inspiringly named Upper Deep Gill Route at Grade II.

By mid-January the following year conditions were good and Davison was back from the Antarctic and keen to do battle with Central Buttress. This time he had Rob Mulvaney with him as he climbed to the Oval to view a thin veneer of ice that had formed down the wall to the right of the Great Flake. With crampon points carefully placed into the ice and axes thrust deep behind the flake he resorted to lay-backing. As his first axe was placed on the top of the Flake the ice stripped under his crampons, and with full body weight suddenly loaded onto the single axe the blade slid along the curved edge of the Flake and off the end. Crampon points scraped down the wall, and in a flash Davison found himself at the base of the flake as remnants of ice tinkled down around him. With the ice stripped retreat was the only option.

The previous day's failure was still in their minds as the pair started up Moss Gill looking for climbable ice. Without a guidebook to hand they didn't know the ice they found was hanging down Harvest, a summer HVS which still sported a point of aid to cross its top slab. The lower slab gave access to ice hanging down the right wall.

Above: Climbers approaching the foot of Moss Gill when in perfect winter conditions. The line of Harvest Crunch takes the prominent white slab just below the darkest overhang in the centre of the picture, then the very narrow slab immediately above this feature.

Right: Andy Mitchell joins Dave Birkett at the belay, just after completing the crux of Harvest Crunch during the second winter ascent. Note the Birkett-shaped impact mark on the slab below the lower overhang!

Davison recalled:

> "I climbed the ice and gained the narrow slab above. Some thin climbing led to below a roof. I was forced to move leftwards into a hanging corner but it was too far left for me to look into it and so I blindly aimed my left axe in the corner and it stuck; but I couldn't find anything for my feet. I gently shifted leftwards not wanting to make any jolting movements which might displace my left axe in the corner, as it was the only point of contact I had. I was now hanging just by my left axe and couldn't find anything for my feet to allow me to make a move up to place the other axe above. I was too weak to do a one arm pull up, so in the end I grabbed the axe with both hands and pulled up on it and then let go with my right hand and hammered in that axe above, before my strength gave out. Thankfully the corner was short and I was soon lying on the ledge above. It was only when I got back to the valley that I discovered what we'd climbed, and so named it Harvest Crunch to distinguish it from the summer ascent. By now the new extended grading system was taking shape and I had a better grasp on the grades so gave it VII, 9 as although it was technical the difficulties were short. Al Phizacklea freed the summer line of Harvest the following summer at 6b and was surprised to see the crampon scratches. Given the lack of holds and the reach required to get round into the corner I was surprised at it being freed in summer." (7)

This route remained unrepeated in winter until 2011 when Dave Birkett and Andy Mitchell managed it, but not without incident. Dave fell from the crux and ended up crashing onto the slab below the overhang he'd been trying to cross, leaving a Birkett-shaped outline in the snow on the lower slab.
A month later Davison was back with Richard Jones. They headed further up Moss Gill, past the chockstone, and this time Clockwork Orange was the target. He recalls:

> "The groove wasn't as friendly as Harvest and didn't seem to have a crack in the back to offer axe and protection placements. I remember getting a 'Friend' in after about 12m but as they tend to come out of verglassed parallel sided cracks I wasn't that happy with it. I moved above it until it looked like the only runner high enough to prevent a ground fall landing next to Richard. I kept moving up and down becoming familiar with the moves and gaining a little height each time before returning to a semi resting place. I couldn't find any more gear and knew I would have to commit to the moves above. But I needed to know how far the 'Friend' was below me and if it was above half way. I'd already avoided asking the question several times and Richard must have sensed what was to come because as I started to phrase the question he unclipped from the belay and positioned himself on the edge of the chockstone ready to jump. It had worked for the Australian climber Kim Carrigan in the summer when he'd fallen off Midsummer Nights Dream on Cloggy so hopefully it would work for me. I just didn't fancy finding out. I don't think I ever finished the question. I made my rehearsed moves then launched up the final section of groove until my axes were sunk into lovely turf on a ledge in the corner." (8)

To distinguish it from the summer route the name was changed to Mechanical Orange, after a Peruvian youth club seen on the shores of Lake Titicaca. The difficult and serious nature of the climbing warranted a high grade; and VIII, 8 was as high as grades reached in 1987.
At some point during the 1986-1987 winter Al Phizacklea, Andy Rowell and Paul Plowright were back filling in gaps, and they climbed the long neglected line of Pollux, III. This may be a rather unmemorable line, and it was climbed in thick mist, but to its credit it comes quickly into condition.

Footnotes

1. Al Phizacklea, author's note for Brian Davison
2. Al Phizacklea, author's note for Brian Davison
3. Jim Fotheringham, telephone conversation with author, 2010
4. Brian Davison, first written for this publication
5. Jim Fotheringham, telephone conversation with author, 2010
6. Bob Wightman, e-mail correspondence to author, 2011
7. Brian Davison, first written for this publication
8. Brian Davison, first written for this publication

Photo: Ed Luke

Paddy Cave battling up the main pitch of Moss Gill Grooves during the second winter ascent.

1987 - 1997

Between Borderline and Birkett

Photo: Al Phizacklea

Looking up from Deep Gill, the central prow of Death Arête is caught in the morning sun, a sight that inspired its name back in 1987, when there were only two established routes on this part of the crag. Swillshark follows the slender rib in shadow on the right.

Overleaf:
A climber on the front face of The Great Flake on Central Buttress. The original line across the front of this feature, Marr's Variation, traversed across to the thin crack to the left of the climber, but now most ascents continue directly from the climber to the crest of the flake.

Photo Ed Luke

Early in 1987 Al Phizacklea wandered up the wide gully of Deep Gill, an area of the crag he hadn't visited since his fellwalking days a dozen years gone. Looking around from the junction where The Great Chimney and Professor's Chimney merge into the gill, he noticed an amazing array of unclimbed rock. To the right of The Great Chimney rose a slender elegant arête, sharp edged and vertical, a wonderful feature reminiscent of the photo of High Noon in the recently published Newman/Wilson book *Extreme Rock*. On the opposite wall of The Great Chimney rose a huge imposing square cut arête overhanging the gully like the prow of a majestic ocean liner. This awe-inspiring feature prompted Phizacklea to mutter John Redhead's prophetic quote from Jim Perrin's article 'The Great Wall Saga' in *Extreme Rock* – 'It'll go – but there's nothing, it's Death!' Al thought: 'Wow! It's a Death Arête'. Little did he know at the time that the name would stick.

Looking across the gully to the sunlit slabby walls of the upper Scafell Pinnacle he noticed a direct line was lacking. At a grass ledge below the slabs Al tied himself to his abseil rope and boldly climbed a little wall to gain the slabs, and then delicately to a ledge.

Here he re-tied into his abseil rope and continued up the slabs, tracing a line through the overlaps to the right of the Central Route. It was perhaps not a true solo ascent as the rope was used as a safeguard against falling into the depths of the gully. The climbing was not too technical, only 4c (with possibly a 5a start), but its bold style prompted the name Bold Eagle.

Phizacklea then wandered around to The East Buttress where he met a group of three Kendal based friends and he teamed up with Ted Rogers to climb Zeus. At the top of the crag he persuaded Ted to walk across to the top of Deep Gill and have a look at the unclimbed 'High Noon' line. Climbing on sight up the slightly lichenous but elegant arête right of The Great Chimney Al reached a good nut placement in a horizontal break at half height, providing encouragement for the upper edge. This was sharper than below, allowing a layback up its left side in a wild situation until a large sloping platform could be reached. He was amazed at the elegance of the climbing, but was tempered by Ted's laconic edict that it was probably only E1. A compromise of E2 was agreed, but it probably still awaits a second ascent for confirmation. A possible reason why it has failed to attract any attention is its mundane name of Swillshark; inspired the following weekend when Phizacklea and Steve Hubbard were reading a copy of *The Beano* in Pete's Eats café in Llanberis (purveyors of true quality reading matter!) Inside the comic, The Bash Street Kids were disgusted by their school dinner; a large vat of pig swill in which was circling the menacing fin of a Swill Shark.

The next major route to be climbed on The East Buttress was the formidable overhanging, brown stained wall between Zeya and the perpetual wet streak denoting the line of Armageddon. This had been investigated by Martin Berzins and Chris Sowden shortly after their success on Borderline, and their abseil inspection required the ropes to once again be clipped into nuts down the route. Martin waited whilst Chris removed the nuts by abseil and prepared for his attempt, watched from the sidelines by Rodney Valentine and Al Phizacklea. The start was a hard pull to gain a small undercut where Berzins slotted in a tiny micro-'Friend' but expended a great deal of effort just to remain in contact with the rock. He fought hard to reach a good hold at the base of the main feature, a slender groove, but the rock fought back harder, resulting in several retreats to the belay. Lacking the knockout punch that day, Martin used a wire for aid to gain the hold, where he placed a crucial runner before advancing quickly up the groove. A particularly stubborn micro nut failed to seat correctly in a slot, but it was persuaded to do so by belting it into place with a karabiner in an act of tiring desperation aided by a number of profanities. From his frantic puffing breaths and cursing it was obvious Martin was struggling to pass a small overlap to reach a resting ledge and runners. Finally, a short gangway just below the belay gave a precarious move to finish, but it had a trickle of water running down its back. This proved to be his undoing, and he peeled off the rock, swearing profusely as he flew earthwards. Martin was held by the runner after a twelve metre fall, after which he swung down to the aid nut to use for a rest and to compose himself before climbing back up to the belay.

This picture captures Martin Berzins just after using the point of aid on the first ascent of Siege Perilous. He returned several years later to climb the route free.

The Seventh Scafell Guide

The seventh series of the Scafell guidebook emerged in 1988, only four years after the previous edition. In effect it was only an updated re-print of the 1984 Scafell, Eskdale and Dow Crag guide with new photographs, and it included seven additional routes to Scafell.

The seventh guidebook to Scafell.

The major innovation, no doubt causing consternation with the traditional old guard, was that for the first time all pitch lengths were given in metric (as a straightforward conversion from feet). More subtle changes were the inclusion of the altitude and aspects of the crags next to the introduction to each crag. Al Phizacklea updated the guidebook, and as Dave Miller had stood down from the editing job, it was completed by his successor Dave Armstrong.

The diagram of Central Buttress.

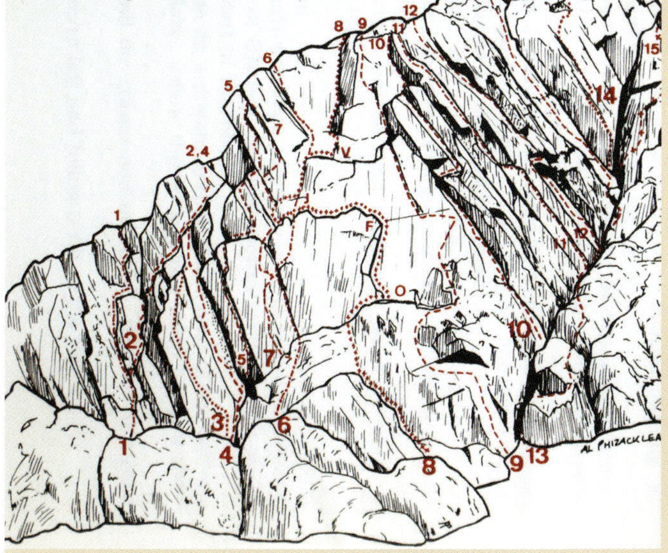

Photo: Al Phizacklea

Chris Sowden and Martin Berzins were the main pair of climbers operating on Scafell in the late 1980's.

Dai Lampard on the thin layback flake of Ixodes.

Photo: Al Phizacklea

The watching pair was stunned into silence (so much for giving support!) realising they had just seen the most inspiring lead they had ever witnessed. Chris Sowden followed through on the top pitch, a stubborn short hanging crack which led up to the White Slab. Martin reluctantly conceded that the route, later to be named The Siege Perilous, deserved to be graded E7, with individual pitches of 6b and 6a, but he was not satisfied with the point of aid. He would return to free the route some time later. The name Siege Perilous derives from the mythical seat around King Arthur's Round Table which could only be sat upon by one who had found the Holy Grail – but if anyone else sat upon it, they died. Berzins' explanation was:

> "I thought it was a really good name for a pokey route, but talk about it being pretentious, or what!" (1)

Phizacklea's next summer visit to Scafell was in 1989 in the company of the enthusiastic Welsh adventurer, Dai Lampard. They started the day's activities by repeating the first pitch of Foxshooter, which took them to the top of The Great Flake on Central Buttress. From here they abseiled alongside a thin crack dropping down the front of the flake; it looked difficult and was rather mossy so they left it as neither had brought a wire brush for cleaning. Phizacklea then suggested a look at the unclimbed rock high in Deep Gill, with the excited promise of a 'Death Arête' as an incentive.

After trudging up, the first line to catch their eye was a deep, unclimbed corner left of Grey Bastion, and this was quickly dispatched despite its lining of lichen. Lampard led the second pitch up to a clean arête, but the problem was gaining access to the arête due to bridging behind a delicately perched pinnacle to reach the holds. It was worryingly unstable; the higher he bridged, the greater was the leverage forcing off the block and it could have fallen at any time. They abseiled nervously back to the bed of the gully, and Phizacklea christened it Doctor Death, HVS, which was the nickname given to the unpopular Managing Director of the Barrow Shipyard at the time. Needless to say this route is probably unrepeated to this day.

Lampard then spotted a tenuous sharp-edged flake pressed tightly against the left side of the 'Death Arête', a quite intriguing line which promised some intense climbing. Following an abseil inspection he shuffled up the flake by a series of thin layback moves. It became a scintillating first pitch to the route called Ixodes, graded E1 or possibly E2, 5b, which is named after some genus of hard-bodied tick, the type responsible for those irritating bites at Chapel Head Scar, and the cause of nasty infections such as Lyme Disease.

The pair returned to the gully bed by abseiling down a crack system in the overhanging wall to the right of the 'Death Arête', but without a brush they were only able to clear debris blocking the crack with a nut extractor. It gave an excellent route, christened Alamogordo after the test site for the first atomic bomb in New Mexico. The steep, unrelenting nature of the climbing assured a grade of E5,6a. This was the first time three new routes had been added to Scafell in one day by a single team.

Following publication of his article in *Mountain* magazine updating the history of Scafell, Phizacklea realised there was a large unclimbed gap on The East Buttress between Centaur and Caradhras. He studied photographs of the area, but there was only one way to find out whether there were any holds on the line, and that was to have a look; which he did in May 1990. He recalled:

> "It was foggy when I picked up Andy Rowell and John Holden at about half-five, but when we drove over Birker Moor we emerged above the fog into a wonderful, clear atmosphere, with Scafell and all the surrounding hills rising out of the mist 'like islands out of a cotton wool sea'. It was gorgeous, but down at Wasdale it was sopping wet and there were all these damp walkers dressed in waterproofs plodding up towards Brown Tongue.

"They were amazed to see us bombing past them in shorts and T-shirts! The weather was scorching and The East Buttress was bone dry, so without any pratting about I got straight on the wall between The Centaur and Great Eastern Route. The pitches kept on coming; they were naturally clean and full of interest, especially the last one, a strenuous diagonal crack that got us all really pumped. We were dead chuffed because we had found something special, a three pitch E3 on The East Buttress which we led completely on sight." (2)

The Route was given the name Chiron after the first Centaur in Greek Mythology, but Phizacklea felt the route was tainted because he was forced to follow a short section of The Centaur on the first pitch. He later returned with Iain Turnbull to improve the start, making Chiron a sustained four pitch route, with technical grades of 5b, 5c, 5c and 5c.

A couple of weeks later, Phizacklea and Holden were back below The East Buttress to inspect a prominent corner which rose above the apex of The Yellow Slab. From the foot of The Yellow Slab Phizacklea led up the open corner, large capping roof and vertical flake that led spectacularly above the roof to easy ground. This route was named Cerberus after the large three-headed dog that in Greek mythology guarded the Gates of Hades. A similar character later became better known to millions of kids as 'Fluffy', the three-headed dog in Harry Potter and the Philosopher's Stone; but the name doesn't quite have the same ring to it!

The next route to be added in 1990 was The Caution Horses, E5, by Martin Berzins and Chris Sowden. This takes a vicious thin crack in the steep wall right of Lucius and it is a typical thuggish Berzins creation. He described it as being quite short but very bouldery, and containing a tricky sequence of technical pulling up an overhanging start with only one key runner on it before it reaches a belay on Pegasus. Although following the theme of its equine neighbours Pegasus and Lucius, the name is derived from a Cowboy Junkies album.

Above: Al Phizacklea was desperately in need of a style makeover in the late 80's.

Left: Unknown climbers tackling the strenuous upper pitch of Chiron.

Photo: Andy Fowell

Photo: Pam Shawcross

On the same day, and oblivious of Berzins and Sowden on The East Buttress, Al Phizacklea returned with Dave Kirby to 'have a look' at the thin crack to the left of The Great Flake on Central Buttress which he had originally inspected with Dai Lampard. They both soloed up Moss Ghyll Grooves with full racks of gear to reach a convenient abseil point. The crack they were aiming for is actually a drainage line for any water that runs down behind The Great Flake, and therefore it suffers from continual growths of moss and lichen. Despite many attempts, Phizacklea failed to stand on a small finger hold just left of the crack, and it was evident this would be the crux.

Retreating for a brew, Phizacklea decided to take an alternative look at the problem, so he fixed a runner in The Nazgul in order to try the blank wall to left of the crack. This approach resulted in six falls off the searingly small holds before he finally managed to stand on the small foothold and gain the crack. Running out of stamina, he climbed to a good 'Friend', and slumped back onto it for a rest. With bleeding finger tips from the crux Phizacklea was unwilling to repeat the performance, so he resigned himself to complete the route including the 'rest' and let someone else get the glory!

Phizacklea forced his way up the continually overhanging crack; frantically attempting to beat the pump with a dash for the top; but blew it, falling five metres amidst a hail of profanities that shocked watching teams on The Oval. He lowered down to the resting 'Friend' and sat there until his strength returned. Then with the ropes still running through his high runners; he quickly passed his high point and took a belay on a small ledge a few metres below Jeffcoat's ledge.

Dave Kirby followed with a tight rope, but then it became clear that there was the possibility for continuing this new line right to the top of the crag. Al traversed right into the centre of The Great Flake and climbed steadily to its highest point. From standing on this there followed an unprotected committing move up to a shallow scoop. A fall was unthinkable, as the sharp top edge of the flake would split more than a climber's personality if he fell astride it! The scoop led up to The V-Ledge, where they recovered their abseil gear left earlier in the day.

Phizacklea called the difficult first pitch Original Sin, and at E5, 6c, he reckoned he had found the limit of his abilities on the crag. It was to be another nine years before young Craig Matheson free climbed the route via the very hard direct start at E6, 6c, and this direct variation was repeated by Dave Birkett on the following day. Realising that repeat ascents would not continue beyond the first pitch, Phizacklea grafted the upper pitches onto the first pitch of Foxshooter for the guidebook to create a long, sustained and independent E4 up the front of the crag.

In the same summer, the Yorkshire based team of Tony Marr and Mike Took climbed a couple of variations on The Great Flake on Central Buttress. Tony had climbed C.B. several times in the past, and each time he had taken an inquisitive look around on to the front of the flake, so on this occasion he moved out from a sloping ledge onto the front face of the Flake, before climbing up to the top of the Flake thus effectively bypassing the chockstone and the famous crux of Central Buttress. This line had been attempted as far back as 1934 when F.G. Balcombe tried it, before he returned to a more conventional ascent utilising the chockstone. [In his book, *Cumbrian Rock*, Trevor Jones mistakenly suggested that Balcombe had tried the line of Foxshooter, but this was mere 'journalistic licence' and a lack of local knowledge]. When seconding, Mike Took didn't climb straight up, but continued to traverse horizontally before ascending to Jeffcoat's Ledge. Both variations were originally graded HVS.
Tony Marr explains:

> "I'd looked at this line over the years, and each time I did C.B. I'd notice that The Great Flake was much harder than the rest of the route. I'd always wondered what the front face was like. When I climbed it with Mike I led it with a wire brush between my teeth, because the rock was covered with lichen that was like little black caterpillars. It turned out that the front face of the flake was pure pleasure, because I hate laybacks." (3)

Above: Al Phizacklea on the first ascent of Original Sin.
Left: Tony Marr (right) and Mike Took pictured below Central Buttress after repeating their own variation out on the front of The Great Flake in 2006.

Tony felt aggrieved that his ascent didn't capture the attention of the locals, and wondered whether the FRCC had a secret agenda to ignore the efforts of 'outsiders'. But at the time, no-one thought that missing out the historical crux of what was possibly the most famous climb in Britain was a variation worth considering; even the suggestion of avoiding the Flake seemed an almost sacrilegious opinion. However, four years later these variations proved to be the most discussed of items on the FRCC website; but more of this later.

The final new route climbed on Scafell in the summer of 1990 was on The East Buttress and it was by the Ambleside based party animals Paul and Greg Cornforth. They climbed up the steep wall between Leverage and Dyad. The first pitch is rather deceptive; consisting of a series of slight bulges leading to a shallow groove; containing few positive holds, and fewer positive runners. It takes a certain degree of cool to stay focused on hanging onto side holds and smears, whilst aiming for the sanctuary of the Dyad ledge. The second pitch takes a bold arête to the right of the upper section of Dyad, which also provides few runners. At E5, 6a, 5c this is a truly modern test piece, but in reverence to the much earlier Keswick Brothers' Climb, but they astutely called their route The Ambleside Brothers' Climb.

Rob Matheson following The Ambleside Brothers' Climb.

Photo: Ed Luke

Standing a few metres away from the foot of this part of the crag a series of diagonal ledges can be seen rising rightwards from Dyad; these lead to nowhere in particular, but they do form a natural line across the crag. This is the line of the first pitch of Juno, climbed on the first day of June in 1991, hence the name. The crux of this E4, 6a, 5c route is a steep blank corner at the end of the ledges that lead with difficulty to a belay on The Fulcrum. The second pitch links by a long stretch to overcome a blank section of rock and join with the top section of The Ambleside Brothers' Climb. The first ascent was made by the Phizacklea, Holden and Rowell team.

Moving further around to the left-hand end of The East Buttress, and whilst Rowell relaxed in the sun opposite the crag, Phizacklea and Holden went looking at the steep pillar left of South Chimney. The first pitch was a wandering line up some subsidiary mossy slabs, but the main pillar proved to be too steep and bold to be climbed on-sight. They climbed up a shallow groove on its left side, which led pleasantly to a fine finishing flake. This gave them The Eastern Front, a rather obscure E1; but readers should note the steep pillar still awaits a direct ascent.

Walking over the top of The East Buttress, they dropped down into the depths of Deep Gill, where they claimed another route. This is The Unforgettable Fire, HVS, which climbs the slabby corner on the left of the 'Death Arête', and it is named after the U2 album. The upper pitch ends just below the small peaked top of Deep Gill Buttress called Symond's Knott, making the final holds the highest of any rock climb in England. Also completing that third climb made it the second time Al Phizacklea was involved with three first ascents on Scafell in a day.

This part of the crag still held an obvious unclimbed line, which attracted Phizacklea back with Paul Plowright at the end of the summer. They climbed the route on-sight, following the slabs to the left of The Unforgettable Fire to reach the main target; a steep hanging crack in the headwall. A large block is perched against the headwall, above which the crack rises. Starting moves were awkward with more difficult moves up to the huge undercut flake which is such a prominent feature of this wall.

Above: Al Phizacklea and John Holden on Juno.

Right: Al Phizacklea, first ascent of The Unforgettable Fire.

What followed used strenuous undercuts rightwards, rather like a desperate version of the Kipling Groove undercling in Langdale. The vertical extension then leads with memorable jamming to the top. A notable factor about this huge top flake is that daylight is visible behind the crack, for it is an almighty detached block perched above the huge drop of Deep Gill. This gives an unnerving moment as the climber must launch out on those strenuous undercuts, with the nagging doubt that his efforts are lifting the flake off its perch. If the block was ever to drop it would take out anyone in Lord's Rake and probably trundle way down past The Woolworth Boulder. The name The Scarlet Pimpernel was inspired by the taunts of Paul Ross who was to visit the same area five days later.

Paul Ross and Pete Lockey enjoyed a long standing partnership, and together they had been responsible for several classic routes in Borrowdale stretching back to the mid-1950s. By now, they themselves had reached their own mid-50s; but age was no barrier to their determination. Since the 1950s, Paul had wanted to make his mark on the crag, and was worried that Phizacklea 'was now jumping on every available line.' His previous history was one of misfortune; he had missed out on the first ascent of May Day Direct; he had attempted Centaur and The Nazgul but was rained off the crag, and he had tried Talisman, leaving the peg in place. Rossy had spotted his potential route on the side of Deep Gill Buttress one misty day whilst walking his devoted Parson Jack Russell terriers, (a type of dog for which he had just won 'Best in Breed' at that year's Cruft's dog show).

They climbed steeply between the cracks of Gobsite and Xerxes to give a surprisingly awkward route at E2 which they dubbed Swansong. On the day of the ascent Ross abseiled the line to remove any loose blocks, but he kept the cleaning to a minimum. It follows a series of steep corners connected by a continuous crack line, building up to the final strenuous crack to give a memorable pitch. Ross was obviously overjoyed with the result, because three days later Phizacklea learned about his success in the form of a photo of the first ascent, upon the back was Paul's taunting scrawl: 'You missed this one, Al!' His accompanying letter accused Phizacklea of avoiding him on the crags and named him 'the Scarlet Pimpernel'; hence the name of the earlier route.

During the spring of 1992, Phizacklea received a call from Martin Berzins who was looking for a partner to accompany him on a long term project – to free the line of The Siege Perilous. The grade remains at E7, 6b, and it gave Al an indication of life at the top of the tree as he was hauled up on a tight rope. Martin recalls:

> "It was far from ideal conditions; it was a wild day and the weather was totally crap, but the steepness kept the route dry and passers by were looking aghast because we were the only people climbing on the crag." (4)

When the weather improved Phizacklea casually told Martin about this wonderful 'Death Arête' around in Deep Gill. Martin's scepticism soon evaporated as he viewed its incredible line, and although he had written the 1984 guidebook to The East Buttress, he had no inkling that this area of the crag even existed. Taking a careful note of the line, Berzins then led the second ascent of Alamogordo, confirming its quality and grade, but he vowed to return someday.

No further new routes were added that year, but in 1993 the Fell & Rock held a 'Guidebook Climbing Meet' at Brackenclose, where teams were asked to check out various routes in the area. Phizacklea teamed up with Iain Turnbull, but he had nothing other than a new route in mind. His objective was to avoid Right-Hand Edge and take a direct line up the front face of The Pinnacle, passing through two bands of overlaps. He had become aware of this line from photographs published in Gordon Stainforth's spectacular book, *Eyes to the Hills*. The route went exactly as planned, its direct line giving the name Meridian, and a Grade E1, 5b, 5b.

Pete Lockey following Ross' Swansong; a copy of this picture was the one sent to Phizacklea.

Paul Ross.

Iain Newman, the unfortunate victim of the C.B. chockstone, taken below Central Buttress.

'Chance in a million' kills climber as Great Flake chock stone tumbles

Whitehaven News Staff Report

DANGER on one of Lakeland's most popular climbs has risen dramatically following a fatal fall at the weekend.

Iain George Newman, 20, of Hollin Hill, Burnley, died on the flanks of 3,162ft Scafell in West Cumbria.

He was attempting pitch three on Great Flake, part of the mountain's Central Buttress, when disaster struck.

The climb's chock stone, a key feature in scaling Great Flake, was dislodged and crashed down onto Mr Newman with fatal results.

Without the half-ton, man-sized stone, the 470ft pitch — already graded "hard to very severe" — now steps up into the "extreme" category.

Great Flake is one of Lakeland's toughest challenges. When it was first climbed in 1914 the achievement was hailed as a breakthrough in mountaineering.

Now it is likely to be even more difficult to ascend, and is certain to be beyond the skills of all but the most expert climbers.

Insp John Furness, of Egremont police, said: "Anyone planning to tackle Great Flake should be fully aware of this and of the risks involved.

"The chock stone was halfway up the pitch, and its loss makes the climb significantly more dangerous."

Mr Newman's death was described as "a chance in a million" by Bill Pattison, who led 22 members of Wasdale Mountain Rescue Team to the scene of the tragedy.

Mr Newman had been climbing with his friend of four years, Robert Cobbold, of Fosse Close, Blackburn. The pair were roped together, with Mr Newman leading.

Mr Pattison said: "He had a running belay round the chock stone to protect his next move, and he was almost at the top of the Flake when he slipped.

"The rope held, and he was lowered about 50ft down to where his companion was in position.

"Then, against all the odds, the chock stone came away and fell on him, causing fatal injuries.

"It could have missed him or it could have killed them both. What happened was a chance in a million."

Mr Pattison added: "Thousands of people must have fallen over the years on that climb, and the chock stone has always held.

"It was an enormous lump of rock, jammed in a crack, but it must have been loosened by the frost and thaw of the past winter."

Both climbers were highly experienced and well equipped, said Mr Pattison, who praised the efforts of the survivor for doing all he could for his companion both before and after the accident.

Mr Pattison and his team were called out at 6.30 pm on Saturday after other climbers had reported hearing screams and falling rock.

On arrival at Central Buttress, the rescue party lowered the dead climber and his shocked companion off the crag.

The body was carried down the mountain to Standing Stones, where a Sea King helicopter from RAF Boulmer took over.

In Whitehaven on Monday the deputy coroner for West Cumbria, John Taylor, opened and adjourned an inquest into Mr Newman's death.

PC Alison Bell said the climber was certified dead at the scene and had been formally identified by his climbing companion, Robert Cobbold.

Courtesy of Whitehaven News

The chockstone from Central Buttress was found on the scree below the crag. It is very difficult to discern it from the detritus below the crag now it has weathered to a more even colouring.

The following day the same team climbed what they thought was a new direct line up the front face of Pisgah Buttress, where it later transpired that the first two 5b pitches followed Morrison and Fowler's earlier route Hilarity. A third pitch proved somewhat contrived as it was difficult to find an area of unclimbed rock, but the blank wall right of the crack of The Gripe gave a difficult pitch. On the day the entire line of Pisgah Buttress Direct was filled with two dozen bumbling purple-helmeted climbers, who turned out to be Army recruits on their final practice climb before going on a collective Alpine trip. "Bloody hell" commented Iain "Talk about lambs for the slaughter!" a comment which inspired the name of Sacrificial Squaddies for the route at E2.

The only route added in 1994, in June, was a poor, mossy single pitch VS climbed on the left extremity of The East Buttress. The weather was dispiriting and misty, prompting Phizacklea and Barry Chislett to give it the uninspiring name Smeagaidh (pronounced Smeggy).

The entire year was overshadowed by a tragic event when a young climber fell off the layback of Central Buttress. The famous chockstone somehow became dislodged and it struck him as it fell. He died on The Oval before help arrived. This incident has become notorious as one of the freakiest accidents to happen in the history of British climbing. It is perhaps the most tragic accident to occur on Scafell since 1903, yet this may be because it is still fresh in the minds of most of today's climbers. On the 4th of June, Iain George Newman (age 22) of Burnley and Robert Alexander Cubbold (age 24) of Blackburn, two fit and experienced climbers, had intended to climb C.B. They bivouacked at Mickledore the previous night, and despite the clear weather the rocks were still greasy from recent rain. Newman led up The Great Flake, threaded a sling around the chockstone for his runner as thousands of climbers had done before him, and as he proceeded to layback the upper section of the flake he slipped and fell. Amazingly, unbelievably, the chockstone slipped out of its crack causing Iain to fall further down the face, followed by the chockstone. As his fall was arrested by his last runner, the chockstone struck him on his right leg, shattering the femur and severing the femoral artery, sending him into shock. Cubbold lowered him back down to the Oval ledge, where despite a determined effort to stem the flow of blood, Newman passed away before the rescue team could give medical assistance. (5), (6) There have been several inaccurate versions of this event published in the past, some have implied that the stone fell out whilst he was being lowered, or it slipped out after he had been lowered safely onto The Oval.

Aside from the horrific death of young Iain, it was obvious that the route Central Buttress would never be the same again. This chockstone was probably the most famous of its type, holding a unique place in climbing history as generations of climbers had pulled on it, sat on it, used it as a launch platform for the final layback of The Great Flake, and thanked its location when determination for that layback was lacking. The list of climbers who have fallen onto the chockstone is long and distinguished, and it increased with every passing year. Words of derring-do have been written about those who had tied themselves to it, and it had become one of the most discussed pieces of rock over an evening pint back at the pub. Just over eighty years since its first ascent Central Buttress and The Great Flake had irrevocably lost its character, and were clearly never going to be the same again. Now the previously dismissed variations out onto the front of the flake were obviously going to be crucial for the future of the route.

A subsequent search amongst the scree below the crag located the chockstone, its polished exposed section contrasting sharply with its lighter coloured sides that once lay against the flake and the main crag. The chockstone, which would have weighed about 250 kilograms, was approximately 45 cm high, 30 cm wide and 80cm deep; with a section of its back edge broken off in the fall. This was a clean break, with no evidential staining that might indicate that it had previously been cracked. There was nothing to show it had been subject to wear, nor was there any sign of slippage apart from impact scratches where it had fallen. Clearly the chockstone had been held in place by sheer pressure, akin to a piece of steel held in the jaws of a vice. As it takes only a slight reduction in the pressure from the vice to allow the steel to be removed, it may similarly be concluded that the pressure holding the chockstone in place had been reduced.

This can only be explained by acknowledging The Great Flake must have moved a fraction, obeying the natural law that governs the erosive forces on mountains whereby all loose rock will fall to earth at some time. The Great Flake must have settled slightly and thus reduced the pressure on the chock-stone. All it needed was the miniscule impact of a falling climber to pull it free. There would have been no sign of this, and no warning. It could have happened at any time, it was simply an unfortunate coincidence that Iain Newman happened to be there.

Al Phizacklea and Stevie Whittall were the first to repeat the route to check the situation for the guidebook, but their frame of mind was tempered by the pool of congealed blood still covering the Oval ledge. They discovered that there were no further runners at the place where the chockstone once sat, There was another small chockstone set deeply behind where the original had been, but who was going to trust that? Now the stone had gone, starting the layback position for the upper flake had become a very strenuous proposition.

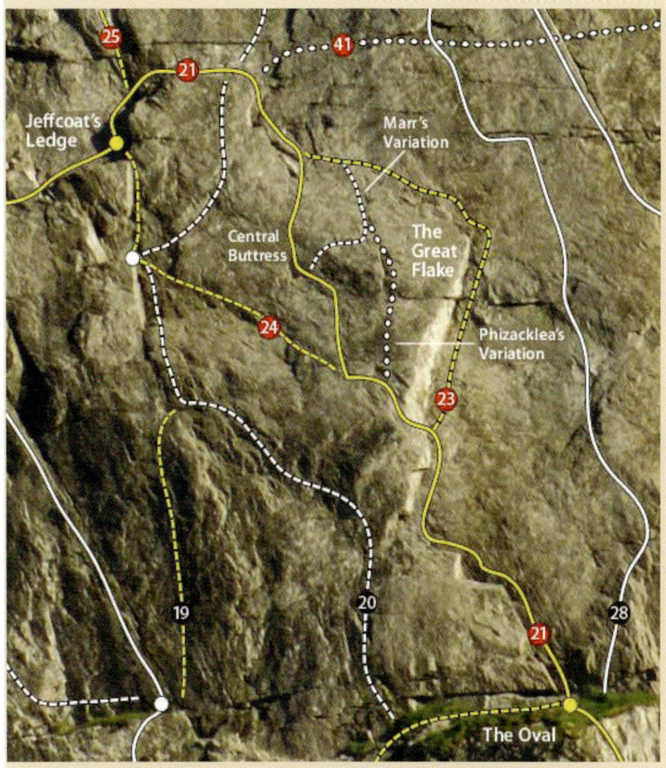

This diagram illustrates the confusion surrounding the numerous variations that now exist across the front face of The Great Flake. The line of Central Buttress as currently described in the 2014 guidebook is numbered 21. This is now considered the normal route.

The original 1914 route is numbered 23. Marr's Variation was the first route across the flake. Phizacklea's Variation was the route described in the 1996 guidebook. Took's Variation is numbered 24. For further details of the other routes please refer to the Central Buttress diagram on page 351.

Dave Parton climbing Marr's Variation of the Great Flake, Central Buttress.

C.B. Sid

1996 saw the death of one of the most famous characters to grace the crags of Scafell. Sid Thompson, who reached the age of 81 before his death, never achieved any fame through climbing nor did he produce any new routes on Scafell; but he became famous, and was known through the climbing world simply as 'C.B. Sid'.

Picture the old man in his seventies, dressed in Dad's Army-style Millets baggy pants held up with wide braces, topped with a battered flat cap and drinking milk from an old Domestos bottle, sitting on The Oval ledge. Here Sid waited alone for the day's first leader on Central Buttress to reach that hallowed grass, who would be surprised to find the ledge already occupied. Sid used to cycle the twenty miles from Maryport and make his way up the hill, and solo up to The Oval in order to hitch a ride up The Great Flake. With a disarming innocence and mild manners, he would kindly ask the team whether he could join them to complete the route, sealing the contract with a bag of sticky wine gums. Only once was he refused; and following this rebuke, the second of the two climbers who had earlier told him where to go, failed on The Great Flake. As second the climber endured the embarrassment of being lowered to the ground, and the leader sheepishly asking Sid whether he could tie onto the rope instead so he could complete the route.

Sid once claimed that he climbed the route 'more than 50 times', but there have been so many climbers who have claimed to have taken him up the route, the actual number of ascents must be many more. The walls of his council house in Maryport were adorned with pictures of his favourite route, including one of himself spread-eagled on the traverse pitch to the V-Ledge, but there were none of him leading The Great Flake. This pitch proved rather too much for him, and despite sometimes repeating it twice in one day he never managed to lead it. Chris Sice and Tony Stephenson once tried to coax him into leading the pitch, and as Chris put it: 'He just had this mental block; he easily had the ability to lead it, but he just couldn't put it together.' The news of the loss of the chockstone was broken to him by Chris Bacon, and Sid sadly realised that he had climbed the route for the last time. This charming man had become a legendary figure as he strove to lead his favourite route, but old age eventually robbed his chance of achieving his dream. (12)

It is clear that a slip from the greasy rock will result in a 12 metre fall and, having witnessed the consequences of this, their resolve was lacking that day. Phizacklea repeated Marr's Variation which followed a thin break onto the front face of The Great Flake, starting from a sloping ledge 3 metres below the chockstone's old location. With footholds as mere smears at this point and the rocks below the feet overhang gently this position has an instant and inescapable sense of exposure. It didn't feel like a HVS, and because of the dramatic transformation from big flaky holds to a huge drop, it was graded E1 in the guidebook.

Marr accused the FRCC of over-grading his line, belittling his addition to the crag and publishing an incorrect guidebook description. A little explanation is in order here - at the time Phizacklea had no description of Marr's Variation and he took a more direct and harder line to that of Marr, and this was the line recorded in the 1994 guide. Phizacklea repeated the route for the latest guide and the description now follows a more direct line than Marr's, but he retained the E1 grade, which was supported by evidence from locals and the C.B. log in *U.K. Climbing*. On the other hand, it should also be noted that Marr and Took are two traditional Yorkshire climbers, raised in the unforgiving gritstone world where HVS has always been regarded as a tough mission, especially for soft mountain men. There was no deliberate intent to disparage Tony's original ascent; the fact was there were no recorded repeats of this line whilst the chockstone was in position and this variation only became significant because it provided the easiest way up the route, not because it was a significant addition to the crag. Back on the original line, it was discovered that laybacking up the Flake can be well protected at E2 with the insertion of a mighty 'Friend 6' behind the Flake.

Central Buttress is still a great route but, as older climbers will remind you, it's not the same route. The history of Central Buttress and its famous flake would not be complete without a few of the many anecdotes of exciting epics that have centred around this feature. Arthur Dolphin fell off when lay-backing up the Flake in nails under very greasy conditions. One witness, Pete Brown recalled:

> "I can remember watching him leap into a layback position in his clinkered boots from the chock-stone on the Flake and he made two moves and his feet … I can hear the noise now as his feet just went out across the face of the rock and he came flying back down again." (7)

Dolphin escaped bruised and badly shaken, but otherwise unhurt. He required assistance down to Brackenclose from Joe Griffin, who said he could only walk slowly as he was in quite a bit of pain. Dolphin rarely fell off and this was indeed a rare incident, but the following day he went to The East Buttress and climbed Mickledore Grooves and Yellow Slab just to ensure he hadn't lost his nerve. Strangely, his main partner on Scafell, Pete Greenwood, also fell off from the same place.
The conditions were poor, and he was climbing the pitch with socks over his rubbers. He omitted to place a runner on the chockstone so he fell directly onto the Oval, bounced off and endured a scaphoid fracture of his wrist before he was held by his second. He climbed back up to the belay, and then reversed the route, climbing down as last man, before walking back to Langdale! (As an indication of his robustness, ten days later he led Hangover in the Llanberis Pass with his broken wrist!)
An anonymous climber fell off under unusual circumstances, as the following note in the Brackenclose book testified:

> "He began to lower down from the chockstone sling, but as soon as his weight came on the sling the knot came undone. He hurtled into space completely missing The Oval. The fall was checked in fine style by his second and third men after he had fallen from 70-80 feet. The rope made a deep groove in the grassy cornice of the Oval otherwise probably nothing could have prevented it from breaking. He was now hanging unconscious in space and our leader [John Ball] whipped down at great speed onto a small ledge below The Oval from which it was just possible to reach the now semi-conscious leader and help him onto the ledge.

"It was ascertained that no bones were broken, and he had only a slight cut to the head. The rest of the team lowered him to the ground and escaped via Moss Ghyll Grooves. The third man had one hand badly burned. The leader was removed to Whitehaven Hospital for an X-ray of his skull and was retained there. Thus ended our attempt on C.B. this holiday." (8)

Ken Jackson also fell from this point in another bizarre accident. After an attempt on the crux of The Great Flake, he retreated back to the chockstone for a rest. Instead of hanging from his waist belt, he decided to stand in the sling looped around the stone, but accidently stood into a loop of the climbing rope between himself and the thread. Ken effectively pulled himself off the rock and he ended up 40 feet lower.

No doubt dozens of climbers could tell similar tales of near-misses from this particular feature and its loss with tragic results over 20 years ago is still keenly felt. The author would like to express his gratitude to Iain's family who wanted this incident recording for posterity; somehow we all feel their loss.

1995 was to be a momentous year; the new Scafell guidebook was in its final phase, and there were many last minute lines to be bagged. Tony Marr and Mike Took returned to The East Buttress and climbed a good route based vaguely on the line of Incubus, but avoiding the stopper section of that route. Bat Out of Hell, originally given E1, climbs rightwards from the start of Incubus over an awkward bulge to gain the stance above the first pitch of Hell's Groove. It then followed the un-climbed main corner line to the left of the second pitch of Hell's Groove, a major drainage line with a waterworn smooth crack down the back. Fortunately for their ascent it was bone dry and the gear on this pitch is excellent, but subsequent ascents have reported that it was like trying to jam up frog spawn. The traverse line of Lord of the Rings was reversed leftward onto the main pillar of Incubus, which was followed to the top. This in effect gave only 20 metres of new climbing in a 60 metre route, but it did open up the lovely upper pillar of Incubus for the mid-grade climber at a sustained 5b standard. It has seen several repeats and it is now considered that E2 is a more accurate grade.

Phizacklea was back on the scene with a last minute guidebook checking team and he was investigating why no route continued directly above the initial slab of May Day Climb. This dirty, mossy groove was partially cleaned and it led to a belay below the leaning upper wall of SOS. In the company of Steve Merry, Phizacklea added a better second pitch up a shallow groove which was followed by a thin crack over the lip of this hanging wall. Thinking this may be the last new route in the guidebook Al christened this E2, 5c, When the Fat Lady Sings, but he happened to be well short of the mark.

The following day Ron Kenyon and Chris King linked a new variation finish to Moss Ghyll Grooves via the crack forming a direct continuation of that line's famous slab pitch. This route which they called Anglo, gives tremendously exposed climbing at E1, 5b, above the line of Saxon's main pitch. However, shortly after this was claimed, Bob Wightman confided to Phizacklea that he had inadvertently soloed a similar exit to Moss Ghyll Grooves after losing his way, but then traversed back to the main route once he realised what he was on was somewhat harder than Mild VS!

One midweek spell in August, Al Phizacklea and Mike Lynch visited Deep Gill Buttress to check out Ross' route Swansong. Phizacklea had still not tired of showing his friends the mighty 'Death Arête' dominating this part of the crag, and as they stood below this feature a pair of ropes whipped through the air and snaked down to the ground. They were astonished that this happened just as they stood there, and they soon found the ropes belonged to none other than Martin Berzins, who appeared above them.

"Trust you to come sneaking up here midweek to check out this line" Phizacklea shouted.
"What the hell are you doing here?" came the incredulous reply.
Martin was clearly stunned to have been discovered. "How did you know I was up here?"
"I'm just making sure you Yorkshire bastards don't nick all our routes!"

Photo: Al Phizacklea

Keith Phizacklea on the first pitch of Bat Out of Hell.

Sid Thompson, known to all as C.B. Sid, photographed at his usual haunt on The Oval ledge.

Photo: Jake Hughes

It was an incredible coincidence and it was followed by good natured banter. It became clear that Martin had thought his quiet midweek inspection would go un-noticed and he had spent the morning abseiling down the continuation groove of Borderline, but it appeared to lack protection. Later that afternoon, belayed by Mike Lynch, Martin attempted to climb the arête. Getting placements for the initial runners was awkward but he managed to locate a 'Friend ½' around the left side of the arête, and he fitted the crucial 'Rock 1' in a blind placement high in a tiny groove to the right. This was strength sapping, and Martin climbed down for a rest on the slab before committing himself and powering up the sustained thin cracks on the right side of the arête. These rise rightwards away from the arête, but he was visibly struggling and resorted to a rest on doubtful gear. After composing himself, he continued to the top but was again disappointed at not completing the line at his first attempt. Berzins returned with Phizacklea at the weekend, determined to lead the route cleanly. Whilst he set about re-cleaning it, Phizacklea wandered down to the area around Sleeping Crack to check a couple of lines for the guide, when he noticed a blank slab that offered possibilities. He abseiled down this slab after soloing the lower section of Grey Bastion and called Martin to join him. He quickly climbed two short separate routes which both led to a convenient abseil point to give Morpheus and Insomnia, names extending the sleeping theme. They were both clean and solid E1's, but they were definitely more of an outcrop type of route which seemed an alien concept on Scafell.

Above: Martin Berzins on his initial attempt on Def Arête, seen here making the difficult placement of the crucial Rock 1 runner.

Below: Martin Berzins's final contribution to Scafell was Def Arête, which ended a nineteen year association with the crags.

Now fully warmed up following the two lines, Martin set off up his intended route. Due to energy sapping efforts on the earlier attempt to affix the 'Rock 1', he had left one in place from the abseil. He quickly made short work of the problem, albeit with a great deal of exertion and cursing, and it seemed that he only just managed to reach the belay without falling off. For a second time, Phizacklea was to endure the delights of a Berzins E7 on the end of a tight rope. When Al scrambled to the top of the crag, Martin found himself unclipping from the belay in a dreamy daze, before realising he was poised delicately right on the brink of the crag. If he had leaned back he would have fallen the full length of the crag into the depths of the gully. To this day he has no idea what was going on as it wasn't a conscious act, he just puts it down to being really exhausted. Martin called the route Def Arête, because it wasn't quite the true arête line, but he realised that it would become the definitive arête if it ever got climbed. Once again, three new routes had been climbed in a single day by a single team.

Two days later a pair of Kendal based ex-army Captains, Nick Wharton and Dominic Donnini, along with Helen Davies, arrived at The East Buttress. Nick was one of the best Cumbrian based climbers around at the time and had gained a reputation as a bold and powerful leader. Sights were set on one of the most obvious lines still unclimbed; the overhanging arête below the upper part of Edge of Eriador. This had been eyed by virtually every visitor to The East Buttress because it soars impressively above the gearing up shelter below the crag, presenting an un-missable challenge. There are two large holds which form notches in the arête, and these were evidently going to be the key to an ascent. There had been a rumour, by then almost a legend, that Jeff Lamb had once attempted the line. In fact he got as far as the second notch on the arête, and placed a wire behind a flake that used to sit there. Returning to the ground, he and Pete Botterill then tested the wire by pulling on the ropes, smartly dislodging the block! He never attempted it again.

Donnini was the driving force for this project. The previous year he had cleaned the line and placed the pegs, the first at the back of the flat ledge by the first large hold, and the second a sawn-down blade just below the second large hold. He had tried the route with Helen Davies but it was quickly apparent to him that reinforcements were desperately required and strong reinforcements at that. He persuaded Wharton that the project had his name written all over it, but it had taken them two previous visits to figure out how to overcome the crux. Wharton recalls:

> "Dom had to drag me up there for the final attempt; I wasn't that keen because I was more interested in doing so many of the other routes that existed up there. We did the route ground up because it was too steep to try it on a top-rope, and the climbing turned out to be tough, really tough. I can't remember how many falls I took, there were quite a few; but at least we did pull the rope down each time.

"The holds weren't at all positive, they were pretty poor really and moving from one to the other involved very dynamic climbing, and I ended up lurching from one sloping hold to another. You had to go a long way above a wire that was pretty poor on that steep bit, but I knew that the angle eased above and a runner was coming up, which was a 'Rock 5' placed sideways in a shallow placement. Above this there was one further hard move before it eased and you reached the ledge on Edge of Eriador. I note that my diary says 'A good hard new route with hard climbing before and after the pegs,' which is a bit of an understatement, really." (9)

Nick named this Entonox after the anaesthetic gas used in childbirth because he was celebrating the fact that he had just become a father. He modestly graded it 'Hard E6', but subsequent ascents have confirmed what many had suspected, that it is a fully blown E7. However, if readers think this was the end of the story of yet another route then they are very much mistaken. In the heat of June 2010, a visit by the hard climbing pair of Ed Brown and Iain Small took up the challenge, and they were the first to attempt this line since the end of the last hard winter. Ed was keen to try something different, so they climbed Edge of Eriador in order to give the route a quick clean.

Nick Wharton.

Ed Brown captured during the fall that dislodged the block from Entonox.

The Eighth Scafell Guidebook

In 1996 another guidebook to Scafell, Wasdale and Eskdale was published. The previous edition, which included the entire Dow Crag and Eskdale areas, ran to a total of 320 pages of text and photographs. This new edition, covering only half the area, amassed an amazing 400 pages of routes, diagrams and photos.

The eighth FRCC guidebook to Scafell.

The geographical split between guidebook areas was necessary due to the sheer volume of new routes. The majority of these were of the short, rather inconsequential variety found on the local outcrops; but thirty were added to the crags of Scafell.
This new volume of the guide included crags in the lower Wasdale Valley and Eskdale, and was a reversion to the area covered by the first guidebook to Scafell. A new innovation for the guide was a photograph on the rear cover, so the only area to contain the purple colour indicating the Scafell area was on the spine of the book.

The author and illustrator was Al Phizacklea, who had drawn a complete new set of diagrams marked with red lines, and for the first time these appeared alongside the appropriate sections of the text.

Iain later explained what happened:

> "Ed climbed up past the first peg and got to the next jug where there are two knifeblades, and was making the move past these when he took a fall. He came back to the ground, took a rest, and pulled the ropes before getting back on it. He moved around the arête and was going for the next big hold when he lobbed off again and rested on the rope. He made the move, but decided against going any further so he climbed back down and just dropped his weight onto his top nut. When the rope came tight, it pulled sideways on the lost arrow peg in behind the first big jug and this levered the entire block off. It plummeted besides me and bounced off down the screes. I was lucky to be stood off to one side when it came off!" (10)

This lower block formed a fairly large incut jug, but more importantly it had held the first runner. The crack behind the block was dirty, indicating that this had been subject to weathering for some time; it certainly wasn't a fresh, clean break. In its place there is now a sloping scoop without any chance of protection, leaving a very hard move to get up to the two knifeblades. This has obviously made the start a lot nastier, but it could be a while before another ascent can confirm whether the grade has increased. What is more worrying for the future of Entonox is the fact that it isn't the first instance of a crucial block coming adrift, and one worries about the integrity of the only remaining jug. It will now take an extremely brave (or absolutely desperate) leader, and a second who has limited interest in reaching old age, to test the pegs which remain in-situ!

The final act before the guide went to the publisher was from evergreen climber Rob Matheson who replaced the peg and repeated the first pitch of Ringwraith directly without the detour right along the handrail. Within days, news that the route had been scrubbed had spread and it received several repeat ascents, and built up a reputation for being the best E5 on the crag, if not The Lakes. Andy Mitchell led the route early in 2012, brushing away the dry algae as he progressed, and pronounced that an on-sight ascent without any preparation or previous knowledge of the route deserves an E6 grade.

Within weeks Colin Read returned with Graham Swainbank to put the new guide out of date. This veteran team had for the past few years been touring the major crags of The Lakes and finding some quality mid-grade routes in areas that were considered to be fully developed. Their ascent of Zenith on Scafell Pinnacle is such a case. Read spied a direct line on an old photograph, and commented:

> "If you stand at the bottom of The Pinnacle and look up at the Heavens above you, that's the line it takes." (11)

The route links a series of overlooked corners and grooves that had been bypassed by earlier explorers, and gives another sustained VS up this part of the crag. He describes it as an eliminate that can't help touching other routes but it contains continuously interesting climbing on excellent rock. This part of the crag is formed of naturally clean rock which suited the on sight style of the first ascent.

Footnotes

1. Martin Berzins, FRCC audio recording 2009
2. Al Phizacklea, first written for this publication
3. Tony Marr, e-mail correspondence with the author, 2010
4. Martin Berzins, e-mail correspondence with the author, 2011
5. Interview with Rob Cubbold and Harold Newman by the author, 1996, with additional e-mail correspondence with Harold Newman (Ian's father) in 2009
6. The rescue team were alerted by a group of passing walkers hearing Cubbold's shouts for help from the Oval ledge. They rang for assistance from their mobile phone, one of the earliest recorded instances of a rescue team being raised in this way. Fortunately, there was an RAF Seaking helicopter already on exercise in another part of The Lakes, and they airlifted the rescue team directly to Mickledore. The team managed to reach the causality within 50 minutes of the alarm being raised, but sadly Newman had already passed away. With thanks to Julian Carradice.
7. Pete Brown, telephone conversation with the author, 2009
8. The Brackenclose Logbook, 1937 - 1959
9. Nick Wharton, e-mail correspondence with the author, 2010
10. Iain Small, telephone conversation with the author, 2011
11. Colin Reid, FRCC audio recording 2008
12. With thanks to Tony Greenbank for this article

8th Scafell Guidebook (contd.)

By a perhaps unfortunate coincidence Phizacklea was also the editor of the FRCC guidebooks at the time, hence the appearance of a rather insular one-man publication. He rather timidly copped out of the controversial graded list by merely listing the routes of each grade in the sequence they appeared in the guide, instead of in order of difficulty.

A section of the East Buttress diagram that illustrated the 1996 guidebook.

This was due to a lack of consistent information returned from questionnaires sent out to known activists. There were many routes that were unrepeated, and those that were never seemed to attract any consensus of difficulty. Phizacklea felt any attempt to set the routes in order of difficulty would result in erroneous information, which would produce criticism. Damned if you do – damned if you don't. Such are the quandaries of the guidebook writer!

Photo: Al Phizacklea

The late winter snows below Moss Gill provide a perfect cooler for your bivouac beverages...

1998 - 2006

Dave Birkett - King of the Hill

Dave Birkett, looking smarter than usual, ready for a visit to 10 Downing Street in October 2008.

Overleaf:
Dave Birkett on the first ascent of Welcome to the Cruel World, one of his E9's on the East Buttress.
Photo Mark Glaister

Readers will realise how throughout the history of climbing any rise in standards stems from the combination of new technology (better boots, harnesses and wire runners) and the appearance of a pioneer who seems to be comprehensively better than his predecessors. Examples of these include O.G.Jones, Colin Kirkus, Don Whillans, Joe Brown and Pete Livesey. In the early 1990s, there emerged from Langdale a young climber who has utterly dominated the climbing scene in The Lakes ever since; David Birkett.

Being the grandson of Jim Birkett, and nephew of Bill Birkett, Dave is the third generation of top class climbers who were all born in the very heart of The Lakes and who all live, or lived, within a mile of their birthplace. There has been no other family within British climbing able to claim the distinction of being as local as the Birketts. From such an impressive lineage, it is unsurprising that Dave seems to be somehow genetically superior on hard, unprotected rock than any other climber. Dave is rough-hewn, as rugged as his native fells, and just as tough. He is well known amongst the Lakeland farming community as the man who rescues crag-fast sheep. Dave reckons he has successfully rescued more than 600 sheep from the crags over the years, and in all that time he has 'lost' only two ewes. He unashamedly proclaims that he is 'the best sheep-rescuer in the world', a claim that few could refute, or challenge. I once met him, or more exactly, heard him on Mickledore when I was on Scafell Crag, his distinct nasal drawl enquiring as to our wellbeing, as he always does. "What are you up to?" I enquired, thinking he was prospecting a new line on one of his solo mid-week visits to the crag. "Nay, just cum up fra' Langd'l an' rescued a yow of't crag, ah'm off t' Crinkles now to pull another off that ah've heard's cragfast." And so off he dashes, down to The Great Moss and over to the Crinkle Crags, just an easy day off work spent running miles over the fells rescuing any unfortunate sheep that gets reported as stuck. He's certainly a legend amongst the local Dales farmers.

Alistair Lee, the renowned film-maker, remains awed by Dave and described him thus:

> "Dave Birkett is a man with a big presence. When I stand next to him I'm always surprised to see I'm as tall as he is as he makes me feel so small when he walks in the room. His bounding stride, hands like shovels and that steely glint in his eyes all add to the climbers' answer to Clint Eastwood." (1)

Colin Wells described him perfectly:

> "Birkett is wiry rather than muscular with a bottle-brush of a barnet and a dazzling white smile that contrasts with his dark tan. He sounds as he looks – fizzing with energy." (2)

Since the 1980s Dave has amassed a hugely impressive total of hard new routes, including twelve routes of E8 and four at E9; and in between he has repeated many of the country's hardest climbs. This is a truly remarkable record, and it is difficult not to over-hype with repetitive superlatives.

His tactics for preparing the routes may seem over-complicated and unethical to older generations, but the repeated abseil inspections, practises using a shunt, and top-roping are all part of the preferred modern tactic of 'headpointing'. This involves practising the route to a point when it can be led straight from the ground at the first attempt, which is vitally important; failure on some of Dave's routes could be potentially fatal; and fatal really means fatal! In 1998 Dave set his sights on the remaining unclimbed lines on Scafell.

The large square-cut corner of Lost Horizons is the dominant feature of The East Buttress. It sits slap bang in the centre of the crag. It overhangs above the base of the crag, but it also leans across it, and gives an optical illusion of lying back at an amenable angle. It is only the drops of water falling from above that indicate the true degree of its steepness; to a casual observer these seem to defy the laws of gravity.

Situated on either side of this corner are two equally steep, sharp-edged arêtes rising in parallel as an extraordinary natural sculpture which is almost architectural in its perfection. These unclimbed arêtes were the next obvious challenges in the history of Scafell.

Al Phizacklea remembers how, in the mid 1990s, he was sitting in The Lover's Leap Café in Stoney Middleton (trying to re-live his youth), when he overheard two customers on the table behind mention '… the arête left of Lost Horizons …' He strained his ears for further clues and casually looked around, but he didn't recognise either of them. The fact the route was discussed in the social heart of Peak District climbing indicated its significance as a prize to the wider climbing world. This arête was one of the most notable and impressive unclimbed lines in Britain, stunning in its elegance, awe-inspiring in its potential. Its ascent was evidently going to involve a breakthrough in standards of difficulty and seriousness. Birkett had also noticed the arête, as he recalled:

> "After the last edition of the guidebook it was blindingly obvious that the last great, great lines were to be found on Scafell, and this arête was one of the great challenges of the Lake District. I first kind of mentioned it to my uncle Bill that I was going to go up there to have a look one day, and he said 'Oh, don't bother, we checked that out years ago, and there's all these horizontal quartzite breaks that run all the way through that part of the crag where you can escape into the E4,' and he kind of put me off really. Later in that year I went on a trip to the Himalaya with John Dunne and a couple of other climbers, and John said something that made me think that he knew more about this route. I thought I've got to go up there and do it before him, because if he does it, he'll make out that it's the best thing since sliced bread, as he always does." (3)

Dave Birkett repeating New Horizon for Alistair Lee's biopic 'Set in Stone.'

Photo: Alistair Lee

Dave Birkett visited the crag with Andy Hyslop in 1998, where as part of the preparation, Andy led the corner of Lost Horizons directly through the upper slot previously avoided by a leftwards traverse. This awkward direct version went at E5, 6b; it is rather surprising that such an obvious variation hadn't been climbed before.

The story of the ascent of the arête, which was given the name of New Horizons, is best described in Dave's own words:

> "I went there and all of a sudden you're gobsmacked as to how steep it was, and if there had been any horizontal breaks leading off onto the E4 then it would have been a complete joy. It was obvious straight away that the protection was poor and it would be a very committing climb, maybe French F7c+, but you have to make a 6c move when there's a good chance you're going to die. If you're lucky, you'll just swing back into the corner and hit the ledge, in either case you won't be walking back down from the crag." [laughs] (4)

Dave is typical of the modern generation who effortlessly and unconsciously swap grading systems between traditional English and French 'F' grades normally used for bolt protected climbing, which generally indicate the sustained nature of the moves. He continues:

> "I got a group of three pegs in just before the crux; three very marginal tap-in knife blades linked together that kept pulling out when I tested them. The way I did this was to have a back-up rope from the top belay, and I'd just jump off onto them, and they kept coming out. On the third or fourth test they worked, I don't know why, maybe I didn't drop as far that time, but it gave me the psychological break you needed, and I thought OK, I can do this. I did it on my next try; it was a beautiful climb up a magical line, I gave it E8, 6c, but it has the chance that you might die.
>
> "To think you could escape off it was so far from the truth; once you committed to the moves then you've got to go with it. You traverse onto it very low down and you use vertical layaways for your right hand which are two or three feet from the edge, but all your footholds are on the arête, and it feels like it should be very barn-doory, but it isn't. It's because of the way it overhangs leftwards, it feels like you've got to put a bit of motion into the moves. Your mind tells you that this is a really stupid move and there's a mental feel that you're going to barn-door off so you've got to trust in the knowledge from your practice that you won't. It's a fantastic piece of climbing; it was a great day and a great introduction to the new lines on Scafell. I took the pegs out afterwards because they were so marginal that I thought if anybody wants to do this they can place the pegs themselves." (5)

Birkett returned two years later, his target being the right arête of Lost Horizons, where the protection would be even worse than that on New Horizons. Again Dave practised the ascent by top roping the line several times, as getting the crux sequence wrong was potentially fatal – this takes serious climbing to a whole new level. The route starts with bold 6b climbing up the lower arête protected by a side runner low in Lost Horizons (which wouldn't stop you from hitting the starting ledge should you blow it) to a flat hold on the edge of the arête. This provides the only protection, a thin sling draped across it that gave no guarantee of staying in place. Again, Dave describes the action:

> "My next route was the bleedingly obvious arête on the right which looking at it from the ground you think 'Yeah, another great line to do' and it looks easier, about E6, but when you get down it on a rope, it's the same old, same old.

"Every route on The East Buttress is a lot, lot steeper than it first looks, and despite having one big hold on it, the protection was a lot worse, and you had to make a harder move. I practised it a few times on a top rope and this gives you enough confidence, so when you set off and lead those first moves, you kind of know how it will feel higher up."

Photo: Liam Lonsdale

Jordan Buys engaged on the crux of Talbot Horizon, on the second ascent.

Just as this book was about to go to the printers, news broke of the remarkable repeat of Talbot Horizon by renowned climber Jordan Buys. In August 2016 he inspected and practiced the route on his first visit, and on his second he led it with little problem. He made the following comment on the crux of the route:

> "The move involved releasing a bomber heel hook and getting into a ridiculously awkward position in order to slap for a sloper. The other thing is the angle of the arête, it is very weird, it feels like it is trying to throw you off all the time. The gear is only so-so, I reckoned it was probably best not to fall off."

This is a very impressive repeat, which may be the start of breaking down the mythological status of Dave Birkett's routes on Scafell.

"After I climbed it my mate Graeme Lee said 'Oh, you didn't tell me you were going to have to jump for a hold!' because there's one section where your gear is just a sling on that sloping hold, and you're moving around the arête where the only thing holding you in is a heel toe combination on a bit of a lock. The height I am, I couldn't reach the next hold with my foot on, so to enable me to get into the position I had to make a quick move to get to these sloping holds by taking off my foot and kind of hop a little bit, but you cut loose and swing free. This is obviously the crux move, and I thought if you come off that move you are definitely a complete gonner. I thought at the time, and I still do, that maybe this is the most serious thing I've ever done, but you know the risks and this gets you inspired by it really.

"I called this route Talbot Horizon which carries on the horizon theme, but I get a bit of stick about it sometimes. I called it that because on one of the days I was up there trying it with Dave Turnbull, the head of the BMC, and this lad Cameron, who I spent a few weeks climbing with while he was on an exchange visit from the USA. Anyhow, Dave said 'If you climb this, you'll have to call it Talbot Horizon' which was a bit of a joke, and we were laughing and rolling around being daft. Cameron had no idea what we were laughing at, so we told him, but being American it fell on stony ground and he didn't get it. So at the end of the exchange he went back, and two weeks later he fell off a climb and died. I got on incredibly well with this guy, and it was kind of like – one minute you're climbing and having a laugh, and the next thing you know he's fallen and died, so the route was named in memory of Cameron and that magic moment all three of us had on that day. Bill got some excellent photos of me which were set up with Martin Armitage holding the ropes that I'd rigged up around the corner. Some routes you don't mind getting back on to them, but without the side rope there's no way I was going to get back on that route!" (6)

The crux of Talbot Horizon is a committing swing on terribly sloping holds; Dave Birkett repeated this for the camera with a side runner out right.

Not unsurprisingly, Birkett gave the route a grade of E9, 6c. He did admit later that it was a more serious proposition than Breathless, John Dunne's test piece on The Napes, which was originally graded E10, but at the time of writing there has been no other ascent to confirm its grade. Sometime later, Dave was asked a direct question following one of his public slide-shows, and it put him awkwardly on the spot. "What do you consider is the hardest route in the Lakes, Dave?" After some deep thought, he quietly replied "If you are talking about the most serious route in the Lakes, then it has to be Talbot Horizon, no doubt. But if it's the hardest move I've ever done on a route, then it has to be Welcome to the Cruel World, it was bloody desperate."

The 2001 foot-and-mouth epidemic ensured that there were no other routes added to the Scafell Crags until 2002 when Dave Birkett laid siege to the thin crack right of Borderline; which he named Welcome to the Cruel World. This was the hallowed line that had attracted much interest over the years; it was even rumoured to have been climbed with a single aid point by Chris Sowden, and it had engaged the attention of some major activists, with Ben Moon and Adam Hocking reputedly trying it. The effort of preparing the route taxed even Dave's resolve, but again he best tells the story:

"I'd looked at it two or three times in the past, and it's such a mission coming down that part of the crag, and when you get there, you think that the new bit of climbing isn't really all that long, and is it really worth it? As you go down, the route doesn't last very long – there's quite a few long moves at the start, and a long move at the end before you reach easy ground, but there's a section of about 15 feet which is incredibly hard. I never managed to do those moves when I was practising it on a top rope, I almost thought it was impossible but something in my mind thought no – there are actually some features here. Then all of a sudden it's in your mind that it's one of the last great lines; and if I'm not going to do anything else I'm going to put all my efforts into doing this route, even if it takes me all year.

"I had a long spell in South Africa where I did a lot of climbing, so I was incredibly fit, and then I had a trip to Fontainebleau for two weeks for the purpose of getting bouldery strong. I concentrated fully, which I'd never done before, and I even got down to ten stone to do the route.

The crux of Welcome to the Cruel World involves hanging off a single small finger-tip jam on a very overhanging wall with minimal footholds.

"When I got there with some friends early that spring, I managed to do the four or five individual moves that make up the crux first time on the top rope. I came back later when I tried to link them and then I knew it was on – so I ended doing it over three or four days of cleaning it and trying it. There is climbing on it which I don't normally do; it was more kind of a sprint, a 100 metre dash rather than a stamina route which I prefer really, so I had to change my whole style of climbing to do it. I don't think I even chalked up on it; I just got on it and went for the top.

"I placed all the gear on the lead, except for the top piece which was hard to place. It was psychological; I thought that trying to get it in might stop me from climbing it that day. You could probably not bother placing it and you wouldn't hit the ground, but I left it in place from the top rope. There's four other pieces of gear and it's all good, especially at three-quarters height where there's such a gobsmacking 'Rock 7' that goes in and down, you'd need a wagon to pull the crag over with that one! It's one of those routes which is safe and you'll take a bit of a fall but you're never going to kill yourself on it.

"So you do the lower section of the route as a warm up before you come down and test the gear, then you're into the crux. You've got to do a mono [one-finger] move on an undercut to another mono pull on steep rock; there are two ways of doing that last awkward move. I was tired, I had a little bit of a power drain on it and I wanted to use a sidepull crimp, but it was easier to hang off a mono from the little finger, which was the only finger to go in. It felt more positive pulling down rather than pulling sideways off the crimp, which also takes more power. Its harder doing the one finger pull and you're more likely to hurt something, but there's less chance of falling off it, you've just got to bear down and it's all just a bit gnarly on your fingers, that's one reason why it's called Welcome to the Cruel World. It's also a musical album from an artist called Ben Harper, and I was really into his stuff. It was a very impressive line, but I lowered off from the top of The Yellow Slab because it just seemed silly to do some French 8b+ climbing lower down only to force a contrived HVS upper section." (7)

Photo: Al Phizacklea

Dave Birkett surveys his kingdom below The East Buttress.

Dave gave the route a grade of E9, 7a, the only route on Scafell to be given such a high technical grade. He was belayed on the first ascent by his wife Mary Jenner. The task of checking and cleaning these potential new routes was usually a solitary affair for Dave; he would walk up from Wasdale with a full rucksack including three ropes, and set up his abseil, then shunt, clean and practise the moves without meeting a soul all day. Each of these routes required three or four visits, a lonely but painstakingly dedicated task. Dave thrives on being amongst the hills, and the crags of Scafell epitomise this devotion towards the unfashionable high mountains of The Lakes. The following comment amply illustrates this enthusiasm:

"When spring comes, you're itching to get up there as soon as possible. When you drive over Hardknott and down Eskdale, you notice that the primroses are out when they're not in Langdale, and you think 'Yeah, spring's here!' and that puts you in a positive mood in itself. It's hard to get anyone out for this new routing so you go there on your own on the shunt – they're some of the best days I've had out, practising these routes on my own. I usually solo up something like Great Eastern with a couple of ropes tied to my back, because it's pretty much the easiest way of getting to the top of the route. Mind, there's been a couple of times when it's not felt right and I've gone back down, you think it's just a kind of madness, here I am trying to do the first ascent of an E9, and I'm backing off a VS!" (8)

The next route to fall to the unstoppable Birkett was the groove forming the extension to Borderline, the same line examined by Berzins seven years earlier. The name of the route, Another Lonely Day, reflects those solitary days of cleaning:

"When I was trying Welcome to the Cruel World it was blindingly obvious that the real line to do there was the extension to Borderline, it's the line where Borderline should have gone. It's the perfect line up a blank piece of rock, an offset banana-shaped corner that's got just enough holds and just enough gear to make it kind of possible at that grade; it's a magical pitch to climb. On the first day I could do all the moves and I knew it was going to be easier than Welcome to the Cruel World, so after a couple of days up there I had got it sussed. The next weekend was nice so we went up there with friends and top-roped it, then I went back midweek with Mary to do the first ascent.

"I did it in two pitches because you daren't extend any of the gear you get in, in case you drop from the crux and hit the rampline of Ichabod on the swing; and if you did it in one pitch you'd experience a bit of rope drag. It would be a better route to do it in one, but once you get onto the ledge you're quite happy to take a belay in case you force your luck and you blow it, then you'd have to do that bottom bit again. Anyhow, on the first ascent it started raining and the top bit was wet, so the following week I returned with Graeme Lee and abbed into the ledge and we did the top pitch, which was an E6 in its own right.

Photo: Bill Birkett

Photo: Al Phizacklea

Above: Dave relaxes with Mary at home.

Left: The crux section of Another Lonely Day.

> "When you climb the lower part of Borderline there are kind of slots behind the flake where you can get your fingers in; it's all steady but in a steep position. When you get to the peg, and Borderline goes left, these slots run out and you have to kind of layaway off the edge of the arête of the shallow corner. It's so steep there, the wall must overhang about 25 degrees but in your favour is the reasonable footholds, and the key to success is finding the correct sequence of using these footholds as your handholds are not really there. There's a twenty foot section of very powerful French 8a climbing, where you have a kind of back-hand severe layaway, and it's one of those routes where once you start the sequence you're very much committed to it even though the moves start to get easier. So you're moving up, leaving your gear behind, which is an 'R.P.' about two foot above the peg, and there's no more protection until you do the move right along the lip of the overhang just below the ledge. There's another 'R.P.' there and a very poor peg, which are linked together, but if you fail to clip them you're going to be very close to smacking into the ramp below. It's kind of touch and go at that point. I gave it E8, 6c and 6b. I just think that this is the best trad route in Britain. It's got everything, the quality of the line is unsurpassable and the actual climbing flows really well, and if I had to pick my all-time favourite route it would be this one." (9)

The Easter weekend of 2003 will always be remembered as giving a dry and balmy start to the year, and the crags of Scafell were thronged by an enthusiastic band of climbers, mostly from around the Keswick region. They took advantage of the weather by bivouacking below the crag, and many of the now classic hard routes on the crag were repeated: Ringwraith, Zeya, Cullinan and Shere Khan were all ascended in a jovial spirit that was reminiscent of those halcyon days of the late 1970s.

Part of this group was young James McHaffie (known throughout the climbing world as Caff), the prodigiously talented son of Ray McHaffie. He had noticed the possibility of extending Berzins' Judas Priest on the main face, so late in the evening he soloed Central Buttress, just to look across at the wall. This was his only preparation for the route. Judas Priest had by now lost its peg runner, and that left just the doubtful micro-runners. Undaunted, he led it on-sight, and added an upper pitch as a direct version of the top arête of Saxon. Colin Downer belayed him for the ascent, but admitted that he barely dared to watch his intrepid leader:

> "There were no runners, he never abseiled it or anything and the rock was quite lichenous. Tight rope? Of course I had! It was bloody desperate, and I came off on the leftwards traverse. It was a suicide mission!" (10)

Nothing new from Caff, then!

McHaffie named this new and improved variation The Rob Halford Finish, which raises an already audacious route to a bold E6, 6a, 5c, and it is the hardest on-sighted new route on the crag. Readers may or may not know that Rob Halford was in fact the lead singer of Judas Priest; clever!

Later in the year, Wes Hunter and James McHaffie returned to the crag, and claimed a new route just right of the Pinnacle Face on the steep bounding wall above the lower section of Deep Gill. Wes had noticed this line some time earlier following a descent of Deep Gill, and due to its rather remote location, he decided to lead it on sight. Unfortunately, all he achieved was a repeat of Bill Birkett's Edge Hog from 1971. It must have seemed like a new route because it may have been 30 years since it was last climbed.

Higher up Deep Gill, Dave Birkett finally cracked the true line of 'The Death Arête', which naturally became the name for this new E8 route.

"It's a funny place, Deep Gill. It's such a spectacular route to get to the top of Scafell for a walker, and there's this beautiful, blindingly obvious arête which I saw in a photo in a FRCC journal. I thought Martin had taken the easiest natural line, and although it is a great line, it isn't actually anything to do with the arête itself. When I started to check it out, I placed a couple of pegs to hold me in position. You need these when you're on a shunt, because a wire can pull out and you'll go swinging across the crag and you'll shit yourself to be honest! The pegs were just to hold the rope; there's none in now, but it did cause a bit of a laugh at the time.

"There was a group of Fell & Rockers coming down Deep Gill and they took offence at me knocking in the pegs, and I could hear them mumbling 'What's going on down there?' and 'That's not allowed!' One of them said 'Maybe it's one of the Phizackleas from Barrow,' and he asked me if I was Alan, and I said no. So all these murmurs started up again, and another said 'who are you, then?' and I said David Birkett; and it was all 'Oh well, yes, yes, that's OK then,' as though only the Phizackleas or the Birketts were allowed to put in pegs and nobody else was! It was really kind of funny in a bizarre way.

"The route shares the same hidden 'Rock 1' as Berzins used on Def Arête, and actually the crux of his route is placing that nut. It's a good 'Rock 1' if you place it right, but you can't see if it's in right until you're moving past it onto the arête where you do the crux move, that's why I gave it E8, 6c.

Birkett on Death Arête, filmed for 'Set in Stone.'

> "Rob Fielding thought it was technically harder, but I'm five foot ten and a half inches tall with a six feet five inch wingspan, so I think I may just have a tiny bit more reach sideways than what he has. Once you do the crux move it's only French 7b or E6 to the top, there are small wires and micro-cams available for protection, if you have the strength left to place them." (11)

During the filming of Alastair Lee's documentary Set in Stone, Colin Wells witnessed Birkett repeating this route, and he wrote the following which superbly describes Birkett's controlled climbing style:

> "He starts a mazy, technical sequence up rock which hangs out over space like the prow of a ship. There's no wild insanity to his movement, he climbs with controlled precision, each foothold carefully keyed with a toe, each handhold gripped with a firm intent. On the bulging rock he is now gecko-ing up miles above his last wire, the climb despatched with an economy of effort and no dramatics". (12)

It's all rather reminiscent of his granddad Jim!

The same film also captures Dave on the first ascent of The Return of the King climbed in 2006; another bold fingery E9, 6c which climbs the blank wall between Welcome to the Cruel World and Overhanging Grooves Direct. Once again, the route is best described by Dave:

> "Between the natural lines is this whole sheet of magnificent rock with holds on it which is funny, because the crack to the side has no real features or footholds. Adam Hocking had been trying the crack to the side before I climbed it, and he mentioned that the wall to the right would go so I went up early that year on my own to see if you could escape off it. When I looked down it I thought 'Bloody hell, young Adam was right, it's absolutely wow!' I could see what to do, but I had to wait for it to become a bit warmer. I tried it two or three times, but I was almost blinded by trying to do it too direct; I was struggling to do a move and it felt like an E10. Then it dawned on me that anybody in their right mind would go out right then back left a little because that's where the holds take you, and it was a lot easier.
>
> "This was just at the time when Alistair Lee got in touch with me about making a film about the Lake District, so I thought I could use this one as a test of Al's nature, to see whether he's capable of getting up the hill. I had made the mistake of trying it a little too much on the top-rope, so when I went back the next day to do the first ascent I was too tired, I should have had a couple of days rest. Maybe it's not as hard as I graded it, and it might be the one route that may come down a grade in time." (13)

Adam Hocking leading Return of the King. This is the only occasion that a Dave Birkett route on Scafell has been repeated.

Photo: Dom Bush

The film commentary states that some of the gear is good, and some is pre-placed. From the comfort of our armchairs we can witness the effort required merely to stay in contact with the rock. What it doesn't state is that Dave placed the lower gear from the ground as part of his warm up routine for the route, nor does it convey the steepness of the rock; it's simply awesome. On his attempts to top-rope the line he had been unable to link the sequence, and the hope was that the extra adrenalin from the lead would enable him to string it together. Dave laughed with satisfaction and relief upon reaching the belay, admitting that the crux was a full-on move, and at the top he was so tired he couldn't get any strength back. His final comment was that he was glad it was all over - but also glad it was a fight, really. It was never going to be anything else:

> "I called this line The Return of the King, which was a little bit tongue in cheek. It is the last book in the Lord of the Rings trilogy, but obviously there's a part of me that after ten years of doing first ascents on Scafell I felt like I was the king of Scafell. Deep down you get a kind of feeling that this is my domain, this is my home. So time will pass, it's as much my own ego as following a theme " (14)

The difficulty of inspecting routes on The East Buttress can be judged from Adam Hocking, during his preparation for repeating Return of the King.

Dave was again belayed by his wife Mary Jenner, who provides steady and focussed encouragement during what must be very stressful situations. When she was asked about her role belaying Dave on such a potentially serious route, she replied:

> "It's horrible. I hate it really, you've got to concentrate so much all of the time, and it's quite draining both emotionally and physically. It didn't seem as bad on Return of the King, as some of the really serious routes he's done because there was some sort of gear on it. After he finished that route, David suggested that we should go and climb Saxon, but I just felt too knackered to even contemplate climbing that day." (15)

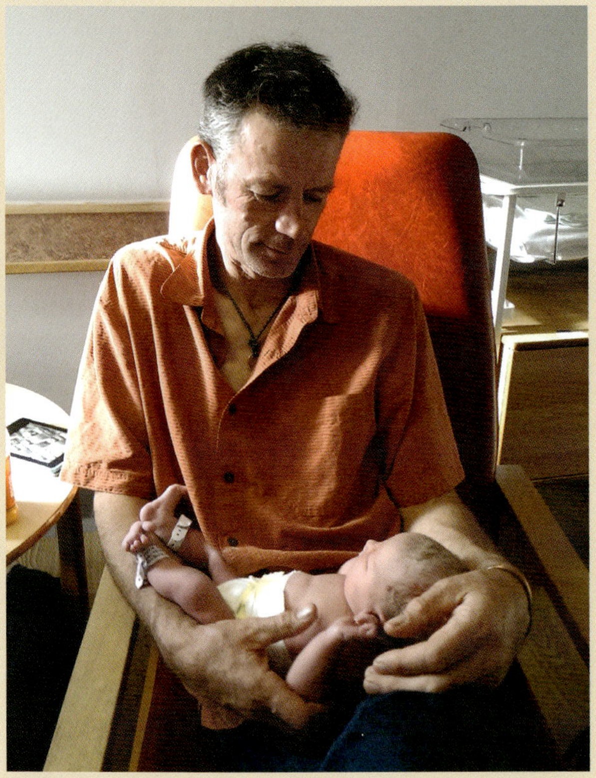

"Eh Mary, what do I do wi' this?"
Dave with May, the latest member of the Birkett family, June 2015.

It is interesting to note Mary never once mentioned the possibility of Dave falling or getting hurt, it seemed as though failure was not an option when he climbed. This is typical of Dave's routes; bold, strenuous and deadly serious, and with a fair quantity of long spans between holds, a package designed to intimidate future suitors.

Despite the seriousness of this route, it became the first to receive a repeat ascent of what later became dubbed as 'The Birkett Super Routes'. It was young Adam Hocking, following return to his native Keswick in 2011, who made this daring breakthrough, although incredulously the media only apportioned the same accolade for his achievement as it did for a repeat of some three-move boulder problem. Such is the way of modern climbing.

Hock again practised the route from a top-rope, and he explained:

> "I left two wires in, the same as Dave. One is low down and hard to place, the other is hard to get it in, and it's not great but it is just by the crux. The first section leaving the pegs to the first pre-placed wire is worrying and you have to clip this off a poor pinch. I found a different way on the crux which was less moves and a little more direct." (16)

The Return of the King was repeated again, this by Scottish activist Dave MacLeod, who has been pushing the limits of the upper grades across the country over the past decade. He inspected the route on his first visit in June 2016 and led it clean, placing all his runners on the lead a couple of days later. His report states :

> "I sussed out the line, give it a quick clean and top roped it first try after trying the moves once. I was aware that both the previous ascents used preplaced gear and I could see why! The crucial small wire placements were right in the middle of the crux sections. So placing them on lead would basically be the crux of the route."

As is usual with the friendly rivalry that exists between the different climbing regions of the country, Dave also came up with the following disparaging comment on the unrepeated Birkett lines on the crag, stating:

> "The other E9s on Scafell look 2 star. Good but not that good. There's better lines in Scotland to go at."

Time alone will tell...

Footnotes

1. Alistair Lee, 'Repeat Offender', *Climb Magazine*, no.67
2. Colin Wells, 'Already in Heaven', *Climb Magazine*, no.21
3 - 9. Dave Birkett, FRCC audio recording 2008
10. Colin Downer, telephone conversation with the author, 2010
11. Dave Birkett, FRCC audio recording 2008
12. Colin Wells, 'Already in Heaven', *Climb Magazine*, no.21
13 - 14 Dave Birkett, FRCC audio recording 2008
15. Mary Jenner, conversation with the author, 2010
16. Adam Hocking, e-mail with the author, 2012

015

Bitter -
imbing through the Nineties and Beyond

Above: John Holden prepares to cautiously step across the big drop on the first ascent of Deep Gill Integrale.

Right: Lower Deep Gill Buttress as seen from the Pinnacle. The upper team are on the final pitch of Deep Gill Integrale, and the lower team are on the second pitch of Great Western.

Overleaf: Andy Mitchell belays Dave Birkett from the Yellow Slab stance on the first ascent of Never Ever Say Never.
Photo: Ed Luke

After the frenetic winter activity through the latter half of the 1980s there foll poor winters where the mild westerlies prevented the forming of any true win spell of cold weather in January 1990 brought the crags briefly into condition advantage of the offerings. He explored the long diagonal rake rising from th first investigated as part of Sod All. His second, John Holden, was not an ent and had not used his long shafted straight picked axe (nicknamed The Alpens years. Though the nature of the climbing was easy, it became suddenly expos abruptly and the crag dropped away vertically into the deep trench of The Gr steep pinnacle of the upper pitch of the summer line of Jacob's Ladder, led w to the top to complete a line they named Deep Gill Integrale. At Grade III, th the most exciting situations for its standard anywhere in The Lakes.

Phizacklea returned in November 1990 with Andy Rowell for an early start to a variation to Sod's Law which they named Sodom, Grade V. The main pitch across some blank slabs where some committing thin moves led with difficulty of Deep Gill Integrale.

Once more, another prolonged sequence of poor winters during the early 199 development on Scafell. Al Phizacklea started the 1994/95 winter season by p Donnini to join him on The East Buttress, abseiling down to the foot of The V team who were attempting the slab route.

The open chimney line which was the Original Finish for the summer Overhanging Wall route had not been climbed in winter, and on this occasion it was barely in condition. Half way up the pitch Al called down to Dom to watch the rope carefully, to which Dom turned to the second on the White Slab and muttered "He's mad! He's going to kill himself! There's no ice!" However there was just sufficient ice, but not quite as thick as Donnini would have liked. The climbing was fairly straightforward at Grade V, but with an awkward step where the chimney narrows.

After several years exploring other Lake District crags, 1995 saw Brian Davison return to Scafell where he repeated Deep Gill Integrale and Slingsby's Chimney Route unaware of previous ascents, and with Colin Wells he added Low Man by the right wall of Steep Gill, V, and Great Western, a very fine and sustained IV, on the Deep Gill Buttress. The following year Davison and Nick Green delicately crossed the slabs of the Deep Gill face of the pinnacle before following a grassy frozen corner to the top of the High Man to produce Centre Route, VI. A few days later Keith Phizacklea and Steve Merry used the well iced cracks of Tia Maria, V, to give a beautiful but quite tricky climb out of Mickledore Chimney on The East Buttress.

The following season started early for Phil Dowthwaite and Steve Edmondson with a November ascent of the S-shaped gully winding its way up the right side of The Shamrock, to create Twisting Gully, IV. With the winter guide going to press the three chimneys at the start of the Integrale, Eye Spy, V, Dharma Armour, III, and Chimney Stack, V, were all climbed on the same day by Davison and Nick Hewitt just after New Year 1997. Their frantic activity ensured the routes sneaked into an addendum in the guide. Ironically for the winter activists, its release heralded a slump in weather and activity for the next few years.

The icefall down The East Buttress is legendary but ephemeral; some tales of long ago tell of a continuous line of ice that forms the full height of the crag. In reality it is two icefalls, one from a weep down the lower pitches of the summer line Gold Rush which readily forms most cold winters, and it offers an attractive approach onto the ramp line above taken by Great Eastern. The second ice-fall forms from the top of the buttress and runs down the corner of Overhanging Grooves. This takes longer to form and rarely grows sufficiently to reach the Yellow Slab area at the bottom of the corner. There is always a gap between the two icefalls meaning some of Great Eastern, including its crux, has to be mixed climbing to link the two falls. Great Eastern had its first winter ascent in 1960 by Kendall and Douglas. Little was known about the route and despite known attempts in the 1970s it probably hadn't had a second ascent until a misty day in 1999 when Davison and Hewitt headed over Mickledore. Davison recalls:

> "I didn't have any particular route in mind when we went over. It was very misty and so we walked over to kill time, hoping the cloud would lift and give us a view of the crag. When I saw the ice at the bottom of Gold Rush I though it was worth climbing and seeing where it would lead. I always carry a warthog with me and that was our only piece of ice protection as all the rest was a rock rack for mixed climbing. We climbed the icefall to Great Eastern to under a steep headwall, and kept getting glimpses of ice through the mist. I moved on but as the climbing became steeper and with limited visibility I had to admit I couldn't see where I was going and there wasn't enough ice to climb. Down-climbing, I returned to the junction and crossed the ramps of Great Eastern to finish a misty day on the East Buttress". (1)

Rush East, as this line was called, can be viewed as an alternative Direct Start to Great Eastern or a failed attempt on the main icefall of the buttress, that due to poor visibility had been rushed at. Either way it was a good day's climbing on The East Buttress. With the century drawing to a close, December 1999 saw Phil Dowthwaite and P. Smalley once again making the most of early conditions at the top of Deep Gill with an ascent of Jacob's Ladder; the stepped corner line right of Great Chimney. This was to be the last new winter route of the decade on Scafell.

Photo: Al Phizacklea

Above: Looking down the final pitch of Sodom into the depths of Deep Gill, climber Andy Rowell.

Below: The cover of the 1997 winter guide to the Lake District, was the third edition of the original Cicerone Guide. It was jointly written by Bob Bennett, Bill Birkett and Brian Davison.

Photo: Ed Luke

Steve Ashworth in action.

Rich Cross on the difficult main pitch during the first winter ascent of Xerxes.

Photo: Steve Ashworth

Over the next few years a new generation of winter climbers emerged. Steve Ashworth had established himself as one of the leading young activists. With ascents of some of the hardest winter routes in the Lake District to his credit, he had the Girdle Traverse on his mind. Steve had climbed the Scafell Girdle Traverse in summer with his father, who had expressed a positive wish not to do it in winter. Undeterred and knowing there was another winter climbing guide in preparation Steve had been in contact with author Brian Davison. He knew that he would be fast and know the crag, and Brian was renowned for a fondness for sideways movement. With nevé on the ledges and the crag to themselves on a beautiful still day in March 2005, the setting couldn't have been better. The pair set off from the start of Botterill's Slab to cross to The Oval, and Davison recalls:

> "The first two pitches I led involved me down-climbing into Moss Gill and then Steep Gill so on both occasions I ended up lower than where I'd started; the kind of leading I like. The route had a sting in its tail though. The traverse from The Crevasse was poorly protected for the second, and the next two pitches had some thin, technical grade 8 moves before easier climbing led to the top of the High Man, reached in time to watch the sunset. It had been a perfect day." (2)

Steve's memories bring forth the image of a young apprentice being given a life lesson by the old wizard:

> "I felt like some young pretender with my leashless axes and monopoints standing next to Brian with his slightly more dated gear. It was a great route, one of the best I've done, the conditions were so good that it all seemed to pass in quite a relaxed manner. Neither of us had a camera that worked with us, so you'll have to appreciate the temperature inversion, alpenglow picking out Gable in the early evening and glistening nevé on the crest of the Pinnacle." (3)

While some of the climbable ice at the top of The East Buttress had previously been gained from abseil approaches, the steep nature of the climbing there, particularly on the lower section, means few routes have been climbed in their entirety from bottom to top. On opening his winter portfolio on the crag with Mark (Ed) Edwards in March 2006, Dave Birkett proved on ice to be not only the master of rock. They made a bold attempt to climb the summer rock line of SOS where the summer route gives a much harder start to May Day Direct. It climbs a steep groove and a mossy wall, and Dave made a determined and strenuous lead to join the dots of frozen moss and gain the belay of May Day Direct. Dave describes their epic attempt:

> "We did it over two visits; two days. The first time we did it, we were going up and falling off, going up and falling off, and the more times you went up you lost the ice in the back of the little placements that had been frozen up, and you're on this E5, 6b with these axes, and there's one or two placements which are behind juggy flakes, it was almost as easy in winter as it is in summer. One thing about the start, with the deep snow, was you thought you could fall off and not go over on your ankle on the stones at the bottom." (4)

It was a considerable achievement, but they failed to complete the route to the top of the cliff. The pair reported the hard climbing they had done as far as the belay, and their efforts were reported in the 2006 *Lake District Winter Climbs*. With the top portion of May Day Direct already climbed from an abseil approach the whole line still required a complete ascent from bottom to top in a single push. Having shown what was possible the pair were keen to get to grips with the line before others could claim the first ascent, and so were first out of the blocks in January 2007. Dave once again joined the dots of moss to climb the first pitch of SOS at a hard technical Grade 10. The corner of May Day Direct was not iced up, so they trended left to finish up a groove to the right of the original May Day Climb finish. This start up SOS stands as one of the hardest winter routes in the Lakes at (IX, 10).

Andy Turner in the restricted groove higher on Xerxes, note the leashless axe and how this system allows the climber to select and place gear without having a viciously sharp tool swinging around your legs, as was common twenty years earlier.

The winter guide produced in 2006 was the first joint production between the Fell and Rock Climbing Club and Cicerone Press. Written by Brian Davison and edited by Steve Reid, this edition contained an impressive 460 pages of information. This was the first winter guidebook to the area that utilised photo topos throughout, many of the crag photos were taken in a single day from a chartered helicopter.

Scafell had to wait until an early cold snap in December 2008 to receive its next addition; Xerxes on the Deep Gill Buttress. Climbed on the wall that contains Sod's Law and Sodom, the trio of Rich Cross, Andy Turner and Steve Ashworth spent all day discovering that this area of the crag offers sloping ledges and hard to place protection and isn't as friendly as the more central sections. They awarded their route Grade VIII.

Only three new winter routes were climbed over the decade up to 2010. However that winter proved to be a long one with conditions lasting from mid-December 2010 to mid-March 2011 and a bumper crop of routes being climbed. The first to mark his card was Dave Birkett who during a sunny Saturday at the end of January found himself once again on The East Buttress. Dave and his wife Mary wandered leisurely around the buttress taking photographs and discovered the mythical East Buttress icefall fully formed in all its glory. Their route for the day was decided.

> "When we went there that day we thought it wouldn't be there, but when we turned the corner, there it was, and bloody hell, it was gobsmacking! We didn't get the earliest start that day, and when we got there it was full in the sun." (5)

They progressed up the first icicle of Gold Rush and the ramps of Great Eastern to the bottom of the Yellow Slab, and the start of the steeper ice. But progress was slow and with the steep ice looming above them the pair decided to abandon the route.

> "It was thawing quite hard, and it was quite dangerous where Mary was belayed, because it was right in the line of the main fall and there were bits of ice dropping off and catching the rock just above our heads!" (6)

Mary had had enough of standing around in the cold, and while Dave was keen to return for a re-match she preferred to take up an offer to climb on gritstone the following day. Dave spent Saturday night calling round for a climbing partner. Phoning Dave McGimpsey's house he enthused about a secret line on The East Buttress which was in condition. He was doubly disappointed when Dave announced he had already arranged his climbing for the following day and that Brian Davison was sitting next to him in the living room. Birkett stopped giving out information and promptly hung up. Fortunately he was able to find Andy Mitchell ensconced in his local pub and tried to persuade him to partner him the next day. Al Phizacklea was also in the pub, and he convinced a slightly dubious Andy by saying that this was going to be the most significant winter route for years. Phizacklea had originally photographed the icefall in 1981, and wrote on the picture the legend 'This is it!' By sheer coincidence, he had photographed The East Buttress that very afternoon from 2 kilometres away from Eskdale, and when he zoomed in the photograph, the green clad figure of Birkett could be discerned on the screen. A hurried phone call also persuaded young photographer Ed Luke to cancel his plans for the next day in order to record the ascent on camera.

Above: The actual picture that Phizacklea had in his workplace for over 20 years, he never did see the icefall form over that period.
Left: A close up of the picture Phizacklea took of The East Buttress which shows Dave Birkett on the section of Great Eastern which leads to the base of the mythical icefall.

The pair abseiled into the belay on Great Eastern Route and climbed the remaining few pitches of steep ice. Again Birkett's ascent is best described by himself:

"The move onto Yellow Slab was kind of steep, and on the first attempt you didn't know what it was going to be like and I was playing about on a half inch of ice that was separated from the rock, and it kind of spooks you a bit. The next day it was re-frozen to the rock and it took little precise placements with the axes and it gave you some sort of confidence. You couldn't smash away at it, you just tap away, tap away until you find something. On the photographs it seems that there's a bucket load of ice on the slab, but it was just that type of snow with an icy crust on it.

"On the main pitch, the first 7 metres of climbing up to a visible nut placement was incredibly kind of balancy, and technically this was the hardest part, all bridgy on small holds, it was amazing. When I got the wire in I settled down, and above it seemed to get easier and more straightforward, but steeper and more scary, if you know what I mean. There was a long run out bit in the middle, which has thin ice on one side of a shallow groove and icy knobbles on the other, and I'm thinking 'will I hit the ledge from here?' I found two of these icy knobs which formed a V in between and I put a hex in between them and it felt quite good. Above there I spent half an hour working to get a couple of wires in, I don't know how long I took to do that pitch, Andy probably thought I took a lifetime!

"I belayed on a ledge on the right, and Andy led the top pitch. He didn't touch the top icicle, and at the time I felt a bit disappointed he avoided it, but I never questioned him at the time but it was a great lead to get to the top. The Icicle was only a couple of feet away, it was barrel shaped and probably weighed a tonne, I know a cubic metre of water weighs a tonne, and it was much bigger than that, and it was hanging there just like a bloody great hornet's nest. There wasn't much holding it there at the top, it was only about this wide (holding his hands abut a foot apart) and you didn't know how much holding power there is there. It would be nice to know a bit about the holding strength of ice at different temperatures, and how much thaw you need for the free hanging weight to take over?" (7)

The route, given the name of Never Ever Say Never by Dave, is graded overall VIII, with a technical pitch of 8. One of the climbing magazines enhanced the climb's reputation by giving it the strap line of 'England's hardest winter route?' across its cover. But there was trouble afoot. According to the Scottish winter climbing code, which is strongly supported by Brian Davison (who was the current editor of the SMC guidebooks), this ascent was a failure. Under these Scottish rules it could not be recorded because it hadn't been climbed in a single push. Brian was working on an updated edition of the winter guide, and he wanted to exclude this route on the grounds that the ethics of winter climbing were being devalued. Following some protracted discussions through e-mails and over a few pints with the Fell & Rock Guidebook team Brian reluctantly included it into the guide with the caveat that whoever climbed it in a single day would also be recorded in the first ascent list.

Photo: Ed Luke

Dave Birkett starting off the crux pitch of Never Ever Say Never.

Paddy Cave, an enthusiastic new name on the Lake District winter climbing scene, already had a string of new routes throughout the district to his credit, but it was the often in condition Deep Gill Buttress that offered him and Ed Luke a chance to stamp their names on Scafell in mid-February 2010. The steep groove at the start of the summer line Ixodes forms the meat of their winter foray Into the Wild, VII, and offers some hard technical Grade 9 climbing to the prominent ledge system which was followed off rightwards.

Photo: Dave Willis

Above: Paddy Cave.
Below: Paddy Cave on the winter ascent of Ixodes, named Into the Wild.

Photo: Ed Luke

Paddy explains:

> "It was the first time I'd actually been into the depths of Deep Gill on Scafell, the scale of the walls was impressive and the angular rock features seem to lean in on you as you make your way up the narrow line of the Gill. Arriving at the base of the route, it was just visible above in the mist, it looked steep and without a lot for the feet once on the right wall. However, the flake and crack line looked very do-able and protectable as well, and the walls of the Gill were white with frost.
>
> "The slab leading to the flake on the steeper right wall looked straight forward, once on it though it proved to be quite insecure with sloping foot holds and no good gear. Moving up and placing a small high wire gave some security to inspect the flake on the wall to the right. Hoping the rock was about to become a lot more helpful I took a blind hook in the crack behind the flake and placed a blind nut. The nut felt convincing though, good enough to torque the other axe above and commit to the flake. Immediately the angle changed, but with it the gear comes good, place a cam into the crack above and away you go. The lack of good foot holds and parallel nature of the crack meant that a sort of laid back torque combo seemed the best bet. To lean forward would release the torque and send the tools down the crack. Some great climbing and good gear leads up to a small ledge and rest below a groove. Next, some wild bridging up towards a slot out left for a cam, the reach out forcing a wild position above the Gill and a view down to Ed, hood up below in the wind. The cam, once placed, finished a run out above the rest ledge and gave me some gear to step back right into the groove. The summer route avoids this probably due to the seepage, this however gave some very thin ice at the back and allowed steady progress up and left to the belay ledge. Safe!
>
> "On the belay I tried to think of a pitch I'd enjoyed more, it was as good as any I could think of. What made it all the better was that I had not seen it before the day, and the atmosphere of the Gill added to the route and the great climbing. Ed came up to the belay confirming what I'd thought about the quality of the pitch; we both agreed, 'awesome'". (8)

Shamrock Buttress is often neglected but can offer some excellent climbing and is a good way to gain access to routes higher on Scafell. Ian Armstrong and Jeff Graham certainly thought so at the end of February 2010 as they took to the Tower Buttress following the chimneys on the left side of the steep lower buttress and then to the base of the second tower before moving up easier snow to Lord's Rake. Unsure of the grade, a VI was settled on; but time will tell.

A short while later Brian Davison and Dave McGimpsey walked up to Scafell on a warm March morning to find the obligatory fang of ice on The Shamrock opposite The Woolworth Boulder had formed and was waiting for their attention. As usual the ice hadn't touched down making the whole structure far weaker. Davison recalls:

> "I'd been walking past that icicle for so long I thought it was time I climbed it. I've seen it fatter and nearer the ground but the bottom fringes could be touched from the ground and I thought I could climb up an icy groove in the rock to gain access to the main climbable ice. The main worry would be the whole thing collapsing during the initial moves. I gained a rock runner but couldn't get any protection above my head or move further up the rock so it was time to commit to the ice. With axe placements as high as I could get them I pulled up and wrapped one leg around the base of the ice. I was hoping that would offer some support to the icicle when I kicked and hopefully prevent it from fracturing above. After dropping the first ice screw I managed to place one and moved out onto the front of the ice. Each step took me nearer safer climbable ice but also further from gear that would protect me if it all collapsed. Above it opened into a snowfield and a second smaller icefall, the second pitch, before we picked up Armstrong and Graham's footprints from the previous weekend". (9)

Paddy Cave on the Shamrock Icefall, the latticework axes will no doubt raise an eyebrow from traditionalists!

The Shamrock Icefall offers a combination of technical mixed climbing and precarious ice climbing which, while never desperate, does offer (VII, 7) climbing under the serious condition in which it is usually found. When told of the ascent, Steve Ashworth said the icicle had been snapped off at the top of the buttress when he visited earlier in the week. A few days of perfect freeze-thaw conditions at the right altitude had brought it into condition very quickly, and indeed as news of the ascent spread it was attempted the following day but without success.

The line of Botterill's Slab takes the darker diagonal line up the centre of this picture, and the line of Botterill's Corner is the broken looking diagonal break on the left. Collier's Groove follows the stepped line running from bottom left to the upper section of Botterill's Corner. Note the condition of The Great Flake on C.B.

Having completed the icefall, Davison and McGimpsey moved up along Rake's Progress to Tricouni Slab. Keswick Brothers' climb shares its first pitch with Collier's Groove up the left side of the slab to a large ledge where the two separate. A failed ascent in 1910 had been erroneously included in the guide book by an over enthusiastic editor keen to include historic ascents. Even keener was Davison who wanted to put things to rights. The left side of Tricouni Slab offered well protected, balancy climbing with the turfy corner of the slab just out of reach to the right.

This means there are now three variations offered by Tricouni Slab in winter. The original one climbed by Al Phizacklea climbs the initial slab and its continuation, which is actually the line of Botterill's Corner throughout. The second ascent of Tricouni Slab by Victor Saunders and Jim Fotheringham follows the summer finish, traversing rightwards at the higher grass ledge into the final chimney section of Botterill's Slab. This third winter version, Collier's Groove, VI, 6, starts up Collier's Climb and takes the continuation of the groove above to link in with the upper section of Botterill's Corner.

The following day of what proved to be probably the best weekend of the winter saw numerous parties crawling across Scafell. There hadn't been so many people winter climbing here in thirty years, let alone a weekend. The nice thing was that everybody was trying all manner of routes, not just the established classic gullies. The route for the day for Davison and McGimpsey was to venture up the projecting rib at the left side of the lower buttress, at the narrowest point of the West Wall Traverse. The summer line starts up a steep crack just right of the rib but with arms feeling the effects of the previous day Davison opted for a less strenuous-looking start up the corner of Doctor Death at the back of the first bay left of the arête. The corner proved steep, protection difficult to place, and the traverse right across sloping ledges insecure. A large prominent spike on a ledge left of the arête felt anything but secure when it was eventually reached, but the rest of the route was more amenable and gave Doctor Grey at a precarious (VII, 7). Thus one of the busiest and most pleasurable winter weekends ever experienced on Scafell came to an end.

By the following weekend, winter was losing its grip on The Lakes and so Scafell was the only place to be. Investigations during the intervening week had ascertained that the groove line left of Collier's Climb, spotted the previous year, was unclimbed in summer and winter. With a strong northerly wind blowing, Davison and McGimpsey set off to put this right. They teamed up once more and started up Collier's Original Start to the left of Tricouni Slab to produce Collier's Left Hand Variant, VI. By now the thaw had set in so the pair hurried over to Deep Ghyll Buttress to try and dash up the summer line of Upper West Wall Climb, VI. The top was reached with ice stripping from the face.

Winds were stronger on the following day so the pair contented themselves with a snowy Deep Gill solo of the corner at the right side of Impunity Slabs. This Impunity Corner, III, was sufficiently high up to have survived the thaw. A glissade ensured the valley was reached in only thirty minutes and the longest winter for 30 years ended with a tally of eight new climbs being added to Scafell and proof The East Buttress' mythical ice line is climbable when it comes into condition. Hopefully it won't be another 30 years before it sees a complete ascent.

The following winter saw an attempt on the most obvious remaining prize on The East Buttress, the perennial wet area where the summer routes Armageddon and Moonday are found. Paddy Cave and Steve Ashdown looked at this in the middle of a bitterly cold and very windy spell. The ice was tantalisingly brittle when placing screws which put them off committing to the steep icicles that were obviously going to be the crux. They did have an incentive to push on, as Dave Birkett was waiting at the base of the crag, ready to capitalise on their lack of resolve. Dave was invited to have a look, but he conceded that the freezing cold day meant that the conditions were the only winner that day. Steve reckoned it was the best he'd ever seen The East Buttress in winter, the ice was blue like an animated Disney fantasy, the sort of conditions you only see once in a lifetime.

Dave returned with Mary in December of that year and found the crag once again in brilliant condition, "with loads of ice and icicles hanging off it, there was a thick column near the bottom and icicles that felt more like Canada than Cumbria." (10).

The first pitch consisted of an initial easy angled slab of immaculate ice which gave access to a small cramped belay. Above the belay ledge things got a bit thinner, with a hoared-up corner system that led to the foot of the White Slab, where they took the classic Minotaur finish to round off the climbing. This route is rarely in condition but at last the line of the legendary 'Armageddon icefall' which have been the source of many tales over the years has been climbed, and it must rank as one of the best winter lines in the Lakes. They gave the name Moondance to the route.

A combination of good conditions and an increase in the numbers of winter climbers dramatically increased the number of routes being climbed. Many routes climbed originally in the 1980s received repeat ascents, some such as Moss Gill Grooves and Bridge of Sighs having only their second or third ascents while others like Botterill's Slabs received so many ascents in a day it is accepted as having definitely reached the iconic status of modern winter classic. Recent guidebooks have shown what Scafell has to offer, tempting winter climbers to now make the walk up to Scafell in winter rather than drive past to Scotland.

Photo: Mary Jenner

Dave Birkett at the belay ledge on the first ascent of Moondance.

The fifth winter guidebook

In 2012 the FRCC, in partnership with Cicerone Press, produced the fifth winter guide to cover this area, and in most respects this is merely an update of the previous edition. By using a slightly larger format and a stricter adherence to the editing of the text, the team managed to keep the number of pages the same as the previous guide, despite an increase of 220 described routes. The guide was updated by Brian Davison and edited by Steve Scott.

The 2012 winter guide to the Lakes.

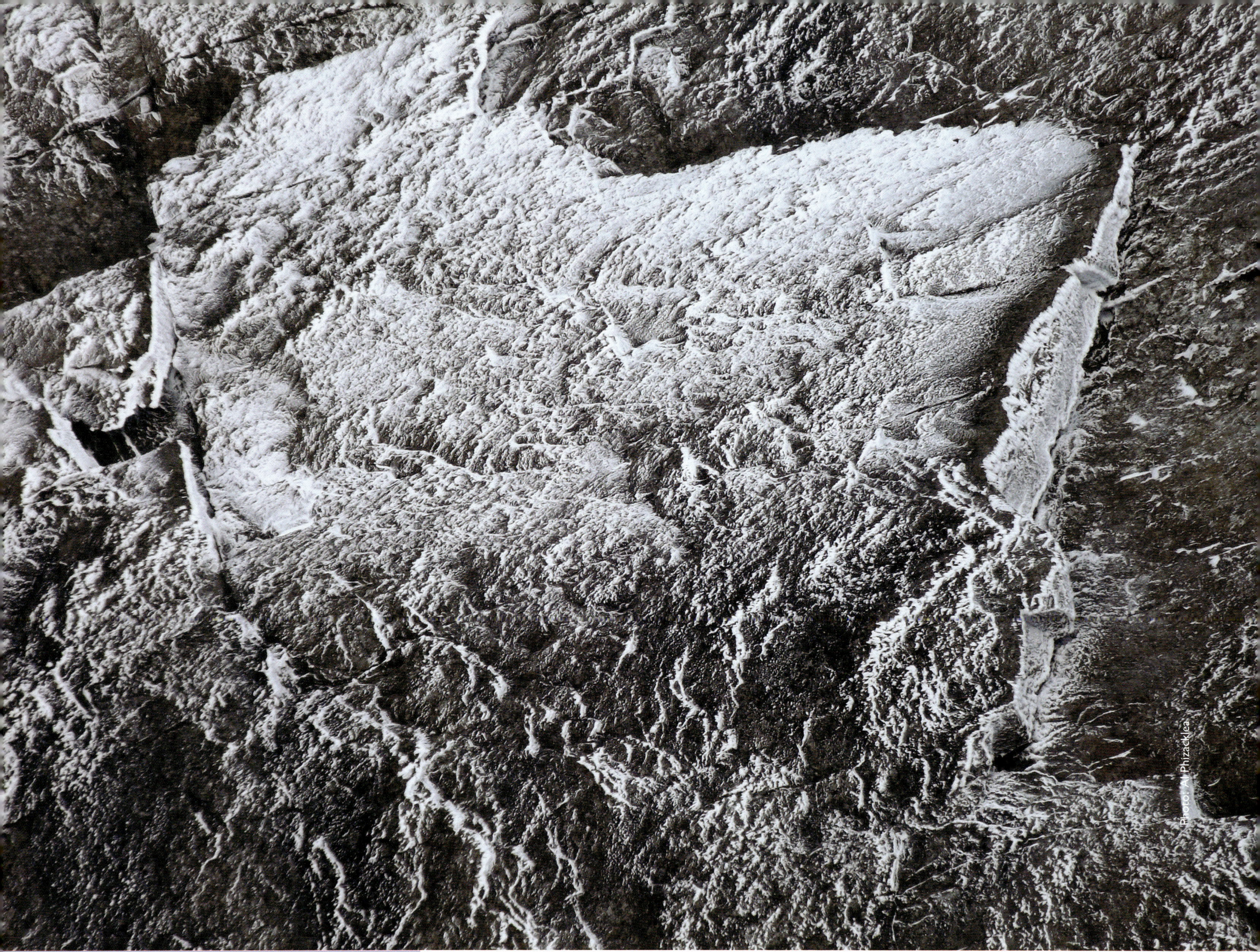

An unusual pattern of hoar frost defining the Great Flake of Central Buttress.

Footnotes

1. Brian Davison, first written for this publication
2. Brian Davison, first written for this publication
3. Steve Ashworth, e-mail to the author, 2011
4. Dave Birkett, FRCC audio recording, 2008
5. Dave Birkett, FRCC audio recording, 2010
6. Dave Birkett, FRCC audio recording, 2010
7. Dave Birkett, FRCC audio recording, 2010
8. Paddy Cave, e-mail to the author, 2011
9. Brian Davison, first written for this publication
10. Dave Birkett, telephone conversation with the author, 2015

2007 - 2015

The Never-Ending Story

There followed a four year lull in development on the crags; a period when people took stock. A sombre thought evolved that any future new routes would require someone better than Dave Birkett to climb them, but what seemed to have been overlooked was just how much scope there was on smaller and more obscure sections of the crag.

Typical of this new wave of the smaller routes were Seasonal Adjustment Disorder and Collier's Climb Left-Hand, discovered on the short wall between North Climb and Collier's Climb, close to Mickledore. It was an area Brian Davison had come to know over the winter, because unusually the second of the routes was originally first ascended under snow and ice before being climbed in summer. A mere three weeks after his winter ascent, Brian cajoled the other members of his team to follow him up the firm nevé snow slope below Mickledore to attempt his first proposed route; a short ramp line rising above the highest point of Rake's Progress. It suddenly dawned on his partners, Susan Jensen and Mike Cocker, why Brian had acquired the nickname of 'Mad Brian' amongst local climbers. The crag was damp and greasy; it had been drizzling the day before and there were still patches of snow on the ledges; not the best conditions to climb a new route on sight.

A slimy spell of climbing later when Brian was close to the top of the route, a hillwalker dressed in full winter regalia complete with ice axe and crampons, looked up from the snow slope below Mickledore and cast a speculative eye over the scene above him.

> "I say," he enquired incredulously, "What route are you on?"
> "It hasn't got a name yet. It's a new route" offered Brian.
> "What will the guidebook writer say, it's still winter!"
> "I am the bloody guide book writer" retorted Brian.
> The walker emerged from the snow slope onto the sunny, dry top of Mickledore, where Al Phizacklea and Pippa Cocker were taking photographs in the warm spring sunshine. It was so pleasant and windless, they were both in T-shirts.
> "Doesn't he realise its winter?" asked the puffing walker, with a look of dismay over his red face.
> "Nay, it's spring now" noted Phizacklea.
> "May I offer a name for this route? It should be called Seasonal Psychosis, because you don't know what season it is!" And with that the walker trudged along the warm dry ridge of Mickledore, complete with crampons and ice axe. As he passed it was noticed he had a fork and spoon protruding from his anorak pocket. Luckily he never heard the departing comment:
> "It's difficult to decide which one of them is suffering from psychosis." (1)

The route is an awkward HVS, and the encounter offered the inevitable name of Seasonal Adjustment Disorder. Davison and Jensen immediately started up a second route; the one Brian had climbed in winter. They followed the first pitch of Collier's Climb, and then finished up the delightful set of ramps to its left. This route was named less flamboyantly but equally descriptively as Collier's Climb Left-hand, and with the first pitch being the crux at VS, 4b, it gives a better finish to the original route. A notable aspect for the day was that Sue Jensen had never been to Scafell before, so she became possibly the only climber to climb two new routes on their first visit to the crag.

The preparatory work for this book had taken Al Phizacklea several years to complete; not that it was difficult to do, it was a mixture of lethargy and personal issues that gradually extended the original completion deadline. This was further exacerbated by the demand for a new guidebook to the crag, and this gradually took over his time. Marking up the crag photographs with the lines of the routes is usually the most satisfying aspect of guidebook work, and this also proved the case.

Photo: Al Phizacklea

Sue Jensen carefully watches Brian Davison struggling with the greasy rock on Seasonal Adjustment Disorder.

Overleaf: Dave Parton and Scott Young plan their day following a bivouac on the grass shoulder opposite The East Buttress.
Photo: Al Phizacklea

He was marking up the lines on a picture of the front face of the Pinnacle, when a notable gap right of Hopkinson's Gully caught his eye:

> "I thought 'Silly sod, I've missed a route off the diagram' so I looked through the guide, but there was nothing in the area. Then I thought 'Oh heck, I've missed a complete route out of the last guidebook, what a stupid thing to do!' or words to that effect. I flicked through the previous edition, and just as I was leafing through the 1974 guide to find this elusive route did the penny drop – there was no route up this part of the crag! I felt like a right dope for not realising straight away! So I immediately rang John Holden and suggested a pint at his local, where I showed him the marked-up photograph and pointed out the unclimbed gap. We immediately vowed that we would have a look at it on the first warm weekend of the spring. I never sent that diagram off to Phil Rigby who was generating the electronic version of the diagram for fear he would spot it himself and tip off the Carlisle team of a potential unclimbed line on the crag." (2)

Al Phizacklea approaches the first belay on the immaculate rock of Low Man by the Jubilee Line.

Photo: Andy Mitchell from the Holden collection

The fine weekend came in May 2012 during a fortuitously dry spell that occurred just before the arrival of one of the wettest and worst summers on record. Phizacklea and Holden climbed the route without inspection up the superbly rough rock of the Pinnacle to create a three pitch HVS. This was the weekend of the Diamond Jubilee of the Queen's accession to the throne, and despite John's ardent republican views it was given the resplendant name of Low Man by the Jubilee Line.

Photo: John Holden

The first ascent of Waiting Wall.

The following spring of 2013 was fine and warm, and Phizacklea returned to Scafell with Joe Holden and Tommy Moore. Joe's dad, John, had been unwell the previous day, and had decided that an early start would be unwise so he arranged to come up later in the day. Following a photographic session on The Pisgah, they decided to wait around the foot of the crag for John to arrive. Phizacklea had long admired the short steep wall that rose above the footpath that ran along the foot of the crag which formed a barrier below the grass of the Pinnacle Terrace. A quick ascent resulted in Waiting Wall, HVS, the first route to be claimed on this wall. At 14 metres, this is one of the shortest routes on Scafell, and would not look out of place on a minor crag in a valley such as Eskdale or Borrowdale; it is quite an alien concept for this crag. However, this opens up an opportunity for anyone who wishes to make their mark by adding half a dozen new routes to Scafell.

The main aim of the plan for that day was to plug another notable gap on the photo diagram of The Pinnacle, this time on the Deep Gill Slabs area. Young Joe has a well documented aversion to getting out of bed at 4.30 am, so while he curled up under some jackets at the base of the crag to catch up on his cherished beauty sleep, John arrived at the crag and replaced him on this ascent. A perfectly straight line to the left of Woodhead's Climb gave an excellent sustained route directly up the slabs and over the upper overhangs at HVS, 4c. The name of High Man by the Central Line had been proposed many months before to complement their earlier route up the Pinnacle.

Photo: John Holden

Al Phizacklea climbing High Man by the Central Line.

Photo: Al Phizacklea

Andy Mitchell steps across the crux traverse of Black Rider on the Shadowfax wall.

Photo: Al Phizacklea

Craig Matheson.

The fine weather of 2013 saw several activists attempting various lines on the crag with the usual preamble of cleaning and inspecting, but there had been too many visitors to conduct these activities in secrecy. News had spread and the expectation arose that there was to be some new routing on the crag and so on one Saturday in July these teams all arrived independently, but knowing that the others would inevitably be there.

First off the mark was Andy Mitchell and Nathan Pike, who had cleaned off the slender ramp immediately to the right of the shallow groove of Shadowfax. Phizacklea had attempted this line in 1990 but this had ended in a face-slapping fall which ended his desire for the route, so he made an arrangement with Andy to make sure he was on hand to record the ascent. This is the most direct line on this wall, as it links several of the prominent diagonal breaks to give a fingery but quite precarious E5 6b. Named Black Rider to maintain a 'Lord of the Rings' link to the Ringwraith theme, it is now considered to be the best line on this face.

Moving around to The East Buttress, Rob Matheson was determined to climb through the inverted 'V' overhang on the wall to the right of May Day Direct, a prominent feature that had been on his radar for decades. He approached it by starting up Edge of Eriador, before continuing directly through the roof and finishing up a thin crack, which had been climbed as a dryer variation to May Day Direct in the past. Although it provides a link between existing lines, the additional climbing makes it a worthwhile addition to the crag at E3. The name of this route also maintains the Tolkein theme, Rise of Angmar, commemorating the ascendency of the witch-king; the Lord of the Nazguls. The author was mortified when Rob pointed out that the name in the new guidebook was wrong, where it appears as 'Rise of Agmar'.

Rob's belayer was his son Craig. He is one of these intense young men who thrive on an exhaustive training regime, which has gained him a reputation of being a climber who is endowed with incredible strength. After climbing Rise of Angmar they went around the crag to view a project between Trinity and Incubus, a tenuous, thin crack up a seemingly blank wall that Rob had been interested in over the past few years. Craig had attempted the line previously, but this day he completed the ascent to give Thy Will Be Done, which was given a grade of E8, 6c. The climbing was of an unusually fingery nature for Scafell, with meagre protection from dubious micro wires, which Craig described the ascent as:

> "Bloody desperate, you can hardly hang on anywhere until you get to the flake. It's as hard to get the gear in as to do the climbing itself, there's almost a two-handed dyno half way through the sequence."
>
> Rob added
> "It'd be easier if we'd placed pegs in the crack because it's only protected by R.P. 1 and 2's. The whole thing is full-on in your face – big time!" (3)

Thus Craig became the only climber apart from Dave Birkett to climb a new E8 on Scafell, forming a very select group indeed. The fact that a young pretender had the audacity to directly challenge Dave to his crown was not long overlooked, and the following year Dave returned to repeat the line.

> "Yeah, there was a kind of competitive feel to it; I had to repeat his route before he repeated one of mine. I had been working at Chelsea [Dave had been landscaping at the Flower Show] and it kind of fired me up to have a look so I went up there three times , twice to check it out on the shunt then I went and did it with Will. It's maybe kind of better protected than the other E8's up there but it has that fingery cranky climbing that suits me well. (Dave was heard saying to someone that it was the only E8 on Scafell that you wouldn't die trying). I always say that I'm not a competitive person, but it seems that I bloody well am!" (4)

Photo: Al Phizacklea

Rob Matheson prepares to pull through the inverted 'V' roof on Rise of Angmar.

Craig Matheson tries to rest on the first ascent of Thy Will be Done, just before committing himself to the upper flake. The picture is a still from a video where the camera was set up inside a shoe!

It had taken a prolonged spell of dry weather to dry out Dave Birkett's latest project on The East Buttress. This climbs the steep brown wall just right of Siege Perilous; a line graced by two old pegs, which were possibly the remnants of an old Martin Berzins project. Dave had previously inspected the line so the ascent seemed a certainty. He certainly made short work of it, because the long run-outs between the gear and the good holds were no place for hesitancy. At E7, 6b this is the easiest of Dave's seven routes on Scafell, but don't expect an easy ride. He explained why he called it Back to Black, "It was partly in respect for Amy Winehouse, but every time I went to try it the lichen had re-grown and everything had gone back to black." Dave's belayer for this ascent was his considerate wife Mary, and when he got back to the ground he gave this revealing comment:

> "The climbing feels harder than it is, but there just isn't enough hard climbing to be harder than E7. I was getting pretty tired up there – you tend to grip a lot tighter when you're frightened". (5)

Al Phizacklea felt a sense of frustration that he was missing out on the action because of his role at the crag that day as roving photographer. He decided to wander over to Red Gill Buttress to try to work out the line of a route for the guidebook; it had been one he was unable to find in the past. There was also the local knowledge that there were of a couple of unclimbed lines on this buttress; there had to be some sort of incentive to endure another ascent of Lord's Rake.

The first route lay up a delightfully rough rib to the left of Red Gill, and was called Red Gill Edge. The second ascended the main central corner on Red Gill Buttress itself and was given the equally uninspiring name of Red Gill Corner. Both routes were Severe, but both give very pleasant climbing which combined with the existing routes in the vicinity would enable a climber of that standard to have a very productive day. These two lines brought the total of new routes added to Scafell on a single day to six, a record for these crags.

Rob Matheson, now in his 64th year, showed a defiant attitude to old age with his bloody-minded ambition and determination to climb whilst others of his age have long since retired to their carpet slippers and crown green bowling. He visited The East Butterss several times throughout the spring of 2014 to inspect the steep direct start to the Arête finish of Phoenix, which takes the leaning pillar between Phoenix and Ichabod. The slim groove which forms the crux in the lower part of the route was often commented upon because it is very prominent in a photograph on page 172 of *Cumbrian Rock*. This had been inspected several times before, but the sheer effort of inspecting and cleaning the rock below the overhanging prow proved too much except for the stubborn and determined effort of the Matheson team. Rob described it as being the most awkward route to prepare he's ever encountered due to the difficulty of swinging in and placing nuts to keep the rope close to the rock. The day of the first ascent was a chilly, breezy day in early May, and Rob and Craig had not intended this to be a serious attempt; just another practice session because he recorded that the air temperature was only 2° Celsius. "It just felt right, I thought I'd have nothing to lose by having a go, I was going to blame the cold weather on any failures that day." (6)

The resulting route was named Barad-Dûr after one of the towers in The Lord of the Rings trilogy, and it is an impressive E6, although the technical grade is not high at 6a. Rob describes reaching the slim hanging groove as "bold, strenuous and potentially perplexing, not the sort of thing you can do on-sight easily." Readers will recall how Matheson was on the first ascent of Phoenix Arête Finish in 1976. This ascent gives him the honour of becoming the climber with the longest period of developing the Scafell crags, which spans an incredible 38 years.

Dave Birkett returns to The East Buttress for his ascent of Back to Black.

Rob Matheson, the active pensioner.

Nick Warton and Steve Scott lead the team up Central Buttress on 20th April 2014, on the centenary day of the first ascent. For the original Abraham photograph (see page 106), the camera was set up at the end of the crest at the top of Shamrock Buttress but the eroded state of Lord's Rake prevented the modern team setting up this picture in exactly the same location.

Photo: Henry Iddon

Photo: Ron Kenyon

Henry Iddon and Steve Ashworth set up the original camera that was used by the Abraham brothers during the centenary ascent of C.B.

Rob Matheson high on a repeat ascent of Barad Dûr.

The Central Buttress Centenary meet

Over the Easter weekend of 20th April 2014, the FRCC celebrated the 100th anniversary of the first ascent of C.B. with a well attended meet at Brackenclose. Some came for the historical association, some came for the launch of the new guidebook and some came for the beer and food, which was produced (and consumed) in abundance! The guests of honour were two of Herford's nephews, Kit and Ted Braunholtz, who seemed somewhat overwhelmed at the attention their uncle received, and they walked to Hollowstones to witness the ascent teams. The route itself was climbed by teams led by Nick Wharton and John Lynch, the latter leading the front of a very wet Great Flake when caught in a sudden shower, whilst several others 'hitched a ride' up the pitch in the immortal style of 'C.B. Sid'. Other notable guests who attended the meet were Pete Moffatt, who at the grand old age of 90 still managed to get up the fells, he first climbed C.B. in 1945, and you may recall that he actually helped to build Brackenclose some 77 years earlier! Previous guide writers Ron Miller, Mike Burbage and Bill Young were also present at the guide launch.

The entire procedure was photographed by Henry Iddon, his team carried the original Abraham's plate glass camera up to the crag to recreate the 1914 first ascent photograph on the centenary day. As plate glass negatives are now unavailable, he managed to obtain some specially commissioned large format film from Eastmans, at a huge expense, which had to be loaded between the original plate glass holders. This presented a problem - he only had 3 slides available for exposure, and this old camera had no light metre, a restricted apeture range and no shutter settings. The exposure was determined by the original method, estimating the length of time between removing and replacing the lens cap. Henry had three attempts to capture this moment in history and it was pure guesswork, but the one second exposure was amazingly accurate to create an excellent photograph.

The ninth Scafell Guidebook

The latest guidebook to Scafell is a very different departure from the earlier guides in many respects. Firstly it is larger than the previous guide, measuring 183mm by 122mm; the previous guides were 171mm by 108mm, giving an increase in page area of 20%. The flexible laminated plastic cover, a feature of the FRCC guides since the 1960's has been replaced by a softer plastic card with the cover photo printed directly onto it, thus keeping abreast with other guidebook producers.

The ninth guidebook to Scafell commemorates the centenary of the first ascent of C. B.

This change has not been welcome by everyone, as these new covers are less hard wearing than the earlier type, and they delaminate when they get wet. The main change with this edition of the guide is the use of full colour crag photo diagrams throughout, a tremendous improvement according to the previous illustrator Al Phizacklea, but again others lament the passing of the old pen and ink sketches. Don Sargeant was drafted in by the guidebook team to create these crag diagrams. These diagrams have been updated and reproduced in this book.

So as the cold, unsteady summer of 2015 ended and the tourist families drifted back to their lives of work and shuttling little Johnny and Sarah on the school run, September turned out to be warm, sunny and delightfully peaceful. Al Phizacklea and Keith Phizacklea decided to inspect the slender ramp between The Hanging Chimney and Collier's Climb, which satisfied Keith's desire to tick off The Hanging Chimney, another example of a typically neglected and obscure route that he loves to collect. Following a difficult struggle up the old line that was supposed to be HVS (where E2 was nearer the mark), Al used this opportunity to grab what he described as a 'superior finish' to Davison's 2010 line Collier's Climb Left-Hand by traversing right onto the clean upper slab at an unchanged grade of VS. The line of the slender ramp was checked and dismissed due to its obvious difficulty, and as they agreed "The ramp might be the same angle as Botterill's, but it's also the same angle as Shadowfax, without any of the holds and the runners". (7)

Somewhat deflated by this failure on his first possible new route, Al persuaded Keith to follow him up Lord's Rake to inspect his second project, one that had fascinated him for years. Every time he had walked up to Scafell, he couldn't help but notice the hanging crack which was visible in the steep wall behind Shamrock buttress. The first time he had discussed the possibility of this area of crag was with George Smith back in 1983, and it had even attracted a comment from Dave Birkett who curiously pondered the overhanging nature of the rock. This area, which he christened 'Back O't Shamrock' seemed somewhat of an enigma, he couldn't even be sure the route was feasible as there was a holdless overhanging wall guarding the base of the crack, but could you reach it by traversing in from the right? Even the approach seemed problematical, facing the climber with either a very unappealing scramble from below up a long slimy gully, or an abseil from above. Finding the top of the crag involved an airy traverse across from Lord's Rake below Red Gill Buttress which left you peering down the steep rocks below with no idea where the crack line was. This uncertainty added a wonderful 'spice' to the prospect, and so by abseiling down on a single 8mm rope Al found himself on a grass ledge dominated by a tremendous overhanging crack and a hanging corner above. This was a dream position so rare in modern cragging, this sort of excitement and anticipation can only be found nowadays by exploring sea cliffs for the first time. The climbing was delightful, the delicate traverse leftwards to reach the crack contrasted delightfully with the perfect jams and gear in the main crack itself. Although only 30 metres long and VS, the adventurous approach and the perfection of the route ensured that Al gave it three stars when he recorded it on the FRCC website. They gave it the somewhat cheeky name of The Barrow Brothers' Climb, as both lads had endured years of other climbers commenting that 'I met your brother at such-and-such crag the other week', despite the fact that the two are not related.

As the setting sun bathed Red Gill Buttress in its glow, Al and Keith managed to grab one last new route up an easy crack which led to the central arete of the buttress. This was led somewhat uneasily on minimal gear and mossy rock at HVS to give Red Gill Rib, which as far as this historical section is concerned, was the last line to be added to the crag.

What does the future hold for Scafell? The obvious unclimbed lines of decades ago have all been claimed, but there are some snippets that still remain for somebody. On The East Buttress, the corner line above the start of Shere Khan and the short corner left of Equinox are obvious. The steep wall left of Borderline has been inspected, as has wall the right of Talisman, and the upper tower avoided by Eastern Front will be challenging. On Scafell Crag, there are possibilities left of The Hanging Chimney, and would anything fill the gap between the top pitches of Ringwraith and The Nazgul? For those who love obscure and somewhat unclean rock, there's a surprising amount of rock to the left of Slingsby's Chimney, as there is further up the the Deep Gill flank of the Pinnacle to the right of Edgehog. The 'discovery' of Back O't Shamrock will undoubtedly result in a handful of steep routes on this area. The history of Scafell has yet to be finished, so as the author listens to the steady patter of rain in the darkness outside, he is contemplating the arrival of next spring and yet another walk up Brown Tongue to savour the delights of Scafell Crag. It is comforting to think that someone could write these exact same words in fifty years time from now, when a new generation of climbers yet to be born will continue this never-ending story.

Footnotes

1. Al Phizacklea, first ascent reminiscence, 2010
2. Al Phizacklea, 2013
3. Craig & Rob Matheson, post new route comments, 2013
4. Dave Birkett, telephone conversation with the author, 2014
5. Dave Birkett, post new route comment, 2013
6. Rob Matheson, post new-route comment, 2014
7. Al and Keith Phizacklea, comment below the crag, 2015

Photo: Keith Phizacklea

The ninth Scafell Guidebook (continued)

Another notable difference to the old guide is the use of Harvey maps to depict where the crags lie rather than a hand-drawn map. The guidebook only covers half the area of the previous edition, describing the Scafell and Wasdale crags only, as the Eskdale section has been split off to create a new joint Eskdale / Duddon valley guide. There have been 20 new routes added to Scafell since the last guide, including all seven of the Dave Birkett 'super routes', but the new layout still requires 331 pages to cover the smaller area. The editor of this new guide is Steve Scott, who cajoled the writing team of Al Phizacklea (Scafell) and Ron Kenyon (Wasdale) to complete the manuscript in time for the Centenary of the first ascent of C.B. The book was 'officially' launched at the club's C.B. Centenary celebration at Brackenclose.

Al Phizacklea jamming up the crack on The Barrow Brothers' Climb.

Author Al Phizacklea and editor John Holden having a brew on top of Pikes Crag, with Scafell Crag in the background.

Scafell

Landscape, Rocks and Structure

Landscape

The high ground of the central Lake District is an undulating plateau, dissected by valleys. The 50 highest Lakeland summits have a mean elevation of 875m and the 100 highest tops average 825m. Scafell (964m) is at the end of a broad ridge in the centre of the upland area.

The landscape was created during and after a period of regional glaciation. The core of mountain is volcanic rock, containing numerous igneous intrusions. The lines of paths, scrambles and climbing routes on the upper slopes were created as less resistant rock types and structures eroded. The geological history of the rocks takes us back in time to the episodes of tectonic plate collision and mountain building hundreds of millions of years ago.

As a geological time frame for this chapter, Palaeolithic man was painting the walls of caves in Spain and France while what is now The Lake District lay beneath an ice cap resembling the one currently covering central Greenland. Homo sapiens has existed as a species for about a million years. The Lake District volcanic rocks were erupted about 450 million years ago and estimated age of the earth is something more than 4000 million years.

Mountains in the topographical sense are transient phenomena. After the ancient tectonic plate collision and mountain building events known as the Caledonian Orogeny which deformed and metamorphosed the rocks of Scafell, erosion removed all traces of elevated ground and The Lake District area became a sea bed.

After erosion to sea level and cover by marine sediments of various ages, The Lake District finally re-emerged as an upland during the Tertiary Period some 30 million years ago. Uplift occurred at about the same time as the beginning of the Alpine Orogeny and as plate movement began to open the Atlantic Ocean by rift faulting.

Overleaf: The northern aspect of Scafell as viewed from Wasdale with rock structure highlighted by snow. Photo: Al Phizacklea

(Fig. A) The glacial coves of the Scafell Range which fed ice to the Eskdale Glacier. The arrows show the direction of flow ice leaving the corries.

Glaciation

Within the last 2 million years, northern Britain has been buried beneath continental-scale ice sheets on numerous occasions. The hill and valley topo-graphy of The Lake District was created by erosion during and after the most recent (Devensian) glacial episode which began about 28000 years ago. At its maximum extent about 24000 years ago, the ice sheet was more than a kilometre thick and covered the whole of northern Britain and Ireland, together with surrounding seas. The Lake District upland acquired its gently-undulating, summit plateau beneath the ice cap. Ice movement was influenced by underlying structure and ice streams flowed outwards from central Lakeland, into the Vale of Eden, the Solway Firth, through the Irish Sea and eastward over the Pennines. Boulders, termed 'erratics', of Shap Granite and other rocks were carried eastward as far as County Durham.

As the ice cap melted, it was succeeded by individual glacier streams which excavated 'U-shaped' valleys along lines of geological weakness. Scafell is bounded by two such valleys, Wasdale and Eskdale. The over-deepening of these valleys by ice flow excavated the hollow of Wastwater, the deepest of the lakes. The ice also deposited moraines (rock debris), including those which impound Wastwater. and other lakes.

There is evidence that localized corrie glaciers and plateau ice fields reappeared in the central fells between 12800 and 11700 years ago. This was the last significant glacial activity although in some high corries, patches of ice may have re-formed as late as the 'mini ice ages' of the Middle Ages and eighteenth century.

The large valley glaciers were supplied with ice from corrie basins. (Fig. A). These are the hollows on hill-sides which are such a characteristic feature of British hills. Scafell's corries include Hollow Stones, Foxes Tarn and Greencove. The Scafell Crag, Pikes Crag and Shamrock cliffs are the back walls of the Hollow Stones Corrie which fed ice to the Wasdale Glacier. Ice also flowed south-eastward from Mickledore into upper Eskdale. Over-deepening of corries by ice scour provided locations for tarns. Corrie exits are commonly peppered with hummocks made of moraine debris deposited as ice melted. Isolated blocks were transported on a glacier surface and left 'stranded in transit', by melting.

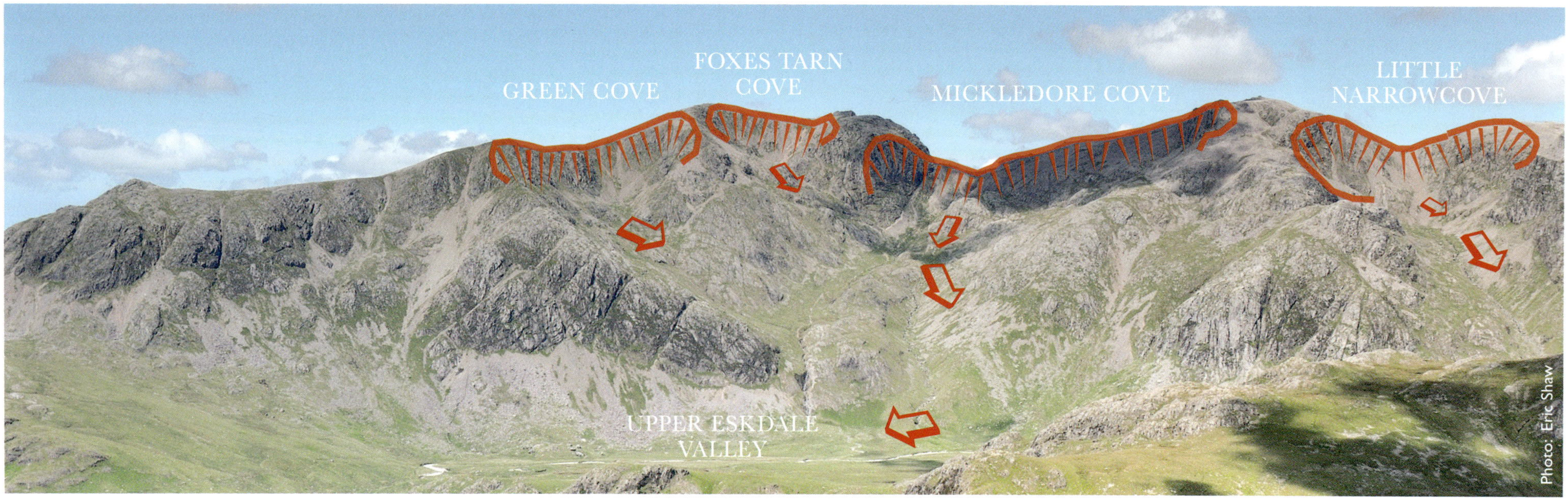

Ice moves by a mixture of internal flow and slippage across its rock base, lubricated by water flowing between a glacier and underlying rock. The grinding motion of fragments beneath the ice leaves striae or grooves, scored into 'ice-polished' rock slabs. Erosion occurs by combinations of abrasion at the base of a glacier and undercutting of corrie headwalls and flanking cliffs. The mechanism of corrie excavation by freeze-thaw splitting of rock creates an apron of scree and steepens the back-wall crags. Some debris falls on to the ice but much accumulates along the edges of the glacier as lateral moraines. Where walls of two corries erode back into each other, ridges are transformed into sharp arêtes. Mickledore, was created this way as were the famous Striding Edge on Helvellyn and Blencathra's Sharp Edge.

Glacial action was the dominant mechanism which shaped the morphology of hills and valleys throughout the central Lake District.

Post-glacial Processes

Erosion has continued since the end of glaciation. Water and weather are now the most important agents. The upper parts of the western and southern flanks of the hill are smoothly convex and partly covered by a vegetated veneer of rock fragments. The middle and lower slopes are thickly blanketed by scree and glacial debris. The debris cover is dissected by gullies and stream valleys (locally known as gills). Rates of erosion are partly self-regulating. Accumulating debris blankets mantle bedrock and then are themselves removed by run-off. The beds of drainage channels are the few places where bedrock can be observed on the lower slopes.

After glaciation, the climate was one of permafrost, similar to arctic tundra, in which the ground was permanently frozen below summer melt depth. Permafrost produces characteristic features which can be seen on many hills.

Photo: John Moore

(Fig. B) Rake End fell, behind Brackenclose hut. Recent mass movement caused by land slipping of surface soil, vegetation and rock debris. Note the detachment scarps, debris fans and 'rippled' texture of ground caused by soil creep when saturated.

Among the most important are soil-creep, heaving to surface of stones and flowage of saturated fine material as mud flows.

Permafrost was followed by the current milder climatic pattern of seasonal melt and freeze. The 'jacking' action caused by the expansion of water as it freezes in rock cracks and fissures adds to scree debris fields which form below the crags. Scafell, like all Lake District hills, is eroding continuously. Run-off water has produced 'V' shaped valleys in glacial debris and softer rocks. Lingmell Gill below Hollow Stones is a good example (GR 195 074). Enormous quantities of rock fragments are moved by the streams which drain the mountain.

Widespread land-slipping during post-glacial wet periods, continues on a small scale on steeper slopes (Fig. B). Landslip scars, with trains of debris below them are widespread. Grassy slopes, contoured by 'sheep-track ripples' are indicators of on-going mass creep movement of the soil and vegetation cover, rather like crumples in a sliding carpet. The banks of Lingmell Gill below Hollowstones show mass movement on the over-steepened slopes of a 'V' shaped valley (GR 195 074).

Catastrophic events periodically supplement the continuous processes. These include flash floods and earthquake vibration. Dramatic rock falls, landslides, debris flows and flash floods which move thousands of tonnes of debris happen during and after major storms. Catastrophic flash-flood events in recent decades have left debris trains in many parts of Lakeland (Fig. C).

(Fig. C) Fresh scree washed out of a gully below the Shamrock following a severe cloudburst in 1958.

The frequency of catastrophic events is assessed in terms of probability in relation to time. Flash floods and earthquakes, for example, have repeat frequencies of decades but more serious events take place on a time scale of centuries or millennia. The absence of records of a major catastrophic event in recorded human history doesn't mean that it won't happen! Human history is too short to predict catastrophic geological events.

Outwash fans formed by continous run-off and flash flood events have created aprons of debris which cover large parts of the floor of Wasdale. The Lingmell Gill debris fan obstructs and diverts Lingmell Beck from the middle of the dale towards the foot of Yewbarrow. Examples of the large flash flood boulders can be seen in the Lingmell Gill bed near the footbridge (GR187 073).

On a geological timescale, landform change in Lakeland is happening both continuously and rapidly as shown by the recent collapse of blocks in Lord's Rake gully*. (Fig. D) *the block collapsed in July 2106.

Photo: Al Phizacklea

(Fig. D) This block fell across the head of The Lord's Rake and remained wedged there for 14 years. The fractured nature of the block indicated a lack of structural integrity which eventually caused its collapse in July 2016 where it now forms an unstable blockage in the Rake below.

Bedrock Geology

The rocks of Cumbria were deposited in a wide variety of ancient environments which included deep-ocean troughs, volcanic terrain, deserts, shallow seas and coastal marshes, whose forests were subsequently transformed to coal. The district has been planed to sea level on numerous occasions since the bed rocks of Scafell were created. The upland is surrounded by younger strata, including limestone, coal measures of Carboniferous age and Permo-Triassic age 'red bed' desert.

Lakeland is a block of sedimentary, igneous and lightly-metamorphosed rocks, formed more than 450 million years ago. The older rocks, are two belts of lightly-metamorphosed sedimentary strata and one of volcanic rocks. The sediments were mudstones and sandstones. The volcanic rocks are collectively known as Borrowdale Volcanic Group and form the higher ground and the major rock-climbing crags.

All three belts of rock were deformed by folding and faulting and modified by pressure and heat (metamorphism) while buried at depths of several kilometres, during the Caledonian Orogeny, a period of tectonism, caused by plate collision. Beneath most of The Lake District is a subterranean batholith ridge of granite, emplaced towards the end of the Caledonian Orogeny. The Eskdale Granite is part of this huge intrusion.

Scafell Volcanic Rocks

Scafell consists mainly of volcanic ashes, lavas and inter-layered sediment-ary strata of the Borrowdale Volcanic Group. The volcanic and sedimentary strata have been intruded by igneous rocks from sources deep in the crust. Small garnet crystals are found in some volcanic lavas and igneous intrusions.

The Borrowdale Volcanic Group and many of the main igneous intrusions are chemically and mineralogically typical of rocks formed near the boundaries of colliding tectonic plates. They include andesite volcanic rocks together with intrusive and volcanic members of the granite family, and relatively small amounts of basalt.

Volcanic rhyolite and dacite are similar in chemical and mineral compos-ition to granite which contains large amounts of silica and aluminium and has relatively low iron content. In contrast, basalts are rich in iron and magnesium but have lower silica content. Andesite is intermediate in chemical composition between the granite and basalt rock types.

Part of a dacite lava flow forms impressive crags of the north and east faces of Scafell. Below the crags, the volcanic and sedimentary layers are less resistant to erosion and have weathered to form open slopes, where bedrock is mostly obscured by rock debris, soil and vegetation. Many interesting examples of volcanic and volcano-sedimentary rocks derived from erosion of the volcanoes can be found as boulders in the beds of becks, as fragments in stone walls and among the blocks used for path improvement (although not all the latter are of local origin).

(Fig. E) Mickledore, Scafell Crag and Lord's Rake indicating the framework of fault lines that have sculpted this area.
The crags are mainly Scafell Dacite Lava.
SCF: Scafell Crag Faults; MG: Moss Gill Fault; SG: Steep Gill Fault; DG: Deep Gill Fault; LRF: Lord's Rake Fault; MCF: Mickledore Chimney Fault; EBF: East Buttress Fault; MFCZ: Mickledore Fault Crush Zone.
(The area between the lower four fault lines defines the Mickledore Fault Crush Zone).

The major rock types

Pyroclastic Breccias and Agglomerates

Pyroclastic breccias and agglomerates result from explosive eruptions in which consolidated rock fragments are ejected into the air from a volcanic vent. They contain angular and rounded fragments up to a metre in size and are relatively common in the Borrowdale Volcanic Group. The larger and heavier fragments fell relatively near their eruptive source while finer material spread further in the wind. Agglomerates, pyroclastic breccias and coarser ashes weather to rough surfaces in which the shape of contained fragments can be seen. This rough surface of the rock provides the friction we rely on for climbing.

Tuffs

Tuffs are deposits of volcanic ash ejected from a vent by explosive volcanism. This is one of the main Scafell rock types. In some cases the fine-grained ash has probably been carried some distance from its source vent by the wind. It is deposited as a blanket, covering the surface on which it falls. As a result, tuffs become layers or lenses in a volcanic pile. Some fine-grained, compact tuffs were used for stone tools at manufacturing sites on the slopes of Scafell Pike above Mickledore.

Pumice

Pumice consists of lava fragments, mainly dacite and rhyolite composition which have expanded by sudden loss of gas during eruption. The lava globules' response to sudden reduction in confining pressure as they leave the vent is similar to the expansion of popcorn. Pumice produced by active volcanoes is often seen floating on the sea and lake surfaces after an eruption. Tuffs can be a mixture of fine-grained lava fragments and pumice. Many of the Borrowdale Volcanic Group ash eruptions were probably similar to those of Vesuvius which buried Pompeii in Roman times.

Ignimbrites (Pyroclastic flows)

Inter-layered with the tuffs, agglomerates and breccias are layers of fine-grained, compact 'welded tuff', interpreted by volcanologists as ignimbrites. Ignimbrites which are also known as pyroclastic flows are erupted as clouds of incandescent dust particles, pumice fragments and globules of molten lava. They cascade down the flanks of a volcano, behaving like an air-borne avalanche. Temperatures inside an ignimbrite particle cloud can reach 1000°C or more. They come to rest as a semi-molten blanket, which slowly cools.

As the ignimbrite consolidates, the still ductile fragments fuse together to produce a hard 'welded tuff'. Commonly, ground water or streams buried by ignimbrites 'boil off' as fumaroles and hot springs. Fossil ignimbrites have a characteristic appearance in which flattened shards, slivers of pumice and globules of lava weather out to produce a distinctive texture known as fiamme (Fig. F).

Ignimbrite flows are among the most dangerous and lethal of volcanic events. An ignimbrite eruption cascading down the flank of Vesuvius engulfed Herculaneum with excruciating consequences for the inhabitants.

Volcanoclastic sediments

Volcanic ashes are sometimes eroded before consolidation and transported as sediment by rivers. They are re-deposited as volcanoclastic sand or mud sediment layers in lakes or pools. The 'sedimentary' strata include ash fragments and lava grains. In some cases they have delicately laminated layering (Fig G). Submarine slumping and sliding of unconsolidated volcanic 'muds' produces contortions of the laminations (Fig. H).

(Fig. F) Weathered volcanic ignimbrite deposit showing slivers of molten or ductile lava (fiamme), deposited in an incandescent volcanic dust avalanche and flattened by the weight of material above. This has been weathered out from the volcanic dust matrix to leave cavities.

(Fig. G) Minor faults and fractures dislocating volcanic sediments: fine ashes and tuffs probably re-deposited as lake sediments.

(Fig. I) Scafell East Buttress showing the surface traces of the East Buttress Fault (EBF), Mickledore Chimney Fault (MCF) and Mickledore Fault Crush Zone (MFCZ). The buttress consists of dacite lava. The lava is cut by numerous chimneys and cracks which mark the courses of crudely columnar jointing and small faults. The face is approximately the plane of the fault, the line of which can be followed as a crack filled by clay gouge along the foot of the crag. Crushed rocks have been removed from the Mickledore Fault Crush Zone by glaciation, exposing the fault as the face of the buttress.

Right: (Fig. H) Contorted layers of volcanic ash and dust which have been 're-worked' and deposited as 'volcanic sediments' in a lake or river pool. The contortions (folding) were caused by small scale submarine land-sliding of the unconsolidated volcanic tuff and ash grains. This block is in the foot-path to Hollow Stones, 50m west of the 'Woolworth' Boulder.

Lavas

The Scafell volcanic pile contains several types of lava. Scafell Crag, The East Buttress and Pikes Crag are remnants of a massive dacite lava flow, in places more than 100m thick. The lava flow has been traced several kilometres from Scafell to Great Gable where it forms the Napes crags. The rock climbs of Scafell, Pikes Crag, Lingmell and Great Gable are on this rock. The lava is fractured by crudely columnar joint fissures which form many of the steeper cracks and chimneys (Fig. I).

Andesite and rhyolite lavas also occur. Some of the rhyolites contain flow banding and fragments, created when broken crusts were re-incorporated into the melted rock. Inter-layered among the tuffs and ignimbrites in the lower part of the mountain are more lavas, including basalts. Outcrops of dark, compact basalt can be seen on the bridleway which leads from Wasdale National Trust campsite to Burnmoor Tarn (NY 183065).

Climbers are aware that certain crags seem to be dirtier than others, and these can be the home for copious quantities of moss, grass and lichens. Other crags, however seem to be naturally 'clean' and free of such vegetation. Those climbers who regularly produce new routes certainly notice the difference, due to the amount of preparation and cleaning required. Al Phizacklea noted "If a crag is naturally clean when you climb on it, it will always remain clean," and that lighter-coloured crags tend to be cleaner than darker crags. It has become evident following the 'discovery' of new crags since the 1960's (such as Goat Crag and Great End crags in Borrowdale) that these crags can revert back to their uncleansed natural state within a decade. There are a two main reasons for this, aspect and geology. North facing crags receive little sunlight, therefore they retain moisture longer than south facing crags, and plants require moisture to thrive.

Mineral nutrients released by chemical weathering promote the colonisation of the rock surface by mosses, lichens and algae. The darker rocks (andesite and basalt) which have a higher iron content are more susceptible to such colonisation than the lighter coloured rocks that contain more silica and aluminium such as dacite, rhyolite and granite. This is evident around the lower part of Scafell Pinnacle, where a slight change in rock colouration defines the boundary between 'dirty' rock and the clean lower slabs taken by Jones' Route Direct and Hopkinson's Cairn Direct routes.

Intrusive Igneous Rocks

Granite and Granitic Porphyry

After the volcanic events, thousands of cubic kilometres of molten granite magma, rose slowly through the crust and emplaced itself in the lower part of the volcanic pile beneath Scafell (granite is less dense than its host rocks). This is the Eskdale Granite intrusion (Plate 1, sections A-A and B-B, page 345). On the Eskdale side of the hill, the slopes above Boot, Bleabeck Bridge and the Woolpack Inn are granite. In Wasdale, granite is exposed in the river bed near Wasdale Head and on the south flank of Scafell in Hardrigg Gill (NY193053).

Granite contains large amounts of silica and aluminium but has relatively small amounts of iron and magnesium minerals. If the magma melt cools slowly, deep in the crust, large crystals form.

If the melt carrying some large crystals is injected into a dyke fissure and cools quickly, the result can be a rock with large crystals scattered through a fine-grained matrix known as porphyry. A dyke of porphyry with large feldspar crystals (Fig. J) can be seen in Lingmell Beck just above the footbridge (NY 189073). Porphyry is one of the by-products of magma crystallization and commonly occurs in and near large granite bodies.
The main episodes of volcanism and related intrusion in the Scafell area took place about 450million years ago. Emplacement into the volcanic pile of the Eskdale Granite and the porphyry dyke intrusions were among the last episodes of igneous activity.

Basalt and Andesite Dykes, Sills and Pipes

Basalt and andesite magmas were injected into cracks, fissures and faults in the volcanic rocks during and after volcanism, creating dykes which cut across the layering and sills intruded between layers. The intrusions include a basalt dyke in the Lord's Rake Fault and garnet-bearing andesite pipes (Plate 1, Geological Sections A-A and B-B).

(Fig. J) A porphyry dyke of fine grained granitic rock containing large isolated crystals of Feldspar (a sodium/calcium/aluminium silicate mineral). This rock intruded into a fault or fracture cutting volcanic rocks. The contact between the granitic dyke and the surrounding volcanic rock can be seen in the bed of Lingmell Beck 200m upstream from the Brackenclose footbridge.

Volcanic Setting
Current geological opinion is that the rocks of the Borrowdale Volcanic Group in the Scafell area are remnants of eruptions from vents associated with a volcanic caldera. A caldera is a circular depression, tens of kilometres in diameter, formed by subsidence during and after draining of a chamber of magma beneath the volcanic complex above.

Calderas have volcanic vents in and around them and contain many fumaroles and thermal springs. The central subsidence area is commonly a sub-circular basin in which water accumulates as lakes and pools. The Yellowstone National Park area in the USA is a caldera, similar in many ways to that postulated for the Borrowdale Volcanic Group in the Scafell area.

The Borrowdale Volcanic Group is a rare example of volcanism on land, preserved and exposed in such a way that a cross-section of the rocks below the caldera can by re-constructed.

Tectonic Structure

To understand the internal structure of Scafell, it is necessary to appreciate the geological definition of 'mountains'. Mountains are created by tectonic processes in 'orogenic belts'. These are swathes of terrain, thousands of kilometres in length, in which rocks are compressed, deformed and subsequently rise to form topographically elevated terrain. They are created along lines of collision between global tectonic plates as is happening in the Alps and the Himalayan ranges. The rocks of The Lake District were involved in collision and subduction of a tectonic plate south of the site of the present day Lake District between 400 and 385 millions of years ago.

While buried during the later stages of the Caledonian Orogeny which affected areas from Scandinavia to the Appalachian Mountains in America, rocks were metamorphosed, folded and dislocated by faulting. Temperature and pressure during metamorphism caused minerals to re-crystallize and change their chemistry. Using the physical chemistry of metamorphic minerals, it is possible to estimate that the Borrowdale Volcanic Group was buried to depths of at least three or four kilometres during deformation.

One result of compression and metamorphism was transformation of tuffs and fine-grained volcaniclastic sedimentary rocks to slates with a cleavage or parting which can be split for commercial use. Lakeland slates have been traditionally used for building and ornamental purposes and are the basis of the 'slate' quarrying industry.

The orogeny ended with intrusion of the granite batholith which underlies northern England. All that remains of the Caledonian Orogenic belt are its folded and metamorphosed foundations.

Folds and Faults
All the bedrocks of the central Lake District were compressed, crumpled and folded during the Caledonian mountain building events. The remains of one of these folds is a trough-shaped syncline in the dacite lava layer which caps Scafell (Plate 1, Geological Section A-A). When buried at depths of several kilometres for long periods of time under the pressures and stresses of orogenic conditions, rocks buckle and deform 'plastically'.

There are similarities between the behaviour of rocks subjected to long periods of compression under high confining pressures, and the toy-material 'bouncy putty'. If a ball of 'bouncy putty' is left at rest, it 'flows' to form a pool. The putty also has elastic properties which enable it if struck sharply to fracture. Rocks show similar combinations of ductile and brittle properties while undergoing deformation.

In addition to folding, the Caledonian deformation caused widespread faulting. Faults are shear fractures whose dislocations can bring rocks of different character into juxtaposition. Faults can operate as single fractures or as complex belts of multiple, sub-parallel structures, known as 'crush zones'. Both types can be seen on Scafell.

Single strand faults weather to gullies, chimneys or rakes. Examples include Deep Gill (DG), Steep Gill (SG), Moss Gill (MG) and Mickledore Chimney (MCF) (see Plate 2). Professor's Chimney and the Jordan Gap, which separates Scafell Pinnacle from the main mountain are parts of the Steep Gill (SG) fault.

Photo: Al Phizacklea

(Fig. K) Lord's Rake Faults.
The floor of the gully (fault zone) contains a basalt dyke, almost entirely buried by scree debris. The walls of the gully are cut by numerous joint fractures many of which are parallel to the faults. Note the fractured boulder which is wedged across the head of the rake.

Erosion along the Scafell Crag Faults (SCF) created the face of Central Buttress, Rake's Progress Ledge and the footpath along the base of the crag from Mickledore to Lord's Rake (Fig. E). Lord's Rake Fault was intruded by basalt magma as a dyke, erosion of which created a broad gully (Fig. K).

Fault movements crush and grind rock to a granulated powder known as 'gouge' which is susceptible to weathering. Soft gouge can be seen in the East Buttress Fault fracture along the base of the crag and in the recesses of Moss Gill and other gullies (Fig. L). In places the walls of fault-line gullies still carry the scoring scratches caused by grinding movements. These grooves and scratches are called 'slickensides'. Their orientation gives an indication of the direction of slippage during the most recent movements.

In contrast to well-defined single-strand faults, the Mickledore Fault Crush Zone (MFCZ) is a 250m broad belt of brecciated rock and gouge which runs from Hollow Stones through Mickledore towards the Esk. The crush zone includes several distinct fractures, notably The East Buttress Fault (EBF), which crops out as a groove along the base of the crag (Fig. I). The crushed rock gouge has eroded to create the gullies whose broken rocks form the unpleasantly unstable scrambles from Hollow Stones to Mickledore.

Fault fractures provided channels for magma, allowing access of dykes of granite porphyry, basalt and other intrusive rocks and to thermal waters which circulated through fissures, depositing veins with quartz, small quantities of metallic and other minerals. Fluorite crystals (CaF_2), haematite (Fe_2O_3) and other minerals can be found in the Mickeldore Crush Zone. Weathering of the hematite causes widespread red staining.

Joints

Joints are among the most common geological structures in the Scafell crags. They are fissures and fractures across which there is little or no lateral displacement. For climbers, they form jamming cracks, finger holds and chimneys.

Joint sets form fracture networks throughout a rock mass. They are created when stress energy is released and rock volume expands. Stress acquired during deformation or burial is released by cooling, relief of compression after tectonic events or by reduction of load as uplift and erosion bring rocks towards the surface. In the case of igneous intrusive rocks like granite or erupted volcanic rocks, fracturing can be triggered by crystal growth or cooling of the magma.

Photo: Al Phizacklea

(Fig. L) Central Buttress is defined at its base by the Scafell Crag Fault (SCF). The Moss Gill Fault has been excavated by erosion to produce the gully/chimney line. Central Buttress is broken by several systems of joint fractures which form slabs, cracks and deidres. A steeply-inclined set of joints form the slabs. Joint fractures parallel to the face and Scafell Crag Faults are responsible for the Great Flake (GF) which is partly detached from the face. A third set of horizontal or gently inclined joints form ledges and terraces including the Oval.

Joints weather to form gullies, chimneys, cracks and flakes. The fractures provide conduits for run-off water which, when it freezes, exerts a 'jacking' force that can destabilize blocks (Fig. D). As these joint-bounded blocks detach and fall, it creates faces and slabs.

Steeply-inclined joint fractures form the classic slab climbing routes on Scafell Crag (Botterill's Slab and Moss Ghyll Grooves) (Fig. L). Rock falling away has left the series of the steeply-inclined ramps which are such a marked feature of the face.

Swarms of joints commonly occur parallel to faults. The chimney fissure which separates the Great Flake from the face is a dramatic feature of the crag. Behind the flake is a joint fracture parallel to the Scafell Crag faults. The fall of the infamous 'C.B. chockstone' may have been in part, a consequence of creeping dilation of the Great Flake crack which will end with the collapse of the flake itself.

The East Buttress and Pikes Crag contain joints of many different orientations but the most obvious group is a set of more or less vertical fractures (Fig. I). Some of these may be 'columnar joints', formed as the lava cooled, by a similar mechanism to that which created the columns of the Giants Causeway in Northern Ireland.

Where it crops out on the Eskdale side of Scafell, the granite is cut by multiple joints, creating a 'blocky' appearance. Horizontal and gently-inclined joint fractures are common in the upper parts of the mountain and on Scafell summit plateau.

Recent Geological Events: Seismicity and Uplift
NW England is one of the most seismically active areas in Britain and faults in The Lake District and surrounding areas are earthquake prone. Recent seismic events include the 2011 Coniston tremors. Shaking during a tremor in 1981 brought about collapse of the Sepulchre block with its associated climbs at Kern Knotts on Great Gable. Many recent earthquakes in NW England are connected with faults beneath the Irish Sea, whose movements may be linked to continuing separation of the Eurasian and North American crustal plates or to release of stress connected with post-glacial uplift. Each seismic event adds an increment of offset to rocks along a fault. Displacements over periods of geological time accumulate into very large displacements.

During and following melting of an ice cap or erosion of rock, the earth's crust responds to removal of 'load' by uplift. This uplift by crustal buoyancy, known as isostasy, occurs rapidly in geological terms.

In Baltic Scandinavia mediaeval boat docking rings in rocks adjacent to harbours have been raised in the last few hundred years, by tens of metres relative to present sea level. Lakeland has been a relatively elevated area for a considerable time but post-glacial uplift has probably enhanced the elevation to some degree as nearby raised coastal beaches demonstrate.

Scafell is a dynamic geological environment in which ongoing processes are punctuated by episodic and occasionally catastrophic events. In geological terms, change continues at a rapid pace.

John Moore.

Photo: Al Phizacklea

Acknowledgements

I extend grateful thanks to my fellow FRCC member, Dr David Stephenson of the British Geological Survey for his patience and hard work proof reading, for his many constructive comments and suggestions and for correction of some of my most glaring errors. I wish to thank the many unacknowledged researchers whose work forms the basis of this description. I appreciated the stimulus given me by FRCC members whose irrepressible enthusiasm for geology was one of the factors which led to the writing of this chapter.

JMcMM.

Glossary of definitions

Agglomerate
A volcanic rock comprising rounded blocks of coarse debris, ejected from a vent by explosive volcanism. Larger fragments commonly occur in a finer-grained matrix of ash.

Andesite
A volcanic rock with a mineral and chemical composition that falls between basalt and granite i.e. less silica than granite and less iron and magnesium than basalt. It is occasionally found in pipes and dykes which may have been the feeders for lava flows. It is a typical volcanic product in areas of tectonic plate collision.

Basalt
This volcanic rock originated from deep within the Earth's crust. It is erupted as lava or fills fractures such as dykes and sills. Basalt is rich in iron and magnesium with relatively low silica content.

Batholith
A huge body of granite found deep underground, commonly hundreds of kilometres in length and width which has risen by buoyancy from the lower crust. Much of northern England, including The Lake District, is underlain by a granitic batholith, of which the Eskdale Granite is part.

Caldera
An extensive, approximately circular, volcanic structure created by subsidence as magma drains from a reservoir beneath.

Cleavage
This prominent fine-grained parting of rock into thin 'slates' is caused by the growth or re-growth of crystals in parallel orientation, during compression and metamorphism. Slates with a well-defined planar cleavage in fine grained rock, can be split to produce roofing slates and other commercial products.

Dacite
A type of volcanic rock that belongs to the granite family that contains a mineral chemistry make up that is between andesite and granite.

Dyke
A steep sheet-shaped intrusion occupying a fissure or fracture.

Feldspar
A major mineral constituent of all the common igneous rocks. The feldspar mineral group is made of aluminium and silica with varying amounts of sodium, calcium and potassium.

Fiamme
Flame-shaped slivers of lava or pumice, found in ignimbrite deposits. The presence of fiamme is one of the diagnostic criteria used to identify ignimbrites.

Fumarole
A steam or thermal water vent which can take the form of a geyser.

Gouge
Granulated rock powder created by grinding movement in fault fractures.

Granite
An intrusive igneous rock which originates by melting deep in the Earth's crust. Granite is rich in silica and aluminium with relatively small amounts of iron and magnesium minerals.

Igneous Rocks
Rocks which originate as a molten melt (magma).

Ignimbrites
Fine-grained deposits of incandescent or molten debris particles from volcanic eruptions, commonly known as pyroclastic flows.

Intrusive Rock
Bodies of rock emplaced in a molten state into fractures and fissures in the Earth's crust.

Isostasy – Crustal Buoyancy
Uplift of the Earth's crust after ice cover removal or erosion of rock. The uplift is caused by buoyancy response as 'load' on the ductile mantle beneath is reduced.

Magma
The general term for molten rock as it moves thorough the Earth's crust.

Mantle
The hot, ductile layer related in composition to basalt from 30 to 100 kilometres below surface, on which the Earth's outer crust 'floats'.

Metamorphism
The transformation of mineral chemistry, crystal structure and growth of new minerals by a combination of heat and pressure during burial deep within the earth. Metamorphic minerals are common in orogenic belts.

Moraine
This is glacial rock debris that was deposited by a glacier to form piles or ridges across the landscape. This was moved in front of the glaciers' 'snout', along its flanks or it formed from debris within the ice.

Orogeny
The process creating deformation and mountain building which occurs when tectonic plates collide.

Pipe
A tubular structure, intruded by igneous rock.

Porphyry
An igneous rock with large crystals in a fine-grained matrix, commonly forming small intrusions.

Pumice
Volcanic fragments which have expanded by loss of gas during eruption to create expanded fragments which float on water.

Pyroclastic Breccia
Volcanic deposits comprising angular debris blocks ejected from the vent by explosive volcanism.

Rhyolite
A volcanic rock corresponding in mineral and chemical composition to granite. Rhyolite is formed when granite magma is erupted at the surface of the earth.

Sill
A horizontal or gently-inclined sheet of igneous rock intruded between stratigraphical layers.

Slickensides
Scratches and scoring on the face of a fault, caused by the grinding motion of movement between the walls of the fault. The orientation of the scratches gives indications of the direction of the most recent movements on the fault.

Subduction
Destruction of a tectonic plate by being forced down into the Earth's mantle during plate collision.

Syncline
A trough-shaped fold. Its complement is an anticline or ridge-shaped fold.

Tectonism
General term for the processes of deformation which occur in the Earth's crust.

Tuff
A rock formed by consolidation of volcanic ash.

Volcanoclastic sediment
Volcanic products (e.g.lavas and ashes) 're-worked' by water erosion, transported in rivers and re-deposited in pools and lakes as 'sedimentary' layers.

Geological Cross Section A-A

(Plate I) Geological cross-sections taken through Scafell. Geological Section A-A: Orientation NNW-SSE. Geological Section B-B: Orientation NE-SW. Key to rock units shown in Sections A and B and Fault name initials.

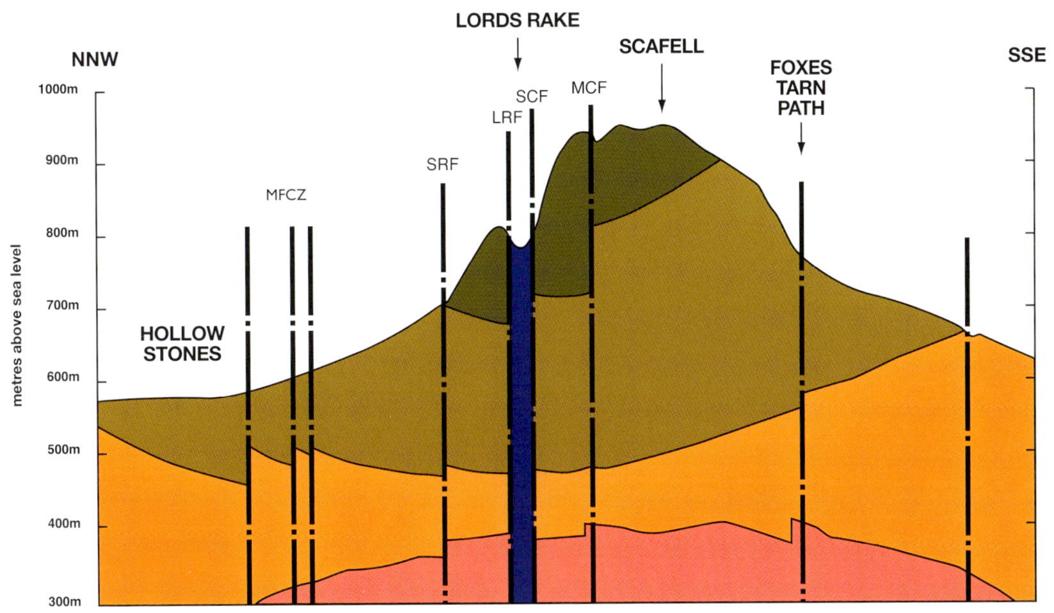

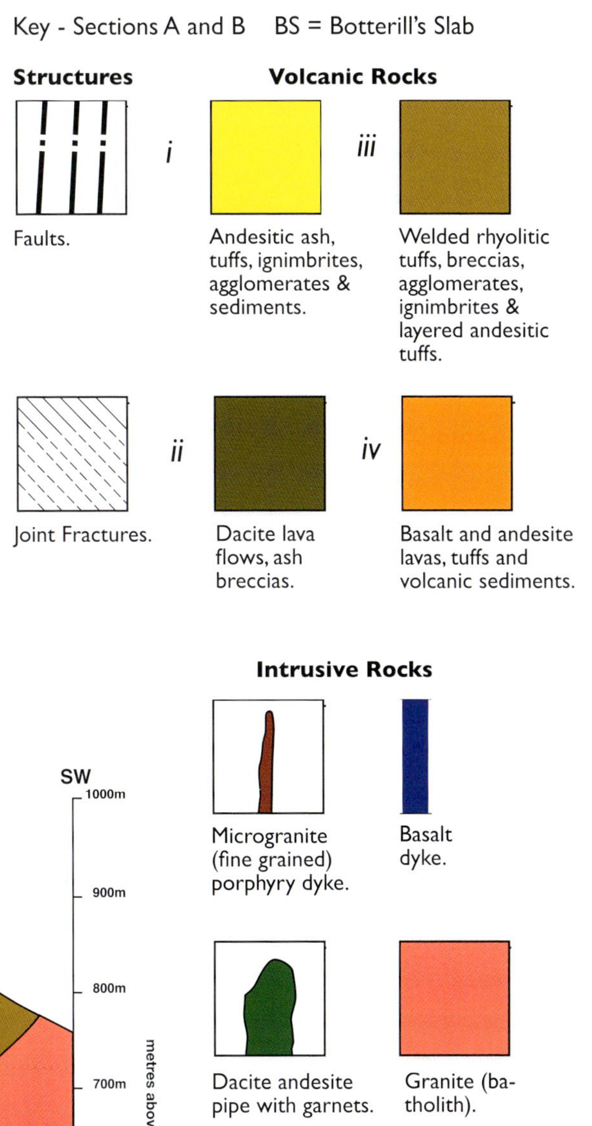

Geological Cross Section B-B

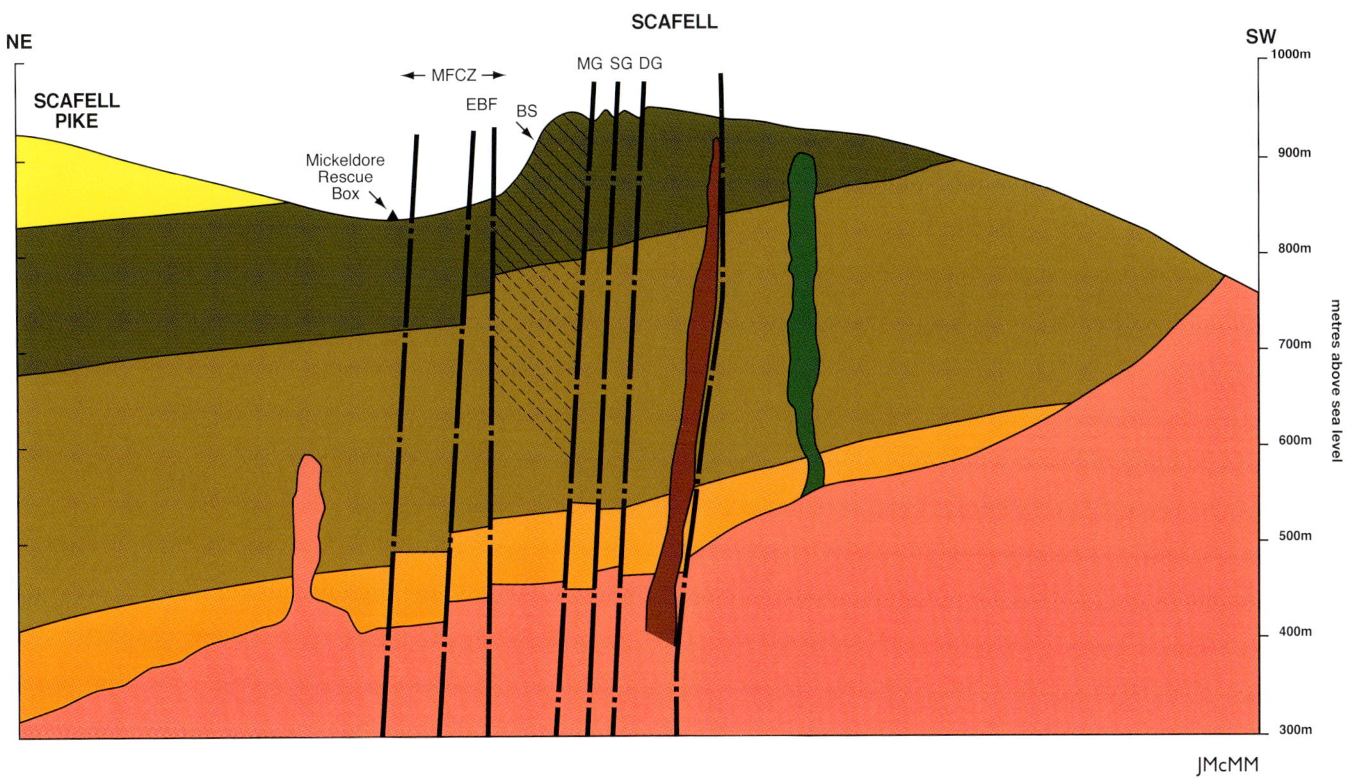

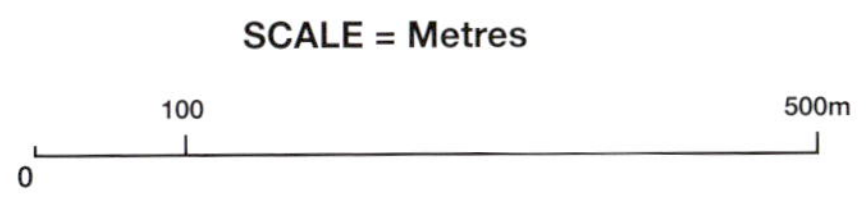

The layered sequence of volcanic units is shown in Plate I: Sections A-A and B-B.

Top: Scafell Pike summit

i Volcanoclastic sedimentary rocks, fine andesitic tuffs, welded tuffs, and ignimbrites (between Mickledore and the summit of Scafell Pike).

ii Scafell dacite lava (Scafell Crag and Pikes Crag).

iii Andesitic and rhyolitic tuffs, breccias and ignimbrites (upper Lingmell Gill).

iv Basalt and andesite lavas, with andesitic intrusive sills, inter-layered with volcanoclastic sedimentary layers (lower Lingmell Gill).

Base: Wasdale National Trust Campsite.

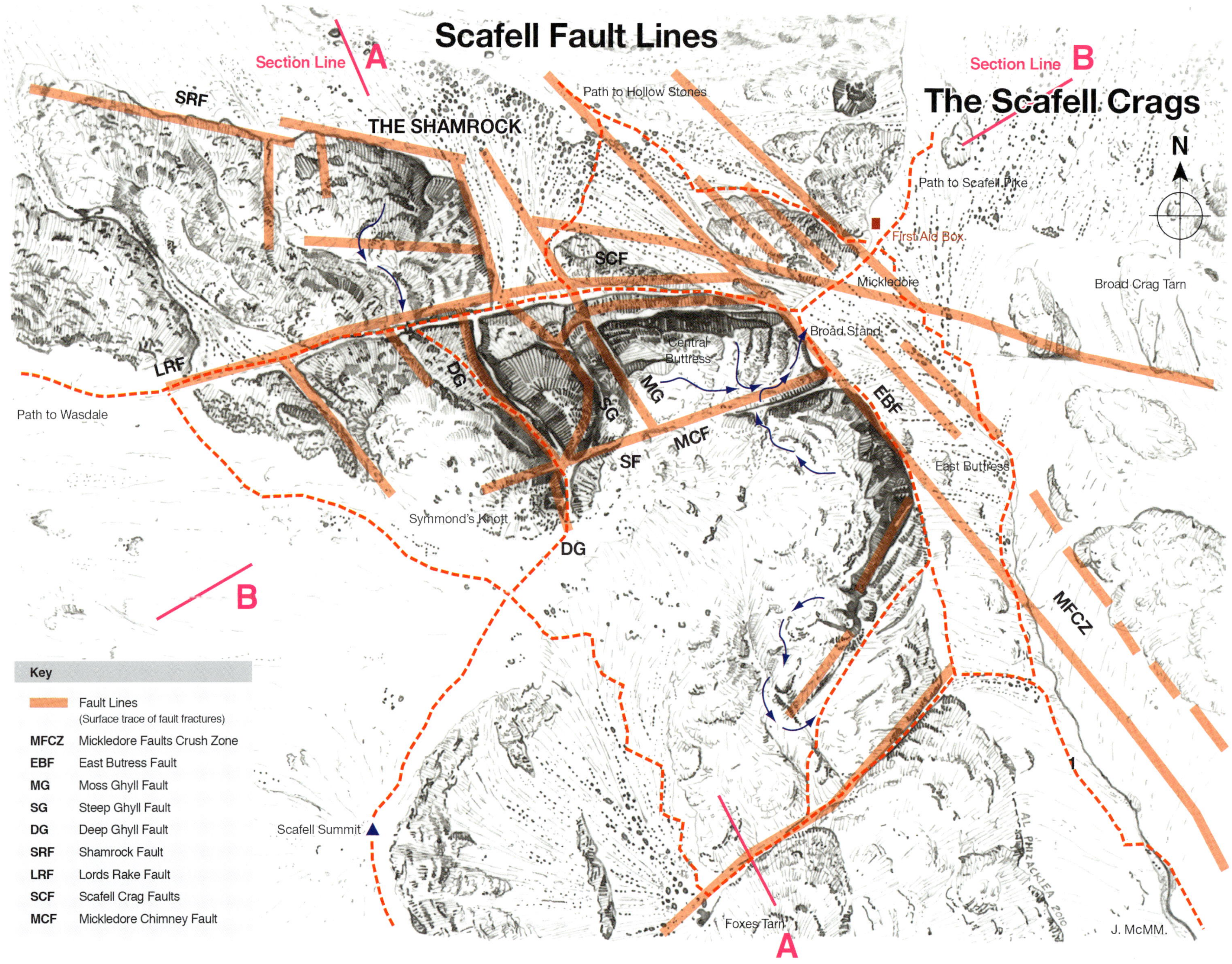

(Plate 2) Map showing a selection of fault lines in Scafell summit area. The upper parts of Scafell are traversed by numerous faults, many of which correspond to topographical features including gullies and chimneys.

Some Notes on Sites of Geological Interest for the Climber.

Broad Stand (NY210 068)
The Scafell Dacite lava which forms Broad Stand is cut by joint fractures. Access from Mickledore is by squeezing through a fissure which has opened behind a joint-bounded block. The awkward crux moves on Broad Stand, which give access to Scafell's upper slopes, involve climbing a joint-bounded block.

Moss Gill, Steep Gill, Deep Gill, Professor's Chimney & Jordan Gap (NY207 067)
These gullies and chimneys have been excavated by erosion along faults. There is crushed and granulated rock powder and gouge in the innermost recesses of the gullies. In Deep Gill, the friable scramble from the West Wall Traverse to the summit plateau, is made up of crushed rock and granulated fault gouge. Slickenside scratches on the walls of the faults, can be seen in Steep Gill. Erosion along the line of the Steep Gill Fault has created Professor's Chimney and the Jordan Gap which separates Pisgah from Scafell Pinnacle.

Pinnacle Face. (NY207 068)
The face is parallel to the Scafell Crag Faults which run along the base of the crag and the Pinnacle Terrace. One strand meets Lord's Rake Fault at the base of Lord's Rake Gully. The Scafell Crag climbs on dacite lava, use joint cracks and fissures.

Central Buttress and the Great Flake (NY208 068)
The face of Central Buttress corresponds approximately, to the plane of one of the Scafell Crag Faults. The Great Flake is a joint-bounded block, almost detached from the main face and kept in place by its weight and friction. The notorious Great Flake chock stone which fell with fatal consequences some years ago had been jammed in the fissure.

Lord's Rake (NY206 068)
Lord's Rake is a deep and unstable gully which contains a basalt dyke, intruded into a fault. The Scafell Crag and Lord's Rake Faults meet in the gully at the base of Pinnacle Face.

Botterill's Slab and Moss Ghyll Grooves (NY208 068)
The steep slabs which form Botterill's Slab and the slab pitches of Moss Ghyll Grooves are members of a group of well-defined, inclined, joint fractures in the fault-bounded block between Moss Gill and East Buttress Faults.

The East Buttress and Mickledore Chimney (NY211 067)
The face of The East Buttress is defined by the East Buttress Fault which runs along the base of the crag. The fault is one of the boundary faults of the Mickledore Fault Crush Zone. The crushed rocks in the valley between The East Buttress and the slopes of Scafell Pike have been removed by glacial and fluvial erosion, leaving a fault face isolated as The East Buttress. Fluorite and other minerals have been found in veins within this fault zone. Mickledore Chimney is a fault line which runs from The East Buttress across the summit plateau to Professor's Chimney and Great Chimney in the flank of Symmond's Knott.

Mickledore (NY210 069)
Mickledore is an arête linking Broad Stand to Scafell Pike. It was created as the headwalls of Hollow Stones Corrie ice and the glacier which flowed north into Upper Eskdale cut back to meet each other forming a sharp ridge. Mineralized thermal waters have introduced quartz and haematite iron minerals into veins along some of the faults. Weathering of the iron minerals has created widespread iron staining.

Scafell Pike Plateau (NY212 072)
Welded rhyolitic tuffs, ignimbrites and volcaniclastic sedimentary rocks crop out and occur as boulders on the routes from Mickledore to Scafell Pike summit. Palaeolithic stone implements made from fine-grained, compact welded tuff can be found in this area.

Hollow Stones (NY202 073)
Part of Lingmell Gill's catchment area is Hollow Stones, a typical glacial corrie. Near the lip of the corrie is the remarkable 'Woolworth Boulder' which may be an erratic transported on the ice surface before being deposited as the ice melted or a massive boulder which slid from the crags above.

Lingmell Gill (NY187 072)
Below Hollow Stones, Lingmell Beck enters a 'V'-shaped valley cut by melt water and enlarged by the stream since glacial times. Incision (down-cutting) and meandering of the steam destabilises its steep banks and numerous small landslips can be seen on the slopes of Lingmell Scars.

Lingmell Gill Footbridge (NY 187 073)
Upstream from Lingmell Gill footbridge the beck is crossed by a dyke of granitic porphyry more than 100m thick, containing large crystals of feldspar. A vertical contact with volcanic rocks can be seen in the bed of gill a few hundred metres upstream from the bridge. Boulders of basalt and andesite lavas and pebbles of the inter-layered beds of volcaniclastic sandstone and breccia can be found in stream debris near the footbridge. Basalt boulders (the darkest-colour rock of the area) are distinctive.

Hardrigg Gill (NY194 054)
Eskdale Granite can be seen in a series of waterfalls in Hardrigg Gill on the southwest flanks of Scafell between Burnmoor Tarn and Broad Tongue. Borrowdale Volcanic Group strata overlie the granite. This is the roof of the intrusion. The volcanic rocks have been 'baked' a hard, flinty consistency by the heat of the underlying granite.

The moraine deposits of Hollow Stones and debris covered lower slopes of Scafell.

Crag Diagrams

Scafell Main Crag Overview

I Waiting Wall. HVS (2013)

Major Features

V The 'V' Ledge

F The Great Flake

O The Oval

HM High Man

LM Low Man

HC Hopkinson's Cairn

Left of Botterill's

1. North Climb. VD. (1869)
2. Seasonal Adjustment Disorder. HVS. (2010)
3. The Hanging Chimney. E2. (1963)
4. Collier's Climb Left-Hand. VS. (2010)

4v. The New and Superior Finish. VS. (2015)

5. Collier's Climb. VS. (1893)
6. The Keswick Brothers' Climb. VD. (1897)
7. Botterill's Corner. MS. (1903)
8. Tricouni Slab. (not illustrated)
9. Burning Bridges (hidden). E5. (1979)
10. Mephisto. E4. (1983)
11. Black Rider. E5. (2013)
12. Subaudition. E3. (1979)
13. Shadowfax. E4. (1976)
14. Botterill's Slab. VS. (1903)

Central Buttress

13. Shadowfax. E4. (1976)
14. Botterill's Slab. VS (1903)
15. The White Wizard. E3. (1971)
16. White Wizard Variation. E3. (1973)
17. Ringwraith. E6. (1977)
18. The Nazgul. E3. (1966)
19. Original Sin. E6. (1990)
20. Foxshooter. E4. (1977/1990)
21. Central Buttress. E1. (1939/1914/1990/1934)
22. Central Buttress New Start. VS. (1921)
23. Central Buttress Great Flake. E3. (1914)
24. Central Buttress Link Pitch. E1. (1990)
25. Central Buttress Pitch 3 Direct Link. HVS. (1957)
26. Central Buttress The Original Finish. VS. (1914)
27. Central Buttress The Bayonet-Shaped Crack. HVS. (1932)
28. Judas Priest. E5. (1983)
29. Judas Priest, The Rob Halford Finish. E6. (2003)
30. Saxon. E2. (1976)
33. Moss Gill Grooves. MVS. (1926)
40. Central Buttress Girdle. E1. (1971)
41. Ring of Air. E2. (1983)
42. Moss Gill. S. (1892)
46. Collier's Chimney. S. (1892)
48. Clockwork Orange. HVS. (1973)

Moss Gill area

30. Saxon. E2. (1976)
31. Saxon - Main Pitch Direct. E4. (1976)
32. Anglo. E1. (1995)
33. Moss Gill Grooves. MVS. (1926)
34. M.G.G.Variation Start. MVS. (1946)
35. Long Stand. VS (1968)
36. Last Stand. E1. (1971)
37. Narrow Stand. HVS. (1959)
37a. Tradesman's Entrance. HVS. (1961)
38. Slab and Groove Route. VS. (1948)
39. Harvest. E2. (1976)
40. Central Buttress Girdle. E1. (1971)
41. Ring of Air. E2. (1983)
42. Moss Gill. S. (1892)
43. The Collie Exit. D. (1892)
44. Chant's Exit. VD.
45. Barton's Exit (not described)
46. Collier's Chimney. S. (1892)
47. Botterill's Exit (hidden, not shown)
48. Clockwork Orange. HVS. (1973)

Pisgah Buttress

1. The Gripe. HVS. (1971)
2. Pisgah Buttress Direct. S. (1898/1911)
3. Pisgah Buttress Original Start (1898)
4. Moses Trod. S. (1963)
5. Hilarity. HVS. (1976)
6. Variation, Sacrificial Squaddies. E2. (1993)
7. Bos'n's Buttress. VS. (1959)
8. Pisgah Ya Bas. HVS. (1971)
9. Steep Gill Grooves. VS. (1945)

Scafell Pinnacle, left-hand side

1. Slingsby's Chimney Route. VD. (1888)
2. The Waiting Room from Steep Gill. MVS. (1919)
3. The Pinnacle Face from Steep Gill. VS. (1919)
4. Leftovers. VS. (1972)
5. The Left Edge. VS. (1960)
6. Bushwhacker. E2. (1984)
7. Hopkinson's Gully. MVS. (1912)
8. Low Man by the Jubilee Line. HVS. (2012)
9. Jones' Route Direct from Lord's Rake. S. (1898)
10. Direct from Lord's Rake to Hopkinson's Cairn. S. (1912)
11. Moss Ledge Direct and Jones' Arête. VS. (1925/1919/1896)
12. Zenith. VS. (1996)
13. Right-Hand Edge and Pinnacle Face Direct. HVS. (1960)
14. Meridian. E1. (1993)
15. Low Man from Hopkinson's Cairn. VD. (1887)

W The Waiting Room
H Herford's Slab
M Moss Ledge

Scafell Pinnacle, Right-Hand side

9. Jones' Route Direct from Lord's Rake. S. (1898)
10. Direct from Lord's Rake to Hopkinson's Cairn. S. (1912)
11. Moss Ledge Direct and Jones' Arête. VS. (1925/1919/1896)
12. Zenith. VS. (1996)
13. Right-Hand Edge and Pinnacle Face Direct. HVS. (1960)
14. Meridian. E1. (1993)
15. Low Man from Hopkinson's Cairn. VD. (1887)
16. Edge Hog. E1. (1973)
17. Caledonian Orogeny. E2. (2004)
18. Jones' Route from Deep Gill. S. (1893/1896)

M Moss Ledge
H Herford's Slab

Scafell Pinnacle, Deep Gill Slabs

19. The Slab Climb. VS. (1962)
20. Bold Eagle. HVS. (1987)
21. Central Route, Deep Gill Slabs. HS. (1920)
22. Jones and Collier's Finish. MS. (1898)
23. High Man by the Central Line. HVS. (2013)
24. Woodhead's Climb. MS. (1907/1913)
24v. de Selincourt's Finish. MVS. (1924-1926)
25. Thompson's Route. VD. (1900)

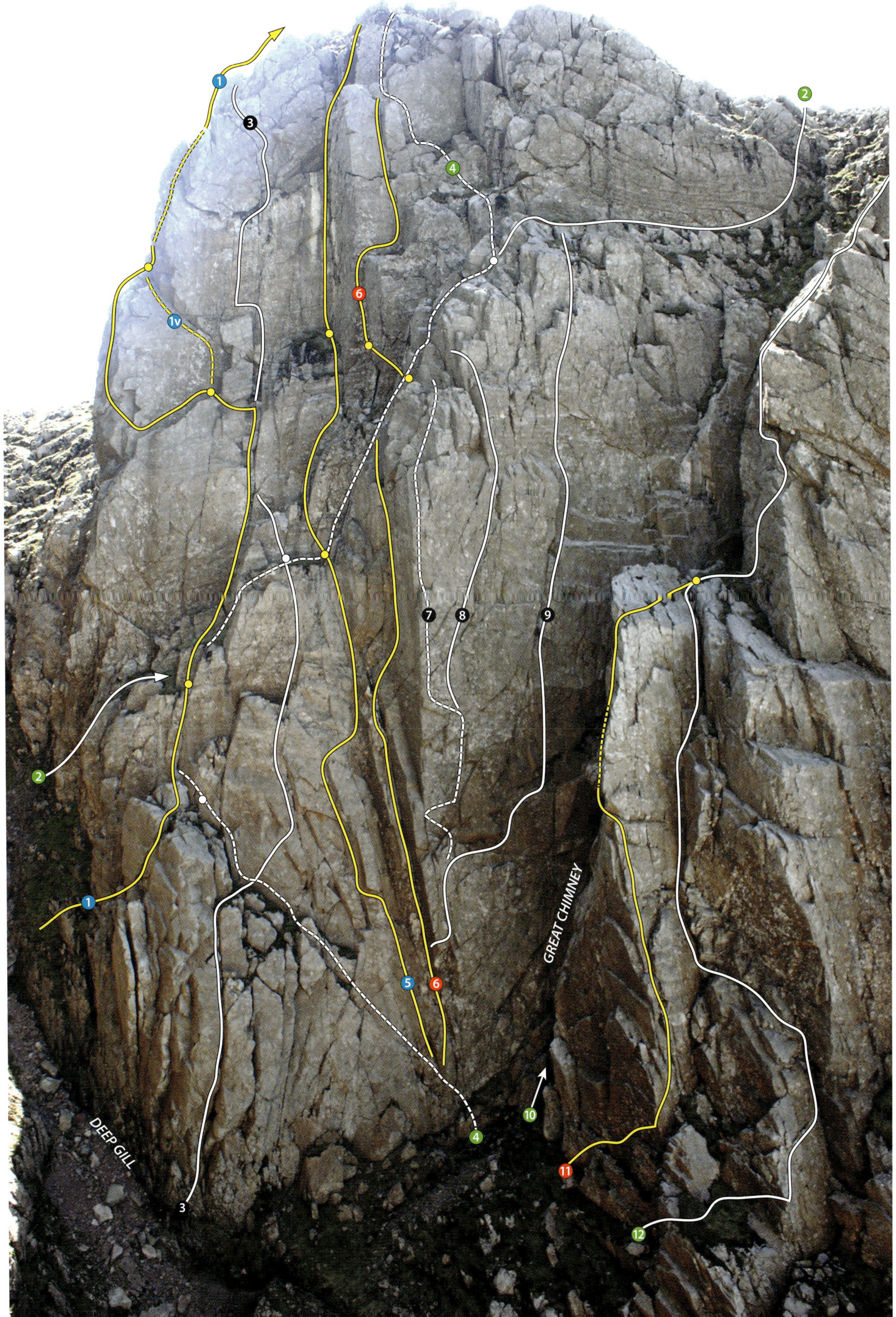

Upper Deep Gill Buttress

1. Upper Deep Gill Buttress. MVS. (1920)
1A Upper Deep Gill Buttress Original pitch 3. VS. (1920)
2. Deep Gill Buttress Original Route. D. (1893)
3. The Scarlet Pimpernel. E4. (1991)
4. Upper West Wall Climb. S. (1911)
5. The Unforgettable Fire. HVS. (1991)
6. Ixodes. E1. (1989)
7. Death Arête. E8. (2003)
8. Def Arête. E7. (1995)
9. Alamogordo. E5. (1989)
10. The Great Chimney. VD. (1895)
11. Swillshark. E2. (1987)
12. Jacob's Ladder. HS. (1936)
13. West Wall Climb (off picture to the right)

Lower Deep Gill Buttress

14. Doctor Death. E1. (1989)
15. Grey Bastion. VS. (1936)
16. Insomnia. E1. (1995)
17. Morpheus. E1. (1995)
18. Sleeping Crack. VS. (1968)
19. Gobsite. VS. (1968)
20. Inamorata Route (not illustrated)
21. Swan Song. E2. (1991)
22. Xerxes. HVS. (1959)

Red Gill area

1. Castor. M. (1925)
2. Pollux. VD. (1925)
3. Moby Dick (not illustrated)
4. Red Gill Edge. S. (2013)
5. Red Gill Wall. S. (1941)
6. Red Gill Corner. S. (2013)
7. Red Gill Rib. HVS. (2015)
8. Red Gill Buttress. HVD. (1922)
9. The Bannister. D. (1925)

The Shamrock

1. Shamrock Eliminate. E3. (1978/1977)
2. Gilt Edge Eliminate. E1. (1969)
3. Silver Lining. VS. (1966)
4. The Tower Buttress. HS. (1925)
5. Shamrock Buttress. VS. (1963)
6. The Rampart. HS. (1938)
7. The Barrow Brothers' Climb. VS. (2015)

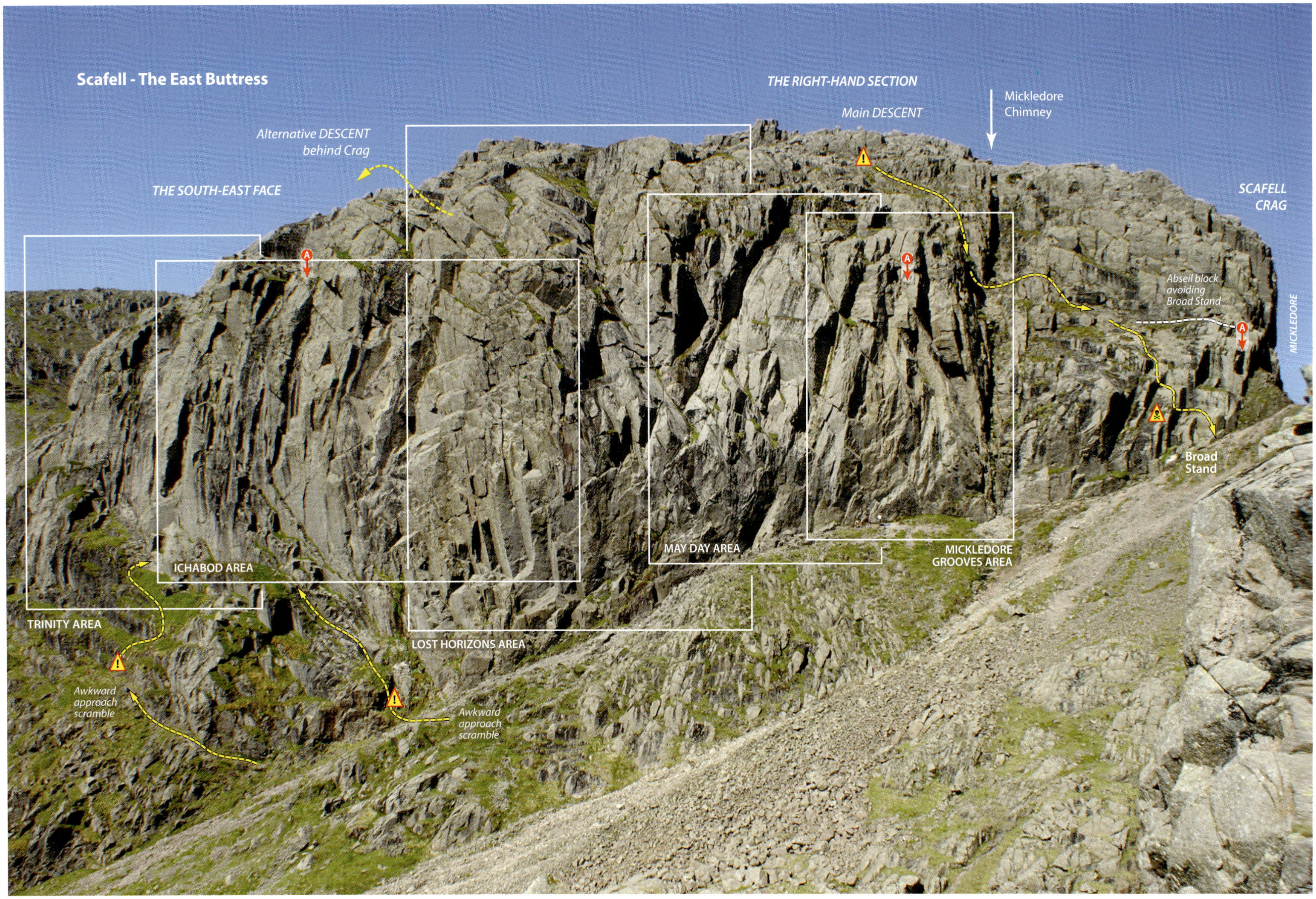
Scafell - The East Buttress
THE RIGHT-HAND SECTION
Main DESCENT
Mickledore Chimney
Alternative DESCENT behind Crag
THE SOUTH-EAST FACE
SCAFELL CRAG
Abseil block avoiding Broad Stand
MICKLEDORE
Broad Stand
MAY DAY AREA
MICKLEDORE GROOVES AREA
ICHABOD AREA
TRINITY AREA
LOST HORIZONS AREA
Awkward approach scramble
Awkward approach scramble

Mickledore Grooves area

1. Absinthe. MVS. (1963)
2. Tio Pepe. VS. (1957)
3. Tia Maria. VS. (1954)
4. Pernod. VS. (1959)
4a. Pernod Direct Finish. HVS. (1971)
5. Strider. E1. (1958)
6. Chartreuse. E1. (1958)
7. Midnight Express. E3. (1979)
8. Aquavit. E4. (1983)
9. Mickledore Arête. E1. (1984)
10. The Fulcrum. VS. (1968)
11. Fulcrum Direct. E1. (1979)
12. Leverage. E1. (1958)
13. Mickledore Grooves. VS. (1930)
14. Barry's Slab Start. HVS. (1936)
15. The Ambleside Brothers' Climb. E5 (1990)
16. Juno. E4. (1991)
17. Dyad. E3. (1968)
19. Edge of Eriador. E4. (1977)
24. May Day Direct. E2. (1959)
87. The Lord of the Rings. E2. (1969)

May Day area

17. Dyad. E3. (1968)
18. Entonox. E7. (1995)
19. Edge of Eriador. E4. (1977)
20. Edge of Eriador - Direct Start. E5. (1984)
21. Rise of Angmar. E3. (2013)
22. S.O.S. E5. (1978)
23. May Day Climb. E1. (1938)
24. May Day Direct. E2. (1959)
25. When the Fat Lady Sings. E2. (1995)
26. Overhanging Wall. HVS. (1933)
27. The Original Finish. VS. (1933)
28. Minotaur. E1. (1968)
29. Moonday, with Doomwatch Finish. E2. (1959/1971)
30. Armageddon. E2. (1960)
31. Shikasta. E4. (1983)
87. The Lord of the Rings. E2. (1969)

Lost Horizons area

26. Overhanging Wall. HVS. (1933)
27. The Original Finish. VS. (1933)
28. Minotaur. E1. (1968)
29. Moonday, with Doomwatch Finish. E2. (1959/1971)
30. Armageddon. E2. (1960)
31. Shikasta. E4. (1983)
32. Back to Black. E7. (2013)
33. The Siege Perilous. E7. (1989)
34. Zeya. E5. (1983)
35. Shere Khan. E5. (1977)
36. Cullinan. E5. (1978)
37. Talbot Horizon. E9. (2000)
38. Lost Horizons. E4. (1976)
39. Lost Horizons Direct. E5. (1998)
40. New Horizons. E8. (1998)
41. Equinox. E4. (1978)
42. The Centaur. HVS. (1960)
42a. Centaur Direct. E1. (unknown)
43. Great Eastern Route. VS. (1932)
45. Chiron. E3. (1990)
87. The Lord of the Rings. E2. (1969)

Ichabod area

38. Lost Horizons. E4. (1976)
40. New Horizons. E8. (1998)
41. Equinox. E4. (1978)
42. The Centaur. HVS. (1960)
43. Great Eastern. VS. (1932)
44. The Yellow Slab. HVS. (1933)
45. Chiron. E3. (1990)
46. Cerberus. E3. (1990)
47. Gold Rush. E1. (1969)
48. Caradhras. E5. (1978)
49. Overhanging Grooves Direct. E3. (1975)
50. Overhanging Grooves, Original Finish. HVS. (1963)
51. Forbidden Colours. E4. (1979)
52. The Return of the King. E9. (2006)
53. Welcome to the Cruel World. E9. (2002)
54. Another Lonely Day. E8. (2002)
55. Borderline. E7. (1986)
56. Roaring Silence. E3. (1979)
57. Ichabod. E2. (1960)
58. Mythical Kings. E4. (1979)
59. Barad Dur. E6. (2014)
60. Phoenix. E2. (1957/1967)
61. Phoenix, Original Finish. VS. (1957)
62. Phoenix, Ash Groove Finish. E3. (1984)
63. Phoenix, Arête Finish. E2. (1976)
64. Morning Wall. MVS. (1933)
65. Zeus. E3. (1974)
66. Zeus Direct Start. E4. (1982)
67. Pegasus. HVS. (1952)
68. Chimera. E1. (1969)
69. The Caution Horses. E6. (1990)
70. Lucius. E5. (1978)
71. The Almighty. E5. (1981)
72. Hell's Bell's. E4. (1981)
73. Hell's Groove. E1. (1952)
87. The Lord of the Rings. E2. (1969)

The Trinity area

64. Morning Wall. MVS. (1933)
67. Pegasus. HVS. (1952)
68. Chimera. E1. (1969)
70. Lucius. E5. (1978)
71. The Almighty. E5. (1981)
72. Hell's Bell's. E4. (1981)
73. Hell's Groove. E1. (1952)
74. Bat out of Hell. E2. (1995)
75. Incubus. E5. (1972)
76. Thy Will be Done. E8. (2013)
77. Trinity. HVS. (1955)
78. Talisman. E2. (1978)
79. The Holy Ghost. E2. (1965)
80. The Gremlin's Groove. VS. (1945)
81. Variation Start. VS. (1963)
82. Slime Chimney. VD. (1925)
83. South Chimney. HVS. (1945)
84. Eastern Front. E1. (1991)
85. Smeaghaidh. VS. (1994)
87. The Lord of the Rings. E2. (1969)

Central Buttress, winter

1. North Climb. III. (1899)
2. Collier's Left-Hand Variant. VI. (2010)
3. Botterill's Corner. IV. (1986)
3v. Collier's Groove. V. (2010)
4. Keswick Brother's Climb. IV. (1986)
5. Botterill's Slab. V. (1984)
6. Central Buttress (Disputed). (1986)
7. Moss Gill Grooves. VII. (1985)
8. Harvest Crunch. VII. (1987)
9. Moss Gill, Collie Exit. IV. (1893)
9v. Variation Start. III. (Unknown)
10. Barton's Exit. V. (Unknown)
11. Mechanical Orange. VIII. (1987)
12. Collier's Chimney. V. (1984)

Pisgah and Pinnacle, winter

1. Moss Gill. IV. (1893)
2. Collier's Chimney. V. (1984)
3. Pisgah Buttress Direct. V. (1937)
4. Restless Natives. VI. (1986)
5. Bridge of Sighs. V. (1986)
6. Steep Gill Grooves. V. (1986)
7. Steep Gill Direct Start. V. (1963)
8. Steep Gill. V. (1891)
9. Slingsby's Chimney Route. IV. (1899)
10. Low Man by the Right Wall of Steep Gill. V. (1995)
11. Hopkinson's Gully. VI. (1986)
12. Moonbathing. VI. (1986)
13. Jones' Route Direct from Lord's Rake. VII. (1984)

The following routes are on Deep Gill Buttress

3. Into the Wild. VII. (2010)
4. Great Chimney. IV. (1986)
5. Jacob's Ladder. V. (1999)
6. West Wall Climb. IV. (1986)
7. Doctor Grey. VII. (2010)

Deep Gill Buttress, winter

1. Upper Deep Gill Route. II. (1986)
2. Upper West Wall Climb. VI. (2010)
3. Into the Wild. VII. (2010)
4. Great Chimney. IV. (1986)
5. Jacob's Ladder. V. (1999)
6. West Wall Climb. VI. (1986)
7. Doctor Grey. VII. (2010)
8. Great Western. IV. (1995)
9. Xerxes. VIII. (2008)
10. Sod's Law. VI. (1984)
11. Sodom. V. (1990)
12. Sod All. III. (1986)
13. Eye Spy. V. (1997)
14. Dharma Armour. III. (1997)
15. Chimney Stack. IV. (1997)
16. Deep Gill Integrale. III. (1990)
17. Castor. III. (1990)

The Shamrock, winter

1. Red Gill. II. (Unknown)
2. Cascade Direct Route. III. (1969)
3. Cascade. III. (1963)
4. Pillar Variation. IV. (1972-1974)
5. Easy Gully. I. (Unknown)

5v. Variation. II. (Unknown)

6. Twisting Gully. IV. (1996)
7. The Tower Buttress. VI. (2010)
8. Shamrock Icefall. VII. (2010)

The East Buttress, winter

1. Mickledore Chimney. III. (1891)
2. Direct Finish. IV. (1963)
3. Tia Maria. V. (1996)
4. S.O.S. IX. (2007)
5. May Day Direct. VI. (1984)
6. Overhanging Wall. V (some aid). (1985)
7. Overhanging Wall Original Finish. V. (1994)
8. Minotaur. IV. (1984)
9. White Slab. III. (1984)
10. Moondance. VII. (2010)
11. Great Eastern Route. V. (1960)
12. Rush East Start. V. (1999)
13. Never Ever Say Never. VIII. (2010)

Scafell Crag at dawn as viewed from Pikes Crag.

A list of first ascents

(1802 – 2015)

For the first time, all routes on Scafell Crag, The Shamrock and The East Buttress are brought together in a list in chronological order combining both winter and summer first ascents, details of variations, and free ascents.

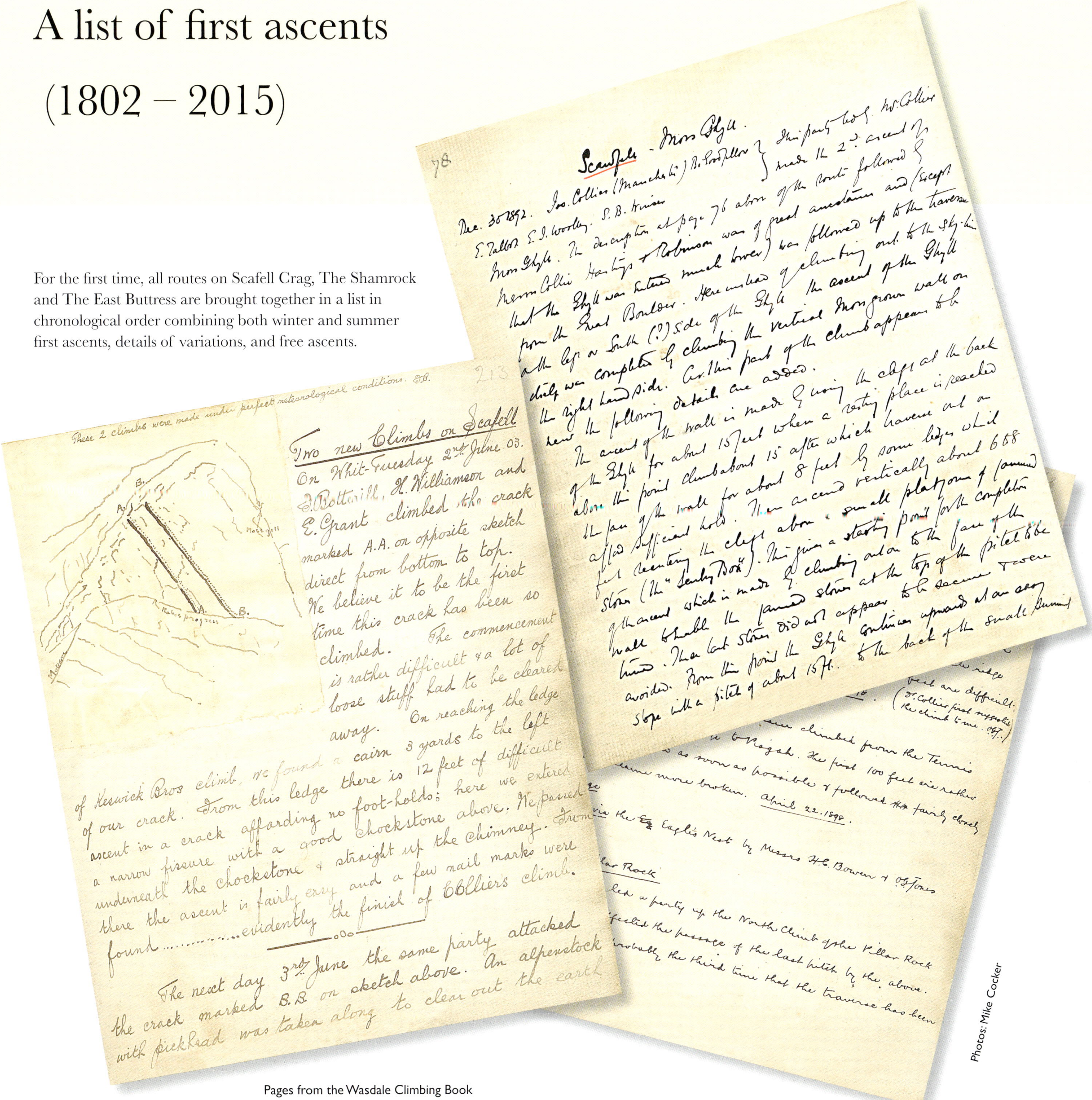

Photos: Mike Cocker

Pages from the Wasdale Climbing Book

Scafell Crags: A list of first ascents

Note – (W) indicates the first winter ascent.

1802 5 Aug — Broad Stand (descent) S.T. Coleridge (solo)

Early 1800's — Broad Stand Unknown, possibly T. Tyson, J.V. Towers

1859 19 Apr (W) — Broad Stand J. Tyndall and ANO

1869 — Mickledore Chimney C.W. Dymond

1869 — North (Penrith) Climb Major J. P. Cundill (solo)

1882 Jan / Feb (W) — Deep Gill C. Pilkington, L. Pilkington, E. Hulton

1884 Aug / Sept — Deep Gill W.P. Haskett Smith, C. Cookson

1884 3 Sept — Scafell Pinnacle (From Jordan Gap) W.P. Haskett Smith (solo)

1884 24 Sept — Steep Gill, Low Man-High Man W.P. Haskett Smith, J.W. Robinson

1887 17Aug — Professor's Chimney J.W. Robinson, H.R. Proctor, W.S. Corder

1887 Sept — Low Man from Hopkinson's Cairn E. Hopkinson, C. Hopkinson, A. Hopkinson, W.N. Tribe

1888 15 May — Steep Gill H. Wooley (solo)

1888 15 July — Slingsby's Chimney Route W.C. Slingsby, G. Hastings, E. Hopkinson, W.P. Haskett Smith

1891 3 April (W) — Old Professor's Chimney A.M. Marshall, H.B. Dixon, W.I. Beaumont, A.G. (Gwynne?)

1891 19 Apr (W) — Mickledore Chimney O.G. Jones, W.E. Sumpner, C.G. Munro

1891 21 Apr (W) — New Professor's Chimney O.G. Jones, W.E. Sumpner, C.G. Munro

1891 25 Dec (W) — Steep Gill J.N. Collie, W.L.W. Brodie, E.W. Marshall

1892 26 Dec — Moss Gill, (Collies Exit) J.N. Collie, G. Hastings, J.W. Robinson

1892 30 Dec — Moss Gill, (Collier's Chimney) J. Collier and party

1893 9 Jan (W) — Moss Gill O.G. Jones (solo)

1893 2 April — Hopkinson's and Tribe's Route C. Hopkinson, W.N. Tribe

1893 2 April — Collier's Climb J. Collier, S.B. Winster

1893 12 Sept — Mickledore Chimney Direct W.H. Fowler

1893 1 April — Deep Gill Buttress Original Route J. N. Collie, G. Hastings, J.W. Robinson

1894 9 May — Crowley's Route E. A. Crowley (solo)

1894 April — Parson's Gully Revd. T.C.V. Barstow

1895 23 Sept — Great Chimney V. Blake, A.W. Southall

1896 20 April — Jones' Route from Deep Gill O.G. Jones, A.P. Abraham, G.D. Abraham

1897 12 July — Keswick Brothers' Climb G.D. Abraham, A.P. Abraham, J.W. Puttrell

1898 19 April — Jones' Route Direct from Lord's Rake O.G. Jones, G.T. Walker

1898 22 April — Jones and Colliers Climb O.G. Jones

1898 22 April — Pisgah Buttress O.G. Jones, G.D. Abraham A.P. Abraham

1898 5 Sept — Moss Gill (Barton's Exit) C.W. Barton and party

1898 10 Sept — West Wall Climb J.W. Robinson, T.H. Doncaster, W.H. Blunt

1899 8 Apr (W) — North Climb C.W. Barton, G. Barton, F. Cowley, F. Davey

1899 11 Apr (W) — Slingsby's Chimney Route C.W. Barton, G. Barton, F. Cowley, F. Davey

1900 1 June — Thompson's Route P.S. Thompson, P.A. Thompson

1903 2 June — Botterill's Corner F.W. Botterill, W. Williamson, J.E. Grant

1903 3 June — Botterill's Slab F.W. Botterill, W. Williamson, J.E. Grant

1903 3 Sept The accident on Scafell Pinnacle

1903 The Wright Brothers achieve the world's first powered flight

1907 24 Aug — Woodhead's Climb A.G. Woodhead, W.L. Collinson

1907 Dec (W) — Botterill's Slab G. Winthrop Young, H.V. Reade

1909 10 June — Moss Gill (Botterill's Exit) F.W. Botterill and party

1910 Easter (W) — Keswick Brothers' Climb (incomplete) T.C. Ormiston-Chant, E. Scantlebury

1911 6 July — Pisgah Buttress Direct S.W. Herford, F.M.J. McConechy

1911 Sept — Upper West Wall Climb J. Laycock, H.B. Gibson, S.W. Herford

1912 RMS Titanic sinks on its maiden voyage

1912 17 April — Direct from Lord's Rake to Hopkinson's Cairn S.W. Herford, G.S. Sansom

1912 19 June — Hopkinson's Gully S.W. Herford, G. S. Sansom

1912 14 Sept — Scafell Girdle S.W. Herford, G.S. Sansom, W.B. Brunskill, H.B. Gibson

1913 10 July — Woodhead's Climb pitch 2 S.W. Herford, S.F. Jeffcoat

1914 20 April — Central Buttress S.W. Herford, G.S. Sansom, C.F. Holland

1914 – 1918 First World War

1919 7 July — The Bad Corner H.M. Kelly, G.S. Bower, E. Kelly, R.E.W. Pritchard

1919 28 July — Right Wall of Steep Gill C.F. Holland, H.M. Kelly, C.G. Crawford

1919 30 July — Waiting Room from Steep Gill C.G. Crawford, H.M. Kelly, C.F. Holland

1919 30 July — Jones' Arête from Hopkinson's Cairn C.G. Crawford, H.M. Kelly, C.F. Holland

1919 5 Aug — Pinnace Face from Steep Gill C.G. Crawford, C.F. Holland

1920 23 May — Upper Deep Gill Buttress H.M. Kelly, R.E.W. Pritchard, G.S. Bower

1920 29 Aug — Central Route, Deep Gill Slabs H.M. Kelly, R.E.W. Pritchard, G.S. Bower

1921 20 Aug — Central Buttress New Start C. Frankland, B. Beetham

1922 10 Sept — Red Gill Buttress W. Eden-Smith, H.M. Kelly

1923 5 Aug — Central Buttress Traverse Variation, Fives Court to Botterill's Exit H.B. Lyon, T.R. Burnett, M. Barker, H.P. Cain

1924 First guidebook to Scafell

1924 Mallory and Irvine disappear on Everest

1924 - 1926 — Woodhead's Climb, de Selincourt's Finish M. de Selincourt, A.N. Other

1925 14 April — Castor H.M. Kelly, R.E.W. Pritchard

1925 14 April — Pollux H.M. Kelly, R.E.W. Pritchard

1925 5 June — Slime Chimney C.D. Frankland, B. Beetham, A.W. Wakefield, J. Wright

1925 18 June — The Bannister B. Eden-Smith, H.M. Kelly

1925 3 Sept — Intermittent Chimneys R.E.W. Pritchard, H.M. Kelly, B. Eden-Smith

1925 3 Sept — Tower Buttress H.M. Kelly, R.E.W. Pritchard, B. Eden-Smith

1925 6 Sept — Moss Ledge Direct F. Graham, G.M. Wellburn

1926 1 July — Moss Gill Grooves H.M. Kelly, B. Eden-Smith J.B. Kilshaw

1930 24 May — Mickledore Grooves C.F. Kirkus, I.M. Waller, M. Pallis

1931 Aug — Central Buttress free J.M. Edwards, W.W. Stallybrass, M. Pallis

1932 21 Aug — Great Eastern Route M. Linnell, S.H. Cross

1932 6 Oct — Bayonet Shaped Crack M. Linnell (solo)

1933 23 July — Overhanging Wall M. Linnell, A.T. Hargreaves

1933 13 Aug — Morning Wall A.T. Hargreaves, W. Clegg, M. Linnell

1933 10 Sept — The Yellow Slab M. Linnell, H.B. Pearson

1934 June — Central Buttress Direct Finish F.G. Balcombe, J. Wright, J.R. Files

1936 20 June — Jacob's Ladder A.T. Hargreaves, S.H. Cross

1936 21 June — Grey Bastion S.H. Cross, A.T. Hargreaves, R.E. Heap

1936 20 Sept — Barry's Traverse R.V.M. Barry, C.G.T. Collin

1936 Second Guidebook to Scafell

1936 First T.V. programme broadcast by the BBC

1937 (W) — Pisgah Buttress Direct A.T. Hargreaves, S.H. Cross, A.M. Nelson

1938 16 April — The Rampart S.H. Cross, H.M. Kelly, A.M. Nelson, C.J. Astley-Cooper

1938 1 May — May Day Climb R.J. Birkett, C.W. Hudson, C.R. Wilson

1938 7 Aug — East Buttress Girdle R.J. Birkett, L. Muscroft

1938 18 Sept — Tricouni Slab A. Mullan, L. Mack

1938/1939 — Overhanging Wall free R. J. Birkett, L. Muscroft

1939 26 July — Central Buttress Direct Start A. Mullan, H. Thompson

1939 – 1945 Second World War

1941 22 June Red Gill Wall A.T. Hargreaves, S.H. Cross, R.E. Hargreaves, A.M. Cross

1945 28 July Steep Gill Grooves R.J. Birkett, T. Hill

1945 29 July Gremlin's Groove R.J. Birkett, T. Hill, L. Muscroft

1945 8 Aug Morning Wall free A.R. Dolphin, A.B. Gilchrist

1945 6 Sept Overhanging Wall free D. Birch, J. Wilkinson

1945 12 Aug South Chimney R.J. Birkett, T. Hill

1946 July Moss Gill Grooves Variation Start T.G. Pierson, M.H. McFarlane

1948 28 Aug Slab and Groove Route R.J. Birkett, L. Muscroft

1950 End of petrol rationing

1952 17 May Pegasus A.R. Dolphin, P. Greenwood

1952 24 May Hell's Groove P. Greenwood, A.R. Dolphin

1953 Queen Elizabeth II coronation; the first Ascent of Everest by Ed Hillary and Sherpa Tenzing Norgay

1954 5 June Tia Maria H. Drasdo, K. Finlay

1954 J.R.R. Tolkein's The Lord of the Rings published in three volumes 1954 - 1955

1955 5 June Trinity D.D. Whillans, J. Sutherland

1955 Aug Pegasus free R. Miller, P. Moffatt

1956 Third guidebook to Scafell

1957 2 May Tio Pepe G.J. Sutton, E.D.G. Roberts

1957 9 June Central Buttress pitch 3a Direct Link R. McGregor, L. Clarke, J.P. Moody

1957 1 Aug Phoenix R. Moseley, D.M. Adcock

1958 3 May Chartreuse R. Smith, D. Lever

1958 3 May Leverage R. Smith, D. Lever

1958 Summer Strider R. Miller, ANO

1959 4 April Pernod G. Oliver, F. Carrol

1959 21 June May Day Direct G. Oliver, L. Willis

1959 Summer May Day Direct free L Brown, ANO

1959 21 Aug Bos'n's Buttress H.I. Banner, L.J. Griffin

1959 22 Aug Narrow Stand H.I. Banner, J.P . O'Neil, L.J. Griffin

1959 30 Aug Xerxes L. Brown, C.E.M. Yates

1959 13 Sept Moonday L. Brown, J. Gerrard

1960 21 April Armageddon L. Brown, G. Lund

1960 21 May The Left Edge. L.O. Kendall, D.W. English

1960 21 May Right-Hand Edge J. J.S. Allison, C. J.F. Rawbotham

1960 21 May Direct Finish, Pinnacle Face C.J.F. Rawbotham, J. J.S. Allison

1960 28 May Ichabod G. Oliver, G. Arkless, L. Willis

1960 30 June The Centaur L. Brown, S. Read

1960 12 Dec (W) Great Eastern Route L.O. Kendall, J. Douglas

1960 14 Dec (W) Mickledore Chimney Direct Finish J. J.S. Allison, L.Kendall

1961 1 Sept Tradesman's Entrance H.I. Banner, G. Dyke

1962 7 June Phoenix free D. Miller

1962 Summer The Slab Climb J. J.S. Allison, R. J. Mansfield

1963 Jan (W) Steep Gill Direct Start J. J.S. Allison, L.Kendall

1963 28 Feb (W) The Cascade, Shamrock R. Byfleet, R. Blain, C. Whalley

1963 1 June The Hanging Chimney J. J.S. Allison, R.J. Mansfield

1963 5 June Impunity Slabs D.N. Greenop, E. Ivison (not described)

1963 June Overhanging Grooves J. J.S. Allison, C.H. Mitchell, D. Moy

1963 July Moses Trod L. J. Griffin, J. Wilkinson

1963 July Absinthe L. J. Griffin, J. Wilkinson

1963 1 Aug Shamrock Buttress L.J. Griffin, J. Wilkinson

1963 2 Aug Gremlin's Groove Variation Start L. J. Griffin, J. Wilkinson

1964 16 May The Inamorata Route D.N. Greenop, J. Wilson

1964 Sept Ichabod free T. Sullivan, L. Brown

1965 April The Holy Ghost C.J.S. Bonington, M. Thompson

1966 12 June Silver Lining D.W. English, J. Wilkinson, R. Valentine, L.J. Griffin

1966 12 July The Nazgul L. Brown, K. Jackson

1967 18 June Phoenix top pitch A.G. Cram, W. Young
Led free shortly after by K. Wood

1967 Fourth guidebook to Scafell

1968 1 June Gobsite T. Martin, J. Wilson

1968 5 June Sleeping Crack G. Milburn, D. Gregory

1968 16 June The Fulcrum K. Jackson, J. Adams

1968 16 June Minotaur S. Clark, G. Oliver, H. Loughram, G. Lowes

1968 June Dyad K. Jackson, C. Read

1968 11 Aug Long Stand E.N. Cross, N.J. Soper, G. Dyke, G. Valentine

1969 30 Jan (W) Shamrock, Cascade Direct R. Bennett, R. Lavender

1969 7 June Chimera W. Young, A.G. Cram

1969 14 June Gold Rush A.G. Cram, W. Young

1969 14/15 June The Lord of The Rings J. Adams, C. Read

1969 Neil Armstrong walks on the Moon

1969 16 Aug Gilt Edge Eliminate C. Read, R. Lake
Top pitch P. Moffatt, P. Hogg, late 1940's

1969 First e-mail sent between two computers

1970 Summer Gold Rush free J. Adams, C. Read

1971 22 May Pisgah Ya Bas R. Valentine, J. Wilkinson, B.R. Fuller

1971 23 Aug Central Buttress Girdle C.J.S. Bonington, M. Thompson

1971 11 Sept The White Wizard C.J.S. Bonington, N. Estcourt

1971 12 Sept Doomwatch Finish A.D. Barley, A. Roach

1971 12 Sept The Gripe R. Valentine, J. Wilkinson, D. Pogson

1971 Sept Pernod Direct Finish P. Braithwaite, D. Little

1971 Sept Last Stand H.I. Banner, M.P. Hatton

1972 20 May Central Buttress Girdle Variation I. Roper, C.H. Taylor

1972 26 Aug s Incubus C. Read, J. Adams

1972 28 Aug Hell's Groove Direct Finish J. Adams, C. Read

1972 28 Aug Doomwatch free J. Adams, C. Read

1972 28 Aug Banner's Exit H.I. Banner, M. Foggan

1972 29 Aug Leftovers R. Bennett, R. Lavender

1972 7 Oct Last Stand Start J. Lamb, W. Young, A. Hunter

1972 - 1974 (W) Shamrock, Pillar Variation W. E. Pattison, A. W. Dunn

1973 5 May Clockwork Orange M.J. Burbage, W. Young

1973 16 June Edge Hog T.W. Birkett, M.R. Myres, C.J. Richardson

1973 25 Aug White Wizard Variation Finish C. Read, W. Robinson

1974 Fifth guidebook to Scafell

1974 29 June Dyad free J. Lamb, P. Botterill

1974 30 June Zeus J. Lamb, P. Botterill

1974 summer The Nazgul free T. Dick (unconfirmed)
1975 25 May Silk Cut Slab E. Spofforth, J. Wilkinson
1975 31 May Moonday free J. Lamb, S. Clegg
1975 11 June The Nazgul free P. Botterill, S. Clegg (confirmed)
1975 23 June Sowker J. Ratcliffe, E. Spofforth
1975 July Overhanging Grooves Direct J. Adams, C. Macquarrie
1976 29 May Hilarity M. Morrison, M. Fowler
1976 7 July Shadowfax P. Botterill, S. Clegg
1976 10 July Saxon J. Eastham, E. Cleasby
1976 17 July Saxon pitch 1 R. Matheson, E. Cleasby
1976 17 July Phoenix Arête Finish R. Matheson, E. Cleasby
1976 28 Aug Harvest A. Stevenson, H. Charlton, C. Sice
1976 Aug Saxon Direct M. Berzins, C. Sowden
1976 Sept Lost Horizons P. Livesey, J. Lawrence
1976 White Wizard free M. Berzins, G. Higginson
1977 22 May Ringwraith pitch 1 M. Berzins, R.H. Berzins, C. Sowden
1977 28 May Ringwraith pitch 2 M. Berzins, R.H. Berzins
1977 28 May Foxshooter pitch 1 M. Berzins, R.H. Berzins
1977 28 May Shere Khan pitch 1 E. Cleasby, R. Matheson
1977 29 May Shere Khan pitch 2 R. Matheson, E. Cleasby
1977 29 May Edge of Eriador R. Matheson, E. Cleasby
1977 29 May Overhanging Grooves Direct free M. Berzins, R.H. Berzins
1977 19 June Shamrock Eliminate pitches 2-5 R.G. Hutchinson, J.W. Earl
1977 7 July White Wizard pitch 3 Direct P. Botterill, J. Taylor
1977 Elvis Presley dies (allegedly!)
1978 20 May Shamrock Eliminate pitch 1 R.G. Hutchinson, J.W. Earl
1978 28 May Talisman P. Botterill, J. Lamb, J. Taylor
1978 28 May Cahadras pitch 1 J. Lamb, P. Botterill
1978 29 May Cahadras pitch 2 P. Botterill, J. Lamb
1978 29 May Equinox pitch 1 J. Lamb, P. Botterill
1978 3 June Armageddon free P. Whillance, D. Armstrong
1978 4 June Equinox pitch 2 P. Botterill, J. Lamb
1978 17 June Cullinan R.H. Berzins, M. Berzins
1978 13 July Lucuis pitch 1 P. Botterill, J. Lamb
1978 16 Aug S.O.S. pitch 1 J. Lamb, P. Botterill
1978 26 Aug Lucuis pitch 2 J. Lamb, P. Botterill
1978 26 Sept S.O.S. pitch 2 P. Botterill, J. Lamb
1979 1st Lakes Winter guidebook
1979 11 June Mythical Kings J. Lamb, R.H. Berzins
1979 12 June Fulcrum Direct P. Botterill, J. Lamb
1979 17 June Roaring Silence R.H. Berzins, J. Lamb, M. Berzins
1979 17 June Forbidden Colours M. Berzins, R.H. Berzins, J. Lamb
1979 12 July Burning Bridges J. Lamb, P. Botterill
1979 14 July Subaudition R.H. Berzins, M. Berzins, J. Lamb
1979 15 July Midnight Express P. Botterill, J. Lamb
1979 Summer Shere Khan free R. Fawcett
1980 9 April Moby Dick S. Dougherty, T. Glendenning
1981 10 Aug Hell's Bells J. Lamb, P. Botterill
1981 28 Aug The Almighty P. Botterill, J. Lamb
1982 15 May Incubus free M. Berzins, C. Sowden
1982 15 May Zeus Direct Start M. Berzins, C. Sowden
1982 2 June Lost Horizons free R.H. Berzins, M. Browell
1983 18 June Aquavit C. Sowden, M. Berzins
1983 19 June The Lord of the Rings Variation Finish A. Phizacklea, R.E. Wightman
1983 31 July Zeya M. Berzins, C. Sowden
1983 9 Aug Shikasta E. Cleasby, R. Matheson
1983 Aug Ring of Air M. Berzins, C. Sowden
1983 Aug Mephisto M. Berzins, C. Sowden
1983 Aug Judas Priest M. Berzins, C. Sowden
1984 Sixth guidebook to Scafell
1984 21 Jan (W) Jones' Route Direct from Lord's Rake A. Phizacklea, E. Cleasby
1984 15 Feb (W) Botterill's Slab A. Phizacklea, D. Kay
1984 18 Feb (W) May Day Direct (top pitch) A. Phizacklea, E. Cleasby, S. Swindells
1984 18 Feb (W) The White Slab (top pitch) A. Phizacklea, E. Cleasby
1984 18 Feb (W) Collier's Chimney T. Furniss, J. Fotheringham
1984 1 Mar (W) Minotaur (top pitch) A. Phizacklea, D. Geere
1984 24 Mar (W) Slime Chimney J. Fotheringham, S. Howe
1984 9 June Mickledore Arête R.J. Kenyon, C. King
1984 8 July Bushwhacker A. Phizacklea, R. Knight
1984 August Phoenix, Ash Groove Finish J. Dowthwaite, P. Dowthwaite
1984 Summer Edge of Eriador Direct Start P. Dowthwaite, J. Dowthwaite
1984 21 Dec (W) Sod's Law A. Phizacklea, G. Smith
1985 19 Jan (W) Moss Gill Grooves B. Davison, R. Jones, A. Perkins
1985 28 Nov (W) Overhanging Wall J. Fotheringham, G. Bonington
1986 3 Jan (W) Great Chimney J. Fotheringham, G. Bonington
1986 4 Jan (W) Botterill's Corner A. Phizacklea, G. Smith
1986 Jan (W) Keswick Brothers' Climb J. Fotheringham, V. Saunders
1986 9 Feb (W) Age Concern S. Howe, J. Grinbergs, D. Kay, M. Lynch
1986 9 Feb (W) Steep Gill Grooves T. Stephenson, K. Murphy, L. Rutland
1986 16 Feb (W) Hopkinson's Gully R.E. Wightman, M. Lynch
1986 16 Feb (W) West Wall Climb D. Kay, S. Howe
1986 19 Feb (W) Restless Natives D. Kay, J. Grinbergs
1986 19 Feb (W) Bridge of Sighs S. Howe, T. Stephenson, P. Andrews
1986 22 Feb (W) Moonbathing A. Phizacklea, D. Richards
1986 1-2 Mar (W) Central Buttress (disputed) T. Brindle, A. Moore
1986 2 Mar (W) Impunity Slabs A. Phizacklea (solo)
1986 2 Mar (W) Sod All A. Phizacklea, M. Lynch
1986 16 Mar (W) Upper Deep Gill Route A. Phizacklea (solo)
1986 26 June Borderline C. Sowden, M. Berzins
1986 2nd Lakes Winter guidebook
1987 11 Jan (W) Harvest Crunch B. Davison, R. Mulvaney
1987 14 Feb (W) Mechanical Orange B. Davison, R.A.L. Jones
1987 26 April Bold Eagle A. Phizacklea
1987 26 April Swillshark A. Phizacklea, E. Rogers
1988 Seventh guidebook to Scafell
1988 18 June Harvest free A. Phizacklea, R.E. Wightman
1989 27 May Shadowfax Variation Finish A. Phizacklea, R.E. Wightman

1989 24 June The Siege Perilous M. Berzins, C. Sowden
1989 8 July Doctor Death A. Phizacklea, D.R. Lampard
1989 8 July Ixodes D.R. Lampard, A. Phizacklea
1989 8 July Alamogordo A. Phizacklea, D.R. Lampard
1989 The Berlin Wall falls (serves them right for using cheap Eastern European labour!)
1990 28 Jan (W) Deep Gill Integrale A. Phizacklea, J.L. Holden
1990 5 May Chiron A. Phizacklea, J.L. Holden, A. Rowell
1990 26 May Cerberus A. Phizacklea, J.L. Holden
1990 17 June The Caution Horses M. Berzins, C. Sowden
1990 17 June Original Sin A. Phizacklea, D. Kirby
1990 17 June Foxshooter pitches 3 & 4 A. Phizacklea, D. Kirby
1990 18 July Central Buttress Variation Marr's Variation A. Marr
1990 18 July Central Buttress Variation The Link M. Tooke
1990 25 July The Ambleside Brothers' Climb P. Cornforth, G. Cornforth
1990 Nov 25 (W) Castor A. Phizacklea, A. Rowell, P. Plowright
1990 28 Nov (W) Sodom A. Phizacklea, A. Rowell
1991 First use of World Wide Web opens to the public – What would you do without it?
1991 1 June Juno A. Phizacklea, J.L. Holden, A. Rowell
1991 1 June Eastern Front A. Phizacklea, J.L. Holden
1991 1 June The Unforgettable Fire A. Phizacklea, J.L. Holden, A. Rowell
1991 3 Sept The Scarlet Pimpernel A. Phizacklea, P. Plowright
1991 8 Sept Swan Song P. Ross, J. Lockey
1992 24 May Siege Perilous free M. Berzins, A. Phizacklea
1993 5 June Chiron Variation Start I. Turnbull, A. Phizacklea
1993 5 June Meridian A. Phizacklea, I. Turnbull
1993 6 June Hilarity Variation Sacrificial Squaddies A. Phizacklea, I. Turnbull
1994 2 Jan (W) Overhanging Wall, Original Finish A. Phizacklea, D. Donnini
1994 11 June Smeaghaidh A. Phizacklea, B. Chislett
1995 12 Mar (W) Low Man, Right Wall of Steep Gill B. Davison, C. Wells
1995 21 Mar (W) Great Western B. Davison, C. Wells
1995 23 June Bat Out of Hell A. Marr, M. Tooke
1995 28 June When The Fat Lady Sings A. Phizacklea, S. Merry
1995 29 June Anglo R.J. Kenyon, C. King
1995 17 Aug Morpheus A. Phizacklea, M. Berzins
1995 17 Aug Insomnia A. Phizacklea, M. Berzins
1995 17 Aug Def Arête M. Berzins, A. Phizacklea
1995 19 Aug Entonox N. Wharton, D. Donnini, H. Davies
1995 23 Aug Ringwraith Direct R. Matheson, K. Phizacklea
1996 Eighth guidebook to Scafell
1996 24 Feb (W) Tia Maria K. Phizacklea, S. Merry
1996 28 Feb (W) Centre Route B. Davison, N. Green
1996 5 Aug Zenith G.L. Swainbank, C. Read
1996 24 Nov (W) 1996 24 Nov (W) Twisting Gully P. Dowthwaite, S. Edmonson
1997 3rd Lakes Winter guidebook
1997 2 Jan (W) Eye Spy B. Davison, N. Hewitt
1997 2 Jan (W) Dharma Armour N. Hewitt, B. Davison
1997 2 Jan (W) Chimney Stack B. Davison, N. Hewitt
1998 19 May Lost Horizons Direct A. Hyslop, D. Birkett
1998 19 May New Horizons D. Birkett, A. Hyslop
1999 12 Jan (W) Rush Finish, Great Eastern Route B. Davison, N. Hewitt
1999 summer Original Sin free C. Matheson, K. Phizacklea
1999 11 Dec (W) Jacob's Ladder P. Dowthwaite, P. Smalley
2000 28 May Talbot Horizon D. Birkett
2002 Spring Another Lonely Day D. Birkett
G. Lee seconded pitch 2
2002 19 April Welcome to the Cruel World D. Birkett
2003 18 April Judas Priest Rob Halford Finish J. McHaffie, C. Downer
2003 Aug Death Arête D. Birkett, R. Fielding
2004 9 Sept The Caledonian Orogeny W. Hunter, J. McHaffie
2005 8 Mar (W) The Girdle Traverse S. Ashworth, B. Davison
2006 3 June The Return of the King D. Birkett
2006 4th Lakes Winter guidebook
2007 25 Jan (W) S.O.S. Mayday Finish D. Birkett, M. Edwards
2008 3 Dec (W) Xerxes R. Cross, A. Turner, S. Ashworth
2010 30 Jan (W) Never Ever Say Never pitch 1 D. Birkett, M. Jenner
2010 31 Jan (W) Never Ever Say Never pitch 2 D. Birkett, A. Mitchell (disputed)
2010 12 Feb (W) Into the Wild P. Cave, E. Luke
2010 27 Feb (W) The Tower Buttress I. Armstrong, J. Graham
2010 6 Mar (W) Shamrock Icefall B. Davison, D. MacGimpsey
2010 6 Mar (W) Collier's Groove B. Davison, D. MacGimpsey
2010 7 Mar (W) Doctor Grey B. Davison, D. MacGimpsey
2010 13 Mar (W) Collier's Left-Hand Variant B. Davison, D. MacGimpsey
2010 13 Mar (W) Upper West Wall Climb B. Davison, D. MacGimpsey
2010 14 Mar (W) Impunity Slab Corner B. Davison, D. MacGimpsey
2010 10 April Seasonal Adjustment Disorder B. Davison, S. Jensen,
A. Phizacklea, M. Cocker
2010 10 April Collier's Left-Hand Climb B. Davison, S. Jensen
2010 Dec 4 (W) Moondance D. Birkett, M. Jenner
2012 26 May Low Man by the Jubilee Line A. Phizacklea, J.L. Holden
2012 5th Lakes Winter guidebook
2013 8 June Waiting Wall A. Phizacklea, T. Moore, J.L. Holden
2013 8 June High Man by the Central Line A. Phizacklea, T. Moore, J.L. Holden
2013 20 July Black Rider A. Mitchell, N. Pike
2013 20 July Rise of Angmar R.M. Matheson, C. Matheson
2013 20 July Thy Will be Done C. Matheson, R.M. Matheson
2013 20 July Back to Black D. Birkett, M. Jenner
2013 20 July Red Gill Edge A. Phizacklea (solo)
2013 20 July Red Gill Corner A. Phizacklea (solo)
2014 Ninth Guidebook to Scafell
2014 3 May Barad-Dûr R.M. Matheson, C. Matheson
2015 10 Sept Collier's Climb Left-Hand Superior Finish A. Phizacklea, K. Phizacklea
2015 10 Sept The Barrow Brothers' Climb A. Phizacklea, K. Phizacklea
2015 10 Sept Red Gill Rib A. Phizacklea, K. Phizacklea (var)

The Wasdale valley.

Scafell

Profiles of the leading historical activists

The following profiles are of the major activists and climbers who have been instrumental in developing the crags on Scafell. The only rules for inclusion in this section is that they must have made a significant contribution to the history of Scafell, and secondly, they must no longer be alive. I don't wish to embarrass my climbing friends and those I have come to know over the course of preparing this book. So if you still have the capacity to read this you can count yourself lucky that you are not amongst those included below.

G. D. Abraham and A. P. Abraham

George Dixon (1872-1965) and Ashley Perry Abraham (1876-1951) were native Keswick brothers who established themselves as the leading mountain photographers of the era. Their contribution to recording the crags, routes and characters of the day was immense, and it provided a huge source of material for this book. They produced several books on Lake District mountains, together with others that covered Scottish, Welsh and Alpine climbing. Their main contribution to the crags of Scafell is the quaintly named Keswick Brothers' Climb but, typically for that time, that name was not of their choosing. They were sometimes looked down upon for their lack of 'formal' education, but they were smart cookies and far from the country bumpkins that some had suggested. Ashley was a chess champion, and he was elected the first President of the Fell and Rock Climbing Club when it was formed. George was a keen motorist and he was the first to cross Wrynose and Hardknott passes in 1913, long before they were covered in tarmac and any green lane regulations. They were physically dissimilar, George was blessed with 'sturdy Cumberland legs' and always led when the brothers climbed, whilst Ashley was described as bandy legged and his family used to say 'he couldn't stop a pig in an alley'.

H. Banner

Hugh Banner was born just outside of Liverpool in 1933. He started climbing when at Bristol University and he soon gained a reputation for being an audacious climber on the worrying Avon Gorge, by establishing several bold routes such as Desperation, E1. He frequently soloed routes of a high standard and became known to the wider climbing world after repeating many of the Rock and Ice classics in Wales. He proved his mettle after adding Troach, E2, on Cloggy. He was less fortunate on Scafell; his best contributions were Bos'n's Buttress and Narrow Stand in the company of his old mate Joe Griffin. He seemed strangely attracted to the remaining lines around Moss Gill, where his routes Last Stand and Banner's Exit were soon usurped by better and more direct versions, leaving Banner as a rather forgotten pioneer. He established the HB Company which produced high quality micro-wires and micro-cams. Since his death, this has merged into the DMM Company. Hugh loved fast motorbikes, but a horrific accident at the age of 67 resulted in the loss of a leg above the knee. Undaunted, he used his engineering skill to enable him to operate the clutch and gear change from the handlebars, it seemed nothing could hold him back. That was until a brain tumor put an end to it all in 2007.

R. J. Birkett

Robert James (Jim) Birkett was born in April 1914 in Little Langdale and spent almost his entire life living in the valley. He was always interested in the fells, firstly through egg collecting, and then he developed his desire to climb which he did without the support of any climbing clubs. He added May Day Climb on Scafell just over a year after starting climbing – at E1 this was the hardest route in The Lakes at the time, an admirable demonstration of his natural ability. He gained a reputation for being a master of nailed boot climbing, and some have the impression that is all that Jim ever climbed in, but it transpires that he sometimes climbed in rubbers. Other major additions to Scafell include the East Buttress Girdle, Gremlin's Groove and Slab and Groove.

A. R. Dolphin

Arthur Rhodes Dolphin was born just outside of Bradford in 1924 and as a child he excelled at athletics, running and cricket. It was fortunate for the climbing world that he discovered gritstone, and he was to dominate Almscliff for several years by climbing such classics as Great Western, Birdlime Traverse and Overhanging Groove. In the Lakes, he established Kipling Groove, Deer Bield Buttress and Sword of Damocles, raising the technical standard of the area and becoming something of a local legend. On Scafell he added Pegasus and Hell's Groove with Greenwood, and he may have become one of the greatest climbers of his era had he not been killed whilst descending from the Dent du Géant in the Alps in 1953.

P. Greenwood

Pete Greenwood was born in Bradford in September 1931. He was a very talented ballroom dancer, but he took up climbing after being faced with a challenge that "If you think you're tough, you should try climbing!" Apparently, his competitor top-roped a VS at Ilkley, to which Greenwood retorted that a rope was unnecessary, and promptly soloed it! He was a member of the climbing group of young working class climbers who became known as 'The Bradford Lads'. During the early 1950's, they hitch-hiked every weekend to The Lakes and usually ended up in Langdale. Greenwood became a brilliant climber, often in poor conditions (Kneewrecker Chimney and Deer Bield Crack were both climbed under deep snow). His contributions to wider Lake District climbing include Sword of Damocles on Bowfell and Thirlmere Eliminate and Last Laugh on Castle Rock, Thirlmere. Typically for the period, Greenwood smoked excessively and drank heavily (It was claimed that he had smoked half a million cigarettes and drank 20,000 pints in his lifetime, figures he recently confirmed as being correct). A rather short climber, he was nick-named 'Rubberlegs' due to his supple but strong physique, but it was the friendship with Arthur Dolphin that marks his place in Scafell History. They climbed Pegasus and Hell's Groove, the latter being made possible by Pete's lead of the first pitch. A strong willed and opinionated climber, once he made a decision, he stuck to it. He suddenly gave up climbing at the height of his achievements the week before becoming married, and in February 2000 he decided to give up smoking, going from sixty a day to nothing. "I'd made up my mind, and that was it. I never even craved another fag; it was just sheer will power." He eventually succumbed to a long illness and died in February 2010, aged 78.

Hopkinson family

This not-so-merry band of five brothers emerged from the nouveau-riche district of South Manchester, where the family made its fortune servicing the booming industrial economy. John (1849-1898; Electrical engineer), Alfred (1851-1939; Professor of Law), Charles, (1854-1920; Engineer), Edward (1859-1921; Electrical engineer) and Albert (1863-1949; Surgeon) were hard working, frugal and not prone to self-promotion, and they left few records of their climbing exploits. Their name lives for evermore in the annals of Scafell history because Edward, Charles and Albert built a cairn on a prominent ledge on Scafell Pinnacle, which bears their name to this day. Due to a long-standing misunderstanding of an early winter probe on the Pinnacle, they were credited with partially descending what was christened Hopkinson's Gully in their honour, although it transpires they never actually set foot on the route.

A. T. (Bert) Hargreaves

Born in Stockport in 1903, Albert Thomas Hargreaves graduated from his local outcrops to The Lakes, where he led the first ascent of Deer Bield Crack. On Scafell, he led Morning Wall, Jacob's Ladder and Red Gill Wall, and was on the ascent of Overhanging Wall with Linnell. Hargreaves climbed the second ascent of Steep Gill in winter with his wife and Sid and Jammie Cross, a great achievement. Hargreaves wrote the 1936 FRCC guidebook to Scafell and his contributions formed the framework of the 1956 guide. Apparently he was a man of very few words, but despite this brevity of speech he could deliver a scathing rebuke to anyone who annoyed him. A.B. Hargreaves said of him "He was a strange sod, was A.T., he never said two words when one would do. He wasn't funny, there wasn't a funny side to A.T., he was always very serious." He worked as a commercial traveller for Nestlé's Milk and therefore had the use of the company car, which enabled him to climb widely around the country. He and Frank Heap 'exchanged' wives in 1934 and Bert lived with Ruth Hargreaves for the rest of his life. They took patronage of The Burnmoor Inn at Boot in 1946, which was taken over by John Heap, the only child of Ruth Hargreaves, in 1956. Many people still fondly remember John's Austrian-born wife Josie, who remained at the inn until she retired in the early 1980's. Bert should not be confused with Alan Bennet Hargreaves from Blackburn, the two were not related. A.T. was killed in a ski-mountaineering avalanche above Overgurgh in Austria in 1952.

W. P. Haskett Smith

Walter Parry Haskett Smith was born in Kent in 1859, and was a naturally gifted athlete, apparently becoming the first person to clear 25 feet in the long jump, a world record for the time. He first visited Wasdale Head in 1882, and during his 2 month stay he was introduced to the higher peaks and crags of the area by F.H. Browning. Haskett Smith (correctly un-hyphenated) is generally credited for being the first to rock climb for the sake of it, without any ulterior motive for progressing to the greater ranges. He is often referred to as 'The Father of Rock Climbing', giving the impression that he invented the sport, which is not the truth. He climbed many of the gullies around The Lake District but became immortalised with his solo ascent of Napes Needle in 1886. On Scafell, Haskett Smith was the first to reach the top of Scafell Pinnacle, first by the short side, then by a flanking ascent from Steep Gill, and he was part of the Slingsby's Chimney Route team. His book *Climbing in the British Isles* published in 1894 was perhaps the first ever climbing guide, although it was written in a typically Victorian descriptive prose, and quite unlike any modern guidebook. Haskett Smith is often regarded as the first of the true climbing heroes of Britain. He died in 1946.

S. W. Herford

Seigfreid Wegdewood Herford, born in Aberystwyth in 1892, was a gifted and intelligent child. But possible autism led to him having a difficult upbringing. One of the ways that Siegfreid coped with this was through physical energy; he had a very active childhood which transformed him into a lithe and powerful adolescent. His introspective nature, formidable brainpower and natural athleticism were the making of a superb and natural climber, a 'rock athlete' of the Edwardian era. During his time at Manchester University he climbed frequently on gritstone with Laycock and Jeffcoat, but it was at Wasdale, and particularly the crags of Scafell, where he will be forever remembered. Along with Sansom and Brunskill, he climbed the Upper West Wall Climb, Hopkinson's Gully, and the Girdle Traverse. He also led the second ascent of Botterill's Slab, but it was the ascent of Central Buttress which made his name legendary. Shortly afterwards, the Great War intervened, and it seemed Herford wanted to shake off the ignominy of having both a German name and a German mother. After a spell in the Ambulance Corps, he joined the 24th Royal Fusiliers, where he would perish in the trenches from a rifle grenade early in 1916. His spirit would seem to live on at Wasdale, where several tales of 'Herford's Ghost' have emerged through the years.

C. F. Holland

Cecil Fredrick (Charles) Holland was born at Chiswick, Middlesex in January 1886. The son of a vicar, his education covered the Holy Scriptures, Greek and Latin literature and history, political history and geography, and he emerged from university with a BA in 1907. Holland was typical of the well educated middle class Edwardian climbers who were active at this time. He served in the war as a lieutenant with The Gloucestershire Regiment, where he was awarded the Military Cross and Bar, but he was wounded in his upper arm, which resulted in limited movement in later life, though this did not deter his climbing ambition. Holland was a very influential figure in the Wasdale climbing scene, being involved in a supporting role for the first ascent of Central Buttress, and leading several new routes on the Pinnacle face during the revival after the war. He was also involved in the ascents of Sodom and Gomorrah on Pillar Rock with Harry Kelly. Holland wrote the first guidebook to Scafell in 1925 and many articles for the FRCC. He was short in stature but had a memorable face which was said to resemble a 'Notre Dame Gargoyle' and a Rabelaisian laugh that got louder after two or three pints. Sounds like our sort of guy. He was a headmaster of various schools throughout his career (including the appropriately named Rock Preparatory School at Reigate) until his retirement in 1939. During the Second World War he was accepted to help Frank Smythe train Commandos in mountain warfare at Braemar, by subtly altering his birth certificate. The truth came out after he was caught bouldering along the side of Winchester Cathedral, his unquenchable lust for climbing being his final undoing. He died at Exminster in 1968.

O. G. Jones

Born in London in 1867, Owen Glynne Jones became one of the most influential of the Victorian activists at Wasdale, where he made his first visit aged 23. Although he only established 4 new main routes and a series of variations to existing routes on Scafell, with his ascent of Jones' Route Direct from Lord's Rake he became the first climber to seriously probe the smooth slabs on the open faces that did not rely on chimneys or cracks for progress. This suggests that his potential for developing the area would have been huge had his life not been cut short at the age of 32. He was said to be short, short-sighted but immensely powerful. One act credited to him was to complete three one-armed pull-ups using only three-fingers but with George Abraham lifted off the ground under his other arm. If this is true, he must be the strongest climber that ever lived, because I doubt any of today's well-honed activists could match that feat. Jones wrote the first guidebook to the area that categorised routes into grades of difficulty (*Rock Climbing in the English Lake District)*, thus starting the British grading system we still use today. He died on a guided ascent on Switzerland's Dent Blanche in 1899.

H. M. Kelly

Born in Manchester in 1884, Harry Mills Kelly was something of an enigmatic character when it came to his private life. He never spoke about his employment and it is unclear what he did for a living, but he certainly was not short of money. Even after his death, none of the obituaries mentioned what Kelly did. There is even some confusion about his name; one biographical book actually names him Harry Moss Kelly. He had a reputation for being a strong and complex figure, and he had an intimidating personality but a rather sardonic sense of humour. One example of this was during the visit of the German climbers in 1936 (the team that used pegs on the Direct Finish to Central Buttress) who were guests at a Rucksack Club evening dinner. The German guests were singing Teutonic songs accompanied by a mandolin, when during a silent pause, Kelly said in a loud voice "I reckon a Jew's harp wouldn't be very popular here!" Throughout the evening, the Germans in turn suddenly stood to attention and proclaim a loud 'Heil Hitler' with the accompanying salute, to which the others would respond likewise, the British hosts retained a polite but embarrassed silence. Not Kelly, he bided his time and, at an appropriate moment he sprang to his feet, gave a mock Nazi salute and yelled "Heil Hitler!" Dead silence prevailed. The leader of the Germans, the 6 foot 6 ins. white whiskered Rickmers, slowly unwound to his full height and replied in loud, stern tones "Zat is not for you to say!" He then took a small note pad out of his pocket, licked the end of a pencil and said "For zat, you vill go in my little black book. Vot is your name?" to which the president of the club shouted out "Don't tell him, Kelly!" (Actually the last bit about the note book was made up, but you can just imagine the atmosphere). Later in life, Kelly was to edit the climbing guidebooks for the Fell and Rock between 1938 and 1964. By the time he was eventually deposed from this post by peer pressure from the remainder of the guidebook team, Kelly had reached the age of 80 - he just couldn't let go, it was his life. He was a very influential climber of his day, championing the use of rubber shoes and pioneered the gardening of routes from above prior to an ascent. His new routes around Wasdale read like a tick-list of classics, Tophet Wall, Grooved Wall, Sodom, Gomorrah and Rib and Slab Climb, and are lasting evidence of his skill as a pioneer. He climbed many routes on Scafell, including Upper Deep Ghyll Buttress, Central Slabs, Tower Buttress; but the most famous one which stands as his testimonial is Moss Ghyll Grooves. Kelly eventually passed away in 1980 at the ripe old age of 96.

C. F. Kirkus

Colin Fletcher Kirkus was born in July 1910 in Liverpool and he attended the local West Kirby Grammar School before graduating to Liverpool College. Colin spent many years walking in the Welsh hills with his family, where he started climbing by soloing routes, sometimes with hair-raising epics! He joined the Wayfarers' Climbing Club in 1928. It was said that Colin had an extraordinarily long reach for his height, which gave him an edge over other climbers. His first ascent list includes Great Slab, Pedestal Crack and Curving Crack on Clogwyn d'ur Arddu, Lot's Groove on Glyder Fach, Nose Direct on Dinas Mot and Pinnacle Wall on Craig yr Ysfa. Kirkus stamped his name on Scafell with the first ascent of Mickledore Grooves, the first route on the East Buttress. This put Kirkus at the top of the climbing spectrum in the 1930's. He was passed up for a place on the 1933 Everest Expedition, but in that year he went on a Himalayan expedition and climbed Bhagirathi III, a technically difficult climb for its day. The tragic accident on Ben Nevis which resulted in the death of Linnell affected his climbing career, and he never pioneered a hard route afterwards. In 1941 he published a climbing instruction book called '*Let's go Climbing*!', which became a classic of its type. During the Second World War, he joined the R.A.F. as part of the Pathfinder Force, marking targets from an obsolete Wellington bomber. He was lost without trace on one such raid over Bremen on September 4th 1942.

J. Lamb

Jeff Lamb was born on a council estate in Carlise in 1946. His parents had no interest in outdoor activities, so Jeff's first outings were with the scout group. His first serious climbing was after he met John 'Moony' Moore in the Cally pub, and the following day he led Gimmer Crack in the heavy rain. Poor conditions did not dampen his enthusiasm. He had the determination to climb as much as possible and he was never deterred by any route, regardless of its reputation. He became very strong through his work as a carpenter, coupled with the discovery in the early 1970's of the Armathwaite outcrops, where he pioneered many of the classic routes and boulder problems. He loved the challenge of climbing a route in a better style than had previously been ascended and this led to his nickname of 'The Jackal'. His involvement in Lakes climbing is almost legendary, a selection of his classic first ascents are Trilogy, White Noise, Sacrificial Crack and Running on Empty; whilst on Scafell he added a fine selection of desperate routes like Zeus, Caradhras, S.O.S., Mythical Kings and Burning Bridges.

J. Lamb (continued)

He was the top Lakes-based climber operating on Scafell in the era between 1978 and 1981. Jeff moved out to Australia in 1981, returning briefly to marry Maureen. Shortly after arriving back in Oz he became the victim of a hit and run accident. It was whilst awaiting compensation through the courts he was killed at a nearby crag. His death in 1983 was never fully explained; he was found dead in his car with serious head injuries, whether this was from a stone dislodged by his abseil rope or thrown without intent from the top of the crag by someone was never established. Fittingly, his ashes were scattered under The East Buttress of his beloved Scafell.

M. Linnell

Maurice Linnell was born in Stockport in June 1909. His family moved to Kendal when he was ten, where he attended Stramongate School and formed a climbing group, much to the dislike of the headmaster. He was accepted by Manchester University where had studied chemistry and also formed the Manchester University Mountaineering Club. It was whilst climbing at the local crags that he met A.B. Hargreaves and Alf Bridge, who introduced him to Colin Kirkus. These two made several important first ascents including Birthday Crack, Curving Crack and Narrow Slab on Clogwyn d'ur Arddu, the impressive and extensive crag on the northern slopes of Snowdon. Linnell was described as 'a very ambitious and intense person who did not like to be thwarted by failure to get up something'. He had a lithe physique, with a mop of black hair that flopped across his round steel rimmed spectacles; but he was always immaculately dressed. He often wore a suit for climbing 'Last year's office suit is this year's climbing suit'. Linnell's ability opened up The East Buttress with ascents of Great Eastern, Overhanging Wall and The Yellow Slab. He was one of the best climbers of his period, and would have become famous had his life not been cut short in a tragic winter accident with Colin Kirkus on Ben Nevis in 1934.

P. Livesey

Born in Huddersfield in 1943, Pete Livesey was an outstanding athlete, orienteer, canoeist, caver and climber; he excelled at everything he tried. Much has been written about his exploits within this book so there is no point in repeating them here, but there was a darker side to Livesey's climbing that was not analysed with any scrutiny in his biography *Fast and Free* by Sheard and Radtke. There is nothing about the chipped holds on Athanor and Nagasaki Grooves in Borrowdale, the mystery of the unchalked crux of Blitzkreig, the false claims of free ascents of Lost Horizons and The Cumbrian, and what exactly did 'self belay' on Nagasaki Grooves and Dry Grasp entail; away from the eyes of witnesses? They aren't even hinted at; it was all completely ignored, leaving Livesey the target of insinuation and accusation by those who have no right to censure his name (such as myself). It must be said that his sole contribution to Scafell, Lost Horizons, is probably one of the most compelling and aesthetic lines in the country which still claims its fair share of failures amongst the climbing elite. He died in 1998 of cancer.

J. W. Robinson

A true dalesman, John Wilson Robinson was born in 1857 at Lorton, just south of Cockermouth. He was a keen fellwalker who had a taste for adventure, and this inevitably led him to meet the early climbers who were based at Wasdale Head. Although his home was 15 miles away, he would frequently walk over Scarth Gap and Black Sail passes to the Wastwater Hotel, where he would meet the guests at breakfast, embarking on a full days climbing on the crags and rounding this off by walking back home in the dark. It is a measure of his personality and widespread knowledge of the fells that allowed him to be integrated into that highly educated group as a peer. Robinson was involved with the first ascent of Needle Ridge and Kern Knotts Chimney, and on Scafell he was part of the team that pioneered West Wall Climb and Moss Gill. He recorded over 100 ascents of Scafell Pinnacle and 20 winter ascents of Deep Gill – that must have taken an awful lot of walking to achieve. He became a vice-president of the FRCC when it was formed in 1906, but he died of bowel cancer the following year aged 50.

G. S. Sansom

George Samuel Sansom was born in London in 1888, where he studied zoology at the University College, gaining a Doctor of Science degree. He became a keen photographer, and he was a pioneer in the use of colour photography and stereo photography. He first visited Wasdale Head in 1908, and made frequent visits thereafter, climbing with various partners such as the Abrahams and Botterill, where he gained a reputation for being a 'quick and neat climber'. Sansom formed a formidable partnership with Herford, whom he met in the summer of 1911, and between them they added Direct from Lord's Rake to Hopkinson's Cairn, Hopkinson's Gully, the Girdle Traverse and of course Central Buttress. Sansom spent much of his time in the Amazon forest, studying rare animals, often with scientific instruments that he had crafted by his own skilled hands. During the war, he transferred from the St. John Ambulance Brigade to the Royal Flying Corps, where he won the Distinguished Flying Cross. Sansom continued to visit Wasdale Head between the wars, and he always repeated his favourite route, Hopkinson's Gully. He also maintained his love of flying at Brooklands Flying Club, where he was affectionately known as 'The Professor'. He was the last link with the pre-war activists of Wasdale until his death in 1980 at his home at Godalming in Surrey.

R. C. Smith

Robin Clark Smith was probably the finest climber to emerge from Scotland in the 1950's, despite being born in Calcutta in 1938. His family moved to Edinburgh when he was eight, which was a cultural disadvantage when he first came face to face with the tough Glaswegian members of the Creag Dhu club. However, his bold and seemingly reckless approach to climbing and the prevailing conditions earned huge respect, and he became a legend in his short lifetime. In Scotland his routes are modern classics; Shibboleth, The Needle, The Bat, Orion Face Direct and Smith's Route are testament to his foresight and skill. His major contribution to Alpine climbing was the first British ascent of the notorious Walker Spur with Gunn Clarke. One little recognised fact of Smith's forays into The Lakes was a possible first ascent of The Central Pillar on Esk Buttress. He had attempted it early in 1962 with Moriarty, Graham Tiso and Ronnie Marshall, but was defeated on the top pitch by darkness. According to Moriarty, in what transpired to be a 'death bed confession', he adamantly claimed that he and Smith returned a fortnight later and completed the route. This was before Crew's ascent, and shortly before Smith left for his expedition to the Pamirs, where he died with Wilf Noyce. Moriarty was so distraught with his friend's death that he never recorded the route, but Smith was more than capable of climbing it and the claim has some substance, but no evidence. Smith's visit to Scafell in the summer of 1959 with Derek Lever resulted in Chartreuse and Leverage, but this incident was such a shock to the locals that it sparked a major new wave of development on the crag.

D. D. Whillans

Donald Desbrow Whillans (1933-1985) needs no introduction to the readers of this book, but if you do desire more knowledge of this legendary character please read Jim Perrin's biography *The Villain*. Apart from the overgrown, overblown 'classic' of Extol, the only good new route he added to The Lakes was Trinity on The East Buttress of Scafell. Whillans was said to have a natural eye for a good line, but some doubt this reasoning because to reach Trinity he must have walked past The Centaur, Ichabod and Phoenix – but he did climb the fourth or fifth ascent of Ichabod some time later. Like all good rock stars he died far too young; succumbing to a heart attack aged 52.

Members gather at the Central Buttress centenary event at Brackenclose, April 2014.

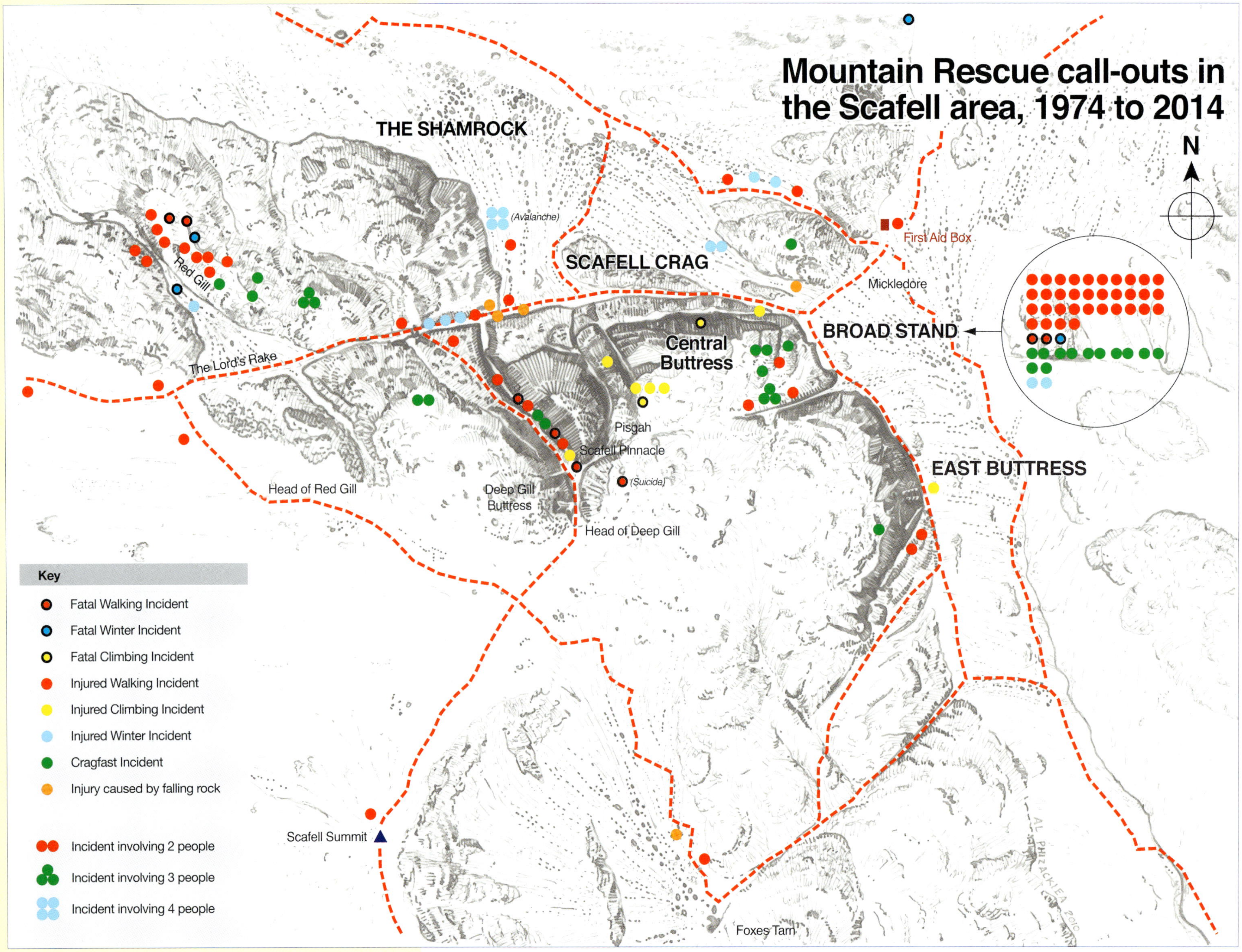

A review of the last 40 years

The accompanying map illustrates the type and distribution of accidents around Scafell and the Scafell crags that have involved the services of the Wasdale Mountain Rescue Team. The Wasdale MRT was created in 1968 and provides emergency assistance in the Wasdale and Eskdale valleys of West Cumbria. It is made up of volunteers from the Seascale, Gosforth and Egremont areas who are on call 24 hours a day, 365 days a year; rain or shine. These unpaid, unrecognised people willingly give up their meals, the pub and social lives; often at great personal discomfort and inconvenience to their family members to help a climber or walker in trouble on the fells.

Scafell Accidents (continued)

The map indicates the different incidents that have occurred on Scafell since 1974, as extracted from the records available. The clustering of accidents around certain parts of the mountain is evident – it is unsurprising to find that Broad Stand has been the scene of half the total accidents, in fact this place is so notorious for being the 'centre' of accidents that it is surprising that there have only been 3 fatalities. The other interesting 'black spot' which is not so well known is around the lower part of Red Gill, near the western end of Lord's Rake. This is a wide scree funnel that suggests a short cut to the valley for the unwary, but which narrows savagely near the bottom, forcing its victims onto the steep, wet hillside where the inevitable accidents occur. The Lord's Rake, Deep Gill and the West Wall Traverse area is another that has had its share of incidents over the years, where the steep, loose nature of the ground gives little chance of emerging unscathed from a simple trip or fall.

There have been two fatal rock climbing accidents over the 40 years. The loss of the chockstone on Central Buttress has been documented within this book, and the other was a climber involved in a fall whilst retreating from Moss Gill. In fact, Moss Gill is the location of the majority of rock climbing accidents on the crag, probably because of its popularity as an 'alternative' route to be attempted when conditions are poor, as the guidebook states "A route for all seasons, which can be ascended in any conditions…". Might this be a salutary lesson for guidebook writers and editors? One point must be made for clarification – the category of 'walkers' also includes rock climbers who have slipped during their descent from the crag; these incidents have not been classed as climbing accidents.

The number and types of incidents have changed over the years and this needs some explanation. There are more people on the fells now than there were 40 years ago, and this has given rise to an increase of about 20% in the average rate of call-outs per year. The major shift over the past 20 years is that accidents now represent less of the total workload and there has been a marked increase in the number of crag-fast or stuck people who are unable to extricate themselves from difficulty. This is mainly due to the advent of the mobile phone. Years ago, before you could telephone for help, if you found yourself in difficulty, you had to get yourself out. Recently there has been a big rise in stranded people who simply ring the police, sit tight and await their rescue – no bad thing if they are genuinely in peril (it is possible that some accidents are being avoided), but in many instances it is due to a lack of 'hill sense' and simply an expectation that help will always come at the push of a button. It is this attitude that has led to the large increase in calls to the rescue team and, along with the '3-Peak' challengers who ascend Scafell Pike throughout the summer months, is pushing the patience of the rescue teams to breaking point.

I am indebted to Julian Carradice for the information used to create this map. Julian has been a long-time member of the Wasdale Rescue Team; he was team leader between 1999 and 2012. He compiled the figures from the annual reports from the team, except for 1975 as that data was not available for inclusion. Julian's personal experience, which includes the breakdown of his marriage, is typical of the stresses that these volunteers are facing from the increasing demands of call-outs. Reluctantly, this caused him to leave the team in 2012, though he is still an active member of the Cumbria Ore Mines Rescue Unit, a specialist team operating under the wing of the Lake District Search and Mountain Rescue Association. Happily, I can report that he was awarded an MBE in 2013 for his services to Mountain Rescue, a well deserved accolade. Thanks Julian, and enjoy your climbing.

Helecopter evacuation of an injured climber from close to Hollow Stones.

Susan Jensen.

John and Val Holden.

Acknowledgements

This book is not a single handed venture; it is the result of the combined efforts of many friends within the climbing world, and in particularly the members of the Fell and Rock Climbing Club which should be affixed with the word 'of the English Lake District Limited' to give it its full official and legal title. There have been many who have given their valuable time and considerable and hugely valued experience in such varied fields as publication, diagram formatting and even posing (if that is the right term) on the rock for photographs.

I would particularly like to thank Mike Cocker, who wrote the early history of the crag based on the research he made for his earlier publication the *Wasdale Climbing Book*. His careful and crafted research, along with meticulous eye for detail has resulted in the initial part of the book leading up to the ascent of Central Buttress. Brian Davison wrote the winter climbing sections, following a bizarre exchange of e-mails which he sent from a research vessel caught in the middle of a mighty storm in the South Atlantic Ocean! John Moore wrote the geological section from a climber's prospect, rather than filling it with the usual textbook gobbledygook of synclines and anticlines. Julian Carridice, an old friend and past leader of the Wasdale Rescue Team, spent much of his precious time filtering details from old rescue team reports to compile the details of the accident statistics over the last 40 years. I would also like to thank Tony Greenbank for allowing me to alter his notes on C.B. Sid. The superb talents of Don Sergeant transformed my photographs into the fantastic diagrams published within; his care and attention to detail have also graced the Fell and Rock guidebooks for years. Other contributors who should be credited are Jamie Lamont, who transformed the maps and geological diagrams into what you see within, and Ben Ransom compiled some late illustrations which I used throughout the book.

I am indebted to the Committee members of the Club who have given consent for financial backing for this project following the sad death of our original publishing mentor, Peter Hodgkiss. There are possibly hundreds of people who have sent e-mails, photographs, and notes to me, or who have rung up with some long forgotten snippet of information which often led down another path of research. Finally, to the editing team, the long-suffering editing team, how many thanks I owe you all. This started with Sue Jensen until her 'gap year' from work, where the Himalaya and the Alps proved too much of a calling, where the final crafting was taken up by Doug Elliott and John Holden. For a final sanity check, we employed the eagle-eye of Max Biden, who did an amazing job of picking out dozens of typing errors that had eluded both the contributors and the editing team, his contribution was small but vital. Thank you to Tom Prentice for his valued suggestions on editing style. This team finally moulded my rambling script into the finished product, where the final vote of thanks goes to Chris Sherwin, who designed, page set and juggled the pictures into the form you have in your hands. To all these people, I would like to express my deep gratitude; you have all made a contribution, however small.

This book would be very much poorer without the contributions made by the following climbers who were interviewed at length for this book. They happily gave their time and many mugs of tea and biscuits to myself and Mark Scott, the Oral Archivist for the FRCC. Their words and memories have made this book special, so my heartfelt gratitude extends to: Johnny Adams, Jeff Allison, Bob Berzins, Martin Berzins, Bill Birkett, Dave Birkett, Jack Carswell, Chris Bonington, Pete Botterill, Arthur Brookes, Les Brown, Ed Cleasby, Syd Clark, Geoff Cram, Peter Greenwood, Joe Griffin, Rob Matheson, Ron Miller, Pete Moffatt, Geoff Oliver, Colin Read, Chris Sowden, Stan Thompson, Rod Valentine, John Wilkinson and Bill Young.

Acknowledgements (continued)

Thanks for those who contributed photographs; unfortunately, not all contributions could be published:
Bob Allen, Steve Ashworth, Robin Beadle, Bill Birkett, Shaw Brown, Mike Burbage, Dom Bush, Chris Carter, John Cheesemond, John Cleare, Julian Cooper, Brian Cropper, Rob Cubbold, Dennis English, Mark Glaister, Ann Greedy, Tony Greenbank, John Hartley, John Holden, Jake Hughes, Henry Iddon, Ken Jackson, Mary Jenner, Dave Kay, Les Kendall, Alistair Lee, Mike Lynch, Ed Luke, Rob Matheson, Jimmy Marshall, Dave Miller, Andy Mitchell, Lawrence Monckton, John Moore, Keith Phizacklea, Stephen Reid, Ian Roper, Paul Ross, Andy Rowell, Eric Shaw, Pam Shaw-cross, David Sykes, Dave Willis, Graham Willison, Roonie Wood-Johnston, John Woodhouse, Bob Wightman, Ken Wilson and Bill Young.

Acknowledgements for the letters and e-mails from:
John Allen, Rick Bennett, Bob Berzins, Martin Berzins, Max Biden, Dorothy Buffey, Mike Burbage, Robin Campbell, Paddy Cave, Ed Cross, John Cross, Steve Dean, Mike Dent, Ian Dewhurst, Glyn Edward, Paul Exley, Mick Fowler, Ollie Geere, Brian Griffiths, Andrew Hall, Joy Hodgkiss, Peter Hodgkiss, Ken Jackson, Dave Kay, Ron Kenyon, Helen Killick, Dave Kirby, Dai Lampard, Jill Lawrence, Adam Lincoln, Peter Lucas, Tony Marr, Angela Mellor, Harold Newman, Tim Pickles, Audrey Plint,.Stephen Reid, Dave Rhodes, Jancis Richards, Stan Roberts, Paul Ross, John Sheard, Elspeth Smith, Carole Smithies, Angela Soper, Jack Soper, David Stephenson, Terry Sullivan, Derek Walker, Ian Whitmey, Bob Wightman and George Wostenholm.

Additional thanks to those whom spoke to me in the pub, or on the phone, some were even at the crag!
Allan Austin, Albert Ainsworth, Des Birch, Gerald Bonington, Alistair Brightman, Peter Brown, Valerie Brown, Ginger Cain, Richard Courchee, Jimmy Cruickshank, Claude Davies, Colin Downer, Phil Dowthwaite, Harold Drasdo, John Earl, Jim Fotheringham, Mark Gorin, Fred Gough, Dennis Gray, Tony Greenbank, Ray Greenhall, Alan Greig, Don Greenop, Gordon Higginson, Adam Hocking, Wes Hunter, Mary Jenner, Les Kendall, Chris King, Mike Lynch, Mick Lovatt, James McHaffie, Tom Meredith, Terry Parker, Keith Phizacklea, Guy Plint, John Porter, Norman Rimmer, Mick Ryan, Chris Sice, Iain Small, Eric Spofforth, Tony Stephenson, Jack Thornton, Tom Waghorn, Nick Wharton, Pete Whillance, Robin Whitworth, Graham Willison, Al Wilson, Joe Wilson and Ken Wilson.

Special thanks to the following members of the Fell and Rock Climbing Club who have contributed invaluable sections of this book, this is their work:
John Barrett, Max Biden, Mike Cocker, Brian Davison, Doug Elliott, Tony Greenbank, John Holden, Susan Jensen, Ron Kenyon, Tim Pickles, Phil Rigby, John Robinson, Mark Scott, Chris Sherwin, Eleanor Sherwin, Peter Smith OBE and David Stephenson.

Strangely, I would also like to extend my gratitude to the doctors and nurses at Whitehaven Hospital, and also the members of Furness and Duddon Mountain Rescue Team who were there when I needed them the most.

Doug Elliott.

Max Biden.

Selected climbing guidebooks to Scafell

FRCC Guidebook Series 1 1924. Scawfell Group, C.F. Holland, Ed. R.S.T. Chorley
FRCC Guidebook Series 2 1936. Scafell Group, A.T. Hargreaves, Ed. H.M. Kelly
FRCC Guidebook Series 3 1956. Scafell Group, A.T. Hargreaves, A.R. Dolphin, R. Miller, Ed. H.M. Kelly
FRCC Guidebook Series 4 1967. Scafell Group, G. Oliver, L.J. Griffin, Ed. J. Wilkinson
FRCC Guidebook Series 5 1974. Scafell Group, M. Burbage, W. Young, Ed. J. Wilkinson
FRCC Guidebook Series 6 1984. Scafell, Dow and Eskdale, G. Willison, M. Berzins, R. Matheson, E. Cleasby, Ed. D. Miller
FRCC Guidebook Series 7 1988. Scafell, Dow and Eskdale, A. Phizacklea, Ed. D. Miller & D. Armstrong
FRCC Guidebook Series 8 1996. Scafell, Wasdale and Eskdale, A. Phizacklea, Ed. A. Phizacklea
FRCC Guidebook Series 9 2014. Scafell and Wasdale, A. Phizacklea, R. Kenyon Ed. S. Scott
Cicerone Press Lake District Winter Climbs, 1980. R. Bennett, A Hyslop, T.W. Birkett (plus reprints 1982, 1985, 1986)
Cicerone Press Lake District Winter Climbs, 1997. R. Bennett, B. Davison, T.W. Birkett
Cicerone / FRCC Lake District Winter Climbs, 2006. B. Davison, Ed. S. Reid
Cicerone / FRCC Lake District Winter Climbs, 2012. B. Davison, Ed. S. Scott

Selected reference books

Hard Rock. Ken Wilson, (Hart-Davies, 1975)
Classic Rock. Ken Wilson, (Granada, 1978)
Extreme Rock. Ken Wilson and Bernard Newman, (Diadem Books, 1987)
Cold Climbs. Ken Wilson, Dave Alcock, John Barry (Diadem Books, 1983)
Cumbrian Rock. Trevor Jones and Geoff Milburn, (PIC Publications, 1988)
Welsh Rock. Trevor Jones and Geoff Milburn, (PIC Publications, 1986)
A Century on the Crags. Alan Hankinson, (Dent Publications, 1988)
Lakeland Rock. Adrian Bailey, (Weidenfield and Nicholson, 1985)
A Guiding Hand. Doug Elliott, (Ernest Press, 2006)
Lakeland's Greatest Pioneers. Bill Birkett, (Robert Hale Ltd, 1983)
Hands of a Climber. Steve Dean, (Ernest Press, 1993)
Don Whillans. Don Whillans and Alex Ormerod, (Heinemann, 1971)
The Villan. Jim Perrin, (Hutchinson, 2005)
And Nobody Woke up Dead. Jan Levi, (Ernest Press, 2006)
The Black Cliff. Peter Crew, Jack Soper and Ken Wilson, (Kaye and Ward Ltd, 1971)
Climbing in the Dark. Ken Jackson, (Private publication, 2006)
The Central Buttress of Scafell. Graham Wilson, (Millrace Publication, 2004)
Let's Go Climbing. Colin Kirkus, (Thomas Nelson & Sons, 1941)
Climbing at Wasdale. George Sansom, (Castle Cary Press, 1982)
The Wasdale Book. Mike Cocker, (Ernest Press, 2006)
Scafell, Portrait of a Mountain. Bill Birkett, (Frances Lincoln, 2007)
Wasdale records book, 1919 – 1927, (FRCC archives)
Brackenclose Log Book, 1960 – present, (FRCC archives)
Brackenclose Log Book, 1937 – 1960, (FRCC archives)
Who's Who in British Climbing. Colin Wells, (The Climbing Company Ltd, 2008)
Rock Climbing and Mountaineering. C. Brumming, (Forbes & Forbes, 1946)
Park Gate (Coniston) climber's log book, 1932 – 1955, (FRCC archives)
Memories of Dolphin. Tom Greenwood, (Green Woods 2009)

I have not referenced all the climbing club journals used for reference in this book, but I would like to thank all the clubs for permission to use their material.

On top of Deep Gill Buttress, as viewed from the head of Deep Gill in winter time.

May Pickles practices for a quick exit from Brackenclose in the 1940s.

Publication of this book has been supported by a legacy from May Pickles.

May began walking in the Lakes and Yorkshire Dales around 1940,
and was introduced to the FRCC when she met her husband, Charles.
She became an active club member from 1980 to her death in 2013, making many friends.
Charles joined the club in 1936 and served as President from 1976 to 1978.
They lived in Yorkshire where May was a local historian and writer.
Both had a particular fondness for Wasdale.

FELL & ROCK CLIMBING CLUB

A history of climbing on Scafell

by Al Phizacklea and Mike Cocker

with additional contributions from Brian Davison and John McMMoore.